AF574019

BOOKS EDITED BY FRANCIS COLEMAN ROSENBERGER

SEVEN VOLUMES OF

Records of the Columbia Historical Society of Washington, D. C.

"*Rosenberger has invigorated the Records and placed them on a high level.*"

KENNETH R. BOWLING in *The North Carolina Historical Review*

Virginia Reader: A Treasury of Writings from the First Voyages to the Present

"*This readable anthology contains over eighty selections about Virginia or by Virginians, spanning some three and a half centuries of literary, intellectual, social and political history. A good many of the selections are all too little known, out of print, or difficult to obtain . . . a happy balance between the familiar and the unfamiliar, between the traditional and the uncommon . . . should appeal to specialist and layman alike, to non-Virginian as well as Virginian . . . admirable anthology.*"

WILLIAM PEDEN in *The New York Times Book Review*

Jefferson Reader: A Treasury of Writings About Thomas Jefferson

"*Francis Coleman Rosenberger, alumnus of 'Mr. Jefferson's University' and member of the Virginia bar, has steeped himself in Jeffersoniana and with keen discrimination has selected for his anthology the writings about the Master of Monticello which give not a composite biography but a likeness in three dimensions. . . .*"

THOMAS PERKINS ABERNETHY in *The New York Times Book Review*

American Sampler: A Selection of New Poetry

Selected for typography and design by the American Institute of Graphic Arts as one of the Fifty Books of the Year

"*A volume to be valued by lovers of fine books.*"

LAWRENCE FERLING in *The San Francisco Chronicle*

The Robinson-Rosenberger Journey to the Gold Fields of California, 1849–1850: The Diary of Zirkle D. Robinson

Selected for typography and design by the American Institute of Graphic Arts as one of the Fifty Books of the Year

"*Most interesting diary of a trip from the town of Virginia in Cass County, Illinois, overland to California.*"

JOHN FREDERICK DORMAN in *The Virginia Genealogist*

Records

of the Columbia Historical Society
of Washington, D.C.

1973-1974

Color photograph by Russell A. Crouse

Homer Tope Rosenberger, President of the Columbia Historical Society since 1968, painted from life by the Washington artist Mary Elizabeth King (Mrs. Archibald King) in Washington, D.C., May–June, 1950.

Records

of the Columbia Historical Society of Washington, D.C.

1973-1974

Edited with an Introduction by

FRANCIS COLEMAN ROSENBERGER

ILLUSTRATED

Published by the Society

DISTRIBUTED BY THE UNIVERSITY PRESS
OF VIRGINIA

Copyright, 1976, by the
Columbia Historical Society
1307 New Hampshire Avenue, N.W.
Washington, D.C. 20036

The Records for 1973–1974
Whole Number Volume 49
(the 49th separately bound book)

International Standard Book Number 0–8139–0641–5
Library of Congress Catalogue Card Number for series 1–17677

PRINTED FOR THE SOCIETY AT THE WAVERLY PRESS, BALTIMORE, MARYLAND

Distributed by
The University Press of Virginia
Box 3608, University Station
Charlottesville, Virginia 22903

Contents

Introduction

This volume of the *Records*, for 1973–1974, is somewhat smaller than its immediate predecessor, the volume for 1971–1972. It should perhaps be noted that this is not because of any falling off in the quality or in the variety of manuscripts availabe to the editor. On the contrary, there appears to the editor to be a steady increase of interest in and a professionalism of research into many aspects of the intellectual and cultural history of the Washington area. This volume is smaller only because of the Society's limited financial ability to pay the printer —and the work of the authors and the chores of the editor continue to be uncompensated except for the satisfaction of making the essays available in print. Perhaps some of our readers will welcome a less bulky volume.

Members of the Society should keep in mind that in 1974 a portion of the Society's funds was alloted to support the separate publication of the *Historic American Building Survey: District of Columbia Catalog* scheduled to be distributed in 1975.

The critical reception of the successive volumes of the *Records* by members of the Society, by the scholarly community, and by a slowly growing public, continues to be gratifying. A few comments on preceding volumes are quoted, as is our practice, in the Advertisement pages at the end of the book following the indexes.

As in preceding volumes, the editor's Introduction provides a convenient place for a word of biography about the authors of the papers.

OLIVER W. HOLMES (born 1902), author of *Suter's Tavern: Birthplace of the Federal City*, has long been active in the Columbia Historical Society, has served as a member of its Board of Managers, and is a member of its Advisory Committee on Historical Research. He edited the 1951–1952 volume of the Society's *Records* and the 1953–1954 portion of the combined 1953–1956 volume of which Cornelius W. Heine edited the 1955–1956 portion. He grew up in Minnesota where he was born, received his B.A. from Carleton College, and went on to Columbia University for graduate work in American history. His Ph.D. dissertation was on "Stagecoach and Mail from Colonial Days to 1820" and he has published a number of articles on this subject, among them "Stagecoach Days in the District of Columbia" in the 1948–1950 volume of the *Records.* He came to Washington in 1936 as one of the employees of the newly established National Archives where he served for the next thirty-six years in many capacities, the last ten as Executive Director of the National Historical Publications Commission. Upon his retirement in 1972, *A Tribute to Oliver W. Holmes,* a handsome volume designed by P. J. Conkwright and printed by the Princeton University Press, was assembled by his friends and reprinted his essay "Shall Stagecoaches Carry the Mail?" which was first published in *The William and Mary Quarterly* in 1963. His interest in stagecoach lines out of the District of Columbia led him to go through contemporary newspapers noting references to taverns, particularly those in Georgetown. His article "The Colonial Taverns of Georgetown" in the 1951–1952 volume of the *Records* and his article on Suter's Tavern in this volume are some of the products of that research. He has also written extensively in the field of archives administration and has served as president of the Society of American Archivists.

DAVID J. BRANDENBERG (born 1920), co-author of *The Duc De La Rochefoucauld-Liancourt's Visit to the Federal City in 1797: A New Translation,* is Chairman of the Department of History at American University in Washington, D. C. He was graduated from Bowdoin College, Brunswick, Maine, in 1943 with a major in English and American Literature. He studied at Columbia University from 1946 to 1948 and received an A.M. degree in 1947 and a Ph.D. in 1954 in the Modern History of Western Europe. His dissertation dealt with agricultural reform in Eighteenth Century France. He taught in elementary and secondary schools in 1943–1946, and in the College of General Studies, Columbia University in 1947–1948. He came to American University as an Instructor in 1948. He has published in professional journals and is the author of the sections that deal with the early modern period of European history in *A History of the Western World* by S. B. Clough and others, published by D. C. Heath and Company in 1964. Over the years he has been working on a new translation and annotated edition of La Rochefoucauld-Liancourt's *Voyage dans les États-unis d'amérique.* He received a Fulbright grant in 1959 for research in France on La Rochefoucauld-Liancourt, and research in the correspondence between La Rochefoucauld-Liancourt and DuPont de Nemours regarding the original publication of the French edition of the *Voyage* has been aided by a grant from the Eleutherian Mills Historical Library, Greenville, Wilmington, Delaware. He wishes to acknowledge also that Yvette Castro Kornfeld has rendered important service by preparing a first-draft translation of much of the *Voyage,* that several generations of graduate students at American University have contributed to research for the annotation and that the University's Office of Graduate Studies and Research has made funds available to help in the work.

MILLICENT H. BRANDENBURG, co-author of *The Duc De La Rochefoucauld-Liancourt's Visit to the Federal City in 1797: A New Translation*, received her B.A. degree, magna cum laude, Phi Beta Kappa, in 1943 from Elmira College, New York, where she majored in English and French literature. She spent the next year studying American and European history at the University of Chicago, completing the course work and thesis, but not the comprehensives, for an M.A. After her marriage in 1944, she devoted herself to raising the Brandenburg children, teaching in elementary and secondary schools, and some community activities. In 1964 she received an M.A. in painting, art history and criticism at American University. The following year she began working in a special part-time program for professional women at the United States Atomic Energy Commission, Germantown, Maryland, as a research assistant in the Office of the Historian. She worked for the next six years as a researcher, editor, and historical analyst in the Commission's historical programs in its Division of International Affairs, during part of the time at the United States Embassy in Paris. In 1971 she served as a legislative assistant to Congresswoman Bella Abzug of New York. She has been a guest lecturer and academic counselor at American University, and for the past several years has devoted much of her time to picture research for an illustrated edition of *A History of the Western World* by S. B. Clough and others, and working on the translation and editing of La Rochefoucauld-Liancourt's *Voyage dans les États-unis d'amérique.*

HAROLD KIRKER, author of *Charles Bulfinch and the Washington Unitarian Community, 1818–1830*, is Professor of History at the University of California at Santa Barbara. He is the author of *The Architecture of Charles Bulfinch*, published by the Harvard University Press in 1969, and the co-author with James Kirker of *Bulfinch's Boston*, published by the Oxford University Press in 1964. His volume *California's Architectural Frontier: Style and Tradition in the Nineteenth Century*, first published by the Huntington Library in 1960, was reprinted by Russell and Russell in 1970 and published in a paperback edition by Peregrine Smith in 1973. He contributed the essay "California Architecture and Its Relation to Contemporary Trends in Europe and America" to the volume *Essays and Assays: California History Reappraised*, published by the California Historical Society in 1973. He is a fifth-generation Californian and received his Doctorate from the University of California at Berkeley in 1957.

CHRISTIAN F. FEEST (born 1945), author of *Lukas Vischer in Washington: A Swiss View of the District of Columbia in 1825*, has worked at the Museum für Völkerkunde (the Museum of Ethnology) in Vienna, Austria, since 1963 and since 1966 has been Curator of the Museum's North American Indian Collections. He was in Washington in 1972 and 1973 as a Post-Doctoral Fellow in Anthropology at the Smithsonian Institution. He was born in Braunau, Czechoslovakia, and has lived in Austria since 1946. He studied anthropology and linguistics at the University of Vienna where he received his Ph.D. in 1969. He is the author of numerous publications in English and German on Eastern North American Indian ethnohistory, among them "The Virginia Indian in Pictures, 1612–1624" in the *Smithsonian Journal of History* and "Seventeenth Century Virginia Algonquian Population Estimates" in the *Quarterly Bulletin* of the Archeological Society of Virginia.

WILLIAM A. BATE (born 1945), author of *Thomas Ewbank: Commissioner of Patents, 1849–1852*, is the Editor of *American Studies: An International Newsletter*, published by the Council for International Exchange of Scholars, Washington, D. C., and is a Ph.D. candidate at George, Washington University. He received his A.B. from the State University of New York in Albany in 1966 and his M.A. from Union College, Schenectady, New York, in 1971. He taught from 1966 to 1971 at the Shenendehowa Central Schools, Elnora, New York, and was a Graduate Teaching Fellow in American Civilization at George Washington University in 1973–1974.

ELIZABETH STEVENSON (born 1919), author of *Olmsted on F Street: The Beginnings of the United States Sanitary Commission*, won the Bancroft Prize for her *Henry Adams: A Biography*, published by Macmillan in 1955. A paperback edition of the biography was published in 1961. Other books by her are *The Crooked Corridor: A Study of Henry James*, published by Macmillan in 1949, of which a paperback edition was published in 1961; *A Henry Adams Reader*, published by Doubleday in 1958, reprinted by Peter Smith in 1968; *Lafcadio Hearn*, published by Macmillan in 1961; and *Babbitts & Bohemians: The American 1920s*, published by Macmillan in 1967, of which a paperback, *The American 1920s*, was published in 1970. She has also written the Introduction to the Collier Books edition of Jane Austen's *Pride and Prejudice* and has published book reviews and articles in the *Virginia Quarterly Review*, *South Atlantic Quarterly*, *New York Times Book Review*, *Nation*, *Commentary*, *Booklist*, and *Atlanta Journal*. She attended the public schools of Great Falls, Montana, and Atlanta, Georgia, and received a B.A. degree, magna cum laude, with majors in History and English, from Agnes Scott College, Decatur, Georgia, in 1941. She was employed in the Statistics section, Georgia Division, of the Southern Bell Telephone and Telegraph Company in 1941; was an auditor with the Georgia regional offices of three wartime agencies of the Federal government, Central Administrative Services, War Production Board, and War Assets Administration, from 1942 to 1947; and was a Library Assistant, Order Department, Atlanta Public Library, from 1947 to 1956. She was Assistant to Emory College Dean, Emory University, from 1960 to 1974, and in 1974 became Research Associate, Institute of the Liberal Arts, Emory University. Her honors and awards include Phi Beta Kappa, a Guggenheim Fellowship in 1950–1951 for a study of Henry Adams, a Guggenheim Fellowship in 1956–1957 for a study of Lafcadio Hearn, a Rockefeller Fellowship to supplement addition to second Guggenheim Fellowship for travel to Japan on Hearn research, four Emory University Committee grants for study of the American 1920's and of Olmsted, and a National Endowment for the Humanities summer stipend in 1974 for Olmsted study. She served as a Judge in biography for the National Book Awards in 1960.

DONALD BEEKMAN MYER (born 1937), author of *Unbuilt Bridges of Washington, D. C.*, has been a Registered Architect in the District of Columbia since 1972. He has worked with the United States Commission of Fine Arts, involved with both historic preservation and design review for new public buildings, parks, and monuments, since 1965. From 1968 to 1970 he was on leave from the Commission to work with the Washington architectural firm of Keyes, Lethbridge and Condon. From 1962 to 1965 he worked for the National Park Service in Washington, Philadelphia, and Cape Cod as a Supervisory Architect in restoration and administration of local Historic Buildings Survey projects. He received a Bachelor of Architecture degree in 1961 from the University of Illinois and a Master's degree in Architectural History there in 1962. He has lectured at the Smithsonian Institution and George Washington University, has contributed to professional journals, and is the author of *Bridges and the City of Washington*, Government Printing Office, 1974.

ROBERT BELMONT FREEMAN, JR. (born 1951), author of *Design Proposals for the Washington National Monument*, was graduated from Yale University in 1972, magna cum laude, Phi Beta Kappa, receiving a B.A. degree in the Study of the City and History of Art. Since 1972 he has been living in Philadelphia, where he is completing work on a Master's degree in Architecture at the University of Pennsylvania. He was born in Washington, D. C. and grew up in Arlington, Virginia, and in Brussels, Belgium, where his family was on assignment with the United States Embassy. As an undergraduate at Yale, he was a planning intern with the National Capital Planning Commission. More recently he has been employed by the Historic American Engineering Record and the Historic American Buildings Survey, working on recording projects in Morgantown, West Virginia, and Charleston, South Carolina. During the academic year 1974–1975 he will be studying in Europe under Dales and Woodman Travelling Fellowships, given by the Graduate School of Fine Arts of the University of Pennsylvania.

KENT AHRENS, author of *Constantino Brumidi's "Apotheosis of Washington" in the Rotunda of the United States Capitol*, teaches at Randolph-Macon Women's College, Lynchburg, Virginia. Research for his essay was conducted during the 1973–1974 academic year under the auspices of a grant from the National Endowment for the Humanities. He received his A.B. from Dartmouth College and his Ph.D. in the history of American art from the University of Delaware. He spent the academic years 1968–1969 and 1970–1971 in residence at the National Gallery of Art Washington, D. C. as a Samuel H. Kress Fellow and as a Chester Dale Fellow respectively. In the summer of 1968 he lectured for the Extension Program of the University of California at Los Angeles. From 1971 to 1974 he was a member of the faculties of the Florida State University and the Florida State University Study Center in Florence, Italy.

RUTH L. BOHAN (born 1946), author of *The Farragut Monument: A Decade of Art and Politics, 1871–1881*, is a doctoral student in American Studies at the University of Maryland. She received her B.A. from the University of Illinois in 1969 and her M.A. from the University of Maryland in 1972. She was an Analyst for the Defense Department before commencing her studies at the University of Maryland. She is the co-author with David H. Bowman of "Herman Melville's *Mardi, and a Voyage Thither*: An Annotated Checklist of Criticism" in *Resources for American Literary Study*, Spring 1973.

JAMES BORCHERT (born 1941), author of *Alley Life in Washington: An Analysis of 600 Photographs*, is Acting Assistant Professor of History and Community Studies, and a Fellow of Crown College, University of California, Santa Cruz. He received his B.A. from Miami University in 1963 and holds Master's degrees from Indiana University and the University of Cincinnati. He is currently a Ph.D. candidate in American Studies at the University of Maryland and received a Smithsonian Fellowship for 1974–1975 to return to Washington to complete his dissertation on Washington alleys. He has taught at Alabama A. and M.

University and the University of Maryland. He contributed to the 1971–1972 volume of the *Records*.

PAUL A. GROVES (born 1935), author of *The Development of a Black Community in Southwest Washington, 1860–1897,* is an Associate Professor in the Department of Geography of the University of Maryland at College Park. He received his Ph.D. in Geography from the University of California at Berkeley in 1969. His recent publications in the field of historical geography include "The 'Hidden' Population: Washington Alley Dwellers in the late Nineteenth Century" in the *Professional Geographer* and, with Edward K. Miller, "The Evolution of Black Residential Concentrations in late Nineteenth Century Cities" in the *Journal of Historical Geography.* He is a Member of the Advisory Committee on Historical Research of the Columbia Historical Society.

SUSAN H. MYERS (born 1943), author of *Capitol Hill, 1870–1900: The People and Their Homes,* has worked since 1971 at the Smithsonian Institution where she is now a Museum Specialist in the Department of Cultural History. She was born in Washington, D. C., attended Washington-Lee High School, Arlington, Virginia, and in 1964 received a B.A. degree in Art History from Mary Washington College, Fredericksburg, Virginia. She is a Master's candidate in the Department of American Civilization at George Washington University.

RODERICK S. FRENCH (born 1931), author of *Chevy Chase Village in the Context of the National Suburban Movement, 1870–1900,* is Professor of Philosophy at George Washington University and is Coordinator of the University's Humanities Development Program. He has been responsible in the latter position for the systematic development of new courses throughout the University which relate academic disciplines to the city of Washington. He is one of the organizers of the Annual Conferences on Washington, D. C. Historical Studies, sponsored jointly by the University and the Columbia Historical Society, and he is the General Editor of the new monograph series devoted to Washington as an urban center, *GW Washington Studies.* He has been active in the oral history movement in the Washington area and is a member of the George Washington University Committee on the Bicentennial. He earlier served as Director of Youth and Student Work for the World Council of Churches in Geneva and was Special Assistant to the Director of the Office of Public Affairs in the Peace Corps. He received his undergraduate degree in philosophy from Kenyon College, a Bachelor's degree from Episcopal Theological School, Cambridge, Massachusetts, a Master's degree in church history from Union Theological Seminary, New York, and a Ph.D. in American Civilization from George Washington University. He is a Member of the Advisory Committee on Historical Research of the Columbia Historical Society.

THOMAS J. CANTWELL (born 1939), author of *Anacostia: Strength in Adversity*, did the research for two exhibits on the Anacostia area of Washington, D. C. for the Anacostia Neighborhood Museum and has produced a videotape documentary for the Museum. He attended the public schools of Bristol, Virginia, received his Bachelor's degree from Randolph-Macon College in Ashland, Virginia, and a Master's degree in media technology and learning systems from Federal City College in Washington, D. C. He has designed and produced educational material for students in the mountain area of southwest Virginia, in the then newly independent African nation of Malawi, and in low-income areas of Washington, D. C. He works as a training materials and audio visual specialist with the National Drug Abuse Center.

HAL S. CHASE (born 1943), author of "*Shelling the Citadel of Race Prejudice*": *William Calvin Chase and the Washington* "*Bee*", is Assistant Professor of History at Simpson College, Indianola, Iowa, and Director of the Simpson College Venture Fund, the faculty development program. He received his B.A., cum laude, in American Civilization from Washington and Lee University in 1965, his M.A. in American History from Stanford University in 1966, and his Ph.D. in American Civilization from the University of Pennsylvania in 1973. He taught at the University of Pennsylvania in 1967–1969, at Mt. Vernon College in 1970–1972, and at North Carolina Central University in 1973–1974. He has published in a number of professional journals.

MAURINE BEASLEY (born 1936), author of *Kate Field and* "*Kate Field's Washington*"*: 1890–1895*, received a B.A. degree in History and a B.J. in Journalism in 1958 from the University of Missouri, where she was awarded membership in Phi Beta Kappa, scholastic honorary fraternity, and Kappa Tau Alpha, journalism honorary fraternity. She was a staff writer for the *Kansas City Star* from 1958 to 1962. She received a M.S. in Journalism, with high honors, in 1963 from the Columbia University Graduate School of Journalism, New York, where she was awarded a Pulitzer Travelling Fellowship, the Theta Sigma Phi Prize, and the Sevellon Brown Award in the history of journalism. She was a staff writer for the *Washington Post* from 1963 to 1973, with a leave of absence in 1964 for travel and study in Europe and in 1972 for graduate study. She received a Ph.D. in American Civilization from George Washington University in 1974. She lectures at the University of Maryland College of Journalism and is working on a book on American women journalists. She is married to Henry R. Beasley.

HELEN L. HOROWITZ (born 1942), author of *The National Zoological Park: "City of Refuge" Or Zoo?*, is Assistant Professor of History at Scripps College, Claremont, California. She received her B.A. degree from Wellesley College in 1963, her M.A. from Harvard in 1965, and a Ph.D. in American Civilization from Harvard in 1969. She was a Teaching Fellow at Harvard from 1964 to 1967, an Instructor in History at the Massachusetts Institute of Technology in 1969–1973, a Visiting Assistant Professor of History at Union College, Schenectady, New York, in 1970–1972, and a Post-Doctoral Fellow in American and Cultural History at the Smithsonian Institution, Washington, D. C., in 1972–1973. Her essay here on the National Zoological Park was researched and written while she was at the Smithsonian. She has published in the *History of Education Quarterly*, and a book on the subject of her doctoral thesis, "*Culture and the City*": *Cultural Philanthropy in Chicago, 1890–1917*, has been accepted for publication. She is married to Daniel Horowitz.

J. KIRKPATRICK FLACK (born 1937), author of *Scientific Societies in Gilded Age Washington*, is Associate Professor of History at the University of Maryland, College Park, and in 1974 held a Senior Fulbright-Hays Lectureship in American History in India. He received his B.A. degree from Albion College, Michigan, in 1959, studied at Exeter College, Oxford University, in 1961, received his M.A. from Wayne State University, Michigan, in 1963, and his Ph.D. from Wayne State University in 1968. He was an Instructor in 1965–1966 at Wayne State University, a Lecturer in 1967–1968 at the University of Maryland, and Assistant Professor at Maryland in 1968–1974. He has published in professional journals and a book on *The Intellectual Community in the Capital City, 1870–1900* has been scheduled for publication.

CHARLES MERRILL MOUNT (born 1928), author of *The Works of John Singer Sargent in Washington*, is distinguished both as a painter and as a biographer and contributed to the 1971–1972 volume of the *Records*. His *John Singer Sargent: A Biography* was first published by W. W. Norton and Company in 1955. A British edition was published in London in 1957. A Kraus Reprint edition was published in New York in 1969. He is also the author of *Gilbert Stuart: A Biography*, published by Norton in 1964, and *Monet: A Biography*, published by Simon and Schuster in 1966. He attended Columbia University, studied painting under John Carroll at the Arts Students' League, and has worked as a portrait painter in France, Italy, England and Ireland. He has contributed to a number of professional journals and has lectured at many museums and galleries including the Corcoran Gallery of Art in Washington. In the early 1960's he represented the Corcoran to gather pictures in Europe for its Sargent exhibition. He has held a Guggenheim Fellowship in history and a research grant from the Archives of American Art.

MARCIA M. MATHEWS, author of *George Biddle's Contribution to Federal Art*, contributed "The Art of Henry O. Tanner" to the 1969–1970 volume of the *Records*. She has taught art history at Wellesley College, Duke University, and Morehouse College. She holds degrees from Tulane University and Wellesley College and did graduate work in art history at the Institute of Art and Archaeology in Paris. She has published articles on art in both scholarly and popular magazines and is the author of three books: *Richard Allen* (1963), *Henry Ossawa Tanner: American Artist* (1969), and *The Freedom Star* (1971).

HOMER TOPE ROSENBERGER (born 1908), author of *The Economic Development of Washington: An Introduction*, has been President of the Columbia Historical Society since 1968. A native of Pennsylvania, he was graduated from Albright College, Reading, Pennsylvania, in 1929, received his M.A. from Cornell University the following year, and his Ph.D. from Cornell at the age of 24 with a dissertation on "Public Utility Regulation in Pennsylvania" in 1932. He worked for many years with the Federal Government in Washington, first with the Bureau of Prisons, Department of Justice, and later with the Bureau of Roads, Department of Commerce. He was awarded an LL.D. by Albright College in 1955. He has published widely in professional journals and his books include *What Should We Expect of Education?* (1956), *Letters From Africa* (1965), *The Pennsylvania Germans, 1891–1965* (1966), *Adventures and Philosophy of a Pennsylvania Dutchman* (1971), *Man and Modern Society* (1972) and *Mountain Folks: Fragments of Central Pennsylvania Lore* (1974). He has in press *The Philadelphia and Erie Railroad: Its Place in American Economic History*, a comprehensive volume scheduled for 1975 publication.

JOHN NOLEN, JR. (born 1898), author of *Some Aspects of Washington's Nineteenth Century Economic Development*, was active for many years in city planning in the Washington area. He was City Planner and Director of Planning for the National Capital Park and Planning Commission from 1931 to 1951 and Director of the National Capital Planning Commission from 1951 to 1958. He was born in Ardmore, Pennsylvania, received a B.S. degree in Civil Engineering at the Massachusetts Institute of Technology, and studied at Harvard, the University of Cincinnati, and the University of Pennsylvania. He is a member of a number of professional societies and continues to work as a Planning Consultant.

ROGER W. ALLEN (born 1915), author of *A Summary of Twentieth*

Century Economic Development of the District of Columbia and the Washington Metropolitan Area, is the Statistician for the Business Research Division of the Chesapeake and Potomac Telephone Companies with headquarters in Washington, D. C. He received a B.S. degree in Business Administration from the Virginia Polytechnic Institute and a M.C. majoring in economics from the University of Richmond. He began work with the Chesapeake and Potomac Telephone Company of Virginia in 1936 and advanced through various positions with the Virginia company until 1966 when he transferred to Washington, D. C. He is a member of the National Association of Business Economists, the National Federation of Financial Analysts, and other professional organizations.

WALTER F. MCARDLE (born 1915), author of *The Development of the Business Sector in Washington, D. C., 1800–1973*, is the President of the McArdle Printing Company, Inc., Silver Spring, Maryland, and Past President of the Metropolitan Washington Board of Trade. He has been active in many Washington area business and community posts. He is a member of the board of the First National Bank of Washington and of the Hamilton Federal Savings and Loan Association and is a trustee of the Washington Consortium of Universities. He was born in Brooklyn, New York, and received a B.S. degree from St. Francis College there.

WALTER A. SCHEIBER (born 1922), author of *Washington's Regional Development*, has been the Executive Director of the Metropolitan Washington Council of Governments since 1966. He is a graduate of Swarthmore College and Columbia Law School and has a Master's degree in Political Science from the University of Pennsylvania. He was a practicing attorney in New York State from 1947 to 1954 and for the next ten years served as a City Manager in Pennsylvania and Maryland. Before his appointment to his present position with the Council of Governments he was the Executive Vice President of a Washington area industrial development firm.

GARY F. HEURICH (born 1957), author of *The Christian Heurich Brewing Company, 1872–1956*, is so far as the editor knows the youngest writer ever to publish in the *Records*. He delivered his excellent paper before the Society on February 20, 1973, three months before his sixteenth birthday. He is a senior at Landon School, Bethesda, Maryland, and plans to attend Bucknell University, Lewisburg, Pennsylvania. He is the grandson of Christian Heurich, Sr., about whom he writes, and the son of Christian Heurich, Jr., and is a life member of the Columbia Historical Society.

DOROTHY CLARK WINCHCOLE, author of "*Do You Remember —?*", was the author of "The First Baptist Church in Washington, D. C." in the 1957–1959 volume of the *Records* and of " 'The General' ", a tribute to U. S. Grant, 3rd, in the 1966–1968 volume of the *Records.* She is the daughter of Allen C. Clark (1858–1943), who was President of the Columbia Historical Society from 1916 to 1943, and the sister of the late Elizabeth C. Clark, who was long the Chronicler of the Society. She has served as a member of the Board of Managers of the Society and of its Executive Commitee.

EMIL A. PRESS (born 1904), author of *Growing Up In Swampoodle,* has long been active in the Columbia Historical Society and is a member of its Board of Managers. He was born and grew up in Washington and received a B.S. degree from the George Washington University in 1935. He retired from the District of Columbia government after 43 years of service and for the past ten years has been on the engineering staff of Metro.

WILLIAM H. PRESS (born 1906), author of *Another View of Swampoodle,* has like his brother Emil long been active in the Columbia Historical Society and is a member of its Board of Managers. He was born and grew up in Washington and received a B.S. degree from the University of Maryland. He was associated with the Board of Trade of Metropolitan Washington from 1936 to 1971 and during much of that time was its Executive Vice President. He was appointed Chairman of the National Capital Planning Commission in 1973.

FRANK MILLER SMITH (born 1903), author of *The Washington Temple: A New Landmark,* is a newspaperman whose by-line was long familiar to readers of the former *Washington Times* and *Washington Times Herald.* He was born in Cumberland, Maryland, attended school there, and went on to Johns Hopkins University and Randolph Macon College. He was chief editorial writer for the *Washington Times Herald* at the time the *Times Herald* merged with the *Washington Post* in 1954. He had earlier served over the years as city editor, Capitol Hill reporter, White House correspondent, and feature writer for the *Times Herald* and before that as political columnist, city editor, literary editor, radio editor, and reporter for the *Washington Times.* Before his long association with the *Times* and the *Times Herald,* he served as a reporter for the former *Washington Herald* and *Washington Daily News* and he began his newspaper career as a young man as a reporter for the *Cumberland Leader* and the *Baltimore Sun.* After the death of the *Times Herald,* he worked for some years on the staff of the National Association of Manufacturers. He is an accredited correspondent for the Church News section of the *Deseret News,* published in Salt Lake City, Utah, and for other church publications of the Church of Jesus Christ of Latter-Day Saints.

This volume of the *Records* has benefitted from papers from two special activities of the Society. The first was the Columbia Historical Society Washington Economic History Institute, organized by William H. Press, a member of the Board of Managers of the Society and the Chairman of the National Capital Planning Commission, which was held at the Cosmos Club on September 19, 1973. The second was the First Annual Conference on Washington, D. C. Historical Studies, sponsored by the Columbia Historical Society and the George Washington University, and organized by three members of the Society, Professor Roderick S. French of George Washington University, Professor Letitia W. Brown of George Washington University, and the editor of the *Records*, which was held at the Martin Luther King Memorial Library on January 11 and January 12, 1974. Papers delivered at the Institute and at the Conference, as are papers delivered at meetings of the Society, are so identified in an unnumbered footnote at the bottom of the first page of the text of the paper.

Two typographical errors in the preceding volume of the *Records* seem to the editor to be serious enough to be mentioned and corrected here. Unaccountably the illustrations on pages 635 and 640 were transposed in printing, with the result that the captions under them should be transposed to identify them correctly. (The profile, of course, is the painting and the full face is the photograph.) The editor will swear the illustrations had their proper places in final page proof. No more easily explained, the beleaguered Alexander R. Shepherd somehow became Andrew R. Shepherd on pages viii, xix, and 845, although he has his proper identity elsewhere in the volume. Editorial and printing gremlins are pesky creatures whose only redeeming value is to engender editorial humility.

As in the 1969–1970 volume of the *Records*, the editor is grateful for a generous special gift which has made possible the use of a color frontispiece in this volume which otherwise would have been beyond the limits of the editor's budget.

Lastly, I am deeply indebted to my wife, Astra, without whose help and understanding in organizing my limited time at home, after long and busy days at other work at the office, it would not have been possible for me to assemble and edit this volume.

FRANCIS COLEMAN ROSENBERGER

Washington, D. C.
December 1974

Suter's Tavern: Birthplace of the Federal City

OLIVER W. HOLMES

A. BIRTHPLACE OF THE FEDERAL CITY

What was there about Suter's Tavern, more than about scores of taverns like it, including several others in Georgetown at the time, that makes its story of continuing interest today? Surely I do not need to explain to an audience of the Columbia Historical Society that Suter's Tavern has always seemed especially important because it was the birthplace of the "Federal City" which was soon to be named "Washington." If you do not like the idea of the capital city of our nation being born in a tavern, it may please you to know that John Suter's own name for his tavern throughout the years of his tenancy was the "Fountain Inn." This was its sign, and a popular one it was in its day for there were Fountain Inns in Baltimore, Annapolis and Alexandria, to name only neighboring towns, and later there were to be several east of Rock Creek in the new Federal City itself. Tavern signs were useful for directing strangers to an hostelry, but the more popular the landlord made his house, the more his name became associated with it in the records of the day.[1]

To emphasize the importance of Suter's it will be necessary to quote passages from the words of the "Founding Fathers"—passages that have been printed again and again but which are necessary to set the stage. First among these must be the entries in President Washington's diary for Monday, Tuesday and Wednesday, March 28–30, 1791.

This is an extensive revision, making use of additional sources, of a paper read before the Columbia Historical Society on April 14, 1964. For information and assistance in research the author owes special thanks to Mary Jane Lethbridge, Mathilde D. Williams and Robert W. Lyle.

[1] This dual nomenclature can easily make for confusion in using and interpreting contemporary records such as memoirs and newspapers. One has to learn that the Fountain Inn and Suter's Tavern are the same, but be on the alert also because new landlords often continued to use an old sign when it had become famous. Also when landlords moved into new buildings they often took their old signs with them so we cannot be sure a "Green Tree" or "Indian King" will always be in the location where we first met with it.

Monday, 28th. Left Bladensburgh at half after six, and breakfasted at George Town about 8; where, having appointed the Commissioners under the Residence Law to meet me, I found Mr. Johnson one of them (and who is Chief Justice of the State) in waiting—and soon after came in David Stuart, and Dan'l Carroll, Esqrs. the other two. A few miles out of Town I was met by the principal Citizens of the place and escorted in by them; and dined at Suter's tavern (where I also lodged) at a public dinner given by the Mayor and Corporation—previous to which I examined the Surveys of Mr. Ellicot who had been sent on to lay out the district of ten miles square for the federal seat; and also the works of Majr. L'Enfant who had been engaged to examine and make a draught of the grds. in the vicinity of George Town and Carrollsburg on the Eastern branch making arrangements for examining the ground myself to morrow with the Commissioners.

Tuesday, 29th. In a thick mist, and under strong appearances of a settled rain (which however did not happen) I set out about 7 o'clock, for the purpose above mentioned, but from the unfavorableness of the day, I derived no great satisfaction from the review.

Finding the interests of the Landholders about George Town and those about Carrollsburgh much at variance and that their fears and jealousies of each were counteracting the public purposes and might prove injurious to its best interests, whilst if properly managed they might be made to subserve it, I requested them to meet me at six o'clock this afternoon at my lodgings, which they accordingly did.

To this meeting I represented that the contention in which they seemed engaged, did not in my opinion comport either with the public interest or that of their own; that while each party was aiming to obtain the public buildings, they might by placing the matter on a contracted scale, defeat the measure altogether; not only by procrastination but for want of the means necessary to effect the work; That neither the offer from George-town or Carrollsburgh, seperately, was adequate to the end of insuring the object. That both together did not comprehend more ground nor would afford greater means than was required for the federal City; and that, instead of contending which of the two should have it they had better, by combining more offers make a common cause of it, and thereby secure it to the district; other arguments were used to show the danger which might result from delay and the good effects that might proceed from a Union.

Dined at Colo. Forrest's to day with the Commissioners and others.

Wednesday, 30th. The parties to whom I addressed myself yesterday evening, having taken the matter into consideration saw the propriety of my observations; and that whilst they were contending for the shadow they might loose the substance; and therefore mutually agreed and entered into articles to surrender for public purposes, one half of the land they severally possessed within bounds which were designated as necessary for the City to stand with some other stipulations, which were inserted in the instrument which they respectively subscribed.

This business being thus happily finished and some directions given to the Commissioners, the Surveyor and Engineer with respect to the mode of laying out the district—Surveying the grounds for the City and forming them into lots, I left Georgetown, dined in Alexandria and reached Mount Vernon in the evening.[2]

Thus, at Suter's Tavern, where he spent three days and two nights, the Father of his Country carried to a successful conclusion the complicated negotiations with the owners of lands between Rock Creek and the Anacostia River that resulted in our National Capital being located here. Had he not succeeded in bringing them to favorable terms it would almost certainly have been located elsewhere. To the articles of agreement, signed by the President and the original proprietors on this occasion, the original of which is in the National Archives, the name of the tavern keeper, John Suter, is subscribed as a witness. On the basis of this agreement Major Pierre Charles L'Enfant was directed to make detailed plans for the new city and to recommend locations for the Federal buildings.

For the next three months Washington was on an extended tour in the Southern states as far as Georgia, but, rumors having reached him that some of the proprietors had become dissatisfied with their bargain, he again stopped in Georgetown on his way to the temporary capital in Philadelphia, and again spent his days and nights at Suter's while he adjusted complaints and checked the progress of surveys and plans. This time he tied the bargain down by getting signed deeds of trust from all the proprietors. Again, we read from his diary:

Monday, 27th. Left Mount Vernon for Georgetown before Six oclock;—and according to appointment met the Commissioners at that place by 9—then calling together the Proprietors of those Lands on which the federal City was proposed to be built who had agreed to cede them on certain conditions at the last meeting I had with them at this place

[2] This text is the version of John C. Fitzpatrick in his edition of *The Complete Diaries of George Washington,* Vol. IV, pp. 152–155. One of the best summaries of these proceedings is that by Louis Dow Scisco, "A Site for the 'Federal City': The Original Proprietors and their Negotiations with Washington," in the *Records of the Columbia Historical Society of Washington, D. C. 1957–1959* (1961), pp. 123–147. See also H. Paul Caemmerer, *A Manual on the Origin and Development of Washington,* (1939). The three Commissioners whom Washington had appointed were Thomas Johnson, David Stuart, and Daniel Carroll of Rock Creek (not of Duddington as Fitzpatrick has it in a footnote). The three Commissioners or their successors were to govern Washington until 1802.

but from some misconception with respect to the extension of their grants had refused to make conveyances and recapitulating the principles upon which my comns. to them at the former meeting were made and giving some explanation of the present State of matters and the consequences of delay in this business they readily waved their objections and agd. to convey to the utmost extent of what was required.

Tuesday, 28th. Whilst the Commissioners were engaged in preparing the Deeds to be signed by the Subscribers this afternoon, I went out with Majr. L'Enfant and Mr. Ellicot to take a more perfect view of the ground, in order to decide finally on the spots on which to place the public buildings and to direct how a line which was to leave out a Spring (commonly known by the name of the Cool Spring) belonging to Majr. Stoddart should be run.

Wednesday, 29th. The Deeds which remained unexecuted yesterday were signed to day and the Dowers of their respective wives acknowledged according to Law.

This being accomplished, I called the several subscribers together and made known to them the spots on which I meant to place the buildings for the P: and Executive departments of the Government—and for the Legislature of Do.—A Plat was also laid before them of the City in order to convey to them general ideas of the City but they were told that some deviation from it would take place—particularly in the diagonal streets or avenues, which would not be so numerous; and in the removal of the Presidents house more westerly for the advantage of higher ground—they were also told that a Town house, or exchange wd be placed on some convenient ground between the spots designed for the public buildgs. before mentioned.—and it was with much pleasure that a general approbation of the measure seemed to pervade the whole.

Thursday, 30th. The business which brot. me to Georgetown being finished and the Comrs. instructed with respect to the mode of carrying the plan into effect I set off this morning a littel after 4 Oclock in the prosecution of my journey towards Philadelphia; and being desirous of seeing the nature of the Country North of Georgetown, and along the upper road, I resolved to pass through Fredericktown in Maryland and York and Lancaster in Pennsylvania . . .[3]

Perhaps we can imagine the relief felt by Washington as he passed up High Street (now Wisconsin Avenue) in Georgetown toward Williamsburg, as Montgomery County Court House, now Rockville, was then known, and on to Frederick, 43 miles, for the night, making his

[3] Fitzpatrick, *Diaries,* IV, pp. 199–201.

way to Philadelphia by what was then known as "the upper route." The work of creating a new capital for the nation could now begin in earnest, and Suter's was the center of activity. Andrew Ellicott, the nation's leading surveyor, who had in fact made his headquarters at Suter's from February on, had by the time of Washington's first visit completed the survey of the District's boundaries, and was beginning to lay out the main avenues, cooperating with L'Enfant in preparing his map, and getting ready for the first sale of lots in the new city which, it had been announced, would be on October 17th. The notices of the sale were immediately inserted in nearby newspapers, and newspapers throughout the nation were requested to copy. Major L'Enfant, the engineer and planner of the Federal City had made his headquarters at the Tavern since his arrival, March 9th. Here, coming in from his rides over the area, he dreamed his dreams of the future city and endeavored to catch them in sketches and plans on his drawing board.

How many of the assistants of Ellicott and Major L'Enfant also stayed at the tavern we do not know; probably most of them found other quarters, but surely they came and went, and many of the necessary conferences were held there.

Suter's was also the meeting place of the three Commissioners under whose direction, when Washington was absent, all other activities were supposedly ordered. L'Enfant insisted however that his subordination to the Commissioners was contrary to his understanding with his old General, and when Washington finally made the relationship clear, L'Enfant felt he had no recourse but to resign, for he and the Commissioners were not seeing eye to eye.[4] We know many of the people who came and went from the tavern in these days from the minutes of the Commissioners' meetings and from the letters to and from them that are to be found today in the National Archives and the Library of Congress.

The next meeting deserving particular mention is that of September 8, 1791, when Thomas Jefferson and James Madison met with the Commissioners. Washington had asked his Secretary of State and Madison, then one of Virginia's Senators, to stop over on their way from Philadelphia to their homes to discuss a whole host of questions that had arisen. The two travellers arrived the night before, and, although I have nowhere found a definite statement of their lodging place, it seems likely that it was Suter's, and almost certainly they met the Commissioners there. In fact, Jefferson, a few days later wrote from

[4] The best account of these differences and L'Enfant's activities generally, heavily documented, is in H. Paul Caemmerer, *The Life of Pierre Charles L'Enfant* (1950).

Monticello to Andrew Ellicott and asked the surveyor to offer to hire Mr. Suter's houseboy, Billy.[5] This did not work out but Billy was not forgotten because in 1794 we find Bartholomew Dandridge, then serving as Washington's secretary, writing to John Suter from Philadelphia saying that the President would be glad to employ Billy, whose time with Suter had then expired. The terms of the employment offered were $8.00 a month and a full suit of livery clothes annually.[6]

There had been much talk that the announced sale of lots in October was premature, but it was decided at this meeting to go ahead with it. It was also at this meeting that the decision was arrived at to name the 10-mile square Federal District the "District of Columbia" and the new Federal City to arise east of Rock Creek the "City of Washington." It was decided further to designate the streets by numbers in one direction and by letters of the alphabet in the other. We are thus still governed by decisions made at that meeting and shall be indefinitely into the future.[7] We might read Jefferson's brief report to Washington written that evening, probably in Suter's Tavern.

> We were detained on the road by the rains so that we did not arrive here till yesterday about ten o'clock; as soon as horses could be got ready we set out and rode till dark, examining chiefly the grounds newly laid open, which we found much superior to what we had imagined,—. . . we have passed this day in consultation with the Commissioners, who having deliberated on every article contained in our paper and pre-admonished that they should decide freely on their own view of things concurred unanimously on, I believe every point with what had been thought best in Philadelphia.[8]

And the next event at Suter's that deservies special mention is this first sale of lots, begun on the 17th as advertised and continued for three days.[9] One might suppose that some temporary structure could have been erected for this event over on the grounds of the new city, but there would have been no place for the purchasers to lodge except in Georgetown. These purchasers were not only from the neighborhood but "from the Eastward" and "from Carolina and Norfolk" ac-

[5] Nineteenth Century copy in the Edgehill-Randolph papers, University of Virginia.

[6] John C. Fitzpatrick, ed. *Writings of Washington,* Vol. 33, p. 434.

[7] See the letter of the Commissioners to Major L'Enfant, September 9, 1791, as published in H. Paul Caemmerer, *The Life of Pierre Charles L'Enfant,* p. 167.

[8] Saul K. Padover, *Thomas Jefferson and the National Capital* (Washington, 1946), p. 68.

[9] This advertisement can be seen in the Georgetown *Weekly Ledger* for July 2, 1791. It is followed by the line, "The Printers throughout the United States are requested to insert the above in their papers."

Courtesy of Charles Francis Adams
and the Frick Art Reference Library

Thomas Jefferson in 1786 by Mather Brown (1761–1831).

Replica, painted by the artist in London in 1786 for John Adams, of the lost original portrait painted from life in London in the spring of 1786 and received by Jefferson in Paris in 1788.

cording to Commissioner Stuart's report to Washington.[10] The sale seemed to go as well as expected despite inclement weather which must have forced much of the activity inside. The Commissioners promptly, two days later, approved payment to Suter of £ 6, 18 s, 9 d. "for wine and wood furnished at the sale of lots on the 17th, 18th and 19th inst." [11]

We know too little of what went on within the tavern walls in this exciting year, and I cannot present all the details of what is known. Ellicott continued to make it his headquarters in 1792, carrying on his own work and taking over much of that of L'Enfant. We know from Jefferson's account book that he stopped there again on July 18, 1792, on one of his trips between Monticello and Philadelphia, for his entry reads: "Shuter. lodgg, brkft, &c 4.9. sevts 15. 5.05." [12] The Commissioners also continued to meet there but they may also have set up an office elsewhere on the block in addition for they are paying rent "for Robert Peter's House." We know, of course, that Robert Peter was the owner of the tavern all the time it was occupied by Suter, but it seems unlikely that Suter's Tavern was meant when the words "Robert Peter's House" were used. This is a detail that has never been satisfactorily cleared up.[13] Perhaps a more intriguing problem is the raid that was somehow carried out on L'Enfant's quarters while he was absent in Philadelphia. His papers, maps, plans for the public buildings, and accounts, were carried off, and, except for the map, which Samuel Davidson returned to him some years later, the rest has never come to light. L'Enfant always blamed the Commissioners for this raid on his quarters, but it is clear that they never had these papers nor access to them. It seems more likely that this affair was engineered by certain dissatisfied proprietors for reasons not entirely clear. But what happened has been a well kept secret, and, at the present stage of our in-

[10] Quoted in Wilhelmus B. Bryan, *History of the National Capital,* Vol. I, p. 159, who cites the original as located in the Washington Papers, Library of Congress.

[11] Commissioners' "Proceedings," Vol. I, p. 53, in the National Archives. In December Suter also submitted a bill to the Commissioners for Ellicott's and L'Enfant's rooms and board to that date totalling Ł 110, which the Commissioners paid on January 9, 1792. *Ibid.,* 74–75.

[12] This "Account Book," as it has usually been called is in reality a journal of expenditures which enables one to follow Jefferson around from day to day. The original for this period is in the New York Public Library, but I have used the copy with the "Jefferson Papers" project at Princeton University through the courtesy of Julian Boyd.

[13] Robert Peter's home was on lot No. 69, a lot also on the east side of Wisconsin Avenue, but further south and separated from the tavern lot (No. 51) by lot No. 52. It was about where the Presbyterian Church is now. But Peter probably had other houses he could rent on the many lots he owned in what was already being called "Peter's Square."

vestigations, we are unable to pronounce any man guilty.[14] It must have been a very embarrassing event for John Suter at best, and he must have wondered at times if he were really in control of his house.

Surely enough has been said about this old inn in the exciting years of 1791 and 1792 to make you curious as to its earlier and later years. Washington's more famous visits in 1791, for example, were not his first to Suter's. His earliest recorded visit is noted in his diary as on August 1, 1785, when he came up to a meeting of the "Potowmack Company" and "dined at Shuter's Tavern." [15] That Company had been organized just in May with Washington as its first President. Again he notes in his diary for October 22, 1787: "Went up to a meeting of the Pot'k Company at Georgetown. Did the business which called the Com'y together, dined at Shuter's Tavern, and returned as far as Abingdon at night." [16] In 1790 we find the following news item in the *Times and Potowmack Packet* for September 15th:

> Last Saturday about eight o'clock in the morning, arrived here from Bladensburg, where they lodged the preceding night, the President of the United States, his Lady and Suite, on their way to Mount Vernon. The members of the Potowmack Company of Alexandria, and this place, met their illustrious President at Mr. John Suter's and notwithstanding the fatigue of a long journey, his Excellency proceeded to business respecting the navigation of the Potowmack.

The Manuscript "Proceedings" of the Potowmack Company, now located in the National Archives, do not in this first period specify the meeting place of the directors other than in Alexandria or Georgetown, but it seems likely the Georgetown meetings in these earlier years were regularly at Suter's as they were noted to be in later years when meeting places were specified in the minutes of the Company.

Washington's last meeting at the tavern in the interests of this Company was on August 6, 1795, after John Suter had died. Mrs. Suter was carrying on. A notice in the July 3rd issue of the *Columbian Chronicle* announced the meeting in the following words:

---

[14] See L'Enfant's affidavit, sworn to before William Thornton, February 8, 1803, as published in Bessie W. Gahn, *George Washington's Headquarters in Georgetown* (1940), p. 43. The original is in the Digges-Morgan L'Enfant Collection in the Manuscript Division, Library of Congress.

[15] J. C. Fitzpatrick, ed., *Diaries of George Washington,* Vol. II, p. 394.

[16] *Ibid.,* Vol. III, p. 257. It seems likely that he may have attended additional meetings of the Potowmack Company in Georgetown before he was elected President of the United States, when it became more difficult. For the history of the Potowmack Company and its importance in that period as a predecessor of the Chesapeake and Ohio Canal, see Mrs. Cora Bacon-Foster, *Early Chapters in the Development of the Potomac Route to the West* (1911).

> The stockholders in the Potomac Company are requested to attend their General Meeting at the house of Mrs. Suter in George-Town on the 3d day of August next. Matters of great consequence to the company will be proposed; particularly a plan for enlarging the capital, for the purpose of finishing the work and opening the navigation of the Shannandoah River . . .

Washington did not get to this meeting until the 6th, it having been adjourned from day to day. He noted in his diary that he lodged that night "at Mrs. Suter's." [17] He was no longer president of the Company; his long time secretary, Tobias Lear, who had often represented him at meetings, was now president. Suter's appears almost to have been the Maryland office of the Potowmack Company in these years. Notices may be found from time to time in the newspapers, for instance, of the sale of shares in the Company at Suter's. The first such notice is in the *Maryland Gazette* for May 3, 1787, but as late as January 20, 1795 the *Columbian Chronicle* was carrying a notice that shares of delinquent holders of Potowmack Company stock would be sold "at the House of the widow Suter" in Georgetown. In this same issue of the *Chronicle* Sarah Suter, the widow, and John Suter, Jr., the son, were, as executors, giving notice that those having "just claims against the estate of John Suter, dec." and those "in any way indebted to said estate" should present their claims or make immediate payment. For John Suter had died the previous November at his farm "Earnhill" in Montgomery County near Rockville.

B. THE TAVERN'S ROLE IN THE TOWN OF GEORGETOWN

It was at the November 1783 session of the Montgomery County Court that John Suter had been first bonded to keep "an ordinary or public house of entertainment in Georgetown," Georgetown being then, of course, in Montgomery County.[18] No record of any earlier license issued to John Suter has been found, although his brother, James Suter, had since 1777 been keeping a tavern on a tract called "Aberdeen," located on the Georgetown-Frederick road about 13 miles from Georgetown and one mile this side of Rockville.[19] John Suter's name also appears a number of times in Montgomery County

[17] Fitzpatrick, ed., *Diaries of George Washington,* Vol. IV, p. 237; and "Proceedings" of the Board of the Potowmack Company, Vol. I, p. 55, in the National Archives (Record Group 79).

[18] Records of the November 1783 Session of the Montgomery County Court, p. 164, in Rockville. Records of the August 1784 session show John Suter bonded again.

[19] James Suter's license was granted by the August 1777 Court, the first court sitting in newly established Montgomery County (Court Record, 1777–1781, page 6). No record of his having an earlier license was found in records of Frederick County, from which Montgomery County had been set off. In 1774 James Suter had offered to the public by way of a lottery 50 lots in his new town called "Aberdeen," where he was

Court records in 1777, notably as one of two persons standing surety for Ninian Beall's tavern on Seneca Creek, and in 1778 as surety for Lodoweek Yost, another Montgomery County tavern keeper. In these years, however, John Suter himself appears to have been a farmer, and he appears to have kept his farm through all the years from 1783 to 1794 while he presided as landlord of the Fountain Inn in Georgetown.[20] Many tavern keepers found it advantageous to own a farm in connection with their tavern.

It is my belief that Suter took over what had been Georgetown's most famous colonial tavern, the King's Arms, built about 1760 by Joseph Belt on lot 51 of the original Georgetown survey, which lot fronted 133 feet on the east side of present day Wisconsin Avenue just north of the canal. Belt operated this tavern until 1775. He was succeeded by John Beall who in turn continued as host until 1782.[21] Meanwhile in 1779 "the lot and houses where Mr. Joseph Belt formerly kept, and Mr. John Beall now keeps tavern" were advertised for sale in the *Maryland Journal and Baltimore Advertiser* (issue for October 26) and the land records in Montgomery County record purchase by Robert Peter.

In November 1782 Ignatius Simpson informed the public "that he had just opened *Tavern* in the House that was formerly occupied by Mr. John Beall in Georgetown." [22] But Simpson's license was not renewed. Instead John Suter received his first license in November 1783. Unfortunately I have found no notice as specific as Simpson's above that Suter took over from Simpson, but it seems significant that the Commissioners of Georgetown who had been meeting many years only with Belt and Beall, and with Simpson in 1783, recorded meeting in 1784 "at the House of Mr. John Suter." [23] Thus it seems likely that

expecting a new road from Bladensburg to meet that from Georgetown. *(Maryland Journal,* January 20, 1774).

[20] As early as 1771 John Suter was advertising for sale in the *Maryland Gazette* (issue for December 26) land on the Muddy Branch in Montgomery County "containing by Patent 196 acres." The farm he appears to have had while keeping the tavern, however, is the one his widow and son offered for "public sale, at the Fountain Inn in Georgetown," described as "That beautiful and well-improved seat . . . known by the name of Arnhill, containing 205¼ acres . . . situated . . . 18 miles from George-Town . . . and 3 miles from Montgomery Court House." (*Columbian Chronicle,* March 3, 1795.) The farm name is usually given as "Earnhill."

[21] Further documentation for all this is to be found in my article, "Colonial Taverns of Georgetown," written in 1950 in the hope that it would provide background for Suter's and other Georgetown taverns of the Federal period. It was published with extensive footnotes in the *Records of the Columbia Historical Society of Washington, D. C. 1951–1952* (1955), pp. 1–18.

[22] Notice in *Maryland Journal* (Baltimore), December 10, 1782.

[23] "Minutes of the Georgetown Commissioners," old volume, now in the Manuscript Division, Library of Congress, in which volume the place of meeting is recorded year after year.

Suter's Fountain Inn was located in the same building as Belt's King's Arms. Further proof will be presented, but leaving the question of location aside for now let us review happenings at Suter's to understand the place the tavern had in Georgetown's life.

We have mentioned the important meeting at Suter's Tavern of the Commissioners for the Federal City and also those of the members and officers of the Potowmack Company. We probably have not said enough about meetings there of the Georgetown Commissioners, seven in number, who governed until 1789 when the Maryland General Assembly provided for a mayor, recorder, six aldermen and ten common councilmen. Robert Peter was the first mayor—from 1789 to 1798. We find that in this period the tavern was also a frequent meeting place of the first Masonic lodge in the present District of Columbia which had been chartered by the Grand Lodge of Maryland in 1789 as "Lodge No. 9." [24] A news item in the Georgetown *Weekly Ledger* for June 26, 1790 gives one picture of the tavern in this role:

> On Thur. last assembled at their Lodge-Room in this town, Lodge No. 9 of Ancient York Masons, to celebrate the festival of St. John. At 11 o'clock A. M. they proceeded in procession to the Presbyterian meeting-house, where an excellent discourse was delivered by the Rev. Mr. Balch. . . . After divine service, they returned in Masonic order to the house of Mr. Suter, and partook of an elegant dinner, prepared on the occasion. The utmost harmony and good order prevailed thro the day and friendship and brotherly love shewn conspicuous in every breast. They were joined by a number of their brethren from Alexandria, and other lodges, in commemorating the day.

Another account of this same event appeared in the June 30, 1790 issue of the *Times and Potowmack Packet,* Georgetown's first newspaper. Its editor, Charles Fierer, was the first master of Lodge No. 9. Reverend Stephen Bloomer Balch, founder and first pastor of the Presbyterian Church in Georgetown, was also a member of Lodge No. 9, as was John Suter.[25]

Of greater interest perhaps than an occasion like the above is the story of the laying of the cornerstone of the White House. James Hoban, architect of the White House, happened to be another member

---

[24] The first Masonic Lodge in the *then* district of Columbia was of course the Alexandria Lodge, chartered in 1783.

[25] Masonic background for Georgetown and the District of Columbia may be found in a 71-page pamphlet entitled *Federal Lodge No. 1,* published in 1943 by that Lodge and in another pamphlet entitled *The Laying of the Corner Stone of the White House* (9 pages, 1949) published by Potomac Lodge No. 5 (which considers itself the lineal descendant of Lodge No. 9 of Maryland) consisting of a report prepared by R. Baker Harris, a Past Master of that Lodge. See also Allen C. Clark, "Rev. Stephen Bloomer Balch, a Pioneer Preacher of Georgetown" in the *Records of the Columbia Historical Society,* Vol. 15 (1912), pp. 73–95.

of the Georgetown Lodge, which took charge of this ceremony. The only known contemporary newspaper account of this event, which took place on October 13, 1792, is found in an issue of the Charleston (South Carolina) *City Gazette* for November 15, 1792. According to this account "the procession was formed at the Fountain Inn, Georgetown" and proceeded "to the president's square" where "The ceremony was performed by brother Casaneva, master of the lodge, who delivered an oration well adapted to the occasion," and:

> After the ceremony was performed they returned, in regular order, to Mr. Suter's Fountain Inn, where an elegant dinner was provided, and the following toasts given in honor of the day:
>
> 1. The fifteen United States.
> 2. The President of the United States.
> 3. Our worthy brothers.
> 4. District of Columbia: may it flourish as the center of the political and commercial interests of America.
> 5. The city of Washington: may time render it worthy of the name it bears.
> 7. The French nation: a happy issue to their struggles for liberty and justice.
> 8. Marquis de la Fayette.
> 9. The masonic brethren throughout the universe.
> 10. The Rights of Man and the author of Common Sense.
> 11. The fair daughters of America.
> 12. The memory of those who have bled in the cause of liberty.
> 13. General Wayne and the western army: may their efforts be crowned by a speedy and honorable peace.
> 14. The governor of the State of Maryland.
> 15. The governor of the State of Virginia.
> 16. May peace, liberty and order extend from pole to pole.[26]

Lodge No. 9 played an important role also in the laying of the cornerstone of the United States Capitol on September 18, 1793, but no reference has been found to any dinner afterward at Suter's Tavern.[27]

---

[26] This quotation is as published in Potomac Lodge No. 5, *The Laying of the Corner Stone of the White House,* pp. 2–3, and omits the 6th toast. I have not seen the Charleston *City Gazette* for November 15, 1792, the only copy of which is reported to be in the Charleston Library Society. The Charleston *City Gazette* may have carried this item because Hoban was a resident of Charleston when he submitted his design for the White House. The name of the master of Lodge No. 9 at this time was Peter Casanave, not "Casaneva."

[27] *Ibid.,* pp. 4–7. Early in 1797 the reconstituted lodge after 22 meetings ceased to work, and no other lodge was chartered in Georgetown until 1806, which lodge with the establishment in 1811 of the Grand Lodge of the District of Columbia became known as Potomac Lodge No. 5. It is considered the descendant of the first Georgetown lodge and has custody of the minute books of the second lodge, which worked in the years 1795–1796.

This does not mean there were not other dinners on less important occasions, but unhappily Lodge No. 9 ceased to work in 1794, James Hoban having established and become the first master of a new lodge east of Rock Creek (chartered as Lodge No. 15 of Maryland). Georgetowners, including John Suter, petitioned for the Georgetown lodge to be reconstituted, which it was in 1795 as Lodge No. 19 of Maryland. Although Suter died late in 1794, his son, John Suter, Jr., took a very active part in the meetings of the reconstituted lodge, the minute books of which have been preserved by present Potomac Lodge No. 5 in its Georgetown meeting hall. Unfortunately those of the pioneer lodge, No. 9, are not known to be in existence.

As to events of a different kind taking place at Suter's, it should be of interest that the Georgetown *Times and Potowmack Packet* for November 25, 1789 presents the scheme of a lottery to raise $1,509 for the purpose of finishing the church on the road between Georgetown and Bladensburg known then and since as the Rock Creek Church. The names of the ten managers of the lottery, all of Georgetown, were listed and readers were informed that "as soon as the Tickets are sold, the Lottery will commence drawing at Mr. John Suter's at Georgetown." Many Georgetowners were at that time members of this historic church.

We find many advertisements of real estate sales to take place at Suter's. Some may found in Alexandria, Annapolis and Baltimore newspapers before the first Georgetown newspaper made its appearance in 1789. For instance, the *Maryland Gazette* of Annapolis, for March 22, 1787, carries notice of a sale "at the house of Mr. John Suter" of nearly 120 acres, which "Said land adjoins the addition to Georgetown and binds on the river for upwards of 3000 feet." In the early 1790's we find such notices in Georgetown papers nearly every month. A few examples may be offered. The *Times and Potowmack Packet* for April 21, 1790 has a notice that "by virtue of a Deed of Trust" from Col. John Murdock "sundry lots of valuable woodland . . . near this place will be sold to the highest bidder on April 22, 1790, at Suter's Tavern in this town." An issue of the same paper for September 15, 1790 contains a notice of a sherriff's sale of many farms and tracts of land the first day and of certain Georgetown lots the second "at John Suters, in Georgetown."

The *Times and Potowmack Packet* for December 22, 1790 has a notice of the sale "at the house of Mr. John Suter in Georgetown" of the "lot or acre of ground on which the old warehouse formerly stood." Just the previous month the same paper had carried a notice that certain subscribers appointed by the Court were ready to contract with workmen to erect a new warehouse "contiguous to the Old Inspection" in Georgetown and would on December 14 meet those interested "at Mr. Suter's Tavern" to offer the job of building it to the lowest bidder.[28] Then in April 1791 Robert Peter was offering for sale certain described buildings on lot No. 43 "situated near the center Warehouse which makes it a very convenient stand either for a Store or Tavern." The sale, he added, will be "On the first Monday in June next, if fair, if not the next fair day, for *ready money*, to the highest bidder," and "will commence at Mr. Suter's tavern at half past three o'clock in the afternoon." [29]

Often extensive tracts of land in Montgomery County were involved in these notices of public sales at Suter's. For example, a 517 acre tract is advertised in the Georgetown *Weekly Ledger* for March 19, 1791; and the same newspaper in its July 23, 1791 issue announces the sale of Magruder's and Beall's "Honesty," containing 337 acres about one mile above the Little Falls and five miles from Georgetown. But these sales are not limited to land in the newly established District of Columbia or Maryland or Virginia. The *Weekly Ledger* for January 28, 1792 has a notice of William Bayly, a Georgetown real estate speculator of this period, offering for sale 14,540 acres of land on Oconee River in Georgia "to the highest bidder at the house of Mr. John Suter in Georgetown."

We should not be surprised to find a notice in the *Weekly Ledger* (for September 17, 1791) of a sale at Suter's on October 18, "if not sold privately before that," of 25 or 30 "likely Negroes belonging to the estate of John Murdock" by his executors. Yet no notice of additional sales of slaves at the tavern has been noticed by this writer in newspapers examined until 1795 when the *Columbian Chronicle* of August 25 gives notice of the sale of several Negroes belonging to Jeremiah Orme "at Mrs. Suter's Tavern in George-Town." Perhaps we can draw the conclusion that public sales of human property at the tavern were not as frequent as those involving real estate.

We find the tavern contributing to the cultural life of the town by selling tickets to the theatre of the day. In August 1790 we find McGrath's Company of Comedians advertising their performances of *The Beggar's Opera, The Tragedy of Douglas, The West Indian,* a two act comedy of Garrick and other short plays, with "Tickets at three-quarters of a Dollar each, to be had at Mr. Suter's and Mrs.

[28] *Times and Potowmack Packet* for November 17, 1790.

[29] Georgetown *Weekly Ledger* for April 9, 1791.

White's Taverns." [30] And in October of the same year there is a notice of "the new American Company" presenting the "*Tragedy of Jane Shore,* a humorous dissertation on jealousy delivered by Mrs. McGrath, & a farce." Again, "tickets at Mr. Suter's and Mrs. White's Taverns. No money taken at the door." [31] As late as 1794 the McGrath Company was advertising a presentation of *Richard III* with an "afterpiece" to be "The Prisoner at Large; or the Irish Wedding." We are further told that between the play and the afterpiece there would be "An Interlude of Dancing—a Hornpipe by Mr. Kelly and a favorite song by Mrs. Fitzgerald." Tickets were still available at Suter's, but it is not known where the plays were presented.[32] We do however find a notice in the *Columbian Chronicle* for December 3, 1793 that "The dancing assemblies commence this evening at Mr. Suter's."

Also Suter's, in 1792, became the Georgetown headquarters of "an extensive *Circulating Library* . . . consisting of upwards of one thousand volumes; selected from the most approved Authors, both Ancient and Modern" which had been started by John Lockwood who had a bookstore in Fairfax Street in Alexandria. Subscriptions were to be received "by Mr. John Suter in Georgetown" but how much of the Library was kept there is not made clear. Lockwood stated, however, "The public may be assured that no Books tending to corrupt the morals of youth will ever be admitted into the above mentioned *Circulating Library*—on the contrary, every exertion shall be made to render it of general utility to the rising generation." [33]

Suter's Tavern also played an important part in the organization of the first bank in the District of Columbia, appropriately named the Bank of Columbia, chartered December 28, 1793, by the state of Maryland (the second bank chartered by that state). One will find in issues of the *Columbian Chronicle,* in February and March 1794, notices "that the subscribers to the said bank are requested to attend, in person or by proxy, at the house of Mr. Suter, in George-Town, on Thursday the 20th day of March next, for the purpose of electing 12 directors for the term of one year thereafter." The *Columbian Chronicle* for March 25 reports on the first meeting, March 22d, of the di-

[30] Notices in issues of the *Times and Potowmack Packet* for August 4 and 11, 1790, and the *Weekly Ledger* for August 14, 1790.

[31] *Times and Potowmack Packet* for October 27, 1790. Notices of a tavern in Georgetown run by Mrs. Jane White are found in newspapers from 1790 to 1794, but the writer has not determined its location. It seemed to be more of a boarding house. Dancing lessons were given at her house and on one occasion a French gentleman advertised teaching drawing and painting at her house. See *Times and Potowmack Packet* for May 26, 1790, and the *Weekly Ledger* for May 15, 1790, for examples.

[32] *Columbian Chronicle* (Georgetown) for February 25, 1794.

[33] *Weekly Ledger,* September 22, 1792.

rectors thus chosen, who had in turn unanimously chosen Benjamin Stoddert as their President. Samuel Hanson, publisher of the *Chronicle,* was chosen cashier. The first meeting of the directors may also have been at Suter's, but unfortunately the *Chronicle* news item does not tell us. The bank was needed not only for Georgetown businessmen but to handle the accounts of the District Commissioners and paper connected with speculative lot purchasing in the new city of Washington. In his will, brought in for probate in November of 1794, Suter mentions "my bank stock in the Bank of Columbia." [34]

Keeping a well-known tavern had its occasional problems. In the *Maryland Gazette* for May 30, 1793 may be found the following notice:

> A story having been propagated injurious to me, that the French minister [Edmond Genet] has met with insult at my house; justice to myself obliges me to declare, in this public manner, that so far from there being any foundation for this story, the minister did not put up at, nor was he in my house, during the short time he remained in this town, on his route from the southward toward Philadelphia.
>
> George Town, May 24, 1793.
>
> John Suter.

Genet, the new minister of the French Republic to the United States, had landed in Charleston, South Carolina, early in April and travelled by land to Philadelphia where he arrived in the middle of May. He was, of course, met everywhere by opposing opinions as to his mission, but the background for Suter's notice remains a mystery.

The following newspaper notices illustrate some other problems of a tavern keeper, the first to be found in the *Times and Potowmack Packet* for October 14, 1789:

> Five Guineas Reward will be given to any Person, who shall convict a *curious* customer of breaking open and taking letters committed to the charge of the subscriber, and deposited at the Bar of the Fountain Inn.
>
> John Suter.

The second is from the issue of the same newspaper for December 22, 1790:

> "Four Dollars Reward"
>
> Stolen out of the Stable of the Subscriber, last night, an English made Saddle, almost new, with a double flap, small plain Silver Bosses, pad covered with red, striped saddlecloth bound with red. Whoever will bring the Thief and Saddle to me, shall have the above Reward, or Two Dollars for the Saddle only.
>
> John Suter

[34] Recorded in Montgomery County Probate records, Liber C, folio 178.

And in the *Weekly Ledger* almost a year later (issue for November 26, 1791) we find the following insertion:

> John Suter Respectfully thanks those Gentlemen who have favored him with their custom since he commenced keeping Tavern in this town. A number of his customers being much in arrears, proves very injurious to him, he earnestly requests all such to settle with him before the 15th day of January next, or he must, in justice to himself take such steps as will be very disagreeable to him—He cannot give them any further *credit.*

But John Suter was to have more serious matters to worry about by 1794. According to family tradition he developed cancer, and leaving the tavern to his wife and son, he returned to his Montgomery County farm, where he died early in November.[35]

The death of John Suter did not at once make much difference in the running of Suter's Tavern, as it was still known when continued by his widow, Sarah Suter, for the following year (1795). She undoubtedly had help from their son, John Suter, Jr., but widows often proved to be very successful tavern keepers on their own. She was probably responsible in part for the reputation the place had achieved. The Commissioners for the District of Columbia again met there on January 9, 1795, according to their "Proceedings." [36] The Directors of the Potowmack Company voted on June 12, 1795 to meet on the 4th Monday in each month alternately in Alexandria and Georgetown, the next meeting to be at Mrs. Suter's tavern in Georgetown.[37] This was to be the meeting, already mentioned, that Washington attended.

Something new is noted in the arrival in town in June 1795 of a dentist, a Dr. Fendall, whose "residence will be at the House of Mrs. Suter." A few weeks later he announced his intention to leave about July 18th.[38] This was typical of the itinerant practitioners of the day. Another, a Doctor Beziers, who boasted of having practiced his profession in Europe for some years and later with Mr. Gardette, a dentist in Philadelphia, announced in April 1796 that he may be consulted at the tavern "for a few days." [39]

---

[35] John Suter's very interesting will was probated November 23, 1794, with his widow and John Suter, Jr. as executors. It may be found in the Montgomery County records at Rockville. (Wills, Liber C, folio 178.) Five children are mentioned, three sons, Alexander, John Jr. and Robert, and two daughters, Volinda (who married Alexander Smith) and Margaret (who married a Patterson).

[36] Vol. I, p. 352.

[37] "Proceedings" Vol. I, p. 49, in Potowmack Company records in the National Archives.

[38] *Columbian Chronicle,* June 19 and July 7, 1795.

[39] *Ibid.,* April 26, 1796.

One of the most interesting developments, looking backward, was ushered in by a notice in the *Maryland Gazette* for June 4, 1795 that "books will be opened, at the house of Mrs. Suter in George-Town on the first Monday in July next, to receive subscriptions to the number of 400 shares at $200 each share" for the first bridge across the Potomac River. It was not to be at Georgetown, of course, but up at Little Falls where the river was narrower. A little later it was announced in the *Gazette* that Timothy Palmer, "an artist eminently distinguished by the bridges he has lately built over the rivers Merrimack in Massachusetts and the Piscataqua in New Hampshire," had been engaged to construct this first Potomac bridge. On July 30, 1795, the *Maryland Gazette* carried a notice that a meeting of the subscribers to the Georgetown Bridge Company "is requested at the house of Mrs. Suter in George-Town on the 2d Tuesday in September next to elect 3 directors for managing all concerns of the Company for the present year." Subsequent meetings of the Georgetown Bridge Company were held at this tavern under later proprietors. The first bridge at this site, a wooden one, was opened in 1797 and had a life of seven years before it collapsed. The Company built a second wood structure, designed by Theodore Burr, a bridge engineer who had achieved fame for his truss design, but this was carried away within six months by a flood. Eventually, in 1805, the Company constructed one of the first suspension bridges in the nation, known as the "Chain Bridge," which lasted until 1840.[40]

The association of the Suter family with the Fountain Inn came to a close at the end of the year 1795. A number of Georgetowners had subscribed to the erection of a new tavern which they felt to be a needed improvement in the town. It was appropriately named the Union Tavern and was completed late in 1795, at a cost of $16,000, on the northeast corner of present M and 30th Streets (then Bridge and Washington Streets). John Suter, Jr. and Samuel Huff formed a partnership and became the first landlords of this new establishment, and Mrs. Suter, who presumably did not wish to compete with them, gave up the old Fountain Inn.[41] Huff died unexpectedly in January 1798 and Suter, as the surviving partner, continued to run the Union

[40] The history of the Georgetown Bridge Company, as presented in a memorial to Congress in 1826, is printed in 19th Congress, 1st Session, *Senate Document No. 86*.

[41] The best contemporary description of the new Union Tavern, to be the leading Georgetown tavern for a generation, is to be found in the *Centinel of Liberty* for February 18, 1800, when the trustees advertise it for sale. The partnership of Huff and Suter is mentioned in the same paper for November 17, 1797, when it was announced that it was being dissolved "by mutual consent," with the business to be conducted in the future by Huff. His death changed the picture, however. See the notice by John Suter, Jr., "surviving partner," in the *Centinel of Liberty* for February 20, 1798.

Tavern alone until February 1801, when Charles McLaughlin took over.[42] One has to realize that occasional newspaper references from 1796 to 1800 to Mr. Suter's tavern are not to the Fountain Inn. John Suter, Jr. in a notice in the *Washington Federalist* for December 31, 1800 requested all persons indebted "to the late firm of Huff and Suter" and "to the estate of John Suter," his father, "or to the Subscriber" to make immediate payment as "He is determined to move from this State." This is the last of the Suters as tavern keepers in Georgetown.

C. LATER HISTORY OF THE FOUNTAIN INN

Meanwhile, the Fountain Inn had continued to operate under different landlords. The first after Mrs. Suter was Clement Sewall and one could cite a number of newspaper notices of happenings there through 1796—sales of Negroes and lands (including a mill seat on Rock Creek), tickets in the Washington lottery #2 (lotteries for lots east of Rock Creek were becoming common), the newly organized Georgetown militia corps dining there on Washington's birthday "after many accurate firings in honor of the day" and others.[43] But Sewall was understandably attracted to the new City Tavern, completed late in 1796 and still standing today on the south side of M Street just west of Wisconsin. He became its first landlord, moving in by December when we have notices of both the Georgetown Corporation and the Georgetown Bridge Company meeting with him.[44] Clearly the Fountain Inn was to have another major competitor.

Who was to be the next landlord? We find the following notice,

[42] McLaughlin had been in charge of the City Tavern and was a partner in the stage lines running from Georgetown to Baltimore and to Frederick when he purchased the Union Tavern, which he ran until his death in 1806. See the writer's article "Stagecoach Days in the District of Columbia" in the *Records of the Columbia Historical Society of Washington, D. C. 1948–1950* (1952), especially pages 19 and 37.

[43] Notices referring either to the "Fountain Inn" or "Sewall's Tavern" may be found in issues of the *Columbian Chronicle* for February 24 and April 8 and 26; in the *Centinel of Liberty* for June 17 and 24 and July 8; and the *Washington Gazette* for July 6 and 11; all in 1796. Thomas Twining, an English traveller in America in 1795, recites an interesting stagecoach trip from Baltimore to Georgetown through the rain, which required them to lower all the leathern curtains of their coach thus rendering the interior "very dark and oppressively hot." They were happy to descend from their "prison" at the "Fountain Tavern." He follows with compliments for the landlord (Thomas Twining, *Travels in America 100 Years Ago* [New York, 1894] p. 97). Thus the Fountain Inn continued to be Georgetown's stage coach tavern as it had been under the Suters. By 1800 the Union Tavern had become the main headquarters for stage lines.

[44] Notices of both these meetings are to be found in the *Centinel of Liberty* for December 23, 1796.

dated December 16, 1796, in a number of issues of the *Centinel of Liberty:*

> The Subscriber informs the public and his friends in general that he has opened a Tavern at the Fountain Inn, lately occupied by Mr. Clement Sewall. Those who choose to call on him will be thankfully received and well entertained.
>
> Henry Medley[45]

It is interesting that we find advertised for sale, in the *Centinel of Liberty* for January 27, 1797, "Lot No. 48 near Medley's Tavern . . . with its improvements." Lot 48 was on the west side of Wisconsin Avenue almost directly across from Lot 51 on the east side where I believe Suter's Tavern to have been located. Medley got the Georgetown Corporation meetings back at the Fountain Inn in March and May[46] but the September 29, 1797 issue of the *Centinel of Liberty* carries notice of the death of Henry Medley. Clearly the Fountain Inn was in for a depressed period. I have been unable to find any certain data on the occupancy of the Fountain Inn for the later months of 1797, or for 1798 and 1799, a period for which there are unfortunately few newspapers in existence.

It was not until the last of June, 1800, that the *Centinel of Liberty* carried a notice under the heading "Sign of the Ship" which ran for several weeks. Francis Kearns who signs it begs leave to inform the public "that he has rented the tavern formerly occupied by Mr. Suter, called the Fountain Inn, where he has laid in all kinds of liquors of the first quality and every other accommodation necessary for travellers." He added that he would accommodate 6 or 8 gentlemen boarders and keep a few horses. For the first time the old tavern has a new name. And it may be significant that to identify it Kearns goes back to "Mr. Suter," ignoring all proprietors in between. It may be significant that the July 29, 1800 issue of the *Centinel of Liberty* carries a notice of a public sale of a dark grey horse "at the Sign of the Ship, High Street, Georgetown." That should help, when associated with Kearns' announcement of the month before, to fix the location of Suter's Tavern as being on High Street (present Wisconsin Avenue).

It is important to note next that the *Centinel of Liberty,* for November 7, 1800, carries a notice of the following Monday "being the

[45] *Centinel of Liberty,* January 13, 1797.

[46] Georgetown Corporation minutes, 1800–1805 [in Manuscript Division, Library of Congress].

day for holding an election for electors of President and Vice President throughout this state," and that "voters of that part of Montgomery County lying within the territory of Columbia comprising the 5th District are informed that the election for that district will be held at Mr. Kearns' Tavern, Georgetown where it was held for representatives to the assembly last month." This notice was signed by William D. Beall, John Threlkeld, and Thomas Corcoran as judges of the election. This, of course, was "the election between Mr. Jefferson and Mr. Adams for the Presidency" which Christian Hines described so vividly in his *Recollections* and remembered as "held in Suter's Tavern in Georgetown in the year 1800" which "was a one-story frame, and stood on High Street [Wisconsin Avenue] between Bridge [M Street] and Water [K] Streets and a little east of the Canal bridge." Mr. Hines was 19 years old in 1800, and he worked for and lived with Mr. Joseph Green who had "moved his family down High Street to opposite Mr. Suter's Tavern" where "he carried on the soap and chandler's business." [47] Apparently the establishment, no matter who the landlord might be, was still known in the community as "Suter's Tavern." Also an advertisement for a strayed or stolen horse later in 1800 refers to "Mr. Kearns' Fountain Inn." [48] Had the "Sign of the Ship" been abandoned? We find no later references except to "Kearns' Tavern." We may read in the *Federalist,* for February 28, 1801, that "Ordinary keepers and Retailer's Licenses will be granted by the Mayor's Court, on Monday next at Kearns' Tavern." The Georgetown Corporation again met "at the tavern of Francis Kearns" in April and June, 1801.[49] The June 17th meeting was especially concerned with the membership of the "Commission of Paving" which was to have responsibility for converting the natural roadways of Georgetown to graded and paved streets.

Again, unhappily, we read in the *Washington Federalist* (October 22, 1802) of the death in South Carolina of Francis Kearns "formerly a resident of Georgetown." We have found no reference to any other landlord looking after the old inn for the two years from July 1801 through June 1803. Perhaps these gaps can be filled in some day, but it will require additional research. We are happy to find in the issue of the *Washington Federalist for* July 8, 1803 the following announcement of a new period of life for the old Fountain Inn:

---

[47] Christian Hines, *Early Recollections of Washington City* (Washington, 1866), pp. 5–9 and 88–90.

[48] *Centinel of Liberty,* November 14, 1800, advertisement of Dennis Cochran.

[49] Georgetown Corporation minutes, 1800–1805 [in Manuscript Division, Library of Congress].

> Anchor Tavern
> and
> Oyster House
> (Late the Fountain Inn)
>
> George Pitt having taken and entered upon the above Inn and fitted it up at a considerable expense respectfully solicits the patronage and support of his late friends, when a resident at the Eagle Tavern, those who frequented the Fountain Inn, and the public in general.

Pitt operated the Anchor Tavern, or the "Golden Anchor" as it was sometimes referred to, or just "the tavern of George Pitt," from this date until his death in May 1816, making it for these 13 years almost as much of an institution in Georgetown as was Suter's Fountain Inn, but a very different one.[50] Previously, as mentioned in his notice, Pitt had been the proprietor of the Eagle Tavern, which, in a notice dated January 28, 1801, he had described as a "Beer, Beefsteak and Oyster House," located in a house "lately occupied by Messrs Dodge and Tenney opposite the Lower Ferry" which "he has fitted up in the neatest and most comfortable manner." He further described this as "the first attempt of the kind made in Georgetown," [51] and apparently it was this ambition to carry on a special beefsteak and oyster house that he now transferred to the old Fountain Inn.

Pitt's advertisements over the years are especially interesting and reveal an educated man about whom one would like to know more. He could quote the ancients, Dr. Johnson, the Marquis of Condorcet, William Godwin and others on the merits of the oyster and he advised temperance for his patrons while advertising his very special liquor supply.[52] In a notice in 1805 of the necessity of putting his business on a cash basis, he refers to himself as the "worn out oysterman." [53] In 1808 he informs Georgetowners and others that his tavern:

> has been completely repaired and improvements added as to make it comfortable and convenient for the weary traveller—retired apartments for the philosopher or man of business—an extensive view of that beautiful island belonging to General John Mason, river Potomac. A copious and elegant garden with rural and public walks and arbours for the desponding lover to meditate on the object of his affections—and the man

[50] Pitt's death notice is in *The Messenger and Town and City Gazette* for May 19, 1816.

[51] *Georgetown Museum Advertiser,* January 28, 1801. Before coming to Georgetown Pitt had been in charge of a tavern on the upper ferry over the Anacostia River in Washington. See *Centinel of Liberty,* January 21, 1800.

[52] *Washington Federalist,* September 26, 1804.

[53] *Ibid.,* September 2, 1805.

of pleasure to pass away a dull and tedious hour. And its being in the centre of the town, near the banks and other offices and the nearest tavern to *commercial characters,* renders his situation more convenient to the planter, farmer and man of business; and gives it a decided preference over any other—to which add the keeping of good and attentive servants, the best of regulations in his house; liquors equal to any in the Union; good beds, wholesome diet, moderate charges, and a determination to use every exertion in his power to give general satisfaction.[54]

Other newspaper notices reveal that, despite the importance of newer taverns in the town, the Anchor Inn had become an important meeting place for Georgetowners themselves. Elections to the Common Council of Georgetown were held there and also for members of the Board of Alderman.[55]

The War of 1812 led to the formation of a number of volunteer organizations that seemed to make George Pitt's Anchor Inn their meeting place. One of these was the Columbian Hussars, commanded by John Peter. A meeting was requested at "Mr. Pitt's Tavern" on June 23, 1813 for a company court martial case, another in May 1814 "to elect officers," and a general meeting on June 22, 1814.[56] Notices of meetings of the Georgetown Field Artillery, the Light Infantry Company, and the Georgetown Rifle Company are also to be noted.[57] We cannot give details of these and other meetings. We can note only that *The Messenger* for May 29, 1816 announces a "Public Sale" of "all the goods and Chattels of the late George Pitt, deceased, consisting of all his Household and Kitchen Furniture, Beds, Bedding, and Bedsteads, bar utensils, his stock of fine pale ale, also a Negro man." The sale was to take place at 10 a. m., June 1, "at the late residence of the deceased, Sign of the Golden Anchor Tavern."

Someone must have continued keeping the tavern open for we find a notice for the Georgetown Rifle Company to meet July 27,

[54] *Ibid.,* October 1, 1808.

[55] *Federal Republican,* February 22 and December 20, 1814; February 18 and July 4, 1815; and *The Messenger* for May 25, 1816, are examples. No effort has been made to locate all such examples. A notice in the *Federal Republican* for February 8, 1815 notes that George Pitt was paid $11.00 for two elections held at his house the previous year.

[56] *Federal Republican* for June 21, 1813, and May 13 and June 17, 1814. For details on the Columbian Hussars and other militia companies in Georgetown, see Frederick P. Todd, "The Militia and Volunteers of the District of Columbia, 1783–1820" in the *Records of the Columbia Historical Society of Washington, D. C. 1948–1950* (1952), pp. 379–439.

[57] *Federal Republican* for September 20, 1813; July 25 and August 11, 1814; and January 4, 1815.

1816 "at early candle-light at the Anchor Tavern nearly opposite Mr. Simm's Tavern." [58] In 1818 they were meeting "at Mr. Eno's . . . at early candle-light" [59] and Mr. Eno seems to have been the proprietor in these years for in *The Metropolitan* for July 21, 1821 we are informed "Mr. Howard has taken out a tavern license for the venerable stand, nearly opposite to Mr. Semmes, formerly occupied by Mr. Eno . . ." Perhaps we might emphasize the word "venerable" for it will appear again, and it may be of interest that in the following August we find a notice requesting members of the Mechanical Fire Company "to meet at Mr. Howard's Tavern, opposite Semmes' Hotel *Tomorrow Evening* at early candle-light." [60]

But we cannot note all references to this old tavern. Let us move ahead to 1824 when, in its issue for August 24, *The Metropolitan* has an editorial on Lafayette's arrival in New York and his possible visit to Georgetown. "If happily the Marquis should indulge any reminiscence of a former period," the editor writes, "he will at once recognize the old inn where he stopped in his youth, which still stands unhurt amid the decay of ancient buildings, as if to perpetuate the recollection of an event which always associates something dear to our hearts." In October of that year Lafayette did visit Georgetown, whereupon *The Metropolitan* informs us: "The General looked in vain to recognize one spot, one house that he had before visited; all had passed away and were replaced by splendid buildings and improvements; not a vestige could he trace, save the old Inn which was venerable even in its ruins." [61]

We find no other references to this "venerable" tavern for the next ten years. Perhaps it was in "ruins" and was no longer operated as a tavern. Part of the lot was involved in the construction of the Chesapeake and Ohio Canal. We skip ahead to the issue of *The Metropolitan* for May 1, 1835 in which we find the following notice signed by Thomas Wright, then a prominent Georgetown auctioneer: "On Monday, the 4th of May next . . . I shall sell by order of the Corporation without reserve the old building, formerly Pitt's Tavern, situate on High Street adjoining the Bridge over the Canal, with all the

[58] *The Messenger* for July 24, 1816. The reference to "Mr. Simm's Tavern" is again to Joseph Semmes' Columbian Inn on old lot No. 49 on the west side of Wisconsin Avenue almost opposite although a little south of lot No. 51 on which the Anchor Tavern was located.

[59] *The National Messenger* for May 4, 1818. In its issue for February 14, 1817, this paper had a notice of an election for eleven members of the Board of Common Council of the Georgetown Corporation to be held "at Mr. Eno's Tavern."

[60] *Metropolitan* for August 7, 1821; also August 21, 1821.

[61] *Ibid.* for October 19, 1824.

back buildings, to be removed by the purchaser within fourteen days from the day of sale." Although no further record has been found of this sale, it would seem likely that it chronicles the end of the story for the King's Arms, the Fountain Inn, and the Golden Anchor.

D. WHERE WAS SUTER'S TAVERN?

Why is it so difficult to settle the location of Suter's Tavern? If we can no longer have the old wooden building itself, certainly we should determine the site and place there an appropriate plaque telling residents and tourists in the coming Bicentennial years: "This was the place." But the office of National Capital Parks will tell us there is already a marker at the northwest corner of Congress and K Streets on land now owned by the Federal Government. And earlier there were inscriptions on the walls of the "Old Stone House," also known as "Washington's Headquarters," on the north side of M Street. Actually, it was the publication in 1940 of Bessie W. Gahn's book, *George Washington's Headquarters in Georgetown,* assuming to prove that Suter's Tavern and therefore "Washington's Headquarters" (whatever was meant by that term) was in the "Old Stone House" that, arousing my skepticism, prompted me to begin checking records and newspapers. Also because Suter's was the first stopping place in Georgetown for stagecoaches, I was anxious to pin down its location in connection with an article I had in mind.[62] I had to admire the amount of research Mrs. Gahn had for the first time conducted into original sources, yet still I questioned her interpretations and her conclusions. She so wanted to prove that the "Old Stone House" was Suter's Tavern.

I looked on with approval when Cornelius Heine, working as an historian with the National Capital Parks, proved in a brilliant example of historical research that the "Old Stone House" was never Suter's Tavern despite the fact that it was hoped by many that Mrs. Gahn's thesis could be authenticated.[63] Actually there was a strong movement to get the Federal Government to purchase the property as an historical site of national importance, but the Park Service, primarily because of Mr. Heine's research, acquired it instead because of its "architectural merit" as an example of a colonial building in early Georgetown.

But to help to prove that the "Old Stone House" was not Suter's

[62] This was my article, "Stagecoach Days in the District of Columbia," in the *Records of the Columbia Historical Society of Washington, D. C. 1948–1950* (1952), pp. 1–42.

[63] Cornelius W. Heine, *The Old Stone House,* (106 pages, processed by National Capital Parks, Washington, D. C., 1955).

Tavern, Mr. Heine felt he had to find a different location for the tavern. To my dismay he decided that the real site was at the northwest corner of K and 31st Streets (formerly Water and Congress Streets) where the Park Service placed its plaque in 1955. In the 1955 announcement of the National Park Service and in Mr. Heine's book, *The Old Stone House,* three reasons were advanced for accepting this site. They were:

1. The "written reminiscences of Mary Suter," great granddaughter of John Suter, who had, according to Mr. Heine, stated that the tavern was on that corner;

2. A photograph which Mr. Heine came across in the prints division of the Library of Congress, which had pencilled on its back the words "Suter's Tavern" and showed detail of the roof of Grace Episcopal Church in the background which exactly matched that in a picture the Park Service photographer made from the same spot; and

3. A notation on an original tax assessment list, 1793–1798, found in the County Assessor's office at Rockville, which described property owned by Peter Casanave as being "opposite Suter's Tavern;" and Mr. Heine locates as one of Casanave's Georgetown properties, a Lot #1, on the south or water side of K street opposite the supposed tavern site.

Taken together, these three items of evidence were deemed sufficient in the words of the announcement to "prove conclusively" that the site of the tavern had at last been determined, and on the basis of this statement, presumably, the present marker was placed on the site.

Let us examine these three arguments in this order, which is the order, Mr. Heine implies, in which he made his discoveries.

First, as to Mary Suter's "reminiscences." On page 53 of *The Old Stone House* these are quoted as follows:

> . . . It was in this long low building, at what is now the northwest corner of Water and Congress (31st) Street, that Washington purchased the site for the capital. In later years it became an oyster house and a restaurant, but in these early days it was the last proud word in tavernkeeping.

Authority for this quotation is given in a footnote as "Mary D. Suter, 'Biography of John Suter,' Washingtoniana Section, District of Columbia Library." This rather strange 2-page typed copy of what purports to be a letter Mary Suter sent her cousin in 1920 has pencilled on it at the top a note by Miss Edith Ray Saul, long chief of the Washingtoniana Section, to the effect that an unsigned popular article in the feature section of the *Sunday Star* for December 26,

1920 is the source for the information on Suter's Tavern. Mary Suter was doubtless responsible for the last part of the letter which consisted of accurate family history. The words Mr. Heine attributed to her appear to go back to an 1896 clipping, also in the Washingtoniana Division, signed by J. S. Tucker, where we read, "It stands today on the northwest corner of Water and Congress, or Thirty-first streets, and is now occupied as an oyster house and restaurant." It appears from other similarities that the 1920 newspaper writer used the Tucker article as a source.

Second, as to the picture, there is in the library of the Columbia Historical Society a letter in Mary Suter's own handwriting to John Clagett Proctor, dated March 17, 1928, commenting on an article printed in the *Sunday Star* of February 19th in which Proctor had referred to Suter's Tavern. Her words are:

> The picture which you show of the tavern must be imaginary, as my father was born in 1828 and he had never seen it. Surely the small building that has been presented so often lately was too diminutive to accommodate the many guests assembled there.

The picture to which Mary Suter referred, and which appeared with Proctor's article, is the same one Mr. Heine found at the Library of Congress. It is of a very small building, which was standing on a tiny lot on this northwest corner until it was torn down early in this century. And it does have the word "oysters" on it, but I do not think that proves anything as to its antiquity or historical association. On the back of the picture the words "Suter's Tavern" are pencilled followed by a question mark which was not mentioned in the literature put out by the Park Service. These words could have been put there by any keeper of such pictures in a newspaper "morgue," which may have been the source for this.

Thus the first two bits of evidence adduced for this location prove to be based merely on newspaper stories dating back to the final decade of the last century.

Only the third reason submitted involved a contemporary document or primary source. This was an original assessment book for Montgomery County for the years 1793–1797, in the custody of the County Assessor at Rockville. One portion of this volume was headed "An account of the Lotts and Houses in George-Town by Joseph Sprigg Belt assessor for 1793." In it are two entries for Peter Casanave, an important citizen of the day, as follows:

1 House and Wharf	800 £
1 ditto opposite Suters	300 £

In *The Old Stone House* the word "Tavern" is added within quotation marks after "opposite Suters," but it is not found in the original. Mr. Heine assumes Casanave's house is south of modern K Street because he has concluded Suter's Tavern is north. But this is before the causeway, running straight east from the foot of Wisconsin Avenue where the modern K Street is now, was constructed. The only street then in this area was Wapping Street shown on all Eighteenth Century maps, including the original survey of Georgetown, as running northeast from the foot of Wisconsin Avenue at a compass reading of North, 70° East, so that it intersected Congress Street 128 feet further north than the present intersection of K and Congress. Actually Wapping went northeast along the old shore line which was then farther inland. It is true that Thomas Sim Lee, William Deakins, Jr. and Peter Casanave did own what land existed on the river side of Wapping Street in the early 1790's. It was part of the acreage known as "Frogland" in the early records. If this were the tract meant I believe it would have been mentioned by name, and that all three of the owners' names would have been listed. The entire site of the building shown in the photograph submitted as proof by the Park Service would have been on the water side of Wapping Street in Suter's day.[64]

The 1798 assessment book for Georgetown happens to be in the custody of the Maryland Historical Society in Baltimore.[65] It is more specific in its locations of owners' lots and buildings and describes the latter in detail because even windows were counted and taxed. Robert Peter is shown as the owner of lot No. 68 in the original survey, the large one at the northwest corner of the intersection of Wapping and Congress Streets, but there were no buildings on it.[66] It would seem

[64] The best map on which to study this relationship is the large official "Map of Georgetown in the District of Columbia Prepared from Survey and Other Data under an Act of the Legislature, Approved Dec. 28th, 1871." This map was prepared in the office of the Surveyor for the District of Columbia and has the boundaries of "Old Georgetown," that is the original survey, superimposed in red on the modern map, using the old survey declinations of the needle in plotting it. Wapping Street as shown on this map and on the original survey is a feature of all contemporary maps of Georgetown down to the "Map of Georgetown with the Additions" prepared by Francis Fenwick, Surveyor of Washington County, in 1814.

It should be added that both John Suter and Peter Casanave owned lots in other parts of Georgetown at this time, although I must admit that I have not been able to locate the two that were opposite each other. The 1793–1797 assessment book was not specific in its locations.

[65] The writer has a microfilm copy. Patrick Magruder was the assessor.

[66] This was the most southeasterly lot in what was becoming known as Peter's Square. Robert Peter already in 1798 owned at least 9 of the 12 lots in it. He had purchased lot 68 as well as lot 67 bounding 68 on the north and 71 bounding it on the west and going all the way to Wisconsin Avenue. Lot No. 68 was valued at only $900, less than any other lot on the square.

there would be if Suter's Tavern were down here under the hill, a very unlikely place in my opinion for a tavern so prominent as Suter's in the 1780's and 1790's.

I would like to place the tavern in our imagination up the hill on lot No. 51 on the east side of Wisconsin Avenue, the only other place offering serious contention and the site that I obviously prefer. What does the 1798 assessment book say about this large lot, 133 × 202 feet, owned by Robert Peter? It has on it a "wood dwelling house 30 × 30, 1 story, 8 windows 5 × 2½—1 house 2 story wood 16 × 24 8 windows 5 × 2½ a kitchen 1 story wood 16 × 24 3 windows 4 × 2½ 1 Brick stable 1½ story 24 × 50."[67] The whole, consisting of four buildings, three of wood and one of brick, was valued at $6,000. Although the word "tavern" is not used, the facilities, especially the large stable and the kitchen, seem suitable for a tavern. The name of no occupant is given, but this is one of those years after the Suters left when we do not know who was landlord. The tavern may have been vacant. Only two lots on Peter's Square had a comparable valuation, one of them being Robert Peter's own home on lot No. 69, the second one south from No. 51 with a two story brick house, 33 × 40, on it plus other buildings and also valued at $6,000. One can from this assessment book trace the nature of all the buildings in 1798 on Peter's Square as well as of those on the west side of Wisconsin Avenue. One is tempted to compare the buildings on lot No. 51 with those on part of lot No. 49 on the west side (facing 53 feet on Wisconsin Avenue and 200 feet back on the north side of Cherry Street) where Isaac Pollock had just completed the Columbian Inn. This now had on it "1 Brick House 3 stories 38 × 53 21 windows 3 × 6 21 windows 3 × 5. Pk [plank ?] House 2 stories 25 × 25 7 windows 3 × 5 1 Pk Stable 20 × 50 1 story 1 Brick Smoke House 10 × 10." All these new buildings were also valued at only $6,000. One may be interested in the similar dimensions of the stables for these two taverns. But the Fountain Inn now clearly had, along with the City Tavern and the Union Tavern, another formidable rival. If it were unoccupied in 1798, this may be part of the explanation.

The "City of Georgetown Assessment Records, 1800–1807," are in the National Archives and are arranged alphabetically.[68] I am tempted

---

[67] These assessment volumes are not paged but entries run roughly alphabetically by owners' names. The wording of entries appears confusing at first, especially since the different buildings and their features are not more clearly separated by punctuation.

[68] The records of the Georgetown City Government, 1800–1879, are in the National Archives, Record Group 351. They include assessment records 1800–1818 after which there seems to be a gap of some years.

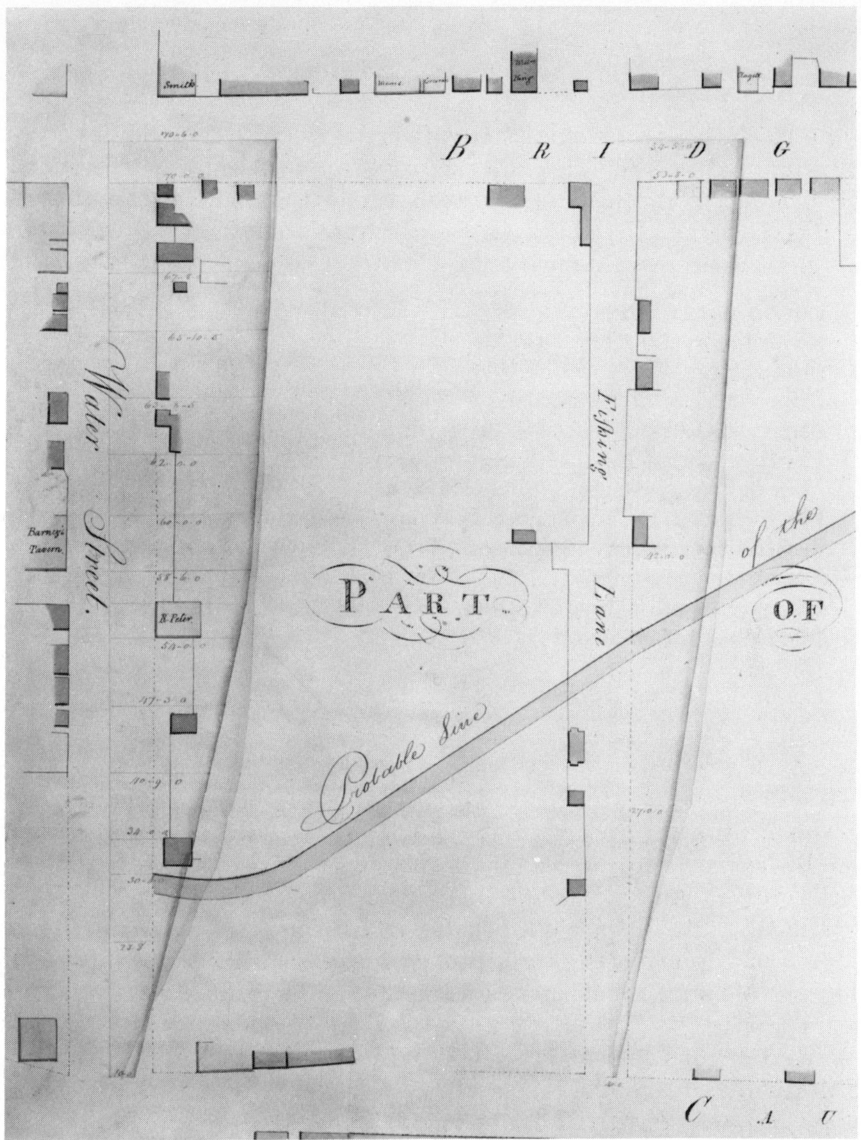

Photograph courtesy of the Library of Congress

Section of 1800 King-Latrobe map showing buildings.

Part of sheet 4 of King-Latrobe map entitled "Plans and Sections of the Proposed Continuation of the Canal at the Little Falls of the Potomac to the Navy Yard in the City of Washington."

This small section of a large map was selected to show buildings as of 1800, when Nicholas King made his survey, on streets bounding "Peter's Square" (today bounded by 31st Street, M Street, Wisconsin Avenue and K Street).

Suter's Tavern, on the east side of Wisconsin, might be expected to be labelled, just as "Barney's Tavern" is on the west side and a little south, but no keeper is known in 1800 until June when Francis Kearns informs the public "that he has rented the tavern formerly occupied by Mr. Suter."

to quote all real property listed under "Robert Peter, Senior" because he died in 1806 and the picture after distribution to his five sons becomes complicated. The list's implications are better understood if it is remembered that in these years Water Street was the name of present Wisconsin Avenue below M Street.

1 Lot on Water Street	800
1 Lot Improved on Jefferson Street	1000
3 Lots on Jefferson Street	1000
1 Improved Lot on Beall Street	600
1 Improved Lot on Water Street—Stable	3260
1 Improved Lot on Water Street—Tavern	2864
½ Lot on Water Street	528
1 Lot Improved on Water Street—Your dwelling	5088
1 Lot Improved on Water Street—Cromwells	1500
1 Lot on Bridge Street	1340
1 Improved Lot on Bridge Street—Daniels	1940
1 Improved Lot on Bridge Street—Lonys	1119
1 Lot on Fishing Lane	445
1 Lot on Wapping Improved—Stone House	4380
	21125

As will be seen in this list the lots are not numbered as in the 1798 assessment, nor do they have the details as to buildings. Apparently the old tavern building was becoming less valuable than the newer brick stable. Significantly, the lots on Fishing Lane (Congress Street) are still not valued high enough for any tavern to be located there. It is my opinion that the unimproved lot on Fishing Lane valued at $445 is No. 68 on the corner of Wapping and Fishing Lane that was vacant in 1798.

Robert Peter's lots in Peter's Square after his death appeared to be all divided into five lots to give his five sons each their share. Thus lot No. 51 was divided into five lots: number 15 coming into the possession of George Peter; 16 which Thomas Peter inherited; 17 which David Peter inherited (all three fronting on Wisconsin Avenue); and two back lots, 18 and 19, which I have not traced. It is significant, I feel, that in the Georgetown Assessment volumes for 1813–1815 and 1815–1818 we find Thomas Peter who inherited the middle of the three lots on Wisconsin Avenue, charged with "pt. family square O T [meaning "Old Town"] 44.8 Water [Street, meaning Wisconsin Avenue] ptr [?] Pitt's Kitchen." [69] Such an entry

[69] Page 12 in the 1813–1815 volume and page 15 of the 1815–1818 volume, both in the National Archives. One is disappointed not to find reference to other buildings

would mean little if we did not know Pitt was then located in the old Fountain Inn.

There were in those days no numbers on homes and business buildings in Georgetown to which potential customers could be directed so we find business notices like that of Ben Ellinwood advertising his furniture store "Opposite Mr. Suter's Tavern." [70] In 1791 George Stevens who had been keeping a store and advertising imported goods gave notice that he had "for sale a small House, nearly opposite Mr. Suter's Tavern, in this town, now occupied as a Barber's shop; it will answer a small family, or may be converted into an Attorney's Office, etc., subject to a small ground rent." [71] And one cannot omit mentioning the notice of John Suter, Jr., in the *Weekly Ledger* for September 22, 1792, that he was commencing the clock and watchmaking business at the sign of the Regulator, "directly opposite the Fountain Inn." Would all of these business places have been opposite the tavern if it had been down on the southeast corner of Peter's Square? It would seem that the west side of Wisconsin Avenue would have been a more natural location.

Mentioned earlier in this paper is the reference in Christian Hines' *Early Recollections of Washington City* to Joseph Green, who "opposite Mr. Suter's tavern . . . carried on the soap and chandler's business." It will be seen that I go along with Allen C. Clark who, in his studies of Suter's Tavern, said: "Christian Hines knew where it was for he in his boyhood lived close by it." [72] Actually Hines lived with the Green family for a number of years. We might note that Mrs. Green was still living in the area in 1809, for a deed of that year refers to "part of lot 49 . . . upon which Mrs. Green now resides." [73]

Some sites can be discovered only by the digging of archeologists. But the site of Suter's Tavern, if there is still a question, is more likely to be determined by the further digging of historians and archivists in additional contemporary published sources, in collec-

---

of the tavern, but buildings were not being accounted for in detail as in the 1798 assessment volume. This mention of Pitt's kitchen seems added simply to help identify the lot.

[70] *Times and Potowmack Packet,* August 11, 1790.

[71] *Weekly Ledger,* June 18, 1791. Notices of Stevens' store, which was at a different location at least part of the time, may be found in the *Times and Potowmack Packet* for November 25, 1789, and July 21 and November 17, 1790. In 1792 Richard Ober was advertising an extensive assortment of imported goods at his store "nearly opposite Mr. Suter's Fountain Inn." (*Weekly Ledger,* December 15, 1792.)

[72] *Records of the Columbia Historical Society,* Vol. 26 (1924), p. 193.

[73] Deed registered in Liber W, folio 376, in Register of Deeds Office, District of Columbia.

tions of personal manuscripts, some of which may not yet be available to the public, and in repositories of public records. Publication of this paper was postponed in the hope that I could turn up more information, and I have. But there is more digging to be done than any one person can be expected to do. I only hope that in presenting some of my findings I have provided an accurate outline of the tavern's history into which discoveries by searchers of tomorrow can be fitted more easily.

After this essay was in page proof, news was received from Dr. and Mrs. Robert S. McCeney of Laurel, Maryland, of two portraits in their possession: one of John Suter, the tavern keeper, and another of his wife Sarah and their daughter Margaret. They have sent us copies so attractive that we greatly regret not being able to add them to illustrations in this volume, but we do hope to reproduce them in a future volume of the *Records*. Perhaps other pictures and documents will be found that will result in a supplementary article on Suter's Tavern. We invite contributions that will help complete the tavern's story in the coming Bicentennial years.

The Duc De La Rochefoucauld-Liancourt's Visit to the Federal City in 1797: A New Translation

DAVID J. BRANDENBURG
AND MILLICENT H. BRANDENBURG

La Rochefoucauld-Liancourt's *Voyage dans les États-Unis d'amérique, fait en 1795, 1796 et 1797*, in eight volumes, is an often cited but little read source book for the federalist period of United States history.[1] Published in the spring of 1799 by DuPont de Nemours in Paris, the work is a very rich document about America that was carefully prepared by its distinguished author and painstakingly edited by the DuPonts on the eve of their emigration to the United States. Interestingly enough, an authorized German translation of the first half of this work appeared in Hamburg at least six months before the French edition was released;[2] further, the first installment of an unauthorized English translation was published not more than three months after the DuPont volumes appeared.[3]

Copyright, 1975, by David J. Brandenburg and Millicent H. Brandenburg.

[1] François-Alexandre-Frédéric duc de La Rochefoucauld-Liancourt, *Voyage dans les États-unis d'amérique, fait en 1795, 1796, et 1797* (8 vols., Paris, 1799). For an examination of the use, non-use and misuse of this work by American historians, see David J. Brandenburg, "A French Aristocrat Looks at American Farming: La Rochefoucauld Liancourt's *Voyages* [*sic.*] *dans les États-Unis*," in *Agricultural History*, Vol. 32, no. 3, 1958.

[2] De la Rochefoucauld Liancourt, *Reisen in den Jahren 1795, 1796 and 1797 durch alle der belegenen Staaten der Nordamerikanischen Republik; imgleichen durch Ober-Canada und das Land der Irokesen. Nebst zuverlässigen Nachrichten von Unter-Canada. Aus der Französischen Handschrift übersetzt.* (3 vols., Hamburg, 1799). This publication was part of a series of travel books—*Neuere Geschichte der See-und Land-Reisen*—published by Benjamin Gottlob Hoffman. Although the date of publication indicated on the title page is 1799, at least the first two volumes appeared late in 1798. See Christian Gottlob Kayser, *Vollständiges Bücher-Lexicon enhaltend alle von 1750 bis zu Ende des Jahres 1832 in Deutschland . . . gedruckten Bücher* (Leipzig, 1834), III, 482.

[3] Duke de La Rochefocault-Liancourt, *Travels Through the United States of North*

Photograph courtesy of the John Ross Robertson Collection Metropolitan Toronto Public Library, Toronto, Canada

François-Alexandre-Frédéric, Duc de La Rochefoucauld-Liancourt. Engraving signed T. Goutère sc.

When Liancourt's work appeared in 1799, it was poorly received, especially by Americans, most of whom read the pirated English

America, the Country of the Iroquois, and Upper Canada, in the Years 1795, 1796, and 1797, trans. H. Neuman (2 vols., London, 1799). The publisher of this quarto edition was Richard Phillips. In 1800 he republished the work in a four-volume octavo edition. The title page and translator's preface of the first volume of the 1799 edition are silent regarding the document from which the translation was made; but in the preface to the second volume of the 1799 edition as well as in the 1800 edition appears the following: "This translation has been faithfully made, without alteration, from the last Paris Edition. . . ." This statement can be correct only as regards the second half of the translation.

translation made by H. Neuman and published by Richard Phillips in London. Those who objected to its wealth of detail called it ridiculous; others resented its political bias. Nevertheless, it went through two editions in English—a fact which virtually destroyed the overseas market for the French volumes. Neither the DuPonts nor the author profited from the sale of the French or the English editions.

WHY A NEW TRANSLATION?

In a letter to his English friend and sometime model, Arthur Young, Liancourt revealed that he had thought of arranging for an English edition of his work but had given up the idea.[4] We can only imagine his chagrin when the Neuman translation appeared.

This English translation was an amazing feat. The first half of it must have been made from the less-than-perfect German translation that came out before the DuPont edition—indeed, errors appear in the German which are repeated in the English but do not appear in the French. The second installment, somewhat more accurate, seems to have been done from the French. Neuman, the English translator, was known at the time for his multi-lingual dictionaries and his English translations of German works. The entire task of translating the eight volumes of some three hundred pages each, not to mention setting the type, correcting proofs, printing and binding, was done in less than eight months time. (It took DuPont and his sons over a year to edit, print and publish the French edition.) One is reminded of Dr. Samuel Johnson's comment about a woman preaching: "It is not done well; but you are surprised to find it done at all."

Neuman's English translation was filled with errors, omissions and garbled renditions of the names of people and places. Reading it against the original French of La Rochefoucauld-Liancourt today, however, one is struck not so much by these errors and omissions, as by the fact that the French idiom of this noble son of the Enlightenment seems much closer to modern workaday English than to the flowery and somewhat stilted language current in the London of George III. It is chiefly for this reason that, rather than simply editing the Neuman English version, we have embarked upon an entirely new translation from the French. Needless to say, this has added considerably to the length of time and the amount of effort expended on the project. (As of this date, the entire eight volumes have been trans-

[4] LRL to Arthur Young (ALS), April 10 [1798 or 1799]. "As for my Voyages, I am sorry for the trouble you did take about it. I will renounce to sell it in England, and when printed in France, it shall be translated and mutilated as they please." British Museum, Additional Manuscripts, Young Papers.

lated and the basic research for the notes is completed. The first three volumes are ready for publication.)

In his correspondence with the DuPonts,[5] Liancourt mentioned that he had collected illustrations for his work. Evidently these never materialized. As students of the period know, such illustrations are difficult to come by today. There were few artists working in America and what they produced has largely disappeared.

ABOUT THE AUTHOR

François-Alexandre-Frédéric de La Rochefoucauld-Liancourt (1747–1827) was born into a continuously distinguished French noble family.[6] His traceable ancestry dated back to the Eleventh Century and included notable soldiers, statesmen, ecclesiastics, courtiers and men and women of letters. His father, a La Rochefoucauld known as the duc d'Estissac, was in great favor with Louis XIV and was Grand Master of the Royal Wardrobe. His mother was a great-great-granddaughter of François VI de La Rochefoucauld, author of the famous *Maximes*. Liancourt's maternal aunt, the duchesse d'Enville, to whom he dedicated his *Voyage*, was a cultivated lady who gathered about her many of the French "social scientists" of the last half of the Eighteenth Century. She was much admired by Benjamin Franklin and Thomas Jefferson. Her son, Liancourt's cousin and friend, worked closely with Franklin and Jefferson during the American Revolution and again later when these American ministers were publicizing America in France. A tradition of intellectual activity and concern with social, political and economic problems runs through the family history; and many members of the family believed in the educational value of travel.

Young Liancourt had the beginnings of a literary education in a French *collège*. At age sixteen he left school to enter the army. By age twenty-three he was married, had two living sons, and was colonel of a dragoon regiment. After his father's death he became Grand Master of the Royal Wardrobe. Despite the demands of his military and courtly duties, he also managed to become involved in reformistic activities of several kinds: social, agricultural and industrial.

During the French pre-revolution and the early stages of the Revo-

[5] The business correspondence regarding the publication is remarkably complete at Eleutherian Mills Historical Library, Greenville, Wilmington, Delaware, among the papers of DuPont de Nemours.

[6] For a biography and for the family background, see Ferdinand-Dreyfus, *Un philanthrop d'autrefois: La Rochefoucauld-Liancourt, 1747–1827* (Paris, 1903), and Jean Marchand, *Iconographie et isographie de la maison de La Rochefoucauld* (no date, no place).

lution itself, Liancourt took a prominent place among the liberal nobles who welcomed the opportunity for progressive change that events seemed to offer. With his cousin he was an active member of the group of liberal activists known as the Committee of Thirty that played during 1788 an important role in ensuring that a revolution would, indeed, take place in France. With several other members of his family he was elected to the Estates General of 1789. As revolutionary tendencies became more violent, radical and republican, Liancourt found himself passed by. He made the political mistake of continuing to support Louis XVI (who probably did not understand the aspirations of this liberal monarchist), with the result that the rising republican Left came to consider Liancourt a counter-revolutionary.

In August 1792, at the time of the attack on the king in Paris, he deemed it wise to flee the country. After some frightening experiences he arrived in England. His cousin, the duc d'Enville, was not so wise nor so fortunate and was stoned to death by a mob a few days after Liancourt's emigration.

THE TRAVELS

Liancourt spent more than two years in England, where he had many friends; but in the autumn of 1794 he found living in a country that was at war with France excessively painful and decided to go to America. Accordingly, he collected letters of introduction to prominent people in America and sailed from London on an American ship on September 28, 1794. On board he passed himself off as a Swiss in fear of the ship's capture by a French cruiser. After a long and tiresome crossing (more than sixty days), he arrived in Philadelphia.[7] He spent the winter of 1794–1795 in that city, where he was well received and where he found several old friends and colleagues, Talleyrand among them.

In the spring of 1795 he set out on his American travels, always returning to winter in Philadelphia. His first trip took him through Pennsylvania to western New York, to Niagara Falls, Upper Canada, back to New York State, to Albany and across Massachusetts to Boston. Thereafter he visited the "Province of Maine" twice, travelled through Rhode Island, Connecticut and New Jersey, and sailed from Philadelphia to Charleston, South Carolina, whence he made an

[7] Liancourt's journal of his crossing and of his first winter in Philadelphia has been edited by Jean Marchand, *Journal de voyage en amérique et d'un séjour à Philadelphie, 1 octobre 1794–18 avril 1795* (Baltimore, 1940). This is a lively and detailed, if abbreviated, diary.

excursion into Georgia. On his way north, he saw tidewater Virginia, visited Thomas Jefferson at Monticello, crossed into the Valley of Virginia and followed the Shenandoah River to Harpers Ferry and thence back to Philadelphia through Maryland. His next to last trip led him from Philadelphia through Wilmington, Delaware, across the Eastern Shore and Chesapeake Bay to Annapolis and the Federal City.

During all of these travels he was never without his notebook (at least one of his friends—Talleyrand—found his eternal asking of questions and writing of notes a trifle foolish). Moreover, he freely borrowed material from the journals written by friends and acquaintances, notably Moreau de Saint-Méry, another French *émigré* who kept a bookstore in Philadelphia; John Guillemard, a wealthy young English amateur geologist who accompanied Liancourt on some of his travels; and du Petit-Thouars, a French naval officer, who also travelled with Liancourt.

After his return to Europe—he sailed from New York for Hamburg about the end of August 1797—Liancourt hired secretaries to prepare a manuscript and got in touch with DuPont de Nemours, then still at his printshop in Paris, about publication. After some hesitation, DuPont decided to undertake the project. The result was that the *Voyage* appeared as an eight-volume work in the revolutionary month of Germinal Year VII (March–April 1799), nearly a year before Liancourt was permitted to return to his native land.

THE FEDERAL CITY

By the time of his trip to the Federal City, "Mr. Liancourt," as he was known in America, had already come to know many of the principal actors in the drama that was being played out on the shores of the Potomac. He had been to dinners and balls at the Philadelphia home of Robert Morris whose increasing financial difficulties Liancourt viewed with alarm. He also knew Thomas Law, the rich Anglo-Indian who played an important part in the development of the capital; and he had met Morris' unfortunate associate, John Nicholson, who was soon to die in debtors prison. In addition, he had heard the gossip circulating in Philadelphia regarding the plans and progress of the Federal City and the frenzied real estate speculation that the project engendered. (In view of these facts it is surprising that Liancourt fails to mention the name of Pierre Charles L'Enfant.)

The passages that follow are excerpted from our new translation from the French of Volume VI of Liancourt's *Voyage* as published by DuPont de Nemours in 1799.

Voyage to Federal City in 1797

Boredom and melancholy drive me from Philadelphia and lead me to seek peace of mind and diversion in travel. This time, I am heading for the Federal City. I shall be more lonely than ever on this trip, for my faithful dog Cartouche is too old and weak to come along. Thus do our sources of comfort fail us when our need is greatest.

I leave on the 26th of March 1797.

* * *

From Upper Marlboro to Eastern Branch Creek [present-day Anacostia River], the land rises gradually showing the usual exhausted fields and poor crops. From the top of the hills that border the Eastern Branch, one discovers the Potomac River, from far above Georgetown all the way to Alexandria. One can also see the Eastern Branch over five or six miles of its course, and one has a perfect view of the location of the new city, all its public and private buildings perfectly visible. The view is wide and impressive, sufficiently framed by the heights above the Potomac, so that the eye may take in all its details without wandering off into the distance.

Upper Marlboro is the seat of Prince George's County, which has a population of twenty-two thousand, of whom twelve thousand are slaves. The tobacco grown here in great abundance is considered the best in Maryland.

It is noteworthy that in this county, as in most counties in this state, the older towns and villages are all built on rivers at the points where they become navigable. For a long time the only commodity exported was tobacco, and inspection houses built at these points served as the nuclei for other houses.

One crosses the Eastern Branch on a rather good boat—unfortunately too flat and much too small for the number of horses it carries. I crossed with ten horses and a carriage, and was most apprehensive until we reached the other side. This river is more than three-quarters of a mile wide at the crossing point. After crossing it, one enters Federal City—or, rather, the site of Federal City, for as yet the very things most lacking in this capital of the United States, this metropolis of North America, are houses.

But because of its destiny, or the anticipated destiny of this city, it is bound to become the focal point of the country, and of great importance to the domestic policies of the United States. I shall describe it in such detail and in such a way as to help the reader understand the background of this ambitious project, the means employed for its execution, its present state and the fate which everything I have observed leads me to predict for it.

FEDERAL CITY

Soon after the Constitution of the United States was drawn up, its partisans (and at that time nobody had yet been charged with not being one) believed that the perfect complement to the federal system they advocated would be the creation of a seat for the general government at some centrally-located spot where it would be independent of any one state and under the sovereignty of the Union. In this way, they could avoid any conflicts between the federal laws and those of any one state which might have a different set of laws and judiciary system. If the general government were to be located in one state, the jealousy of the others would be excited, thus sowing the seeds of disunion. Neither Philadelphia nor New York are centrally situated; and, having to travel farther than their northern colleagues, southern congressmen would become discontented, thus destroying the harmony it was so important to maintain. Finally, this sovereign government, whose existence was still a sort of fiction, might acquire an appearance of reality if it were established in a territory which belonged to itself alone and where it could exercise all its sovereign functions without obstruction. Such were the chief and very plausible reasons that persuaded Congress to adopt this idea.

In July of 1790 it passed a law,[1] the principal provisions of which are:

(1) To accept as the permanent seat of government for the United States a territory not to exceed ten miles square at the junction of the Potomac River and the Eastern Branch or Connogechegue [Connogochegue],[2] with the proviso that the sovereignty of the state to which this piece of land now belongs will in no way be curtailed until the date fixed for the establishment of the general government on this site, or until Congress has by law decided otherwise;

(2) To authorize the President of the United States to appoint and pay the fees of three commissioners to survey, measure and define the

[1] This law was the so-called "Residence Act," signed by George Washington on July 16, 1790. François-Alexandre-Frédéric de La Rochefoucauld-Liancourt (hereafter abbreviated as LRL) compresses its six articles into five. The full text is to be found in H. Paul Caemmerer, *A Manual on the Origin and Development of Washington* (Washington, D. C., 1939), 7.

[2] *Ibid.* In the words of the act, "... on the river Potomac, at some place between the mouths of the Eastern Branch and the Connogochegue. . . ."

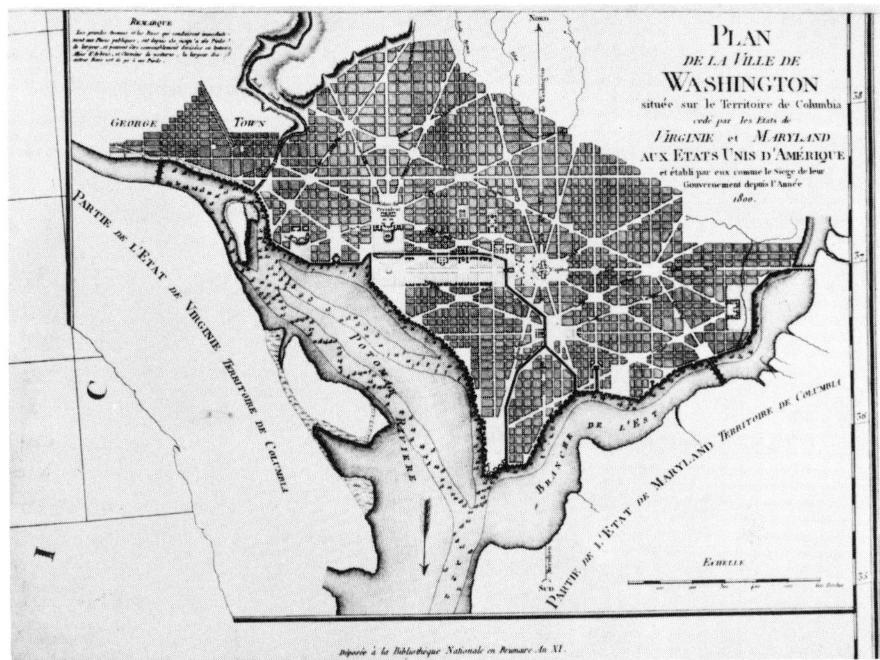

Photograph courtesy of the National Archives, Washington

Plan de la Ville de Washington. Copy, with French titles, of Andrew Ellicott's 1792 "Plan of the City of Washington."

The French caption notes that the map was "deposited in the Bibliothèque Nationale" in 1802.

boundaries of this district, subject to the above limitations, these three commissioners being required to work under the direction of the President of the United States and being able to act only when at least two of them are present;

(3) To authorize the commissioners to buy or accept as much land on the east bank of the Potomac as the President deems necessary for the use of the general government, and to order them to have such buildings as are needed to receive the Congress, the President and the public officials of the United States government ready for occupancy by the first Monday of December, 1800, all according to plans approved by the President;

(4) To authorize and request the President to accept all gifts of money made for the purpose of contributing to the expenses of these acquisitions and for the buildings;

(5) To declare that on the first Monday of December in the year

1800 the government of the United States shall be transferred to this district and place mentioned above; to order that all government offices, with their responsible officials, be moved to this place, and that, thereafter, said offices shall function in that place and no other; and to allocate as necessary sums from import and export duties for the payment of the expenses incurred in so moving.

Passed when Congress still met in New York, this law also provided that the United States government should be moved to Philadelphia and remain in that place until the first Monday of December, 1800, the date on which it was to be transferred to its permanent location.

At that time Congress was assured of the favorable disposition of the states of Virginia and Maryland, both of which, having previously debated the issue within their own legislatures, had offered to cede those parts of their respective territories needed for the establishment of the general government. Being centrally located, removed from the perils of possible aggression by a foreign enemy in time of war, well positioned to become a large trading center that could be easily and safely supplied, and blessed with a healthy climate, the location could not have been better chosen.

The states of Virginia and Maryland, both aware of the great advantages of having the seat of the United States government on the territory that had been chosen, were intensely interested in the success of this great project. Virginia gave the Union $120,000 and Maryland gave $72,000 to promote the execution of the plan.[3]

The proprietors of the land on which the city was to be built were even more anxious to see it constructed. They gave half of the territory to the Union; that is to say, they gave title outright to one-half the lots which eventually would be included in the city. They also freely ceded the land required for the streets and public spaces, on condition that they should receive eighty dollars for each acre made into public parks.[4] Those lots to which the owners retained title, and those that had been given to the government, were to be distributed

[3] LRL's figures are correct. A few months before his visit to the new Federal City, however, President Washington was urgently appealing to Governor Stone of Maryland for additional funds. John Reps, *Monumental Washington: The Planning and Development of the Capital Center* (Princeton, 1967), 26.

[4] The original proprietors were not quite so cooperative as LRL suggests. George Washington had to intervene personally to get them to cede this land, lest "whilst they were contending for the shadow, they might loose the substance. . . ." John C. Fitzpatrick, ed., *The Diaries of George Washington*, 4 vols. (Boston, 1925), IV, 154. The names of the original owners are listed in Louis Dow Scisco, "A Site for the 'Federal City': The Original Proprietors and their Negotiations with Washington," *Records of the Columbia Historical Society of Washington, D. C. 1957–1959* (1961), 145.

Photograph courtesy of the National Archives, Washington

Territory of Columbia. Drawn by Andrew Ellicott, based on the first topographical survey of the District of Columbia, and published in 1793.

alternately, so that the owners and the government should share equally in the advantages and disadvantages of the location of each lot or block—for sometimes the distribution of the land was organized by alternate blocks and not by lots.

On 6 March 1796 a law was passed authorizing the commissioners to borrow, on the approval of the President of the United States, a sum of $300,000 to cover the cost of the project voted in 1790, with clauses stating that they could not borrow more than $200,000 in any one year, that the interest should not exceed 6 percent, that the sums borrowed were to be repaid by 1803, that the city lots that could be disposed of, but had not yet been sold, should serve as collateral and eventually be used to repay the loan. The United States agreed to pay off any remaining debt, if necessary. Under this law, the commissioners were obliged to render to the Secretary of the Treasury a semiannual accounting of the expenditures for which the borrowed money was used.

And thus the commissioners have had at their disposal $192,000 donated by Virginia and Maryland and $300,000 from the loan authorized by the Congress. In addition, they had the money from the sale of the town lots belonging to the United States. They were authorized to sell these lots under certain rules and restrictions set by the President of the United States.

Navigation on the Potomac is interrupted at several points along its course from Cumberland (located 192 miles from the site of the new city), especially by a large waterfall fifteen miles above Georgetown and by another, smaller one six miles closer to town. In 1784, a company called the Potomac Company[5] was incorporated by the state of Virginia and authorized to collect tolls on the various canals that would have to be built. The establishment of the general government on the banks of the Potomac led to increased interest in, and more activity on these languishing works. The company's capital, which had consisted of five hundred shares, worth $444 each, was increased to six hundred shares in 1795. Thus it had $270,400 at its disposal for the improvement of nagivation on the Potomac. Moreover, the states of Maryland and Virginia interested themselves even more directly in the success of this company and bought up a rather large number of shares. When this work is completed, the produce of an immense territory, which today must be transported overland to Philadelphia and Baltimore, will find a quicker and cheaper outlet along this great river. The new city will acquire thereby a sure supply of goods for consumption and trade, and these will add still more to the natural advantages of its location.

The Point separating the Potomac from the Eastern Branch[6] is

[5] About this time the name of this company, of which Washington was the first president, was changing from "The Patowmack Company" to the modern spelling used in this translation. See Corra Bacon-Foster, "Early Chapters in the Development of the Potomac Route to the West," *Records of the Columbia Historical Society*, Vol. 15, (1912), 123–322, esp. 185–187. The reader will recall that this company had nothing to do with the Chesapeake and Ohio canal organized later. The canals built by the "The Patowmack Company" were on the Virginia side of the river and only around the falls. There are still remains of them at Great Falls and at Seneca.

[6] The "Point" mentioned here is present-day Fort McNair, at that time the southernmost tip of Federal City. Modern Haines Point is part of the complex of East and West Potomac Parks, developed on filled land in what was formerly a much wider Potomac River.

difficult and even dangerous to round at certain times of the year, and the Eastern Branch is deeper and more convenient for vessels. Therefore, it is important to connect the Potomac with the Eastern Branch and thus avoid the Point. Besides, to extend internal navigation would be a great advantage to the city. In 1798, the state of Maryland authorized the establishment of two lotteries to raise funds for the building of a canal.[7] These lotteries are each worth $175,000, of which 15 percent, that is, $26,250, has been allocated for the canal.

These are the various arrangements, laws, financial operations and sums of money employed so far for the establishment of Federal City. It is planned that the city will extend for more than three miles along the banks of the Potomac and the Eastern Branch and will contain 4,124 square acres.

In America, where more than anywhere else the desire for wealth is the dominant passion, there are few operations that fail to fall into the hands of speculators. Since the establishment of the Federal City presented such great opportunities, it has not been free of them.

Mr. Morris was the first to see the possibility of great profit. Joining forces with Messrs. Nicholson and Greenleaf[8] soon after the town plans had been drawn, he bought all the lots he could lay his hands on, either from the original owners or the commissioners—that is, any lots that any of these people would sell at the time. He has bought six thousand lots from the commissioners, at eighty dollars each. Each lot measures 5,265 square feet.[9]

Under the terms of the deal made with the commissioners in 1793,

---

[7] Mention of these lotteries of 1798 indicates that LRL's discussion of Federal City was written some time after he spent six days there in 1797. L'Enfant's original proposal included a plan for an inland waterway or canal which also appeared on the Ellicott map of 1792. The canal was eventually constructed and used for about fifty years, but it fell into disrepair and became more of an open sewer than a waterway in the latter half of the Nineteenth Century. (The stone house at the corner of 17th Street and Constitution Avenue, N.W. is all that remains today of its former lock system.) See Cornelius W. Heine, "The Washington City Canal," *Records of the Columbia Historical Society of Washington, D. C. 1953–1956* (1959), 1–27; William Tindall, *Origin and Government of the District of Columbia* (Washington, D. C., 1907), 215; W. B. Bryan, *A History of the National Capital*, 2 vols., (New York, 1914–1916), I, 151, 243, 493–494.

[8] Robert Morris (1734–1806), financier of the American Revolution, and John Nicholson (1757–1800) of Philadelphia were partners in many land schemes at this time. James Greenleaf (1765–1843) of Massachusetts had been appointed United States consul in Amsterdam in March of 1793. He returned to Washington in September of that year, and Morris and others anticipated that he would be able in Holland to sell shares in the Federal City properties. Greenleaf represented himself and Robert Morris in the great land sale of December 21, 1973 described by LRL here. Allen C. Clark, *Greenleaf and Law in the Federal City* (Washington, D. C., 1901) 72–90; Proceedings of the Commissioners, I, Record Group 42, National Archives and Records Service, Washington, D. C. (Hereafter RG 42, NARS.)

[9] LRL's figures are substantially correct except that half of the 6,000 lots sold for £35 each, or about $115.

it was agreed that, of the six thousand lots Mr. Morris was buying from them, fifteen hundred would be in the northeast section of the town, and the 4,500 other lots would be located in places to be chosen by Mr. Morris and his company. It was also agreed that Mr. Morris would build 120 two-story brick houses on these lots within the space of seven years,[10] that he would not sell any of these lots before the first of January 1796, and that all sales should carry the same specifications for house construction as stated in his contract. Finally, it was agreed that payments in full should be made, beginning on the first of May 1794, at the rate of one-seventh, or $68,000 per year, the total being $480,000.

The number of lots bought by Mr. Morris from the original owners was about the same and the price identical. The conditions of payment are of no historical interest and, as a matter of fact, were different in each case.

This is the only sale made on a large scale by either the United States commissioners or private owners to one man or one company. Hoping to sell at a higher price, the commissioners waited for the time when the demand for lots should increase and their own needs should become more pressing. Private owners thought along the same lines, and both the commissioners and the owners saw in the sale to Mr. Morris a way to stimulate the settlement of the town: Mr. Morris would be interested in immediately reselling some of the lots. At that time, his credit and financial situation gave him the means of success, thus immediately adding to the number of persons interested in the swift completion of the enterprise.

Indeed, in the first eighteen months Mr. Morris has sold approximately one thousand lots.

The laying of the foundations of the Capitol and of the President's house stimulated the first purchasers to hope that great numbers of new buyers wishing to locate in the new town would soon come flowing in or, at the least, feel that the situation was attractive enough to encourage further speculation. The press published rosy descriptions of the town, with premature announcements of its development—in other words, all the usual charlatanism by which merchants in all the countries of the world try to make their wares seem more attractive. These skills are widely known and much practiced in this new world.

Those who bought up a large number of Mr. Morris's lots were Mr. Law and Mr. Dickinson, both lately arrived from India and ex-

[10] The correct figure was 70 houses, or ten a year for each of the seven years.

ceedingly rich, General Howard and General Lee and two or three wealthy Dutchmen; but no one purchased more lots than Mr. Law, who bought 445 of them.[11] They paid at least $293 for each of these lots or, rather, five pence (Maryland currency) per square foot, for they were not exactly the same size. Several were sold for up to six, eight or ten pence per square foot, latecomers paying the higher prices and the location of the lots having some effect on their prices.

Some of these gentlemen, either to gain control of a complete block, or for speculative motives of their own, bought up several commissioners' lots on their own, for the same price. The acquisition of the latter carried with it the obligation to build, as was the case in Mr. Morris's contract with the commissioners. Six hundred lots were sold in this way. Each purchaser chose his lots according to his ideas of the best location and the best chance of quick development. Thus the locations favored by these sub-buyers were those in the vicinity of the Capitol and the President's house, near Georgetown and along the Potomac River, on the Point and in the area near the Eastern Branch. This is true of most of the lots they bought, since no one was able to buy all the lots he wished in the areas he favored and expected to be the first developed. They all believed, however, that the plans for the city would soon be fulfilled.

This view was then widely shared. Both the President and the commissioners held this opinion so fully that a regulation prohibited the farming of any part of this enormous tract of land. Only gardens could be planted, and at one time the building of wooden houses, or even one-story houses, was forbidden. This rule, it is true, was quickly revoked and the original owners have retained the right to fence and cultivate the tracts of land they have not sold.

One of the greatest and cleverest speculators in Philadelphia, Mr. Blodget, had acquired a large number of lots. Under the pretense of helping the development of the town, but actually for the purpose

---

[11] "Mr. Dickinson" was evidently William Mayne Duncanson of England and India who invested between $60,000 and $70,000 in the Federal City. Bryan, *A History of the National Capital*, I, 245. "Light Horse Harry" Lee or General Henry Lee (1756–1819) of Virginia, a famous cavalry leader during the American Revolution, helped to put down the so-called "Whiskey Rebellion" in 1794 while serving as governor of Virginia. *Dictionary of American Biography*, XI, 17–108. John Eager Howard (1752–1827) of Maryland, another hero of the American Revolution, was governor of Maryland, 1788–1791. At this time (1797) he was a United States Senator, having refused Washington's offer of the Secretaryship of War in 1795. *DAB*, IX, 279. Thomas Law (1759–1834), an Englishman, came to the United States in 1793 ready to spend the great wealth he had acquired as a representative for nearly twenty years of the East India Company in India. *Dictionary of National Biography*, XI, 676–677. LRL says more of Law below.

Photograph courtesy of Charles Merrill Mount

Mrs. Thomas Law by Gilbert Stuart.

Photograph courtesy of Charles Merrill Mount

Thomas Law by Gilbert Stuart.

of waiting while others engaged in development, he set up two lotteries. The main prize in the first lottery was a fine tavern,[12] located between the President's house and the Capitol, worth fifty thousand dollars. The three principal prizes in the second lottery were three houses to be built near the Capitol, worth twenty-five thousand, fifteen thousand, and ten thousand dollars respectively. These lotteries required no special authorization, for they occurred before the passage of a Maryland law prohibiting unauthorized lotteries. They were, in fact, warmly supported by the commissioners, who saw in them a means of encouraging the development of the city. It seems that these lotteries had the effect Mr. Blodget hoped for; in other words, he made a lot of money and was the only one whose hopes were not disappointed.[13]

Mr. Morris and those who purchased from him were not so quickly successful in their speculations. After having admired the beauty and magnificance of the plan of the city for a while, people began to realize that it was too vast, that it was gigantic in view of the circumstances of the United States at the present time and for years to come, even should no unforeseen event arrest the advance of their prosperity. It became evident that for many years this large expanse of land would not be covered with buildings, as had been hoped. Thus each landowner, convinced at last that the town could only develop by degrees and that a start would have to be made in one section or another, and wishing to see this development begun in the section where he owned the most lots, acted accordingly. From that time on, there were no common interests, and a great rivalry spread among the owners. Each one started building in his part of town, hoping to enhance the possibility of attracting new arrivals. Each vaunted the advantages of his section to the detriment of the others. The public press no longer spoke of the beauty of Federal City, but of the beauty of this or that section of Federal City.

---

[12] The cornerstone of "Blodget's Hotel," as this "tavern" came to be known, was laid with great fanfare in 1793. Isaac Weld, a contemporary English traveller, described it as "a large building of brick, ornamented with stone; it stands between the president's house and the capitol. In the beginning of the year 1796, when last I saw it, it was roofed in, and every exertion making to have it finished with the utmost expedition. It is anything but beautiful." The building accidentally burned to the ground in 1836. *Records of the Columbia Historical Society of Washington, D. C. 1957–1959* (1961), f.p. 122; Isaac Weld, *Travels through the States of North America*, 2 vols. (London, 1807), I, 84–85.

[13] The lotteries of Samuel Blodget, Jr. (b. 1755), founder of one of the earliest insurance companies in the United States, were not successful—in fact, they seem to have ruined him. See Aaron M. Sakolski, *The Great American Land Bubble* (New York, 1932), 154–156.

The commissioners[14] were not immune to this mercenary competition. Two of them owned lots near Georgetown, and, even had they not, their relations with that already existing city could not fail to influence their opinion as to which part of Federal City should be developed first. The various interests were concentrated in four main areas, each of which hoped to attract the largest number of buildings.

The inhabitants of Georgetown, who had bought a good number of lots in their vicinity, contended that the support of an already existing town would be a great help to the new city. They boasted of the port of Georgetown, arguing that trade already established there would be a great advantage to commerce in the new city.

Owners of lots near the Point insisted that their location was the most airy, the healthiest, the most beautiful, and that it was the most convenient for commerce, since it benefits from the nagivation on two rivers and is equidistant from the Capitol and the President's House.

Owners along the Eastern Branch disparaged the port of Georgetown and the banks of the Potomac as having no shelter from winter's ice; they disparaged the Point as being between the two rivers and thus having the advantages of neither. They boasted that their port was deep and secure, never frozen, and sheltered from the prevailing winds. They extolled their proximity to the Capitol, the seat of government, the place where all Members would have to convene at least once a day, and which was never more than three-quarters of a mile from the most remote lots on [New] Jersey Avenue where the Eastern Branch promoters held their land.

The owners of lots surrounding the Capitol said that Federal City would not necessarily become a commercial town, that its principal object was to house the Congress, and that therefore it was important to build as many houses as possible around the Capitol and to extend them as far as possible towards the President's house, which though of secondary importance was still the chief building after the Capitol. Finally, they said that it was important to connect these two centers of government by a series of roads and buildings for the convenience of Congress.

With these arguments each owner hoped to sell the houses he

[14] The original commissioners appointed by Washington in 1791 were Thomas Johnson of Frederick, Maryland, Dr. David Stuart of Virginia and Representative Daniel Carroll of Maryland. They were succeeded in 1794 and 1795 by Gustavus Scott, William Thornton, and Alexander White. RG 42, NARS; *Records of the Columbia Historical Society*, Vol. 17 (1914), 1n.

built in the section in which he owned the most property, but he built few houses and with a certain caution, fearing that his rivals' interests would prevail over his.

The commissioners in charge of construction of the public buildings were accused by the landowners whose interests were not in Georgetown of showing partiality to Georgetown at the expense of the three other rival sectors by working more diligently on the erection of the President's house (which is closer to Georgetown), of planning to house government officials there, and of neglecting the Capitol.

Advocates were found for each of these views concerning the best location for starting the city's establishment, even among those who had no vested interests and whose only concern was the advancement of the public interest; but public interest was not the concern of the rival parties.

This state of affairs still prevails. The President's house is so far advanced that it can be roofed this year.[15] The wing of the Capitol building that has been started (for the plans for this edifice are so huge that two-thirds of the total construction has been put off indefinitely) can be roofed next year.[16] A hundred and fifty houses are scattered over the vast surface of the projected city. Some thirty or forty, still set very far apart, are grouped in each rival sector.

That the present chaotic state of affairs is common knowledge doubtless prevents new purchasers from presenting themselves. It also complicates matters for the present owners, among whom Messrs. Morris, Nicholson and Greenleaf are further constrained by the current state of their affairs. All their property has been attached as security for their debts.[17] Thus they are prevented from investing any

---

[15] ". . . [T]he President's house, will be covered this autumn, or to speak more correctly perhaps, . . . is *now* receiving its cover . . ." wrote George Washington from Mt. Vernon in the spring of 1797. However, the work was not completed before the end of the year. A handwritten note to the commissioners, dated November 29, 1797, from John Kidgeley begins: "Gentlemen if you please I will cover the roof the President' house in the best manner. . . ." Washington to David Humphreys, June 26, 1797, *Records of the Columbia Historical Society,* Vol. 17 (1914), 196; "Proposals and Estimates, 1795–1816," RG 42, NARS.

[16] On November 18, 1797, George Hadfield, superintendent of the work on the Capitol, reported that "part of the entablature and the balustrade, are only wanting to complete the whole of the intended elevation. The brick work is also raised as high as the roof . . ." U. S. House of Representatives, 58 Cong., 2nd Sess., *Documentary History of the Construction and Development of the United States Capitol Building and Grounds* (Washington, D. C., 1904), 78.

[17] Although we do not know just when LRL wrote this statement, by July of 1797 Greenleaf was in jail and Morris and Nicholson were hiding out from their creditors in their country houses near Philadelphia, "in hourly dread of being taken." Morris was not imprisoned until February 15, 1798. Nicholson died in the Philadelphia Prune Street

more money, either to straighten out these difficulties or to fulfill their obligations to build. Last year they had built, or started to build, about forty houses on various locations in this projected city.

It is said that because of this combination of circumstances few new houses will be built this year—or, at least, this is feared by those who are most concerned with the development of the city. There have been no, or very few, sales of lots. The chief landowners are more discouraged and there is discord among them. These are not the best conditions for promoting a successful enterprise, especially one that has enemies in the state of Pennsylvania, where people are not happy to see Congress about to elude them. In parts of Maryland and Virginia, the tendency to concentrate the largest public expenditures in this area is resented. Each individual would prefer to see this spending closer to his area of interest.

The disinterested person who studies the plan[18] for the siting and the boundaries of this great projected city does not even have to know all the aggravating circumstances I have just mentioned to reach an unfavorable conclusion regarding the practicality or even the possibility of this whole project. The conception of a capital for the government of the United States, independent of any single state, is a great and noble idea. As I have said, the location of the town has been well chosen. My only objection is that it might have been wiser to place the Congress far away from a maritime town to insure it against the real danger of being influenced in its deliberations by commercial interests. The plan has been well conceived and cleverly, even magnificently drawn; as a matter of fact, it is the very magnificence of the conception that gives it its dreamlike quality.

As I have already explained, the plan of the city comprises 4,124 acres, of which 712 have been set aside for the sixteen avenues which are to be named after the sixteen different states and for other, lesser streets and for public squares and parks. The remaining 3,412 acres, divided among the original owners and the Union, contain 23,000 house lots, not including 3,000 square feet of lots suitable for wharves. The price of the latter has been fixed by the commissioners at twelve to sixteen pence per foot of frontage by eighty feet of depth. Some, but not many, have already been sold.

debtors prison in 1800 while Morris was still there. See Eleanor May Young, *Forgotton Patriot Robert Morris* (New York, 1950), 225–237 and *passim*. The quotation is from a letter of Eliza Wescott to Thomas Law, July 27, 1797, Thomas Law and Eliza Parke Custis Law, Miscellaneous Papers, 1796–1835, Library of Congress Manuscript Collection, Washington, D. C. (Hereafter cited as Law, Misc. Papers, 1796–1835, LC MS).

[18] LRL probably studied the Ellicott plan published in 1792 in Philadelphia. L'Enfant had been dismissed in 1791 by Washington, and he took his drawings with him. Reps, *Monumental Washington*, 22.

The Capitol is a mile and a half distant from the President's house, and about three-quarters of a mile from the river beside which merchants, if they come, will settle with all their business interests. Aside from the inconvenience, which will increase as time goes on, of having the Capitol so far from the President's house, three hundred houses would be required to fill in this space, and that would mean one single street lined with buildings. Others would have to be built around the Capitol and the President's house to accommodate people working in these buildings. Thus, a calculation that five hundred houses are necessary to make this connection is an underestimate. And, again, all one would have is a single street—on which not one house has yet been built.

This section of town might be convenient for Members of Congress, and it will no doubt have a few stores and a tavern or two. But this is not the place where business people will settle, or those looking for a pleasant spot to live. Furthermore, this is the area in which the present owners are least interested in building, because most of their lots are in more distant locations. If the space between the two main buildings is not filled, communication will be impractical in winter, for it is difficult to believe that the United States will go to the expense of paved streets, sidewalks and street lamps on such a large expanse of uninhabited space.

Connecting any of the other four sections with either of the principal government buildings would require more than two thousand houses, and then all the other sections would remain devoid of houses and so isolated as to form separate and distinct hamlets.

Doubtless every city has started from a small nucleus of houses around which others have gradually been built. But here there are two centers, separated by a mile and a half; and this place is supposed to be a complete city, ready to receive the President, Members of Congress and the foreign dignitaries who will convene here once it becomes the seat of government. As a town it should be fashioned so as to provide all these public officials with a certain measure of comfort, which they will all be disinclined to do without, having enjoyed in Philadelphia as much comfort as is to be had in all America.

There are those who say, as I have heard repeatedly, that once the government has been installed here those material comforts that may be lacking at the outset will quickly abound. They forget that those who are attached to this government and who will come here in its train, already disenchanted with the idea of this keystone of federalism, will lose all patience when they realize that they lack the simplest and most necessary conveniences.

Local investors are not showing much insight in exhibiting so little concern for the comfort of all these public officials while counting on the decision taken by Congress to move here in 1800. If (as some doubt but as I believe will happen) the government, in order to comply with its decision and justify the expenses incurred, does move here in 1800, the general discontent of all those involved will assure that their stay will be a temporary one, and it may have even more serious effects. There is less public spirit in this part of the world than in Europe—or at least the kind of public spirit which inspires people to sacrifice personal interests to national interests, even for the sake of promoting a great national project.

What people here call convenience, ease or comfort may not be exactly what a European would understand by those words. Be that as it may, people want it, like it and will have it. One cannot say that they are pushing the idea of comfort to extremes when they wish to be preserved from falling into mud holes for lack of paved roads, or from breaking their necks for lack of street lights. This sort of incovenience will endure here for many years, given the size of the city's plan and the great distance between the two centers of public affairs.

In starting a new town, it is normal for the first owners and first inhabitants to pool their efforts to insure the success of the enterprise. Here everyone is divided. There is no common effort because, in truth, the various interests are really different; consequently the efforts of each individual are wasted as far as the common weal is concerned. Each person who acquired lots from the commissioners on conditions that he build is trying to get rid of this clause. The Messrs. Morris, Greenleaf and Nicholson are exempt in fact from complying with the clause because of the unhappy state of their affairs. Those who bought from them are seeking to profit from the impossibility of their being prosecuted by not fulfilling the conditions for which the former are the primary warrantors. The commissioners, with more or less good will towards the lot owners, sometimes waive the clause and sometimes insist it be complied with. They feel that if the conditions of sale were to be exactly fulfilled in the six or seven hundred lots they have sold, they would only find that that many brick houses, thinly spread out over the immense city plan, would have little effect in hastening its development.

If a town should arise here for commercial reasons, it would begin in the area best suited to trade. It would expand more or less quickly, as word of its success spread. Each of its new inhabitants, having an interest in seeing the town develop, and each inhabitant having come of his own volition, would bear without complaint the hardships of a growing town. They would know that the latter would gradually disappear, because their trade and their profits would give them patience. In this town things are different. The city has as its base a union of different states; and although this base is not unsteady, there is little doubt that it has been sufficiently attacked to stimulate caution among those who wish to speculate on its solidity. Trade is a very secondary consideration and, again, the sector of the city appropriate to commerce is so far away from the seat of the government that two or three towns could easily fit between them.

The majority of the Members of Congress will arrive discontented and they will take up residence grudgingly. Those who are already inclined to be opposed to the Federal Government and consequently to the creation of a Federal City will find, in the great expenses already incurred and the still greater ones that will be required, free play for their dissatisfactions. In the general discomfort, these will be shared increasingly by others. The influence of private interests on public affairs in every country of the world cannot be questioned —to do so would be to show little understanding of human nature.

Besides, there are so many good reasons why the Union will not remain intact for very many years, and there are so many indications of this, that it is hard to believe that this Federal City will ever develop even a tenth of its territory before the inevitable rupture—which can be hastened by a thousand circumstances.

These thoughts are in the minds of many Americans, whether they fear or hope to see them come true. They have impeded the progress that otherwise could have been predicted for this Federal City.

For all the reasons I have detailed as succinctly as I could, it is impossible to believe that, as projected and begun, the Federal City will ever develop to the point where it will become a pleasant place to live for the kind of people who are destined to inhabit it.[19]

* * *

There is still one more thing to be said about this place of which I have spoken at such length. The population of Federal City, at this point, is very small,[20] and the inhabitants are so spread out that, even

[19] LRL's gloomy conclusions about the Federal City are all the more remarkable in view of the sanguinary predictions of Isaac Weld. The Federal City, Weld wrote, "will become the grand emporium of the West, and rival in magnitude and splendour the cities of the old world." Weld, *Travels,* I, 80. It has, in fact, taken nearly two hundred years for such enthusiasts' dreams to begin to come true.

[20] In the spring of 1796, Isaac Weld thought the population numbered about 5,000, "including artificers, who formed by far the largest part of that number." Weld, *Travels*, I, 86.

if they were not fully preoccupied by their feuds and speculations, it would still be hard for them to socialize. It is as if they were living in the country, where neighbors see very little of one another. Workmen and merchants all live in Georgetown, so that is where everybody goes for supplies. The few stores open in Federal City are very expensive and miserably stocked, and the few available workmen are unreliable and very expensive to hire. Meat is extremely hard to come by, especially beef, as is any butchered meat for that matter (if I am to judge by the six days I spent there, during which I never saw any). Eggs are occasionally brought in from the country, but again not very often. In fact I have not seen, even in the most backward parts of America, a place so lacking in provisions of this kind.

The Capitol building and the President's house are handsome constructions of white, beautifully-worked stone. I am not very fond of the type of architecture found in these two buildings. The stone used is a kind of hard granite, yet not hard enough to be resistant to frost. It is extracted from a quarry near the Potomac, thirty miles below the town.[21] At the same distance, but up-river, there are quarries of beautiful white and red-veined marbles and a slate quarry. Lime is found near the Potomac too, but some thirty miles further upstream. Work on the interior canal, for which a lottery has just been opened, has not been started yet. It is believed that this will be quickly built: workmen will start excavating in a month. Two small creeks run through the town; their waters can be conveyed to any part of it. Those of Tyber Creek, which rises a few miles from town at seventy-eight feet above its level, can be piped to the top of the highest buildings.

* * *

MR. LAW

I stayed all my time in Federal City with Mr. Law, and saw his great happiness in his wife, whom he married last year.[22] She combines gentleness, good manners and a pretty face, with a healthy, wise

[21] A quarry on Hissinston Island in the Potomac near Acquia, Virginia, was purchased for $3,192 for the purpose of furnishing sandstone for the Capitol and President's house. Other quarries in Acquia were leased. Bryan, *History of the National Capital,* I, 171, 231.

[22] Thomas Law, aged 39, married 19-year-old Eliza Parke Custis, granddaughter of Martha Washington, on March 21, 1796. That year, Law took his bride to his new home at what is now 6th and N Streets, S.W., where LRL also must have stayed. In the spring of 1797 Washington visited the Laws here on his way from Philadelphia to Mt. Vernon after his retirement from the presidency, as did Louis Philippe of France and other important French visitors. John A. Carroll and Mary W. Ashworth, *First in Peace* (New York, 1957), 447; Clark, *Greenleaf and Law,* 236–237, 242. Clark cites a diary of 1797 by Thomas Law which the present editors have been unable to locate.

and honest mind and all the domestic virtues. I cannot congratulate him equally on his speculative ventures, in which he has so quickly bought up a great number of lots in this new town and decided to settle here. It seems to me he could have more wisely invested the great fortune he had accumulated through many years of toil and care in India. He is getting more and more deeply involved in the affairs of this city, with no guarantee of success. He once had a fortune much larger than any of the great American fortunes. He could live handsomely on his income. He could have been happy and made others around him happy. His temperament is that of a kind, loyal philanthropist; but, of his own volition, he has jumped into a morass of contradictions, operations, problems and anguish that is preventing him from enjoying his fortune and is, moreover, endangering it. He himself is not convinced he will succeed: he lacks confidence, and is far from being a greedy man. But in his enthusiasm he closes his eyes to the unfavorable signs that he cannot help but see, and every day sinks deeper and deeper into trouble. His life will consequently not be as happy as he deserves.[23]

[23] LRL's prediction was quite accurate. Law had many handicaps in the American world of business, for "As a foreigner, and particularly as an Englishman, Mr. Law could never possess any political weight in the country . . ." His young wife left him, and although he was never bankrupt like so many of his contemporaries who were caught in the maelstrom of the French Revolution and Napoleonic wars, his investments did not turn out well. An undated letter written by Law in a shaking hand near the end of his career is especially poignant: "When you see my friends in England, you will learn how I was respected and loved by them & adored by the natives [of India] — . . . I find myself breaking fast, calamities disappointments and misconstructions shake my nerves and enfeeble me . . ." Among his many accomplishments, Thomas Law was a poet. Clark, *Greenleaf and Law,* 238; Law, Misc. Papers, 1796–1835, LC MS.

After this essay was in page proof, we learned of the existence of a manuscript version of the equivalent of 15½ pages of the French text as printed. The manuscript, which is filed with the Holland Land Company Papers, Volume 280, no. 32, in the Gemeentearchief, The Netherlands, appears to have been made in America from a manuscript made available by LRL to Theophile Cazenove, who was the agent in the United States for the Holland Land Company. Needless to say, the nature of the excerpt would not have encouraged the Holland Land Company to invest in Federal City. This information was supplied by William Stinchcombe who is currently in Amsterdam.

Charles Bulfinch and the Washington Unitarian Community, 1818–1830

HAROLD KIRKER

Charles Bulfinch has been identified with Boston more consistently than any American architect with any other American city. Born in Boston in 1763, he watched the Battle of Bunker Hill from the roof of the family mansion in Bowdoin Square, graduated from the Boston Latin School, and attended college in nearby Cambridge. When he returned home in 1787 from the Grand Tour, he expressed his intention to settle down for life in Boston and devote himself to architecture and public service. And for the next thirty years, Bulfinch designed practically every important building in Boston and served permanently as chairman of the Board of Selectmen and superintendent of police. Thus, the capital of Massachusetts in the period 1787–1817 is known historically as Bulfinch's Boston. Nevertheless, Bulfinch himself described the twelve years he spent in Washington both personally and professionally "the happiest years of my life." [1] This period commenced with Bulfinch's appointment as Architect of the Capitol and his departure from Boston in January, 1818.

At the time Bulfinch arrived in Washington, five designers and five presidents had impressed their diverse personalities upon the yet unfinished Capitol. The latest in the architectural line was Benjamin Henry Latrobe, named Surveyor of Public Works in 1803. Latrobe had taken considerable liberties with Dr. William Thornton's original design. And although these were the masterful alterations of a brilliant professional, Latrobe's work was impaired by political and personal enmities and the burning of the Capitol during the War of 1812. President James Monroe, aware of the political

Delivered at the First Annual Conference on Washington, D. C. Historical Studies, sponsored by the Columbia Historical Society and George Washington University, January 11, 1974.

[1] Charles A. Place, *Charles Bulfinch, Architect and Citizen* (Boston, 1925), 279.

Courtesy of Fogg Art Museum, Harvard University
Gift to the University by Francis V. Bulfinch

Charles Bulfinch in 1786 by Mather Brown (1761–1831).

necessity of completing the building, also understood the need to turn the work over to someone with administrative as well as architectural talents. While on his Good Will tour of New England in 1817, the President was so impressed by Bulfinch's combination of patience and tact in administration and experience and taste in design, he offered him the post of national architect with a salary of $2,500 a year. Bulfinch perfectly understood his task. "I shall not have credit for invention," he wrote early in his first year of residence, "but must be content to follow in a prescribed path." [2] Bulfinch continued in Washington until the summer of 1830 "in pursuits congenial to my taste, and where my labors were well received." [3] These labors included not only completion of the Capitol and laying out the grounds but the organization of the Washington Unitarian community and the design of its first church.

Bulfinch tells us the reasons he judged the Washington experience the most satisfying in a long and active life were personal as well as professional. In regard to the latter, nothing suggests better the immense general appreciation of the completed Capitol than Mrs. Francis Trollop's contemporaneous admission that it would take "an abler pen than mine to do . . . justice [to its] beauty and majesty." [4] Such praise was surely welcome to the modest but often disappointed architect. Equally important to his sense of well being was Washington society, and particularly the growing Unitarian community among which the Bulfinch family exerted the strongest lay influence in the first decade of its history. But the maturation of that community, like the completion of the Capitol itself, was a slow and often painful labor. In one of his first letters from Washington, Bulfinch wrote: "There are a number of places of public worship, of various denominations, but all agreeing in circulating the most Trinitarian and Calvinistic opinions." [5] The Unitarian principles, currently sweeping his native Boston, were in Washington either unknown or ridiculed. But this was only a decade since the men of Unitarian leanings gained ascendancy in the Harvard Divinity School and the denomination, which came to be known as "Boston's religion", was still in its infancy. The Bulfinch family, however, was among the initial American converts, and two of the architect's finest New England buildings—the Church of Christ in Lancaster and New South in

---

[2] Ellen Susan Bulfinch, *The Life and Letters of Charles Bulfinch, Architect* (Boston, 1896), 214.

[3] Place, *Bulfinch,* 279.

[4] Francis Milton Trollope, *Domestic Manners of the Americans* (London, 1832), 175.

[5] Bulfinch, *Life and Letters,* 218.

Boston—were designed for Unitarian congregations. At the same time, several of Bulfinch's earlier churches, notably the Federal Street Church planned expressly for his friend William Ellery Channing, completed the transition from the Congregational to the Unitarian service.

One of the first religious services the Bulfinches attended in Washington was in Latrobe's enchanting little Church of St. John, which stood within the shadow of the blackened and burned-out White House. Latrobe's concern in the building of this church—supplying not only the design but writing the hymn for the dedication—was similar to Bulfinch's deep personal involvement in many of his Boston commissions. The minister of St. John's, however, did not share his architect's tolerance; he was outspoken toward all who did not tread the Episcopal path and was particularly violent in his denunciation of the new Unitarian creed. Jonathan Mason, one of Bulfinch's principal Beacon Hill patrons and now Congressman from Massachusetts, appealed unsuccessfully to the wardens of the church to temper the harshness of their minister's attacks on other Christian faiths and particularly the one shared by himself and so many other statesmen from "the neighborhood of Boston." Secretary of State John Quincy Adams, the leading Unitarian in Washington at the time, was highly critical of what he held to be the narrow-minded parochialism preached in the Lafayette Square church. In a diary entry of December 23, 1821, relating to the Unitarian Jared Sparks' investiture as Chaplain to the House of Representatives, Adams noted that the rector of St. John's "preached a sermon of coarse invective upon the House, who, he said, by this act had voted Christ out-of-doors." [6] However, Adams left to Sparks the business of answering the Christian critics, and the Chaplain's conspicuous success in this endeavor owed considerably more to his universally acknowledged social gifts than any zeal for theological argument. But Charles Bulfinch, whose tolerance and patience were a legend in Boston, maintained a genuinely friendly relationship with the minister of St. John's. He recorded this friendship in his letters, noting that the minister consulted him frequently and seriously on the subject of enlarging his church. Although we do not now what advice Bulfinch gave regarding what he called "this beautiful little church", it is certain, and unfortunate, that Bulfinch's always generous inclination to continue an earlier designer's "prescribed path" was not followed in the additions of 1842 and 1883.

[6] Allan Nevins, ed., *The Diary of John Quincy Adams, 1794–1845* (New York, 1951), 272.

In the first years of his Washington residency, Bulfinch also attended Sunday services in the hall of the House of Representatives that later served as the Supreme Court chamber. These services were likewise conducted in the Episcopal form but the sermon considerably less inflammatory than that offered in St. John's at the other end of Pennsylvania Avenue. Nor was the ritual of the Episcopal church alien to Charles Bulfinch as it was to his fellow Bostonians of Puritan extraction. Bulfinch's maternal grandfather, Charles Apthorp, contributed a thousand pounds to the building of King's Chapel in 1749 for the Anglicans of Boston and secured the design of the church from his friend Peter Harrison. But shortly after the conclusion of the War for Independence, King's Chapel became the first distinctively Unitarian church in America. The Bulfinch and Apthorp families were among this pioneering congregation that adopted a new religious service in 1785 modelled after the one developed in the earliest Unitarian chapel in London. Yet despite its English origin, Unitarian historians maintain that the movement in America developed logically, as it did regionally, from Congregationalism. This was certainly true of the experience in King's Chapel, whose young lay minister, James Freeman, shared New England's traditional reservations regarding the Trinity. This uneasiness was also felt by Dr. Thomas Bulfinch and his son Charles, who are listed among the half-dozen most prominent members of King's Chapel at the time of its defection. Thus, from its beginning, American Unitarianism was a matter of Bulfinch family interest. This concern was transferred, after 1818, from Boston to the nascent Washington community.

There was no Unitarian church among the twelve houses of public worship in Washington when Bulfinch took up his duties as Architect of the Capitol. However, a group largely composed of English Unitarians held private meetings at Georgetown as early as 1815, and two years later met for public Sunday services in the school established by the English Unitarian émigré John Wright. The *Georgetown National Messenger* of June 5, 1818 reported that Sunday services were held both morning and afternoon in the school on Bridge (now M) Street and estimated the membership of the Georgetown Society at 150. But the founding of a Unitarian community in Washington itself was preceded by events in nearby Baltimore, which, for the first time, brought Unitarian religious principles to national attention. In 1816, Bulfinch's minister at King's Chapel in Boston, the Reverend James Freeman, came down to Baltimore to deliver three lectures on religious liberalism. The result was the formation there of a strong Unitarian congregation and the construction, in the fol-

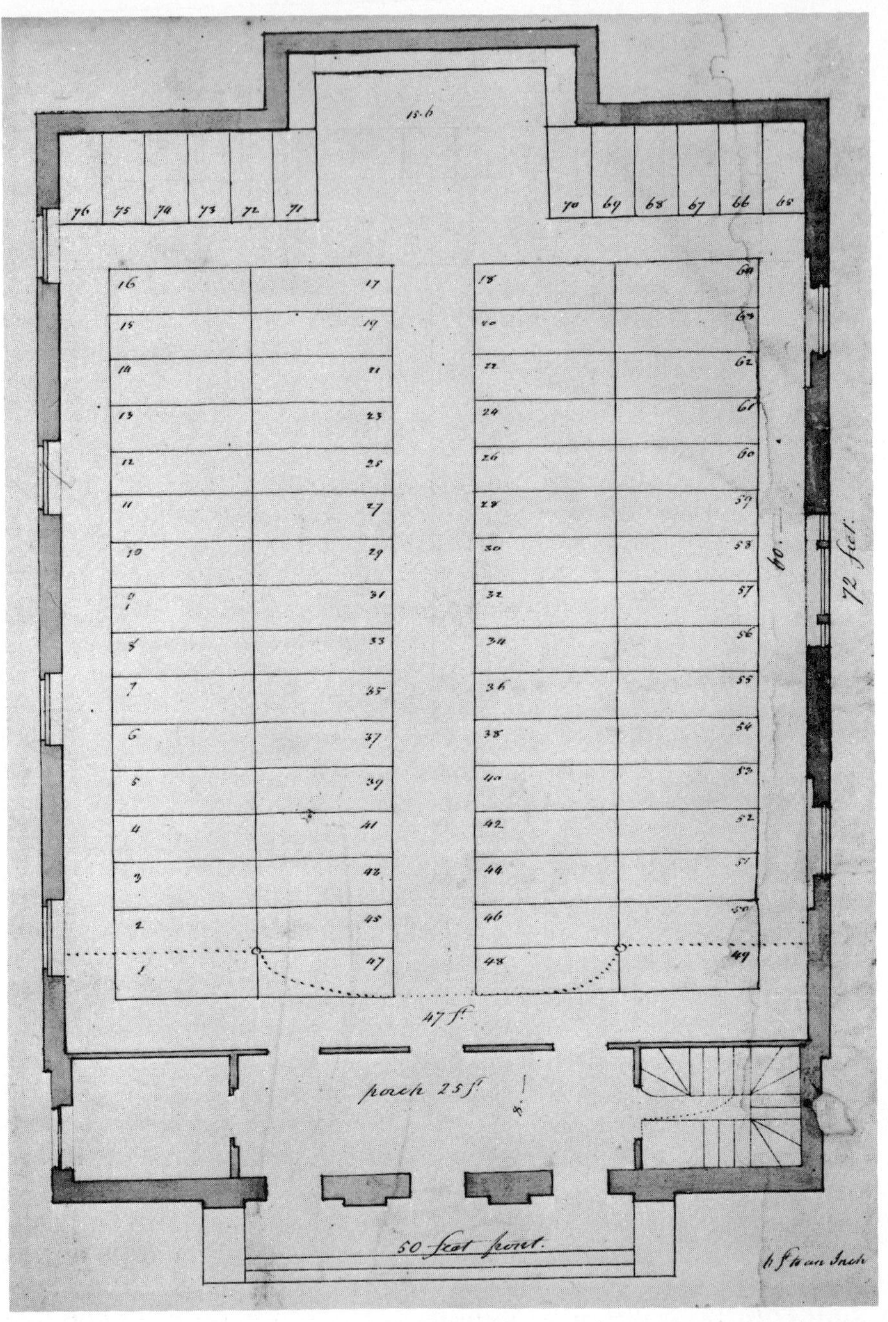

Library of Congress

Bulfinch's preliminary plan for the Unitarian Church in Washington, D.C.

lowing year, of the superb church still standing on the corner of Charles and Franklin Streets. It was to this church that the young but already famous Jared Sparks was called to minister early in 1819. The sermon delivered at Sparks' ordination in Baltimore by William Ellery Channing—universally known as "the Pentecost of American Unitarianism"—attracted wide popular attention, not only in Maryland and Washington but throughout the Republic. Channing's sermon was significant in setting forth in the clearest terms the fundamental tenets of the Unitarian creed. These tenets had an enthusiastic advocate in Jared Sparks who took upon himself the task, begun by James Freeman of King's Chapel, of spreading "Boston's religion" into the Southern states.

In February of 1820, Edward Everett, another New Englander who, like Sparks, served as a future president of Harvard College, delivered a notable sermon in the Chamber of the House of Representatives. The sermon was important in focusing local interest in the Unitarian creed, especially among some of the men in high government position. Partly as a result of this, Jared Sparks was appointed Chaplain to the House of Representatives in the following year. There was still much opposition to the selection of a Unitarian to this post, but Sparks' nomination was successfully defended by two of Monroe's cabinet members, the Unitarians John Quincy Adams and John C. Calhoun. The election of Sparks as Chaplain to the House on December 10, 1821 was regarded at the time as a critical contest between religious liberalism and orthodoxy. The men of orthodoxy, having successfully driven the Unitarian Dr. Thomas Cooper from the initial professorship of the University of Virginia two years before, entered the battle with great vigor and violence. Sparks, who believed that the clergy of Washington generally opposed him, attributed his victory to the men in government, both elected and appointed, who supported his cause. The political climate of the Era of Good Feelings and the new Chaplain's immense charm and growing reputation prevented every subsequent attempt to unseat him. The contest was absolutely crucial to Washington's emerging Unitarian community, whose formal organization took place in the same year as the controversy over Sparks' election.

But even before the battle over Sparks' confirmation, a Washington (rather than Georgetown) Unitarian congregation was meeting weekly in the "long room" over the public bath on C Street. A first notice of this place of public worship was given in the *National Intelligencer* of June 2, 1820, where we are further told the room was a comfortable one seating about eighty people. The *Intelligencer* was owned by two

Unitarians, brothers-in-law Joseph Gales, Jr. and William Winston Seaton, who, along with Robert Little, were among the twenty-seven founders of the Washington church. Little, refusing to use the title Reverend even after he became the first minister in 1821, shared the pulpit in the "long room" with Jared Sparks, who traveled down from Baltimore almost every Sunday. By 1823, when Sparks had resigned both his Chaplaincy and the Baltimore church to become editor of the *North American Review,* thereby embarking upon a distinguished secular career, the Washington congregation was well settled in the new Bulfinch church located about one-half mile northeast of the Capitol. And although the Unitarian community continued to be plagued with financial woes, the years of religious and political harassment were over.

On July 31, 1820, at a meeting held in the "long room" with Bulfinch's son Thomas acting as secretary, it was proposed and adopted that "measures be taken for erecting a place of divine worship upon Unitarian principles in the City of Washington." [7] At a second meeting held the following week, the democratic character of the church government was assured by a resolution providing that the minister and all church officers be elected directly by the congregation and committees serve only for specific purposes and for limited periods. The actual organization of the church, however, was delayed for more than a year because of financial difficulties. It was not until November 11, 1821 that the First Unitarian Church, Washington, D. C., was formally constituted and Robert Little elected minister. In the meanwhile, the Bulfinch sons, Thomas and George, were engaged in a national fund-raising campaign whose appeal seems to have gone largely unheeded outside of Boston. Then, as now, Unitarians were convinced, in the view of the Washington church's first minister, "that truth is best left to make its own way." [8] Nonetheless, probably one thousand dollars was raised among the New England churches, notably in the neighborhood of Boston; in addition, the Baltimore and Charleston congregations contributed perhaps one-third that amount.

The official biographer of Washington Unitarianism has stated that the First Church has always counted among its members "an unusual number of persons prominent in national and community life." [9] This is certainly true of the twenty-seven men who organized

---

[7] Memorandum of Thomas Bulfinch, August 1, 1820, All Souls Church archives, Washington, D. C. Courtesy of Dr. Laurence C. Staples.

[8] Quoted in Laurence C. Staples, *Washington Unitarianism: A Rich Heritage* (Washington, D. C., 1970), 6.

[9] *Ibid.,* 15.

the Church in 1821. John Quincy Adams was the most important founding member during the church's crucial first decade as well as its most articulate lay exponent. Adams was a Unitarian before there was a church of that faith in Washington. Like his cousin and fellow founder, William Cranch—and indeed like Cranch's cousin and fellow founder Charles Bulfinch—Adams brought to the capital a well defined religious philosophy. As early as 1812, in a diary entry from St. Petersburg, he neatly summed up (for himself at least) the great Unitarian question:[10]

> The Trinity, the Divinity of Christ, the whole doctrine of atonement, all miracles, the Immaculate Conception of Jesus, and a devil mantaining war against Omnipotence, appear to me all as contrary to human reason.

This reliance upon reason in religion gave to Adams, as to that other Unitarian president Thomas Jefferson, a tolerance not supportable to early Nineteenth-Century orthodox Protestantism. It also enabled him to steer clear of the schisms which later developed within his own church. So far as can be known, Adams' views were precisely those held by the founders generally, and they were succinctly summed up in a letter from the then Secretary of State to George Sullivan in 1821—the year in which the First Unitarian Church, Washington, was formally constituted.[11]

> The only importance of religion to my mind consists in its influence upon the conduct; and upon the conduct of mankind the question of Trinity or Unity, or of the single or double personal nature of Christ, has or ought to have no bearing whatsoever.

At the time Adams made his observations the Trinitarian controversy was fifteen hundred years old, and little insight was expected either from St. John's on Lafayette Square or in the "long room" on C Street. Adams and the other founders wisely left the business of spiritual rebuttal to the worldly Jared Sparks, for whom Unitarianism was a stepping stone to a wide and distinguished career.

On the list of church founders in 1821, the name of John C. Calhoun follows that of John Quincy Adams. Four years later, Calhoun was still following Adams, this time as Vice President of the United States. Although raised a Presbyterian, Calhoun gradually shook off his Calvinist orthodoxy until, in his student days at Yale, "he ceased

---

[10] C. F. Adams, ed., *Memoirs of John Quincy Adams* (Philadelphia, 1874), II, 356.

[11] Worthington C. Ford, ed., *The Writings of John Quincy Adams* (New York, 1917), VII, 90.

even to profess Christianity." [12] But Calhoun remained an intensely religious man. Prior to the completion of the First Unitarian Church, he and his wife were often in attendance at St. John's on Lafayette Square. It is not known whether Calhoun was brought to Unitarianism through his contacts with John Quincy Adams and Jared Sparks but his conversion was complete. He was the author of the unfulfilled prophecy: "Unitarianism is the only true faith and will ultimately prevail over the world." [13] On a more substantial level, Calhoun was a church founder, contributed materially to the erection of the Bulfinch building, and maintained a pew in that austere edifice.

Among Washington Unitarianism's founding families, only the Galeses exerted an influence on the same scale as that of the Bulfinches. Joseph Gales, Sr., his son Joseph, Jr., and son-in-law William Winston Seaton, were the first to sign the Church articles of incorporation. Joseph Gales, Sr. was the patriarch of American Unitarianism, having fled England in 1794 as a result of his outspoken support for Joseph Priestly and Thomas Paine. He settled first in Philadelphia, where he won immediate fame for his verbatim daily reports of the Congressional proceedings in the *Independent Gazetteer*. In 1799, Gales moved to Raleigh, North Carolina, when he founded the weekly *Register*, served a long term as mayor, and helped establish the Unitarian society in Charleston, South Carolina. After his retirement, Gales resided in Washington where his son and son-in-law owned and edited the *National Intelligencer*, famous to historians for its half-title, *Annals of Congress*. Joseph Gales, Jr. reported the debates from the Senate; his brother-in-law William Winston Seaton did those from the House. Both editors served as mayor of Washington, Seaton for an unprecedented five terms (1840–1850).[14] Seaton's well known political independence was put to the test in the controversial Presidential election of 1824, when he supported William H. Crawford instead of fellow founder John Quincy Adams. But Crawford, although not a church member, had contributed to the construction of the Bulfinch building and Seaton's act can therefore not be regarded as apostasy. Furthermore, it was presumably to Crawford, Secretary of the Treasury in Monroe's cabinet, that the appeal was made to secure a "livelihood" in the Treasury Department

[12] Margaret L. Coit, *John C. Calhoun* (Boston, 1950), 21.

[13] Quoted in Jennie W. Scudder, "Historical Sketch of the Unitarian Church of Washington, D. C.," *Records of the Columbia Historical Society of Washington, D. C.*, 13 (1910), 169.

[14] Two of the other early mayors of Washington, Richard Wallach and Robert Chew Weightman, were among the forty-six gentlemen who joined the church after it was organized in 1821.

Library of Congress

Bulfinch's preliminary front elevations for the Unitarian Church in Washington, D. C.

for Robert Little, the Unitarian church's first and consistently underpaid minister. The Seaton's Washington house was famous for decades for "a rich cellar and a heavy table", and was the constant resort of John Quincy Adams, John C. Calhoun, Daniel Webster, and Justice Joseph Story of the Supreme Court—fellow Unitarians not always united in political fellowship.[15]

Midway down the list of founders appears the name of William Cranch, a favorite cousin of Mrs. Charles Bulfinch and a close childhood friend of her architect husband. The son of a judge of the Court of Common Pleas of Massachusetts, Cranch maintained simultaneously a friendship with John Adams (his uncle), who appointed him assistant judge of the First Circuit Court in 1801, and Thomas Jeffer-

[15] It was said of Webster that he "attended divine worship [in the First Unitarian Church] when he wasn't worshipping the Constitution or himself." Quoted by William Tindall, "Homes of the Local Government," *Records of the Columbia Historical Society of Washington, D. C.*, 3 (1900), 295.

Library of Congress

Bulfinch's preliminary side elevation for the Unitarian Church in Washington, D. C.

Library of Congress

Bulfinch's section for the Unitarian Church in Washington, D. C.

Library of Congress

The Unitarian Church in Washington, D. C. Watercolor, dated 1839, attributed to August Kollner.

son, who elevated him to the head of the judiciary of the District of Columbia in 1806. For the next fifty years Cranch was a man of action and legend in Washington, where he and his family gave indispensable social comfort and assistance to several generations of Bulfinches residing in the nation's capital. Among the papers relating to the early Washington Unitarian community is a letter from Cranch to Secretary of War Joel R. Poinsett, dated April 2, 1838, recommending the Reverend Stephen Greenleaf Bulfinch, then minister of the Unitarian church, for a government clerkship.[16] Cranch probably also served as the reconciling link between John Quincy Adams and Charles Bulfinch. For apart from their deep mutual concern with Washington Unitarianism, there seems to have been little personal warmth between President Monroe's Secretary of State and his Architect. Nevertheless, all three were absolutely essential to the organization and administration of the First Unitarian Church: Adams as the ranking founder and most articulate lay spokesman; Bulfinch as architect and head of a family preeminent in church organization and finance; Cranch as permanent secretary, chairman of the Committee of Management and, upon occasion, church organist.

[16] Archives of All Souls Church.

As previously noted, the decision to erect "a place of divine worship upon Unitarian principles in the City of Washington" was taken in July 1820. Construction of the church edifice, however, was held up until the Society's formal organization in November of the following year. The First Church, for which Bulfinch gratuitously furnished the plans (he and his family were among the chief subscribers to the building fund), was dedicated on June 9, 1822. The delay in church construction was the usual one of flagging finances. Both the future minister, Robert Little, and the architect's son Thomas were sent canvassing among every likely source. Little concentrated upon New England, which he visited in the summer of 1821, relying heavily for support upon Bulfinch's old friend William Ellery Channing and the architect's son-in-law Joseph Coolidge, Jr. Thomas Bulfinch made the rounds of the Federal City, where he seems to have been most successful with Thomas Law, who gave $650 to the building fund. Law, the son of the Bishop of Carlisle, came to Washington in 1794 and his name is among those later appended to the list of founding members. But Law's was a rare benefaction; from the first the Washington community was plagued with financial difficulties—and indifference. According to his biographer, Jared Sparks was "deeply grieved" that no Unitarian clergymen came to Washington from New England to attend the ordination of Robert Little, although invitations "had been sent to all the brethren in the vicinity of Boston." [17] Indeed, the Washington church was dedicated with only the neighborly assistance of a lay member from Philadelphia. But even worse than indifference, money was not forthcoming. As Bulfinch himself said, the construction of the Washington church was "hampered by every consideration of economy", and this fact accounts for his unsatisfactory design compromises.[18] The dismal state of finances is evident too in the declining salary paid to the first minister: $1,000 in 1822 (just one-half of that paid Sparks by his Baltimore congregation); in 1823 it dropped to $830. By the time Bulfinch's son, Stephen Greenleaf Bulfinch, became minister (1838), the stipend was only $600—which explains Judge Cranch's attempt to procure him a "living" in the War Department.

The site selected for the First Unitarian Church, a slight elevation at the northeast corner of Sixth and D Streets, was considered at the time to be in "an aristocratic neighborhood." This situation reflected not only the social status of the congregation but was convenient to

[17] Herbert Baxter Adams, *The Life and Writings of Jared Sparks* (Boston, 1893), I, 196.

[18] Place, *Bulfinch,* 264. The cost of constructing the church was $9,291.15; the building lot $1,161.20. Archives of All Souls Church, Washington, D. C.

the homes of many of the founding members. The Bulfinch family, for example, resided one-half block to the north on Sixth Street. The First Unitarian Church, Washington, was the last of nine documented churches Bulfinch designed and the only one erected outside of Massachusetts. In this final ecclesiastical commission, Bulfinch returned to the Doric order of his first Boston church (Hollis Street) and the meeting-house design of his early country churches in Pittsfield and Taunton. The absence in this design of the brilliant innovations of his mature work, such as the Church of Christ at Lancaster, resulted from the "consideration[s] of economy" noted by the architect. A study of the drawings preserved in the Library of Congress, which include site and floor plans, alternative exterior and interior elevations, and drawings for the dedicatory tablet and entrance gates, show that Bulfinch only reluctantly accepted the final scheme with projecting bell tower continued through the porch. The effect of this extrusion upon an otherwise handsome portico was unfortunate. The interior of the church, however, fully justified the contemporary press appellation of "architectural elegance." [19] Bulfinch's surviving elevations reveal an austere but beautiful composition of recessed round-headed windows similar to those introduced thirty years earlier in his first Boston houses. The plan shows that the church was designed to seat about 350 people in 76 box pews and a small gallery over the entrance porch. Some among the congregation undoubtedly felt that the dozen pews placed in a line along the altar end of the church abutted perilously upon the minister's pulpit, but economy was the controlling factor in all matters of design.

Bulfinch negotiated with Paul Revere's son Joseph for the casting of the bell of approximately a thousand pounds which arrived "warranted with suitable usage for one year." [20] The thankless task of raising the purchase price—forty cents per pound—was undertaken by the architect's son George. In July of 1822, the sum was finally subscribed, primarily due to a $100 contribution by President Monroe. The Revere Bell was the only one in the capital to toll the execution of John Brown in 1859, and for this defiant act was officially silenced until the Civil War when it again rang out to record Union victories.[21] The bell, although guaranteed by its maker for only one year, has hung successively in three church towers, and today, one hundred and fifty years later, continues to call the Unitarians of

[19] *National Intelligencer,* June 12, 1822.

[20] Staples, *Washington Unitarianism,* 9.

[21] In the Civil War, the Bulfinch Church, like most religious institutions in the Federal City, served as a hospital for wounded troops.

Library of Congress

Unitarian Church in Washington, D. C. Photograph showing alterations made after 1865.

Washington to Sunday service. In 1827, five years after the bell was lifted into place, the entrance gates were installed and the church completed. The gates, made in Philadelphia by Samuel Richards, were inspired by William Strickland's design for the Second Bank of the United States. The design of the gates was Bulfinch's last attempt to impose the Greek Revival style upon the civic and religious architecture of Washington.

Although Bulfinch returned to Boston in 1830, his connection with the Unitarian church in Washington continued for another decade. The first minister died in 1827 and was succeeded by three young men trained at the Harvard Divinity School which included Stephen Greenleaf Bulfinch, appointed the church's fourth minister in 1838.

The youngest of the architect's sons, he served in Atlanta and Pittsburgh before coming to the nation's capital where he ministered until 1844. His parents visited Washington in the fall of 1838 and remained through the following spring. During this period, Bulfinch supervised a number of improvements and repairs for the church. It is possible that these included the design for the semi-circular steps, which, however, were not constructed until many years later. Bulfinch's building continued in religious use through the third-quarter of the Nineteenth Century, although the neoclassical proportions were seriously marred by the addition of Gothic buttresses. The final Unitarian service was held in the church on May 27, 1877. Three years later the building was sold to the District of Columbia for $20,000 and converted to a police court. The Bulfinch structure was pulled down in 1900; the site is today occupied by the Office of the Recorder of Deeds.

All that now survives as testament to Bulfinch's services to the Washington Unitarian community is a silver flagon long used in the Communion service and designated by the Church as "one of its most precious possessions." [22] This flagon, an earlier work from the shop of Paul Revere, was presented to the architect in 1787 in gratitude by the congregation of the Hollis Street Church in Boston. The plan Bulfinch gratuitously gave for that church was the first of many gifts culminating more than three decades later with the design for the First Unitarian Church, Washington. It was consistent with Bulfinch's generous nature that, when he and his wife returned to Boston in 1830, he presented to their Washington Church its most historic relic. This chaste but elegant flagon can be taken as symbolic of the life of service and devotion which Charles Bulfinch brought from Boston to the nation's capital and which the Washington Unitarians hoped to foster in their community when the Bulfinches moved among them.

---

[22] Staples, *Washington Unitarianism,* 21.

Lukas Vischer in Washington: A Swiss View of the District of Columbia in 1825

Translated and edited by

CHRISTIAN F. FEEST

Until a few years ago, Lukas Vischer was known almost only to Swiss art historians as a member of a circle of amateur artists in Basle in the early years of the Nineteenth Century, and to students of Mexican antiquities as the collector of an interesting collection of mainly Aztec stone sculpture and pottery. Then research by the Austrian Mexicanist Ferdinand Anders on the history of Vischer's collection resulted in the discovery of two sketchbooks of watercolors and pen and ink drawings and a set of American diaries in the Vischer family archives at Wildenstein castle near Bubendorf, Basel-Landschaft.

Following this discovery I was asked by Anders to make a study of Vischer's pictures of Creek Indians, painted in 1824, which are among the earliest Creek pictures known to have been painted in the Creek Nation. My contribution, which included the annotated transcript of Vischer's Creek diary, together with Anders's work on Vischer in Mexico, was published in 1967 in a volume portraying Vischer as an artist, traveller, and collector.[1] It was the first time that a portion of Lukas Vischer's North American diaries was published, but it presented only the entries for one week in 1824. The whole set of diaries, however, covers without a break the full period of Vischer's residence in the United States from 1823 to 1828. Consisting of 17 volumes filled with the author's minuscule handwriting, it presents an enormous amount of detailed observations of American life during an interesting period of

Christian F. Feest spoke before the Columbia Historical Society on October 16, 1973.

[1] Ferdinand Anders, Margarete Pfister-Burkhalter, and Christian F. Feest, *Lukas Vischer: Reisender-Künstler-Sammler*, Völkerkundliche Abhandlungen 2 (Hannover, 1967).

Courtesy of Peter L. Vischer

Lukas Vischer in 1838. Portrait in Vischer family archives at Wildenstein.

American history.[2] Although the general interest in Vischer's diary was plainly apparent from the first time I had a chance to look at it, my only action so far has been to publish all materials relating to the American Indians contained in those volumes.[3] As an anthropologist (though one with a strong taste for history) I did not feel at that time that I was in a position to prepare a useful edition of

[2] I wish to thank the owner of the Lukas Vischer papers, Mr. Peter L. Vischer, for his kind and continuing interest in my work on his great-great-granduncle's diaries, for his permission to study them in 1968 in Vienna and in 1974 at Wildenstein castle, and for his permission to publish parts of them here.

[3] Christian F. Feest, "Lukas Vischers Beiträge zur Ethnographie Nordamerikas", *Archiv für Völkerkunde* 22: 31–66 (Wien, 1968).

the full diary. On the other hand, it was clear that few American local historians, who might have the greatest interest in the data, would be able to make use of the manuscript. It is written not only in German, but in a German script which today even those to whom German is a native language may find a little hard to decipher.

During my appointment as a Smithsonian Fellow for 1972–1973, I was encouraged by Wilcomb E. Washburn to prepare a translation at least of those parts of the diary relating to the District of Columbia. At the same time the Virginia Historical Society indicated its interest in publishing the much longer Virginia section.[4]

Lukas Vischer was born in 1780 into a patrician family of Basle, a family with strong ties to the silk ribbon industry, considerable political power, and an interest in the arts. The family's art collection was one of the most important in all of Switzerland. While Lukas's elder brother Peter was destined to inherit the factory, Lukas apparently had considerable time for his hobbies. When at the age of 42, Vischer left Switzerland for the New World, his decision was prompted by difficulties with his family who thought that it might be better for Lukas to leave the country for a while. In America, however, he was usefully employed in making business contacts and opening new markets for his family's industry. But most of his time he appears to have spent in travelling and exploring American society.

He arrived in the United States in June 1823 and took up residence in Stamford, Connecticut. In October he moved to Philadelphia with the intention to stay there over winter, but in December he was persuaded to take a boat to Charleston, South Carolina, where he remained until the end of February 1824. Subsesequently he crossed the South via Savannah, Georgia, the Creek Nation, to Montgomery, Alabama, down the Alabama River to Mobile and finally to New Orleans. In May 1824 he went up the Mississippi and the Ohio to Pittsburgh and across Pennsylvania to Philadelphia where he made his headquarters until September 1825. During that time he visited New Jersey, New York, Maryland, the District of Columbia, and Virginia, and explored various parts of Pennsylvania. In September 1825 he paid a short visit to

[4] The officers of the Virginia Historical Society have kindly agreed to my proposal to publish those parts of the diary relating to Washington separately from those relating to Virginia, although Vischer's second visit to the nation's capital forms an integral part of his tour of Virginia, the diary of which is to be published at a future date in the *Virginia Magazine of History and Biography*.

Montreal and Quebec and afterwards settled for 40 weeks in Boston. During the summer of 1826 he toured Nova Scotia and New Brunswick. The rest of his time in the United States, Vischer had his headquarters in New York. Early in 1828 he finally left for Mexico via New Orleans. After five years in the United States, he stayed for ten years in Mexico, travelling widely and collecting and painting more extensively than in the years before. On the other hand, less diaristic material survives for this period. He returned to Basle in 1838 and died two years afterwards at the age of 60.

His diary was not written for immediate publication, although internal evidence discloses that such was probably his long range goal. Internal evidence also shows that his entries were not made daily, but at a later date on the basis of notes taken. He was generally interested in the social conditions of all classes, but had, of course, a special concern for the French and German element (both Swiss and non-Swiss) in the American population. His attention was frequently directed to minorities of all sorts, including social, racial, cultural, and religious minority groups. But his main interest was probably in art. It is therefore not surprising to learn that the only piece of his writing ever published during his lifetime was a well-informed, critical survey of art and artists in the United States, published in 1828 in a German journal devoted to America, whose editor he had met in Philadelphia.[5]

Vischer's judgments may at times seem to be overcritical, but his observations are always fresh and personal and at times amusing. His continuing concern for facts and details makes his diary an interesting source for local history.

Vischer paid two visits to the District of Columbia, both in 1825. In January he accompanied a certain J. G. Hess of Zürich, whom he had met earlier in Philadelphia, on a tour to Baltimore and Washington where he stayed two days. The second visit spanned ten days and was part of a much longer stay to Virginia which Vischer made in the company of the Italian count Carlo de Vidua, a son of the Prime Minister of the King of Sardinia. Vidua's letters from America which describe the same trip were published in Italy in 1835 and have recently been translated into English.[6] If proof for Vischer's ability as an observer is desired, a comparison with Vidua's letters amply provides it.

---

[5] Eduard Florens Rivinus, ed., *Atlantis* 4 (Leipzig, 1827).

[6] *Lettere del Conte Carlo Vidua*, ed. by Cesare Balbo (3 vols., Torino, 1835); Elizabeth Cometti and Valeria Gennardo-Lerda, "The Presidential Tour of Carlo Vidua with Letters on Virginia", *Virginia Magazine of History and Biography* 77(4): 387–406 (Richmond, 1969).

In translating the following texts, an attempt has been made to retain as much as possible of Vischer's style and flavor. If the English at times may seem to be unusual, it should help to remind the reader that these are indeed the observations of a foreign visitor.[7]

FIRST VISIT, JANUARY 20–21, 1825[8]

January 20

In the morning between 7 and 8 we traveled by mail stage ($4 for 37 miles) to Washington, through mostly thin, sandy country, and unsightly villages one of which (where we had breakfast) had been rechristened Waterloo.[9] In another one, situated on the eastern branch of the Potomac (presumably Bladensburg, 6 miles from the capital) one of our travel companions pointed out to us the road on which the British had advanced in 1815, and the hills over which the Americans had retreated.[10]

Washington

As soon as we came to Washington we found the Capitol, went around it and down Pennsylvania Avenue and took our lodging at the Indian Queen, at Brown's.[11] This lower road or roads which extend slantwise from the Capitol for about one mile to the vicinity of the house of the President, already have an urban appearance. They are on both sides bordered with houses, mostly containing small shops. But as soon as one turns left from this road, one enters a kind of desert extending to the river, through which one reaches the governmental docks.[12] Turning to the right, however, one passes through streets which though laid out according to plans have as yet no connection with one another. Between the habitation of the President and Georgetown there is also a proper street, containing some not unsightly houses mostly used for lodgings. In general, however, there are besides the government's buildings only small unimportant houses, from which it may be seen that neither have rich individuals settled here, nor is that place particularly suited

---

[7] Marginal notes in the diary (except when they contain additions to the running text) are printed here as italic captions in the text.

[8] Diary no. 6.

[9] Waterloo in eastern Howard County, Maryland, on U.S. Highway 1 which closely follows the old post route between Baltimore and Washington. The sandiness of the land is also noted by Traugott Bromme (*Reisen durch die Vereinigten Staaten und Ober-Canada* [3 vols., Baltimore, 1834–1835], II, 195).

[10] 1815 is an error: General Ross defeated the Americans on August 24, 1814.

[11] The "Indian Queen" is mentioned also by William Owen in 1824 (*Diary of William Owen*, ed. by W. Hiatt [Indianapolis, 1906], 39).

[12] The Navy Yard, visited by Vischer in June.

for the acquisition of wealth, both of which appears perfectly natural taking into account the unfriendliness and poverty of those parts.

Surroundings

The surroundings in the back of the town are broken and mostly covered with thin woodlands.

Georgetown

Georgetown can more than sufficiently supply the people of the vicinity with their needs. This town, containing about 7,000 inhabitants, is compact, on uneven ground, situated close to the Potomac, just at the point where the river fleeing the coercion of mountaineous banks enters an open plain and—just like a youth freed from his warden's supervision, commits debauches. Between the Virginian banks and the city lies a beautiful island.[13] The situation of the place has something romantic about it. From the upper part of it one may enjoy a wide view across the river, which includes Mount Vernon, the place of General Washington's home and grave. Georgetown contains a stately college[14] and a nunnery[15] which is opened to visitors once a week.

Banks

Of course, there are also several banks here, one of which boasting a Greek exterior stands on top of a slope. But this on second glance miserable, petty offspring which had never reached full maturity has caused the death of its mother. The architects wasted the whole capital of $45,000, whereupon the Bank of the United States, probably as the foremost creditor, bought the monster in public auction for $10,000. The houses of this old town almost extend to those of Washington. We visited there a certain Mr. Willcox.

January 21

Our first excursion on this day was to the Columbian College to visit the young Dr. Staughton[16] who had come over from Europe

[13] Theodore Roosevelt Island.

[14] Visited during the second visit; see below.

[15] The old Clarist convent, also known as the "monastery", was established in 1801, and the building sold in 1805 to Bishop Neale who established a visitation convent there (Richard P. Jackson, *The Chronicles of Georgetown, D.C. from 1751 to 1878* (Washington, 1878), 226–228; see also Bromme, *Reisen,* II, 208). Vischer mentions it again without visiting it in June.

[16] The front fly leaf of Diary no. 6 has the following note in English: "Dr. F. [sic] Staughton, 10th Street, nearly opposite the Globe hotel, about 8 doors above the Pennsylvania Avenue." The young Dr. Staughton is below identified as James M. Staughton.

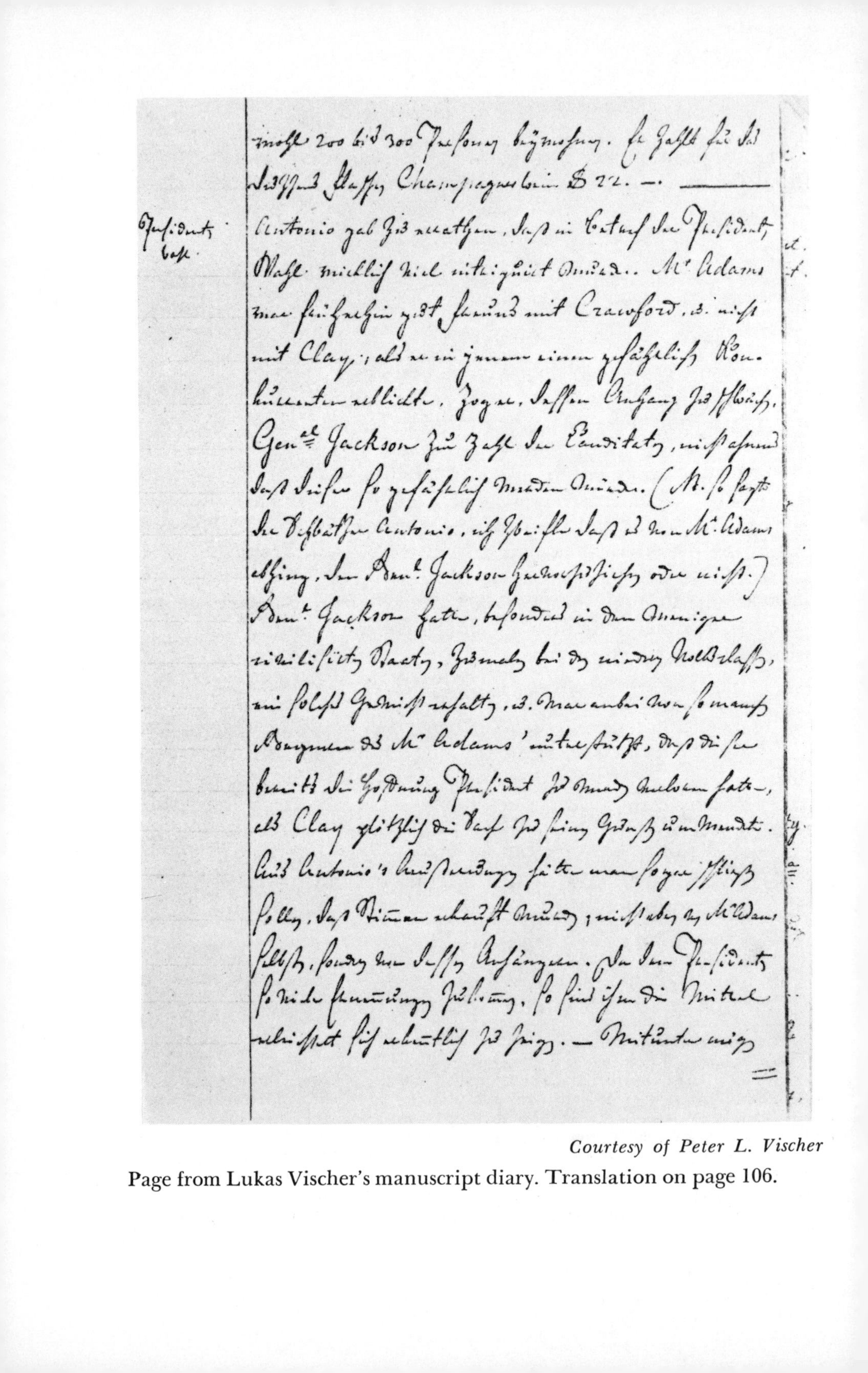

Courtesy of Peter L. Vischer

Page from Lukas Vischer's manuscript diary. Translation on page 106.

together with Mr. Hess. We took a hackney-cab for $1 for both of us; the price for excursions within the city as fixed by the government is 25 cents per person. Columbian College[17] is situated on the woody hill one to two miles from the city. It consists of a main building with several adjacent buildings. This year another main building is to be erected. The institution originated three and a half years ago. At the present time the number of pupils is 130. Two students live together in a study and two small bed rooms, a special room is reserved for newspapers. The old Dr. Staughton,[18] the president of this place of learning and formerly a clergyman in Philadelphia, received us very kindly, showed us the building, the far extending view from the battlement of the roof, and the young museum, wherein the chemical apparatus and the beautiful scientific instruments are the most important items.

Dr. Staughton

His son, doctor of pharmacology, lives in the city; his excellent education is crowned by modesty.

Patent Rooms[19]

This amiable young man led us to the rooms in the house of the Postmaster General, in which the many models are kept, which were submitted for the purpose of receiving a patent. The supervision over this rather peculiar collection has been entrusted to a mechanic, Keller of Schaffhausen.[20] This compatriot went out of his way to point out and explain to us the more remarkable pieces.

King's Gallery of Paintings[21]

Afterwards Dr. Staughton conducted us to the exhibition of paintings of the painter King, which consists for the main part in

---

[17] For more details about the Columbian College which later became George Washington University, see Vischer's account during his second visit, below.

[18] William Staughton (1770–1829) was president of Columbian College between 1822 and 1829 (*Dictionary of American Biography* [*DAB*], ed. by A. Johnson, [New York, 1946], XVII, 539–540).

[19] Visited again by Vischer and Vidua in June. For contemporary descriptions of the Patent Office see Bernard Duke of Saxe-Weimar, *Travels Through North America, in the Years 1825 and 1826* (2 vols., Philadelphia, 1828), I, 173–175, and Bromme, *Reisen*, II, 200.

[20] "Under Dr. Thornton, a Swiss is employed whose name is Keller, a very able mechanic, and inspector of the model room, who explained everything to me." (Saxe-Weimar, *Travels*, I, 175); "Mr. Keller, a Swiss, is employed as the attendant of the model room." (Bromme, *Reisen*, II 199–200).

[21] Charles Bird King (1785–1862) is today best remembered as the artist who painted Indian delegations visiting Washington (Groce and Wallace, *The New-York Historical Society's Dictionary of Artists in America, 1564–1860*, [New Haven and London, 1957], 370).

portraits or copies of paintings made by the owner, but occasionally also contains products of rather good artists, among which, however, I did not notice any one which would deserve special notice or inclusion into a renowned collection.

Capitol

Afterwards we went together to the Capitol, saw there the portrait of General Washington by R. Peale,[22] which was on display without charge and on which I have commented on Christmas Day, and also two of the four big historical paintings of the old Trumbull,[23] which are destined to decorate the hall of the Capitol.

Senate

We stayed for a while in the chamber of the Senate. The senators were sitting there quietly and decently with uncovered heads.

Jackson

General Jackson[24] was occupied with folding a letter; he was called to the door and it struck us all as strange how he always bowed as he passed the audience, regardless of the fact that nobody seemed to take notice. So we usually fall into extremes when we try to act contrary to our natural character. The demagogue was made embarrassed, the man who had called him to the door was a rough Kentuckian who—doubtlessly heartened by a few glasses of brandy—was plainly taking up his idol's time to be admitted to the Senate. But the benches on the sides, which are reserved for distinguished visitors only, were already fully occupied, and the General thirsting for the presidency did not permit himself to send the impudent or confused man to the gallery, the most suitable place for him. Finally an attendant of the house helped him over his embarrassment by telling the Kentuckian he should himself look for a place to sit. Now the peasant seated himself on the seat of a senator, and after he was directed to move away from thence, he

[22] Rembrandt Peale (1778–1860); his portrait of Washington was seen by Vischer in Philadelphia when it was displayed by Peale after its completion on December 25, 1824 (Groce and Wallace, *Dictionary* 493–494; *DAB* XIV, 344–347).

[23] John Trumbull (1756–1843) executed four large historical paintings for the Capitol Rotunda: Declaration of Independence, Surrender of Burgoyne, Surrender of Cornwallis, Resignation of Washington at Annapolis (Groce and Wallace, *Dictionary,* 637–638; *DAB* XIX, 11–15).

[24] Andrew Jackson (1767–1845), 7th President of the United States (*DAB* IX, 526–534). This was after the disputed 1824 election in which Jackson had received the largest share of the popular vote, but before the inauguration of John Quincy Adams.

placed himself right in front of Miss Wright, but was also pushed from there farther to the back of the room. The chamber of the Senate receives all its light from above which lighting corresponds with the dignity of this assembly.

Chamber of the Representatives

The chamber of the Representatives is far more spacious and brilliant, surrounded by pillars of grey, domestic marble. Besides the lighting from above there are windows at the sides draped with scarlet curtains. As colorful and confusing as the chamber is itself, just so colorful and chaotic were the proceedings in the room. The Representatives present themselves in perfectly informal dress, in topcoats, cloaks, with walking sticks, and all of them—except for the period when they harangue—have their hats on. In general they do not behave themselves differently from the way they are used to in their characteristic rudeness. Almost no notice is given to the

Photograph courtesy Architect of the Capitol

Interior of the Hall of the House of Representatives painted by Samuel F. B. Morse in 1822.

The date of this picture was given as 1825 in the 1969–1970 volume of the *Records* (1971) at page 205. More recent research seems to establish 1822 as the correct date.

speaker, except when he is one à la mode, which appears to me to be one of the most offending insolences. There is a continual roving around, walking up and down, and even those who sit or rather lie, are talking with one another. Blowing one's nose with the fingers in this magnificent hall laid out with precious carpets is nothing unusual; I was myself witness of it.

Library Building

We also viewed the magnificent room of the library; the Capitol building did not meet my expectations, although it is a costly, spacious building. Built of white stone on the top of a slope rising 78 feet above the city, I judge it as not being built in a noble and grandiose style; the windows—round, square, pointed, oval—look to me like a sample card. The central dome appeared to me to be proportionately too high. Towards the city there are two basements above one another. The entrance is a small door. The interior of the building appeared to me to be badly built and dark.[25]

House of the President

The house of the President, built undoubtedly by the same architect,[26] appealed even less to me. Mr. Hess had a letter for the President's daughter. An unsightly servant opened the doors. The lady had gone out for a drive. We let us be shown to the reception rooms and marvelled at their small dimensions. Only every 14 days, on Wednesdays, there is an assembly at the President's; visitors wishing to be admitted leave their cards in the morning at the house of the President and thereupon get an invitation. A garden not too well cared for surrounds the building.

Office Buildings[27]

In the vicinity are several spacious government offices built of bricks. Their ground floors do not rise sufficiently from the ground. In this part of the city the construction of a spacious inn is said to be planned by a group of stockholders.

---

[25] The Capitol is discussed in more detail below.

[26] The White House was indeed built after plans by James Hoban.

[27] The State Department, Treasury, War Department, and Navy Department were built "in a line with and at the distance of 450 feet from the President's house." (David B. Warden, *A Chorographical and Statistical Description of the District of Columbia* [Paris, 1816], 36; for a later and more detailed description see William Q. Force, *Force's Picture of the City of Washington and its Vicinity* [Washington, 1848], 78–83).

Theater

In the evening we visited the theater; this, of course, does not compare with the country but rather with the capital and is consequently small. At the same time there was also a performance of the circus.

Painter Wood[28]

I visited the painter Wood who was formerly a goldsmith and became a painter of his own accord. His main field is miniature painting, but he also does sketchy portraits in watercolor and those I like pretty well. I find them spirited and tasteful, and have an even greater estimation for the artist, because he became everything he is on his own.

Keller, the mechanic, told me about the presence here of a son of the former provincial governor Jenner[29] of Berne; I saw this man, neither his appearance nor his behavior gives witness of noble birth. He told me he had formerly been an officer in the British service, had come to America in hopes of being employed as an engineer. Without success he had tried to apply for such an employment in southern America, and here they also give him little hope, so that he now plans to sell the mathematical instruments which he had brought along from Berne, and go to Pittsburgh and New Orleans as a merchant. This man told me about one called Brodbeck[30] from Basle, a good old man who is here employed in the War Department as a servant. Then there is here also a woman from Basle, Mrs. Lehmann, born a Halter,[31] whose husband works as a teacher of the French and German languages at the Columbian College and also teaches fencing.

The inhabitants of the capital are said to amount to 14,000,[32] and moreover there are another 1,000 visitors during Congress.

SECOND VISIT, MAY 29–JUNE 7, 1825[33]

May 29

From the Little Falls of the Potomac the Count and I proceeded on foot to Georgetown[34] where we arrived a quarter to nine and took

[28] Joseph Wood (ca. 1778–1830) was originally a silversmith who had his studio in Washington since 1816 (Groce and Wallace, *Dictionary,* 699–700; *DAB* XX, 466–467).

[29] Probably Gottlieb Abraham Jenner d.J. (1765–1834) who had been chief of the Berne war department shortly before and during the French occupation (*Allgemeine Deutsche Biographie,* [65 vols., Leipzig, 1875–1912], XIII, 770–772).

[30] Brodbeck is a rather common name in Basle. Vischer visited him during his stay in June. See below.

[31] The Lehmann and Halter (or Halder) families are also mentioned more extensively in connection with the June visit. See below.

[32] Marginal note by Vischer: "According to a new count of 16,605."

[33] Diary no. 6.

[34] A walk of approximately four miles.

lodging for the night in the Columbian Inn at Semmes'. We requested only a cup of tea for which the innkeeper charged us—allegedly according to the custom of this country—37½ cents each for supper.

May 30, Georgetown

After we had roamed through this agreeable little town, looked at the neat Catholic church with its paintings, and refreshed us at the beautiful sight of the Potomac, the island, the bridge, the Capitol, &c., which one enjoys from the upper part of the town, particularly from behind the Jesuit College, we let us be taken to the neighboring Washington and put up in the closely adjacent Franklin House at Gadsby's, where we stayed until June 8.

Gadsby's Hotel[35]

This inn passes for the foremost in the metropolis. Gadsby formerly kept the Indian Queen Hotel in Baltimore and at that time his house is said to have been the best in the United States. Nevertheless he went bankrupt, and now truly starveling conditions reign in his house. All is aimed at pretence. Five chafing-dishes permanently decorate the table; butter and occasionally radish is put upon them. The lunch consisted of a poor soup and two main dishes, roast beef and ham, roast veal and fish, and so on; vegetables scarcely sufficient for two or three persons, almost every day fried chicken which in fact are parched cocks with really not the least to gnaw off. What I liked best were the strawberries for dessert; they are eaten in this country with cream or milk. Gadsby is a scoundrel who wants to do it right by making empty compliments, his bar keeper is a rude, jovial Irishman, his servants are an unruly mob of Negroes. Since I had met with much ado about this house, I found it in reality even more miserable. They were impudent enough to charge me $2 for the room, the same as the Count who had one of the best rooms, but I insisted on lowering it to the fixed price of $1½. Another inconvenience of this inn is its location so far up in the town, closer to Germantown[36] than to the busy part of

---

[35] On I Street, N.W., east of 21st Street (Samuel C. Busey, *Pictures of the City of Washington in the Past* [Washington, 1898], 305). Also mentioned ("Godsby's") by William Owen on November 24, 1824 (*Diary of William Owen,* 39). Vischer's unfavorable description of the hotel is confirmed by an anonymous German visitor of 1830 who refers to the owner as "an Englishman, named Gadsby, a pathetic innkeeper." Georg Lotz, ed., *Wanderungen eines jungen Norddeutschen durch Portugal, Spanien und Nord-Amerika in den Jahren 1827–1831* (4 vols., Hamburg, 1834), III, 22.

[36] Slip of the pen for "Georgetown".

Washington. I had to hurry to get in three quarters of an hour from the Capitol to this place.[37]

City

Washington is similar to a bed of asparagus in which some asparagus stands out here and there, the greater part of which, however, is fallow and occasionally disfigured by weeds. Even Pennsylvania Avenue, the main street, still has many gaps. If, however, the now dispersed buildings were closer together, they would form a considerable town. Even between the Capitol and the Eastern Branch[38] there are already some houses which appear to be a separate village since they are not connected with the center of the city. This quarter may be one of the most agreeable both because of the small river and its opposite bank consisting of gentle hills.

Locality

The locality of the metropolis this time appealed more favorably to me than during my first brief visit in the winter. The cause for the present unpleasant appearance of the city, which also makes staying there disagreeable, is the fact that the greatest part of the space which according to plans is intended for the city has been converted into waste lots. In my opinion a great part of the wood could have been left standing for the time being, at least shady parks here and there, since there is presently no way of knowing when and whether the plan will ever be fully executed. At the present, the low area between the river and Pennsylvania Avenue has a swampy appearance, and the higher ground is a bumpy desert.[39] Despite the poor soil, however, one can see plenty of livestock grazing there; a numerous herd was lying down on Capitol Hill. I thought that similar to the child and childish old man, newly begun and decayed cities present the same picture. But the opposite banks of the rivers, the hill which almost surrounds the upper part of the projected city, the not unromantic surroundings

[37] The distance between Franklin House and the Capitol via Pennsylvania Avenue is slightly more than two miles.

[38] Anacostia River.

[39] Vischer was not alone in his disappointment with what was then to be seen of Washington. William Owen recorded in his diary on November 26, 1824: "The city appeared to be built in an inconvenient manner." (*Diary of William Owen,* 40). The Duke of Saxe-Weimar wrote of his visit in 1825: "I had not formed a great idea of Washington city, but what I saw was inferior to my expectation. . . . This part of the city [near Pennsylvania Avenue] has the appearance of a newly established watering place." (Saxe-Weimar, *Travels,* I, 170). Compare also Bromme, *Reisen,* II, 197.

of Georgetown, and the island[40] lying opposite to Rock Creek possess a natural charm; and if at one time the waste ground will be covered regularly with houses, then nothing could be said against the location of the city. From some viewpoints one can enjoy a beautiful view down the Potomac, one can see Alexandria, Mount Vernon, etc.

Lots

The lots (separated spaces on which the city shall be built) are not expensive, the purchaser, however, has to erect a building on it within a certain period. At present there are still no distinguished private buildings; occasionally there are neat domestic buildings, made of bricks, but none of exceptional size. And the official edifices also merit no admiration.

Post Office[41]

The house in which are located downstairs the Post Office, and upstairs the halls in which are on display the various models submitted for the attainments of patents, is admittedly spacious, and is painted yellow, but bare of architectonic beauty.

Churches, Banks, Theater, Markets

The churches are small, some of them are new and neat, the inns represent little or nothing. The banks are simple, agreeable houses, and therefore contrast favorably, in my opinion, with so many other pompous banks; the theater is modest. The market-halls[42] are boarded up with planks and make a poor sight.

City Hall[43]

Judging from the model on display, the city hall will be a beautiful building with a rotunda. To accelerate its construction, however, the city has been allowed to establish a lottery, the first prize of which was $100,000. The man with whom the city contracted to run the lottery, however, made off with all the money, and the winner of the $100,000 claimed his prize which has been granted to him with interest by various courts of justice. The thief allegedly has meanwhile died in New

[40] Annacostan or Mason's Island, now Theodore Roosevelt Island.

[41] The Old Post Office on E Street, N.W., between 7th and 8th Streets; it burned on December 15, 1836, and a new Post Office building was erected in its place (*Force's Washington,* 83–84).

[42] Probably Centre Market on Pennsylvania Avenue (*Force's Washington,* 34).

[43] On Judiciary Square; construction, after a plan by George Hadfield, started in 1820 but was not completed by 1848 (*Force's Washington,* 31–32).

York, and from his heirs apparently no money is to be had. In this case the proverb "Pride will have a fall" has come true, I believe.

Inhabitants

A city which at best may have 17,000 inhabitants[44] including no rich people, but many needy Negroes and slaves,[45] was far too undeveloped to justify such a costly city hall.

Hospital, Jail

The jail[46] and the hospital[47] conform to the present state of the city. From a different point of view I regarded the buildings of the federal government. In reference to them I have to raise the opposite reproach that they have not been executed with due solidity and thorough artistic skill.

Offices

The four buildings in which the government offices are located look like they are sunk into the ground.

President's House

The house of the President in the center, although made of white stone, does not appeal to me, and appears to me to be of bad taste and built for pretence; the annexes and surroundings also make a poor sight.

Capitol

The case of the Capitol is not much better. Dr. Thornton,[48] presently Superintendent of the Patent Office, is said to have made the plans for this national monument, with secret consultation of, or perhaps under full instructions, however, from a French architect, Mons.

---

[44] Marginal note: "By the end of 1824 the population of Washington is said to have been 16,605."

[45] In 1840 somewhat less than one third of the population was black (43,712 total population, 8,361 free colored, 4,694 slaves). See *Compendium of the Enumeration of the Inhabitants and Statistics of the United States as obtained at the Department of State, from the Returns of the Sixth Census* (Washington, 1841).

[46] The prison was a two-story building, 120 feet long (Warden, *Description*, 36).

[47] ". . . a neat building . . ." (Warden, *Description*, 36).

[48] William Thornton (1759–1828) came to Washington in 1793 after his design for the construction of the Capitol had been accepted. He supervised the construction between 1794 and 1804 and was at the same time one of the Commissioners of the District of Columbia. Between 1802 and his death he was also in charge of the Patent Office (Groce and Wallace, *Dictionary*, 628; *DAB* XVIII, 504–507).

Hallet.[49] Later on several changes have been made. The present superintendent of the construction is Mr. Charles Bulfinch.[50] Such an important, costly, spacious, and well situated building should probably attract the applause of both the experts and the non-experts. I belong to the latter group, and I honestly hope that this may be the reason why the Capitol does not appeal to me.[51] Despite its huge size I find it petty, probably because of its many decorations and variations in the shape of its windows. The rail and the chimneys disfigure the roof. The main cupola appears to me to be relatively too high. I think the whole building should be less compressed and squeezed together, but more extended and light. I cannot abide the narrow little yards in the interior of the block. The corridors and stairs are likewise very narrow and compressed. The round hall in the center of the building is defaced by a round opening in the floor, surrounded by a rail, which was made to illuminate the basement. Even this proud national building was not built for durability but according to American custom for pretence only. The framework of the cupola consists chiefly of wood and brick, the enclosure of the lower cornice of the pillars and along the staircases is made of wood. Unfortunately they do not have good stone even for the pillars; they procure the stone from two localities, that which comes down from the Seneca is hard and good, but cannot be quarried in great quantities, wherefore the greater has to be gotten from Acquia Creek[52] down the river; this freestone is a kind of slender sandstone which soon wears out and breaks, and already many steps of the staircases are broken. In addition, this stone is full of holes, the pillars that are now being made are full of them, and they fill them up. The pillars in the hall of the Congress are made of dark colored marble which is procured 25 to 30 miles down the Potomac. The echo in this round hall is strange; if someone speaks in front of me I hear his voice behind me. In this hall has been placed a big statue representing the Constitution which was made by a young Italian, Cau-

[49] Étienne (Stephen) Sulpice Hallet (1775–1825) won the second place in the competition for the design of the Capitol, was commissioned to revise Thornton's plans and supervise the construction in 1793, but was dismissed in 1794 (*DAB* VIII, 152–154).

[50] Charles Bulfinch (1763–1844), the "architect of the Capitol" was in charge of the construction between 1817 and 1830 (*DAB* III, 245–247).

[51] For an idea of how the Capitol looked in the late 1820's, see Charles Bulfinch's east view of 1828 and Robert King's west view of 1830 in the *Documentary of the Construction and Development of the United States Capitol Building and Grounds*, 58th Congress, 2nd Session, House of Representatives Report No. 646 (Washington 1904), plates facing 294 and 318.

[52] Marvin F. Studebaker, "Freestone from Aquia", *Virginia Cavalcade* 9(1): 35–41 (Richmond, 1959).

sici.[53] This artist is not without talents, but he is arrogant, plays the genius without having been summoned to it by nature, talks much nonsense, and dresses and behaves disorderly. Still another Italian, Capellani,[54] is engaged in stucco-work in the Capitol; he is said to be a very dexterous, modest, and orderly man. We could not see this time the library, the Senate chamber, and Trumbull's paintings, because the attendant was absent. On the other hand I enjoyed with bliss the wide view from the height of the cupola.

Dimensions of the Capitol of the United States, and its Grounds[55]

The grounds within the Iron Railing, 20 acres & ⅛. Length of Foot Walk, outside of railing, ¾ of a mile & 185 feet. The Building is as follows:

Length of front	350 feet
Depth of wings	120 feet
East projection of steps	65 feet
West do. do.	83 feet
Covering 1½ acres, & 1826 feet	
Height of wings to top of balustrade	70 feet
Height to top of centre dome	140 feet
Representative room, greatest length	95 feet
greatest height	60 feet
Senate chamber, greatest length	74 feet
greatest height	42 feet
Great Central Rotunda, 96 feet in diameter, & 96 feet high	
Library, 92 by 34, & 36 foot high	

Navy Yard

In the company of Dr. Staughton's son who like his father was again very friendly and helpful to me, we visited the Navy Yard which is located on the Eastern Branch. The location is beautiful and the buildings fine-looking; everything that is necessary for the equipment, is being manufactured here; for this purpose they have a considerable steam engine.[56] There are about 300 to 400 workers,[57] of which the

[53] Enrico Causici worked on the U.S. Capitol between about 1823 and 1825. The panel over the south door of the Rotunda, showing Daniel Boone fighting Indians, is his work (Groce and Wallace, *Dictionary,* 116; *Force's Washington,* 60).

[54] Antonio Capellano worked in the United States between 1815 and 1827 and was during part of this time employed at the Capitol. His work there includes the relief showing Pocahontas and John Smith (Groce and Wallace, *Dictionary,* 108).

[55] The list of measurements is given by Vischer in English and was probably copied by him from an unidentified source.

[56] According to Warden (*Description,* 62–63) the steam-engine had as of 1816 been lately constructed and was used to drive the forge-hammer. There were at that time

ordinary ones get $1.36, the best smiths $1.52, and the carpenters $2 (during the winter $1½) per day. The man-of-war *Columbus,* a frigate with 74 canons, has been built here. At present there is a frigate with 44 pieces under shelter, which was dragged out of the water onto the dry ground. The small armory is furnished nicely. In the yard there is a marble monument with allegorical figures, in honor of the officers and soldiers who were killed in 1804 during the various attacks on Tripolis;[58] it was made in 1806 by Geo. Charles Micali in Livorno.[59] The figures are poor and, moreover, were mutilated by the British on August 25, 1814.[60]

Capitol

Excerpt from a letter written by an American, Washington, December 7, 1825, and printed in public journals.[61]

The Capitol is nearly finished, at least advanced far enough to give an idea about how it will be after its completion. Generally, it is a magnificent and imposing building; but I do not like the taste that is manifest throughout it. Its interior is stifling, massive, and phantastic. Everywhere usefulness and commodity have been sacrificed to a ponderous, proud splendor. Generally it lacks simplicity, unity, grace, commodity—on the other hand it does not lack dignity. In the field of architecture, whether in reality or in books, I have never seen anything which was in its way more splendid and in addition to it more capricious and useless, than its dark subterranean corridors, inner colonnades, little cupolas, and high passages which lead nowhere and everywhere. The cupola is magnificent. Despite the great disparity of the conditions and of its uses, the Capitol reminded me very much of

only 60 to 150 workers in the Navy Yard, against a former number of 700 to 800. Ferdinand Ernst (*Bemerkungen auf einer Reise durch das Innere der Vereinigten Staaten von Nord-Amerika im Jahre 1819,* [Hildesheim, 1820], 15) says the steam-engine had 13 horse power and was connected with a sawmill and a turnstile. This is confirmed in less detail by Bromme (*Reisen,* II, 199).

[57] White workmen on the steam-engine were paid $1.81 ten years before. Black workmen received only 85 cents. (Warden, *Description,* 64.)

[58] During the Tripoli War, 1801–1805, Stephen Decatur and his men entered Tripoli harbor on February 16, 1804, and burned the U.S. warship *Philadelphia* which had previously been captured by Tripoli.

[59] The statue has been mentioned or described by many visitors to the Navy Yard (e.g., Ernst, *Bemerkungen,* 13; Bromme, *Reisen,* 199; Saxe-Weimar, *Travels,* I, 172; A. Levasseur, *Lafayette in America in 1824 and 1825,* [2 vols., Philadelphia, 1829], I, 178). It was later removed to the west front of the Capitol (Martin, *A New and Comprehensive Gazetteer of Virginia and the District of Columbia* [Charlottesville, 1835], 500).

[60] Rather on August 24, when General Robert Ross burned Washington.

[61] This excerpt appears in the context of Vischer's Washington diary. Dated December 1825, it indicates that either the present text was not written up from the author's notes before December 7, 1825, or "1825" is a slip of the pen for "1824".

Blenheim castle.[62] Vanbrugh,[63] who built this castle, was also given to the same ponderous magnificence, for which reason the following epigram was written for him, which is also suitable for L'Enfant[64] and Latrobe,[65] the original plan makers of the Capitol; Lie heavy on him, earth; for he laid many heavy loads on thee.[66]

Patent Halls

Among the infinite number of submitted models, one can find much absurdity, and some things that have not been invented in the United States but in Europe, which, however, the imitators have submitted as their own inventions. The guard, Keller from Schaffhausen, told me that, and also complained about the bridge-builder Wernwag[67] whom I had met in Harper's Ferry.[68] He had submitted a model of a bridge as his own invention which in fact is but an imitation of a bridge in Switzerland.

Grave of the Van Ness Family

Within the circumference of the city, not far from some of the buildings, there is a new, round building made of bricks, similar to a monument, which is the tomb of the Van Ness family and its descendants.[69] The building is still unfinished. To reach its entrance one has

---

[62] Blenheim castle was built in 1705–1724 commemorating the victory at Blenheim (more correctly Blindheim, near Höchstädt, Bavaria) in the battle of August 13, 1704.

[63] Sir John Vanbrugh (1664–1726), architect and surveyor of Blenheim castle *(Dictionary of National Biography,* XX, 86–94).

[64] Pierre Charles L'Enfant (1754–1825) designed the basic plan for Washington, but had little to do with the construction of the Capitol (*DAB* XI, 165–169).

[65] Benjamin Henry Latrobe (1764–1820) supervised the construction of the Capitol between 1803 and 1811 and again between 1815 and 1817 (Groce and Wallace, *Dictionary,* 385–386).

[66] The epigram is "Epitaph on Sir John Vanbrugh, Architect of Blenheim Palace" by Abel Evans (1679–1737) and is in full:

Under this stone, Reader, survey
Dead Sir John Vanbrugh's house of clay.
Lie heavy on him, Earth! for he
Laid many heavy loads on thee!

(*The Oxford Dictionary of Quotations* [New York, 1955], 202).

[67] Ludwig (Lewis) Wernwag (1769–1843), a native of Württemberg, who came to the United States in 1786. The bridge in question is probably the drawbridge across Frankford Creek, Bridgeburg, Pennsylvania (1811), said to have been the first cantilever type drawbridge; or the bridge across the Schuylkill at Upper Ferry, built in 1812, which with its 240 feet span was the longest bridge in America at that time, being surpassed only by a 410 feet bridge in Switzerland (*DAB* XX, 2–3).

[68] On May 25, 1825.

[69] "The mausoleum, a copy of the temple of Vesta in Rome, on Mausoleum Square, was erected by General John P. Van Ness and contained the remains of David Burnes' family and General Van Ness' family." (*Force's Washington,* 34). See also Allen C. Clark, "General John Peter Van Ness, a Mayor of the City of Washington, His Wife,

to climb up a hill; inside, behind doors that lead underground, there are small vaults to shove the coffins into. I think it formerly belonged to the Burn family, and Miss Burn married a Mr. Van Ness.

Fire-Engines

There are said to be ten fire-engines in Washington.

Beggars

I did not see one beggar.

Catholic School

In the Catholic school or college kept by the Jesuits there are 130 pupils.

Columbian College

Columbian College at present has 142 pupils, of which one is Catholic. The president, Dr. Staughton, and the professor of theology are Baptists. The first mentioned gives every morning an ex tempore prayer and every Sunday a theological sermon. In the chapel or the room for the church service are the images of the patrons of this institution, besides those of Columbus and Vespucius. In the coffee room are the best newspapers, besides American, English, and French journals. The College was built from voluntary contributions and is being expanded in the same way. What the students pay is only for their sustenance and the salaries of the teachers. The present teachers are:[70] Wm. Staughton, D.D., President & Professor of General History, Belles Lettres, Rhetoric, & Moral Philosophy; Thos. Sewall, M.D., Professor of Anatomy & Physiology; James W. Staughton, M.D., Professor of Chemistry; Wm. Ruggles, A.M., Professor of Mathematics and Natural Philosophy; Irah Chase, A.M., Professor of the Learned Languages;[71] Alexander M'Williams, M.D., Professor of Botany; Alexis Caswell, A.B., Tutor & Librarian,[72] and three more teachers.

One of the professors, I believe it was Mr. Chase, was in Germany;[73]

Marcia, and Her Father, David Burnes," *Records of the Columbia Historical Society* 22 (1919), 125–204.

[70] The following section appears in Vischer's diary in English.

[71] Irah Chase (1793–1864) was the second Baptist among the professors. He was ordained to the Baptist ministry in 1817 and headed the Theology department of Columbian College until 1825 (*DAB* IV, 25–26).

[72] Alexis Caswell (1799–1877) taught at Columbian College between 1822 and 1827, the last two years as professor of ancient languages (*DAB* III, 570–571).

[73] Irah Chase visited Europe in 1823–1824 and resided briefly in Halle and Göttingen.

they already have several German classical works, and they intend to order more of them.

Classical Department: 11 pupils are in the Senior Class, 16 pupils in the Junior Class, 10 in the Sophomore Class, 18 in the Freshman Class: 55 pupils in all; most of them are from the District of Columbia and from Virginia.

Theological department, Wm. Staughton & J. Chase, heads of the department.	
Medical students	22
Preparatory school 1st class 33, 2d class 17, 3d class 8	58
Not yet classified	7
Classical department (as above)	55
	142

Two vacations, two months during summer and three weeks during winter. The most necessary expenses of a student, except for clothing, books, pocket money, and vacations, do not exceed $200. In the regulations and laws of the college the following may be found:

The College is not affiliated with any Christian sect. Although church service is being held every Sunday in the chapel, students if requested by the parents or curators, may attend services in another church, but they should not be left to themselves. Visit the city as rarely as possible. Much pocket money is disadvantageous. $10 per year is more than enough. The three teachers eat with the students to keep order; generally, order should be kept. Every student pays $10 for admission to the College and then annually for the first term and for the second term[74]

	First Term	Second Term	Annual
Teaching courses, in advance	$30	$20	$50
Use of the library	$2	$1	$3
Board (only part-payment)[75]	$15	$10	$25
Room and furniture	$9	$5	$14
Bed and linen	$5	$3	$8
Steward's salary	$4	$3	$7
Servants	$3	$2	$5
Shining of boots and shoes	$2	$1	$3
	$70	$45	$115

Laundry 37½ cents per dozen pieces.

[74] Marginal note: "The year is divided into two terms, the first six months long, the second three months and one week."

[75] Marginal note: "Board amounts to $2 or somewhat less per week. Teaching, board, lodging, and service amount to $170 per year; if one calculates $30 for water, heating and light, and damages, this makes $200."

Board, wood, and candles are only calculated and set after it is apparent how much has been spent for them. Similarly, at the end of each term the total of general and private damages for which a student has to pay is set. A book is said to be kept on the behavior of the students. All kinds of games are included among the offences. Throwing of stones is prohibited near the buildings. Servants, weapons, powder, horses, and dogs are prohibited. The students should be in their rooms by 9 o'clock in winter and by 10 o'clock in summer. Cleanliness is strongly recommended, no spitting on the floor. Every damage caused has to be compensated. If the culprit or the culprits are unknown, the costs are divided among the suspects according to the understanding of the committee. Defilement of the walls etc. brings about correction. Smoking in or near the buildings and strong drinks are prohibited. Students are obliged to give information about offences. Clubs and societies are prohibited. Students must not go further than two miles or visit taverns without leave. Fines: absence without leave 25 cents per day, absence from or late arrival at courses not more than 10 cents, keeping library books beyond the period allowed at most 10 cents per day.

Studies: Freshman Class. English, Latin & Greek language; geography; arithmetic & algebra; history and antiquities; exercises in reading, languages, and composition. —Sophomore Class. Geography, history, and the elements of chronology; rhetoric and logic; logarithm, geometry, trigonometry; art of measuring and surveying, nautics, conic sections, & Euclid's Elements. —Junior Class. Natural Philosophy, Astronomy, Chemistry, Fluxions (infinitesimal calculus), Natural History, History of Civil Society, Natural Religion and Revelation. —Senior Class. Natural & Political Law, Metaphysics, Moral Philosophy, & Analogy of Religion to Nature.

Throughout the four years, exercises in learned speech, Criticism, Rhetoric & Oratory.

Besides other letters of recommendation for Washington, the Count had one from the American envoy in Paris, Mr. Brown,[76] for John Quincy Adams,[77] the present President, and one for the present Secretary of State, Mr. Clay.[78] In the absence of the latter he gave it to the First Clerk in the State Department, Mr. Brent. He gave him also the letter for the President and named me as his escort. Mr. Brent told

[76] James Brown (1766–1835) served as minister to France between 1824 and 1828 (*DAB* III, 126).

[77] John Quincy Adams (1767–1848), 6th President of the United States (*DAB* I, 84–93).

[78] Henry Clay (1777–1852), Secretary of State under John Quincy Adams (*DAB* IV, 173–179).

us, we should return the following day, at 1 o'clock p.m., when he would accompany us to the President. So we did.

Office of the Secretary of State

In the office of the State Department they showed us the originals of important documents, among them: Commission of General Washington, dated June 19, 1775, and signed Hancock. The Declaration of Independence. First Confederation, July 9, 1778. Present Constitution, of September 17, 1787; among the signatures I noticed those of Washington, Rufus King, Madison, and Franklin. All kinds of treaties with England, with France as a republic, empire, and kingdom, with Spain, Russia, etc. Presents of the emperors Napoleon, Alexander, and other monarchs, which were received by American envoys and delivered by them according to the Constitution.

President

(June 1, 1825) Mr. Brent then proceeded with us to the residence of the President;[79] as is well known, there are no guards there; we rang the bell, a servant opened the door and led us to the reception room. It is customary here to take off the hat outside the room, and no special etiquette prevails with the President. In the room we found Mrs. Adams with a niece and two gentlemen in boots, who left soon thereafter. Soon Mr. Adams appeared, in a simple, but somewhat negligent dress. The bands to tie his Nanquin pantalons hung down to his shoes. His look was deep and grave. It is said that he welcomes visitors usually in a cold and mute way. We did not find that to be true. Perhaps he made an exception in relation to the Count, and it appeared as if he wished to win him over for his country.[80] He said the first impressions of strangers are usually unfavorable, he referred to travel books, and entered then the field of literature which is said to be his hobby, and found in the Count someone who not only knew the works but also many famous authors in person. They became engrossed in this subject, talking in French, and it was incumbent on me to converse with the two ladies.

---

[79] "Mr. Brent came and introduced Count Vidua, of Turin, son of the Prime Minister of the King of Sardinia, and Mr. Vischer, son of one of the principal magistrates of Basle in Switzerland." (*Memoirs of John Quincy Adams Comprising Portions of His Diary from 1795 to 1848,* ed. by Charles Francis Adams [Philadelphia, 1875], VII, 22).

[80] Vidua wrote that Adams "has the reputation of being extremely cold, reserved, and laconic. I cannot go along with this judgement; he was not only very courteous to me, but the first visit consisted of an animated dialogue of an hour's duration." (Cometti and Gennardo-Lerda, "Vidua", 393).

Mrs. Adams

Mrs. Adams[81] is the daughter of a Mr. Johnson from Fredericks-town, who was American consul in London where Mr. Adams met and married her. There is nothing distinguished in her exterior, but she is very good in conversing. She is said to be somewhat ailing, and therefore sometimes moody. It is said that she is generally not very much liked by other women. But judging from what I have heard, she must be a kind hearted and charitable woman.

Adams's Sons

They have three sons, of whom the eldest is a lawyer in Boston, the second is his father's secretary, and the third is still in college in Cambridge.[82] Of the latter one expects the most, the two elder ones are not distinguished by any talents.

Family

(Mr. Adams's elder brother in Boston is a drunkard, in one of the bureaus in Washington there is said to be one of his brothers-in-law who is in debt.) His venerable father,[83] more than 89 years old, lives on his estate, 8 miles from Boston, and is said to be supported by his son Quincy. After three quarters of an hour we said good-bye. French was spoken most of the time, even though Mr. Brent does not understand this language.

Dinner with the President

Next day we received an invitation of the following contents: "Mr. and Mrs. Adams request the Honor of Mr. Vischer's Company at Dinner on Saturday, the 4 of June at 5 o'clock (The Favor of an Answer is requested)".[84] When we arrived on this day, we found besides the President and his wife, his second son, one nephew and two nieces, several other guests, such as Mr. Appleton[85] from Boston, who soon thereafter was sent to Naples in connection with the claims for dam-

[81] Louisa Catherine Adams (1775–1852) was the daughter of Joshua Johnson (*National Cyclopaedia of American Biography,* V, 76).

[82] Charles Francis Adams (1807–1886) graduated from Harvard in 1825, and later became a member of the Massachusetts General Court, a member of the House of Representatives, and a minister to Great Britain.

[83] John Adams (1735–1826), 2nd President of the United States, resided until his death in Baintree (now Quincy), Massachusetts (*DAB* I, 72–82).

[84] The text of the invitation is given in English by Vischer.

[85] John James Appleton (1792–1864) was in 1825 sent as chargé d'affairs to the Two Sicilies (*National Cyclopaedia of American Biography,* XIII, 392).

ages from Naples; Mr. Murray from New York, Mr. Rensalear[86] from Albany, and Mr. Brent. By chance I came to sit next to the President. The meal was well prepared, more after the French style than the English. (Immediately after the soup the President invited me to drink with him a glass of wine, which I refused according to my habits; afterwards he drank with the Count and then by turns with the other guests.) The ladies left the table first. The gentlemen also did not remain seated for a very long time. After we had removed to the reception room, the other guests soon left. The Count and I remained for tea and when we left Mrs. Adams invited us to visit her sometimes in the evening. Since she spent Monday at the wedding celebration of Baron Maltiz,[87] first secretary of the Russian legation, and Miss Lee, (not being invited out of special favor, since she does not attend social gatherings outside her house), we went there only on Tuesday, the evening before we left.

Visit in the Evening

We found there another gentleman with his wife, both in informal dress, some gentlemen in boots, and Dr. Waterhouse,[88] Professor in Cambridge, in flowery evening dress. Besides wine, orange slices and a kind of lemonade in long-stemmed glasses were served. It was very warm. The guests left only about 11 o'clock, but nevertheless the President, according to his habit, went the following day at 4 o'clock in the morning to bathe in the Potomac; usually he remains in the river swimming and lying on the water for an hour and even longer. From the conversation of the Count with Mr. Adams I remembered the following remarks of the President:

Remarks of the President

In forty years, New York will have 400,000 inhabitants;[89] —There is no people more religious than the Americans, here in Washington there are two Episcopalian, 2 Presbyterian, 3 Catholic, and 1 Methodist churches, and (he added with a smile) even one for the Unitar-

[86] Stephen Van Rensselaer (1764–1839) was president of the Erie Canal Commission between 1824 and 1839 and served as a member of Congress from 1823 to 1829 (*DAB* XIX, 211–212).

[87] "Baron Maltitz, of the same [Russian] legation, who married an American wife some months ago." (Saxe-Weimar, *Travels,* I, 171).

[88] Benjamin Waterhouse (1754–1846), a former professor of medicine at Harvard (*DAB* XIX, 529–532).

[89] The population of New York City was 124,000 in 1820; forty years later the number of inhabitants had increased to more than twice the number predicted by Adams (1860: 814,000).

Photograph courtesy of Charles Merrill Mount

Benjamin Waterhouse by Gilbert Stuart.

Just what Waterhouse chose to wear to the President's House on the warm Washington evening in June 1825 is unclear, but it struck Vischer as curious and inappropriate and he twice comments on it. It has been translated here as "in flowery evening dress" and "dressed in evening clothes" but this does not convey Vischer's sense that Waterhouse's costume was slightly outrageous. What Vischer called it was a flowery night gown, "Nachtrock" in the first instance and "Schlafrock" in the second.

The portrait by Stuart of Waterhouse (in a green coat) was painted in London about 1785 when Waterhouse was 31.

ians; Florida will soon raise itself to statehood;[90] —Since the inhabitants of the South American republics belong to very different classes, it may be somewhat doubtful whether their present constitutions will be able to last; —He did not know whether it was possible to intro-

[90] In fact, it took Florida another 20 years to attain statehood. After the 1823 cession of the Seminoles' lands, prospects for an early date looked good but the Seminoles' reluctance to remove to Indian Territory and the Second Seminole War (1835–1842) held up the process considerably.

duce their Constitution in Europe, but he knew this much, that it would be impossible to introduce the European systems of government here; —Where the English population gains a foothold, the Indians have to disappear. He was, of course, averse to slavery. I talked to him about the state of the art of painting in America, but it appeared to me that he was not interested in this subject. He said that Trumbull's big paintings, except possibly the Signing of the Declaration of Independence,[91] were poor, and he passed a similar judgment on R. Peale's General Washington on Horseback.

Personality of the President

It turned out that Mr. Adams's first house servant happened to be a compatriot of the Count, his name is Antonio, he came with Mr. Adams from Europe and married Mrs. Adams' chambermaid. It appears that Mr. Adams has some affection for this old servant, but he is said never to confide in, and to be without exception and according to American custom stern and cold to his servants. His domestics are 16 persons, mainly Negroes, but no slaves.

His Religion

Even before he became President, Mr. Adams had his pew in several churches. But he never visits the English Episcopalian one. He does not go to church in the morning. In the afternoon he is said to go to the Presbyterian and occasionally to fall asleep there, and in the evening he attends a meeting of the Unitarians, and essentially he keeps with this sect to which also his father adheres.

Mrs. Adams

Mrs. Adams is reproached for being arrogant with other ladies. But it cannot well be expected that she should receive everybody equally friendlily since so many people impudently flock around who cannot have interest for the President and his wife. Tradesmen arrive in the morning with their wives to drop their visiting cards to oblige Mrs. Adams to invite them to the evening parties.

Her Brothers-in-Law

Two brothers-in-law of Mrs. Adams have become bankrupt, one of them is employed by the War Department.

Guests

Even when he was only Secretary of State, Mr. Adams gave weekly banquets for 20 to 22 persons. Antonio thinks that the number of

[91] See note 23 above.

guests will now rise to 40 and that the assemblées in the evening will be attended by 200 to 300 persons. He pays for the dozen of bottles of champagne $22.

Presidential Election

Antonio gave to understand that there was really very much plotting in relation to the election of the President, Mr. Adams was formerly good friends with Crawford,[92] and not with Clay; when the latter appeared to him as a dangerous competitor, he brought in General Jackson as another candidate to decimate Clay's followers, not suspecting that he could become so dangerous. (Note that this is what the gossip Antonio says; I doubt whether it depended on Mr. Adams to bring forth General Jackson or not). General Jackson had gained so much influence, especially in the less civilised states, and particularly among the lower classes, and in addition received the support of some of Mr. Adams's opponents, so that he [Adams] had already lost his hope of becoming president, when Clay suddenly changed the state of affairs to his advantage. From Antonio's remarks one could even have concluded that votes were bought; not by Mr. Adams himself, but by his followers. Since the President has to make so many appointments, it is made easy for him to show his gratitude. —Occasionally also representatives may get themselves into troubles by passionate gambling and thereby become tractable.

Clay

Clay is an arch-gambler,[93] and his sons are also said to follow his example. It is also said that he without modesty frequents mean women.

Embassy in Ghent

Five American delegates were at the congress in Ghent, of which Adams and Gallatin[94] behaved with dignity, while the three others carried on a lewd life. Clay kept himself mistresses, while Bayard,[95] although wealthy, frequented prostitutes and shortly after his return died from a virulent disease. Note: this is what Antonio relates.

---

[92] William Harris Crawford (1772–1834) finished third in the presidential elections of 1824 (*DAB* IV, 527–530).

[93] "He played cards, was fond of horse-racing, and liked good liquor" (*DAB*).

[94] Albert Gallatin (1761–1849), a native of Geneva, Switzerland, was Secretary of the Treasury between 1801 and 1814. After the negotiations in Ghent he served as minister to France (*DAB* VII, 103–110).

[95] James Ashton Bayard (1767–1815) died six days after his arrival from England (*DAB* II, 64–66).

Mr. Adams' Income

Mr. Adams is said to get $7,000 to $8,000 in annual interest. He acquired his wealth by diligence as a jurist and lawyer, by frugality, and a part he also got from his wife. As President he receives a salary of $25,000. Besides, the President on taking his office gets $14,000 for repairs and furnishing of his residence. I had been told that the residence is newly furnished upon a change in the presidency, but I found the same pieces of furniture which I had seen in winter under Mr. Monroe.[96] It was also said that Mr. Adams planned to make ready the great hall which up to now remains unfinished and unused, but his niece denied it and said that the $14,000 would not be sufficient.

Mr. Salomon

When I was in Washington with Mr. Hess in January, he was sorry that we did not have a chance to visit our compatriot Mr. Salomon from Geneva, who is employed in the Treasury Department and came to America with Albert Gallatin.[97] This time I visited him and was kindly received by him. He is an old, stout gentleman; at first he was, like Mr. Gallatin, a farmer in the western part of Pennsylvania; he did not prosper, however, and got a position as a clerk in the Treasury Department with a salary of, I believe, $800, as a result I suppose of Mr. Gallatin's intervention. Of his salary he is said to send $300 to his wife who remained in Pennsylvania and who is, as I was told, somewhat out of her wits. They have no children. Although Mr. Salomon does not get along well with his wife, he appears to be a reasonable and amiable man. He is on particularly good terms with the Russian envoy, and Mr. Maltitz loves him like a father. He lives with a French Swiss who is a confectioner.

Brodbeck

In the same house lives Brodbeck from Muttenz,[98] formerly a soldier, who is employed as an attendant in the War Department with a salary of $500. Although this worthy and kindhearted man sends money to his brother and has spent many dollars on his countrymen, he nevertheless has accumulated a certain wealth, bought a piece of land, and built a small house on it, part of which he lets while living

[96] James Monroe (1758–1831), 5th President of the United States (*DAB* XIII, 87–93). Vischer met him later in June during his trip through Virginia.

[97] On the back fly leaf of Diary no. 6 Vischer noted the two addresses next to one another: "Mr. Salomon, Treasury Department, Washington City. Albert Gallatin, Esqr. New Geneva, Fayette County, Penna."

[98] Muttenz is today a suburb of Basle.

in the other part; he now lives with his niece, a kind girl of about 20 years of age, who has recently come over with the old Mrs. Halder.

Halder Family

I met this woman and her son at Brodbeck's, she showed great joy in seeing me and asked me to visit with her her daughter, Mrs. Lehmann. Oh, what misery I found there. Mrs. Lehmann lives in a new, isolated house which is very wet, and without doubt this is the reason why Mrs. Lehmann and her husband became sick and consequently got into deep misery. The formerly pretty Miss Halder still looks thin and pitiful like a ghost and drinks cow-warm milk. She has pretty children, I think four in number. Her husband earns only little by teaching French and German languages and fencing. Halder who came to welcome his mother will see how he can make a livelihood in Pennsylvania, not only for his mother but also for the Lehmann family. Halder says he was immediately after his arrival disheartened by Mr. Iselin, to whom he had been recommended, had suffered great misery, but now patiently manages to put up with everything. He lives with his wife and her parents in Shepards Town, Post office, Lebanon County.[99]

Stohler

Stohler from Liestal,[100] who had come to see me in Reading, learned from Brodbeck about my presence; he visited me and complained to me about his misery, he lays the blame for it on others, although he is guilty of it himself; I was displeased to see that man in sorrowful circumstances like these.

Georgetown

The Count and I also went back to Georgetown, chiefly to see the Roman Catholic College there.

Roman Catholic College

The same has existed for 30 years.[101] It is a considerable brick building with sixteen windows in a row. The situation is agreeable, the view of the Potomac is exceptionally beautiful, and behind the build-

[99] On the back fly leaf of Diary no. 6 Vischer wrote the address: "Mr. Niclaus Halder, Schäfer's Town, Post Office, Lebanon County, Pensila."

[100] Liestal is a major town of the canton Basel-Landschaft. Wildenstein castle is located at some distance. Stohler is a very common family name in the area.

[101] The Catholic College of Georgetown, now Georgetown University, was founded in 1790 (Warden, *Description,* 106).

ing it is very rural and hilly. 25 Jesuits manage this educational establishment. The president is an American,[102] a big, imposing man, he appears to be a man of intelligence, but to me he seemed rude, and it looked to me as if our visit annoyed him. Under his administration the institution is declining rather than advancing due to a lack of tuition and discipline, it is said. At present there are only 36 students[103] who sleep in one large room. The library contains 7,000 to 8,000 volumes. The museum is still rather unimportant. Nine Jesuits manage the Catholic college in Washington; in all, there are said to be about 80 Jesuits in America. The superior is a Pole.[104] He was present and proved to be very courteous. He spoke with the Count in French, like the President and others.

Curé Niel

We found there also a certain Mons. Francois Niel,[105] curé de St. Louis in Missouri. He showed us an old Roman copper coin with the image of the emperor Nerva,[106] which is said to have been found by an Indian in Missouri. This man will travel shortly to Europe to collect contributions for the missions in Louisiana to which Missouri belongs.[107]

Catholic Church

The Catholic church in Georgetown looks neat both inside and out.[108] We did not visit the nunnery. On a nice building I read the inscription: "The R.Catholic benevolent male School, founded 1817."

[102] Benedict Fenwick (1782–1846) was president of Georgetown College between 1822 and 1825 (Jackson, *Chronicles,* 224; *DAB* VI, 327–328).

[103] By 1830 the number of students had risen again to 164 (Bromme, *Reisen,* II, 208).

[104] Francis Dzierozinski was appointed as superior in 1824 (Thomas Hughes, *The History of the Society of Jesus in North America,* [4 vols., London and New York, 1907–1917], passim). Cf. Joseph C. Osuch, "Patriarch of the American Jesuits", *Polish American Studies* 27 (3/4): 92–100 (1960).

[105] Francis I. Neale (b. 1756), one of six Jesuit brothers, and a former president of Georgetown College, was at the time of Vischer's visit manager of the Jesuits' St. Thomas plantation in Maryland. In 1823, however, he had been connected with the Missouri missions (Hughes, *History,* I, 721, and passim).

[106] Marcus Cocceius Nerva reigned in Rome between A.D. 96 and 98. Finds such as this coin have long stimulated speculations about possible pre-Columbian transatlantic contacts.

[107] Through the Upper Louisiana Concordat of 1823 the Diocese of New Orleans ceded to the Society of Jesus the exclusive care for all missions on the Missouri River and its tributaries, while the Jesuits pledged an immediate start of their mission work; fund raising therefore became a necessity (Hughes, *History,* I, 1021–1024).

[108] Old Trinity Church was remodeled after the new Trinity Church was built in 1849–1850 (Jackson, *Chronicles,* 141).

Weather

On the day we had dinner with the President, the weather was extraordinarily wild and frosty, and on the following day, June 5, it was so cold that they kindled an open fire. Two days thereafter, however, it was very warm, so that one could see many men with umbrellas to protect themselves from the great heat of the sun. Therefore Doctor Waterhouse came to the President dressed in evening clothes, and the President went bathing on the morning of the 8th. In Georgetown, I forgot to enquire about the vinyard of which I frequently had read in the newspapers.

Thomas Ewbank: Commissioner of Patents, 1849–1852

WILLIAM A. BATE

In its Saturday edition of May 12, 1849, the *Daily National Intelligencer* announced to the citizens of Washington that Thomas Ewbank had arrived in the city. The reason for his arrival had been the subject of a notice two days earlier when the paper reported that Ewbank of New York had been chosen by President Zachary Taylor to become the new Commissioner of Patents. The nomination having apparently taken the paper's own correspondents by surprise, the *Intelligencer* quoted an article from the *New York Commercial Advertiser*. Regarding Ewbank's credentials as unimpeachable, the *Advertiser* claimed that there was "no man in the country so thoroughly conversant as Mr. Ewbank with the whole subject of mechanical inventions, and therefore so competent to deal accurately with claims and pretensions of which they are the subject." Noting that Ewbank was "curiously learned in these matters," the article ventured the prediction that the new Commissioner would prove to be "as much at home amid the thousand and one mysteries of the Patent Office as though he had lived in it all his life." Finally, the newspaper expressed its belief that Ewbank was a "perfect novice" in politics, and that his appointment, therefore, could not have been the result of any political influence.[1] In his subsequent three years as Patent Commissioner, Ewbank was to find himself at home among the mysteries of the Patent Office with one notable exception, for it seems that the thousand and first mystery was in fact a political one. For Ewbank, the "perfect novice," it was to prove a mystery he was ultimately unable to solve.

It is difficult to speak of Thomas Ewbank as a man who looms large in the local history of the nation's capital, for there are no monuments

Delivered before the Columbia Historical Society on February 12, 1974.

[1] *Daily National Intelligencer,* May 12, 1849, p. 3.

Thos: Ewbank

Decem: 8. 1866

Courtesy of the American History Division,
The New York Public Library,
Astor, Lenox and Tilden Foundations

Thomas Ewbank. Photograph and signature which appeared as the frontispiece in *North American Rock-Writing, and Other Aboriginal Modes of Recording and Transmitting Thought* which was privately printed in Morrisania, New York, in 1866.

to his memory, no plaques commemorating his achievements—indeed, precious little information to suggest that he did any more than serve in an official capacity in Washington, D.C. during his three years as Patent Commissioner under Presidents Taylor and Fillmore. Yet because the city's history is in large measure the nation's history, the figure of Thomas Ewbank is significant enough to merit more than just our passing notice. Thus, to the extent that a consideration of the scientific and technological changes that marked the decades of the 1840's and 1850's in America must take account of the activities of official Washington and its scientific community, Thomas Ewbank becomes a central figure.

Who, then, was he? The few biographers who have bothered to chronicle Ewbank's life inform us that he was born in Durham, England, in the year 1792, and that he was apprenticed as a young boy to the sheet metal working trade. From 1812 to 1817, he worked as a tinsmith in London where he made cases for preserved meats, and in 1819, at the age of 27, he left England for the United States. According to Joseph Brumbaugh, whose brief biographical sketch of Ewbank appeared in the *Journal of the Patent Office Society* in 1919, Ewbank felt that the English social and political institutions simply "did not allow men to be as useful to each other as they were capable of being," and that in America such restrictions would not exist. From 1819 to 1836, Ewbank resided and worked in New York City where he evidently prospered as a manufacturer of copper tubing, for in 1836 he retired from business to devote himself to the more scholarly pursuits of literature, travel, science, and the history and philosophy of technology and invention.[2]

By our own Twentieth Century standards, the range of Ewbank's accomplishments is impressive. In contrast to our own culture of specialized and narrow vocations, Ewbank displayed a catholicity of interests and a breadth of curiousity that was characteristic of the young and dynamic culture of pre-Civil War America. In this regard, even a brief and partial survey of his activities prior to his tenure as Patent Commissioner testifies to the diversity of his career.

In 1842 Ewbank published what was to be the first of more than sixteen editions of a work entitled *A Descriptive and Historical Account of Hydraulic and Other Machines for Raising Water, Ancient and Modern, Including the Progressive Development of the Steam Engine*. According to Eugene Ferguson, the noted historian of American technology, the book in both its historical and technical detail is

[2] N. J. Brumbaugh, "Thomas Ewbank, Commissioner of Patents," *Journal of the Patent Office Society*, II (September, 1919), pp. 3–11.

often tedious. Yet, as Ferguson states, "Ewbank had read everything in his field and much else besides. Thus a reader ignores Ewbank at his own peril." [3] One of his most famous works, the book soon earned Ewbank a reputation as one of the most accomplished practical scientists of his day.

In 1844 there appeared his second major work, *The Spoon, With Upwards of One Hundred Illustrations, Primitive, Egyptian, Roman, Medieval, and Modern*. Published under the pseudonym of Habakuk O. Westman, the book was satirically offered to the public as an outgrowth of the "Transactions of the Society of Literary and Scientific Chiffoniers." In the publisher's advertisement that preceded the text, the work proposed to "elucidate the origin, history, and value of several primitive devices, which, from their apparent insignificance, have been overlooked by writers on the useful arts; but which have not been without their influence on the progress of civilization." Thus, while there is no evidence to suggest that the work took the American reading public by storm, there was behind the comic mask a serious purpose. In Ewbank's view, the meaning of civilization was to be discovered not only among the declarations of kings and the glories of war, but among the artifacts of daily life as well.

Ewbank's scientific and antiquarian interests were neatly joined in a work published in 1845. The volume was entitled *Specimens of Ancient and Oracular and Fighting Eolipiles: With Remarks on Dragons and Other Fire-Breathing Monsters of Mythology and the Middle Ages, Being a Supplement to His Treatise on Hydraulics and Mechanics*. Although the title is almost explanatory in itself, what Ewbank tried to argue was the proposition that fire-breathing monsters of ancient and medieval legend were primitive forms of steam engines devised by ingenious priest-engineers to exploit the ignorant pagans.

In that same year, Ewbank traveled to Brazil to study the arts of South American Indian culture, thus reflecting his growing interest in the burgeoning field of ethnology. In this connection, it should be noted that if one reads through the city notes of such mid-Nineteenth Century magazines as *The Historical Magazine* or Duyckinck's *Literary World*, one will frequently find Ewbank's name mentioned in conjunction with the American Ethnological Society. Allegedly, Ewbank helped found the society in the mid-1840's, but available evidence suggests that he held no office in the organization until the later years of his life when he served briefly as vice-president. What

[3] Eugene Ferguson, *Bibliography of the History of Technology* (Cambridge, Mass., 1968), pp. 244–5.

is significant about this aspect of his intellectual career is that it reflected the context in which he viewed man's technological progress. That his view of the useful arts was not a one-dimensional one was made plain years later in a brief piece written for another mid-Nineteenth Century magazine, *The American Artisan*. In Ewbank's words:

> We inherit the mechanical alphabet from barbarians, and, considering the times, places, and circumstances in and under which the elements of the world's machinery were disclosed, an account of their origin and early applications would form a brilliant chapter in the romance of history and of the first rude struggles of genius.[4]

But in 1849, the gentleman-scholar, the man of diversified interests and wide-ranging intellect, was about to enter upon a wholly new career. For the moment, at least, history would be without an aura of romance, and while there would be rude struggles, they would not be those of genius. In that year, President Taylor appointed Ewbank to the post of Commissioner of Patents.

It is surprising that American historians have paid so little attention to the United States Patent Office, but in fact there exists no history at all of its accomplishments. Such a lacuna of scholarship is particularly puzzling, since several individuals connected with the Office rank among some of Washington's most notable historical figures, from Superintendent William Thornton, the architect and man of science who was associated with its early history, to the Office's first Commissioner under the Patent Law of 1836, Henry Ellsworth. The list could go on to include such other men as Titian Ramsay Peale, who was himself a patent examiner both during and after Ewbank's tenure, and William Chauncy Langdon, also a patent examiner during Ewbank's administration and a co-founder of the Washington Y.M.C.A. Even more significant is the place of the Patent System in the context of the history of American institutions. The most cursory study of its early activities suggests that the Patent Office had emerged by the mid-Nineteenth Century as one of the most forceful expressions of the American preoccupation with technology and the useful arts, an agency that both democratized and commercialized the inventive impulses of the young Republic at a time when some of its most basic assumptions were taking shape. Since it was at this time that Ewbank assumed his new duties, his tenure becomes one of particular historical importance.

---

[4] *The American Artisan,* December 21, 1865, p. 181.

Specifically, the Patent Office which Ewbank was about to head had undergone an important change, for in 1849 it was placed under the aegis of the newly formed Department of the Interior. This administrative shift was significant for two reasons. First, the new alignment resulted in a policy change that now placed in the Commissioner's hands the final decision on patent appeals which had previously been the responsibility of a larger administrative board. In a decade when economic expansion was proceeding at an accelerating pace, reaching a fever pitch in the Gold Rush of the same year that Ewbank took office, an individual who held the patent on the right invention might well grow rich fast. Thus the Commissioner's powers now seemed greater than ever before, since the decision was now his to insure or deny the applicant for a patent a potential fortune. Consequently, given this combination of the Commissioner's new powers and the pecuniary motives of eager patentees, charge and counter-charge continually filled the air. Increasingly, many came to hold little regard

Library of Congress

Daguerrotype of the Patent Office about 1846 attributed to John Plumbe, Jr.

for the scientific scholar who carefully scrutinized would-be inventions for their historical innovativeness and their scientific merit—for a man, in short, who insisted on reading the Patent Law honestly. Paradoxically, however, the new administrative shift resulted in what proved to be a restriction of the Commissioner's freedom to act, for his increased powers made his position within the executive branch of government increasingly vulnerable to the political maneuverings of his time. The Commissioner's ultimate success, it seemed, would now be dependent in no small degree on how well he could master the science of politics.

According to the evidence surrounding his nomination and eventual confirmation by the Senate, Ewbank stood particularly well with the scientific community of his time. Not only was his nomination supported by his own Mechanics' Institute of the City of New York, but also by the members of the prestigious Franklin Institute of Philadelphia. In addition to these declarations of support, such men as Jonathan Bartlett of Rhode Island, who was a founder of the American Ethnological Society, and a subsequent appointee of President Taylor to the Mexican Boundary Commission, undertook to boost Ewbank's candidacy. In a letter to Alexander Dallas Bache on March 7, 1849, Bartlett spoke of "our mutual friend, Mr. Ewbank" and asked "whether there is a man in the country so well, so completely fitted for the place . . ." Echoing the prevailing sentiment of both the scientific community and of the press and public, Bartlett pointed to Ewbank's accomplishments both as scientific theoretician and practical scientist.[5] Friendships notwithstanding, Ewbank did seem admirably suited for the position on more than one count. He had been a successful manufacturer and businessman; he had broadened his national prespective by travel to a nation not yet dedicated to the rigors of material progress; he had written a classic work dealing in part with the already legendary steam engine; he had published in the *Journal of the Franklin Institute* on several occasions; and, if all that were not enough, he had patented a number of inventions of his own some years before. Here, it appeared, was a candidate who could combine in just proportion both theoretical insight and practical wisdom. Under such leadership and direction as this, it was reasonable to expect that the Patent Office might well serve both as a promoter of material and commercial progress and as an agency for the advancement of the purer aspects of science. Thus,

[5] Letter from John Bartlett to Alexander Dallas Bache, March 7, 1849, *Smithsonian Institution Manuscript Collections, Bache Papers.*

as Benjamin Perley Poore observed, Ewbank's nomination seemed an exceptionally wise one despite the "shameless nepotism" that characterized the presidency of Zachary Taylor.[6]

Of all the achievements of Ewbank's administration, few were perhaps more important than those brought about in connection with the Annual Report of the Commissioner, works numbering into the hundreds of pages which were designed to record the number and nature of all patents granted during the previous year, together with a brief summary on the state of the Patent Office. Upon assuming office in 1849, Ewbank immediately requested the governors of the various states to send to him their state archival material relating to the history and progress of invention. Ewbank's plan was to publish this material in the Annual Reports, thus making them expanded compendia of useful information accessible to the entire nation. Under his direction the Reports would be a key instrument in the nationalization of technological knowledge and practice.

Ewbank intended to go even further. In addition to increasing the scope of the Reports, he had decided to use his first one as a platform from which to argue his own views on the useful arts and manufactures, and on the future of American technological progress. Whereas such previous Commissioners as Burke and Ellsworth had been content to make succinct, *pro forma* statements concerning the state of American invention, Ewbank seized upon the Reports as an opportunity to share and promote his vision of a coming technological utopia. Thus in the first volume of the Report for 1849, he expanded in the following fashion on the development of the mechanical arts in America:

> The study of Nature's mechanisms, of God's own applications of the same principles and materials He has given inventors to work with, is only beginning. The UNIVERSE is before inventors, and all its elements and energies invite their attention.[7]

From his perspective, the world had to begin to think in profoundly new ways. Thus he asserted:

> A habit of modern, it was a passion in former times, to look askant at those who use the hammer or spade, under the fond delusion that the less wise men have to do with gross matter, the nearer they resemble the great spirit; whereas God is the greatest of workers—the chief of artificers. So far from locking up his wisdom in abstractions, he is

[6] Benjamin Perley Poore, *Perley's Reminiscences Illustrated,* Vol I (Philadelphia, 1886), p. 356.

[7] *Report of the Commissioner of Patents for the Year 1849, Part I: Arts and Manufactures* (Washington, 1850), p. 487.

> incessantly embodying it in tangible things; and in them it is that his intelligence, ingenuity, and resource are made manifest.[8]

"What is this world," Ewbank continued, "but one of his workshops, and the universe but a collection of his inventions?" It was a rhetorical question that lay at the very heart of all he would say and do throughout his intellectual and public life. In the Commissioner's view, nature's laws revealed God's preference for the materially useful. Accordingly, man was ordained to discover the truly beautiful or sublime among those inventions and manufactures that were the creative embodiment of natural laws. The greatest of moral truths was that of perpetual progress, the realization of which required only the dedication of enlightened workingmen. At times, it was a vision on whose behalf Ewbank marshalled the most sweeping prose:

> Man rises with the motors. His growth begins with them, and only as he extends their applications or adds to their number, can he increase in real stature. Nothing can compensate for their absence, for nothing valuable can he acquire but through them. Steps of a ladder resting upon earth and reaching to heaven, he is without them an earthworm, with them almost a God. His destinies are and ever must be wound up in them.[9]

Unequivocal in its embrace of the machine as an indispensable instrument of human perfection, such passages as this reveal Ewbank's fervent—almost evangelical—view of the transforming power of machine technology as the divine engine of material and moral progress, and it was just such passages as these that the citizen of 1850 had spread before him in the Commissioner's Annual Report for 1849.

Not everyone was impressed. In particular, Senator Henry Stuart Foote from Mississippi was decidedly distressed by the tone and the rhetoric of this government document. As a Southerner, it is likely that Foote did not share Ewbank's unrestrained faith in the power of the machine; after all, the manufacturing interests of the North were already threatening the peculiar institutions of the South. Furthermore, Foote had learned that Horace Greeley had been so favorably impressed by the first part of the Report that he had written an introduction for a privately printed version of it in which he zealously praised both the Report and its author. Since the abolitionist Greeley was no friend of Foote's, it followed that the Commissioner and his Report were no friends either. Thus when a request for funds for printing additional copies of the Report's second half dealing with

[8] *Ibid.*, p. 487–8.
[9] *Ibid.*, p. 498.

agriculture reached the Senate floor, hot debate ensued over the wild visionary statements of the Commissioner and over whether public funds should be used to support such "propaganda." In part because of the popularity of and demand for the document, funds were ultimately voted for the additional copies, but it seems clear that the episode did nothing to broaden the base of the Commissioner's political support.[10]

For the remaining two years of his tenure, political opposition waxed and waned periodically; charges were continually brought by disgruntled patentees whose applications had been rejected, and certain manufacturing interests sniped away at a Commissioner whose purposes did not coincide with their more single-minded desire for quick profits. Pressures increased from virtually all sides until finally another Southerner, the Patent Office's Chief Agricultural Clerk, Daniel Lee, unleashed a series of attacks on Ewbank's administration that ultimately brought the Commissioner down. The precise reason for the bitter division between them remains somewhat unclear. Perhaps Lee, like Foote, viewed the Commissioner's consuming interest in manufactures as detrimental to the interests of an ever beleaguered South; perhaps Lee was motivated by sheer political ambition; perhaps it was simply a question of personal antipathy. Whatever the case—and it was probably a combination of all three in varying measure—events might have been different had it not been for the death of President Taylor two years earlier, for upon the succession of President Millard Fillmore, the tides of political fortune began to turn slowly but irrevocably against Ewbank. Lee, it seems, had spent some time in Buffalo as a journalist, and Fillmore, who had practiced law in Buffalo, was indebted to the newspaper for which Lee had once worked. This historical coincidence, together with the volatile changes in the political climate following the death of Taylor, made Ewbank's position an increasingly untenable one. Finally, on October 30, 1852, Secretary of the Interior A. H. H. Stuart, acting at the request of President Fillmore, asked for Ewbank's resignation for what he termed "widespread feeling of discontent which prevails in regard to your administration of the affairs of the Patent Office." [11] The science of politics had proved an art after all, and the "perfect novice" had become a sudden casualty in the rude struggle of political battle.

---

[10] *Congressional Globe,* 31st Congress, 1st Session, May 17, 1850, pp. 916–922.

[11] *Records of the Office of the Secretary of the Interior,* Appointments Division, Record Group 48, Box 112, National Archives.

Ewbank's Washington experience was not confined to the mysteries of the Patent Office. While Commissioner, Ewbank served on the special commission that was appointed by the Department of the Interior to "test the several specimens of marble" that had been offered for the extension of the Capitol. Appointed on November 3, 1851, the commission included Ewbank, together with Joseph G. Totten, Joseph Henry, Andrew Jackson Downing, and Thomas U. Walter.[12] As Patent Commissioner, it was probably inevitable that Ewbank should on occasion move among the circles of Washington's scientific elite. In this regard, his association with Joseph Henry comprises one of the more fascinating aspects of Ewbank's Washington years. Although somewhat ambiguous, their relationship provides an important—albeit limited—perspective on the intellectual tendencies prevalent in the Federal City during the mid-Nineteenth Century.

From the beginning, Henry had been unsure of Ewbank's qualifications to become Patent Commissioner, and had recommended others for the post. Yet soon after Ewbank arrived in Washington, Henry, in a letter to J. H. Alexander, indicated that he thought Ewbank would "endeavor to discharge his duties to the extent of his ability. . ." [13] Henry's enthusiasm for Ewbank seems never to have gone beyond the measured approval of that early statement. One of the most salient clues to their relationship, which seems always to have been characterized by a certain distance, can be found in the Henry diaries where, at one point, the Secretary proclaims his determination to divorce himself for the Patent Office and its daily affairs. Certain patentees, it seems, had been eager to secure Henry's blessings on their inventions; and while Henry regarded the Patent Office as an agency of government that could indeed promote the cause of American science, he was apparently bothered by the idea of scientific inquiry and invention undertaken for the primary purpose of commercial profit. This is not to say that Henry was opposed to the applications of science for the purposes of material progress. He was not. Rather, Henry was first and foremost a scientist who saw clear and present dangers in too close an association with the commercial and political implications of Patent Office practice.[14] Ewbank, on the other hand, dedicated as he might be to the purely scientific aspects

---

[12] *Documentary History of the Construction and Development of the U.S. Capitol Building and Grounds* (Washington, 1904), p. 554.

[13] Letter from Joseph Henry to J. H. Alexander, May 17, 1849, *Smithsonian Institution Manuscript Collections, Joseph Henry Collection.*

[14] *Ibid.*, entry for Saturday, April 24, 1852.

of his work, was ineluctably involved with the legal and economic rights of inventors whose first concern was financial gain rather than the opportunity to advance the cause of science either pure or applied. From this perspective, it is not surprising that Henry and Ewbank never enjoyed a particularly close relationship, given their differing professional roles. Added to this was probably a fundamental difference in how each viewed science itself. For Henry, the imperative was the advancement of knowledge; for Ewbank, its spread and democratic application. For Henry, scientific frontiers were to be won by men of inquiring intellect; for Ewbank, by men of deliberate action armed with all the machinery that a sophisticated technology could produce.

Although now unburdened by the concerns of government office, Ewbank continued to play a role in official Washington's scientific enterprises. In 1853 he accompanied his life-long friend and Patent Office librarian, W. W. Turner of New York City, on the Whipple Expedition to the Pacific in search of a railroad route. Ewbank, together with Turner, wrote of the Indian tribes encountered on the expedition, their manners, customs, artifacts and, most important for later scholarship, their language.[15] In 1855, through the auspices of the Smithsonian Institution, Ewbank was invited to write an essay dealing with the Indian antiquities that had been brought back from Chile and Peru by the United States Naval Astronomical Expedition.

In that same year he published what was perhaps his most comprehensive statement of the relationship between man and nature. The book was entitled *The World a Workshop; or, The Physical Relationship of Man to the Earth.* As the title suggests, the leading metaphor was that of the earth as factory and man as factory worker. With Baconian inspiration, Ewbank proclaimed that "we are created for the work we can do—for the useful and productive ideas we can stamp upon matter . . . " In measured phrases that echoed such previous statements as those found in his first Annual Report as Commissioner, Ewbank asserted that "To one great lesson the world is beginning to listen: faith in human power." In addition to theoretical pronouncements on the nature of the earth's origins, the work in large measure devoted itself to an examination of that particular kind of power that evolves when one has hitched his imagination to the powers of the machine.

Then in 1856, following the publication of *Life in Brazil,* there appeared in the city of Washington *A Classified Catalogue* of Thomas

[15] Lieutenant A. W. Whipple, Thomas Ewbank, Esq., and Professor W. W. Turner, *Report Upon the Indian Tribes* (Washington, 1855).

Ewbank's library, or at least that part of it which he was to sell at Joseph McQuire's Auction Sale Room on Tuesday, May 20 of that year. Official Washington having no longer any need for him, the ex-Commissioner was leaving his residence on the east side of 6th Street West between D and E, and returning to New York City.

For the remaining fourteen years of his life, Ewbank continued to think and write on those subjects that had so consumed his interests during his Washington years. In 1858 he published a scientific treatise which purported to examine the nature of physical matter and the idea of force. Two years later two more works—shorter in scope and length—were published. The first was an essay originally read before the American Ethnological Society. Entitled *Inorganic Forces Ordained to Supersede Human Slavery,* the essay argued that the crisis of the Union and the crisis of the American Negro were at bottom a question of labor, and that the issue of slavery should be approached on this basis, irrespective of its moral or political dimensions. Contending that the Negro was an inefficient machine, and that the laws of nature ordained that a technology of inorganic forces would soon render such a labor system obsolete, Ewbank echoed the position articulated ten years earlier in the Patent Office Report for 1849. As he had said then, "Not till mechanical as well as ethical science is fully explored and universally applied can man attain his destiny, and evil be swept from the earth." [16] The second essay of 1860, *The Position of Our Species in the Path of its Destiny,* attempted to establish the view that man's relationship to his physical surroundings was marked by laws of continual change and progress.

In 1866 there appeared his last significant contribution to the world of science, *North American Rock-Writing and Other Aboriginal Modes of Recording and Transmitting Thought.* In this essay Ewbank argued that America represented the material embodiment of a third stage in human history characterized by continual scientific inquiry, and that only in America could such inquiry be freely pursued under the banner of democratic values, unhampered by monarchial institutions. Finally, in September of 1870, at the age of 78, Thomas Ewbank died in New York City.

Ewbank's significance for the student of Washington history in both its local and national dimensions derives from the fact that he served the cause of science and technology at a time when key assumptions and ideas were being formed concerning the place of science and the role that its attendant technology would play in the development

[16] *Op. Cit.,* p. 488.

of the American nation. Certainly it is hazardous to draw too brief a characterization of the intellectual community in which Ewbank lived and worked during his years in Washington, but it is not inaccurate to say that the local community reflected in part the larger one. During this period, as historians have reminded us, there were few institutional rigidities, less a reverence for the traditional than a concern for the possibilities of the new and experimental, and above all, perhaps, an atmosphere of Emersonian self-reliance in which the individual had only to shout loud enough to be heard. In more specific terms, as James Flack has argued, the arrangements for scientific enterprise in the second quarter of the Nineteenth Century tended to be fluid, loose, and open, rather than rigid, inflexible, and closed. Certainly such openness is confirmed by the transient character of such local Washington associations as the short-lived Metropolitan Mechanics Institute, or even the National Institute, which, without the strong hand of a Joseph Henry, eventually dissolved. In short, associations, despite a growing sense of professionalism, were loose aggregations of individuals rather than tightly knit groups of narrow and specialized interests. Given the diversity of such a career as Ewbank's, there is little wonder that such was the case, for assuming that he was more or less representative of his age, what single organization could there have been to meet the needs of a man who was at once a businessman, antiquarian, ethnologist, literary amateur, explorer, historian, manufacturer, and public official?

To be sure, a fully adequate assessment of the impact of Thomas Ewbank on the intellectual and technological developments of mid-Nineteenth Century American culture must await a more extended treatment of his life and career. But it is not premature to suggest that for the student of official Washington history during this period, Ewbank's presence in the Federal City was an important and far-reaching one. In a civilization such as ours, which has come to be virtually synonymous with the very idea of technology, the study of such a man as Ewbank is imperative if we are ever to gain a more complete understanding not only of his times but of our own.

Olmsted on F Street: The Beginnings of the United States Sanitary Commission

ELIZABETH STEVENSON

In June 1861, a slight, crippled man set up a temporary office on a table in one room of the Treasury Building in Washington, D.C. Coming and going about his obscure business, he impressed people by the intensity of his posture and attitude, by the dip and swing with which he propelled himself rapidly on crutches, and by the way he quickly made himself known to important people. This was springtime, and the unfinished streets of the city were invaded by the smells of the blossoming countryside not far away from the Capitol dome at this time being reconstructed in a new style. Across the river, visible from rooftops on the city side, were the flags of the enemy; Frederick Law Olmsted, for he was this new man in the city, had climbed to such an eminence to see the sight. And he had written home to his wife in New York City his forebodings of the difficult days ahead for the overconfident Union.

Olmsted, who had been devotedly supervising the continuing construction of New York's Central Park after sharing with Calvert Vaux in the design of this remarkable parallelogram, was persuaded by the Reverend Henry Bellows, an influential clergyman, to take on the precarious job of directing the work of a new voluntary organization with headquarters in Washington. In spite of a serious injury to his

---

The two illustrations which are published with this essay are from a collection of memorabilia of the United States Sanitary Commission which is now being sorted and catalogued by the Society's Curator of Prints and Photographs, Robert A. Truax. The collection was brought to the attention of Mr. Truax by Winter K. Graves, a member of the Association of Oldest Inhabitants of the District of Columbia, who sought a depository for the material on behalf of its owner, Gershom Bradford, a Washington resident now in his 97th year. Mr. Bradford generously donated the collection to the Columbia Historical Society. The material was originally collected and preserved by the Rev. Frederick N. Knapp, who was active in the Commission in the Civil War period.

From the original in the Columbia Historical Society
Gift of Gershom Bradford

Frederick Law Olmsted, 1863.

On the reverse of the card on which the photograph is mounted is the name and addresses of the photographer: "BROADBENT & CO., 912, 914 & 916 Chestnut Street, Philadelphia."

leg in a recent carriage accident, Olmsted had agreed to leave Central Park and become Secretary General of the United States Sanitary Commission. The charter for the organization had been signed by President Lincoln, but the Commission was an anomaly, a private, volunteer organization, which raised money for its own efforts and received only office space, stationery, and postage from the Federal government. Bellows and his fellow commissioners served the organization without pay and delegated, in this early period, the day-to-day direction of affairs to Olmsted, who had taken a substantial cut in income to do this job. The Commissioners counted on Olmsted's push and ability to organize a headquarters in the capital city and to begin field work for the expected battles yet to be fought. He found almost at once that it would require all of his stubborn audacity to aid the

Federal government, sometimes against its collective will, to improve the health services of the new Union Army.

That same Army strolled about the streets of the city, within sight of the unfinished capitol and the halfreared shaft of the Washington Monument, in a state of cheerful and impudent disarray, many privates sporting straw hats and civilian clothes, their uniforms not yet distributed, jeering at officers instead of saluting them smartly, obviously unready, in the view of the alarmed Secretary General of the United States Sanitary Commission, to face the unknown force gathered just across the Potomac. Olmsted was not happy at all about the state of unpreparedness he found in Washington, D.C. and shared his mordaunt criticisms with his wife Mary, at home in a house on the hill of Mt. St. Vincent in Central Park. Imperturbable in public, he wrote privately, two days before the 4th of July, 1861: "I do not get on very well . . . should not be much surprised to get up and find Jeff Davis in the White House." [1] He saw Abraham Lincoln on a sidewalk one day where the President was walking informally with friends. Olmsted was not impressed. The new President, in his ill-fitting clothes, and with his physical ungainliness, "looked as if [he] would be an applicant for a Broadway squad policemanship." (The anguish and drama of the war years might have been measured in retrospect for Olmsted by the change in his opinion of President Lincoln.)

His fear that the government, its President, and its soldiers were not prepared for attack, seemed borne out by the 1st battle of Bull Run. Olmsted saw the pitiful rout of the army of the Union when stragglers from the nearby battlefield dragged themselves into Washington, flopped down on the streets in disarray, dirty, hungry, thirsty, without the guns they had dropped along the way. Olmsted was disgusted, not so much with the soldiers, as with those who had failed to prepare them for actual fighting. He went beyond his duties as Secretary of the Sanitary Commission and wrote a report generally critical of the state of preparedness of the army; the report was so sharp that it was suppressed, temporarily.

But meantime, Olmsted plunged wholeheartedly into work for the new Sanitary Commission. He organized the work both in Washington and elsewhere and did a great deal of it himself. He began first by enlisting a medical member of the commission to go with him to inspect the filthy, unsanitary hospitals and army camps ringing Washington. He began writing urgent reports to the Army and to the Secretary of War about filthy latrines, dirty food, and the unsuitable

[1] This, and succeeding quotations, from Frederick Law Olmsted Papers, Library of Congress, unless otherwise noted.

swampy ground chosen for camps. He analyzed the poor enlistment procedures which had brought boys, old men, and physically disabled and ill recruits into the Army; he saw them in the camps forlorn and unable to serve. He proposed ways of instituting proper elimination of those physically and mentally unfit at enlistment time. Buttressing these improvised early activities, which were making the Sanitary Commission officers known as enterprising and formidable gadflies, he organized an office force in the city of Washington and enlisted capable and energetic inspectors for the field. These were mostly civilian and medical, but he instituted a tactful cooperation with the activities of the Army medical organization, using its facilities whenever he was able. His organization was designed to serve this unit of the Army; he saw at once that this branch of the Army was pitifully small and weak. He worked behind the scenes in Washington to strengthen this official medical service while enforcing upon himself and his volunteers a policy of getting along with prideful and touchy medical officers.

To extend the influence of the Sanitary Commission into every town and country crossroads of the north, he enlisted and organized the eager, inchoate will to help which existed but had not before had a forceful kind of leadership. These volunteers gathered together clothes, food, medicines, bandages, and whatever else that was designated as needed in careful lists circulated by the Commission. Olmsted set up depots at points which he surmised, as if by a sixth sense, would be at some time within the sound of the gun-rumblings of future campaigns. By September 18, Frederick could write to Mary, his wife, to whom he told all things important to him: "I have completed a *large* organization. . . ."

The gentlemen commissioners in New York City, at this time leaving the entire running of the Commission to their agent Olmsted, could express some satisfaction and even wonder at the celerity and energy he showed in his work. They were finding that his organizing flair, demonstrated already in the greatest public work undertaken by any American city, was no fluke, and that they had chosen the right man for the job. They had as yet not run up against his imperious will when a difference of opinion might chance to arise between them.

Hours of overwork combined with bad news continuing after the shock of Bull Run made Olmsted morose in his judgments. He spoke almost in despair of the sight of "that insufferable beast Wycoff" standing beside Mrs. Lincoln at the White House to hear a band concert on the lawn. Olmsted and others wandered freely the grounds as part of a casual audience on this occasion (September 28, 1861).

Wycoff was known to Olmsted as a political fixer. Olmsted's emotions were as extravagant as his efforts: ". . . The North certainly is not and never can be what we had hoped for it. Vulgarity and poverty of intellect rule. We have no greatness; no heroism; no art."

Olmsted was to soften, if not toward Mrs. Lincoln, at least toward the President, rather soon. On October 17, he wrote painstakingly a hand-printed letter to his twelve-year-old son to make a story of what he was seeing and what he was doing while staying away from his family:

> Dear Charley,
>
> There was a man who had been on picket duty and got nervous and tired. And when he got through, and got some coffee he laid down in his tent with his gun by his side, and his feet out the door of the tent, and he went to sleep and had a dream. He dreamed that Beauregard was comeing. And he woke up, and when he opened his eyes he saw his toes against the sky out of the door, and he thought his toes were Beauregard and a squad of men comeing over the hill; so he pointed his gun, which was already pointed that way, toward them, and pulled the trigger, and shot four of his toes right off. And then I think he woke quite up. And Bishop Clark [one of the Commissioners] saw him in the hospital today, and he only had one toe and that was what he said. And the doctor said he thought it was so.
>
> I went to the White House today and saw the President. He is a very tall man. He is not a handsome man. He is not graceful. But he is good. He speaks frankly and truly and straight out just what he is thinking. Commonly he is very sober but sometimes he laughs. And when he laughs he laughs very much and opens his mouth very deep. He said he was glad to see me and shook hands with me. It seemed as if he was. He did not look proud nor cross but a good sort of fellow.
>
> Give my love to Mother and Charlotte and let me know if anything goes wrong.
>
> Your affectionate father . . .

At about the same time he wrote this letter to his little boy Frederick Olmsted found a more commodious headquarters for the Sanitary Commission than the room in the Treasury Building. This was the old three-story, rambling Adams House at 244 F Street, within easy walking distance in one direction of the Treasury Building and in the other direction of the big bulk of the Patent Office, which before the war was over would be converted into one of the city's many improvised hospitals. The Adams family of Massachusetts owned the house. It had been their city residence—when they were not in the White House—for many decades. John Quincy Adams had purchased it when he became Secretary of State under Monroe. He

From the original in the Columbia Historical Society
Gift of Gershom Bradford

General Office of the U. S. Sanitary Commission, 244 F Street, Washington, D. C., 1862.

The photograph is pasted on the printed card. The inscription in small type at the bottom of the card is: "Entered according to Act of Congress, in the year 1862, by GARDNER & GIBSON, in the Clerk's Office of the District Court of the District of Columbia."

Another view of the headquarters building, and other related photographs, appear in the 1960–1962 volume of the *Records* (1963) with the essay "The United States Sanitary Commission in Washington, 1861–1865" by the late Donald H. Mugridge (1905–1964).

had returned to it when, after his presidential term, he served Massachusetts as a member of the House of Representatives. His widow had lived on in the house till she died. Under the terms of the agreement made with this upstart organization, the Federal government had agreed to furnish quarters for them. The government leased the house and turned it over to the Sanitary Commission. Olmsted took great delight in making the house efficient and comfortable for his and his small staff's use.

The Secretary General now had a sort of castle-keep from which to issue forth on the business of his corps of strong-minded volunteers and underpaid agents pursuing their good work in the midst of the increasingly busy war-time city. Olmsted described the homely housekeeping details of his settling into the Adams House to his wife (October 13, 1861). During one of his absences, his sub-lieutenants had seen to making the house usable. "Found that Knapp and Bloor had got possession . . . had a room freshly papered . . . and bedded, ready for me, opening into a fine board room, which when Board not in session will be my private office or parlor.

"A suite of rooms below for general offices. Three bedrooms above to be fitted for the President [of the Commission], Knapp, and Bloor.

"Keep a good heart and order me home by telegraph when necessary." (This volunteer soldier in the cause was awaiting the news of the birth of a child in the house in Central Park where he had left his family.)

No. 244 was to be a busy doorway on F Street. It fronted the roadway directly. Horses, carriages, wagons stopped to bring or take on supplies. Civilians and military men came and went on important or trivial errands. The house became the center for all the activities of the Sanitary Commission although later an office on Broadway in New York City would become an important meeting place for the Executive Committee. There were to be many depots, warehouses, and subsidiary offices established throughout the north. This was the nerve center of action although the nerve endings were to be always in the crucial areas of destruction and death upon battlefields elsewhere. Here, at least in busy times, Olmsted lived as well as worked. His nominal places of residence were first Willard's Hotel, then the Paris Hotel, a place owned by a freedman and frequented by congressmen, and then, as his father recorded his son's address, "Fredk's Washington address, 185 South B Street, corner of W. 9th, back of Smithsonian." [2]

In the midst of organizing the Sanitary Commission, Olmsted was also undergoing the anxieties of publication. On October 25, the first copy of an English publisher's edition of his book about the South, *The Cotton Kingdom,* arrived. He had written about his travels in the South in two other forms earlier: newspaper articles for the *New York Times* and New York *Herald* and then this journalism condensed into three books. Now, with war fanning even his relatively judicious temper, he had condensed the three books into one and with the help of a well known abolitionist writer, Daniel Goodloe, had pointed up the virtues of the North and the faults of the South a little more sharply than in the original versions. The book was as

[2] Information about Olmsted's addresses in Washington from biographical Notes drawn from John Olmsted's diary in F. L. Olmsted Jr. & Theodora Kimball, editors, *Frederick Law Olmsted: Landscape Architect, 1822–1903.*

much an effort on behalf of the war as his service in the Sanitary Commission. It would sell well.

The author of the new book had little time to go home even when his daughter Marion was born, on October 28. After seeing the mother and child and describing her proudly as "a regular Tom gal," he returned to Washington. He was as bound by war service as any soldier. And he paid for his service in Washington by difficulties at home in New York City. The Commissioners of Central Park reduced his salary by half on January 6, 1862 and decided to sell the house his family was living in on Mt. St. Vincent "for a tavern." He made flying visits to New York and the park and kept the foremen and "park keepers" at their work of completing and maintaining the park even during war time. In spite of personal complications he was more than ever involved in the work and emotion of the war. On January 28, 1862, he wrote his sister Bertha, "It is a good big work I have in hand. . ." and he spoke with fervor and faith of "the low, obscure, mysterious strength of the free and unenlightened people" who were supporting the war.

But in the long dead months following Bull Run, the national government did not give any scope to the fervor of the people. General George McClellan occupied himself so long in fastidious preparation of his great army, with no forays or campaigns to accompany this getting ready, many citizens lost hope. The Commissioners and their agent in Washington were again disheartened. The organization had an enemy in Edwin Stanton, the Secretary of War. He considered them meddlers in his affairs. Olmsted, Bellows, and George Templeton Strong, the able Treasurer of the Sanitary Commission, had to go around this capable and forceful man in order to attain their ends. And it looked, during this winter of their discontent, that Stanton would put them out of business.

Olmsted attended an important meeting at Dr. Bellows' house in New York on February 18, 1862. Strong wrote in his diary for that day, "We propose now to prepare, at least, to put our house in order, wind up our affairs, and resign. Government keeps no faith with us." [3] But President Lincoln, too, had become impatient with the over-finicky carefulness of General McClellan's preparations. Four days after the unhappy meeting of the Executive Committee of the Sanitary Commission, Lincoln issued a general order for a frontal movement by both the Eastern and Western armies of the North. A few weeks later, probably in expectation of a strong movement southward, the Southern army, which had been camped almost against the bridges

[3] George Templeton Strong, *Diary,* III, 207.

over the Potomac, withdrew quickly and silently. The city of Washington and its citizens were made aware that the threatening force standing up against them across the river was thin and weak indeed, and that even many of its gun emplacements were mock wood constructions painted to look like cannons.

Along with some other gentlemen of the organization, Fred Olmsted rode out into the Virginia countryside from which the Confederates had withdrawn, leaving behind them a litter of tents, papers, weapons, all the impedimenta of an army. The little group, on horseback and in a carriage set out together happily and in a mildly adventurous mood, for there might still be snipers in the vicinity. They scattered across the strangely desolate and abused landscape attracted by the odd disjecta of the vanished troops. On a good horse, cheerful at being outdoors and away from a confining desk, Olmsted rode out and away from the sight of the more sedentary members in the carriage. He was soon beyond the others, savoring the cold air, curious about the remains of the army which had threatened the city.

The separated travelers were caught by night too far to return to the city. Those who had lost sight of Olmsted made up their beds on the floor of a half wrecked house, using their coats to cover themselves. Next morning the cold and tired group found Olmsted as haphazardly as they had lost him. "Olmsted met us, bristling with bowie knives and shooting irons picked up on the ground and looking like Robinson Crusoe." [4] Thus, George Strong described the chief of the Sanitary Commission, seeing in him a man happy to have had an adventure away from his office. He had found a snug shelter in the wreckage of the camps. Olmsted greeted his friends with a cheerful grin, not in the least upset by a night in this man-made wilderness. It was probably about the time of this small adventure that Olmsted shed his gentlemanly city clothes and adopted a useful, soldier-like jacket and trousers and a jaunty, visored cap. It was a more suitable outfit for rummaging about shanty-like hospitals and unsanitary camps than what he had been wearing in the office.

The Commissioners and their Secretary General still did not know if they were to have a place in the new activity of which they heard rumblings in Washington. Olmsted, thinking that he might be out of a job, offered his thoughts to Lincoln on "the management of the negroes at Port Royal." Olmsted was concerned that the North not abandon freed Blacks, such as these sea island inhabitants. There were thousands of these laboring people of the great rice and cotton plantations along the coast. The Federal armies had moved in and occupied

[4] *Ibid.*, III, 211.

these barrier islands; the whites had fled from their homes and lands; their "people" were rudderless, and not many citizens of the North cared very much what became of them. They were a burden to the army except in their capacity as cheap and convenient labor. Olmsted thought beyond the situation of the moment. He believed that what was owed to these freed men, contrabands as they were callously called, was a simple, careful guidance in learning to work for wages—the opportunity in this and other ways to learn to be responsible for themselves. His forthright hope was that this would be a training for citizenship. He looked far enough ahead to expect and to wish that these people might attain the full rights of civilized living. But he was realist enough, with his knowledge of Southern actualities, to know that a good outcome for the Negroes would not come easily or quickly. He spent some thought on the subject, wrote out his ideas at some length, and believed that he could justify his ideas in practice, if given the care of these peoples of the coastal islands. He was to raise the issue once again a year later after he had gone through a tumultuous year of field activities away from his desk in Washington. But Olmsted was not to take on the care of the freedmen.

For all at once, in the spring of 1862, two battles, which the Sanitary Commission had been fighting behind the scenes, were won. On April 18, 1862, a bill which the commission had engineered was passed by Congress. "An Act to Reorganize and Increase the Efficiency of the Medical Department of the Army" was not everything Olmsted and the others wished, but it began to adapt the old, creaking organization to the needs of giant armies. The Commission would have an organization with which it could work. Frederick Olmsted announced in a letter to his father that he had given up the Sea Island project. He had a job to do in the Sanitary Commission. The skeleton organization which he had completed this past year in Washington might now go to work in earnest. About the bill he said, "Our success is suddenly wonderfully complete." In addition to their success in the modernization of the Medical Department, they had got their man appointed as its head. "The President yesterday promised to nominate for Surgeon General, Hammond, the very man whom, eight months ago, we picked out as the best man in the corps for the office. . . ."

This was written on April 19, 1862. McClellan was about to make his move, not the campaign southward from Washington which Lincoln had hoped for but a movement by sea to the coast of Virginia, to the "Peninsula" below Richmond, and a move inland with a great and finely trained army, to take the Southern capital and, as the general confidently hoped, end the war quickly and efficiently. Olmsted was strung up with tightly knit energy, ready to plunge into an active part in McClellan's new campaign. He received permission to commandeer old transport ships, convert them to hospital ships, and take his Sanitary Commission into the field of battle. They were to accompany the invading fleet and receive and succor the wounded and the sick from the expected battles. They would then shuttle ships backward and forward from the northeastern ports, taking men off and bringing back medical supplies, food, nursing and surgical help in turn. In the letter in which he told his father about the political successes won by the Commission, he said almost incidentally, "As you will see by the papers, I am getting up floating hospitals. I shall probably take command of the [fleet] in person."

Olmsted set sail with his handpicked doctors, medical students, women volunteers, who would all labor in the weeks ahead as they had never done before, achieving a unity and cheerfulness of purpose under the keen and cool eye of their "chief" in harrowing and exhausting circumstances. These circumstances justified all Olmsted's fear about the unpreparedness of the medical service of the army. This frail voluntary service was, for some weeks, the only barrier between the army and complete disaster and disgrace in the medical care of the northern troops in this campaign.

But this is another story, an episode quite different from the long, grinding year in which Olmsted worked away in Washington, D.C. to prepare the Sanitary Commission for just such an emergency. The Commission was now able to work as its Secretary General had seen that it would have to work—past the edge of human abilities for long days and nights. The preparations had been cleverly made and were to be justified. Olmsted would go out from 244 F Street for another year and a half of war, the hard, bitter early years when the Union had no clear view of victory; the soldiers at Harrison's Landing, at Antietam and Gettysburg and many other battles saw the slight, crippled figure of the Secretary General of the Sanitary Commission, whose arrival usually signalled trainloads of supplies routed through troop movements or wagon loads brought on back roads when the rail lines were blocked. He would cooperate with General Hammond in the creation of new kinds of ambulances for the battlefields, new kinds of pavilion hospitals which were cleaner and easier to manage. He would cajole, threaten, order supplies forward to where the guns were still hot and see that men in need were looked after. The rooms at 244 F Street would hear tales as he came and went in these busy months. And even when Olmsted had gone from the organization, the Sanitary

Commission, created by his efforts from this center in the capital city, continued with ever increasing success to aid the medical department of the army to be better than it had been and to furnish its own kind of unconventional, nervy, needed help to the common man of the Union Army.

Unbuilt Bridges of Washington, D. C.

DONALD BEEKMAN MYER

Pierre Charles L'Enfant based his Baroque city plan for Washington on its special topography cradled between several hills and two great rivers. His original vision was for a city penetrated and serviced by creeks, rivers and a series of canals. Though the Capital did not develop like another Venice or St. Petersburg, its architecturally and historically important bridges have given the city a special appearance.

Washington bridges have been planned through a sequence of economic, political and natural events. Many, however, were never built. These unbuilt bridges are interesting because their engineering and stylistic achievements are untarnished by time, disaster or obsolescence. They are important for the part they play in the city's evolutionary history of planning and appearance. This paper presents some of the most interesting unbuilt bridges designed for Washington, D. C.

THREE SISTERS BRIDGE

Over the Potomac River west of Georgetown

Washington has no older unbuilt bridge than the Three Sisters Bridge. L'Enfant recommended it as his original 1791 Potomac crossing, though shown only as a recommended location for the bridge. Army Engineers surveyed the Potomac in 1857 and recommended two designs for a suspension bridge which would pass high over the Three Sisters Rocks.

Of the designs prepared under supervision of Army Engineer in Charge Alfred L. Rives, one was a single span suspension bridge which dramatically soared through a pair of arched stone towers. An alternate two span suspension structure had two decks—the lower for railroad use and the upper for highway use. The Civil War caused postponement of both schemes and the crossing was not seriously considered again until the mid-Twentieth Century.

Delivered before the Columbia Historical Society on April 17, 1973.

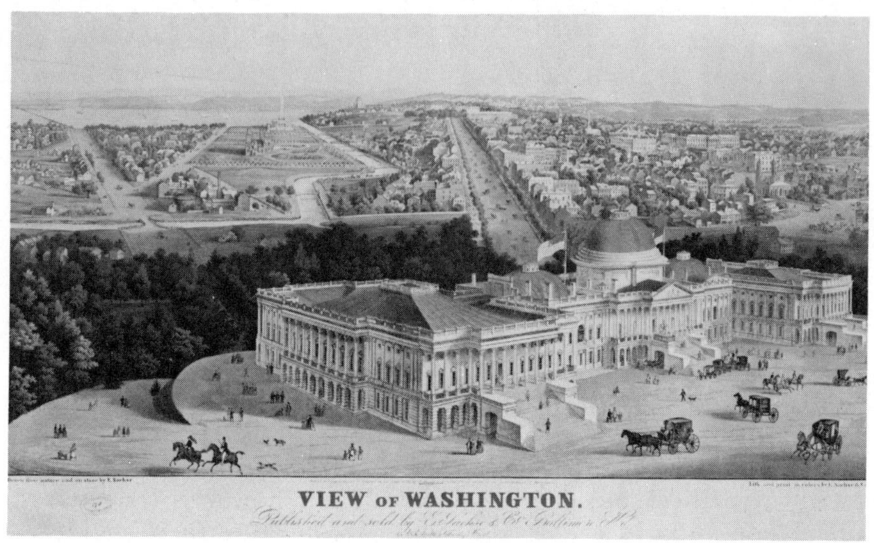

Smithsonian Institution

Mid-Nineteenth Century idealized view of monumental Washington by Edward Sachse showing a combination of proposed and existing bridges over the Washington Canal.

In 1959 the District of Columbia Highway Department discussed the Three Sisters site with the Commission of Fine Arts. The Commission insisted that if constructed the bridge should not detract from the surrounding natural beauty. A design eventually approved by the Commission of Fine Arts in 1967 was developed through a series of exchanges between the Highway Department and the Commission of Fine Arts. Preliminary designs included a multi-piered continuous girder type structure, as well as single arch, multiple-arch, and center-support-cable-suspension structures. The scheme favored through further design development was for an orthotropic steel, single span bridge that would be one of the longest of its kind in the world. Design problems arose with the approaches and the curvature at each end, and the scheme was discarded.

The present, delayed scheme for Three Sisters Bridge has a dramatic 750 foot concrete span, 80 feet high. The structure would have two piers which would gracefully thrust an arch across the river. At

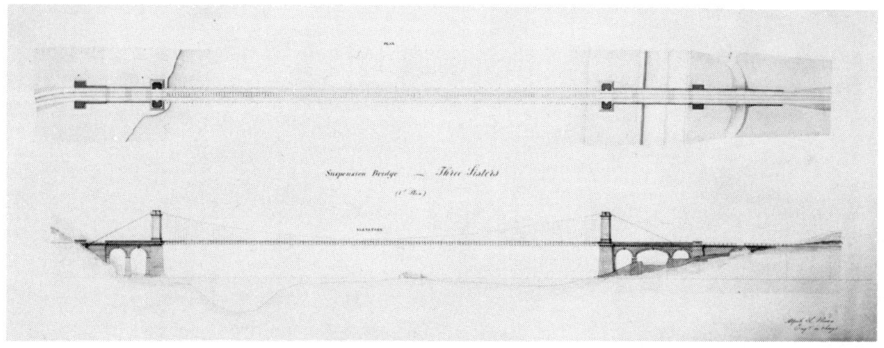

National Archives, Record Group 77

Three Sisters Bridge designed by Alfred L. Rives in 1857 as a single span suspension bridge slung between stone towers. An alternate scheme had two suspension spans and a lower highway level topped by a railroad level.

National Archives, Record Group 77

Three Sisters Bridge suspension towers as proposed in 1857 by Alfred L. Rives.

each end, half arches would sweep away to the shores. Inward slanting sides would provide a rich shadow and reflection pattern. Particular design merit comes from the cantilevered connections between the bridge and the shore highways. If the bridge is constructed, it will be built on a series of concrete girders. The design team included the firm of Howard, Needles, Tammen and Bergendoff, Consulting Engineers, New York City, and Paul Weidlinger, engineer, Cambridge, Massachusetts. The architect is Gordon Lorimer of New York City.

AQUEDUCT BRIDGE

Over the Potomac River at Georgetown

One of Washington's best known early bridges was built on the site of the present Key Bridge. Called Aqueduct Bridge, its function was to carry canal barges across the Potomac from the Chesapeake and Ohio Canal to Alexandria. Aqueduct Bridge was built between 1833 and 1843 with a trussed wooden trough and stone piers. Though the Aqueduct is a part of the rich bridge history of Washington, a less known scheme by Robert Mills preceded it. Mills, who also prepared designs for Washington's water supply, the Capitol, the Treasury and the Washington Monument, recommended an aqueduct in 1832. His designs for a stone-supported wooden trough were exquisitely rendered in water color and extremely detailed, but were never used. Contemporary with Mills' scheme was another untitled watercolor rendering of a stone arched bridge for Georgetown.

As the Aqueduct developed maintenance difficulties through the middle of the Nineteenth Century, Mr. Rives of the Army Engineers suggested a new scheme. His 1857 design showed a lower masonry arched level with canal trough and an upper iron structure for railroad and highway use. None of the grand replacement schemes for the Aqueduct Bridge was built, but the trough was eventually removed and replaced with an iron truss structure over the original stone piers. This eventually became inadequate for early Twentieth Century Traffic and replacement efforts were made again.

Architect Nathan Wyeth's original scheme for the 1923 Francis Scott Key Memorial Bridge was another two level structure. This would have had separate highway and trolley levels. Trolleys could have gone directly from the upper level into the transit terminal at the base of M Street for an interchange with downtown, upper Georgetown, Glen Echo and Virgina lines. The present Key Bridge was built with a single level because of World War I budget and timing problems.

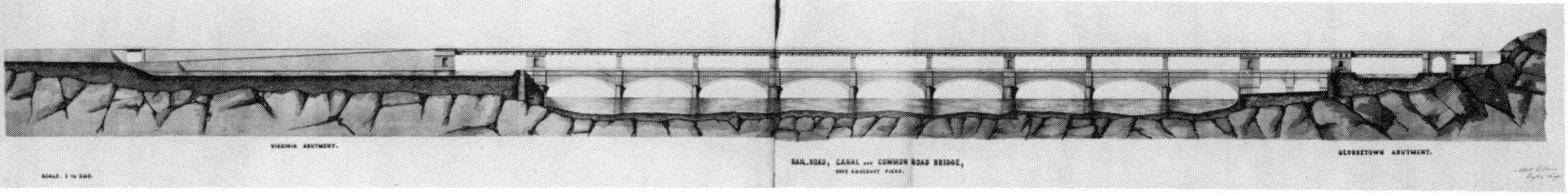

Proposed replacement for Aqueduct Bridge designed by Alfred L. Rives in 1857 with a stone trough level for canal traffic topped by an iron railroad and highway deck.

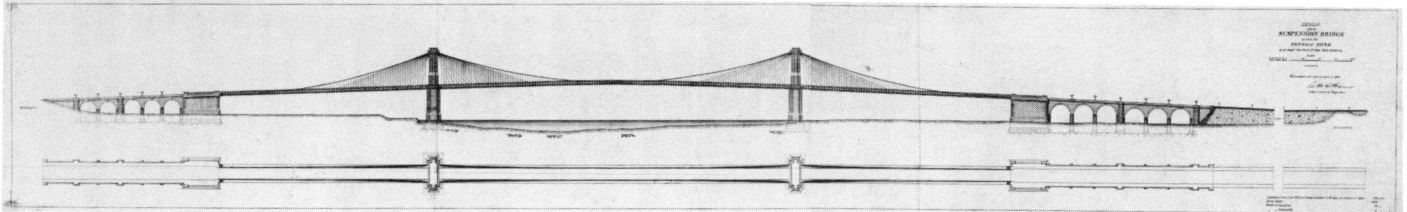

Memorial Bridge designed by Peter C. Hains in 1890, on the alignment of New York Avenue across the Potomac.

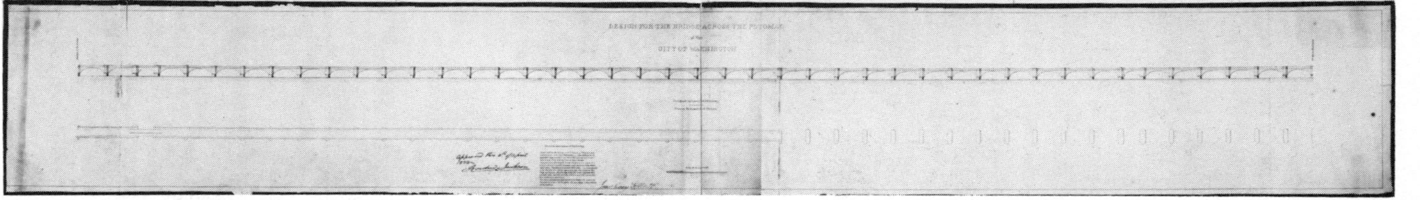

Long Bridge designed in 1833 by James Kearney, and approved by President Andrew Jackson, as a masonry arched replacement for the wooden Long Bridge,

National Archives, Record Group 77

ARLINGTON MEMORIAL BRIDGE

Over the Potomac River between the Lincoln Memorial and Arlington Cemetery

The Memorial Bridge site has one of the world's most distinguished collections of unbuilt bridge designs. Some were strictly utilitarian while others were architectural tours-de-force.

The present simple classical dignity of Memorial Bridge was designed as part of the Baroque city plan, a part of the Mall. This bridge is one of Washington's most successful pieces of architecture. From the initial planning for a bridge at this site to the final setting of the sculpture after World War II there is a 100 year span.

Colonel Peter C. Hains of the Corps of Engineers was the first officially to design a bridge approximately at the Arlington Memorial Bridge site. In 1886 Colonel Hains recommended a multi-span, utilitarian truss bridge. At almost the same time, an arched masonry Lincoln-Grant Memorial Bridge was proposed by Captain T. W. Symons. Another was proposed by Paul Pelz, designer of Georgetown University's Healy Hall and the Library of Congress. Pelz design was an extremely romantic Romanesque Revival tower bridge in honor of U. S. Grant.

Congress authorized another study by Colonel Hains in 1890. This resulted in a multi-million dollar suspension bridge scheme stretching across the 4,500 feet between the foot of New York Avenue and Arlington Cemetery. No action was taken on Colonel Hains' second design.

National Archives

Memorial Bridge designed by Peter C. Hains in 1890, on the alignment of New York Avenue across the Potomac, in honor of U. S. Grant.

Commission of Fine Arts

Memorial Bridge designed by William H. Burr and Edward Casey in 1899, on the alignment of New York Avenue across the Potomac. This competition winning design was abandoned with the decision to align the bridge with the Mall rather than with New York Avenue.

District Engineer Major Charles Davis reported on bridge needs in 1892 and 1895. It was during this period that Congress agreed upon an ornamental crossing concept. This prompted an 1899 authorization to hold a memorial bridge competition.

The competition attracted a dramatic series of colossal monumental designs, all of which ran from the base of Observatory Hill near the foot of New York Avenue across the Potomac to Arlington Cemetery. Designs were submitted by engineers L. L. Buck, William H. Burr, William R. Hutton and George S. Morison. An ornate triumphal arch design by Burr was selected. He prepared the design in conjunction with architect Edward Casey. (Casey had been associated with Morison on Taft Bridge across Rock Creek Park.) The project was not funded by Congress.

Both the McMillan Plan and the Commission of Fine Arts scuttled the Burr-Casey design in a conscious effort at reorienting the bridge location to become a design element of the formal Mall scheme. Thus the bridge was to become a planning element rather than an exhibitionistic work of architecture. Building of the present McKim, Mead and White design started in 1926.

Commission of Fine Arts

Memorial Bridge alternate design 1 by William H. Burr and Edward Casey.

Commission of Fine Arts

Memorial Bridge alternate design 2 by William H. Burr and Edward Casey.

Commission of Fine Arts

Memorial Bridge alternate design 3 by William H. Burr and Edward Casey.

Commission of Fine Arts

Memorial Bridge competition design by William R. Hutton.

Commission of Fine Arts

Memorial Bridge competition design by George S. Morison, the design engineer of Taft Bridge.

LONG BRIDGE

Over the Potomac River from the foot of 14th Street

Unlike its elegant neighbor, Arlington Memorial Bridge, Long Bridge served during most of the Nineteenth Century as a crude utilitarian wooden structure. It is still a utilitarian structure with three highway bridges and a railroad bridge side by side. Soon there will be a Washington Metropolitan Area Transit Authority Bridge added to the complex.

The first wooden bridge was built here in 1809 as a privately chartered toll bridge. Built partly over mud flats with a draw span near each shore, the structure was frequently damaged by floods and ice flows.

Lieutenant Washington Hood prepared several masonry arched replacement designs for Long Bridge in 1832. These were followed in 1833 by an arched masonry bridge design by Lieutenant Colonel James Kearney and approved by President Andrew Jackson. A similar multi-arched structure was proposed by Lieutenant Edward B. White. Each of these designs was based on a large number of small masonry spans with draw or bascule sections.

The 1857 Potomac Bridge study by Alfred L. Rives included designs for Long Bridge as well as for bridges at the Three Sisters and Aqueduct sites. One of Rives' schemes had a multi-arched iron truss. The other was a more traditional masonry arched structure with small arches across the mud flats in the Potomac's center and larger arches over the two channels.

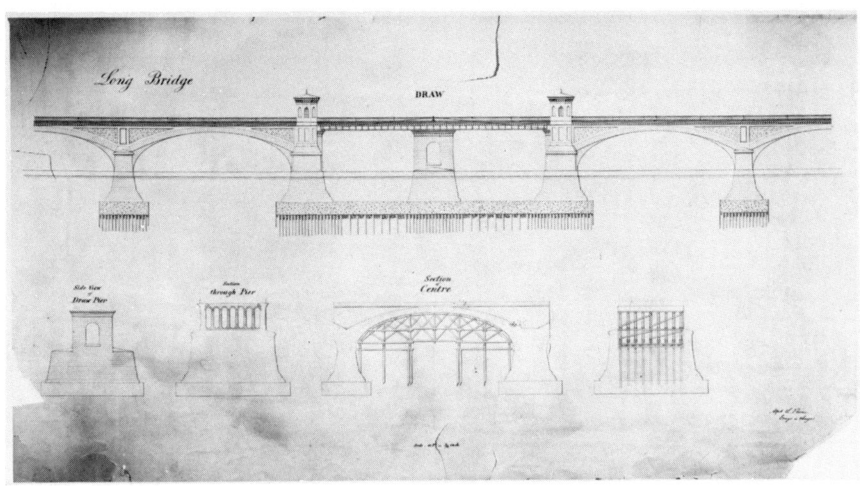

National Archives, Record Group 77

Long Bridge designed in 1857 by Alfred L. Rives as a masonry arched replacement for the wooden Long Bridge.

None of the masonry arched schemes was ever built at the Long Bridge crossing. The Civil-War-scarred wooden bridge was eventually replaced in 1903 by an iron truss structure. This basic scheme had been recommended by Colonel Hains in 1890, about the time he was recommending a suspension bridge for the Arlington Memorial Bridge site.

GREAT FALLS BRIDGE

Over the Potomac River at Great Falls

In 1930 the Congress in the Capper-Crampton Act proposed Potomac-side parkways. The George Washington Memorial Parkway was built, but an elaborate Great Falls Bridge connecting Maryland to Virgina never got beyond the design stage.

MASSACHUSETTS AVENUE BRIDGE

Over the Anacostia River in line with Massachusetts Avenue, S.E.

Massachusetts Avenue, one of the Capitol's primary cross-town axes, was one of the first avenues to extend the formal street pattern of L'Enfant's capital across Rock Creek to the far northwest. At the end of the Nineteenth Century, the concept of running this great avenue across both Rock Creek and the Anacostia River from District

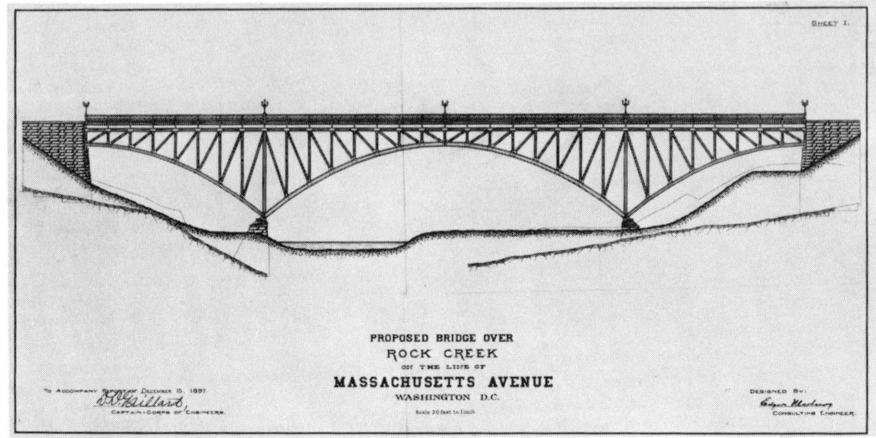

National Archives, Record Group 77

Massachusetts Avenue Bridge designed in 1897 by Edgar Marburg.

line to Distict line was considered. This scheme would have traversed the entire District of Columbia.

A study made by the District Army Engineer, Colonel Charles J. Allen, under an 1897 Congressional authorization recommended extending Massachusetts Avenue across the Anacostia River with a 2,517 foot, $450,000 steel truss bridge for general traffic and trolley use. This project never got beyond the design study, though a right-of-way is still maintained through the D.C. General Hospital grounds.

WASHINGTON PONTE VECCHIO

Over the Washington Channel from Maine Avenue to East Potomac Park

Just as Memorial Bridge and some of the Rock Creek Park bridges were conscious planning elements as well as crossings, a proposed "Ponte Vecchio" from southwest Washington would have linked various pedestrian activities in this giant urban renewal scheme. The project was proposed in 1966 as a shop and restaurant-lined link between East Potomac Park and the Southwest-Maine Avenue commercial strip across the Washington Channel. Since the proposal was not for highway or railroad use, as is usual for a bridge, it was put out to bids by the Department of Interior which hoped to attract private capital. Though no developer emerged to sponsor the project, several interesting designs evolved.

The first design for the Ponte Vecchio was by Washington architect

Chloethiel Woodard Smith. Done for the government in 1966, her design was for a simple linear bridge with a series of irregular straddeling boxes providing the space for commercial activities.

Later in 1968, Kevin Roche suggested a design for the Ponte Vecchio in conjunction with his design for the proposed soaring glass-topped National Aquarium. The Aquarium was to go in East Potomac Park at the end of the original bridge site. The Roche design was a single rectangular appendage to the side of a linear bridge.

The Department of Interior resurrected the Ponte Vecchio scheme in 1970 with a design by Wilber Smith and Associates. This was the simplest scheme of all but the Commission of Fine Arts suggested that a commercial intrusion in conjunction with the other bridges in the Fourteenth Street corridor and so close to the monumental core of the city would be undesirable. At that time the project was dropped.

National Archives, Record Group 77

Aqueduct Bridge designed in 1832 by Robert Mills as a wooden trough supported by stone piers.

CONCLUSION

The planning and growth of Washington cannot be detached from its bridge history. A brief flight of fancy leads to a vision of local bridges that might have been. Imagine a two level Key Bridge, a dramatic Three Sisters suspension bridge, a multi-arched classical Fourteenth Street Bridge and a romantic towered Pelz designed Memorial Bridge all existing at once. Washington would surely be a city of bridges.

Some of the bridges are unbuilt because of cost limitations, others because the designs were too flamboyant. The 1857 effort by Alfred L. Rives of the Army Engineers to study all the Potomac bridge needs at once was commendable. Although none of the bridges suggested by that broad study was constructed, the idea of a bridge master plan is applicable to the future.

BIBLIOGRAPHY

Cosby, Spencer, *Annual Report of the Chief of Engineers,* U. S. Government Printing Office, Washington, 1908.

Department of Highways, Office of Planning, Design and Engineering, District of Colmbia, *Washington Bridges,* Washington, 1956.

Duryee, Sacket, *A Historical Summary of the Work of the Corps of Engineers in Washington, D. C. and Vicinity, 1852–1952,* Corps of Engineers, Washington, 1952.

Emery, Fred A., "Washington's Historic Bridges," *Records of the Columbia Historical Society of Washington, D. C.,* 39 (1938), 49–70.

Historic American Buildings Survey, *Georgetown Architecture, The Waterfront, Selections from the Historic American Buildings Survey Number 4,* Commission of Fine Arts and National Park Service, U.S. Government Printing Office, Washington, 1968.

Horne, Robert C., "Bridges Across the Potomac," *Records of the Columbia Historical Society of Washington, D. C. 1953–1956* (1959), 249–264.

Jacobs, David and Neville, Anthony, *Bridges, Canals and Tunnels,* The Smithsonian Library, American Heritage Publishing Company, New York, 1968.

Jacobson, Hugh Newell, editor, *A Guide to the Architecture of Washington, D. C.,* Washington Metropolitan Chapter, American Institute of Architects, Frederick A. Praeger, New York, 1965.

Mills, Robert, *Water-Works for the Metropolitan City of Washington,* Lemuel Towers, Washington, 1853.

Myer, Donald Beekman, *Bridges and the City of Washington,* Commission of Fine Arts, U.S. Government Printing Office, Washington, 1974.

Myer, Donald Beekman, "Cabin John Bridge: A Washington Landmark," *Journal of Professional Activities,* American Society of Civil Engineers, New York, 1973.

Reiff, Daniel D., *Washington Architecture, 1791–1861, Problems in Development,* Commission of Fine Arts, U. S. Government Printing Office, Washington, 1971.

Spratt, Zack, "Rock Creek Bridges," *Records of the Colombia Historical Society of Washington, D. C. 1953–1956* (1959), 101–134.

Williams, Mathilde D., "The Three Sisters Bridge: A Ghost Span Over the Potomac," *Records of the Columbia Historical Society of Washington, D. C. 1969–1970* (1971), 489–509.

Design Proposals for the Washington National Monument

ROBERT BELMONT FREEMAN, JR.

The simple obelisk on the Capitol Mall gives little hint of the arduous process of design which preceded the construction of the Washington Monument. At the distance of nearly one hundred years since the completion of the monument, it is difficult to imagine that the obelisk design by Robert Mills was once hotly contested and opposed by several serious counterproposals. From the initial suggestion in the Eighteenth Century to build a monument to George Washington until the dedication of the monument in 1884, the debate over the character and appearance of the Washington Monument consumed the time and energy of countless artists, politicians, and concerned citizens. The process of designing the Washington Monument lingered over the major part of the Nineteenth Century, through several distinct phases of American taste and self image. This paper is a discussion of the various designs which were proposed for the Washington Monument. These design proposals fall into two categories: the projects submitted to the initial design competition announced by the Washington National Monument Society in 1836; and the projects formally and informally proposed during the 1876 drive to complete the monument. The various plans provide a valuable catalog of American architectural styles. They offer rare insights into the complex question of Nineteenth Century monumental symbolism. Most important, the design proposals for the Washington Monument chronicle changing tastes of Nineteenth Century America and illustrate the numerous contemporary approaches to the artistic interpretation of the national image.

The proposal to construct a national monument to George Washington has a long history. As early as August 7, 1783, the Continental Congress resolved unanimously "that an equestrian statue of General Washington be erected at the place where the residence of Congress shall be established, in honor of George Washington, the illustrious commander-in-chief of the armies of the United States of America during the war which vindicated and secured their liberty, sovereignty, and independence." [1] The designation of the Federal seat, however, was not accomplished for several years and the monument to Washington was submerged in larger questions. The death of General Washington revived the issue and on December 19, 1799, one day after Washington's entombment, Congress appointed a committee to determine a suitable memorial to the first president. On December 24, 1799, Congress passed a resolution, sponsored by Representative John Marshall, which directed "that a marble monument be erected by the United States in the Capitol, and that the family of General Washington be requested to permit his body to be deposited under it, and that the monument be so designed as to commemorate the great events of his military and political life." [2] President John Adams corresponded with Mrs. Washington; the widow endorsed the idea of a national monument and agreed to the removal of General Washington's remains to the city of Washington but no action was taken on the project. An act of May 18, 1800, in the House of Representatives, would have ordered the erection of "a mausoleum of American granite and marble, in a pyramidal form, 100 feet square at the base, and of proportional height" [3] but the appropriations bill failed to pass in the Senate. Thomas Jefferson during his administration sought to move the project. Jefferson himself suggested that "small temples would furnish good monumental designs." For General Washington he recommended "that commonly called the Lantern of Demosthenes." [4] The temple was not built and growing tensions between the United States and Britain and the subsequent outbreak of war during the Madison administration absorbed governmental attention.

The centennial of George Washington's birth revitalized interest in the Washington Monument project and in 1832 the Congress once again made an application to the proprietors of Mount Vernon for the removal of Washington's remains. This time the Virginia legislature protested and John A. Washington, grandnephew of the General, denied the petition. Thwarted in its attempt to build a public monument and tomb for Washington, Congress instead appropriated $5,000 for the execution of a statue by Horatio Greenough. (The

---

[1] Frederick L. Harvey, *History of the Washington National Monument and the Washington National Monument Society*. (Washington, 1902), p. 4.

[2] Harvey, p. 5.

[3] Harvey, p. 6.

[4] Thomas Jefferson, letter to Robert Mills, March 6, 1826. Cited in Gallagher, *Robert Mills, Architect of the Washington Monument*. (New York, 1935.) According to Stuart and Revett, *Antiquities of Athens* (London, 1762, Vol. I, Chap. IV), "The Lantern of Demosthenes" is an alternate name for the Choragic Monument to Lysicrates.

Greenough statue is today in the Smithsonian Institution's Museum of History and Technology.) In 1833, frustrated by the failure of the government to bring the monument project to fruition, citizens of Washington organized to build the Washington Monument themselves. In September of that year the Washington National Monument Society was founded under the leadership of George Watterston, former Librarian of Congress. Chief Justice John Marshall, friend and biographer of General Washington and an early proponent of the monument project, was elected president of the Society. The Society set up a mechanism to receive private contributions to its building fund. By 1836, $28,000 had been collected and the Monument Society felt sufficiently secure to advertise among American artists for designs for the monument. The design, they directed, should "harmoniously blend durability, simplicity, and grandeur." [5] Several designs considered by the Monument Society during these years are preserved in the Library of Congress and in the National Archives. The slow accumulation of money and the lack of a confirmed site precluded swift execution of any plan decided upon by the Society. Deliberations over the design of the monument were therefore extended and these design proposals represent a span of almost ten years.

The earliest dated and preserved design for the Washington Monument is one by Peter Force (1790–1868), a founding member of the Washington National Monument Society. (Figure 1.) Force was not an architect but a printer, publisher, collector of Americana, and historian, who served as mayor of Washington from 1836 to 1840. Force's design, dated 1837, consists of an immense pyramid. In the interior Force indicates a symmetrical set of chambers entered through portals in the platform base. A high central space of three tiered domes is lit by an occulus in the apex of the pyramid. A second pyramid—the tomb itself—occupies the center of the room. Force is very direct in his architectural symbolism. His design reflects popular agreement on the proprietry of the pyramid as a funerary monument. The Congressional proposal of 1800, as quoted above, specified a mausoleum of pyramidal form to be placed in the Capitol rotunda. Force adopts the idea of a pyramid, moves it from inside the Capitol, and enlarges it to gigantic size. Clearly the primary aesthetic quality of his design is its sheer mass. In his sense of scale and affinity for strong geometric shape, Force parallels on a vernacular level the work of the French visionaries Ledoux and Boullée; and certainly in the vast empty space of the central chamber Force tries to fulfill contemporary criteria for "the sublime."

[5] Harvey, p. 18.

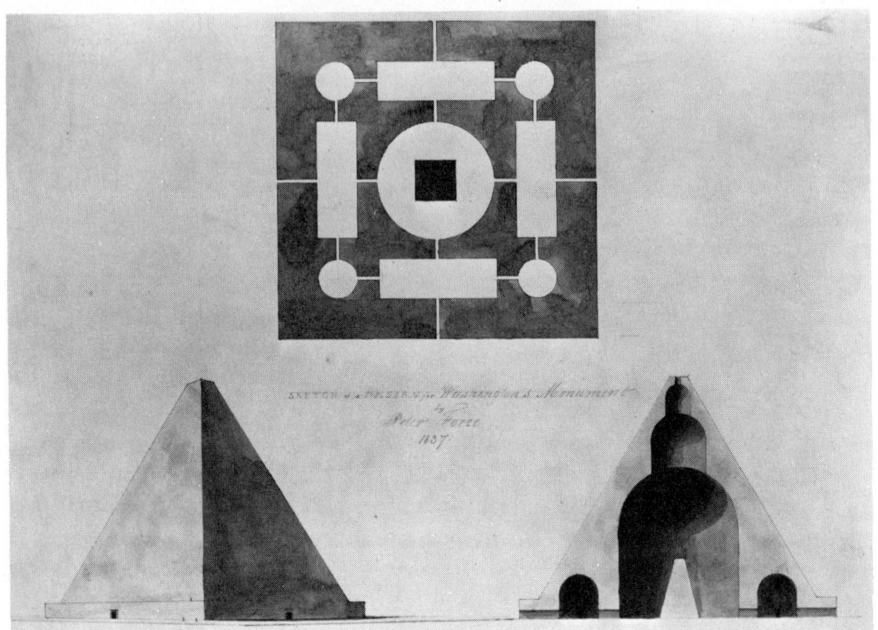

Library of Congress

Figure 1. Peter Force. Design for the Washington Monument. 1837.

Immediately upon the announcement of the competition for the design of the Washington Monument, Thomas M. McClelland of Philadelphia began correspondence with the Monument Society. In January 1836 McClelland wrote to James Madison, then President of the Monument Society, declaring his intention to furnish the Society with a design. In this letter he announced his theme: "Washington in his last farewell address advises us to consider the Union as the Palladium of our Liberty. This is my text and my idea is to raise a Monument emblematic of the Union of these States." [6] The monument would consist of a colossal equestrian statue on a triumphal arch of Gothic order. By March of 1837 McClelland had submitted a perspective of his scheme, which he entitled: "The Palladium, or Washington's Farewell Address, reduced to an architectural structure representing the Union. Embellished with the statues of all the signers of the Declaration of Independence and the Framers of the Constitution of the United States." [7] This first drawing is unfortunately not pre-

[6] Thomas M. McClelland, letter to James Madison, January 23, 1836 (National Archives).

[7] McClelland, letter to George Watterston, March 25, 1837 (National Archives).

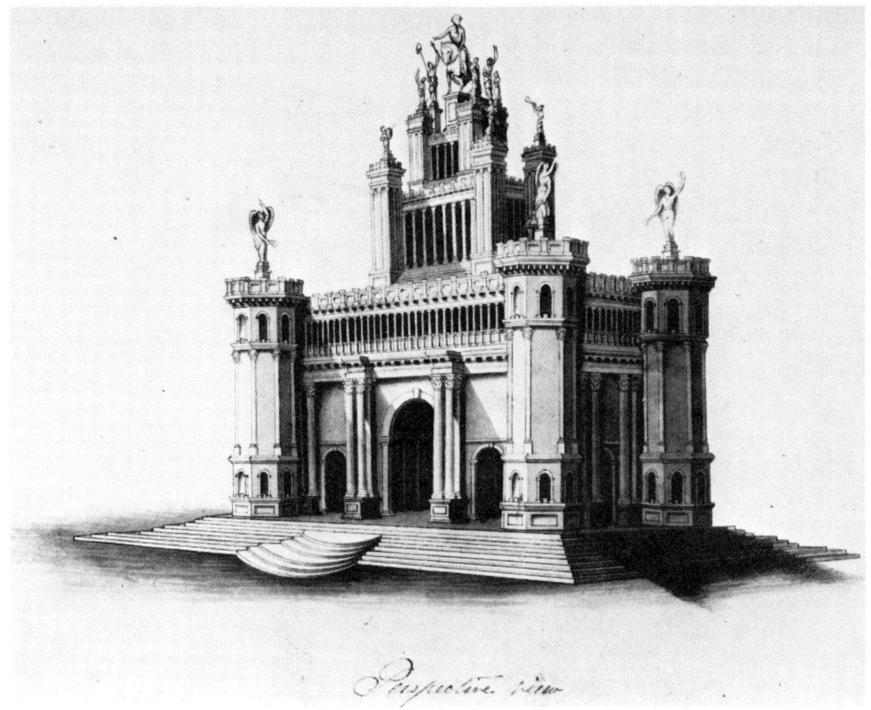

National Archives

Figure 2. Thomas McClelland. "The Palladium." Design for the Washington Monument. About 1837–1840.

served and we cannot see McClelland's monument until after he substitutes the "less expensive" [8] composite order for the Gothic.

The McClelland design as it survives is nonetheless an exuberant composition. (Figure 2.) Many pages of correspondence are filled with the architect's explanation of his sources ("ten of the most if not the most magnificent edifices ever raised by mortal hands" [9]) and the significance of every minute detail of the scheme. Formally and symbolically, the "Palladium" contains distinct strata: "The superstructure supported by the triumphal arch consists of a series of temples representing the Union at different periods. The lower one is intended to be emblematic of our country at the present and which I term the Modern Temple. The upper one is the primitive temple and

[8] McClelland, letter to Washington National Monument Society, October 14, 1837 (National Archives).

[9] McClelland, letter to Washington National Monument Society, March 28 (probably 1837) (National Archives).

is intended to be emblematic of the old thirteen states making an appropriate base for the main group of statues." [10] "The superstructure," he later added, "you may consider as Olimpus or Heaven if you think proper to give flight to your imagination." [11] The iconography of the monument and its decoration is rigorously nationalistic and encyclopaedic in scope. Throughout his letters McClelland stresses the role of his architecture as the material representation of the national spirit as inspired by the words of George Washington, or in the architect's terms: "the giving of a tangible form to an original and complex idea." [12] McClelland's approach to design is that of a linguist. Each architectural element he invests with explicit symbolic meaning and these parts he composes into a complex essay. Unfortunately for McClelland, his labor brought him no return. The Monument Society refused to settle on any design though McClelland wrote frequently urging a decision in his favor. Finally, in June of 1840 McClelland reported that the time and money expended on his patriotic project had ruined him and left him in debtor's prison.[13]

Another competition entry from this period is a design for a large column, signed by E. Barabino. (Figure 3.) Barabino gives his address as 35 High Street, Baltimore, which may explain the similarity of his scheme to the Washington Monument in Baltimore, designed by Robert Mills and dedicated in 1829. The Barabino column is much like the early, more decorated versions of the Mills design as they were published but Barabino's awkward assembly of parts and novel adornments show the hand of an amateur. Barabino includes on his page of drawings a domed temple, an equestrian statue, a fountain, and a funerary urn, but his preferred design he describes as "a column supported by the statues which are represented." [14] "The front portico," he explains, "represents America after the labours and the toils of War—sitting down in *peace* with the Olive Branch in her hand . . . the top part represents Washington on an Arch of Triumph with his name supported by two *fames*—this is an Original Idea as no Romans ever thought of placing their Arches of Triumph on monuments." The artist suggests that the monument be 150 feet high, "or any height the board should think proper" and he adds that "no person could understand the building of it other than myself."

[10] *Ibid.*

[11] McClelland, letter to Washington National Monument Society, Philadelphia, April 13, 1840 (National Archives).

[12] *Ibid.*

[13] McClelland, letter to Washington National Monument Society, Philadelphia, June 9, 1840 (National Archives).

[14] E. Barabino, notations made directly on drawing (National Archives).

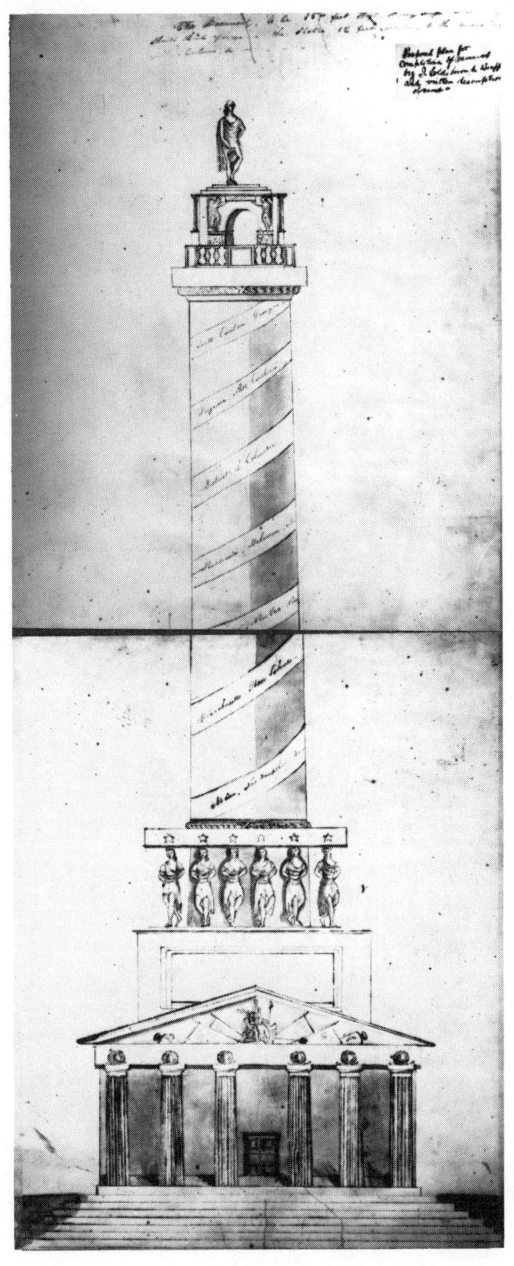

National Archives

Figure 3. E. Barabino. Design for the Washington Monument. About 1840.

Library of Congress

Figure 4. Calvin Pollard. Design for the Washington Monument. 1844.

In 1844 Calvin Pollard of New York submitted a Gothic design for the Washington Monument. (Figure 4.) In New York at this time Gothic churches were being built by Minard Lefever, James Renwick, Richard Upjohn and others. Construction of the most famous American Gothic church, Upjohn's Trinity Church, was begun in this year. There was among New York architects a distinct atmosphere of Gothicism, reinforced by an awareness of artistic developments in England. Pollard's monument reflects the spirit of progressive New York architecture but at the same time his design recalls features of the earliest phases of the Gothic Revival. The stiff symmetrical plan and massing of the tower belong to a classical attitude which the applied Gothic ornament barely masks. In designing a national monument, Pollard was straying from practiced areas of Gothic architecture in America. In 1844 he had few if any local examples of Gothic monument design. British architects were producing Gothic monuments and quite likely Pollard was familiar with G. M. Kemp's 1836 design for the Sir Walter Scott Memorial in Edinburgh, built between 1840 and 1846. The crucial difference between Pollard's monument and a project such as Kemp's—and the source of confusion in Pollard's scheme—is in the symbolism of the Gothic style. Gothic design in the United States had none of the nationalistic overtones which in England made it appropriate for public buildings and monuments. The Gothic in America was considered suitable for such structures as churches, homes, and academic institutions. The only way that Pollard can identify his tower as a monument to George Washington is with an American eagle and a statue of a woman bearing a portrait of Washington.

One important monument design was sponsored by a committee of Congress. During the early years of the Washington National Monument Society, not everyone was convinced that the private organization would be able to bring the project to construction. There were efforts in Congress to authorize Federal financing for the enterprise. On April 12, 1844, Representative Pratt of New York reported for the Committee on Public Buildings and Grounds that "the construction of a 'national monument' has presented itself to their consideration, and they regard it as of deep interest to the American people." [15] In this report and in an expanded version submitted on May 25 of the same year,[16] the committee recommended the erection of a monument

[15] 28th Congress, House Committee on Public Buildings and Grounds, Report No. 434, to accompany Joint Resolution No. 23, April 12, 1844.

[16] 28th Congress, House Committee on Public Buildings and Grounds, Report No. 514, to accompany Joint Resolution No. 33, May 25, 1844.

"to commemorate and illustrate the exploits and virtues of distinguished men" and to honor the memory of the first president. The monument would be set in a landscaped "Monument Square," located due west of the Capitol on the 8th Street cross-axis, and the project would be financed by the sale of lots from the public reservation. The proposal was somewhat broader than for a memorial dedicated exclusively to George Washington, but it was clear that Representative Pratt had the project of the Washington National Monument Society in mind when he drafted his bill. "The construction of this temple," the report states, "will at once carry out the views of a society which has been established in this city for the purpose of erecting a monument to the memory of Washington, and which, it is understood, will apply the funds in its possession toward this desirable object, whenever Congress shall authorize its erection on some prominent portion of the public grounds, from whence the whole city may be overlooked." Of the character of the monument, the Public Buildings and Grounds Committee had a clear vision: "The committee have given their best consideration to the most useful kind of monument architecture, and have come to the conclusion that the *temple form* is the best; and to be built upon such a scale as to be capable of containing the busts and statues of the Presidents of the United States, and other illustrious men of our country, as well as paintings of all the historical subjects which have or may be designed by our artists through ages yet to come." Appended to the report is a lithograph of a suggested monument "designed by the Hon. Zadoc Pratt of N.Y." and naming W. Strickland as Architect. (Figure 5.) One can only speculate as to the relative contributions of Pratt and Strickland to the design but it seems unlikely that an architect of Strickland's stature would have been retained merely to render the congressman's scheme. Further research can perhaps clarify the question of authorship and isolate possible sources of the design. The round temple form was popular with architects of the day and had appealed to Jefferson when he proposed his "Lantern of Demosthenes." William Strickland is known to have been interested from early in his career in the design of a memorial to George Washington. In 1813 he exhibited at the Pennsylvania Academy of Fine Arts a "Design of a Grand National Monument, Commemorative of the Illustrious Washington." [17] From the written description in the catalogue, we can see that the project differs from the 1844 design but that the basic parti is the same: a basement

---

[17] "Catalogue of the 3rd Annual Exhibition of the Columbian Society of Artists and the Pennsylvania Academy." (Philadelphia, May, 1813), p. 19, No. 96. Cited in Gilchrist, *Willliam Strickland, Architect and Engineer.* (New York, 1969), pp. 46–47.

Library of Congress

Figure 5. Zadoc Pratt and William Strickland. Design for a National Monument. 1844.

built around a statue of Washington, a colonnaded rotunda, and a dome crowned by the American eagle. Passage of the bill to construct this temple would have brought the Washington Monument endeavor to a swift climax and, with the landscaping of Monument Square and the development of adjacent lots, would have had a profound influence on the appearance of the capital city. The bill, however, was read twice and tabled, and the Pratt-Strickland monument scheme was buried in the records of Congress.

The design selected by the Monument Society was one by Robert Mills. The date of Mills' design is uncertain. It evidently had not been declared the official design before 1844, but in 1846 it was published as such. The monument consists of an obelisk on a circular colonnaded base. (Figure 6.) From the architect's description[18] we can appreciate the complexity of the original scheme. Entrance to the monument is through a tetrastyle portico of massive Doric order, crowned by "the triumphal car and statue of the glorious chief." Ascending through the portico, one reaches a vast interior gallery, housing statues of Revolutionary heroes. Opposite the entrance is the statue of Washington, "designated as principal in the group by its colossal proportions." Inside and out, the temple base is decorated with carvings, trophies, wreathes, and garlands. By means of "a graded railway" through the central pier under the obelisk, one ascends to the grand terrace. From the center of this terrace rises the obelisk, the lower portion of which is decorated with pictorial bas-relief. Above this the shaft rises unadorned but for a star near the apex, "emblematic of the glory which the name WASHINGTON has attained." The salient feature of the whole scheme is its enormous scale. Mills incessantly emphasizes the dimensions. The pantheon base was to be 250 feet in diameter and 100 feet high, and the columns would exceed those of St. Peter's in size. The obelisk on its base would reach 600 feet, making the Washington Monument the tallest man-made structure in the world.

Mills' design for the Washington Monument is, apart from its scale, typical of the eclectic "assemblist" architecture of the later years of neoclassicism. In the monument Mills uses Greek, Roman, and Egyptian elements in curious juxtaposition. He takes two discrete architectural units—the obelisk and the pantheon—and clips them together. Mills displays greater interest in the symbolic attributes of the obelisk and the pantheon than in their formal or historical harmony. His design for the Washington Monument suggests an es-

[18] Robert Mills, description of the Washington National Monument, Washington National Monument Society, "The Board of Managers of the Washington National Monument Society to the American People." (Washington, 1846.)

National Archives

Figure 6. Robert Mills. Design for the Washington Monument. About 1845.

sentially "linguistic" attitude toward architecture, characteristic of the late neoclassicists (and precisely the attitude of Thomas McClelland in his "Palladium" project). For Mills, different architectural elements are invested with symbolic values and can be assembled to produce a desired effect.

The obelisk is evocative of eternal memorial. By 1840 the Egyptian mode was accepted as the appropriate style for monuments to the dead. Mills hoped that General Washington's remains would be transferred to the monument and he reserved a crypt for his tomb. Thus the obelisk assumes funerary significance directly comparable to the Egyptian grave monuments so common in Nineteenth Century American cemeteries. The pantheon is more complex in its symbolism. By the 1830's the pantheon was recognized as the appropriate form for a national shrine. The pantheon formula—rotunda and portico—was used in Europe for secular temples celebrating national culture and history. The Pantheon of antiquity was the symbolic center of the Roman Empire and, as the burial place of Emperors and heroes, held secular significance in addition to its generalized religious function. The most famous pantheon of the modern world was that in Paris, built between 1757 and 1790. Napoleon designated the building the shrine to honor French heroes. Mills was undoubtedly conscious of the significance of this architectural form. He explicitly stated that the base of the monument "properly may be designated the 'National Pantheon'." [19] The gallery was to contain statues of patriots and panoramic scenes of American history. Mills even suggested that the catacombs beneath the monument be used for the interment of prominent Americans. In total, the Washington Monument could deliver a very particular message. The pantheon base would mark the monument as a shrine to national history and its heroes, while the obelisk would stand as an eternal memorial to Washington whose remains would be preserved in the foundations of the shaft. An informed observer could read this message quite plainly, while others would simply be moved to reverence by the majestic scale of the monument.

The sources of the Mills design for the Washington Monument can be traced easily enough but a more interesting investigation may be into the basis for the acceptance of the design by the Monument Society and for its public acclaim. By 1840 classicism was declining as the universal mode and was approaching eclipse by the revival styles of mid-century. As evidenced by the design of the Washington Monument itself, classical architecture was becoming more eclectic than aca-

[19] Robert Mills, description of the Washington National Monument.

demic and was being used as a tool for the "associational" symbolism that would dominate the Victorian age. During the 1840's classicism was seeking out a new position in the heterogeneity of the American arts. One role in which classical design was to remain secure throughout the Nineteenth and Twentieth Centuries was in the particular classicism of Washington, both city and man. Classical imagery was used in describing and decorating the Federal city from its beginning, and Washington public buildings were exclusively classical until the construction of Renwick's Smithsonian building in 1847. Contemporary critics read into the buildings the democracy of Greece and the imperial grandeur of Rome. Mills himself, as Architect of Government Buildings, contributed more than anyone else to the classical character of the capital. As with the city, so the person of Washington was "classicized" during the first half of the Nineteenth Century. Almost immediately upon his death, Washington was deified in the manner of a Roman emperor. Eulogies to the late president were filled with allusions to ancient personalities and the images which appeared in such abundance, though complex in their iconography, frequently cast Washington in a classical light. It was a safe assumption that the design accepted by the Washington National Monument Society would be classical. Mills, a well-known architect of standard neoclassical background, provided such a design. The broadly accepted propriety of the classical style for a national monument to George Washington helps to explain public acceptance of the Mills design and the ability of his obelisk to survive to completion almost forty years after its conception.

Changing attitudes toward Robert Mills' design reflect the tides of Nineteenth Century American taste. Mills conceived his monument with the mind of a Romantic Classical craftsman. Proponents translated it into mid-century romanticism. The Washington National Monument was to be an eternal memorial to Washington the man and a perpetual monument to national greatness. Just as the pyramids of Egypt and the temples of Greece, so the Washington Monument in centuries to come should stand as testimony to American civilization. In a revealing publication of 1871, issued with an engraving of the Mills design (Figure 7) to muster public support, the Washington National Monument Society expressed its romanticized view of the monument.[20] The authors of the pamphlet compare the monument to the tomb of Cyrus and suggest that as Alexander was moved to awe

[20] Washington National Monument Society, *The Washington National Monument.* (Washington, 1871.)

From "The Washington National Monument"
Washington National Monument Society, 1871

Figure 7. Robert Mills. Design for the Washington Monument. Engraving. 1871.

and respect by the tomb, during his conquest of Persia, so would any future invaders of America be forced to pause and reflect upon the greatness of Washington and his nation. "Future conquerors of the world will, in the lapse of ages, stand in uncovered reverence before the object . . . which commemorates the virtues and achievements of Washington." The "sublime objects" which are national monuments will "in the era of decay and disintegration which ultimately comes to all human organizations" exert a civilizing influence over the troubled people "touching the hearts of tyrants and teaching them tenderness in the name of a common humanity." Throughout the pamphlet runs a strong current of the "cult of ruins," a perverse delight in the anticipation of the destruction of the city and the struggle between civilization and savagery. The image is analogous to the view of an Egyptian obelisk rising from the desert sands or the ruins of Roman palaces on the Adriatic shore, all illustrated so plentifully in contemporary books of antiquities. The crucial factor is that the image is classical. The complex symbolism which had been built up around monuments and memorials was uniquely interpretable in the classical idiom. On this point the Monument Society was quite explicit:

> So long as the arts, the urns, and the utterances of antiquity exert a charm over civilized men, they will protect a fallen people against the violence of such an enemy; and so long as objects, majestic and mysterious, retain their marvelous power over the superstitions of untutored minds, their presence will lend an effective aid in the protection of the defenseless community against the cruelty of the savage.

On July 4, 1848, the cornerstone of the Washington Monument was set with a lengthy and elaborate ceremony. In January of that year Congress had authorized the transfer of the site at the end of the Mall to the Monument Society. As the construction date neared, dispute over the Mills design and its economic practicality broke out. In a compromise effort, the Society decided to postpone a decision on the height of the obelisk and to defer construction of the pantheon until future funding was more certain.

By 1854 the monument shaft had risen to 170 feet. The $250,000 which the monument had cost to this date had totally depleted the Society's treasury. Mills' estimate for the construction of the monument had been $1,250,000 and the Monument Society saw little hope of raising all of the necessary money without public assistance. The Society petitioned Congress for a grant of $200,000 but the appropriation was killed when the Society became involved in a feud with the "Know-Nothing" Party. Work on the monument halted. Periodically through 1859 the Monument Society attempted renewed construction drives but the public response was feeble. The outbreak of the Civil War postponed any progress on the project.

In 1870 the Washington Monument had stood unfinished for sixteen years. As the Monument Society sought Congressional and citizen support, the unfinished monument became a national disgrace. Many writers reported on the sorry state of the monument, scolding the American people for not bringing the project to completion, deriding the Monument Society for pushing such an impractical scheme, or simply poking fun at the whole situation. Mark Twain on an 1867 trip to Washington wrote: "It has the aspect of a factory chimney with the top broken off . . . cow sheds around its base . . . contented sheep nibbling pebbles in the desert solitudes . . . tired pigs dozing in the holy calm of its protecting shadow." The New York Tribune wrote in a July 1, 1875 editorial:

> The appeal for a 4th of July contribution to the Washington Monument will not amount to much. Public judgement on that abortion has been made up. The country has failed in many ways to honor the memory of its first president, but the neglect to finish this monument is not to be reckoned among them. A wretched design, a wretched location, and an insecure foundation match well with its empty treasury. If the public will let the big furnace chimney on the Potomac flat alone and give its energy instead to cleaning out morally and physically the city, likewise named after the Father of his Country, it will better honor his memory.

On the eve of the National Centennial, Congress acted on the Washington Monument project. In August 1876, a joint resolution declared that Congress "in the name of the people of the United States, at the beginning of the Second Century of the National Existence, do assume and direct the completion of the Washington Monument in the city of Washington." [21] The Monument Society ceded its property back to the government and became a semi-official advisory board to a Joint Congressional Commission appointed to manage the completion of the monument.

Robert Mills was in poor health and became despondent after the suspension of the monument project and in 1855 he died. His design was criticized as impractical and hopelessly out of style. Few expected the monument to be finished according to the original plan. The pantheon was tacitly dropped from the plan by the 1870's. It was frequently suggested that the incomplete obelisk be torn down and a new monument started. *The American Architect and Building News* re-

[21] Act of August 2, 1876; 19 Statutes, p. 123. Griffith, p. 98.

ported in 1876 that the Senate Committee on Public Buildings and Grounds "favor the demolition of the unfinished Washington Monument at Washington. They believe that if ever completed it would have but small claim to architectural beauty, but that a memorial arch decorated with statues and carvings representing the growth of the United States would be a more decorative feature in the national capital." [22] While a majority of Americans probably favored the construction of some Washington Monument, there was little popular interest in its particular design. Many professional architects opposed the Mills design. *The American Architect and Building News* wrote in 1876: "It is certain that the general voice of the architectural profession and of cultivated persons throughout the land who have considered the design condemns it unequivocally." [23]

The American Architect and Building News, which began publication in Boston in 1876, was itself instrumental in organizing opposition to the Mills design. Every month between 1876 and 1878 the magazine carried editorials or reports concerning progress of the monument project. In May 1876, the magazine made its editorial position clear:

> It is not to the credit of the country, that its monument to Washington should remain unfinished, and the centennial year is a very fitting time to set our hands to building a monument to him; but we think that the completion of *the* Washington Monument according to the published design would be nothing less than a misfortune. The design is insignificant in idea, characterless, and inharmonious. The obelisk, and the circular colonnade that is to surround it, are altogether incongruous. The grandeur of the obelisk and the elegance of the colonnade would both be thrown away, and each would shame the other. We earnestly hope that no more will be done on the monument till the design has been carefully reconsidered.[24]

The opposition of the architectural press and profession to the original design for the monument emphasizes the shift in taste which had occurred since 1845. The Monument Society, as demonstrated in its publication of 1871, attempted to keep the Mills design alive by reinterpreting it in the language of extreme romanticism but, to most contemporary aestheticians, the austere classical design was dull and uninspiring. The obelisk itself was thought not a bad model but one lacking the necessary detail and archaeological exactness in its proportions to command the proper symbolism. Sheer force of scale was not,

[22] *American Architect and Building News,* March 11, 1876.

[23] *Ibid.,* April 14, 1877.

[24] *Ibid.,* May 13, 1876.

in 1876, a satisfactory aesthetic quality. The analytic symbolism of late neoclassicism was not relevant to the Victorians with their more complex, emotionally-oriented vocabulary of architectural symbols. What was desired of the monument was a design pleasing to the eye and fluent in historical allusion, a design which would reflect the current level of the American arts. *The American Architect and Building News* frequently urged the redesign of the Washington Monument and in July 1877 formally suggested a new architectural competition. The Washington Monument, the editors wrote, would be a project "so conspicuous and so deliberate that it will be accepted by the world as a type of our best progress." Rather than let "this monstrous obelisk, so cheap to design but so costly to execute, so poor in thought but so ostentatious in size" represent the architecture of America, the design should be reopened to competition which would "call forth the best art which the country can produce." [25] A new formal competition did not materialize but in the next several years a number of new designs were brought before the Monument Society and the Monument Commission. *The American Architect and Building News* published some of these designs along with proposals sent directly to the magazine.

Immediately after the Federal Government took over the monument project, the Army Corps of Engineers undertook an examination of the existing portion of the obelisk. They reported that the foundations were in poor condition and inadequate for the completion of the obelisk as originally designed. This finding incited debate as to whether the monument should be reinforced and completed according to the original design, or completed according to a revised plan, or demolished and redesigned entirely. One group of design proposals offered schemes to complete the monument without adding substantially to its mass, and thereby without requiring new foundations. General Montgomery Meigs of the Army Engineers proposed a plan to complete the monument with a simple Italianate observation gallery. (Figure 8.) "The general effect," wrote Meigs, "would be somewhat like the great tower in the public square of the republic of Venice." [26] Meigs suggested that the builders "terminate the structure by a metallic spire about 140 feet in height" which would raise its total height to about 400 feet with minimal added weight or expense. Col. Lewis Cruger of Charleston, South Carolina, suggested that it might not be too late to convert the project to the Gothic style. He sent to the Monument Society a clipping from an 1844 New York

[25] *Ibid.*, July 21, 1877.

[26] Gen. Montgomery Meigs, letter to John R. Blake, June 11, 1877 (National Archives).

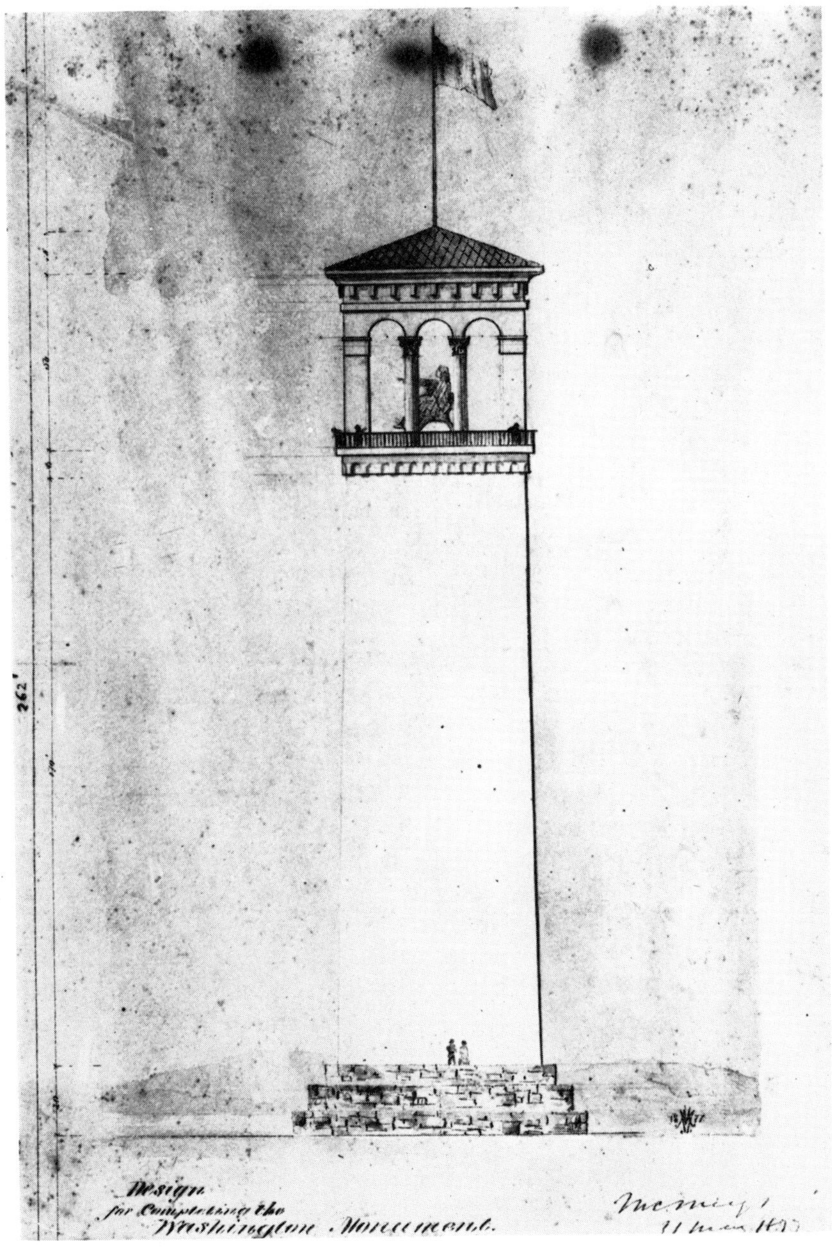

National Archives

Figure 8. Montgomery Meigs. Design for Completing the Washington Monument. 1877.

newspaper illustrating Calvin Pollard's design of that year. "The ornamental parts," wrote Cruger, "can easily be built around the present shaft of the Washington Monument at Washington." [27]

A proposal which received considerable attention in 1877 was that of the sculptor Larkin G. Mead, who wanted to turn the monument stump into the base for an eighty-five-foot statue of George Washington. Similar in conception was a design presented by Paul Schulze of Washington. (Figure 9.) Schulze's design frankly admits the existence of the stump and simply terminates it with a cornice, observation gallery, belvedere, and large statue. The base of the monument he develops with terraces and steps and at the lower corners places allegorical bronze figures. The rustication of the lower masonry, the moldings and details, the statues, and the belvedere are taken from late Renaissance models. The architect Henry Van Brunt reviewed a group of design proposals for the Washington Monument in an 1880 article.[28] Of the Schulze design he wrote: "The whole composition was simple to bareness. . . . It was a workmanlike academical study without high aspiration, but also without straining for originality. It had repose, dignity, and strength."

A design related to that of Shulze, but far more decorative and adventurous, was published in the November 8, 1879 issue of *The American Architect and Building News.* (Figure 10.) The anonymous Californian who submitted it buries the stub of the obelisk in a massive pyramidal base. On top of this he continues the shaft through two stories of observation galleries and tops the structure with a huge "French Style" roof, a tall lantern, and a statue of "America." On the front of the monument is a huge pedimented niche with a statue of Washington. Van Brunt commented that the project "is correctly set forth in the style of the modern French Renaissance, and might have been submitted in the latest architectural concourse of the Ecole des Beaux-Arts." The stepped-back base and chamfer of the lower stories suggest the influence of Mayan pyramids or Hindu temples, but on the whole the design is an exuberant version of the popular "French Style."

The majority of the designs for the completion of the monument were towers. In October 1877, the project engineers, under the direction of Col. Thomas Lincoln Casey, decided that with reinforcement of the foundations the monument could be built to its full intended

[27] Col. Lewis Cruger, note to Washington National Monument Society, undated (National Archives).

[28] Henry Van Brunt, "The Washington Monument," *The American Art Review,* Vol. I, Nos. 1 and 2, 1880; reprinted in *American Art and Collections* (Boston, 1889).

From "American Art and Collections," 1889

Figure 9. Paul Schulze. Study for the Completion of the Washington Monument. 1878.

height. This finding led the Monument Society to reaffirm its faith in the obelisk, but it also prompted several architects to propose alternate tower designs. A study by John Frazer completes the obelisk as a Twelfth Century Italian campanile. (Figure 11.) Frazer handles the style with archaeological correctness and the horizontal banding of contrasting masonry gives the project a Ruskinian flavor. Entrance to

From "The American Architect and Building News," 1879

Figure 10. Design for the Washington Monument. Published in *The American Architect and Building News,* November 8, 1879.

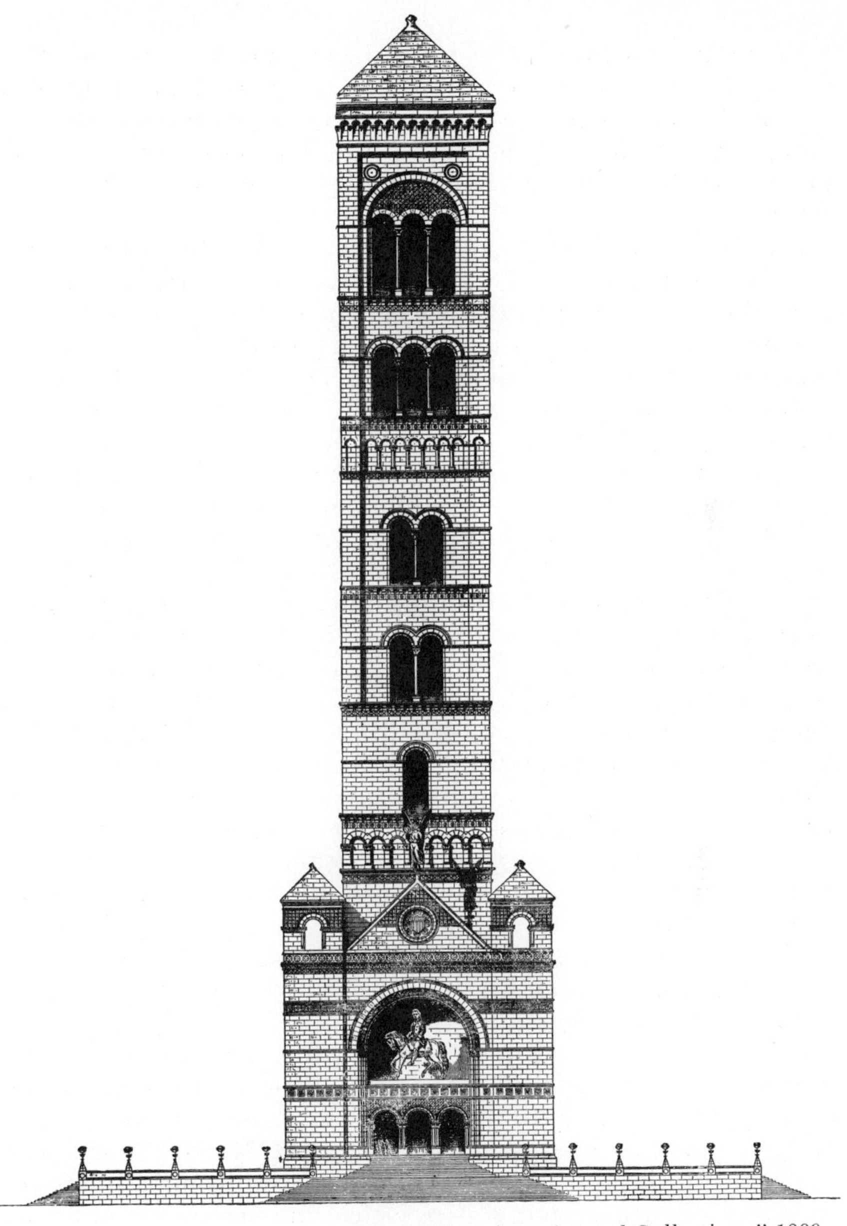

From "American Art and Collections," 1889

Figure 11. John Frazer. Design for the Washington Monument. About 1876–1879.

the monument is through a large arched portal, the top of which contains an equestrian statue of Washington which Van Brunt likened to that of Louis XI at Blois. Van Brunt complains of monotony in this design. As Architect of the Treasury, John Frazer was an ex-officio member of the Joint Commission on the Completion of the Washington Monument.

A design by M. P. Hapgood, published in the March 15, 1879 issue of *The American Architect and Building News,* was in the Gothic style. (Figure 12.) Hapgood was an architectural student from Boston and his project is more an academic study than a serious proposal. His monument design is carefully worked High Victorian Gothic. The tower makes an interesting comparison with the 1844 monument by Calvin Pollard. Pollard's is a free, exuberant interpretation of early Gothic ornament, typical of the first decades of the American Gothic Revival. Hapgood's design is an elegant, studied application of Fifteenth Century Gothic which reflects the High Victorian interest in later styles.

H. R. Searle presented a radically different tower form for the monument. (Figure 13.) Searle's design, which he published and distributed at his own expense in 1877, is basically an obelisk on a stepped base. The obelisk, however, is a distant departure from both the Mills design and the ancient paradigm. Searle was unsatisfied with simple geometry, and ornamented his obelisk, in Van Brunt's terminology, with "audacious but illiterate innovations." The horizontal moldings, fluting, massive Egyptian capital, and pyramidon at top make this a highly original, if not bizarre, composition. The base of the monument appears to be an early example of the influence of Mayan architecture. Searle's monument points out the distant models to which the Victorians looked for their more exotic designs.

The Egyptian obelisk was not ignored as a model for the redesign of the Washington Monument. Early in the centennial discussion on the fate of the project, J. Goldsborough Bruff of Washington addressed a lengthy essay to the Monument Society, explaining the faults of the Mills design and illustrating how an obelisk might be built according to the superior archaeology of 1876. "The very worthy author of the original plan," he writes, "was, as most accomplished architects of the age were, very proficient in the Grecian and Roman, but acquired no other knowledge of other orders than the general terms found in their text books; and of the Egyptian they scarcely knew anything." [29] Bruff would purify the Egyptian architecture of

[29] J. Goldsborough Bruff, "To the Board of Managers of the Construction of the National Washington Monument", 1876 (National Archives).

From "American Art and Collections," 1889

Figure 12. M. P. Hapgood. Design for the Washington Monument. 1879.

Library of Congress

Figure 13. H. R. Searle. Design for the Washington Monument. 1877.

the monument, which required the elimination of the "Grecian pantheon" and the substitution of a simple plinth to accommodate offices, library, and sculpture gallery. Bruff objected to Mills' obelisk "of the spurious Grecian order" with "the depressed pyramidion and proportions of the stela." Bruff redesigned the obelisk and fixed it at 501 feet —one foot taller than the spire on the cathedral at Cologne, then under construction. Taken by itself, the obelisk in Bruff's rendering (Figure 14) resembles closely the monument as it was finally built; but as was Mills, Bruff was unwilling to let the obelisk stand alone. To carry through the Egyptian motif and "perfect the tout-ensemble of our monument," Bruff flanked the entrances with colossal bronze sphinxes. Of his sphinx Bruff wrote: "Rendering it in the true Egyptian style, I have nationalized it by the head and breast of our national bird. Such a figure is symbolical of keen far-sightedness, noble aspiration, energy, strength, courage, and immortality."

The design which gained the most attention and support was that by the sculptor William Wetmore Story. (Figure 15.) Story first presented a design to the Senate Committee on Public Buildings and Grounds in December of 1877. The final version of the Story design, as it was published in *The American Architect and Building News* of February 1, 1879, is an elegant Italian campanile with a pyramidal roof and square porticoed base. In a letter to William W. Corcoran, Story described his study:

> The monument, as it stands, I took as the core of my structure, encasing it with the colored marbles, in which America is so rich, and changing its character into a tower with a portico at its base. In front of this porch, or rather enniched beneath it, I placed a colossal statue of Washington within reach of the eye, so that it could be seen in all its details as the commanding feature of the front. On the opposite side I propose a statue of Liberty,—achieved by Washington for our country,—and on the two sides, two great bronze doors figured over with the principal events of the Revolution, and the portraits of distinguished men of the period, the coadjutors of Washington. Fame on the top of the tower in gilt bronze,—the spiritual essence of his life,—he himself at the base, the corporeal presence.[30]

Story was from a prominent Boston family and since 1859 had lived in an expatriate American artists colony in Rome. His sculpture is exclusively of classical and Biblical subjects and is highly romantic in character. Story's design for the monument is a reflection of his classical and Renaissance interests. It was clear in Story's mind that only an architecture in the Roman tradition could adequately reflect the grandeur of the American culture. The architectural press criticized the Story design; Van Brunt noted that the scheme "depended for its character entirely upon the disposition of forty-four blank

[30] William W. Story, letter to W. W. Corcoran. *American Architect and Building News,* January 11, 1879.

windows." Public reception of the proposal was enthusiastic, however, and members of the Monument Society and the Joint Commission were obviously impressed by the design. In December 1878, the Monument Society resolved to endorse the Story proposal, praising it as "vastly superior in artistic taste and beauty of design to any other modification of the original plan that has been suggested." The Lombard tower, they believed, would "harmonize conflicting opinions and give general satisfaction to the country." [31]

By 1880, 7,037 cubic yards of concrete had been added to the old rubble foundation of the monument and Col. Casey urged rapid completion of the obelisk. The Monument Commission was becoming disenchanted with the Story proposal as the high price of its erection became apparent. Finally in 1880 the Monument Society withdrew support for the alternate scheme and recommitted itself to the completion of the obelisk. The leadership of the Society felt an obligation to finish the monument—or at least the obelisk—according to announced plans. In December 1877 the Society had said that it would be in bad faith to change the design after private donations had built the obelisk to 174 feet.[32] In 1880 the Society returned to this stand and expressed the further conviction that any change in plan "would be likely to postpone the completion of the Monument for another generation, to involve the whole subject in continued perplexity, and to necessitate vastly larger appropriations in the end than have now been asked for." [33] Members of the Monument Society were aware that the completed obelisk would be starkly bare and distasteful to many contemporary critics. They defended the obelisk not on aesthetic merit but by emphasizing its symbolic character, technical strength, and grand scale. "While the structure would make no appeal to a close and critical inspection as a mere work of art, it would give a crowning finish to the grand public buildings of the Capital, would add a unique feature to the surrounding landscape, and would attract the admiring gaze of the most distant observers in the wide range over which it would be visible." [34] Robert Winthrop expressed in 1878 the dilemma facing him as a member of the Washington National Monument Society:

---

[31] Washington National Monument Society, resolution passed at meeting of December 17, 1878 (National Archives).

[32] *American Architect and Building News,* December 15, 1877.

[33] Washington National Monument Society, memorial to Congress, passed at meeting of Society, April 26, 1880, presented to Congress April 29, 1880. Harvey, p. 105.

[34] Harvey, p. 106.

> I am aware that what is called 'advanced art' looks with scorn on anything so simple and bald as an obelisk, more especially when it is made up of a thousand pieces. . . . I recall other obelisks, at home, and abroad which tell their story most impressively. And when I look around and see what 'Advanced Art' has done for us, and done for itself in the myriad of Soldiers Monuments which have been recently erected, I fall back on the simple shaft as at least not inferior to any one of them in effect, and as free from anything tinsel or tawdry.[35]

Economic reasons had by 1873 forced abandonment of the pantheon base. In 1878 Larkin Mead designed for the Society a simple esplanade for the bottom of the obelisk, elements from which were later incorporated in a terrace designed by Edward Clark, Architect of the Capitol. The proportions of the obelisk were also readjusted after 1878. Upon the request of the Washington Monument Commission, George Marsh, United States Minister to Italy, researched the proportions of obelisks and determined that the height of a true obelisk should be ten times the width of the base, thus making the final dimensions of the Washington Monument 55 feet 1½ inches at the base and 555 feet and 5⅛ inches tall. At the same time the pyramidon was made more pointed. In August 1880, President Rutherford B. Hayes set the second cornerstone and the last phase of construction began.

The final design of the Washington Monument is a distant derivative of the design by Robert Mills. Stripped of every relieving element, the bare obelisk is an extreme example of the action of economics and expedience on an architectural conception. The monument stands primarily as a testament to contemporary engineering skill. In the Mills project, the obelisk, pantheon, and ornament were united in a strong symbolic statement. With the removal of all but the obelisk, the intended meaning of the monument was destroyed and little of the original plan remains but a partial formal resemblance. One element of the design which is preserved from the original is the scale. It is evident that in the final plans the sheer power of size is the dominant aesthetic motive. Everyone was conscious of the fact that the completed monument would be the tallest structure in the world. An engraving issued by the Monument Society sometime after 1873, and probably in 1876, shows the streamlined monument design and compares it with famous tall buildings which it would surpass in height. (Figure 16.) The contrast between the Society's highly romantic view

---

[35] Robert C. Winthrop, letter to Senator Justin S. Morrill, Brookline, Massachusetts, August 1, 1878 (National Archives).

National Archives

Figure 14. J. Goldsborough Bruff. "Plan for Completing the Great Washington Monument, Correctly." 1876.

From "American Art and Collections," 1889

Figure 15. William Wetmore Story. Design for the Washington Monument. 1877.

Library of Congress

Figure 16. The Washington National Monument Society. Revised Plan of the Monument. After 1873.

of the monument in 1871 (Figure 7) and this matter-of-fact presentation is striking. The architectural press, bitter over its failure to bring about a redesign of the monument, had little praise for this worship of scale: "The result of plainness, squareness, simplicity, and extreme height will doubtless assert itself to the common mind as a clear achievement (in the vernacular, a big thing), disturbing the spectator . . . with no necessity of analyzing details, no tumult of emotions, and inspiring no thought worthy of thinking."[36] The prospect of a 555-foot structure, however, captured public and official fancy and the monument was promptly dubbed the "Eighth Wonder of the World." (The Washington Monument held this distinction as the tallest structure in the world only until the completion in Paris of the Eiffel Tower in 1889.)

The capping of the Washington Monument on December 6, 1884 (using the world's first piece of architectural aluminum) was an occasion for festivity and oratory. The celebration was as much for the dedication of a new symbol of national greatness as it was for the termination of the long and arduous process of designing and building the monument. The actual construction of the monument had occupied thirty-six years from 1848 to 1884 and the first discussion of the project had begun in the Eighteenth Century. The difficult process of building the Washington Monument had cut across several phases of American taste and self image. The story of the Washington Monument illustrates the difficulties which inevitably arise whenever the realization of a work of architecture is extended beyond the age of its conception, particularly when the work is of such emotional significance as a national monument. To the modern art historian, the design proposals for the Washington Monument provide a valuable catalog of architectural styles and attest to the extreme difficulty for an architect of any period to produce a monumental statement of universal and timeless significance.

BIBLIOGRAPHY

The American Architect and Building News. Boston: Houghton, Osgood, and Company, 1876–1904.

Carrington, Henry B. *The Obelisk, Its Voices; or The Inner Facings of the Washington Monument with their Lessons.* Boston: Lee and Shepard, Publishers, 1887.

Clark, Allen. "Robert Mills: Architect and Engineer," *Records of the Columbia Historical Society of Washington, D.C.* Vol. 40–41. Washington, 1940.

De Zapp, Rudolph. *The Washington Monument.* Washington: Caroline Publishing Company, 1900.

Friedel, Frank and Lionelle Aikman. *George Washington: Man and Monument.* Washington: The Washington National Monument Society, 1965.

[36] *American Architect and Building News,* July 27, 1878.

Gallagher, Helen Mar Pierce. *Robert Mills, Architect of the Washington Monument.* New York: Columbia University Press, 1935.

Griffith, J. Eveleth. *History of the Washington Monument from its Inception to its Completion and Dedication.* Holyoke, Massachusetts: J. Eveleth Griffith, 1885.

Harvey, Frederick L. *History of the Washington National Monument and Washington National Monument Society.* Washington: The Washington National Monument Society, 1902.

Huxtable, Ada Louise. "The Washington Monument, 1836–1884." *Progressive Architecture.* Vol. 38, No. 8, August 1957.

Van Brunt, Henry. "The Washington Monument." *American Art and Collections.* Walter Montgomery, editor. Boston: E. W. Walker and Company, 1889.

Washington National Monument Society. "The Board of Managers of the Washington National Monument Society to the American People." Washington, 1846.

Washington National Monument Society. *The Washington Monument.* ("Views of the Early Patriots Regarding it; Reasons Why it Should Remain on its Present Site; Objects and Uses of Such Structures; An Appeal to the American People.") Washington: W. H. and O. H. Morrison, 1871.

Constantino Brumidi's "Apotheosis of Washington" in the Rotunda of the United States Capitol

KENT AHRENS

One of the most ambitious fresco projects to be undertaken in America during the Nineteenth Century was Constantino Brumidi's *Apotheosis of Washington* (Figures 10 and 11) in the rotunda of the United States Capitol. For over a century now visitors have gazed up in awe at the enormous painting in the eye of the dome. But Brumidi's *Apotheosis,* and the rest of his work in America, received little or no serious study until 1950 when Myrtle Cheney Murdock published her pioneering monograph on the Italian-born artist.[1]

Almost nothing of any certainty is known about Brumidi's life before his arrival in New York in 1852. It is thought that he studied art in the Accademia di San Luca in Rome. A tradition has it that he restored a portion of Raphael's frescoes in the Vatican, but that is probably apocryphal. He did, however, help restore the paintings by Giovanni da Udine in the Logge di San Damaso in the Vatican. Unfortunately, Brumidi's work in the Palazzo Torlonia in the Piazza Venezia, Rome, was destroyed during the construction of the monument dedicated to Vittorio Emanuele II. Following the political upheavals of 1848, Brumidi apparently incurred the enmity of Cardinal Jacques Antonelli, the papal secretary of state, and he was imprisoned. His release was supposedly secured by Pope Pius IX on the condition that he flee the country, which he did. Although Brumidi literature often indicates that he executed a painting in the cathedral in Mexico City, there are no records of such a picture there.[2] He seems to have settled in Washington about 1855.

[1] See Myrtle Cheney Murdock, *Constantino Brumidi. Michelangelo of the United States Capitol,* second edition (Washington, 1965). Also see Charles E. Fairman, *Art and Artists of the Capitol of the United States of America* (Washington, 1927) [69th Congress, 1st Session, Senate Document 95].

[2] Information about Brumidi's work in Italy was the courtesy of D. Redig de Campos,

Brumidi's first opportunity to associate himself with the decoration of the Capitol came in 1855 when Captain Montgomery C. Meigs, whom President Pierce had appointed supervising engineer in charge of construction in 1853, decided to permit the artist to execute a series of frescoes in what was then the House Committee Room on Agriculture. In his annual report Meigs wrote, "One of the rooms of the basement of the south wing is now being painted in fresco. This will enable Congress to see a specimen of this the highest style of architectural decoration." [3] On the ceiling Brumidi represented by allegory the four seasons. And in the east and west lunettes he painted subjects depicting the *Calling of Cincinnatus from the Plow* (Figure 1) and the *Calling of Putnam from the Plow to the Revolution*, respectively. The Cincinnatus panel, which is signed and dated *1855*, was executed first. The Italian artist Giorio Berti had frescoed the legend of Cincinnatus in the Sala di Antonio Ciseri, Palazzo Pitti, and Brumidi was doubtlessly familiar with his design (Figure 2). Although the decorations in this room are among Brumidi's best in the Capitol, they did not escape criticism. The subjects came under attack, but the more fundamental objection lay in the fact that the artist was not a native American. In reply to criticism leveled against him by the editors of *The Crayon* in October 1855, Meigs wrote: ". . . in a fortunate moment an Italian artist [Brumidi] applied to me for employment as a painter of fresco. He asked the use of a wall on which he might paint an example of his skill. . . . I suggested Cincinnatus called from the plough to defend his country.—a favorite subject with all educated Americans, who associate with that name the Father of our Country." [4] Certainly Meigs had a point in terms of artistic precedent.

Monumenti Musei e Gallerie Pontificie, Città del Vaticano. Graciela Reyes Retana, Museo de San Carlos, Instituto Nacional de Bellas Artes, México 1, D. F., searched the records of the collections of the cathedral.

[3] *Report of the Architect of the Capitol,* October 14, 1855, p. 115. For a detailed evaluation of Meigs' achievements in Washington, see Russell F. Weigley, "Captain Meigs and the Artists of the Capitol: Federal Patronage of Art in the 1850's," *Records of the Columbia Historical Society of Washington, D. C. 1969–1970* (1971), pp. 285–305.

[4] Meigs to John Durand, editor of *The Crayon,* October 11, 1856, letter book copy, Office of the Architect of the Capitol. In *The Crayon* (reprinted by Ams Press, Inc.) for July 11, 1855, p. 26, a correspondent identified as "The Leader" reported: ". . . A Roman painter, Brumidi, is decorating one of the new committee-rooms with frescoes. The one already finished by him in a lunette, is Cincinnatus called from the plough—a good composition. . . ." Meigs' letter cited above was in reply to Durand's comments in the October 1856 issue of *The Crayon,* in which he had written in part, p. 311: "The extension of the Capitol at Washington serves to illustrate both national development as well as national shortcomings in Art. . . . The decoration of one of the Committee rooms consists of one subject (among many of different character), taken from the history of ancient Rome. . . . When frescoes are required, we admit the propriety of employing artists who understand fresco-painting, as we have no practitioners in that department of

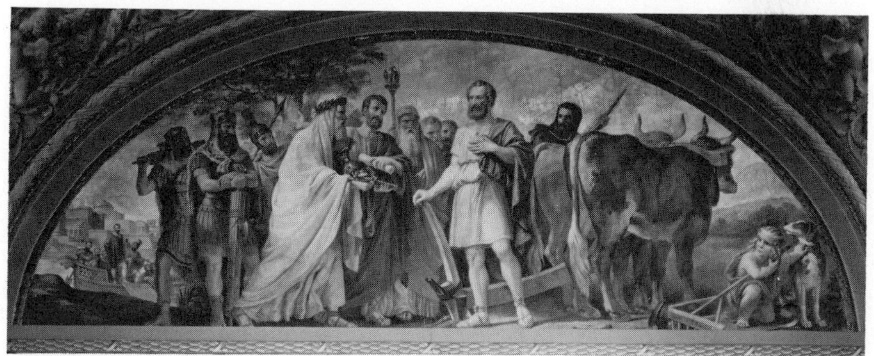

Office of the Architect of the Capitol

Figure 1. Brumidi. Calling of Cincinnatus from the Plow. Fresco. 1855. United States Capitol.

Courtesy Superintendenza alla Gallerie, Firenze

Figure 2. Giorio Berti. The Roman Dictator Cincinnatus Receiving the Senate. Fresco. About 1824–1827 or later. Sala di Antonio Ciseri, Palazzo Pitti, Florence.

In late Eighteenth-Century France Jacques Louis David in his large academic paintings—as for example the *Oath of the Horatii* (1784) or *Brutus, Having Condemned His Sons to Death* (1789)—had sought to equate the political ethics of France with those of antiquity. American painters like John Trumbull seized upon such subjects as his lost *Deputation from the Senate Presenting to Cincinnatus the Command of the Roman Armies* (1784) to draw similar political and philosophical implications about the newly founded United States.

In spite of the criticism which was aimed at the frescoes in the old Agriculture Committee Room and such subsequent panels as *Cornwallis Sues for Cessation of Hostilities Under the Flag of Truce* (1857),[5] Brumidi secured with Meigs' help a foothold in the Capitol by means of these early examples of his art in America.

No doubt it was Brumidi's work which Meigs had in mind when he summed up his own achievements in 1858:

> But little historical painting has thus far been attempted in the Capitol extension. What little has been done has been done with the object of calling attention to the subject, and indicating the mode in which the building admits of decoration by works of art. As public attention has been called to it, my object has been accomplished, and I shall be ready to carry out . . . any plan which the friends of art succeed in passing through Congress.[6]

From 1855 until his death in 1880 Brumidi was engaged sporadically by Congress to help decorate their newly expanded headquarters.

The cornerstone of the Capitol extension was laid in 1851, but it was not until March 3, 1855 that Congress authorized Thomas U. Walter, Architect of the Capitol Extension and New Dome, to replace Charles Bulfinch's wood and copper dome with a new one of iron.[7] The earlier dome had been inspired by Roman models, but Walter's new and lofty one emerged from the European Renaissance-Baroque tradition. As it was finally constructed, Walter's dome consists of a high outer shell and a lower inner shell, culminating in a circular

---

art; but for designs, the chief element of an illustration, we are not so poorly off. We have American artists who excel in design, and they could choose more appropriate subjects, and treat them better, than those accepted and painted on the walls in this building. . . ." Also see *The Crayon,* March 1856, pp. 91–92, and May 1857, pp. 155–56.

[5] Brumidi's *Cornwallis* originally occupied a position on the south wall of the House chamber, but it has been moved to the Members' private dining room, House wing.

[6] *Report of the Architect of the Capitol,* November 15, 1858, quoted from 58th Congress, 2d Session, *House Report* 646 [also called *Documentary History of the Construction and Development of the United States Capitol Building and Grounds* (Washington, 1904)], p. 707.

[7] I. T. Frary, *They Built the Capitol* (Richmond, 1940), pp. 179 and 191–92.

Office of the Architect of the Capitol

Figure 3. An early photograph of Brumidi's oil sketch for the Apotheosis of Washington. Private collection.

opening more than sixty feet in diameter. Suspended between the two shells by means of iron supports is a plaster canopy which carries Brumidi's fresco, the *Apotheosis of Washington* (see Figure 4). Because the opening of the inner dome is smaller than the diameter of the canopy, it is not possible to see the fresco in its entirety from any point in the rotunda.[8]

[8] Until it was closed to the public in the Twentieth Century, it was possible for visitors to ascend the dome. Many guide books noted the fact. DeB. Randolph Keim, *Keim's Illustrated Hand-Book. Washington and its Environs: A Descriptive and Historical Hand-Book to the Capital of the United States of America*, seventh edition (Washington, 1875), p. 77, wrote: "These frescoes cover nearly 5,000 sq. feet. They may be viewed from different points in the ascent of the Dome. As they are approached they

Office of the Architect of the Capitol

Figure 4. Thomas U. Walter. Section through Dome of U. S. Capitol. Pen and ink with watercolor. 1859.

To the best of our knowledge, Walter first formally notified Brumidi of the pending commission for the canopy fresco in his letter of August 18, 1862: "It is intended to have a picture 65 feet in diameter, painted in fresco, on the concave canopy over the eye of the New Dome of the U. S. Capitol. I would thank you to furnish me with a design for the said picture, at your earliest convenience." Brumidi answered Walter's letter on September 8, 1862: "In compliance with the request contained in your letter of the 18th ult. I herewith submit to you my design for the fresco picture to be painted on the Canopy of the new Dome. . . . The six groups around the border represent, as you will see, *War, Science, Marine, Commerce, manufacture,* and *Agriculture*. . . . In the centre is an Apotheosis of Washington, surrounded by allegorical figures, and the 13th original Sister States." [9] On December 24, 1862, Walter wrote Brumidi that his design had been approved by himself, by the Commissioner of Public Buildings, and by the Secretary of the Interior. But Walter went on to say that the artist's estimated cost of $50,000 was too high. Three days later Brumidi replied that he would undertake the project for $40,000.[10] That figure was finally found to be satisfactory to all parties concerned and on March 11, 1863, Walter formally notified Brumidi of the terms of the agreement: ". . . I have the honor to inform you that your design for painting the *Canopy* over the eye of the aforesaid new Dome is adopted. And, in as much as Congress had made the appropriation for the completion of that work, you are hereby authorized to proceed at once with the aforesaid painting. . . . The painting is to be in real fresco. . . ." [11] Beginning April 1, 1863, the artist was to be paid in monthly installments of $2,000, the total amount not to exceed $40,000.

In April 1862 Congress passed a joint resolution transferring control of the construction of the new dome and the extension from the War Department to the Department of the Interior.[12] Thereafter,

increase in size. Seen from the balustrade beneath the canopy, they are of colossal proportions. Sufficient light by day is thrown in from the openings in the outer shell of the Dome. At night hundreds of gas jets . . . illuminate not only the canopy, but the entire interior of the Dome."

[9] Walter to Brumidi, August 18, 1862, and Brumidi to Walter, September 8, 1862, both in the Collections of the Manuscript Division, Library of Congress.

[10] Walter to Brumidi, December 24, 1862, and Brumidi to Walter, December 27, 1862, Library of Congress.

[11] Walter to Brumidi, March 11, 1863, Library of Congress.

[12] *Report of the Architect of the Capitol,* November 1, 1862, p. 604. On May 15, 1861, the Secretary of War suspended work on the Capitol extension and the new dome, and work was not resumed until April 30, 1862 ". . . under the limitations and conditions of the said resolution of transfer. . . ."

Walter submitted all transactions for approval to Benjamin B. French, who was Commissioner of Public Buildings and Disbursing Agent of the Capitol Extension and New Dome, and Caleb B. Smith, Secretary of the Interior. Late in December 1862 Walter wrote to French that he recommended that Brumidi's offer to execute the fresco for $40,000 be accepted. He concluded by writing, "The grandeur of this picture, the great distance at which it will be seen, and the peculiarity of its light will render it intensely imposing." [13] French relayed Walter's recommendation to Smith for his approval. But Smith reasoned that the project needed no official approval from him, ". . . as the work was an incident of the completion of the Dome, and had been included in your [Walter's] estimates [November 1, 1862]. . . ." [14] French elaborated on the discussion between himself and Smith in his journals: ". . . It was approved by Secretary Smith, but he declined giving the order for the contract. . . . At last he asked me if the picture was in the Architectural drawing which was originally submitted. I told him it was. 'Then' said he 'there is no necessity of an order from me, the dome is to be completed according to that plan. . . .' " [15] Elsewhere French made it clear that Brumidi had submitted an *oil* sketch for their approval: "Mr. Smith had the design, painted in oil by Mr. Brumidi, at his house for several weeks, and he expressed his approval of it to me. . . ." [16]

Although formal negotiations between Walter and Brumidi for the canopy fresco were not commenced until August of 1862, existing evidence suggests that the commission may have been offered informally to the artist a number of years earlier. If such is the case, it answers the perplexing question of how Brumidi managed to work out the rather complex iconography and to prepare his pictorial design in less than three weeks.

In 1919 two boxes containing a number of Brumidi's sketches and oil paintings were found in a Washington bank vault, where they may have been placed by Brumidi's wife Lola in the Nineteenth Century. According to Murdock, one of the boxes contained "1 Sketch for Dome Ceiling" and "1 Circular Canvas, Design for Ceiling of Dome." [17] We have no other information about the former. The pres-

---

[13] Walter to French, December 29, 1862, letter book, Architect of the Capitol.

[14] French to Walter, January 3, 1863, letter book (now removed), Architect of the Capitol.

[15] "Journal No. 10. Commenced Monday, January 1st., 1866," *The Papers of Benjamin Brown French,* January 12, 1866, Library of Congress.

[16] French to John P. Usher, Secretary of the Interior, May 4, 1863, letter book, Architect of the Capitol.

[17] Murdock, pp. 104 and 80–82. Also see "Brumidi Paintings Found in Washington

ent whereabouts of the circular canvas is not known, but until it was sold in the 1960's it hung in a private collection near Washington. Murdock identified an early photograph (Figure 3), which was found in a trunk of Brumidi's son Lawrence, as a photograph of this circular painting.[18] In spite of minor differences in detail, the painting so closely resembles the fresco (Figures 10 and 11) that there can be little doubt that this is the design in oils which Brumidi submitted to Walter for approval in 1862. Although the exact date of this oil sketch cannot be determined, the following discussion will attempt to show that the design which it incorporates had been fully worked out by late 1859.

Meigs' annual report of November 16, 1855, offers us a number of important clues concerning the early progress of the design for the new dome and its decorative system.[19] Although he was not specific about the subject to be represented, he clearly indicated that there was to be a "richly painted" surface above the inner shell. It is not, however, until 1859 that we find any architectural drawings showing the interior of the rotunda as it was finally constructed. One of Walter's drawings from that year showing a cross section of the rotunda leaves no doubt that the design for the canopy fresco as it was executed by Brumidi was already known to the architect (Figure 4).

After Search of Forty Years," *The Sunday Star Magazine Section* (Washington), November 2, 1919. The article mentions the circular oil study, but not the other sketch. Charles Fairman was one of the persons present when the boxes were opened.

[18] Murdock, pp. 93–95.

[19] *Report of the Architect of the Capitol,* November 16, 1855, pp. 117–18: ". . . At the termination of the last session of Congress, an appropriation was made for removing the old dome . . . and for replacing it by one of cast iron. . . . Immediately after the appropriation was made, the study of the details of the exterior and the design for the interior were taken up. The design for the exterior has been revised. . . . The design of the interior was made at the same time with this drawing. . . . The interior of the rotundo will remain unchanged to the height of the stone cornice. . . . Above this cornice a vertical wall will be raised, with a deep recessed panel nine feet in height, to be filled with sculpture, forming a continuous frieze . . . of figures in alto relievo. The subject to be the history of America. The gradual progress of a continent from the depths of barbarism to the height of civilization; the rude and barbarous civilization of some of the Ante-Columbian tribes; the contests of the Aztecs with their less civilized predecessors; their own conquest by the Spanish race; the wilder state of the hunter tribes of our own regions; the discovery, settlement, wars, treaties; the gradual advance of the white, and retreat of the red races; our own revolutionary and other struggles, with the illustration of the higher achievements of our present civilization, will afford a richness and variety of costume, character, and incident, which may worthily employ our best sculptors. . . . Above the frieze the interior will be enriched by a series of attached columns. . . . Above this colonnade a dome will spring, which, contracting to a space of 65 feet in diameter, will . . . permit the eye to see another and lighter colonnade. . . . The whole being closed in at the base of the lantern . . . by a second dome of 73 feet span. This upper dome, lighted by openings around its base, should be richly painted. . . ." [Paragraphs have been merged.]

The architectural drawing is dated *December 9, 1859*, about six weeks after Meigs had been relieved of his duties as superintendent of construction. In the canopy, Washington, flanked by two allegorical figures, is clearly discernible as is the figural group which Brumidi later identified as *War*. The armed figure of *Freedom*, which first appears in Brumidi's fresco designs in Figure 3, was inspired by Thomas Crawford's large plaster model for his bronze *Freedom* (Figure 5) which was exhibited in Statuary Hall for the first time in 1859. The groups flanking *War* in the architectural drawing—*Agriculture* and *Invention*—while not as clearly represented can also be identified. The inescapable conclusion is that as early as December 1859 Brumidi's proposed design for the canopy fresco had been prepared, either as a lost drawing or as the oil sketch (Figure 3).[20]

A number of years ago Vose Galleries of Boston sold another version of the *Apotheosis of Washington* by Brumidi (Figure 7) which differs markedly from the previously mentioned oil sketch and from the finished fresco (Figures 3, 10 and 11). In all probability it was an early solution for the canopy design which was later for one reason or another rejected. The tondo is beautifully executed, and it reveals the full power of Brumidi's style. The center of the composition depicts three putti supporting a flag-draped portrait of Washington which is flanked by two allegorical figures—*Liberty* and *Victory-and-Fame* as they were later to be identified. Similarities between this central group and Antonio Capellano's *Fame and Peace Crowning George Washington* (Figure 8), formerly over the east entrance of the rotunda, are too close to be coincidental. The central group in Brumidi's painting is surrounded in the heavens by thirteen large female figures who represent the original states. A number of them hold a banner reading "E. Pluribus Unum." And there is little doubt that each of the thirty-three stars represents a state of the Union. We feel, therefore, that this version of the *Apotheosis of Washington* was executed in 1859 after Oregon had entered the Union as the thirty-third state. Compared to the later *Apotheosis* (Figure 3), neither the pictorial design nor the iconography is as complex. The figural group below the rainbow (traditional symbol of divine promise) probably represents the forces of tyranny being crushed by the eagle of the republic. Absent is armed *Freedom*. The three putti probably symbolize the abundance of American agriculture, but the significance of Mercury cannot be exactly determined. Brumidi seems to have taken his inspiration for the representation of Washington from a type of Roman

---

[20] Fairman, pp. 204 and 208, hints that he felt Brumidi expected to receive the canopy commission before he did.

Office of the Architect of the Capitol

Figure 5. Thomas Crawford. Plaster model for Freedom. About 1856–1857. Smithsonian Institution, Washington. Compare with Figure 6.

Office of the Architect of the Capitol

Figure 6. Brumidi. Detail of the figure of Freedom in the fresco the Apotheosis of Washington.

funerary monument which had been especially popular in the Eighteenth Century, as, for example, Pietro Bracci's *Tomb of Cardinal Carlo Leopoldo Calcagnini* (1746) in San Andrea delle Fratte, Rome. In those monuments the deceased was represented by a painted image, which was supported by elements of architecture or by allegorical figures.

In his 1855 report (See note 19) Meigs was not specific about the decoration for the dome, but he elaborated on the scenes of American history which were to be portrayed in the proposed marble reliefs of the frieze. He had hoped that these reliefs would ". . . worthily employ our best sculptors in its execution. . . ." But for reasons of economy it was finally decided to decorate the frieze with frescoes instead of marble, and the commission was given to Brumidi in the 1870's. The work was left unfinished at his death in 1880, and Filippo Costaggini was later commissioned to execute the rest of Brumidi's panels. Brumidi's sketch, which is on display in the crypt, is signed and dated *C. Brumidi 1859* on the reverse side of the first section

Vose Galleries of Boston, Inc.

Figure 7. Brumidi. The Apotheosis of Washington. Oil on canvas. 1859. Private collection.

Office of the Architect of the Capitol

Figure 8. Antonio Capellano. Fame and Peace Crowning George Washington. Sandstone. 1827. United States Capitol.

Office of the Architect of the Capitol

Figure 9. Brumidi. America and History, and Landing of Columbus, detail from the artist's sketch for the Capitol Rotunda frieze. Brown washes highlighted in white. 1859.

(Figure 9). At least the earlier sections of the long sketch seem to have emerged contemporaneously with the designs for the canopy. The perplexing question remains of why the painter should have concerned himself with the frieze in 1859 when the plan was clearly to have that section of the rotunda decorated in sculptural relief.[21] While the 1859 architectural drawing (Figure 4) accurately projects Brumidi's design for the canopy as it was finally executed, the frieze is filled with a classical battle scene which bears no relationship to either Meig's description or to Brumidi's sketch. Since no sculptor had yet been selected to receive the commission and no plans were yet drawn up, it is not surprising that Walter's drawing should have represented a generalized classical scene. But Brumidi seems already to have had aspirations as early as 1859 of receiving commissions for both the canopy and the frieze. Perhaps he saw himself as the artist who would prepare the designs for the frieze and coordinate the work

[21] For a discussion of the proposed frieze sculpture, see Fairman, pp. 252–255. In order to save money, Crawford suggested to Meigs that the reliefs be executed in plaster, since they would be protected from the weather. Although the article is not wholly reliable, the *Sunday Star, op. cit.,* reported: "The designs for this great historical belt were made in 1859 and were approved by Gen. Meigs. Owing to the disinclination of Congress to become financially interested in art, the work was not commenced until May, 1878, nineteen years later." In all likelihood that information was given to the *Star* reporter by Fairman.

of the sculptors. In 1866, the year the *Apotheosis* was unveiled, Brumidi submitted to Edward Clark, Walter's successor, his plans for the fresco designs he hoped would eventually fill the frieze.[22]

In spite of the personal differences between them, which often flared into open hostility, both Meigs and Walter must have agreed that the political climate in Washington in 1859 was not right for publicly offering Brumidi the commission for a large and expensive fresco in the new dome.[23] In the late 1850's a group of American artists, angered in part by Meigs' continued patronage of Brumidi in the Capitol, submitted to Congress a memorial demanding that an art commission be established to oversee all government art projects. Congress bowed to their demands, but the commission proved ineffective and in 1860 Congress moved to abolish it.[24] During the years immediately preceding the Civil War, Congress grew increasingly wary of spending public money on painting and sculpture and moved toward severely restricting funds for art. It was, however, willing to permit the construction to continue. In April 1862 Congress gave control of construction to the Department of the Interior with the following provision: "That no money heretofore appropriated shall be expended upon the Capitol until authorized by Congress, except so much as is necessary to protect the building from injury by the elements and to complete the dome." [25] Since the canopy had to be painted while the scaffolding was up, Walter was able to avoid any collision with Congress by incoporating funds for the fresco into his budget for completing the dome (see note 27).

Although Brumidi was officially given the canopy commission in March 1863, nearly two and one half years more passed before he commenced work on the actual fresco. The reasons were simple enough. The new dome was still under construction and, as Walter

[22] *Report of the Architect of the Capitol,* November 1, 1866, p. 3.

[23] Meigs was relieved of his duties as superintendent of construction on November 1, 1859, by order of John B. Floyd, Secretary of War. On February 27, 1861, Meigs resumed charge of the Capitol extension and new dome for a brief period. He was not in charge when Walter opened negotiations with Brumidi in August 1862. Raymond L. Stehle argues convincingly that by the early 1860's Meigs and Emanuel Leutze had formulated an elaborate plan for decorating the Capitol, including the rotunda. See Stehle's unpublished *The Life and Works of Emanuel Leutze* (1972), chapter 6. Copy in Columbia Historical Society Library, Washington, D. C.

[24] The memorial was published in *House Report* 198, Appendix A, 35th Congress, 2d Session. Also see 58th Congress, 2d Session, *House Report* 646, pp. 744–49, 770–77, and 780. And see *The Crayon:* April 1858, p. 117; May 1858, p. 148; February 1859, pp. 57–8; April 1859, p. 127; May 1859, pp. 157–60; June 1859, p. 195; and July 1859, p. 220.

[25] *Report of the Architect of the Capitol,* November 1, 1862, p. 604. For a more complete history of the role of Congress as a patron of the arts during the period, see the annual reports of the Architect of the Capitol.

explained to the contractors in 1864, it was not possible for Brumidi to begin his fresco until all of the iron work above the canopy was completed.[26] And, of course, it was necessary for the artist to prepare his large working sketches in order to transfer his designs onto the canopy. The slowness of the construction and the artist's unhurried working procedure seem to have been beyond the comprehension of John P. Usher, who succeeded Caleb Smith as Secretary of the Interior. When Usher learned that no formal contract with Brumidi existed, he ordered Benjamin French to inform the artist that after May 8, 1863, no more funds would be paid to the artist.[27] Fortunately, Walter intervened, and Usher rescinded his order in July.[28] But again in November, Usher suspended payments to Brumidi: "$10,000 . . . has already been paid to Mr. Brumidi. I am of the opinion that the progress which has been made does not justify any further payments at present." [29] His decision was issued in spite of Walter's annual report only five days earlier that Brumidi was at work on the cartoons.[30] Apparently Brumidi received no further payments for more than a year. In 1864, Clement West, French's successor, wrote Usher that the cartoons were complete and that the artist was ready to commence work on the acutal fresco. West requested authority to resume payments to the painter.[31]

Once begun the frescoing seems to have progressed smoothly and by November 1865 Edward Clark, Architect of the Capitol, was able to report:

> The picture over the eye of the dome is all painted in, but the artist is unwilling to have the scaffolding removed until the plastering is thoroughly dry, and the picture toned. As it will at times be viewed by

[26] Walter to James, Fowler, Kirtland, and Company, March 21, 1864, letter book, Architect of the Capitol.

[27] French reported to Usher, May 4, 1863, letter book, ". . . there is no 'contract' in the general acceptation of the meaning of that term. An *agreement* was made . . . which was not consummated until March the 11th. (after an appropriation was made by Congress for the painting). . . . In the estimates of the Architect submitted to the Secretary of the Interior Nov. 1. 1862 is one for completing the New Dome of $200,000. The details of that estimate . . . included the picture by Mr. Brumidi." See French to Usher, May 8, 1863, letter book, and French to Brumidi, May 8, 1863, letter book (removed). Office of the Architect of the Capitol.

[28] In his letter (copy) of July 7, 1863, Architect of the Capitol, Usher wrote to Clement S. West, the new Disbursing Agent, ". . . I have concluded that it [Brumidi's fresco] is a part of the original plan and that it is the will of Congress that it should be executed."

[29] Copy of a letter from Usher to West, November 6, 1863, letter book, Architect of the Capitol.

[30] *Report of the Architect of the Capitol,* November 1, 1863, p. 673.

[31] West to Usher, December 3, 1864, letter book, Architect of the Capitol.

gas-light, he wishes to have the opportunity of trying it by this light before dismissing it from his hands.[32]

The scaffolding was taken down in January 1866, and a number of Brumidi's old acquaintances came to look. French was pleased, as was Meigs who wrote Brumidi a flattering letter:

> I yesterday visited the Capitol to see your great painting, and I congratulate you upon the completion of this magnificant work.
>
> I find the drawing and coloring most agreable and beautiful. The perspective is so well managed that I doubt whether any one not well acquainted with the construction of such edifices as the Dome could determine by the mere use of his [tear in paper] the form and position of the [tear] on which it is painted.[33]

Most newspaper reviews—for example, the *Daily National Intelligencer* for January 17, 1866—were laudatory.

The year the fresco was open to public inspection, Samuel D. Wyeth published a comprehensive description of it in his famous guidebook *The Federal City*.[34] Wyeth had access to the office of the Architect of the Capitol and there is little doubt that his intepretation of the fresco is an accurate one.

Against the infinite heavens we see George Washington in glory, flanked by *Liberty* on his right and *Victory-and-Fame* on his left. The thirteen original states revel in glory with him. Besides apotheosizing Washington, the fresco represents the United States prospering under the protection and guidance of the gods. Mercury offers Robert Morris gold to finance the Revolutionary War. Minerva, goddess of wisdom, instructs the inventors Benjamin Franklin, Samuel F. B. Morse, and Robert Fulton. The goddesses Ceres, Flora, and Pomona assist Young America (wearing a red liberty cap) in gathering a rich

---

[32] *Report of the Architect of the Capitol,* November 1, 1865, p. 5. Brumidi signed and dated the fresco *1865*. See Clark to James Harlan, Secretary of the Interior, April 14, 1866, and May 29, 1866, both in letter books, Architect of the Capitol. The letters deal with problem of whether the fresco was yet finished. In his report of November 1, 1866, p. 2, Clark wrote: "... it [the fresco] is not finished, as the artist intends to soften down the harshness at the joinings of the plastering. He was under the impression that these imperfections would disappear when the surface became dry. He holds himself in readiness to do the proper toning and blending whenever the scaffolding is in place for the painting of the vault of the rotundo." The work was never carried out: see *U. S. Statutes,* 45th Congress, 3d Session, Chapter 182, 1879, p. 391; *Congressional Record—Senate,* 45th Congress, 3d Session, February 28, 1879, p. 2078; and *Congressional Record—Senate,* 46th Congress, 2d Session, February 24, 1880, pp. 1075–76.

[33] Meigs to Brumidi, January 19, 1866, letter book, Architect of the Capitol. For French's reaction to the fresco, see his journals, *op. cit.*

[34] S. D. Wyeth, *Description of Brumidi's Allegorical Painting Within the Canopy of the Rotunda* (Washington, 1866).

Office of the Architect of the Capitol

Figure 10. Brumidi. Apotheosis of Washington. Fresco. Completed 1865. United States Capitol.

harvest with a newly invented reaper. Neptune clears a path through his domain for a chugging steamboat.

Such elaborate iconographical programs—especially those praising the achievements of papal families as, for example, Cortona's *Glorification of Urban VIII's Reign* in the Palazzo Barberini—were a familiar part of Brumidi's Roman background. His treatment of the dome, which opens by illusion into infinite space, with the figures arranged in circular designs around the heavens, also emerges from Italian Renaissance-Baroque tradition. Brumidi was certainly influenced by such earlier masterpieces as Correggio's *Vision of Saint John the Evangelist* in San Giovanni Evangelista, Parma, and Lanfranco's

Office of the Architect of the Capitol

Figure 11. Brumidi. Apotheosis of Washington. An early photograph of the fresco.

Virgin in Glory in San Andrea della Valle, Rome. Unlike those frescoes, however, Brumidi's composition is static.

In the one tondo (Figure 7) Brumidi represented Washington by a painted image modeled roughly after a Gilbert Stuart portrait. In the other oil sketch and in the fresco (Figures 3 and 10), however, Brumidi painted Washington as if he were alive in the heavens.

Brumidi's selection of Horatio Greenough's statue of Washington (Figure 12) for his model was ingenious. By so doing, he strengthened his illusion of Washington ruling from Mount Olympus. Greenough's statue was commissioned for the rotunda but it received so much

Smithsonian Institution, Washington

Figure 12. Horatio Greenough. George Washington. Marble. 1833–1841. Smithsonian Institution.

criticism from a public which did not understand it that in 1844 it was removed to the Capitol grounds. Wyeth wrote of the statue:

> It certainly does not embody a visible realization of the idea existing in the heart of the nation of the "great chief." We do not think of

The Peale Museum, Baltimore

Figure 13. After Rembrandt Peale. Apotheosis of Washington. Stipple engraving by David Edwin (1776–1841).

> Washington as a half-naked Roman, sitting in God-like state, like Jupiter. . . .
>
> A foreign writer thus speaks of it:—"Nothing can be more human, and at the same time more God-like, than this colossal statue of Washington. It is a sort of domestic Jupiter. . . ."[35]

As Wayne Craven pointed out a few years ago, Greenough had based his statue on Quatremère de Quincy's early Nineteenth-Century reconstruction of Phidias' *Jupiter* or *Zeus*.[36] Besides glorifying Washington, Greenough's statue implies the continuation of Greek ideals in the political life and philosophy of this country. While avoiding the sculptor's representation of Washington as semi-nude, Brumidi's work embodies the ideals that Greenough sought to convey to the American public in his statue.

Other allegorical representations of Washington can be found in the art of America, and occasionally of Europe, in the Nineteenth and late Eighteenth Centuries. As early as about 1784, for example, John Trumbull, in a drawing which is now owned by the Avery Architectural Library, Columbia University, treated the subject of Washington's apotheosis. Rembrandt Peale popularized the notion of Washington's apotheosis in a lithograph showing him being borne into the clouds above Mount Vernon (Figure 13). But Brumidi's fresco remains one of the major achievements of academic painting in America at mid-century.

---

[35] S. D. Wyeth, *The Federal City; Or, Ins and Abouts of Washington,* third edition (Washington, 1868), pp. 43–44.

[36] Wayne Craven, "Horatio Greenough's Statue of Washington and Phidias' Olympian Zeus," *The Art Quarterly,* XXVI (no. 4, 1963), pp. 429–40.

The Farragut Monument: A Decade of Art and Politics, 1871–1881

RUTH L. BOHAN

When the memorial to David Glasgow Farragut in Washington was unveiled on April 25, 1881, one of the most intricate alliances between art and politics in the city's history came finally to an end.[1] Spanning nearly a decade, the planning and execution of the monument was a saga of artistic ambition, personal and political influence, and elaborate maneuvering. Sculptors, Senators and Representatives, officers of the Army and Navy, cabinet members, even the Admiral's widow, were caught up in activities which often forced more important aesthetic concerns into the background.

As the most distinguished naval commander during the Civil War and the first Admiral of the United States Navy, Farragut was a person of immense accomplishment and reputation. While in command of his flagship *Hartford,* he had successfully achieved the bloodless surrender of New Orleans in 1862 and two years later supervised the capture of the Confederate defenses in Mobile Bay.[2] With his death on August 14, 1870, plans for erecting a memorial in his honor flourished. Within five days of his funeral, arrangements were underway in New York for the erection of a medallion portrait of the

[1] This paper was originally written for a course offered by the University of Maryland in conjunction with the Smithsonian Institution and taught by Dr. Wilcomb E. Washburn of the Smithsonian in the fall of 1973. In addition to Dr. Washburn, I would like to thank Dr. Lois Fink, also of the Smithsonian, for suggesting the topic; and James C. Brown and Harry Schwartz of the National Archives for their assistance in locating research materials; and to express my special thanks to Michael Richman of the National Trust for Historic Preservation who read the manuscript and offered valuable suggestions and encouragement.

[2] For a biography of Farragut see: Loyall Farragut, *Life and Letters of David Glasgow Farragut* (New York: Appleton, 1891); Charles Lee Lewis, *David Glasgow Farragut: Our First Admiral* (Annapolis: United States Naval Academy, 1943); A. T. Mahan, *Admiral Farragut* (New York: Greenwood Press, 1968); C[harles] O. P[aullin], "David Glasgow Farragut," *Dictionary of American Biography* (New York: Scribner's, 1943), Vol. VI, pp. 286–291.

Office of the Architect of the Capitol

Marble statue of Abraham Lincoln by Vinnie Ream in the Rotunda of the United States Capitol.

Admiral in the Church of the Incarnation where Farragut had worshipped.[3] By January 1871, a much grander scheme was being formulated in the Nation's Capital with the young Washington sculptress Vinnie Ream considered a likely candidate to secure the commission.[4]

Born in the prairie town of Madison, Wisconsin, in 1847, Vinnie Ream spent her early youth in western Missouri where her father was a government surveyor before the family moved to Washington during the Civil War. Shortly after her arrival in Washington, she was introduced to the sculptor Clark Mills, became fascinated with the art of sculpture, and was soon devoting all of her energies to it. Her career was launched when she received permission to make a life study of President Abraham Lincoln while she was still in her teens and a novice in her profession. Her bust of the President was so highly admired that on August 30, 1866, one year after his death, she was commissioned by Congress to construct a full-sized marble statue of the martyred President. With this commission, the first of its kind ever granted by the Congress to a woman, Vinnie Ream became a youthful celebrity in the Capital where she beguiled Washington officialdom with her charm and captivating good looks.[5]

In early 1871, she began work on a portrait of the late Admiral Farragut based on personal recollections and photographs generously supplied by the Admiral's widow.[6] Praised as an excellent likeness by

---

[3] The sculptor Launt Thompson was commissioned to execute the portrait which was unveiled in December 1873. Farragut, *Life and Letters of David Glasgow Farragut,* p. 391; "Memorial to Admiral Farragut," *New York Times,* December 11, 1873, p. 5. A second monument, commissioned in December 1876, was designed and executed by Augustus Saint-Gaudens with the collaboration of Stanford White in the execution of the pedestal. It was erected in Madison Square on May 25, 1881. An early photograph of the Saint-Gaudens monument is published in the *Records of the Columbia Historical Society of Washington, D.C. 1971–1972* (1973), p. 564.

[4] "Formal Unveiling of Vinnie Ream's Statue," unknown newspaper, January 15, [1871], Box 9, Miscellany, Scrapbook 1864–1876, Vinnie Ream Hoxie Papers, Manuscript Division, Library of Congress. The Hoxie papers are hereafter indicated V.R.H.P.

[5] For a biography of Vinnie Ream Hoxie see: A[deline] A[dams], "Vinnie Ream Hoxie," *Dictionary of American Biography* (New York: Scribner's, 1943), Vol. IX, pp. 317–318; Richard L. Hoxie, *Vinnie Ream* (Washington: Press of Gibson Brothers, 1908); Gordon Langley Hall, *Vinnie Ream: The Story of the Girl Who Sculptured Lincoln* (New York: Holt, Rinehart and Winston, 1963); Harold E. Miner, *Vinnie and Her Friends,* unpublished MS, Archives of American Art, Microfilm Roll No. 297, Washington, D. C.; "Vinnie Ream," In Thurman Wilkins, ed., *Notable American Women, 1607–1950,* Vol. 3 (Cambridge, Mass.: Belknap Press, 1971), pp. 122–123.

[6] Virginia L. Farragut — Vinnie Ream, November 13, [1872?], Committee Papers, Committee on Public Buildings and Grounds, SEN 42A-E18, Records of the United States Senate, Record Group 46, National Archives Building. Hereafter this collection will be indicated SEN 42A-E18; the Committee on Public Buildings and Grounds will be indicated CPBG; the National Archives Building will be indicated N.A.; and after the first reference, all individuals will be indicated by their initials only. Vinnie Ream met the Admiral once briefly when he visited her studio. "Farragut," *Evening Star,* April 25, 1881, p. 1.

both Mrs. Farragut and her son Loyall,[7] the bust prompted speculation that young Vinnie Ream hoped to duplicate her success with the Lincoln bust and secure a second Congressional commission. That there was a basis for such speculation is suggested by later testimony of both Mrs. Farragut and General William Tecumsah Sherman that the sculptress was eager for such an award and was personally instrumental in urging Congress to initiate appropriate legislation.[8] However, the extensiveness of her role in these early negotiations with Congress cannot be documented from available records.

Whatever her role, Vinnie Ream was not alone in seeking such a commission. A similar bid was put forth by Dr. Horatio Stone, the physician-sculptor with a studio at the Washington Navy Yard. Like Vinnie Ream, Stone had also commenced work on a model of the late Admiral. He claimed to have met Farragut in Rome while the latter was in command of the Mediterranean squadron and received permission "to make studies of his figure and countenance" from which he had already "composed the sketch model for a colossal statue." [9]

Stone apparently approached Representative Nathaniel P. Banks of Massachusetts in hopes of securing a commission for himself. It seems almost certain that Banks had Stone's model in mind, and not Vinnie Ream's, when, on December 11, 1871, he introduced a joint resolution in Congress calling for the erection of a public monument to Farragut "after a design moulded from life." [10]

Banks' resolution was referred to the Joint Committee on Public Buildings and Grounds for consideration. The Joint Committee, totalling fifteen members, was composed of a Senate and a House Committee. The Senate half, chaired by Senator Justin S. Morrill of Vermont, included Senators Lyman Trumbull of Illinois, Charles Sumner of Massachusetts, Simon Cameron of Pennsylvania, Cornelius Cole of California, and John P. Stockton of New Jersey. The House half, chaired by Representative George A. Halsey of New Jersey, included Representatives James N. Tyner of Indiana, James H. Platt,

[7] Elizabeth Kilham, "Vinnie Ream at Home," magazine unknown, date unknown, pp. 663–664, Box 6, Miscellaneous, Miscellany, V.R.H.P.

[8] VLF — William Tecumsah Sherman, July 31, 1874, General Correspondence, Vol. 37, p. 4842, General William Tecumsah Sherman Papers, Manuscript Division, Library of Congress. The Sherman Papers are hereafter indicated W.T.S.P. VLF — George M. Robeson, November 20, 1874, Senate Executive Document No. 31, p. 4. Senate Executive Document No. 31 is hereafter indicated Sen. Ex. Doc. 31. WTS — GMR, December 23, 1874, Sen. Ex. Doc. 31, p. 3.

[9] Horatio Stone — George A. Halsey, January 11, 1873, House Resolution 2017, 42d Congress, Records of the United States House of Representatives, Record Group 233, N.A. Hereafter this collection will be indicated H.R. 2017. Mrs. Farragut questions Stone's claim. VLF — VR, November 13(?) or March 25(?), SEN 42A-E18, R.G. 46, N.A.

[10] *The Congressional Globe* (42d Congress, 2d Session) (Washington: Globe Office, 1872), p. 55.

Columbia Historical Society Collection

Vinnie Ream.

This photograph in the Columbia Historical Society collection is undated but a handwritten note on the reverse of the original is as follows: "Vinnie Ream as she looked when Lincoln posed for her in the White House."

Jr. of Virginia, Jackson Orr of Iowa, Charles B. Farwell of Illinois, Walter L. Sessions of New York, J. Lawrence Getz of Pennsylvania, Erastus Wells of Missouri, and Eli Perry of New York.

On the advice of Representative Banks, Stone introduced himself to the Joint Committee and made known the existence of his model. In a letter to Halsey, the sculptor asserted that his work had been "approved by all naval officers who have seen it, or knew the original" (presumably referring to the late Admiral) and enclosed testimony from members of Farragut's staff affirming "the merits of the sketch." [11]

[11] HS — GAH, January 11, 1872, H.R. 2017, R.G. 233, N.A.

A related request for a memorial to Farragut was received from the Department of the Navy. "[S]igned by nearly all the officers of the Navy, including all of the staff of the late Admiral Farragut," [12] the Navy's petition gave solid backing to the drive for a Farragut monument and undoubtedly influenced the Joint Committee in its decision to proceed.

Rather than immediately to award a commission, as Stone had hoped, however, the Committee proposed an open competition. On March 25, 1872, a resolution was reported allowing artists sixty days in which to submit models and authorizing the Joint Committee on Public Buildings and Grounds to select the one "that in their judgment shall be the most faithful likeness in form and features, and the most appropriate to commemorate the deeds and character of the said Admiral . . . (at a cost not exceeding twenty thousand dollars)." [13]

The resolution as reported was amended to lengthen the time for the submission of models from sixty days to nine months, setting the deadline as January 1, 1873. It was argued that only artists who had already begun work on their models would be able to meet a sixty day time limit and that by granting more time more artists would be able to compete.[14] (In the middle of December 1872, the date was pushed ahead another month to February 1, 1873.[15])

To assure that the Committee obtain a design "that we shall not be ashamed of," to quote Senator Morrill,[16] a second amendment was adopted on April 5, 1872, which stipulated that the Committee could reject all models if, in its estimation, none of them was "worthy as a tribute of the nation to the naval hero whose memory it is supposed to commemorate." [17] The resolution as amended was approved on April 16, 1872.[18]

By early January 1873, models began to arrive at the Capitol, coming from points as far west as the Pacific coast and as far east as Germany and Italy. In all, thirteen artists competed: Joseph Drischler, Moses Ezekiel (who submitted two models), J. Wilson MacDonald, Fisk Mills, Theodore Mills, C. Ostener, B. M. Pickett, Vinnie Ream, Randolph Rogers, Horatio Stone,[19] Giovanni Turini, Olin

[12] *The Congressional Globe* (42d Congress, 2d Session), pp. 1959–1960.

[13] *Ibid.*

[14] *Ibid.*

[15] *The Congressional Globe* (42d Congress, 3d Session), pp. 294, 339.

[16] *The Congressional Globe* (42d Congress, 2d Session), p. 2061.

[17] *Ibid.*, p. 2206.

[18] *The Congressional Globe: Appendix* (42d Congress, 2d Session), pp. 821–822.

[19] Although disavowing the formal competition, Horatio Stone had his model on display at his studio at the Navy Yard where the Committee came to inspect it. "The Farragut Statue," *Evening Star,* February 18, 1873, p. 1.

Levi Warner and Edward Watson (who submitted only a photograph of his model).

Arranged on scaffolding in a basement corridor in the northeast section of the Capitol building, the models of Farragut were said to present "about as funny a sight as one would desire to see." [20] Most were small, ranging in size from nine inches to just over three feet in height,[21] but in their execution exhibited great diversity. The poses ranged from quiet and contemplative to wildly aggressive, with the skills of the artists covering an equally wide range.

Most of the sculptors emphasized that their models were only "sketches," created to give the idea but not the complete detail of a finished statue. Moses Ezekiel termed it "neither practicable nor customary to produce in a sketch model for a public monument more than the kernel of a future finished production" and urged the Committee to consider only the broad outlines of his model and not its specific details since the "finish of a work of art is in comparison a mechanical process." [22]

Other artists worked diligently to produce as detailed and finished a model as possible. Horatio Stone's model, for example, one of the two heroic-sized entries,[23] was praised by an officer in the Navy as

> a grand conception—grandly carried into effect. Farragut the hero... stands as though amid the din of battle he grasped the situation, and with firm undoubting mein, knew himself the master. In suspended motion—every muscle, every nerve is life itself.[24]

Other Navy officers, including the late Admiral's fleet surgeon, termed the model "true to life" in both "form and figure" and affirmed that the "pose and animated actions, representing Farragut in the moment of giving an order, are also true, and in our judgment, unsurpassed by similar works." [25]

Also impressive was the model submitted by Vinnie Ream. Although badly damaged in transit from her studio at 235 Pennsylvania Avenue to the Capitol building, her eight-foot figure of Farragut was

---

[20] Midge, "Washington," St. Louis *Times,* February 5, [1873], Box 9, Miscellany, Scrapbook 1864–1876, V.R.H.P.

[21] *Ibid.;* and Millard F. Rogers, Jr., *Randolph Rogers: American Sculptor in Rome* (Amherst; The University of Massachusetts Press, 1971), p. 218.

[22] Moses Ezekiel — CPBG, December 1, 1872, SEN 42A-E18, R.G. 46, N.A.

[23] Vinnie Ream was the other.

[24] A Naval Officer, "The Farragut Statue," Letter to the Editor, *National Republican,* February 28, 1873, p. 4.

[25] Capt. Dan'l Ammen, Paymaster Edward T. Dunn, and Surgeon General J. M. Foltz — Nathaniel P. Banks, December 11, 1871, H.R. 2017, R.G. 233, N.A.

able to be repaired and placed on exhibit with the other models.[26] Despite this adversity, her entry received praise from both President Ulysses S. Grant and General William Tecumsah Sherman. Grant termed her model "first rate" [27] and Sherman asserted that it was "decidedly . . . the best likeness and recalled the memory of the Admiral's face and figure more perfectly than any of the models there on exhibition." [28]

The Graphic echoed these sentiments, declaring that in her model, Farragut's

> countenance wears what we can only call a double expression habitual to him, which was produced by the anomaly of a smiling mouth, with forehead and eyes of unusual sternness of expression. The face is alert, yet thoughtful, and the position, erect with one foot resting on a coil of rope, is suggestive of both action and repose.[29]

A Virginia newspaper went so far as to suggest that as the only female contestant, Vinnie Ream should be given the award outright.

> [I]f her male contestants were controlled by a high sense of knight-errantry and true gallantry, such as stimulated the age from which they drew their inspiration, they would retire from the area of rivalry and leave the brave and classic little woman the undisputed claim to the patronage of Congress.[30]

Much of the success of the design of Vinnie Ream's model can be attributed to the naturalness and watchful grace in the pose of Farragut. Artists who attempted to depict the Admiral in more aggressively dramatic poses fared less well. Randolph Rogers, seeking to depict an actual event in Farragut's life, portrayed him as he had appeared during the battle of Mobile Bay—tied to the mast of his ship. Rogers wrote:

> I have represented him [Farragut] as in the *top* and lashed to the mast

---

[26] Her model was accidentally dropped by workmen as it was being transported to the exhibition hall in the Capitol, but the Committee allotted her space in a corridor of the Capitol in which to make repairs. By working night and day, she was able to complete the task by the middle of February. V.V., "The Farragut Models," Boston *Daily Advertiser,* February 12, 1873, Box 8, Miscellany, Scrapbook 1871–1878, V.R.H.P.; VR — CPBG, February 17, 1873, SEN 42A-E18, R.G. 46, N.A.

[27] "A Short Speech by General Grant," [*Evening Star* ?], no date, Box 8, Miscellany, Scrapbook 1871–1878, V.R.H.P.

[28] WTS — Eli Perry, February 18, 1873, Box 1, General Correspondence, 1873, V.R.H.P.

[29] "Miss Ream's Farragut Statue," *The Graphic,* April 30, [1873?], Box 8, Miscellany, Scrapbook 1871–1878, V.R.H.P.

[30] S.M.Y., no title, *The Valley Virginian,* Staunton, Va., December 12, 1872, Box 8, Miscellany, Scrapbook 1871–1878, V.R.H.P.

> with speaking trumpet in his left hand and pointing the way with his right ... I simply wish to convey the idea that he was *lashed aloft,* with his heart bared to the storm of shot and shell, that is the way the people recall him.[31]

Despite Rogers' efforts to achieve historic accuracy, the St. Louis *Times* labeled the pose "too dreadful to contemplate" [32] and the *Evening Star* complained that

> it is not the figure of Farragut or the face either and the position is not a pleasant one to be perpetuated, the Admiral being tied around the waist by a particularly heavy rope to the broken stump of a particularly stout mast.

In place of a national hero, it concluded, Rogers had depicted "martyrdom at the stake." [33] Paradoxically, however, the *Star* also regarded Rogers' model as "[a]rtistically the best and most spirited figure," [34] referring undoubtedly to the technical competence with which the sculptor executed his model and not to the aesthetic quality of the pose. Despite the overly aggressive stance of his model, Rogers' entry did exhibit a quiet refinement in its technical execution which was totally lacking in other models as, for instance, that executed by Edward Watson.

The photograph Watson submitted of his as yet unfinished model demonstrates both his inferiority as a sculptor and designer and his amateurish architectural talent. Concerned primarily with the architectural aspects of his entry, believing "that monuments in public grounds should partake of some degree of architectural beauty," Watson ignored the modeling of his figure of Farragut which resembles a small toy soldier. He channeled his efforts into the construction of a massive and overpowering architectonic pedestal which was to be adorned "with the appropriate inscriptions which will commemorate more of the deeds & character of Admiral Farragut than can be done by allegorical sculpture alone." [35]

---

[31] Randolph Rogers — CPBG, November 25, 1872, SEN 42A-E18, R.G. 46, N.A.

[32] "The Farragut Statue," *Evening Star,* February 3, 1873, p. 1. J. Wilson MacDonald, too, depicted the Admiral lashed to the mast of his ship and his model, too, was labeled "grotesquely absurd" and the artist accused of having depicted "the old sea king ... in acrobatic position on the top of a column holding a rope in the attitude of throwing it to a trapeze performer." In answer to such criticism, however, MacDonald replied that "[h]istory and posterity will look for the 'historical Farragut' and ... in this particular instance nothing will do so well as an active, vigorous figure." Wilson MacDonald — GAH, February 16, 1873, SEN 42A-E18, R.G. 46, N.A.

[33] "The Farragut Statue," *Evening Star,* February 3, 1873, p. 1.

[34] *Ibid.*

[35] Edward Watson — CPBG, January 20, 1873, H.R. 2017, R.G. 233, N.A.

The University of Michigan Museum of Art
Gift of Randolph Rogers

Proposed Monument for Admiral Farragut by Randolph Rogers (1825–1892). Original plaster model, one-third life size.

National Archives

Proposed Monument for Admiral Farragut by Edward Watson.

Similar in overall scheme to the model by Moses Ezekiel,[36] Watson's design merits the same criticism that was leveled against Ezekiel's. Accused of presenting "a good deal of pedestal and precious little Farragut," the latter's model was likened to

> one of those huge pyramid cakes that form centre pieces for wedding and party supper tables. In fact we have often seen genis [sic] of the confectioner's art, that excelled it in grace, symmetry and delicate beauty.[37]

Whatever the artistic abilities of the various sculptors, however, few were confident enough to let their models speak entirely for themselves. Most tried in some way to bolster the appeal of their entry and to win favor with the Committee. Several agreed to alter their models to represent more accurately the character and deeds of the Admiral,[38] to achieve a more accurate likeness,[39] or to eliminate those features for which their models had been criticized.[40] They also

---

[36] By the artist's own description, Ezekiel's model consisted of four allegorical figures, representing Union and Peace in the front and War and Fame in the rear—figures which he proclaimed "convey at once the object of the monument"—several fountains and fourteen steps, all surrounding an elevated figure of Farragut. He had even designed two models of Farragut, but stipulated that "the one in action with mantle" be placed on the pedestal during the exhibition. ME — CPBG, December 1, 1872, SEN 42A-E18, R.G. 46, N.A.

[37] Midge, St. Louis *Times*.

[38] Moses Ezekiel agreed to add to his already busy model scenes in either basso or alto relief "of the most heroic incident in the life of the late Admiral . . . without additional charge" based on the drawings he submitted. H. Ezekiel (Moses' brother) — CPBG, February 21, 1873, SEN 42A-E18, R.G. 46, N.A.

[39] Most of the artists were at a disadvantage when it came to modeling an accurate portrait of the Admiral. Mrs. Farragut generously came to the assistance of two of the artists, lending Vinnie Ream her favorite photograph of the Admiral and Giovanni Turini the "Admiral's costume and parafrenalia [sic]." "Farragut," *Evening Star,* April 25, 1881, p. 1; VLF — VR, November 13, [1872?], SEN 42A-E18, R.G. 46, N.A.; Giovanni Turini — CPBG, December 23, 1872, SEN 42A-E18, R.G. 46, N.A. Randolph Rogers, however, who received no such assistance, wrote to ask the Committee's indulgence. Claiming to have had only "scanty materials" available to him as he prepared his model, he agreed to make alterations to achieve a better likeness if given "the best photograph [of the Admiral] . . . that could be found in America." He made it clear, however, that he stood behind the general design of his model regardless of any minor inaccuracies. "I think my model is more than good," he commented. RR — CPBG, November 25, 1872, SEN 42-A-E18, R.G. 46, N.A.; RR — Henry B. Anthony, November 30, 1872, as reprinted in Millard F. Rogers, Jr., *Randolph Rogers,* p. 130.

[40] Responding to the adverse criticism leveled against his model, Wilson MacDonald assured the Committee that it would be "very easy to make [his figure] less dramatic and to improve it in every way in the next model." He justified the pose of his model, however, asserting that it was "always best to make the sketch vigorous and strong so that the intention of it may be plainly seen." WMcD — GAH, February 16, 1873, SEN 42A-E18, R.G. 46, N.A.

deluged the Committee with letters from prominent persons attesting to their talent as artists and to the superiority of their model.[41]

The greatest number of these testimonials were in support of Vinnie Ream, who had copies of them made, one for each of the Committees, so that she could circulate the originals among her friends and eventually display them in her studio.[42] She was supported by letters from such friends and associates of the late Admiral as the Commander of the United States Navy, S. A. Kimberly; Farragut's Secretary, James E. Montgomery; John J. Cisco; General John A. Dix; and Benjamin H. Fields. Mrs. Farragut also acknowledged in several letters the ability of the young sculptress, remarking in one letter that "I do not think it *possible* your art would accomplish a more perfect work than you have done in delineating the features and expression of my dear husband." [43]

Always ready to help the young sculptress in her efforts to win the approval of the Committee, Mrs. Farragut had faith in the value of her letters supporting her friend, concluding that "nothing further I can do will be of the slightest service." [44] General Sherman, on the other hand, also a close and trusted friend of the sculptress, advocated more aggressive action. On February 20, 1873, he wrote his young friend:

> I think you had better finish the small clay model at your own room, by Monday next and then place it along with the models in the vestibule with a label 'Vinnie Ream'. Don't argue with any of the Committee the reason why you add this small bust to the large model, because it is eloquent in itself and will silence anyone that may attempt to argue

[41] In one such letter, LeB. Gillet acknowledged his support of the model submitted by Olin L. Warner and, since the artist was not well known in the United States at that time, gave a brief account of the sculptor's previous accomplishments abroad, in hope of enhancing Warner's chances with the Committee which he felt would "be slow to give the commission to one who has not already a reputation" in this country. LeB. Gillet — R. H. Duel, January 28, 1873 (forwarded to Halsey), H.R. 2017, R.G. 233, N.A.

[42] This fact was determined by an examination of the records of both the Senate and House Committees as well as from the following sources: J. Hott — VR, February 20, 1873, Box 1, General Correspondence, 1873, V.R.H.P.; J. L. Alavies — VR, February 26, 1873, Box 1, General Correspondence, 1873, V.R.H.P.; "Vinnie Ream," St. Louis *Republican,* June 1, 1878, p. 9, Box 6, Miscellaneous, Miscellany, V.R.H.P.; Harley Quinn, "Vinnie Ream," *The Inter-Ocean,* March 27, 1875, Box 8, Miscellany, Scrapbook, 1871–1878, V.R.H.P.

[43] VLF — VR, November 13, [1872?], SEN 42A-E18, R.G. 46, N.A., This and other testimonials supporting Vinnie Ream are reprinted in Hoxie, *Vinnie Ream,* pp. 31–39. Presumably, however, Mrs. Farragut was basing all of her judgment on the bust of the Admiral that Vinnie Ream had modeled in 1871. When her letter was written, she had not seen the eight foot model. VLF — WTS, July 31, 1874, General Correspondence, Vol. 37, p. 4842, W.T.S.P.

[44] VLF — VR, February 4, 1873, H.R. 2017, R.G. 233, N.A.

National Archives

Sketches by Moses Ezekiel for scenes "of the most heroic incident in the life of the late Admiral" which he offered to add, in either basso or alto relief, to his model of a monument for Farragut.

that a small model [like those submitted by almost everyone else] cannot express a likeness as well as a large one.[45]

The young scuptress apparently had come to the same conclusion on her own, perhaps hoping that the small bust would compensate

[45] WTS — VR, February 20, 1873, Box 1, General Correspondence, 1873, V.R.H.P.

for the damage still visible on her larger model. She had already placed the bust on exhibit by the time she received Sherman's letter.[46]

Not to be outdone, Wilson MacDonald, who, recognizing Vinnie

[46] In a letter to Representative Samuel S. Cox, dated February 20, 1873, the same day as Sherman's letter, Admiral David D. Porter told of seeing the bust on display and commented that "in my opinion, the bust of Miss Vinnie Ream is the only likeness of the Admiral in the lot, and a very good one it is." David D. Porter — Samuel S. Cox, February 20, 1873, Box 1, General Correspondence, 1873, V.R.H.P. Presumably this bust was a copy of the bust Vinnie Ream had modeled of the Admiral in 1871.

Ream as a front runner from the beginning, had vowed that she would not get the commission "without something of a tussle," [47] followed suit with his own bust of Farragut, which he claimed to have modeled in twelve hours "simply to show that it is not a very difficult matter to make a likeness when one has plenty of material from which to work." [48]

With the contestants jockeying for position, the Committee began its deliberations to select the most satisfying model. On February 4, 1873, shortly after most of the models had been installed in the exhibition hall, the Committee heard brief oral presentations from several of the artists or their representatives. Among those who spoke were Ostener, Warner, Turini, Fisk Mills, MacDonald and Ezekiel's brother.[49]

Hopes were high that a winner would be promptly announced, with Vinnie Ream and Horatio Stone considered the most likely candidates for the award. As days went by with no word from the judges, however, it became increasingly clear that they were having difficulty in making a decision. After two weeks, on February 18, the *Evening Star* wrote that it was "not unlikely" that the Committee might follow its prerogative and reject all models.[50]

The vivacious Vinnie Ream, worried by the indecision of the judges, asked Sherman to try to sway two members of the Committee, Senator Cameron and Senator Morrill, to vote in her favor. The General responded that it

> would hardly be right for me to seek out Mr. Cameron and urge him to any definite course of action; but if I see him I will endeavor to do so in such a way as to make him feel that it is his own thought. Men don't like to be *advised,* unless they themselves seek it, but sometimes you can put the proposition so that the thought seems original and then they catch at it like a greedy fish at bait.

---

[47] WMcD — SSC, December 8, 1872, SEN 42A-E18, R.G. 46, N.A.

[48] MacDonald also sent the tools he had used to model the bust. WMcD — Justin S. Morrill, February 27, 1873, SEN 42A-E18, R.G. 46, N.A.

[49] At this time also, the Committee received a letter from Horatio Stone informing them that he was withdrawing from the competition because he could not get his model ready in time. "The Farragut Statue," *Evening Star,* February 4, 1873, p. 1. In view of the fact that Stone had had a model ready for the Committee over a year before, when he first pursued the possibility of a Congressional commission, this letter remains a puzzle. His withdrawal, however, seems to have been more of a protest against competitions in general, which he considered beneath a man of his stature and accomplishment, than an actual refusal to be considered for the Farragut commission, since he did allow the Committee to visit his studio to inspect his model, a gesture which caused open dissension among the other competitors. VINDEX, "The Farragut Statue," Letter to the Editor, *New York Times,* March 10, 1873, p. 5; "The Farragut Statue," *Evening Star,* February 18, 1873, p. 1.

[50] "The Farragut Statue," *Evening Star,* February 18, 1873, p. 1.

He added that perhaps his brother, Senator John Sherman of Ohio, being their colleague, might be in a better position to "say this word." [51]

When the Committee voted on February 27, 1873, Vinnie Ream was still several votes short of winning. Although on firm ground with the House Committee, which selected her as the first choice after only two ballots, she was not able to muster the necessary votes from the Senate Committee, which was deadlocked in a three-way tie among Stone, MacDonald and herself.[52] When a second vote, taken on March 1, two days before the close of the session of Congress, failed to break the stalemate,[53] Chairman Morrill of the Senate Committee reported to his colleagues in the Senate that

> [w]hile the committee are ready to concede that there is considerable merit in many of the models presented, they have not been able to agree that any one is entirely worthy, and therefore . . . reject the whole.[54]

With this announcement, further consideration of the Farragut monument was postponed for nearly a year.[55] The matter was not reopened until February 12, 1874, two months after the new Congress convened. At this time, Wilson MacDonald submitted to the Committee a proposed amendment to the joint resolution passed by the previous Congress. In effect calling for a direct award and an end to further competition, MacDonald's proposal called for the Secretary of the Navy "to contract with Wilson MacDonald Sculptor of New York to execute the statue and pedestal and erect the monument," provided that his model be approved by a special three-member committee composed of the Secretary of the Navy, the Secretary of War, and the Architect of the Capitol.[56] MacDonald assured the Committee that under the terms of this new proposal, "the government

---

[51] WTS — VR, February 25, 1873, Box 1, General Correspondence, 1873, V.R.H.P.

[52] "The Farragut Statue," *Evening Star,* February 27, 1873, p. 1.

[53] "The Farragut Statue," *Evening Star,* March 1, 1873, p. 1.

[54] *The Congressional Globe* (42d Congress, 3d Session), p. 2016. Chairman Halsey made a similar report to the House on March 3, 1873. U. S. Congress, 42d Congress, 3d Session, House Report 97.

[55] The only inquiry into the matter during this period came from sculptor Augustus Saint-Gaudens of New York. He had heard that there was to be a second competition in February 1874 and expressed his desire to compete. Augustus Saint-Gaudens — A. B. Mullett, May 12, 1873, Files of the Office of the Architect of the Capitol. Montgomery Gibbs warned him away from pursuing this course, however, stating: "Don't waste any time modelling a statue of Farragut—nobody will get that to do except a man who can intrigue at Washington." Montgomery Gibbs — ASG, May 22, 1872, as quoted in a letter to the author from John H. Dryfhout, Curator, Saint-Gaudens National Historic Site.

[56] "A joint resolution amending joint resolution of April 16, 1872, relating to a statue of the late Admiral Farragut," [by J. Wilson MacDonald]. SEN 42A-E18, R.G. 46, N.A.

can lose nothing," since in payment he requested only two hundred condemned bronze cannons and "having plenty of time to prepare a model, I can do such an one as will be acceptable." Furthermore, he said, if Congress would act immediately, he could have the statue ready for the Philadelphia Centennial Exhibition to be held in 1876, just two years away.[57]

Although the Committee chose not to accept MacDonald's proposal, it was encouraged to reexamine the terms of the resolution passed by the previous Congress. Less than two weeks after receiving MacDonald's, the Committee drew up a proposal of its own. It delegated to the Secrteary of the Navy the sole responsibility for selecting the artist. It was designed to bypass a choice by Congressional committee and to avoid another stalemate such as that in the previous Congress.[58]

Since Vinnie Ream had no influence with the Secretary of the Navy, George M. Robeson, this proposal was unsatisfactory to her supporters in Congress. They immediately began to work out an arrangement that would be more favorable to her. On March 3, 1874, Representative Godlove Orth of Indiana informed her that her "friends in the House, upon consultation," had agreed to suggest the names of the General of the Army, the Secretary of the Navy, and Mrs. Farragut as "proper persons upon whom to devolve the duty of selecting the artist." He assured her that it was "understood that the Committe having charge of the subject, cordially acquiesce in this suggestion." [59]

Requiring the concurrence of only a majority of the committee members,[60] the proposal was well designed to assure Vinnie Ream the prize, since both General Sherman and Mrs. Farragut were certain to vote for her.[61] To justify this arrangement to the Congress, Representative Stephen W. Kellogg of Connecticut explained that the Joint Committee on Public Buildings and Grounds had chosen the General of the Army

> because he was so intimate with Admiral Farragut and knew him so

[57] WMcD — JSM, February 12, 1874, SEN 42A-E18, R.G. 46, N.A. It is not clear whether MacDonald intended to have his statue displayed in the Philadelphia Exhibition or merely to have it finished by that date.

[58] *The Congressional Record* (43d Congress, 1st Session), (Washington; Government Printing Office, 1874), pp. 2030–2031.

[59] Godlove Orth — VR, March 3, 1874, Box 1, General Correspondence, 1874, V.R.H.P.

[60] *The Congressional Record* (43d Congress, 1st Session), p. 2031.

[61] Mrs. Farragut, who had not yet seen Vinnie Ream's model, reasoned that even should it "fail to please the public . . . it is not in the power of the artist to desecrate the memory of an immortal hero—his true monument is history." VLF — WTS, July 31, 1874, General Correspondence, Vol. 37, p. 4842, W.T.S.P.

Library of Congress

Vinnie Ream working on the plaster model of Farragut at the Washington Navy Yard.

well, and . . . Mrs. Farragut; for if any person on earth ought to know a statue that resembles our great Admiral it should be Mrs. Farragut.[62]

Representative Samuel S. Cox of New York, however, questioned the wisdom of delegating such authority to so untrained a group.

---

[62] *The Congressional Record* (43d Congress, 1st Session), p. 2031.

> Why should the Secretary of the Navy be an especial judge of art? Why should the honored widow of the Admiral Farragut simply decide on the resemblance of a stone statue to her husband, and call it art? Why should General Sherman, who is accomplished in many ways, be an especial judge of art? At least, from this time forward, let us select men who are artists [to decide matters of art].

Cox suggested that the names of two highly respected painters, "Albert Bierstadt and Edward Church," [63] be included on the committee. While not sculptors, these individuals were both "men of rare taste," said Cox, and eminently qualified to judge the intrinsic merit of a work of art. When the proposal came to a vote in the House, however, Cox's suggestion was rejected and Kellogg's adopted.[64]

In the Senate, still another amendment was proposed. This, by Senator Morrill, would have substituted the Admiral of the Navy (David D. Porter) for the General of the Army (William Tecumseh Sherman). Since Porter had praised Vinnie Ream's model in the previous competition, the reason for wishing to substitute him for Sherman, also a supporter of Vinnie Ream, is unclear. Whatever Morrill's reason, when a vote was taken on June 22, 1874, this amendment, too, was rejected.[65]

Although no artist was named in the resolution, it was obvious to everyone, including Secretary Robeson, that Vinnie Ream would be awarded the commission. Robeson, therefore, delayed a vote by his committee. The sculptress once again sought help from her friends in Congress. One whom she contacted, Senator John Ingalls of Kansas, dubbed her "the biggest and most delightful fraud I ever met," but readily agreed to be of assistance. "Nobody eludes you," he chided, "but the laughing old sailor Robeson, and I have no doubt you will conquer that big three decker."[66] Representative Orth, on the other hand, declined, citing the impropriety involved in a member of Congress attempting to influence a Cabinet officer. "In endeavoring to serve," he reasoned, "I might injure your cause." [67] Even Sherman warned against making any rash moves that might antagonize Robeson, declaring that "we must not break with him even if I have to come back all the way from St. Louis." [68]

That, in effect, is what Sherman had to do in order for the com-

---

[63] Cox was probably referring to Frederic Edwin Church. Both Church (1826–1900) and Bierstadt (1830–1900) were primarily landscape artists.

[64] *The Congressional Record* (43d Congress, 1st Session), p. 2031.

[65] *Ibid.*, pp. 5251, 5255, 5336; SFF, "Vinnie Ream," *Daily Star Journal*, Springfield, Ill., July 2, 1874, Box 8, Miscellaneous, Miscellany, V.R.H.P.

[66] John Ingalls — VR, July 15, 1875, Box 1, General Correspondence, 1874, V.R.H.P.

[67] GO — VR, October 11, 1874, Box 1, General Correspondence, 1874, V.R.H.P.

[68] WTS — VR, September 24, 1874, Box 1, General Correspondence, 1874, V.R.H.P.

National Collection of Fine Arts
Smithsonian Institution
Gift of Brigadier General Richard L. Hoxie, 1917

Portrait of Vinnie Ream by George Peter Alexander Healy (1813–1894). Oil on canvas.

mittee to act. In November 1874, Sherman returned to Washington and, on the nineteenth of the month, the three-member committee held its first formal meeting at the Arlington Hotel. From there they visited the various public monuments in and around the city and examined the models for the statue of Farragut "as were already prepared in the city." [69]

[69] "Minutes of the proceedings of the commission on the Farragut Statue," Sen. Ex. Doc. 31, p. 5.

Since Robeson contended that in this second competition, the judges were to choose a sculptor

> by the general and ordinary tests of their executed and known works, cultivated and mature experience, general artistic reputation, and admitted standing and ability in their profession,[70]

this tour of the city's monuments was apparently designed to acquaint the committee members with the work of some of the more prominent sculptors of the day. It seems likely that some artists were considered solely on the basis of their general reputations as artists without any stated interest on their part in receiving the Farragut commission—this in spite of Robeson's statement to both Sherman and Mrs. Farragut that the committee "should not consider the claim or pretensions of any artist who stood on their dignity and claimed that to compete by a model was not artistic." [71] In this group were Joseph Alexis Bailly, Thomas Ball, Larkin G. Meade, Randolph Rogers (who had submitted a model in the initial competition of 1873), William Wetmore Story, John Quincy Adams Ward, "and other distinguished sculptors of the country." [72]

Even among the eight artists who expressed a definite interest in obtaining the commission, it is not clear how many actually submitted models. All eight submitted "propositions," presumably specifications outlining the terms under which the artist would agree to execute the monument, but it is not indicated in them how many of these "propositions" may have been accompanied by models.[73] The eight artists were Henry K. Brown, J. Wilson MacDonald, Clark Mills, E. D. Palmer, Vinnie Ream, Franklin Simmons, Horatio Stone and Launt Thompson, only three of whom, MacDonald, Ream and Stone, had entered the first competition.[74]

When a vote was taken, General Sherman and Mrs. Farragut, as expected, held firm for Vinnie Ream and Secretary Robeson favored Launt Thompson.[75] The Ream model, Robeson declared, had been "substantially rejected" by the Congressional committee and was

[70] Statement of GMR, December 26, 1874, Sen. Ex. Doc. 31, p. 4.

[71] WTS — VR, November 14, 1874, Box 1, General Correspondence, 1874, V.R.H.P.

[72] "Minutes of the proceedings of the commission on the Farragut Statue," Sen. Ex. Doc. 31, p. 5.

[73] Only Vinnie Ream is known for sure to have submitted a model, probably the one submitted in the earlier competition, which the Farragut Committee examined on its tour of the city's monuments. VR, "Proposal," Sen. Ex. Doc. 31, p. 5.

[74] "Minutes of the proceedings of the commission on the Farragut Statue," Sen. Ex. Doc. 31, p. 5.

[75] Launt Thompson was the second choice of both Sherman and Mrs. Farragut. *Ibid.*, p. 6; WTS — GMR, December 23, 1874, Sen. Ex. Doc. 31, p. 3; VLF — GMR, November 20, 1874, Sen. Ex. Doc. 31, p. 4.

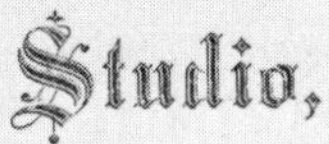

Studio,

235 Pennsylvania Avenue,

Washington, D. C.

If you would be interested in observing the progress thus far attained in my statue of Admiral Farragut, I would be pleased to have you call, and at your early convenience.

Vinnie Ream,

Sculptor.

Columbia Historical Society Collection

An invitation from Vinnie Ream to view in her studio the progress on her statue of Admiral Farragut.

therefore not suitable to be considered by the present committee. In addition, he contended that she did not meet the criteria under which the present group of judges were to select the winner.[76]

Despite Robeson's views, Vinnie Ream had officially won, having been agreed upon by a majority vote. Robeson, however, refused to acknowledge her position and tried to persuade Mrs. Farragut to

[76] Statement of GMR, December 26, 1874, Sen. Ex. Doc. 31, p. 4.

change her vote. The Admiral's widow was unyielding, declaring that "my word is pledged to Miss Ream, who alone deserves the reward of energy even if her model did not excell all." [77] But it was not until January 28, 1875, more than two months after the committee had voted, that the Secretary of the Navy finally capitulated, under pressure from Vinnie Ream's friends in Congress,[78] and agreed to allow the sculptress to sign a contract.

The contract provided that the statue of Farragut was to be ten feet in height, cast in "the best quality bronze," and erected upon a granite pedestal "similar in style and equal in quality" to that supporting the statue of General Winfield Scott at the Soldiers' Home. For her work, the sculptress was to receive $5,000 in advance, $5,000 upon finishing a full plaster model, and $10,000 upon the satisfactory completion of the monument, including the base.[79]

With contract in hand, Vinnie Ream triumphantly set out about her first order of busness—to find a studio large enough to accommodate the massive figure on which she would be working. Not until July 1875 was her search successful and then only at the expense of buying an entire house, the one directly behind her own on Pennsylvania Avenue. By removing the second story floor she was able to create a working area two stories tall[80] and with the aid of scaffolding could have all parts of her model within easy reach.[81]

Although her original model was of heroic proportions, because of the damage it had incurred prior to the initial competition it could not serve as much more than a rough guide in the rendering of the final statue. The construction of a new model required starting virtually from the beginning, although the finished design was said to be an "exact counterpart" of the original, only larger.[82] In modeling the figure, the sculptress labored for two years on the construction of a nude model, making sure that every detail was satisfactorily rendered before attempting to apply the drapery. Convinced that the quality of the nude determined the quality of the work as a whole, she con-

[77] VLF — WTS, January 25, 1873, General Correspondence, Vol. 38, p. 4950, W.T.S.P.

[78] Powell Clayton — VR, January 27, 1875, Box 2, General Correspondence, 1875, V.R.H.P.

[79] "Copy of Contract," Sen. Ex. Doc. 31, pp. 1–2. The suggestion that the pedestal be modeled after that of the Scott was offered by Vinnie Ream in her proposal to Robeson's committee. VR, "Proposal," Sen. Ex. Doc. 31, p. 5.

[80] WTS — VR, August 26, 1875, Box 2, General Corresopndence, 1875, V.R.H.P.; "Vinnie Ream," St. Louis *Republican,* June 1, 1878, p. 9, Box 6, Miscellaneous, Miscellany, V.R.H.P.; "Art Notes," *Evening Star,* April 20, 1878, p. 1.

[81] Emily Edson Briggs in the Philadelphia *Times,* April 25, 1881, as reprinted in Hoxie, *Vinnie Ream,* p. 41.

[82] "Farragut," *Evening Star,* April 25, 1881, p. 1.

tended that the "art of draping is the art of concealing and revealing, and requires refinement of taste and good judgment rather than artistic skill." [83]

Sherman advised her to proceed with caution. Aware that this was to be his friend's first attempt at casting a large statue in bronze, he warned: "Take your time . . . [and do] not hesitate to employ any assistance you may need in the details and drapery." He urged her to consult with Mrs. Farragut "on any and all occasions, and be guided by her judgment." [84]

By October 1877, the statue was "far enough advanced to easily distinguish the features of the old Admiral" [85] and by the following April the *Evening Star* reported that the sculptress expected to have the model ready for the foundry in June and hoped that it would be ready for erection by winter. At that time the clay model had been completed and a plaster model, divided into five sections, made from it.[86] The figure was judged of excellent workmanship and said to be a tribute to the integrity of the committee which had selected Vinnie Ream to execute the monument:

> [T]he Great Naval Captain . . . [stands] on the deck of his flagship, the 'Hartford,' before the capture of New Orleans . . . The face and pose of the old hero combine to tell at once the story of his character and that of the great task before him, and which for the time being commands his soul and all his faculties.[87]

With the model so close to completion, the question of which foundry to entrust with the task of making the bronze casting grew ever more pressing. While there were several, both in the United States and abroad, capable of doing the work, the *Evening Star* emphasized that Vinnie Ream's "patriotic impulse prompts her . . . to have the work done in this country" and predicted that the matter would be decided soon.[88] Despite this prediction and the sculptress'

[83] V[innie] Hoxia [sic], "Sculpture for Women" in *Report of the International Congress of Women,* Vol. 2. June 24–30, 1909 (Toronto: George Parker and Sons, 1910), pp. 355–356.

[84] WTS — VR, February 25, 1875, Box 2, General Correspondence, 1875, V.R.H.P.

[85] "Vinnie Ream," newspaper unknown, October 29, 1877, Box 8, Miscellany, Scrapbook 1871–1878, V.R.H.P.

[86] The figure was divided as follows: "The head separates from the neck or body just below the line of the coat collar; the body in turn is divided laterally under the sword-belt, while the legs are cut in the same way just within the lower part of the coat skirts. In addition to these divisions, the large glass is removable." "Art Notes," *Evening Star,* April 20, 1878, p. 1.

[87] *Ibid.*

[88] *Ibid.*

desire to have the casting started by the summer of 1878, no decision was made for more than a year.[89]

In mid-1879, it was decided to have the work done at the foundry of the Washington Navy Yard. Since the Navy Yard had never before cast an object of this size and nature,[90] her choice seems an unusual one and it may have been influenced by her marriage in May 1878 to Lieutenant Richard L. Hoxie. Assigned to the Corps of Engineers in Washington, Hoxie was familiar with the operations at the Yard and may have suggested it to his wife. In any case, she made her own arrangements, submitting a formal request to the Secretary of the Navy, then Robert W. Thompson, in June 1879. She advised Thompson that she had "conferred with the Naval officers at the Yard, and find that they have ample facilities and are desirous of undertaking the work." In making the request, she agreed to accept "the usual conditions" that the work be done at her own expense "and without prejudice to the current work at the Navy Yard." [91]

The request was granted on July 28, 1879[92] and the sculptress assigned a studio in the Dahlgren Ordnance Building with several men to assist her.[93] To facilitate the casting, her ten foot plaster model of Farragut was surrounded by a moveable platform, operated by a giant block and tackle attached to the overhead beams. Here the sculptress supplied the finishing touches to her model to the delight of the sailors at the Yard who followed the progress with great enthusiasm. One admirer even embroidered a sailor's cap for her to wear as she worked.

At the suggestion of the Engineer in Chief at the Navy Yard, Willam H. Shock, the bronze for the casting came from the propellors of the Admiral's flagship *Hartford* and was used for both the statue

---

[89] This delay was probably due in part to her concurrent involvement in other projects. While working on the Farragut she was also working on busts of Senator David Davis of Illinois, the Honorable L. Q. C. Lamar, General George A. Custer and Captain J. B. Eades. *National Republican,* no date, no title, Box 8, Miscellany, Scrapbook 1871–1878, V.R.H.P.

[90] "Farragut," *Evening Star,* April 25, 1881, p. 1.

[91] VRH — Robert W. Thompson, June 9, 1879, Records of the Secretary of the Navy, Miscellaneous Letters Received, Microfilm Publication M124, Roll, 609, Letter 354, R.G. 45, N.A.

[92] RWT — James C. Febiger, July 28, 1879, Naval Records Collection of the Office of Naval Records and Library, Subject File NH, Box 242, R.G. 45, N.A. Hereafter this collection will be indicated N.R.C.

[93] William H. Shock, Chief of the Bureau of Steam Engineering at the Navy Yard, was assigned to supervise the procedure while the work was cast under the specific direction of the Chief Engineer, William B. Brooks, with the assistance of Samuel Gelston, foreman of the foundry. Briggs in Hoxie, *Vinnie Ream,* p. 40.

National Archives

Proposed improvement in base of Farragut Statue, approved and signed by Alexander Ramsey, Acting Secretary of the Navy, and Viriginia L. Farragut, December 22, 1880.

and the mortars adorning the pedestal. A Frenchman named Stinach was hired to make the mould for the casting. He felt that an extremely fine grade of sand, one not readily available in this country, was required and arrangements were made to have the sand shipped from

France. He chose also to cast the figure in six sections rather than five as the sculptress had anticipated.[94]

The adjustments to the plaster statue, begun in the fall of 1879, were carried out simultaneously with work on the pedestal which, in accordance with the specifications in the contract, was patterned after the pedestal of the Scott monument at the Soldiers' Home. In January 1880, the sculptress wrote the Secretary of the Navy that the granite for the pedestal had been cut and the casting in bronze was "now in progress." She predicted that both would be ready by March 1880.[95] As it turned out, however, the casting took nine months and the statue was not ready for installation until September.[96]

In anticipation of the installation, Farragut Square, the site designated for the monument, one of the seventeen original parks provided for in L'Enfant's plan for the city, which had been named for the Admiral shortly after his death in 1870, had been extensively landscaped with trees and flowering plants. At the time the statue was installed on September 29, 1880, the Square was the handsome center of one of the most fashionable sections of the city.[97] The monument, placed in an ellipse in the center of the square, was designed to face southeast toward Lafayette Park and the White House just two blocks away. Elevated on a pedestal of smooth granite approximately seven feet square and twelve feet high, the heroic sized figure of Farragut was covered with sail cloth to await its official unveiling.[98]

It soon became apparent, however, that the base was "wholly insufficient and inadequate in size for the proper presentation" of the statue, and Congress was urged to appropriate supplementary funds

---

[94] The statue was divided into six sections as follows: head and shoulders together; each arm separately; lower torso, legs and plinth together; sword; and the marine glass. "Farragut," *Evening Star,* April 25, 1881, p. 1; no title, no date, *Evening Star,* Box 9, Miscellany, Scrapbook 1864–1876, V.R.H.P.

[95] VRH — RWT, received January 13, 1880, Records of the Secretary of the Navy, Miscellaneous Letters Received, Microfilm Publication M124, Roll 613, Letter 84, R.G. 45, N.A.

[96] "Farragut," *Evening Star,* April 25, 1881, p. 1; Briggs in Hoxie, *Vinnie Ream,* p. 40.

[97] George J. Olszewski, *Farragut Square* (Washington: United States Department of the Interior, 1968), pp. 3–6; United States Office of Public Buildings and Grounds, *Annual Report of the Chief of Engineers,* 1870–1871 (Washington: Government Printing Office, 1871), p. 978; *ARCE, 1873,* p. 5; *ARCE, 1877, Appendix KK1,* p. 8, *Appendix KK2,* p. 10. In 1879, shortly after their marriage, the sculptress and her husband built a house at 1632 K Street overlooking Farragut Square. For an account of the military career of her husband, Richard L. Hoxie (1844–1930), see Roland M. Brennan, "Brigadier General Richard L. Hoxie, United States Army, 1861–1930," *Records of the Columbia Historical Society of Washington, D.C. 1957–1959* (1961), pp. 87–95.

[98] "The Farragut Statue," *Evening Star,* September 29, 1880, p. 1.

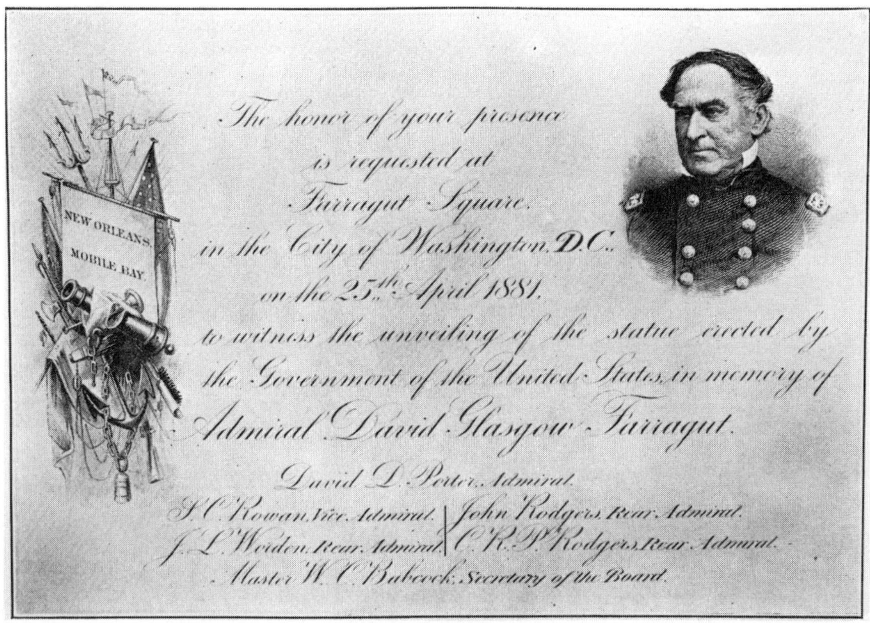

The honor of your presence
is requested at
Farragut Square.
in the City of Washington, D.C.
on the 25th April 1881.
to witness the unveiling of the statue erected by
the Government of the United States, in memory of
Admiral David Glasgow Farragut.

David D. Porter, Admiral.
S. C. Rowan, Vice Admiral. | John Rodgers, Rear Admiral.
J. L. Worden, Rear Admiral. | C. R. P. Rodgers, Rear Admiral.
Master W. C. Babcock, Secretary of the Board.

Vinnie Ream. Printed for private distribution. Press of Gibson Bros., Washington, D.C., 1908

An invitation to attend the unveiling of the Farragut Monument on April 25, 1881.

for the construction of an additional pedestal. The matter was referred to the Committee on Naval Affairs,[99] which on December 21, 1880, approved an additional $5,000 to raise the height of the pedestal nine feet. The problem, as explained by Representative Benjamin W. Harris of Massachusetts, was that the difference in topography between Farragut Square and the location of the statue of General Scott at the Soldiers' Home had not been sufficiently considered when the decision was made to pattern the pedestal for the Farragut on that of the Scott. The Scott monument stood on the crest of a natural rise, unlike the level site in Farragut Square, with the result that the Farragut monument appeared too close to the ground. Harris hastened to add that the fault lay with the government and not with the sculptress whose responsibility was only for the figure of Admiral Farragut.[100]

Plans for an addition to the pedestal, to be composed of three tiers

[99] *The Congressional Record* (46th Congress, 3d Session), p. 16.

[100] *Ibid.*, pp. 27–28. Nevertheless, Vinnie Ream was the one to suggest that the Scott pedestal serve as the model for the Farragut.

of large blocks of rough-hewn granite,[101] were approved by the Acting Secretary of the Navy, General Sherman and Mrs. Farragut[102] and arrangements made for the additional granite to be shipped from a quarry in Rockland, Maine.[103]

Pending the arrival of the granite, revised plans were made for the dedication ceremonies. Originally scheduled to coincide with the Presidential Inauguration on March 4, 1881, the unveiling was rescheduled for April 25, the anniversary of the surrender of New Orleans to Farragut.[104]

Informing the sculptress of the change,[105] Admiral David D. Porter, the head of the Board of Admirals in charge of the arrangements for the ceremonies, explained:

> We don't want to make the ceremonies in honor of Admiral Farragut secondary to anything else . . . . whatever honors are shown will be to the memory of Farragut and will not be mixed up with any political affair. . . . Give yourself no uneasiness about your statue not being seen by an appreciative assembly. There will be one hundred thousand people to witness the ceremonies and the 25th of April will always be remembered as the great Farragut day.[106]

These sentiments were echoed in the press. As early as April 1, the local newspapers began announcing the plans for the parade route. Soon details regarding the ceremony appeared and, on April 8, the *Washington Post* predicted "Everything Indicative of a Great Time at the Unveiling.[107]

The only serious concern was that the granite for the base was late in arriving. It did not arrive until the twentieth of the month, only five days before the scheduled unveiling. In order that the dedication might proceed as planned, Lieutenant Hoxie assumed command and, with a crew of specially selected men working around the clock, was able to assemble the base and erect the statue by the morning of the ceremony.[108]

---

[101] The addition to the pedestal was the design of William H. Shock at the Navy Yard. VRH — Alexander Ramsey, no date, N.R.C., R.G. 45, N.A.

[102] Mrs. Farragut and the Acting Secretary of the Navy Alexander Ramsey signed the design of the proposed improvement to the base of the statue on December 22, 1880; Sherman signed an identical copy on January 1, 1881. N.R.C., R.G. 45, N.A.

[103] "Farragut," *Evening Star,* April 25, 1881, p. 1.

[104] DDP — VRH, January 28, 1881, Box 2, General Correspondence, 1880 [sic], V.R.H.P.

[105] Vinnie Ream Hoxie, who favored the March 4 date, also wanted a hand in determining the speakers for the ceremonies. VRH — AR, no date, N.R.C. R.G. 45, N.A.

[106] DDP — VRH, January 28, 1881, Box 2, General Correspondence, 1880 [sic], V.R.H.P.

[107] "Farragut Statue," *Washington Post,* April 8, 1881, p. 2.

[108] "Farragut," *Evening Star,* April 25, 1881, p. 1.

UNVEILING THE STATUE OF ADMIRAL FARRAGUT AT WASHINGTON YESTERDAY.

Columbia Historical Society Collection

"Unveiling the statue of Admiral Farragut at Washington yesterday," illustration from *The Daily Graphic,* New York, April 26, 1881.

Vinnie Ream. Printed for private distribution.
Press of Gibson Bros., Washington, D.C., 1908

Admiral Farragut Monument, Farragut Square, Washington, D.C., an early photograph.

Expectations were high as the hour of the unveiling approached. The streets were filled with throngs of colorfully dressed military personnel, many of whom had been assigned to Washington in honor of the occasion. Homes along the parade route and those bordering Farragut Square were festively draped with the national colors. At noon, Federal and city government employees were excused from their work.

The festivities got underway with a large and impressive procession, composed largely of members of the United States Navy, which began to form, appropriately enough, at the Naval Monument near the Capitol. From there, it moved slowly and regally down Pennsylvania Avenue, passed the White House, to Farragut Square. At the site of the unveiling, temporary stands seating between three and four thousand invited guests surrounded the statue on three sides and the general public massed around the perimeter of the park. Among those present were President and Mrs. James A. Garfield; Mrs. Farragut (the house guest of the Garfields); Vinnie Ream Hoxie; the Secretary of the Navy, William H. Hunt, the master of ceremonies; the survivors of Farragut's old commands; and numerous other military and civilian dignitaries. After a brief prayer by Rev. Arthur Brooks, the statue was unveiled by Quartermaster Knowles assisted by Boatswain James Wiley, both members of Admiral Farragut's crew. As the flag draping the statue was lifted, the Marine band played "Hail to the Chief," the drums rolled, and a seventeen gun salute was fired by a naval battery stationed in Lafayette Square.[109]

Accepting the statue for the country, President Garfield stressed the monument's value as a guide for future generations. "It is the singular province of art," he declared

> to break down the limitations which separate the generations of men from each other and allow those of past generations to be comrades and associates with those now living . . . . these heroes come by the ministry and mystery of art, to take their places and stand as the permanent guardians of our Nation's glory.[110]

Similar sentiments were voiced by the two other speakers, former Postmaster General Horace Maynard and Senator Daniel W. Voorhees of Indiana.[111]

[109] For accounts of the ceremonies see: "Farragut," *Evening Star,* April 25, 1881, p. 1; "The Man of the Day," *Washington Post,* April 25, 1881, pp. 1, 4; "Farragut Statue," *Washington Post,* April 26, 1881, pp. 1, 2; "Admiral Farragut's Statue," *New York Times,* April 25, 1881, p. 1; "The Statue of Farragut," *New York Times,* April 26, 1881, p. 2; other accounts are excerpted in Hoxie, *Vinnie Ream,* pp. 40–55.

[110] As printed in the *New York Tribune,* April 26, 1881 and reprinted in Hoxie, *Vinnie Ream,* p. 51.

[111] *Ibid.,* pp. 52–54.

Department of the Interior,
National Park Service, National Capital Parks

Admiral Farragut Monument, Farragut Square, Washington, D.C.

After nearly ten years of planning and preparation, the heroic sized statue of the Admiral was now on public view. With a marine glass in his hand and his foot resting on a block and tackle, the figure of Farragut stood on its original pedestal of smooth granite, surrounded at the four corners by cubes of rough-hewn granite supporting four bronze mortars. Supporting this was the addition to the pedestal, also of rough-hewn granite, whose tiered arrangement formed a base twenty feet wide on each side.

Measuring nearly thirty feet from its base to the top of the Admiral's head, the monument drew praise for its fine portraiture. "The expression is thoroughly characteristic, resolute, watchful, reliant" and the memorial "most noble and impressive," wrote the *Evening Star*.[112] "It is simply Farragut," observed the journalist Mary Clemmer Ames. "Not idealized, or sublimated, or artistically heroic; but just the man himself—alert, vigilant, strong-eyed, strong-nerved, compact."[113]

Somewhat less praise has been accorded the monument by later critics. Adeline Adams judged the work only "fairly representative of the average of its day" [114] and Lorado Taft, in his well known book on American sculpture, lamented the fact that the young sculptress was granted this, her second commission, after so little formal artistic schooling. "With proper training and sufficient continuity of purpose," he wrote, "she might have won something more substantial than notoriety." [115]

While the Farragut commission, like the Lincoln commission, brought Vinnie Ream notoriety, the monument is not without its artistic appeal. It cannot be denied, however, that the young sculptress was selected to construct the memorial to Admiral Farragut at least as much because of the devoted efforts of her many friends in official Washington as because of her own artistic ability. Personal ambition and loyalties often blinded those involved to more important artistic considerations with the result that today her Farragut monument is at least as significant as a political achievement as it is as an artistic achievement.

[112] "Farragut," *Evening Star*, April 25, 1881, p. 1.

[113] Mary Clemmer Ames in the New York *Independent*, May 5, 1881, as reprinted in Hoxie, *Vinnie Ream*, p. 47.

[114] Adams, *DAB*, p. 317.

[115] Lorado Taft, *The History of American Sculpture* (New York: The Macmillan Company, 1903, reprinted 1930), p. 212.

Alley Life in Washington: An Analysis of 600 Photographs

JAMES BORCHERT

I would like to preface my paper with an apology. The alley experience I am going to discuss is much too diverse and varied to be fully covered in the time allotted to me here. As well, the problems of gaining reliable information on that experience are so obvious and monumental that what I have to say should be considered only as very tentative.

Several years ago, Harvard psychiatrist Robert Coles recorded a statement by Peter, a nine-year-old Boston alley resident, that makes an excellent introduction to the paper:

> In the alley it's mostly dark, even if the sun is out. But if you look around, you can find things. I know how to get into every building, except it's like night once you're inside them, because they don't have lights. So, I stay here. You're better off. It's no good on the street. You can get hurt all the time, one way or the other. And in buildings, like I told you, it's bad in them, too. But here it's O.K. You can find your own corner, and if someone tries to move in you fight him off. We meet here all the time, and figure out what we'll do next. It might be a game, or over for some pool, or a coke or something. You need to have a place to start out from, and that's like it is in the alley; you can always know your buddy will be there, provided it's the right time. So you go there, and you're on your way, man.[1]

Houses in alleys in Washington date back to the 1850's. They were the result of an expanding population and the lack of an adequate transportation system and technology to permit dispersal of the population. The pressures created by this situation led to more intensive land use. In New York City, where the pressures were much more in-

---

Mr. Borchert's paper "A Demographic and Photographic Analysis of Alley Life" was delivered at the First Annual Conference on Washington, D.C. Historical Studies, sponsored by the Columbia Historical Society and George Washington University, January 11, 1974.

[1] Quoted in Robert Coles, "Like It Is in the Alley," *Daedalus* 97 (Fall 1968), 1315.

tense, this led to tenements that covered 90 percent of a lot. In Washington, where such pressure was weaker, it resulted in the construction of small houses located on alleys at the rear of large lots. Initially these houses were no more than shacks or sheds rented to the laboring classes of the city. Very soon, however, more substantial dwellings were constructed, either frame or brick two-story row houses. These latter structures became the predominate form of alley house.

Prior to the Civil War, alley housing existed on a limited scale with only 348 heads of household reported in 49 alleys. The residents were, for the most part, white laborers. The rapid population growth resulting from the Civil War greatly increased the numbers of inhabited alleys. By 1871, the city directory reported nearly 1,500 heads of households residing in 118 alleys. The great migration of Freedmen during and after the Civil War, however, reversed the racial make-up of the alleys. While 65 percent of alley residents in 1858 were white, by 1871, 81 percent were black. The great majority of alley dwellers, however, remained unskilled and service workers.

The number and size of inhabited alleys continued to grow throughout the last half of the Nineteenth Century. The Police Census of 1897 reported the total alley population of the Federal City at 17,244 (11 percent of the city's population) residing inside 237 blocks. These inhabited alleys ranged in size from one or two families to more than 400 people. Blacks increased their domination of the alleys, making up 93 percent of the alley population.

A number of forces, however, began to impinge on alley houses from the turn of the century on. The construction of a trolley in the 1890's permitted the beginnings of population dispersal, while a ban on alley house construction stopped further building. Housing reformers, business encroachment on alley land, and the need for automobile garages increasingly diminished the number of alley houses. By 1970, the city directory listed only 20 inhabited alleys with a total of 192 heads of household. The "restoration" of "Foggy Bottom" and Capitol Hill, however, begun in the 1940's, considerably altered the nature of alley residents, with almost half such residents now being middle-class professionals.[2]

Two broad generalizations can be drawn from the popular, reform, and scholarly literature on alley dwellers. As William Henry Jones

[2] This brief history of alley dwelling in Washington is based on my article in the preceding volume of the *Records*. James Borchert, "The Rise and Fall of Washington's Inhabited Alleys: 1852–1972," *Records of the Columbia Historical Society of Washington, D.C. 1971–1972* (1973), 267–288.

THE
BLIND ALLEY OF WASHINGTON, D.C.
SECLUSION BREEDING CRIME AND DISEASE
to kill the alley inmates and infect the street residents.

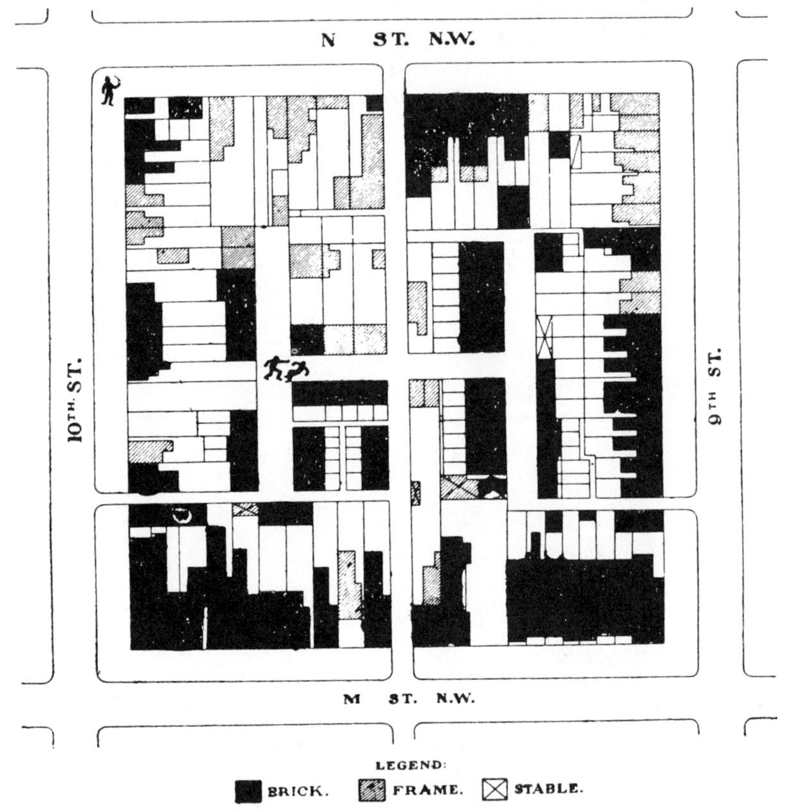

Conversion into minor streets is the effective remedy for the larger alleys.

Complete elimination of dwelling houses is the cure for the smaller alleys.

From Directory of Inhabited Alleys of Washington, D. C., Monday Evening Club, Washington, D.C., 1912

This 1912 drawing is typical of the reformer and scholarly material of the period on the dangers of alley dwellings.

observed in his study of *The Housing of Negroes in Washington, D.C.*, "So closely have the terms *Alleys* and *Negroes* been associated, that in the minds of the older citizens they are inseparable." Secondly, as Jones again observed, "The alleys represent the poorest and least resourceful section of Washington and foster a large percentage of its crime, poverty, disease, immorality and high rate of infant mortality." Illegitimacy, family disorganization, crime and violence were considered the key pathological features of alley life.[3]

The first widely held view, as we have seen, was incorrect. Whites were the first residents of the alleys and continued to reside in alleys, although on a limited scale until recent years. Given this correction, it is perhaps time to reassess the nature of alley life and culture as well.

I would like to begin this tentative reassessment by looking at a twelve block area in Northwest Washington in 1880, based on the manuscript census of that year.[4] The scope will then be expanded to include alley life generally through an analysis of 600 photographs taken by housing reformers from 1900 to 1945, and by drawing on more traditional historical sources.[5] (I might note that these photographs were taken to "prove" the evil alley conditions and the disorganized alley life).[6]

[3] William Henry Jones, *The Housing of Negroes in Washington, D.C.* (Washington, 1929), 40, 46. Several examples of other studies suggest the near universal response of writers on this second point. Ernest Culbertson subtitled his 1922 play *Goat Alley* "A Tragedy of Negro Life." Ernest Culbertson, *Goat Alley* (Cincinnati, Ohio, 1922). Similarly, housing reformers noted that besides the threat of disease from unsanitary alley conditions, there was a far greater danger of fostering crime "by the sure degradation attendant . . . upon blind alleys . . . beyond the pale of decency and morality." Clare de Graffenried, "Typical Alley Houses in Washington," The Woman's Anthropological Society of Washington, D.C., *Bulletin*, 7 (November 14, 1896), 7. Associated Charities Secretary Charles Weller found it "evident that alley houses lack privacy, lack provision for making family life distinct, and a constant seething 'mixup of the population.'" Charles Weller, *Neglected Neighbors* (Philadelphia, 1909), 69. Lastly, a participant-observation study conducted by a doctoral student in the 1930's was entitled, *A Deviant Social Situation: A Court*. Glady Sellew, *A Deviant Social Situation: A Court* (Washington, 1938).

[4] This analysis is based on a larger study conducted by the author. James Borchert, "Race and Place: A Historical Community Study" (unpublished manuscript, 1972).

[5] This analysis is based on a larger study conducted by the author under the direction of anthropologist-film-maker Dr. E. Richard Sorenson of the National Institutes of Health. James Borchert, "Photographs and the Study of the Past" (unpublished manuscript, 1973). These 600 photographs came from a variety of sources: "D.C. Street Survey Collection," the "Farm Security Administration Collection," and the "National Child Labor Commission Collection" at the Library of Congress; "The Lewis Wickes Hine Collection" at the George Eastman House; "The John Ihlder Collection" in the Franklin D. Roosevelt Library; and the National Capital Housing Authority as well as a number of published sources.

[6] The result of this approach was that the photographs were taken of the most "disorganized" and squalid conditions that the photographer-reformers could find. Thus it can be assumed that other alleys and houses reflected no worse conditions and were probably considerably better.

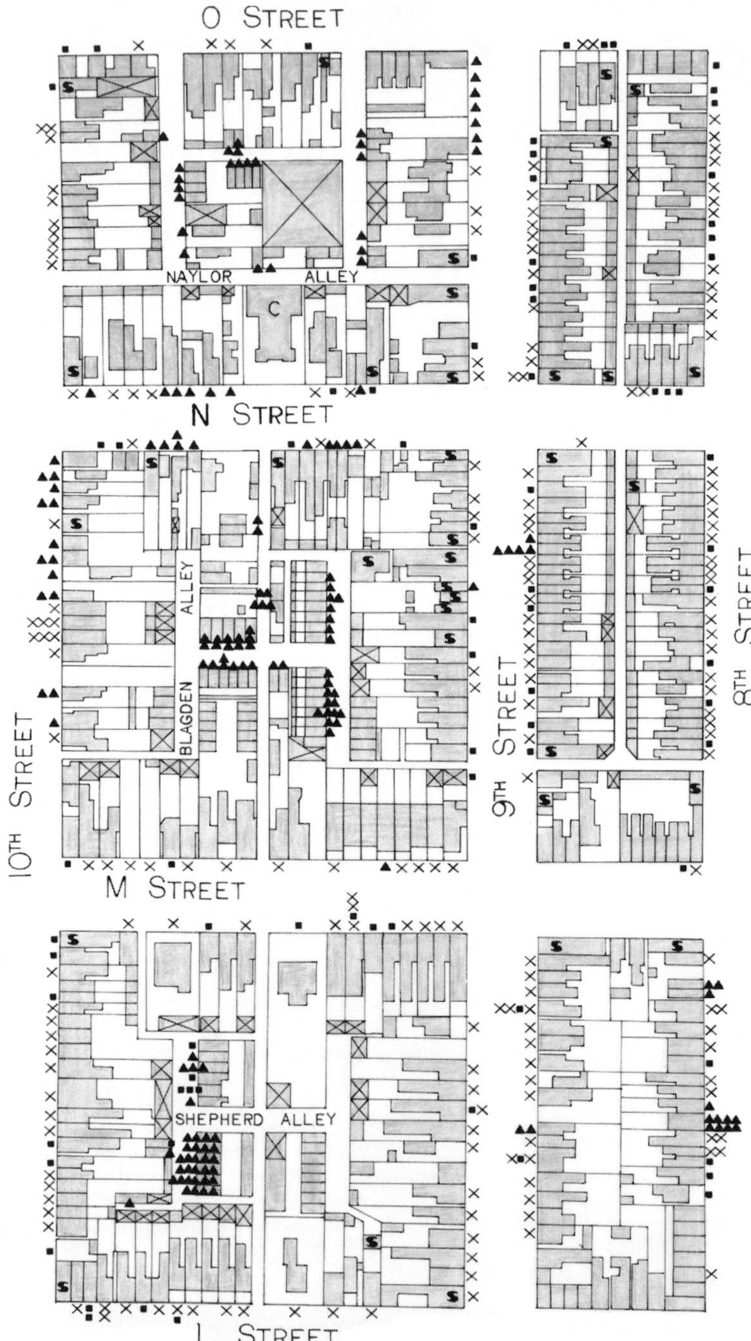
O STREET
NAYLOR
ALLEY
C
N STREET
ALLEY
BLAGDEN
10TH STREET
9TH STREET
8TH STREET
M STREET
SHEPHERD ALLEY
L STREET
S

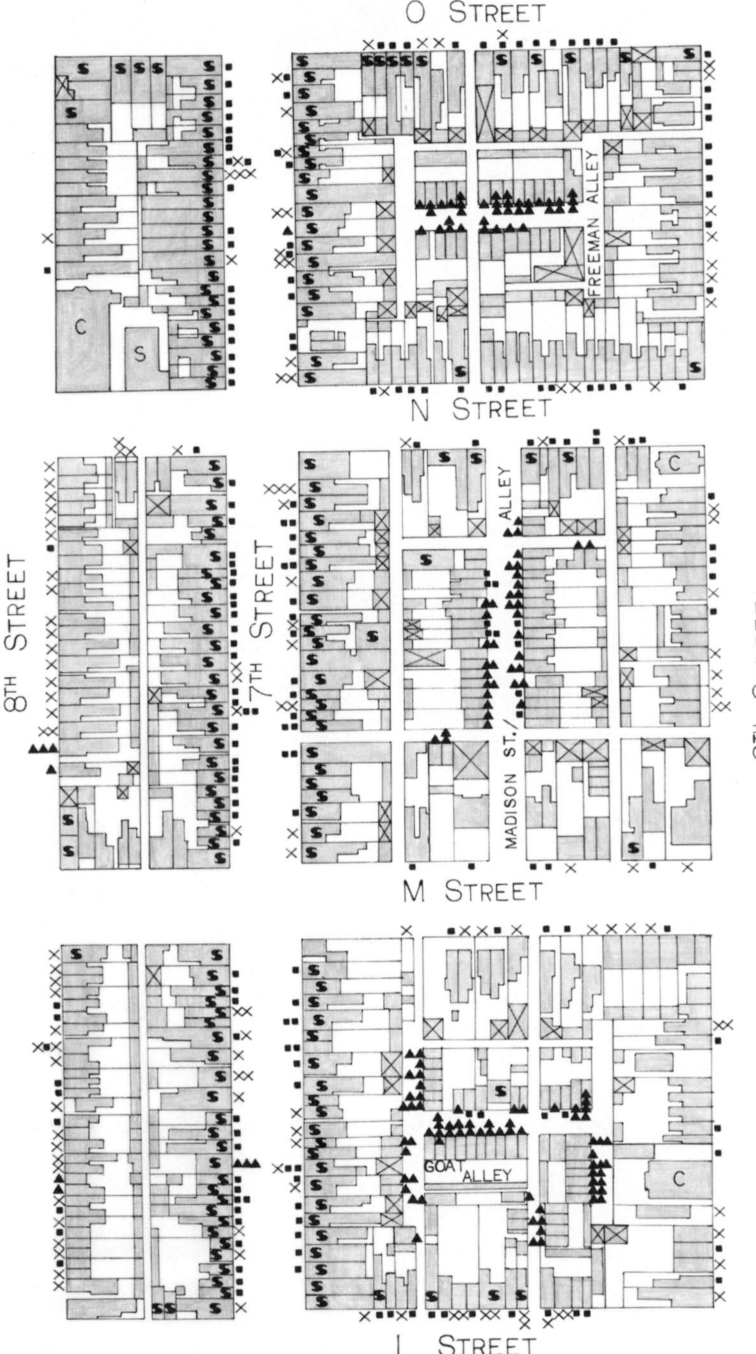
O STREET
N STREET
M STREET
L STREET
8TH STREET
7TH STREET
6TH STREET
FREEMAN ALLEY
ALLEY
MADISON ST./
GOAT ALLEY

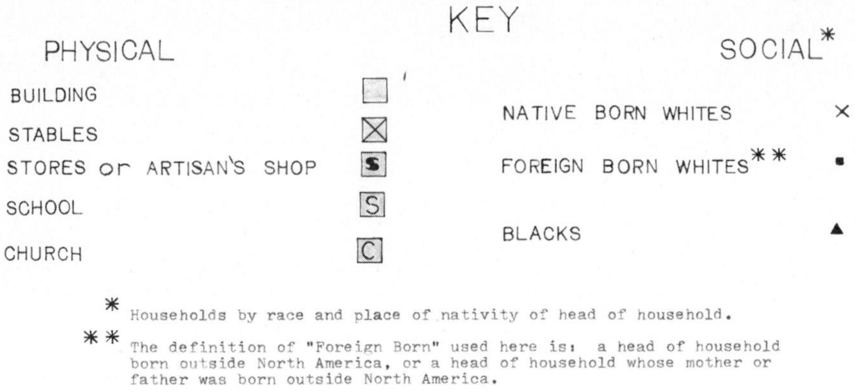

KEY

PHYSICAL		SOCIAL*	
BUILDING	□	NATIVE BORN WHITES	×
STABLES	⊠	FOREIGN BORN WHITES**	▪
STORES or ARTISAN'S SHOP	[S]	BLACKS	▲
SCHOOL	[S]		
CHURCH	[C]		

* Households by race and place of nativity of head of household.

** The definition of "Foreign Born" used here is: a head of household born outside North America, or a head of household whose mother or father was born outside North America.

Map by the author

Map of the sample area studied, between 6th and 10th Streets, L and O Streets, N.W., immediately north of Mount Vernon Square.

Map of area based on *Insurance Maps of Washington, D.C.*, Sanborn Map Publishing Company, New York, 1888, 21. Demographic data based on Record Group 29, Federal Population Census Schedules, 1880, Washington, D. C., Volume 2, Part 2.

The area I chose to study is immediately north of Mount Vernon Square—between 6th and 10th, L and O Streets Northwest. In 1880 these twelve blocks housed nearly 5,000 people. While it was largely a residential area for native born whites and blacks, 7th Street was lined with small shops and stores with the proprietors, many foreign born, living above their place of work. As with the city's population, this area was two-thirds white and one-third black. Although this might suggest considerable integration in housing, in fact the area was highly segregated. Inside the six large blocks were inhabited alleys, Naylor, Blagden, Shepherd, Freeman, Madison and Goat alleys, which housed one quarter of the area's population. Of these alley dwellers 93 percent were black, while of the street residents 91 percent were white. Although a number of blacks, including Mississippi Senator Blanche K. Bruce, owned houses or stores on the streets, the vast majority of black residents of this area lived in the alleys or in a peripheral settlement on 9th Street. This latter group of houses had disappeared by 1888.

The street-alley differences go far beyond racial differences, however. Street dwellers, both white and black, tended to be employed in skilled, white-collar, proprietorial or managerial occupations, with a few professions also represented. Alley dwellers were employed almost entirely—82 percent—in unskilled or service occupations. In contrast to the view of housing reformers who often considered alley residents as indolent, more than 45 percent of the alley population was employed, while of their more affluent street neighbors only 35 percent were employed.

More alley families were headed by a single adult than were street families, but the conclusion that alley families were disorganized does not hold up. The majority of families on both alley and street were nuclear, male headed families. The alley family tended to be younger and smaller than their street counterparts.

Crowding and congestion represent another significant difference between alley and street. While nearly every street dwelling was at least twice the size of the 12 by 20 foot two-story alley house, alley houses averaged over seven persons per house to six for the street. Similarly alley houses averaged nearly two households per house while the street dwellings averaged just over one family.

There was greater similarity in place of birth with 45 percent of both alley and street residents having been born in the city; 50 percent of the alley and 34 percent of the street dwellers were born in neighboring states. Over 50 percent of the alley dwellers had been residents of the city for five years or more. This stands in sharp contrast to the view of reformers who felt alley residents were recent migrants from rural areas who had little understanding of city life. It also compares favorably with the length of city residence of street dwellers.

A composite picture of an alley dwelling family is: a black family, headed by a male between the ages of 18 and 30 who is employed as a laborer. His wife is employed as a servant and they have two to three small children. They have lived in the city longer than five years and share their two-story, two room, brick rowhouse with another family.

Perhaps only a hundred feet away, on the street, a street family is, in a composite picture: white, headed by an older, native born male between the ages of 40 and 49. He is employed as a white collar or skilled worker. His wife stays home to take care of the two- to three-story, brick rowhouse and raise their three to four teenage children.

Although these two families lived close to one another, their contacts were limited. While the street house faced out on the street, the alley house faced in the opposite direction onto the alley. As photographs and fire insurance maps document, the entrance to the interior alley was often obscure and at best unobtrusive, ranging from three to twelve feet wide. Few houses were built on this narrow alley that bisected the block. Most houses were constructed on the blind, thirty-foot H-shaped alley in the interior of the block. This alley and the houses on it were not visible from the street. Because fences and sheds were often located at the back of both the alley and street house,

Farm Security Administration Collection, Library of Congress

Photograph by Ed Rosskam. "Family and their home in an alley dwelling, July 1941."

neither resident was likely to know or interact with his backyard neighbor. The differences in race and class furthered this separation. Alley residents were isolated from their neighbors on the street and from any others who were unaware of the alley entrance or of what lay beyond it.

Despite the claims of housing reformers, many alley houses were well constructed. This is especially true of the brick rowhouses, some of which compare favorably to dwellings on the street. There was, however, wide variation in maintenance by landlords, none of whom were alley residents.

One universal alley feature did account for an indisputable alley problem. The high levels of illness and mortality from certain diseases, often twice that for street dwellers, were directly related to unsanitary and improperly functioning outhouses. These unsanitary outhouses, often located close to the outdoor water hydrant in the tiny backyards, provided excellent breeding grounds for disease. Outdoor plumbing also added an extra hardship for the many alley women who earned their income by doing washing. In some alleys there was only one water hydrant, while in a few it was necessary to go several blocks to obtain water for cooking and washing.

Heat for cooking and heating was provided by wood or coal stoves. Usually there was a stove in each room, whether there were one or two rooms per floor. Common features of the kitchen were large wash boards and buckets and numerous irons used for washing and ironing clothes. While only twelve percent of the females in the 1880 sample were employed as washer-women, the large numbers of irons that appear in kitchen photographs suggest that a higher percentage of these women were probably involved in "commercial washing."

Interior furnishings and their arrangement show little of the disorganization that reformers and scholars allege. While there is wide variation in the quality of furniture, from very ornate and fine pieces to the more common and well used, all show care and concern both with their maintenance and with their placement. Given the limited space in the tiny houses and the overcrowding, much of the furniture had to serve multiple purposes. There are numerous examples of ingenious conversions of single purpose furniture to multiple uses, such as trunk-beds and couch beds. Interiors were kept clean and orderly and often pictures graced the walls. One study reported an average of three pictures per household and these ranged from reproductions of Raphael's "Madonna and Child," DeVinci's "Last Supper," and Gainsborough's "Blue Boy," to calendars with religious or animal motifs and photographs of children.[7]

Perhaps the most interesting aspect of a reassessment of alley life and culture is that which extends beyond the family unit to consider the extent of community organization within the alley. Sociologists have developed two different requirements for neighboring and community to exist: homogeneity[8] and residential proximity.[9] Census data strongly confirms the existence of homogeneity among alley dwellers in terms of race, occupation, age, and place of birth. Similarly, photographs and fire insurance maps confirm both the isolation of alley residents from street dwellers and from the rest of the city as well as the close proximity in the alley of alley houses to each other. The single common entrance-exit to the alley furthered the opportunities for face-to-face contact and interaction. Since the alleys lacked the vehicle

[7] Marion M. Ratigan, *A Sociological Survey of Disease in Four Alleys in the National Capital* (Washington, 1946), 92.

[8] Herbert Gans, *The Levittowners* (New York, 1967).

[9] Leon Festinger, Stanley Schacter, and Kurt Back, *Social Pressures in Informal Groups* (Stanford, California, 1950). For a general review of the literature on neighboring and community see William Michelson, *Man and His Urban Environment: A Sociological Approach* (Reading, Massachusetts, 1970), 168–190.

traffic of the streets as well as non-resident pedestrian traffic, the opportunities for knowing and interacting with one's alley neighbors were even greater.

Sociological theory only suggests the possibilities of interaction, it does not confirm it. Photographic analysis provides help in this regard. Numerous photographs show chairs and benches in front of the alley houses. Evidence of their use, as well as of stoops, stairs and boxes, is strong. Their use was no doubt largely a product of the smallness of the alley houses and the hot, humid summers of Washington, but it furthered the opportunities for interaction and neighboring. With front doors only ten feet apart and less in some designs, and with other houses only thirty feet away across the alley, these conditions suggest that upon entering the alley from one's house one was instantly immersed into the alley world. Unlike suburban houses with private yards and porches to protect the privacy of the occupant, with steps and railing providing a gate-like function to limit or warn visitors, the alley was communal property. Space could not be defined by any physical barrier, it belonged to everyone. One could only retreat to the house or backyard. If the photographs upon which this analysis is based are representative, alley dwellers chose not to retreat to those places. They were found in the alley despite the weather. Few of these photographs were taken for the purpose of showing people. The photographer's interests were to document the physical alley. When

National Capitol Housing Authority

Alley Dwelling Authority photograph. "Fenton Place: 1930's."

Farm Security Administration Collection, Library of Congress

Photograph by Ed Rosskam. "Negroes in front of their homes in the alley dwelling area, July 1941."

Charles Weller added to his caption of Ball Alley that "the usual midday loafers" could be seen, it was not for the purpose of demonstrating neighboring but very clearly for moralistic reasons.[10] The inclusion of "usual" in the caption strengthens the view that the alley was the community center where alley neighbors could meet to exchange gossip, information on jobs, and stories.

The photographs also suggest that males were more likely to congregate in the alleys, at least during the hours when photographers ventured into the alleys (probably during working hours from 8 a.m. to 5 p.m.). Unfortunately few if any photographs appear to have been taken during the early or late evenings when such interaction might be expected to be greatest. Alley men, who had to rely on the unstable day labor market (as suggested by Elliot Liebow's study of such men in a later period[11]), might often be expected to spend non-working days in communion with their fellows in the alley. Women, whose employment was in more stable areas of domestic work and washing, were undoubtedly at work during these hours.

[10] Weller, *Neglected Neighbors,* 82.

[11] Elliot Liebow, *Tally's Corner* (Boston, 1967).

Children appear most often in these alley photographs, and there is evidence that working parents could expect their non-working neighbors to keep an eye out for their children and to take care of them.

Toys and packaged games, not surprisingly, seldom appear, although dolls and toy soldiers were found to be common in a study of one alley.[12] Photographs do show evidence of baseball and other games. Other studies suggest the existence of a number of song games played by alley children.[13] Few teenagers appear in the photographs, which may be accounted for in part by the youthfulness of the alley families and by the necessity for teenagers to work to add to the family income.

One photograph deserves special consideration here. This photograph of Purdy's Court suggests the communal nature of the alley.[14] Here the alley as a gathering place for play, rest, and relaxation, as well as for social intercourse, is strongly confirmed. This near idyllic setting, which to reformers proved the disorganization and degradation of alley life, appears in fact to be one where children could play far from the dangers of the street and where adults could communicate without interruptions from street noise.

The physical environment of the alley promoted community in other ways as well. Because of the relatively small size of the alley community, the propinquity of the houses, and the common alley property, alley dwellers had what Oscar Newman has termed *Defensible Space*.[15] Any outsider entering the alley was clearly visible to alley residents, providing an important form of social control. Some alleys were reportedly "unsafe for an outsider or a white person to enter its boundaries without protection." Similarly, social workers reported that upon entering an alley their activities were closely monitored by alley residents.[16]

Other sources confirm the existence of community in the alleys. In contrast to the view of reformers, who saw turmoil and turnover in the alley population, are the conclusions of a residential mobility and

---

[12] Sellew, *A Deviant Social Situation,* 34.

[13] *Ibid.,* 28–33.

[14] Lewis Wickes Hine, "Purdy's Court, near the Capital, 1908." Photograph in the Lewis Wickes Hine Collection, George Eastman House, Rochester, New York. Reproduced in *Records of the Columbia Historical Society of Washington, D.C. 1971–1972* (1973), p. 272.

[15] Oscar Newman, *Defensible Space: Crime Prevention through Urban Design* (New York, 1973).

[16] Daniel D. Swinney, "Alley Dwellings and Housing Reform in the District of Columbia" (unpublished M.A. thesis, University of Chicago, 1938), 109.

*Farm Security Administration Collection,
Library of Congress*

Photograph by Marion Post Wolcott. "Schott's Court with Senate Office Building in the background, September 1941."

persistence study made of the alley dwellers of six blocks.[17] Those who were heads of household or employed were traced in city directories for the years 1880, 1885, 1890 and 1895. Alley dwellers were found to remain in the city at rates exceeding those found for people in a comparable economic position in other cities. More importantly, one-third of the sample alley residents remained in the same alley from 1880 to 1885. While there are no comparable figures, this appears to be a very high retention rate in contrast to the heavy population turnover experienced by most Nineteenth Century cities and especially high for those who rented rather than owned. This suggests that a sufficient residue of alley residents persisted to permit the socialization of newcomers.

There is also evidence that alley dwellers remained in the alleys not only because of the severe racism which limited the choice of residence and work but also because friends and relatives lived there or

[17] Borchert, "Race and Place," 15–16, Table 12.

because "it had been their 'home' for many years." [18] Others who had moved out of the alley returned to rejoin friends.[19]

Several studies of specific alleys have found an informal social structure usually with one or several people serving as the mediator, consultant and source of help in troubled times. In Union Court, a long time resident was the person "everyone turns to . . . when they are in trouble," while her daughter had "a long record of giving help when needed and knowing what to do 'standing up for herself and the court' in dealing with the world outside." [20] In another alley, sickness and death were met with help and support from fellow residents. "I jes tel you one thing," a Willow Tree Alley resident was quoted, "when any of us gets sick an' dies, we doan ask nobody outside de alley to help us pay de expenses." When an alley resident died, someone immediately started a collection. "The women coming home from a day out at washing or other work are approached and cheerfully contribute a large part of their day's earnings. The men give whatever they have picked up around town that day. During a single hour, they were able to make up a sum of $40 or $50. Out of this amount the undertaker is paid on the spot." Any surplus "goes for beer which is dispensed at the house of mourning." [21] Similarly, a study of Snow's Court observed that "the bulk of the population live 'as one big happy but quarrelsome family.' " [22]

This last observation raises the issue of violence and fighting that was often pointed to as an example of the social disorganization of alley dwellers. While only a tentative hypothesis can be offered, it is possible that the same factors that promoted community in the alleys, the small houses, the proximity, and the lack of physical barriers, also promoted fighting. The lack of personal space, space to which one could retreat and be secure, and the resulting intensity of interaction, could easily lead to confrontation just as it can in a family sharing common quarters.[23] It is entirely possible, however, that such confrontations were closely regulated by the informal social structure and world-view of the alley. If the intensity of conflict grew too great, there was always the possibility of moving from the alley.

It is my conclusion that the conventional view which portrayed

---

[18] Ratigan, *A Social Survey of Disease,* 22.

[19] Swinney, "Alley Dwelling and Housing Reform," 88.

[20] Sellew, *A Deviant Social Situation,* 59.

[21] Washington *Times,* September 11, 1904.

[22] Swinney, "Alley Dwelling and Housing Reform," 90.

[23] Robert Sommer, *Personal Space: The Behavioral Basis of Design* (Englewood Cliffs, New Jersey, 1969); and Edward T. Hall, *The Hidden Dimension* (Garden City, New York, 1966).

alley dwellers as socially disorganized is far from accurate. Certainly alley life was not easy. Nearly every family member over the age of ten was required to go to work to make ends meet. The ends that had to be met included a small house that was probably shared with another family. Inadequate diets and unsanitary outhouses led to a higher expectancy of disease and of an earlier death. On the outside of the alley was a white world that was threatening at best and destructive at worst. To these circumstances alley dwellers responded with a positive and viable lifestyle. That lifestyle was not one of disorganization but of organization and community, constructed for survival in a hostile world and based on sharing and mutual help. It involved also a number of factors which time does not permit me to touch on here. These incuude the preservation and adaptation of a rich cultural heritage that can be seen only dimly now through historical records.[24] As nine-year-old Peter observed, the alley's "mostly dark" but "you can always know your buddy will be there."

[24] These include religion, music, and folklore.

The Development of a Black Residential Community in Southwest Washington: 1860–1897

PAUL A. GROVES

The early role of Washington, D. C. in the developmental history of black residential areas in United States cities has never been explicitly described and analyzed. Studies concerned with the emergence of black residential concentrations ("ghettoes") have generally neglected the last half of the Nineteenth Century, the very period which saw the growth of at least one extensive black residential concentration in Washington. The large black ghettoes of Northern cities have been ascribed to the Twentieth Century developments associated with the massive northward migration of blacks after the turn of the century.[1] Conversely, the study of black residential patterns in the South has centered upon the Ante-Bellum period,[2] though more recently some researchers have examined specific cities in the post Civil War period.[3]

Delivered at the Fir-t Annual Conference on Washington, D. C. Historical Studies, sponsored by the Columbia Historical Society and George Washington University, January 11, 1974.

The author would like to acknowledge the support of a General Research Board Grant from the University of Maryland and to thank Charles Murphy and Joseph Poracsky for preparing the maps.

[1] Allan H. Spear, *Black Chicago: The Making of a Negro Ghetto 1890–1920* (Chicago, 1967); Gilbert Osofsky, *Harlem: The Making of a Ghetto* (New York, 1963); and W. E. B. DuBois, *The Philadelphia Negro: A Social Study*, with an introduction by E. Digby Baltzell (New York, 1967).

[2] Richard C. Wade, *Slavery in the Cities: The South 1820–1860* (New York, 1964) and R. A. Fischer, "Racial Segregation in Ante Bellum New Orleans," *American Historical Review*, LXXIV (1969), 926–937.

[3] John W. Blassingame, *Black New Orleans, 1860–1880* (Chicago, 1973) and Richard Hopkins, "Status, Mobility and the Dimensions of Change in a Southern City: Atlanta, 1870–1910," in *Cities in American History* ed. by Kenneth Jackson and Stanley Schultz (New York, 1972), 216–231.

TABLE 1

Black Population of Selected U. S. Cities: 1860–1900

(1900 rank order) (Population in 000's)

City	1860	1880	1900
Washington, D. C.	14 (19)	60 (34)	87 (31)
Baltimore	28 (13)	54 (16)	79 (16)
New Orleans	24 (14)	58 (27)	78 (16)
Philadelphia	22 (4)	32 (4)	63 (5)
Memphis	4 (17)	15 (44)	50 (49)
Louisville	7 (10)	21 (17)	39 (19)
New York (Manhattan)	13 (2)	20 (2)	36 (2)
Atlanta	2 (20)	16 (44)	36 (40)
St. Louis	4 (2)	22 (6)	36 (6)
Richmond	14 (38)	28 (44)	32 (38)

Figures in parentheses indicate black population as a percentage of total city population.

Source: U. S. Census of Population, 1860, 1880 and 1900.

The more general approach is typified by a recent examination of urbanization and ghetto formation[4] which identifies Baltimore, Washington, Philadelphia, New York, St. Louis, Cincinnati and Pittsburgh as first generation ghetto cities. An examination of the black population of selected United States cities (Table 1) indicates, however, that as early as 1880 New Orleans, Baltimore and Washington had black populations in excess of 50,000 and that Washington was one of the cities where the necessary elements for ghetto formation could be found. Thus, there appears to be a clear case for separating Washington (and probably other border cities such as Baltimore, Louisville and St. Louis) from the more general rubric of the first generational ghetto city and considering it as a city which experienced substantial black residential concentration and segregation at an earlier date than most.

In the second half of the Nineteenth Century there was a group of border cities that attracted large numbers of blacks through short length migration from the South Atlantic States. Of these border cities, Washington, D. C. received the largest influx of black population in the years immediately following the Civil War primarily from the neighboring States of Maryland and Virginia. Washington experienced an addition of 46 thousand blacks to its population between 1860 and 1880 a number unequalled elsewhere in the United

[4] Harold M. Rose, *Social Processes in the City: Race and Urban Residential Choice* (Washington, D. C., Commission on College Geography, 1969), 3–5.

States. The black inhabitants of Washington comprised a large and visible component of the population; 60 thousand blacks by 1880, 87 thousand by 1900. During the last two decades of the Nineteenth Century blacks accounted for not less than one-third of the city's total population. The rapid growth of this segment of the population was of sufficient dimension that by 1880 the city had the largest component of blacks, not just outside of the South, but in the nation as a whole. Thus as early as 1880 more than 50,000 blacks lived in Washington, the approximate level at which black concentrations formed in Northern cities (New York, Philadelphia, Chicago, Detroit, etc.) during the early part of the Twentieth Century.

Together with the two principal characteristics of large absolute numbers of blacks and the high "visibility" of that population (as indicated by the proportion of blacks in the total city population) Washington possessed a third characteristic of import, namely, a significantly weaker slave tradition than the cities of the South. Such a tradition had produced racially mixed residential patterns in Southern cities both prior to and after the Civil War. "The elaborate mechanisms of social distance which existed under slavery left status inequality unthreatened" [5] and hence made residential segregation unnecessary. The tradition of slavery in Southern cities generally operated to delay the physical segregation of the races. In Washington, however, there were more free blacks than slaves by 1830 and by 1860, on the eve of the Civil War, free blacks outnumbered slaves by 3½ to 1. By comparison, in 1860 slaves outnumbered free blacks in Charleston, Louisville, Mobile, New Orleans, Norfolk, Richmond, and Savannah by ratios of between 11:1 and 1.3:1. Only in St. Louis where free blacks outnumbered slaves by 1860 and Baltimore, where that condition had pertained since (at least) 1820, were somewhat parallel conditions to the Washington case found.[6]

Blacks in Washington encountered first, therefore, those factors that led at a later date to the foundation of the massive black "ghettoes" of Northern cities. Consequently, the study of the developmental process pertaining to the growth of black residential areas in Washington in the late Nineteenth Century may provide evidence useful in constructing a general developmental model of the residential segregation of blacks within specific sections of American urban areas.

It is suggested, therefore, that the characteristics of the black popu-

---

[5] Pierre L. van den Berghe, *Race and Racism: A Comparative Perspective* (New York, 1967), 88. See also Wade, "Slavery in the Cities," 277–278.

[6] Wade, "Slavery in the Cities," 325–327.

lation of late Nineteenth Century Washington are shared by only a minimal number of American cities within that time period. Fortuitously, data are available which allow for the analysis and description of this condition. The Manuscript Schedules of the U. S. Census of Population for 1880, the Boyd City Directories for the period, and the District of Columbia Police Census of 1897 allow for the reconstruction of residential patterns by city block. Additional data, which would be useful in a more detailed study than this, are available in the Freedman's Bureau Records, the 1860, 1870 and 1900 manuscript schedules of the U. S. Census of Population, and the various city tax and real estate records.

URBAN HISTORICAL GEOGRAPHY

The urban historical geographer places emphasis on two primary facets of a study of this type. First, like all geographers, he is concerned with the spatial patterning of specific characteristics. The identification of the most suitable spatial unit (blockfront, city block, enumeration district, etc.) to use in analysis therefore becomes paramount. Given a series of options, the preliminary analysis should be undertaken at the level of the smallest spatial unit for which data are available and which provides reasonably congruity for the time period under examination. In this study the basic unit used is the city block for which data for both 1880 and 1897 are available and which enables an examination of the urban historical geographer's second concern, namely, process. This includes questions of why patterns change, the direction of change, and the explanation of such change. These two tenets—the spatial unit of analysis and process—are basic to the approach of the urban historical geographer. The analysis of Southwest Washington that follows depends heavily for its methodology on an appreciation of this approach.

SOUTHWEST WASHINGTON

As early as 1880, using a population count by Enumeration District (a unit averaging about fifteen city blocks in 1880) as a base, several areas of black residential concentration in the District of Columbia had apparently emerged. Three distinct clusters were identifiable in Northwest Washington centered on 19th and R Streets (E.D. 17), Connecticut and L Streets (E.D.'s 37 and 38) and New York Avenue and M Streets (E.D.'s 29 and 42). These clusters contained black populations of 1,446; 2,840: and 2,463 respectively which, in total, amounted to a little over ten percent of all blacks in the city. The largest cluster in Washington, however, was found in the Southwest where 6,060 blacks were resident in E.D.'s 72, 79 and 84. This cluster accounted for about ten percent of the total black population of Washington. It is apparent that less than a quarter of all blacks living in the District of Columbia in 1880 were living in the four defined clusters located in Northwest and Southwest. Many blacks were scattered across the city. Some were living in alleys which were concentrated in the western half of the city;[7] some were residentially dispersed by the nature of their occupations as 'in-residence' servants, nurses, cooks or seamstresses;[8] and some were scattered by virtue of their "acceptance" by whites and thus lived in residences interspersed with those of their white neighbors.

In analyzing the growth of total population and black population for Southwest Washington from 1860 to 1897 (Table 2) two characteristics are of note. First, the area of Southwest during this period exhibited a much faster rate of growth in its black population than the District of Columbia as a whole, and, secondly, the black proportion of total populaltion was consistently higher than was found city wide. By 1897, for example, almost one-half of the Southwest's population was blalck; for the District of Columbia the proportion was closer to one-third. The Southwest, therefore, represented the largest black population cluster in Washington, a city which itself occupied an unusual, though not unique, position in the black urban history of late Nineteenth Century urban America.

SOUTHWEST WASHINGTON: 1860 AND BEFORE

Clues as to the location of blacks in Southwest Washington prior to 1860 are sparse. The general housing stock existent in 1801 was primarily located in the area south of M Street towards Greenleaf's Point; this area contained 58 houses, either in finished form or in the process of construction, of the 98 structures of Southwest Washington.[9] In early Nineteenth Century Southwest the principal source of industrial employment was "the Army Arsenal on Greenleaf's Point

[7] The black alley population of the City of Washington in 1880 was 7,166. Of this total some 5,033 black alley inhabitants lived outside of the four black residential concentrations (E.D's 37, 38, 29, 42, 17, 72, 79 and 84).

[8] While published data are not available for 1880, the 1890 U. S. Census of Population indicates that of 18,773 employed black females in the District of Columbia 10,671 (57 percent) were employed as servants. The respective figure for employed black males was 3,844 (18 percent) of a total of 21,331. A proportion of such servants would have been "live-in" servants at the residences of middle and upper class whites.

[9] "An Enumeration of the houses in the City of Washington made November 1801," *American State Papers* (Misc. Ser. I), 256–257.

TABLE 2

Population Characteristics of Southwest Washington: 1860–1897

	Total Population	Black Population	Percent of Total Population Black
1860*	9,714	1,805	18.5
1870*	17,954	6,697	37.3
1880	19,582	7,342	37.4
1890*	29,089	11,614	39.9
1897	33,193	14,154	48.6

* Figures exclude a small portion of Southwest Washington.

Source: U. S. Census of Population 1860, 1870, 1880 and 1890: District of Columbia, *Board of Commissioners Report 1898.*

on the Eastern Branch, but there, as in privately owned shops, Negroes seldom if ever got as high wages as whites for the same work." [10] One can infer, therefore, that some blacks were living in the Greenleaf's Point area at this early date. By 1825 a small black property owning class had evolved in Southwest. Letitia Brown indicates that

> In the Southwest section the block of original entry became a center of activity and of extensive Negro ownership. Noah Jones acquired three lots in Square 388 between E and F and 9th and 10th Southwest as early as 1824. While Negro homeowners were more scattered in this section than in the Southeast, some concentration occurred between 9th and 10th Streets from Independence Avenue to G Street on the South. Squares 388 and 387 between 9th and 10th and D and F and Square 411 across 9th Street at E became the site of a number of Negro businesses by 1860.[11]

It is worthy of note that the majority of property purchased by blacks after 1825 was in the area to the east of 4½ Street.

The creation of a more specific black population distribution is possible for 1860 (Figure 1). An attempt has also been made to generalize from the Boschke map the built-up area of the Southwest at that time.[12] The source for the location of black residents is Boyd's *Directory of Washington and Georgetown 1860* which identifies 320 blacks by street address and occupation. The presumption is that this is a listing of free blacks, little is documented about the characteristics

[10] Constance McLaughlin Green, *The Secret City* (Princeton, 1967), 27.

[11] Letitia W. Brown, "Residence Patterns of Negroes in the District of Columbia, 1800–1860," *Records of the Columbia Historical Society of Washington, D. C. 1969–1970* (1971), 76.

[12] A. Boschke, *Topographical Map of the District of Columbia* (Washington, D. C., 1861).

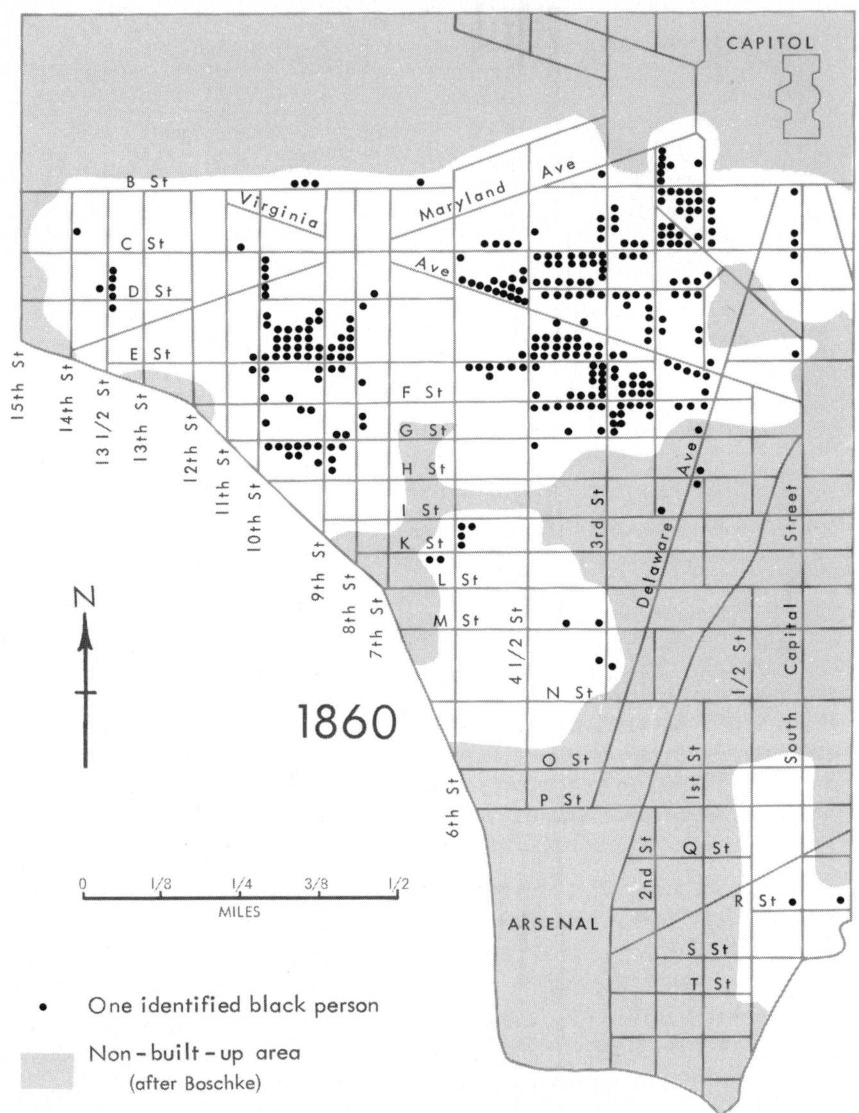

FIGURE 1. Distribution of Black Population: Southwest Washington, 1860. (Source: Boyd's Washington and Georgetown Directory 1860.)

of the slave population at this or at an earlier time. In addition, it seems safe to assume that the Directory source is prejudiced in favor of male blacks and employed blacks.[13] By 1860, two distinct and

[13] Peter R. Knights, "City Directories as Aids to Ante-Bellum Urban Studies: A Research Note," *Historical Methods Newsletter*, II (September 1969) 5–6.

separate clusters of black residences appear to have existed. One was bounded by D and H and 8th and 10th Streets and was roughly synonymous with the concentration of black property owners identified at this date by Letitia Brown. The second, more extensive in size and containing a larger number of blacks, was bounded by Maryland Avenue and G and 6th and 1st Streets. As would be expected, the occupational status of the mapped blacks was low. The overwhelming majority of both males (86 percent) and females (96 percent) was in "unskilled" occupations,[14] the former worked primarily as laborers, porters, waiters and carmen, and the latter as washerwomen.

The growth of a major black residential concentration implies the parallel growth of an institutional and service fabric,[15] part of which may be specifically related to the racial characteristics of the area (black public schools and black churches) but part of which may represent a more general response to a growth in population and attendant consumer demand (retail and service structure). An attempt has been made to graphically indicate certain elements of this service and institutional fabric for Southwest and their spatial relationship to the defined black residential concentrations for 1860 and succeeding dates (Figure 2). The identification of the retail and service areas is the result of aggregating the locations of fourteen separate functions.[16] In 1860, the one area of retail concentration was along 4½ Street between Maryland Avenue and F Street. This is an incipient development with just eight functions being represented by thirteen establishments. In 1860, just two black churches were identified; one at South Capital and B Streets (Israel M.E.) and the other at D between 2nd and 3rd Streets (Zion Wesley Chapel). They were both, as would be expected, close to the developing black residential concentration located immediately to the southwest of the Capitol Building.

SOUTHWEST WASHINGTON: 1880

By using data from the manuscript schedules of the U. S. Census of Population it is possible to recreate with a relatively high degree of accuracy the residential patterns of the Southwest for 1880 (Figure 3).

[14] The occupational classification is derived from that of Stuart Blumin, "Mobility and Change in Ante-Bellum Philadelphia," in *Nineteenth Century Cities: Essays in the New Urban History* ed. by Stephan Thernstrom and Richard Sennett (New Haven, 1969), 165–208.

[15] David Katzman, *Before the Ghetto: Black Detroit in the Nineteenth Century* (Urbana, 1973), 129.

[16] The retail and service establishments mapped were: bakers, druggists, wine and liquor stores, tobacconists/cigar dealers, fancy goods stores, confectioners, clothiers/tailors, undertakers, dry goods stores, boot and shoe stores, butchers, variety stores, watches/jewelry stores and milliners.

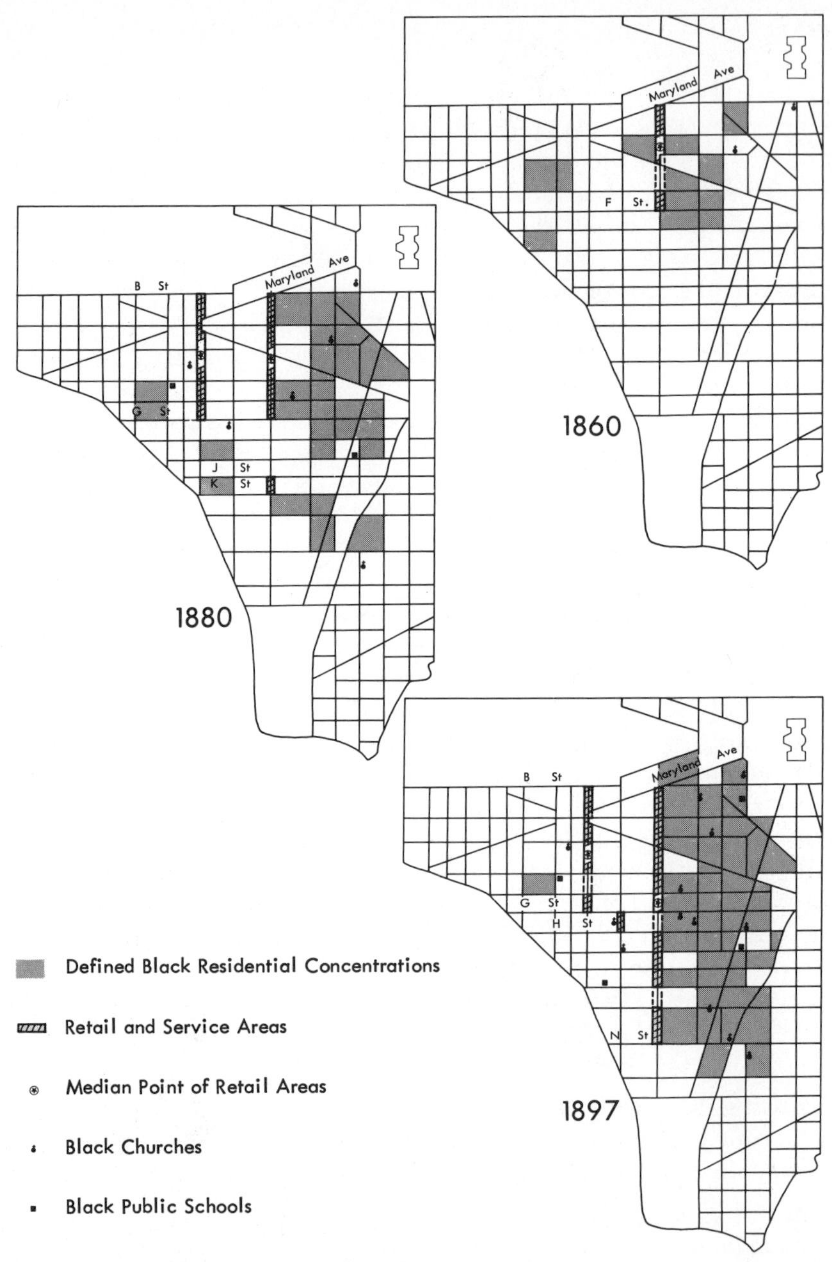

FIGURE 2. Black Residential Concentrations, Black Churches, Black Public Schools and Retail/Service Concentrations: Southwest Washington, 1860, 1880 and 1897. (Source: Boyd's Washington and Georgetown Directory 1860; Boyd's Washington Directory 1880 and 1897: and Report of the Board of Trustees of Public Schools of D. C. 1880 and 1897–1898.)

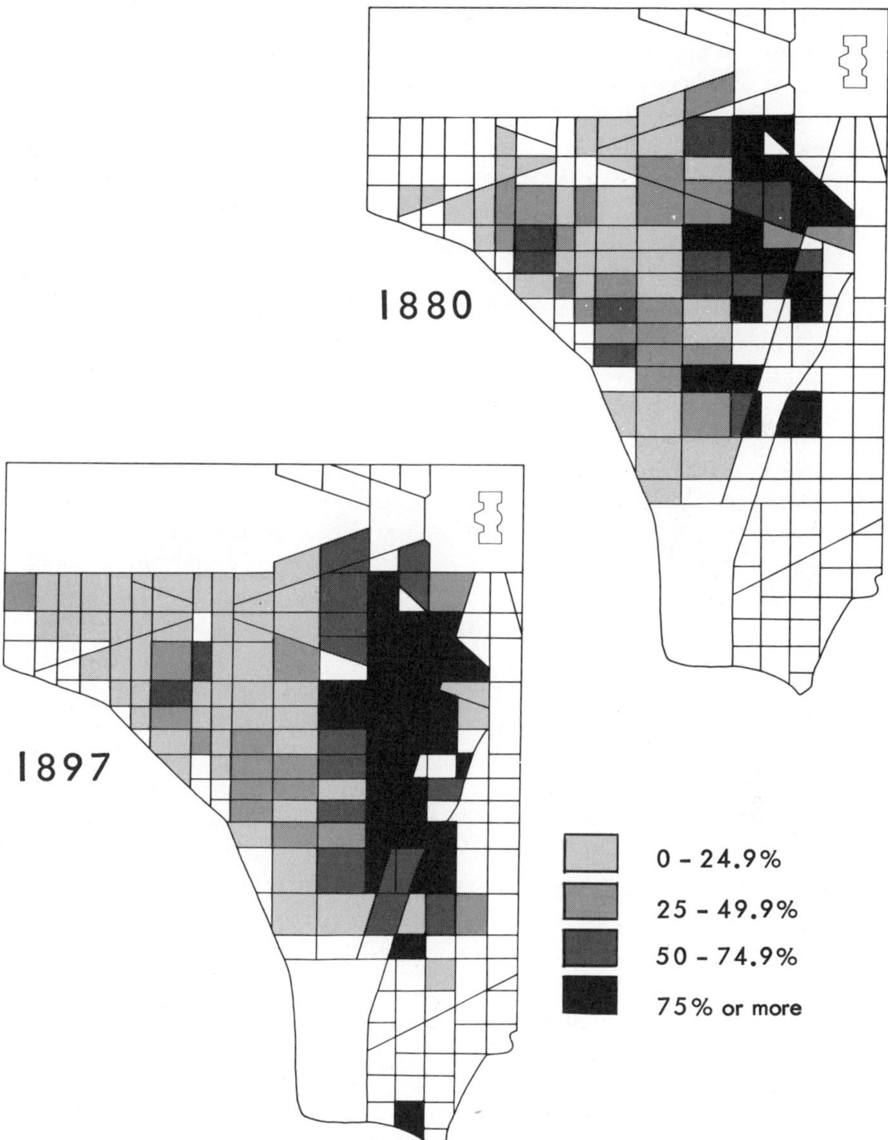

FIGURE 3. Blacks as a Percent of Block Population (Blocks of <50 residents excluded): Southwest Washington, 1880 and 1897. (Source: Manuscript Schedules of U. S. Census of Population, 1880, and District of Columbia, Board of Commissioners Report 1898.)

By that date, the concentration of black population east of 4½ Street is apparent. West of 4½ Street, which was to become an even more important residential barrier with time, only four blocks contained majority black populations. The concentration east of 4½ Street was composed of two major and one minor cluster which had a total area of some twenty-six blocks. The northernmost of these clusters was located north of Virginia Avenue and contained 1,605 blacks (75 percent of total population in the cluster). Immediately south of Virginia Avenue was a second concentration which contained 2,567 blacks (78 percent of total). Finally, there was a minor concentration straddling Delaware Avenue at M Street. This smaller concentration contained 477 blacks (84 percent of total). In total, these three clusters held 4,649 blacks or close to two-thirds of all blacks in the Southwest at this time. Thus, a high proportion of the total black population of Southwest was found in blocks of majority black occupance. In addition, each of these clusters had a core comprising blocks at over 75 percent black occupance and a periphery of blocks with 50–75 percent black occupance. The role of 4½ Street as a barrier to black expansion to the west is indicated by the presence of a number of blocks with less than 25 percent blacks occupance immediately to the west of 4½ Street.

The internal structure of the defined black residential areas of Southwest was characterized by two things of note. First, the blocks with more than 200 inhabitants (black and white) were on the western side of the two major concentrations. Second, that the vast majority of the sizeable alleys (75 persons plus) were found within the black residential areas. Alleys were, therefore, not outliers of the black residential areas but integral parts of them. It is possible that it was alley overspill onto blockfronts which acted to convert blocks (and larger areas) to predominantly black occupance.

The retail and service structure, black public schools and black churches of Southwest are shown in Figure 2. By 1880, the small retail area along 4½ Street had grown and was more fully developed. Between Maryland Avenue and G Street there were 12 functions (58 establishments) represented as compared with 8 (13) in 1860. A second retail area had developed along 7th Street between B and G Streets. It was the 4½ Street complex which was important, however, because of its barrier effect on the expansion of the black residential area to the east. The strength of this barrier was related not just to the presence of retail establishments along 4½ Street, with the majority of their predominantly white owners likely living over the stores. In addition, the street was of above average width[17] and since 1872, the Metropolitan Railroad Company had operated a horse car line running down 4½ Street from Maine Avenue to O Street.[18] The effect of this barrier is further emphasized by an examination of the blockfronts on the *east* side of 4½ Street. From Maryland Avenue to L Street there were ten blockfronts: eight had less than 25 percent black occupance, while two were in the 25 to 50 percent black occupance category. This is a striking break in a residential pattern and indicates a high degree of residential segregation, as well as the need for careful analysis by appropriate spatial units.

By 1880, there were six black churches listed in the City Directory. Four of these were either in the defined black residential areas east of 4½ Street or within one block of same. West of 4½ Street, the Fourth Washington First Baptist, was located on 6th Street in a block with high black occupance. St. Pauls AME, was on 8th Street between D and E and presumably was primarily associated with the small black concentration to the southwest of it.

In the early 1860s, black public schools had begun operation in the District.[19] Therefore, by 1880 we have another institutional indicator. At that date, there were just two black public schools in Southwest. Randall, located at Delaware and 1st Street on the southern periphery of the major black concentration to the north and Bowen, at 9th and E Streets close to the small black concentration to its immediate west.

The 1880 manuscript schedules also give some opportunity to look at the occupational status of blacks in the Southwest. It should be indicated initially that regardless of location, whether it be alley or blockfront, blacks had lower occupational profiles than whites (see Table 3). As would be expected, this distinction between white and black occupational profiles was greater with respect to blockfronts than alleys. Second, blacks within the three major clusters east of 4½ Street had higher occupational profiles than all other blacks in Southwest. For example, within these three areas blacks in "unskilled" positions accounted for 63 percent of all occupied blacks and blacks in "servant" ("live in" and "live out") status accounted for 24 per-

[17] 4½ Street was 110 feet wide whereas the average width of streets in Southwest was between 80 and 90 feet. See District of Columbia, *Board of Commissioners Report 1891* (Washington, D. C., 1891).

[18] LeRoy O. King, Jr., *100 years of Capital Traction* (Washington, D. C., 1972), 8–9.

[19] For a general history of public education for blacks see Winfield Montgomery, *Historical Sketch of Education for the Colored Race in D. C. 1807–1905* (Washington, D. C., 1907) and Lillian Dabney, *A History of Schools for Negroes in D. C. 1870–1947* (Washington, D. C., 1949).

TABLE 3

Southwest Washington: Occupations of Blacks and Whites by Total Area, Alleys and Blockfronts, 1880

	Occupational Groups (percent of total)						
	1	2	3	4	5	6	7
Total Area							
Blacks (3426)	1	3	5	3	66	21	2
Whites (3646)	3	22	30	12	28	3	1
Alleys							
Blacks (885)	—	1	2	4	68	26	—
Whites (79)	—	7	18	3	53	20	—
Blockfronts							
Blacks (2547)	1	4	6	3	65	20	2
Whites (3567)	3	23	30	13	28	3	1

Note: Numbers in parentheses indicate population in each group. Rows may not add to 100% because of rounding.

Occupational Classification: 1—Professional, Executive, Proprietor. 2—Non-Manual. 3—Skilled: Craft or Artisan. 4—Semi-Skilled. 5—Unskilled. 6—Servant. 7—In-Residence Servants.

Source: Manuscript Schedules, U. S. Census of Population, 1880.

cent. Outside these concentrations the parallel figures were 69 percent and 21 percent. This indicates that the more successful blacks, as measured by occupational status, lived within black areas. This is further exemplified by examining the proportion of blacks in professional, non-manual and skilled occupations groups. Within black concentrations those groups accounted for 1 in 10 of employed blacks, outside only 1 in 20.

A marked difference existed between the occupations of blacks living in blockfront locations within the major concentrations as opposed to those outside. Outside the major concentrations there were higher proportions of unskilled workers (69 percent versus 63 percent) and "live in" servants (4 percent versus 0.1 percent), and lower proportions in the professional, non-manual and skilled occupational groups (6 percent versus 10 percent). Alley data indicated little difference on a black versus white basis and this was true with respect to location as well. Alleys within the major concentrations had slightly higher occupational profiles than those outside, but alley populations generally held the poorest inhabitants, from both a financial and occupational viewpoint.[20]

[20] Paul A. Groves, "The 'Hidden' Population: Washington Alley Dwellers in the Late Nineteenth Century," *The Professional Geographer* 26 (1974), 270–276 and James Borchert, "The Rise and Fall of Washington's Inhabited Alleys: 1852–1972," *Records of the Columbia Historical Society of Washington, D. C. 1971–1972* (1973), 267–288.

SOUTHWEST WASHINGTON: 1897

By 1897 a continuous belt of black residential development extended from B Street in the north to N Street in the south. It comprised a core of 29 blocks with more than 75 percent of their inhabitants black with a fringe area of 15 blocks with majority black occupance. This black residential area contained 10,500 blacks (78 percent of the total population) or about ten of every fourteen blacks living in Southwest. In the seventeen years following 1880, the black area not only spatially expanded but also greatly intensified in terms of absolute numbers of blacks. The residential pattern for 1897 (Figure 3) suggests a continuation of the process of black concentration which was evident in 1880, as well as indicating an increasing level of residential segregation. While in 1880 the three black clusters east of 4½ Street had 4,649 black residents, the identical areas contained 6,957 blacks by 1897. The greatest intensification of black population occurred in those blocks that were between 60 and 75 percent black in 1880 (Table 4). In 1897, as in 1880, 4½ Street was a solid barrier to black expansion westward. Again a series of blocks containing predominantly white population faced east across 4½ Street to predominantly black occupied blocks. This condition existed from Maine Avenue in the north to N Street in the south. By 1897, there was little but dispersed black population west of 4½ Street, the notable exception being the alley enclaves located in the blocks between 4½ Street and 6th south of H Street.

The extended black population concentration of 1897 had a solid core of high density blocks containing 200 or more people and overwhelmingly black occupied blocks located north of I Street. This indicates that the most visible black residential area by the end of the century was to be found between 4½ Street, Delaware Avenue, B Street and I Streets.

TABLE 4

Southwest Washington: Major Black Concentration, 1880–1897

Blocks as Defined for 1880	1880		1897	
	Black Population	Black as percent of total	Black Population	Black as percent of total
75 percent or more black	2,535	83.3	4,099	85.4
50–74 percent black	2,116	70.0	2,858	80.5
	4,649	77.5	6,957	82.7

Source: Manuscript Schedules, U. S. Census of Population 1880: District of Columbia, *Board of Commissioners Report 1898.*

By 1897, two district retail areas existed (Figure 2). The 4½ Street retail strip had by this time expanded and ran from Maryland Avenue to N Street; it still operated as the western edge of the black residential area, perhaps even more dramatically so than in 1880. This retail street had grown both spatially and functionally since 1880. The median location of its retail establishments had moved south from Virginia Avenue to a point between F and G Streets and it was now composed of 14 functions and 66 establishments. Conversely, the 7th Street retail area had shown little spatial expansion. As would be expected, the thirteen black churches identified for 1897 showed a high degree of locational association with the identified black residential area; ten of the churches were to be found within that area. By 1897, three black public schools existed in Southwest: two (Randall and Bell) were located within the black residential area, the third (Ambush) was at L Street between 6th and 7th Streets (Figure 2).

CONCLUSIONS

The development of a black residential area in Southwest was a *fait accompli* by 1897. As a result, the Southwest was residentially divided. East of 4½ Street "the population was mostly colored . . . the houses were mostly small and many of them old frames." [21] The area west of 7th Street was mainly "occupied by residences of the middle classes," [22] and had been largely vacated by black population. Only 27 years earlier in 1860, the area west of 7th Street had contained about 25 percent of the located black population.

By 1897, the defined black residential area in the Southwest contained eleven of every fourteen blacks in that quadrant of the city. Such concentration was doubtless aided by the relatively low proportion of "live in" servants in the Southwest, a result of the lack of a white upper or upper middle class residential area. By contrast, some fashionable residential areas could have had black populations of 20 to 25 percent almost entirely as a result of the presence of such "live in" servants.

In the 1860 to 1897 period, the black population of the Southwest expanded in total numbers from about 1,800 to more than 14,000, and this was accompanied by increasing spatial concentration. While the area defined as the 1897 concentration contained close to 79 percent of all Southwest blacks at that date, only about half the blacks in

[21] U. S. Census Office, *Vital Statistics for D. C. and Baltimore, 1890* (Washington, D. C., 1893), 49.

[22] *Ibid.*

1860 lived in that same area. Thus the process of concentration was continuous.

This paper has attempted to examine the relationship of black residential areas in 1860, 1880 and 1897 with regard to retail and service structures, black churches and black schools. The retail structure of 4½ Street played a role, together with the above average width of the street and its use as a streetcar transportation line, in forming a significant western barrier to black residential expansion, a barrier which increased in effectiveness with time.[23] Black churches and public schools were natural institutional reflections of black residential population growth and, as time passed, became more spatially integrated as a result.

It has been suggested elsewhere[24] that black residential concentrations developed through a temporal sequence of (a) dispersal, (b) enclaving/dispersal, (c) emergent concentration, and (d) concentration/expansion. This analysis of Southwest Washington would appear to add credence to this suggestion and may, therefore, provide a useful and testable hypothesis for the analysis of the historical growth of black residential areas in other contexts.

[23] See Homer Hoyt, *The Structure and Growth of Residential Neighborhoods in American Cities* (Washington, D. C., 1939), 68–71 for later examples of this same residential cleavage.

[24] Paul A. Groves and Edward K. Muller, "The Evolution of Black Residential Concentrations in late Nineteenth Century Cities," *Journal of Historical Geography* (April 1975), 169–191.

Capitol Hill, 1870–1900: The People and Their Homes

SUSAN H. MYERS

Residential Capitol Hill, like the residential districts of most of Washington, has been largely neglected by historians, overshadowed by a concentration of interest on its more conspicuous neighbor, the United States Capitol. The purpose of this article is to describe the development of this area, which lies east of the Capitol and is comprised of loosely defined adjacent portions of the northeast and southeast sections of Washington,[1] during the major period of its growth, roughly from 1875 until just before the turn of the century. The article will examine the social and economic position of the residents as well as the architectural styles which appeared there and were a reflection of that community.

During the early decades of the Nineteenth Century, it seemed

---

Delivered at the First Annual Conference on Washington, D.C. Historical Studies, sponsored by the Columbia Historical Society and George Washington University, January 11, 1974.

[1] Washington was designed according to a roughly symmetrical plan with the Capitol at its center and four nonequal districts radiating from that point. Capitol Hill is located in two of these districts, the northeast and southeast, but its extent within these areas is not rigidly defined. The Capitol Hill Restoration Society in 1967 (A Joint Committee of Members From The Capitol Hill Community, Report Prepared by the Committee, *Capitol Hill Prospectus,* Washington, D.C., Capitol Hill Restoration Society, 1967) claimed as large an area as that east of North and South Capitol Streets, north to E Street, northeast and south to the Anacostia River. The Capitol Hill Southeast Citizens Association (*Places and Persons on Capitol Hill,* Washington, D.C., by the Association, 1960), on the other hand, designated only a section between East Capitol Street, South Capitol Street and the Anacostia River as "Capitol Hill." The Capitol Hill Restoration Society is currently working with the National Capitol Planning Commission to establish a more specific definition of the Capitol Hill area. This essay examines an area directly behind the Capitol, bounded north and south by C Streets, northeast and southeast and extending east from the Capitol to Lincoln Park. This area is selected because it provides a large and representative sampling of the types of growth on Capitol Hill during the period under study. The more southerly portions of southeast Washington which are included by the two societies noted above, and which should accurately be included in a definition of modern Capitol Hill, are herein excluded because, as will be seen, much of that area was developed before the period under study and should be considered separately.

obvious that Capitol Hill would become one of the most fashionable and economically influential districts of Washington. From the Capitol south and east to the Eastern Branch, now the Anacostia, River, and especially along New Jersey Avenue, M Street, and South Capitol Street a busy commercial community was developing which many people thought would expand into the main business district and principal waterfront section of Washington, along the then deep channel of that branch of the Potomac.[2] Additionally, the arrival of the Federal government in Washington generated the establishment of a community of Congressmen and Senators living in boarding-houses near the Capitol.[3] Though this was a highly transient society whose members rarely established a permanent home in Washington or even stayed in residence longer than the Congressional term, its presence undoubtedly encouraged the idea that Capitol Hill would eventually be the home of an influential sector of Washington society. Finally, the growth and social activity of the residential district surrounding the Navy Yard, established in 1799, though marginal to Capitol Hill proper, must also have added to its prospects for a future as a fashionable district.

The many changes that took place in Washington during the 1870's had a profound effect on these early expectations about Capitol Hill. These were changes which roused Washington from many decades of governmental neglect of the needs of the residential city and which had the specific effect on Capitol Hill of altering the type of community living there.

Before this time, Washington was a dismal and uninviting spot. Congress appropriated little for the development and maintenance of the city and there was almost no interest in its growth and appearance. It was merely the place where the functions of government were carried out and from which those required to be there in an official capacity fled as quickly as possible. Permanent residences were few, rather boarding houses and hotels provided homes for the highly transient population. Streets and sidewalks were usually unpaved and unlighted; vacant, unkempt lots were a common sight; sewage dis-

[2] Sources on the early commercial development of Capitol Hill include:

Allen C. Clark, "Development of the Eastern Section and the Policy of the Land Owners," *Records of the Columbia Historical Society,* Washington, D.C., Vol. 7 (1904), pp. 118–134.

Charles O. Paullin, "Washington City and the Old Navy," *Records of the Columbia Historical Society,* Washington, D.C., Vol. 33–34 (1932), pp. 163–177.

Zack Spratt, "Ferries in the District of Columbia," *Records of the Columbia Historical Society of Washington, D. C. 1953–1956* (1959), pp. 183–192.

[3] James Sterling Young, *The Washington Community, 1800–1828* (New York: Columbia University Press, 1966), pp. 87–109.

Illustrations from the author

Figure 1. The Frederick Douglass House, now the Museum of African Art, is a handsome example of the influence that the French Second Empire or Mansardic style had on Capitol Hill architecture of the 1860's and 1870's.

Figure 2. Built in 1879, this house with its curvilinear floral details is typical of flat front brick structures of the 1870's on Capitol Hill. It was valued in 1889 at $1,500 and owned by Charles Draper, a messenger.

posal was a constant problem; and the city was far from the grand capital of the republic envisioned by its planners.

One of the first events of the 1870's which prompted a change in the deplorable condition of Washington was the appearance of the notorious Alexander "Boss" Shepherd in both the business and official worlds of the Federal city. Shepherd, a very successful businessman in Washington in the 1870's, gave major encouragement to the economy of the city by his extensive enterprises as a real estate speculator and building contractor, investing large sums of money in building projects in the northwestern sector. In 1871 he was appointed a Vice Chairman of the powerful Board of Public Works and in 1873, when the first governor of Washington, Henry D. Cooke, resigned, he became governor of the city's territorial government.[4] In

[4] One of the many attempts to arrive at a workable scheme of government for the

both offices he exercised a strong hand, undertaking ambitious and extensive public works programs which put the city in great debt and for a time discredited Shepherd, but which nevertheless accomplished essential improvements—street paving, street lighting, improvements to sanitary facilities, and many other long ignored needs of the city. Shepherd's public works programs, along with his ambitious private enterprises, not only improved the appearance of the city but also stimulated interest and confidence in the economic possibilities of Washington and thus encouraged others to invest here.

A second boost to the city's development, and one of even greater importance than the first, was the passage of the Organic Act of 1878, under the terms of which Congress agreed to pay half of the expenses of the Federal city. The primary significance of this act was that it assured the funds necessary for maintaining and improving the city. Perhaps even more important, however, was that this expression of Congressional interest assured the population that the seat of the Federal government would stay in Washington. Insecurity on this point had been a major reason for the retarded growth of Washington from the first day the Federal government moved here and as late as 1869 an attempt was made to move the capital to St. Louis. Finally, with the passage of the Organic Act, there was security that Washington would remain the national city and this assurance soon encouraged many formerly temporary residents to feel justified in establishing permanent homes here. A final advantage of the Organic Act was that it kept taxes low which was no mean factor in further encouraging the many wealthy who had occasion to come to Washington that they should establish a residence here.

A third factor affecting Washington's belated growth was a product of the first two. As the great economic possibilities of real estate became evident during and following Shepherd's investments in the city, and once the continued presence of the government was assured by the Organic Act, the business community of the city finally acquiesced in accepting the fact that it was not in commerce and manufacture but in government and real estate that the prosperity of Washington lay.[5] Manufacture and commerce had never been very successful in Washington and following the events of the 1870's, commerce was virtually abandoned and manufacture retained primarily for products consumed within the city. The choice of real

---

District of Columbia was a territorial form which was initiated in 1871 and abolished by 1874. It was composed of a presidentially appointed governor and upper house, an elected lower house, and a presidentially appointed board of public works.

[5] Constance McLaughlin Green, *Washington, Capital City, 1879–1950* (Princeton: Princeton University Press, 1963), p. 9.

estate and government was a major turning point in Washington's economy and in the city's development generally. In pursuit of these unique Washington "industries," a period of great prosperity took place in the last decades of the century.

The outcome of the events outlined above was the belated growth of Washington into a grand national city, a fashionable center in which it was socially essential to have a residence. Those who had formerly spent the minimum time necessary in Washington, staying in hotels and boarding-houses, now began to establish a formal and often lavish residence here. A great building boom ensued in which the wealthy and even the not so wealthy became real estate speculators, building houses to sell or to furnish and rent. The Federal city rapidly took shape, scores of public and domestic buildings sprang up, streets were paved, trees were planted, and the appearance of the city generally became a matter of interest and pride.

Capitol Hill was affected both positively and negatively by the many changes taking place in Washington in the 1870's. As in the northwestern section of the city, there was the positive effect of an intensive building boom which did not wane until nearly the turn of the century.

The events of the 1870's ultimately also produced the negative effect of turning the city finally and definitely toward the northwest and away from the eastern part of the city. A trend of development toward the east that had been evident in the early decades of the century was reversed during this period and the northwest took priority as the major and most fashionable residential section of Washington.

As the major trend of residential development turned elsewhere, Capitol Hill evolved into a type of community that went largely unnoticed in this city of wealth and fashion—it became a simple and stable middle class society isolated from and largely untouched by the lavish life of the major residential district in the northwest.

In this change, "Boss" Shepherd played a major role. His programs had concentrated very little on Capitol Hill beyond better bridging of the Eastern Branch and some grading of roads, while his major improvements and additions in both public and private enterprise were made in the "West End." This obvious preference for the northwestern section of the city, along with the great advantages that section gained from Shepherd's extravagant investments there, encouraged others to continue the direction of development westward.

Additionally, the business community's acquiesence in the demise of commercial goals for Washington destroyed any hopes for developing the southeast section into a major waterfront district. Even if the interest had persisted, as the upstream areas developed the Eastern Branch silted up to such an extent that continuance of this purpose would have been impossible.

Once the trend began in favor of the northwest, various factors acted to perpetuate the residential patterns as they were set during this period. One of these was the physical isolation of Capitol Hill. Its isolated position on the hill and its location at what quickly came to be considered the "back" of the Capitol had both a physical and psychological effect of separating it from the rest of the city and preventing this district from combining with the more fashionable sections of the city.

In addition, a tendency for public monies to be expended more readily in the northwest than in the northeast and southeast perpetuated the less preferred status of Capitol Hill during the last quarter of the century as the northwest gained prominence.

The silting up of the Eastern Branch and "the enormous and con-

Figure 3. Overwindows from the 1879 catalogue of the Washington company, S. W. Stockstill & Co., National Galvanized Iron Cornice Works.

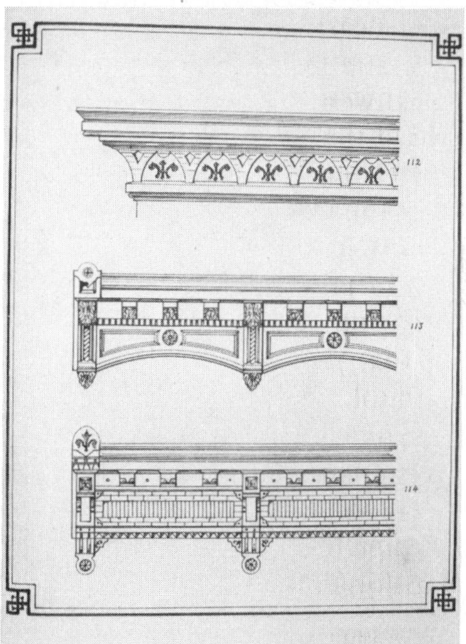

Illustrations from the author

Figure 4. Cornices from the 1879 catalogue of the Washington company, S. W. Stockstill & Co., National Galvanized Iron Cornice Works.

stantly increasing area of marsh along the eastern border of the city" [6] produced a disease breeding menace to the city "daily threatening the health and and well-being of the inhabitants of East Washington." [7] Yet even the influential Board of Trade asked in vain throughout the 1890's for appropriations to improve the dangerously unhealthy condition of the Eastern Branch flats.[8]

In other public projects the same tendency to ignore the eastern city is evident. Street and highway appropriations, for instance, were decidedly in favor of the northwest. In 1882, 68 percent of funds for extension of highways was spent in the northwest while the northeast and southeast together received only 18 percent.[9] By 1887, a *Report of the Committee on Streets, Avenues and Alleys* indicated the continuing preference for the northwest, alleging that funds designated to other sections of the city were often shifted to that district. This document stated that of 1,551,480 yards of concrete pavement laid in the city, about 84 percent was in the northwest and that nearly 75 percent of the unimproved streets were in the northeast, southeast, and southwest as compared with only 25 percent in the northwest.[10]

On the subject of street improvement, Sydney E. Mudd, Congressman from Maryland, charged in the House of Representatives in 1898 that the D.C. Commissioners were advised to act in favor of improvements in the northwest rather than in the eastern sections of the city by powerful people who had interests there; and accused Congress of being generally ". . . very abstemious toward and very negligent of that portion of the city and District lying east and south of this Capitol." [11]

The choice of the northwestern district by the fashionable Washingtonians and the rapid concentration of large and expensive homes there soon left few places in the city for those of a moderate or small income level to live. By the 1870's, the small southwestern section of Washington was near congestion; Georgetown was an old established

[6] Washington Board of Trade, *Annual Reports 1890–1899* (Washington, D.C.: Globe Printing Company, 1899), November 1896, p. 45.

[7] *Ibid.*, p. 15.

[8] Washington Board of Trade, *Annual Reports*, November 1890–November 1899.

[9] John Clagett Proctor, *Washington Past and Present, A History* (New York: Lewis Historical Publishing Company, Inc., 1930), Vol. I, pp. 154–157.

[10] *Report of Committee on Streets, Avenues and Alleys to the Citizens Representative Committee of One Hundred,* Noble D. Larner, chairman (Washington, D.C.: September 20, 1887).

[11] U.S. Congress, House of Representatives, Representative Mudd speaking for the Proposed Extension of Pennsylvania Avenue on the East Side of Anacostia River, June 22 and June 27, 1898.

area; the portion of southeast Washington between the Capitol and the Eastern Branch was relatively grown up; and much of the northwest, while just beginning its period of major development, was reserved for the socially elite of Washington.

Constance McLaughlin Green, citing an article in John Forney's *Sunday Chronicle* which stated "that the capitalists and moneyed men of Washington seeking good opportunities for investment never think of building blocks of small houses within the reach of poor men and government clerks," points out that as Washington became a "city for the rich" those of modest means had great difficulty finding housing. Many were forced to find their accommodations out beyond the northern boundary of the city which was not served by the street railway lines or public facilities.[12]

Capitol Hill, as defined by this study, was one of the few areas within reach of the city conveniences which was still relatively undeveloped and unclaimed by any specific social or economic group. In the 1880's and 1890's it became the city's major residential area for, if not "poor men," certainly for "government clerks" and those of similar middle income level. During these last decades of the Nineteenth Century, Capitol Hill residents included some of the "elite" members of society and a few of the poor but the majority were economically and socially in the middle.

---

[12] Green, *Washington, Capitol City,* pp. 13–16.

Though Capitol Hill was a community for "government clerks" and other groups of moderate income level, many of the houses there are large enough to indicate that the *Sunday Chronicle's* observation that no blocks of small houses were built to accommodate the non-wealthy inhabitants of Washington applied to Capitol Hill to some extent. Nonetheless, middle income people did live on Capitol Hill and were able to afford to live in such large houses for several reasons.

First, regardless of the size of the houses, prices for rent and sale were quite low. Mrs. Green (*Washington, Capital City,* p. 13) notes that $200 per month was an average rental charge in Washington during these decades, but indicates that an average government clerk would pay only about $30 per month. Rents on Capitol Hill, however, rarely reached even this low figure except along the "elite" East Capitol and A and B Streets. More often they were $10 or occasionally even $20 below that figure. Prices for sale of houses were likewise comparatively low.

If the cost of rental or purchase of these houses proved too great for a single family, they sometimes took in boarders. Or, as revealed in the 1889 and 1890 city directories (William H. Boyd, compiler, *Boyd's Directory of the District of Columbia,* 1889 and 1890), expenses were often met by four or five and sometimes more employed adults in the same family living together.

Installment plans for buying houses were popular means of making homes available to low and middle income people. Such agreeable terms as $50 down and the balance $15 monthly, $100 cash and $12 monthly, or even "monthly payments to suit purchasers, if bought this month" (*Washington Star,* May 15, 1880) were offered potential residents of Capitol Hill. Also home loan and building associations grew in number during this period to aid people in the purchase of homes.

Illustrations from the author

Figure 6. Part of a block of houses on the 1100 block of Park Place, N. E., built in symmetrical patterns, probably in the 1870's, on each side of the street. Park Place is on an east-west axis through the center of the square bounded by Constitution Avenue, C Street, and 11th and 12th Streets, N. E., and would have been quite isolated at the date of its building.

Figure 5. Three East Capitol Street houses. The overwindow in the lower left of Figure 3 and the cornice in the center of Figure 4 may have been the models for the details on these houses.

As late as 1870, the direction the city would take was still in question. In that year, M Street and the other areas along the Eastern Branch still housed a busy commercial center. In that year also, such confidence was held in the potential of Capitol Hill to become the fashionable section of the city that Captain Albert Grant, an architect, began building a group of houses known as Grant's Row on A Street, S.E. near the Capitol which were said to be "the most costly and elaborate ever erected east of the Capitol. At the time of its construction it was supposed that this region would become one of the finest residential sections of the city." [13] But Grant was mistaken in envisioning a fashionable Capitol Hill and as a result he suffered serious financial loss in this venture. The frequency with which these houses appeared for sale and rental in the newspapers of the 1880's,[14] when the moderate nature of the community was well established, attests to the near impossibility of disposing of these blocks of houses eventually known as "Grant's Folly."

[13] Charles O. Paullin, "History of the Site of the Congressional and Folger Libraries," *Records of the Columbia Historical Society of Washington, D.C.*, Vol. 37–38 (1937), pp. 173–194.

[14] Advertisements for sale and rental of houses were checked for random dates in the *Washington Star* for 1880, 1881, 1882, 1885 and 1889.

The differences in size and eloquence of design of houses built during the transitional period of the 1870's stress the uncertainty about the area's character. Everything was built from the elaborate "Grant's Folly" to the single block of simple and small houses on Park Place, N.E.[15] Stylistically, too, the evidence of the existing structures shows this to be a decade of varied and sometimes very creative types of architecture. The handsome mansardic style of houses such as the Frederick Douglass House, the flat front brick and occasionally frame houses with varieties of sheet metal overwindow and overdoor designs, and such fine groupings of houses as those on the south side of A Street, S.E. between 6th and 7th Streets representing a style unique on Capitol Hill, all attest to the variety of this decade.

By the 1880's, however, the transitional period was over and the nature of Capitol Hill had more clearly defined itself. The community and the architecture were settling into their characteristic late Nineteenth Century patterns.

The community lost its early Nineteenth Century pretensions and developed, instead, stable, middle class characteristics. By this time few wealthy and prominent Washingtonians were living on Capitol Hill, but had established their residence in the northwestern section of the city. Of almost 4,000 entries in the 1889 *Elite List*[16] only 128 were residents of Capitol Hill.[17] In terms of occupations, the 1889 and 1890 City Directories[18] indicate that very few residents of Capitol Hill were employed at jobs that could be considered "professional" and, in fact, they were rarely employed in any position that might have brought a sizeable income.[19]

---

[15] Park Place is a single block of houses built on a street running through the center of the square bounded by Constitution Avenue, C Street, N.E., 11th and 12th Streets, N.E. In the 1870's it would have stood almost entirely alone in an undeveloped part of Capitol Hill. The frame houses are all small and simple and were built in an architecturally symmetrical pattern which is repeated on each side of the street.

[16] *The Elite List, A Compilation of Selected Names of Residents of Washington City, D.C. and Ladies Shopping Guide* (Washington, D.C.: The Elite Publishing Company, 1889).

[17] Even this low figure may be misleading in determining the number of very wealthy or socially prominent Washingtonians living on Capitol Hill. Mrs. Green notes: "Any well mannered white person, in short, who could afford servants and who meticulously followed the 'cast iron' rules about making calls could be a part or hover on the fringes of Society." (Green, *Washington, Capital City*, p. 84.)

[18] William H. Boyd, compiler, *Boyd's Directory of the District of Columbia* (Washington, D.C.: William H. Boyd, 1889 and 1890). Neither directory was checked in its entirety, rather random alphabetical groupings were selected for examination.

[19] Specific income information about Capitol Hill residents could not be found. The United States Census Records proved of no use for the decades under study. Figures on income were not included in the 1880 records and many of the 1890 records were burned, among them those pertaining to Capitol Hill.

Those who did appear in the *Elite List,* or were noted in the city directories in professional jobs, for the most part strictly segregated themselves along just a few streets—East Capitol, and A and B Streets northeast and southeast—always staying as near the Capitol as possible and almost none ventured farther east from that building than 5th Street or farther north and south than B Streets northeast and southeast.

By 1889 only 19 Congressmen and Senators still listed their residence on Capitol Hill and these were strictly isolated to an immediate two or three block radius of the Capitol, most of them living in boardinghouses.[20]

Conversely, Capitol Hill had few low income or very poor residents. City directories reveal only a small number of Capitol Hill residents listed as "laborer," "domestic," "hustler," "servant," etc. And contemporary sources describing conditions of crime and poverty in the District of Columbia rarely suggest the existence of such problems in the eastern city but almost always refer instead to the southwest and northwest sections. The notorious slum alleys of Washington where the poor and sometimes the criminal lived, did not greatly affect Capitol Hill. Only one alley on Capitol Hill—Schott's Alley which stood between C Street, Constitution Avenue, 1st and 2nd Streets, N.E.—is mentioned in discussions of this problem. A 1912 alleys directory indicates that at that date the total number of alley dwellings in northeast and southeast Washington combined was less than half that in the southwest and only slightly more than a third of that in the northwest.[21] Though representing a later period, these figures appear reliable for this study in light of James Borchert's article on Washington's inhabited alleys which showed little change between the distribution of alleys in the 1890's and the figures shown in the 1912 directory.[22]

Ethnically, too, the community followed a relatively homogeneous pattern. There, as elsewhere throughout the city, there were very few immigrants since Washington's economy did not generate the types of jobs that were attracting immigrant labor to industrial cities. It does, however, seem likely that a community of free Negroes described by Letitia Brown[23] as living in the southeast quadrant by 1860 con-

---

[20] *The Elite List,* 1889.

[21] Thomas Jesse Jones, Compiler, *Directory of the Inhabited Alleys of Washington, D.C.* (Washington, D.C.: Printed through the generosity of Mrs. Medill McCormick, Mrs. William Belden Noble and Mrs. John van Schaick, Jr., 1912).

[22] James Borchert, "The Rise and Fall of Washington's Inhabited Alleys: 1852–1972," *Records of the Columbia Historical Society of Washington, D.C. 1971–1972* (1973), pp. 267–288.

[23] Letitia W. Brown, "Residence Patterns of Negroes in the District of Columbia,

Figure 7. These houses on A Street, S. E., dated 1881, are good examples of the Queen Anne influence in their strong verticality, finely jointed dark red brick, and ornamental brickwork.

Illustrations from the author

Figure 8. The influence of Henry Hobson Richardson's Romanesque style is felt in the stone string courses, round arches at doorways and windows, and massive scale of these houses built around 1890.

tinued to live there into the decades of this study. Additional research is needed to suggest how they might fit into the larger Capitol Hill community.

Most Capitol Hill residents were between the two extremes of wealth and poverty, and the majority were employed at jobs that offered a moderate but adequate income.

The types of occupations found most among Capitol Hill residents fit into three broad categories.[24] The first is related to one of Washington's major "industries," real estate. Very few of the residents of Capitol Hill were engaged in real estate at the level of speculation. It was rather in building the large numbers of structures required by the continuing and rapid growth of Washington real estate that they were

1800–1860," *Records of the Columbia Historical Society of Washington, D.C. 1969–1970* (1971), pp. 66–79.

[24] This was determined from a partial check of *Boyd's Directory* for the years 1889, 1890 and 1895.

employed. The building trades occupied the energies of a large number of Capitol Hill residents as "carpenter," "contractor," "bricklayer," "builder."

A second grouping of Capitol Hill residents were employed by the Federal government. This was rarely at the level of Congressman or Senator, nor was it often as "bureau chief" or other supervisory position. Most were listed at the position of "clerk" and occasionally as "messenger" and "typewriter."

The third category of occupations on Capitol Hill were those serving the community. In this group, a few were attorneys and doctors, but most were grocers, druggists, teachers, and local artisans—tinners, upholsterers, milliners, brassworkers.

The most evident characteristics of this late Nineteenth Century middle class community were its stability and security. Unlike much of the rest of Washington and unlike many of its counterparts in industrial cities, the Capitol Hill community was able to achieve these qualities because of elements unique to the community.

The major factor which made this security possible was Washington's pursuit of its principal "industries," real estate and government, and more particularly the level at which Capitol Hill residents were employed in these enterprises.

Historians have pointed out the problems encountered by workers in industrializing cities. Richard Sennett, for example, in his book *Families Against the City*[25] has explained the effects of industrialism during the latter half of the Nineteenth Century on a lower middle class community in Chicago. The living and working patterns of the residents of this community revealed their intense insecurity and fear in the face of industrialism's competitive and dehumanizing atmosphere.

Capitol Hill residents were relatively untouched by these worries. Washington, with little commerce or industry, was not shaken by the problems of strikes, factories, large corporations, and immigrant labor that threatened so many cities, and the middle class residents of Capitol Hill did not have to contend with the same fears that plagued Sennett's "families."

Capitol Hill residents were even isolated from the unstable aspects of the two non-industrial enterprises of Washington business. While many depended on real estate and government for their livelihood, most were employed at a level which was largely unaffected by the

---

[25] Richard Sennett, *Families Against the City* (Cambridge: Harvard University Press, 1970).

uncertainty and unpredictability which often characterized these enterprises.

Capitol Hill residents who were employed in jobs attached to the real estate industry of Washington were largely working in the building trades which provided a very "safe" income. While the profits of building were not as great as those of large scale speculation neither were the risks as severe. At this level of the real estate boom, Capitol Hill residents were assured an income as long as the need for houses continued and this need showed no signs of disappearing throughout the 1880's up until the depression in 1893, and even after that time it soon revived to almost its former strength.

Washington's other major "industry," Government, provided even greater security to its Capitol Hill employees than did real estate. Before 1883 government employment was subject to the political whim of the spoils system but in that year the Civil Service Commission Act was passed which transferred many Federal positions to a merit system of competitive exams. This act was particularly important to residents of Capitol Hill since it affected primarily those in the lower and middle income jobs and excepted "from examination . . . Persons whose employment is exclusively professional" and "Chief clerks, superintendents and chiefs of divisions or bureaus." [26] The merit system provided assurance of tenure for those to whom it applied and offered surety that they would be able to keep their jobs regardless of political changes. Carroll Wright suggests in *The Economic Development of the District of Columbia* that one expression of the job stability offered by this act was that civil servants felt safe in purchasing rather than renting homes.[27] The Civil Service Commission Act created a general sense of economic well-being and financial security. "Salaries, though very small, meant a regular monthly income" [28] and if wages did not rise rapidly (by 1900 the Federal pay scale was the same as it had been in 1870), they were adequate and steady.

The third major category of occupations on Capitol Hill—those serving the community—offered the same moderate but sure income as the first two. Almost all were small businessmen engaged in local enterprises—"Fine Family Groceries," "Millinery and Dress Making," "Ice Cream Saloon and Bakers," "Druggist and Chemist"—

[26] U. S. Civil Service Commission, *Civil Service Act, 1883* (Washington, D.C.: Government Printing Office, 1883).

[27] Carroll D. Wright, *The Economic Development of the District of Columbia* (Washington, D.C.: Washington Academy of Sciences, 1899).

[28] Green, *Washington, Capital City,* p. 17.

Figure 9. Built probably before the Civil War, this structure was in use in 1889 as a dry goods store owned by Mary Phelan, a widow who lived on Capitol Hill.

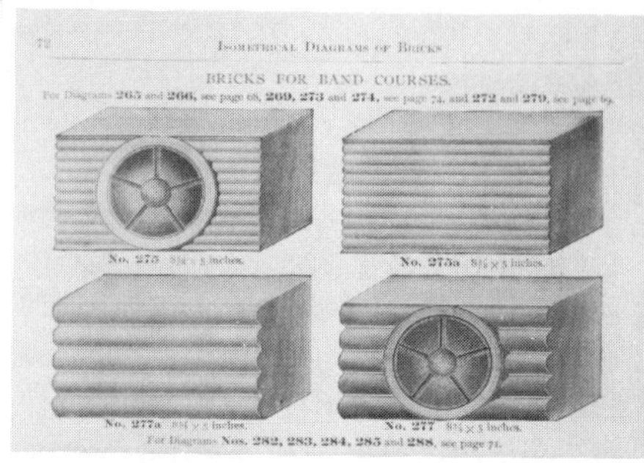

Illustrations from the author

Figure 10. Ornamental bricks No. 275 and No. 277 as shown in an 1890 catalogue of The Peerless Brick Company were among the most popular of the details used on Capitol Hill houses.

located primarily along Pennsylvania Avenue in a five block business district between 2nd and 6th Streets and also in random locations throughout the community, some using their homes as their shops. There is virtually no evidence of large scale enterprise in the immediate Capitol Hill area during this period. In fact, it was not until 1889 that a major bank appeared on Capitol Hill—the National Capitol Bank of Washington which at that time called itself the "only" bank on Capitol Hill.[29] These small businessmen, dependent on the local community and unaffected by more speculative enterprises going on elsewhere in the city, were economically secure as long as the people they served continued to require their products.

As a result of the blending of these economic circumstances, life on Capitol Hill must have seemed very predictable and constant during these last decades of the century when compared with the very transient society of the rest of Washington. An atmosphere of security and stability reveals itself in many ways.

The various institutions of the transient Washington society—boarding houses, rented rooms, hotels, etc.—were largely absent on Capitol Hill. Newspapers for the 1880's and 1890's[30] list very few advertisements on Capitol Hill under "Rooms to Rent" and "Board-

[29] *Illustrated Washington: Our Capital* (New York: American Publishing and Engraving Co., 1890).

[30] Advertisements for sale and rental of houses, for rooms for rent, and boarding, were checked for random dates in the *Washington Star* for 1880, 1881, 1882, 1885, 1889, 1890, and 1891.

ing" as compared with the great numbers of these in the northwest. When they do appear, one finds such restrictions as "low to permanent tenant" [31] and for rent to "reliable and permanent tenants only." [32]

Assessment records suggest that by the last two decades of the century speculation was minimal on Capitol Hill. The 1889–1890 *General Assessment of Real Property in the City of Washington*[33] reveals that individuals generally owned only one or two lots and that these lots were quite often owned by those actually living on the lot. Only occasionally did one person own as many as three to five lots and only four interests owned more than 10 lots; one of these was the unfortunate creditor of "Grant's Folly," the Phoenix Life Insurance Company. Home ownership did not tend to be by the few more wealthy who lived on Capitol Hill as one might expect, but was overwhelmingly by those of the general middle economic level of the community. These ownership patterns hardly suggest the type of transient society characteristic of much of Washington, rather they indicate a permanent and stable community.

The most transient of institutions, hotels, were few on Capitol Hill even though its proximity to the Congress would make one expect the opposite. Guidebooks,[34] newspapers and other contemporary publications rarely mention any major hotels in the eastern city except the Congressional Hotel which was in the older southeastern section of the Hill.

Contemporary sources reinforce the image of a stable residential area. While they rarely mention Capitol Hill directly, they do refer often to the qualities of the government clerks who constituted a large part of that community. An 1884 source noted: "Many are householders, over five thousand, it is estimated, owning comfortable homes of their own, paid for out of their own savings." [35] Carroll Wright, United States Commissioner of Labor and always enthusiastic about the character of the government clerk, wrote: "They have had their influence and no slight one at that, in securing from Congress a recognition of its duties towards the whole body of citizens here. It

---

[31] *Washington Star,* March 31, 1885.

[32] *Washington Star,* 1881.

[33] District of Columbia Assessor's Office, *General Assessment of Real Property in the City of Washington in the District of Columbia, 1889–1890.*

[34] DeB. Randolph Keim, compiler, *Keim's Illustrated Hand-Book* (Washington City: For the Compiler, 1884, 1886, and 1888).

J. H. Soule, *The Pocket Guide to Washington, A Simple and Handy Stranger's Companion at the National Capital* (Washington, D.C.: J. H. Soule, 1881).

Illustrated Washington: Our Capital, 1890.

[35] Joseph West Moore, *Picturesque Washington: Pen and Pencil Sketches* (Providence: J. A. and R. A. Reid, Publishers, 1884), p. 244.

is they in large degree that made Washington attractive. They are public-spirited and interested not in a temporary way but permanently." [36]

Not only the community but also the physical area of Capitol Hill grew and changed in these last decades of the Nineteenth Century. As commercial aims for the far southeastern section of the city, along the Eastern Branch, became less and less a reality, there was no longer any reason to concentrate growth around the river. As a result the extensive building that took place on Capitol Hill during this period was centered around the area directly behind the Capitol and included portions of both the northeast and southeast quadrants where large tracts of relatively undeveloped land were available for building.

By the 1880's the characteristic style of the last decades of the century was rapidly filling the vacant squares. This architecture is of interest both because it represents a change in the philosophy of style and building on Capitol Hill and because it is a reflection of the new community there.

While earlier architecture on the Hill had generally reflected various current modes, the new style was an expression of a specific philosophy of building to which certain formal style elements were added. This philosophy was concerned with brick and the practical, aesthetic and almost moral virtues attributed to building in that medium. Many aspects of the philosophy were expressed in the almost exclusively brick architecture of Capitol Hill during these last decades of the century and its concepts were very well suited to the Capitol Hill community.

While architecture on Capitol Hill has been popularly grouped together under the designation "Queen Anne Style," late Nineteenth Century publications reveal that contemporary interest and knowledge went far beyond this single style.

Late Nineteenth Century builders' periodicals reveal the great interest and the many theories that surrounded brick building during these decades. Even the names of the magazines—*The Brickbuilder* (later the *Architectural Forum*), first published in 1892, *The Clayworker,* first published in 1884—indicate the great popularity of brick. Such periodicals were filled with instructions in and argument over every detail of brick manufacture and construction. Whether bricks should be hand molded or machine molded and, if machine molded, whether they should be wet, semi-dry, or dry pressed, whether air drying or machine drying produced the strongest brick, were frequent subjects of vigorous discussion.

---

[36] Wright, *The Economic Development of the District of Columbia,* p. 181.

Pressed brick fronts which are found on almost all Capitol Hill houses of this period were a particularly popular subject of debate. Pressed bricks were formed under high pressure and the product was a very smooth, fine edged brick of uniform color that became popular in the last decades of the Nineteenth Century for decorative elements and often for non-supporting decorative house fronts. Arguments for and against these pressed brick fronts on both aesthetic and constructional grounds abound. Aesthetically, it was argued that they created an uninteresting and monotonous surface, too smooth and uniform in color. A reply was that pressed brick represented a great technological advance and that it was only resisting change, "looking backward," to reject them in favor of the traditional common brick. Constructionally, they were considered inferior not in themselves, because the intense pressing process produced very strong bricks, but because

Figure 11. Three fine examples of typical late Nineteenth Century Capitol Hill architecture combining the contemporary philosophy of brick building with Queen Anne and Romanesque Revival details. Tan brick in the facade on the left is uncommon on Capitol Hill.

Illustrations from the author

Figure 12. Two examples of the conservative approach to brick architecture which characterizes late Nineteenth Century Capitol Hill houses great and small.

of the way they were utilized in brick fronts. A criticism was that they were not "bonded" or interlocked with the structural wall, in the way that bricks forming a supporting wall would be bonded to one another, but were laid in "blind bond" which meant that the front was more or less free standing, only mortared to the structure, and that the fronts would "crack and shift away from the common brick."

But the overall desirability of building in brick was enthusiastically agreed upon by builders in the late Nineteenth Century. The structural properties of brick were often stressed. A major consideration was that it was cheap, both in manufacture and in construction, and in many cities, among them Washington, clay was readily available. It could be far more easily constructed than stone which required elaborate fitting, was fire-proof, strong and durable, and resisted weathering better than many other materials.

The aesthetic virtues of brick were praised as often and as enthusiastically as the practical. Brickbuilders looked back in history to examples of fine brickwork in Holland, France, northern Germany, northern Italy, and to current "Queen Anne" revivals in England, where brick had served as both a decorative and a structural element. They pointed to the "noble" and "dignified" aspect of structures in this medium and urged American builders to take advantage of brick.

The aesthetic properties attributed to brickwork were carefully defined. Its use and popularity were primarily in reaction to the flamboyant excesses of the Victorian age. It was praised for qualities of modesty and stability and builders in this medium were encouraged to stress the "natural," humble properties of brick. *The Brickbuilder* cautioned in almost every issue that architects and builders should take advantage of the stable, simple, restrained and "straightforward expression" inherent in brick,[37] that they should utilize the "simplest and least expensive treatment . . . which is . . . capable of as much design as a more elaborate and costly affair, and if well treated may be really more beautiful than its more pretentious neighbor." [38]

On Capitol Hill the newly elaborated ideas about building in brick began to express themselves in the early 1880's. Before that time brick had always been a popular building medium there but it had served almost exclusively as a structural element in supporting walls. The front, even if it was constructed of pressed face brick, as some were, was merely a facade upon which overdoor and overwindow decora-

[37] *The Brickbuilder, An Illustrated Monthly Devoted to the Advancement of Brick Architecture,* Vols. I–III (1892–1894).

[38] *The Brickbuilder,* Vol. I, No. 3 (March 1892), p. 17.

tions of wood, copper, or sheet iron were applied and the brick itself was not used as a decorative element. During this period brick took over the decorative as well as the structural functions and soon the entire building, with the exception of metal protective cornices, was made of brick. The result was Capitol Hill's architectural version of the philosophy developed by the brick builders.

In practical terms brick was the perfect building material for homes for people of the moderate economic status of Capitol Hill residents. The low cost of its manufacture along with "the least expensive treatment" created adequate structures that were within the economic range of the members of this society. The structural strength and durability of brick were an added bonus to this community that intended to be a permanent part of Washington.

Aesthetically, Capitol Hill houses adhered strictly to contemporary advice for expressing solidity and restraint in brick building and in some cases even exceeded the most cautious advice of the magazines. The inconspicuous and very simple and massive appearance of these houses is at once an expression of contemporary ideas in brickbuilding and of the community itself.

As was true of other aspects of life in late Nineteenth Century Capitol Hill, the houses were modest yet adequate to their residents' needs. Elaborate structures, that were commonplace in the affluent northwest, were rare on Capitol Hill and tended to appear only on the fashionable East Capitol Street. Variety and innovation were avoided. Advice that "wall surfaces should be generally broad and quiet," with ornament only on cornices, string courses, doors, and windows, that decoration should be only surface patterning not "bold projection," was carefully observed.[39]

Molded ornamental bricks, which formed much of the simple decoration that was used on these houses, were chosen to give a careful and non-individualistic appearance. Contemporary magazines cautioned their readers that the plentiful catalogues advertising decorative brick were lacking in imagination and variety and urged architects and builders to improve the selection of available ornamental bricks. But in comparing the types of brick available in contemporary catalogues[40] with those chosen for Capitol Hill houses it is evident that hardly a tenth of even this limited selection was utilized.

---

[39] *The Brickbuilder,* Vol. I, pp. 3–4.

[40] Washington Hydraulic-Press Brick Company, *Suggestions in Brickwork with Illustrations from the Architecture of Italy, together with a catalogue of Bricks Made by the Hydraulic Press Brick Companies* (Philadelphia: J. B. Lippincott Company, 1895).

Figure 13. Architecture on East Capitol Street, as these two buildings illustrate, was often more elaborate and less conservative than elsewhere on Capitol Hill.

Illustrations from the author

Figure 14. Houses on 8th Street, S. E. which are typical of the style of building on Capitol Hill around the turn of the century when the building boom was beginning to slow.

Simplicity and stability, not change and innovation, characterized the architecture as it did the community.

While Capitol Hill architecture is primarily an expression of theories surrounding building in brick, it also reflects stylistic trends. The two styles which appear the most frequently—Queen Anne and Richardsonian Romanesque—reinforce the architectural and community characteristics which have been described.

The first of these, the so-called "Queen Anne Style," has been popularly used to describe almost any product of the late Nineteenth Century. More accurately, as defined by Elizabeth Aslin in *The Aesthetic Movement,*[41] it should be applied only to a style of brick architecture loosely based on Eighteenth Century vernacular tradi-

[41] Elizabeth Aslin, *The Aesthetic Movement, Prelude to Art Nouveau* (New York and Washington: Frederick A. Praeger, Publishers, 1969).

tions in England which was revived in that country in the late 1860's and gained popularity in America during the 1870's and 1880's. Aslin's theoretical and specific architectural guidelines concerning this style will be utilized here as they apply to Capitol Hill houses.

As defined by Aslin, the Queen Anne Style, as part of the larger "Aesthetic Movement," shared the latter's theoretical focus. This was a "missionary aspect," a desire to be understood not only by the wealthy few but by the general public. William Morris wrote: "I do not want art for a few" and likened the artist working for his own delight to the rich man eating in the presence of "starving soldiers in a beleaguered fort." [42] This revival of Eighteenth Century vernacular building styles in England and America was a reaction against "shams," against the flamboyant Victorian, and in its efforts to reintroduce a more simple architectural style it was an important complement to the theories surrounding brickbuilding generally.

As the changing attitudes in brickbuilding became a part of architecture on Capitol Hill, many of the characteristics of the Queen Anne Style also began to appear—finely jointed dark red brick, tall windows, tall decorated chimneys, quantities of external woodwork, and string courses of ornamental brick. However difficult it may have been to achieve the goals of the "missionary aspect" of this style, it was nonetheless an expressly non-elitist style calling for "simple" and "honest" construction as did the brickbuilders. As such it was made up of both theoretical and stylistic elements that were perfectly suited to express the middle class community of Capitol Hill.

The Queen Anne influence was felt in Capitol Hill architecture well into the 1890's, but in the late 1880's it was joined by a second predominant style—the Romanesque Revival of Henry Hobson Richardson—which added certain subtleties to the existing aesthetic. At this time, external woodwork became less popular, the strong vertical emphasis and other elements of the Queen Anne Style were joined and sometimes replaced by the broad and massive style inspired by Richardson. Here, as with the Queen Anne, qualities attributed to this style were significant in expressing the Capitol Hill community.

Henry Hobson Richardson chose Romanesque architecture as the prototype for his creations not in order to generate a revival of this style but to utilize it as a model from which details and a general "spirit" could be taken and applied to modern society. Architectural historians have had much to say about the monumental and imposing

---

[42] *Ibid,* p. 33.

Illustrations from the author

Figure 15. This simple example of the ubiquitous brick architecture of Capitol Hill was owned in 1889 by John C. Baum, who was a grocer at 401 East Capitol Street. The house was valued in 1889 at $1,600.

yet at the same time ordered and simple structures designed by Richardson and how these were representative of the fast growing and changing late Nineteenth Century American society.[43]

Wayne Andrews in *Architecture, Ambition and Americans* sees Richardson's architecture as a translation of "the fierce ambition of our millionaires."[44] In *Images of American Living,* Alan Gowans, on the other hand, believes that they create "an impression of solidity, an attitude of stability, a mood of security."[45] Whether Andrews or Gowans has accurately described the general spirit and "meaning"

[43] Wayne Andrews, *Architecture, Ambition and Americans* (New York: The Free Press, 1964).

Alan Gowans, *Images of American Living, Four Centuries of Architecture and Furniture as Cultural Expression* (Philadelphia and New York: J. B. Lippincott Company, 1964).

[44] Andrews, *Architecture, Ambition and Americans,* p. 158.

[45] Gowans, *Images of American Living,* p. 352

behind Richardson's architecture, it is the aspect that Gowans describes that is most evident in Capitol Hill's "Romanesque" houses.

Very few houses on Capitol Hill were executed in a style strictly faithful to Richardson's example and very few—almost none—were built entirely in stone which was his characteristic medium. Nonetheless, in details of construction—broad arches, various stone details, and "medieval accents" such as carved decorative elements and turrets—as well as in the general impression of massiveness that pervades most of the houses of the late 1880's and 1890's, there is definite evidence of the influence that Richardson's architecture had on these buildings. These houses are hardly lavish reflections of millionaires but are instead a simple and solid expression of the middle class residents of Capitol Hill. As Gowans has interpreted the choice of the Romanesque style: "They eagerly looked for anything, however symbolic and on whatever scale, that might recall the old lost sense of permanence and belonging." [46] But on Capitol Hill this style, as well as the others described, were chosen not to "recall the old lost sense of permanence" but rather, as suggested throughout this study, reflected the existence of these qualities in this simple community. This community enjoyed an amount of stability and security that was unusual in the last decades of the Nineteenth Century and its architecture was a faithful and accurate reflection of these qualities.

---

[46] *Ibid.*, p. 352.

Chevy Chase Village in the Context of the National Suburban Movement, 1870–1900

RODERICK S. FRENCH

This paper has three main divisions. In the first, Washington's suburbanization is examined in comparison with that of Boston. The second is a study of Senator Newlands' Chevy Chase Land Company as the outstanding example of private initiative in either city. The third analyzes Chevy Chase Village as a community founded in that period.

GENERAL COMPARISON WITH THE GROWTH OF BOSTON, 1870–1900

It sometimes takes a conscious effort to remember that the post-Civil War period is the first epoch of city building in the United States for which any important generalizations about national urban development can be applied to the District of Columbia. Prior to that time Washington belongs to the history of urban planning, thanks to the commission to Major L'Enfant, and to the history of national politics, thanks to the arbitrary location of the capital on the Potomac, but otherwise to the history of towns and villages. The Federal City was urban neither in scale nor in ethos before 1870, but from that moment on Washington does deserve to be included in the study of urbanization in this country.[1]

To give more specific focus to the comparative study of the suburban expansion of the District of Columbia, I will examine our development in relation to that of Boston. Sam Bass Warner's study, *Streetcar Suburbs: The Process of Growth in Boston 1870–1900,* provides an excellent framework within which to identify both common and

[1] This general point can be readily confirmed through an examination of any one of several interpretive works in American urban history. For one example, in terms of the periodization employed by Christopher Tunnard and Henry Hope Reed in *The American Skyline* (Boston: Houghton Mifflin, 1955), Washington has no part in the first four epochs of national city building, pp. 32–117. However, after the Civil War their characterizations of the phases of urban development are quite apt for any discussion of local developments, pp. 118 ff.

distinctive elements in the history of the two cities. Furthermore, within the general narrative of growth in Boston, there is the reasonably well-documented story of Henry M. Whitney and his West End Land Company.[2] This private initiative in real estate and street railways parallels to some degree the role of Francis G. Newlands and the Chevy Chase Land Company in the local suburban movement.

There is of course a significant difference in absolute numbers between the populations of Washington and Boston at both the beginning and the end of this period.[3] However, the rates of growth are quite proportionate: Boston's population increased by 120 percent over the three decades, Washington's by 112 percent. Moreover, the new areas opened up for residential occupation in the two metropolitan centers were comparable in extent. Warner estimates that Boston's middle class enjoyed a sixfold increase in its potential area of settlement in the last third of the nineteenth century.[4] The "annexation" of Washington County in 1871 instantly added six times the area occupied by the City of Washington prior to that date.[5] Street railways not only opened that newly annexed territory to settlement but by 1900 had gone beyond the D.C. line to make many additional tens of square miles potentially accessible to would-be suburbanites.

What is even more relevant than these figures for present purposes is the transformation of the *patterns* of residential settlement which characterized the two cities during this interval. Although one of America's older cities, Boston remained a "pedestrian city" down to the middle of the Nineteenth Century. This meant that the area of significant settlement was confined within a two-mile radius from City Hall. Starting in the 1870's the introduction of improved street railway lines and attendant utilities made possible a progressive extension of the perimeter of dense settlement by one-half to one and

[2] The main source is Louis P. Hager, *History of the West End Street Railway* (Boston, 1892). The book contains several speeches by Whitney and endless statistics on public transportation systems around the world in addition to the narrative by Hager.

[3] The 1870 census gave Boston's population as 250,526 and Washington's as 131,700. The figures reported for 1900 were 560,892 and 278,718 respectively.

[4] Warner, *Streetcar Suburbs* (Cambridge: Harvard University Press, 1962), p. 52.

[5] I am aware that the reasons for instituting the Territorial Government in 1871 and for its abolishment in 1874 were a complex mixture of national and local political considerations. However, from the point of view of urban history I think there is some value in interpreting that action as the equivalent of annexation. Boston annexed Roxbury in 1868, Dorchester in 1870, and West Roxbury in 1873. These actions added slightly more than twenty-five square miles to Boston. Throughout this paper I will be referring only to developments on the Maryland side of the river. "Until street railway lines ran over the Aqueduct Bridge into Virginia in the late nineties, Washington's suburbia included none of the areas beyond the Potomac." Constance McLaughlin Green, *Washington: Capital City, 1879–1950* (Princeton: Princeton University Press, 1953), p. 16.

one-half miles per decade. By the end of the century "the outer limits of convenient street railway commuting stood about 6 miles from City Hall. By transferring one could travel 10 miles and even farther, but good linear service, with cars at ten- to fifteen-minute intervals, ex-

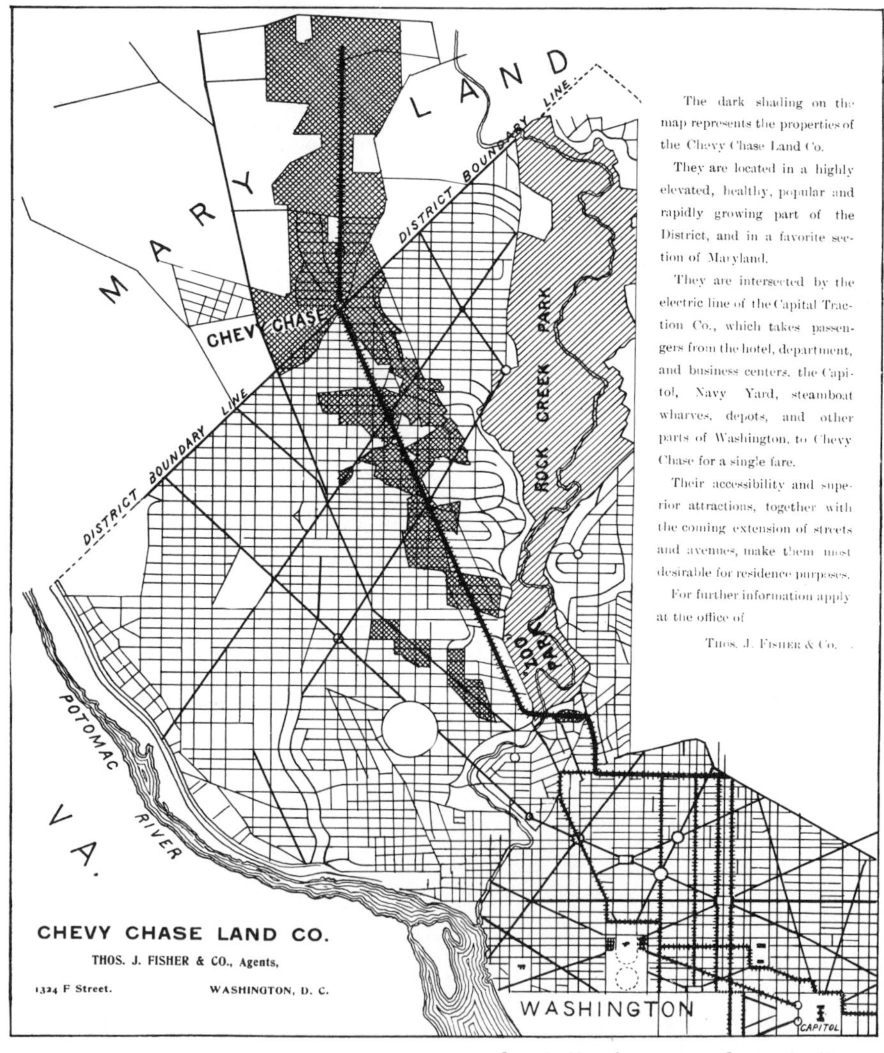

From the Collection of Robert A. Truax

Advertising map of the Chevy Chase Land Co., 1897.

This advertisement links the Chevy Chase Land Co. with its agent Thos. J. Fisher & Co. It appeared in *Greater Washington: The Nation's City Viewed from the Material Viewpoint* published in 1897.

tended only 6 miles out." [6] This six-mile commute took approximately one hour in Boston in 1900.

To gain some idea of the comparable expansion of residential Washington, one can begin with the observation that the 132,000 people living in the District of Columbia in 1870 were similarly concentrated within a two-mile radius of the White House. A circle, or better semicircle, drawn with this two-mile radius embraces Georgetown on the west, LeDroit Park on the north and the Library of Congress on the east. The concentration of local settlement is further emphasized by noting that the total population of Washington County in 1870 was 11,117. This meant that the number of people living in the sixty-odd square miles of the District of Columbia outside the bounds of Georgetown and L'Enfant's Federal City had increased by fewer than ten thousand persons in the seventy years since the founding of the capital.

The facilitating factor in the expansion which was to come, here as in Boston, was the street railway. The first horse-drawn tram line began operation in the District in 1862, ten years later than its counterpart in Boston. However, the technical success and financial profit associated with this innovation touched off an equal "wave of entrepreneurial enthusiasm" in both cities. As a matter of fact, electrification, the high point of this enterprise, was inaugurated in Washington in 1888, one year prior to its appearance in Boston. Furthermore, the range of good commuter service was somewhat larger locally by 1900.

In 1870 the street railways went only as far west as 35th Street in Georgetown and out East Capitol Street to 9th Street. The only line which pushed beyond the original bounds of L'Enfant's City was the branch of the Washington and Georgetown Railroad Company which ran up 7th Street, N.W., to Rock Creek Church Road.[7]

In 1880, although downtown service had proliferated, only two lines had extended the perimeter of "suburban" service. The Columbia

---

[6] Warner, pp. 21, 52.

[7] The indispensable source on early transit routes is William Tindall, "Beginnings of Street Railways in the District of Columbia," *Records of the Columbia Historical Society,* Vol. 21 (1918), pp. 24–86. See also John H. White, Jr., "Public Transport in Washington Before the Great Consolidation of 1902," *Records of the Columbia Historical Society of Washington, D. C. 1966–1968* (1969), pp. 216–230. For a discussion of transit politics, capitalization, management, etc. see the unpublished M.A. thesis by John W. Boettjer, "Street Railways in the District of Columbia" (George Washington University, 1963). For a combination of historical information and a great wealth of photographs and other illustrative material see LeRoy O. King, *100 Years of Capital Traction* (Dallas, Texas, 1973). By far the most useful information on this general topic came from numerous conversations with Robert A. Truax, Curator of Prints and Photographs of the Columbia Historical Society. Mr. Truax gladly shares his extensive knowledge and private collection of materials with any sincere student of Washington.

Railway Company line went out H Street as far as 15th Street, N.E., and the Anacostia and Potomac Company tracks reached the 11th Street bridge.

A great increase in the numbers and lengths of transit lines took place during the next decade. By the end of the year 1890 the Tenalytown Road was completed to the District line. A new route had opened on 14th Street, N.W., up to Park Road, and the Eckington Line had reached the Soldiers' Home. The Anacostia line had crossed the 11th Street bridge and extended service in the Southeast as far as Monroe Street.

By 1900 it was possible and even convenient to work in Washington and live in Glen Echo, Maryland (eight miles west of the White House) or in Seat Pleasant, Maryland to the northeast, or in Congress Heights in southeast Washington. Chevy Chase Circle could be reached in thirty-five minutes in cars leaving every fifteen minutes from the Treasury Department. This service continued on to Jones Bridge Road without necessity of transfer, a distance of nearly eight miles from the White House.[8]

Having sketched in rough outline the story of growth and development in the two cities between 1870 and 1900, it is necessary next to analyze the more specific circumstances and motivations which accounted for this expansion. Warner identifies "three sets of experiences and three associated ideas" which he believes to have been common to most urban Americans in the late Nineteenth Century and to have shaped their behavior in connection with the present subject. The three were: increasing industrialization with the accompanying idea of romantic capitalism, large immigrations which produced nostalgic nationalisms, and the appeal of the rural ideal as an emotional reaction to progressive urbanization.[9]

Simply to observe that the first two of these three broad explanatory concepts were essentially inoperative in Washington reminds us again of the uniqueness of the Federal City. It also means that we must either locate other driving forces to account for our parallel growth or attribute the motive for our suburban expansion to those native Americans who moved here in such large numbers in the latter decades of the last century. Further comparative analysis may disclose the answers.

The prosperity which formed the platform for "fifty years of aggressive expansion" in Boston was the result of industrial developments in the 1840's made possible by the combination of abundant steam

[8] *Post,* May 31, 1903.

[9] Warner, p. 5.

Photograph courtesy of Charles M. Wagner

The Eastern Terminus of the Rock Creek Railway at Florida Avenue, just east of 17th Street, N. W., about 1894.

The street car in the foreground is a Lamokin closed body mounted on a Robinson Radial motor truck. The second car, also built by Lamokin, is mounted on a regular single truck motor truck. Both cars were built in 1892.

power and masses of cheap immigrant labor. This expanded wealth stimulated municipal enterprise and imparted a kind of romantic "enthusiasm for wealth and productivity" to Boston society generally. Washington's relationship to the romantic enterprises of this era was perhaps vicarious but certainly real, as was recorded all too vividly by Mark Twain in *The Gilded Age*.[10] Such prosperity as Washington did

[10] "Many of the characteristics of Gilded Age America could be discerned in Washington. Indeed, the city was a microcosmic reflection of national culture, with fortunes quickly gained, status changes of different social groups, and the effects of these transformations being as visible as in the nation at large." James Kirkpatrick Flack, Jr., *The Formation of the Washington Intellectual Community, 1870–1898* (Ann Arbor: University Microfilms, 1971), p. 19. There are more than literary reasons for a reference to Twain in this context. He had mastered the setting for his scandalous novel during a

enjoy was not the direct fruit of industry, except for the wealth of those members of the new industrial elite who chose to spend the social season in the capital. Far more important for the economic and physical growth of Washington was the fact that the "industry" of permanent government boomed during this period. The number of government employees reached 23,000 in 1890, a figure larger than the total population of the city just fifty years earlier. The size and stability of that federal payroll laid the foundation for Washington's long-delayed emergence as an urban center. The growth and industrial expansion of the country as a whole, of course, was in part responsible for creating the need for this permanent bureaucratic machinery of state.

It is important to differentiate the source of Washington's population as well as its wealth from that of Boston. This becomes decisive for an accurate understanding of suburbanization as a social process. One-third of Boston's population in 1870 was foreign born. That same census lists 3,496 or one percent of Bostonians as being Colored. By way of contrast, only twelve percent of the people living in Washington were foreign born, while one-third of the population was black. This dramatic set of inverse ratios became more pronounced by the end of our thirty-year period and its significance magnified by the growth in numbers. Blacks in Washington doubled in number, thereby maintaining their proportion of the total population, whereas the proportion of foreign born shrank to seven percent. The comparative figures for the two cities in 1870 and 1900 were as follows.[11]

	1870		1900	
	Boston	Washington	Boston	Washington
Total	250,526	131,700	560,892	278,718
Foreign born	87,986	16,254	197,129	20,119
Black	3,496	43,404	11,591	86,702

These simple demographic facts gave rise to profoundly different social outcomes in the otherwise parallel stories of suburbanization in

brief stint in 1868 as secretary to Senator William Morris Stewart. Twain had met and observed the Senator during Twain's days as a young journalist in Nevada. As we shall see in the next section, the link between the Nevada mining fortunes, the national political careers built on those fortunes, and the infusion of Western speculative capital into local real estate was a major factor in Washington's suburban development in the 1880's and 1890's.

[11] For a more complete breakdown of population characteristics throughout this period, see Table A.

the two cities in the late Nineteenth Century. In order to appreciate fully those different outcomes, we must also mention the reluctant but real factor of social class. Warner estimated that between forty and fifty percent of Boston's population was middle class by income, and that perhaps as many as sixty percent belonged to that class "by living habits and aspirations." [12] I suspect that owing to the absence of heavy industry, the negligible foreign immigration, and the educational requirements of government service, at least sixty percent of Washingtonians in this period belonged to a relatively homogeneous middle class. My assumption of homogeneity is based both on the fact that most Washingtonians (black and white) were native to this three-state region and on the general parity of incomes within the relatively narrow range of government salaries in this period.[13]

This similarity in the proportions of the middle class in the two metropolitan areas conceals two decisive sociological discrepancies. First, the great majority of those who constituted that large middle class population in the District were native Americans. Second, an even more overwhelming proportion of them were white.[14] This corre-

---

[12] Warner, p. 8 ff. According to Warner's calculations, the middle middle class made up 15 percent of Boston's population, and it was this block of people most associated with suburban growth. He estimates 5 percent of the population to have belonged to the upper middle class at this time, and 20–30 percent to the lower middle class. Warner, p. 53.

[13] For a variety of cultural and intellectual reasons the precise definition of class is never easy in our society. I can cite examples of the kind of indicators which have shaped my conclusions. For example, thoughout this thirty year period, at least 75 percent of the District's population was native either to the District or to Maryland and Virginia. (This was true for over 90 percent of the black population; but the fact that over half of these persons were newly freed slaves requires a totally separate analysis of the question of class in the black community.) A classification of the District's population by occupation in 1880 was as follows: agriculture, 1,365; professional and personal services, 29,845; trade and transportation, 6,126; manufacture, mechanical and mining, 11,705. Cited in de B. Randolph Keim, *Keim's Illustrated Hand-Book of Washington and Its Environs* (Washington: The Compiler, 1883), p. 10. Civil service payrolls in the period reveal a heavy concentration in a narrow range of middle-level salaries. According to the Civil Service Act of 1883 all jobs paying over $1,800 or below $900 per year were classified as non-competitive. If we take as an example the department with largest local payroll, Treasury, we find the following breakdown for the year 1884: 149 positions with salaries of $2,000 or higher; 1,754 classified employees earning between $900 and $1,800; 304 positions paying less than $900. Further differentiations accentuate the picture of concentration. Of the 149 positions above $1,800, 121 paid between $2,000 and $2,500. All 304 salaries below $900 were within $180 of one another as the range was from $660 to $840. J. H. Soule, ed., *The United States Blue Book* (Washington, 1885), pp. 48–52.

[14] The question of the class composition of Washington's black community is extremely complex. Constance McLaughlin Green emphasizes the existence of pronounced status divisions in *The Secret City* (Princeton: Princeton University Press, 1967), but it

lation of class and race prevented from happening in Washington what Warner describes as the major social result of Boston's suburbanization: the creation throughout the metropolitan area of new residential communities distinguished by "ethnic integration and income separation." [15]

> During the years 1870–1900 one basic pattern organized the whole suburban metropolis: people were separated by income and mixed together with little regard to national origin. Although ethnic concentrations continually appeared, such groupings were strictly temporary and subsidiary clusters subject to the general movement of people by income capability and income identification. Indeed, an observation of the timing and degree of concentration of these clusters provides the historian with a good measure of the democratic openness of Boston society.[16]

The contrast with Washington is almost total and quite melancholy. On the one hand, the relatively few foreign-born residents of the District tended to concentrate in neighborhoods of first or second

---

is hard to gain from that book a sense of the relative size of the different classes. In several conversations, Professor Letitia Brown has stressed that classes in the black community were never so income determined as among whites. Education levels and the general reputation of one's family over several generations counted for more than salary levels. No doubt much more research needs to be done on this point. There are some relevant items of information which can be mentioned. According to Mrs. Green, p. 129, approximately 10 percent of the civil service positions were filled by Negroes in the early 1890's. However, they were over 30 percent of the population at that time and the majority of those employed by the government held lower-level positions, so the significance of that fact is not entirely clear. In the 1900 census, on the other hand, more than one-third of the 23,000 male Negroes over the age of 21 were still classified as illiterate which would indicate a severe lack of qualifications for middle class employment. However, as will be shown, the question of class was virtually irrelevant in any event when it came to the matter of residential areas open to black settlement.

[15] Warner, p. 64. The weight of Warner's conclusion is magnified by the contrasting observation that the pre-1850 Boston "suburbs," that is the towns which were to become suburbs through incorporation, did not separate residence and commerce and industry with the consequence that residential patterns in that earlier period showed a mix of classes in most communities. That diversity was lost through suburbanization. Warner, p. 18.

[16] Ethnic clustering, of course, was neither so minimal nor so transitory in the suburban development of many other major American cities during this period. See the classic study of Chicago by Louis Wirth in chapters 9–13 of *The Ghetto*. This discussion of ethnic suburbanization and class has become a central theme in recent arguments among urban social theorists. Irving Kristol, among others, has attempted to generalize Warner's hypothesis to the point that it becomes the defining element of American urbanization. According to this theory, we should now understand assimilation or Americanization as having meant *embourgeoisement* and dispersal to the suburbs. Because of partisan political interest in minimizing the ethnic divisions in our urban societies, and particulary any correlatons between those divisions and income levels, Kirstol is eager to argue that our cities have always performed this basic function of middle-classification rather well and are even now, belatedly, doing it for blacks. See Kristol's article, "An Urban Civilization without Cities," *Horizon,* 14 (Autumn 1972), 36–41.

settlement inside the boundaries of the old Federal City.[17] And whereas as many as fifteen percent of the District's black people were living in suburban areas (roughly the same percentage as for whites), they were either scattered in still rural districts such as Reno and Mt. Pleasant or concentrated in exclusively black suburbs such as Barry Farms. When blacks did move into previously all-white suburban communities, as they did into LeDroit Park in the mid-1890's, the familiar Twentieth Century process of neighborhood succession went into operation, reversing the racial composition of that community in less than ten years. This local pattern of ethnic segregation was not entirely a consequence of informal social attitudes. Whereas Warner reported that he found no racial or religious covenants in his research into Boston suburbs, Washington's first planned suburb, Uniontown, was restricted to white homeowners by covenant.

However, formal covenants on residential property were not really needed either in the downtown area or the former Washington County. As Mrs. Green has described the process, those few good years of liberty and mutuality which followed the Civil War quickly gave way to disenfranchisement and social exclusion for blacks of whatever class or qualifications. By the 1890's, even the most affluent and genteel Negroes, according to Mrs. Green, "could rarely buy [a house] at all in a conveniently located, orderly neighborhood" in the downtown area.[18] They were forced either to go farther from the center of the city and there to locate in increasingly segregated districts or to join the multitudes in Washington's infamous Alley Dwellings. And, as James Borchert showed in an article in the previous volume of these *Records*, housing in the alleys became even more rigorously segregated after 1870 than was that on the streetfronts.[19]

---

[17] In 1880, for example, of the seventeen thousand foreign born only two thousand were living in the new suburban communities in the old Washington County area. The major foreign-born neighborhoods were in the near Northwest and the Old Southwest. Although Mrs. Green's studies would support this conclusion in general, she does speculate that during the 1850's a fair number of immigrants may have located on the other side of the Anacostia River because housing costs were cheaper there. Constance McLaughlin Green, *Washington: Village and Capital, 1800–1878* (Princeton: Princeton University Press, 1962), p. 183. The absence of census data for the period 1880–1900 on the distribution of foreign born in new suburban areas of the District makes it impossible to be more precise on this point. However, it is clear from Table A that there was *no* movement of recent immigrants to the more remote suburban communities in suburban Maryland.

[18] Green, *Secret City*, p. 127. All of chapter 7 is relevant for its account of the deterioration of race relations in the District in the period under review.

[19] James Borchert, "The Rise and Fall of Washington's Inhabited Alleys: 1852–1972," *Records of the Columbia Historical Society of Washington, D.C. 1971–1972* (1973), pp. 267–288. For an analysis of the 1880 census in this connection see John P. Radford's M.A. Thesis, "Patterns of White-Nonwhite Residential Segregation in Washington, D.C. in the Late Nineteenth Century" (University of Maryland, 1967), esp. chapters 3 and 4.

With respect to the new areas of settlement, it would be a safe generalization for this period that whenever a suburban subdivision was created by a developer, e.g., Brookland, it was segregated. When settlement clusters formed haphazardly over a period of years in the large undeveloped areas of the District, then there was the chance that the two races might live near one another. However, even in the latter instances community life would be organized in segregated institutions. Mt. Pleasant, for example, had a colored Sunday School by 1871. Tennalytown (Tennleytown) had six churches in 1902, two of which were black.[20] Illustrations of this pattern of ethnic concentration are abundant in the censuses taken by the Metropolitan Police Department in the 1890's. Some representative figures are reported below.

	1892[a]	
	White	Black
Anacostia	2,116	106
Brookland	461	—
Hillsdale	141	1,917
LeDroit Park[c]	1,137	49
Garfield	—	226
Tennalytown	520	211
Grant Avenue	198	189

	1897[b]	
	White	Black
Anacostia	2,571	68
Brookland	671	55
Hillsdale	102	2,062
LeDroit Park[c]	1,721	146
Garfield	—	486
Tennalytown	758	369
Territory bounded by Florida Avenue on the south, Rock Creek on the west, 7th Street on the east, and Spring Road on the north	5,986	4,312

[a] *Report of the Commissioners of the District of Columbia, 1892.*
[b] *Report of the Commissioners, 1897.*
[c] This designation when used for census purposes obviously covers a much larger area than the private development of that name.

We can close this line of analysis with two demographic generalizations. (See Table A.) At the end of the thirty-year period the per-

[20] See the appropriate files of newspaper clippings in the Washingtoniana Room of the Martin Luther King Memorial Library, and in the same place the volume of clippings compiled under the title *Suburban Districts.*

TABLE A

	1870	1880	1890	1900
District of Columbia				
Total	131,700	177,624	230,392	278,718
Foreign born	16,254	17,122	18,770	20,119
Black	43,404	59,596	75,572	86,702
Washington City				
Total	109,119	147,307	118,932	220,698[b]
Foreign born	13,757	14,237		
Black	35,455	48,179	69,404[a]	70,284[b]
Georgetown				
Total	11,384	12,578	14,046	15,889[b]
Foreign born	1,020	814		
Black	3,271	3,759	4,030[a]	4,138[b]
Washington County				
Total	11,117	17,753	27,414	41,195[b]
Foreign born	1,477	2,064		
Black	4,678	7,464	11,387[a]	13,903[b]
Montgomery County				
Total	20,563	24,759	27,185	30,451
Foreign born	492	369	352	386
Black	7,434	9,150	9,710	10,054
Prince George's County				
Total	21,138	26,451	26,080	29,898
Foreign born	529	570	590	758
Black	9,780	12,486	11,295	11,985
Boston				
Total	250,526*	362,839**	448,477	560,892
Foreign born	87,986	114,796	158,172	197,129
Black	3,496	5,873	8,125	11,591

* This figure includes Dorchester and Roxbury.

** Including now West Roxbury as well.

[a] The U.S. Census no longer reported ethnic factors of the populations for the old jurisdictions. The figures are taken from the police census conducted in June 1892. This means that the numbers of blacks are slightly higher than the actual counts would have been for 1890.

[b] These figures are taken from the police census of April 1897. The totals are very close to the U.S. Census of 1900 which the District Commissioners believed to have seriously underreported Washington's population.

centage of the population of Washington living in the former County had doubled. The ratio of blacks to whites was virtually uniform in the two jurisdictions, but the residential segregation along ethnic lines was more pronounced at the close of the period than at the beginning. (This generalization does not apply to Georgetown which was undergoing its own evolution during this period. In terms of residential patterns it was the most mixed of the three old jurisdictions in the last years of the Nineteenth Century.)

Continuing our comparative analysis under a different heading, one further result of suburbanization in Boston was that by 1900 it had become "very much a city divided" in terms of zones of use as well as income levels. There was "an inner city of work and low-income housing, and an outer city of middle- and upper-income residences." [21] There are at least two good reasons why this did not happen to anything like the same degree in the District of Columbia. In the first place, there continued to be several premium residential neighborhoods located well inside the old City lines. As a matter of fact, it was the high cost of real estate and of housing in particular which drove many working class and lower-middle class people to find less expensive homes in distant suburbs where land was cheaper but the amenities fewer. In the second place, there was not the same "enthusiasm for a two-part city—a city of work separated from a city of homes" because Washington's inner city was not the usual Nineteenth Century nightmare of manufacturing establishments and grim tenements. Downtown Washington remained, in most of its neighborhoods, an attractive and interesting place in which to live. (Except during summers, a fact which did motivate a seasonal exodus which gradually assumed a permanent character as suburban expansion.) It was not until the physical deterioration and racial polarization of the District reached serious proportions in the mid-Twentieth Century that Washingtonians were really animated by "an enthusiasm for a two-part city."

Although we can assume, therefore, that Washington's middle classes did not develop the same intense hostility toward the city as did their urban contemporaries elsewhere, it would be wrong not to recognize that they also succumbed to the charms and promises of the romantic rural ideal. It is necessary to read only a few samples of the literature prepared by our local suburban developers to be impressed by the strength of the emotional appeal inherent in the vision of a comfortable life in a salubrious natural setting.

This theme made an early appearance in the 1850's in the propaganda designed to lure buyers across the Anacostia into Van Hook's new 240-acre subdivision, Uniontown. The 24 by 130 lots were placed on the market for $60 each in 1854. The announcement in the paper described the lots as "situated in the most beautiful and healthy neighborhood around Washington,—the street will be graded, the

[21] Warner, p. 2.

gutters paved, and edged with shade trees, without charge to lot holders." Van Hook and his partners were assuming, as one historian has said, that Navy Yard workers would like to have a home "with country life adjunct, near their place of business." [22]

A second illustration of this theme can be taken from the brochure circulated at the close of our period by Moore and Hill, Inc., exclusive agents for the Cleveland Park subdivision.

> Cleveland Park . . . is within the District limits, and consequently enjoys every advantage which a downtown resident can claim, and in addition, it is as beautiful a spot and as free from the annoyances of the city as if it were in the heart of the Adirondacks. Its sewerage is the best, its water supply is unlimited, and the water clear and pure; you can have gas or electric light, or both, in your house, just as you prefer; and there is a fire engine for emergency, should it occur.
>
> The park is favored with a special detail of police, to accommodate which there has been erected an attractive little house, which answers at once as a station for the police and suitable quarters for the chemical fire engine which is a part of the District Fire Department. Besides these municipal improvements, there is every blessing of fresh country air, plenty of elbow room, woods and fields, peacefulness, coolness in summer, and comfort in winter.[23]

It is clear that local proponents of the new communities opened up by the street railway interpreted suburban development at least in part in terms of the rural ideal with its emphases "on the pleasure of private family life, on the security of a small community setting, and on the enjoyment of natural surroundings." [24] We shall see further evidence of the power of this ideal in a later section of this paper which deals with Chevy Chase Village.

Before turning to the discussion of Chevy Chase, there is one last conclusion reached by Warner in his analysis of Boston which must be summarized if we are to grasp the full significance of Senator Francis Griffith Newlands' enterprise. Surveying this mass movement to the suburbs accomplished in the last third of the Nineteenth Century in the Boston region, Warner asked himself "who" was responsible for its remarkably orderly accomplishment. To his surprise, the best hypothesis seemed to be the concept of "regulation without laws." An

[22] Charles R. Burr, "A Brief History of Anacostia, Its Name, Origin and Progress," *Records of the Columbia Historical Society,* Vol. 23 (1920), pp. 167–179.

[23] This copy was reproduced in the brochure from an article in the *Post* of May 10, 1903. That article was one of a series of feature stories on all the leading suburbs which ran in the *Post* that year. They constitute a particularly eloquent record of the vogue of this rural inspiration of the suburban movement.

[24] Warner, p. 14.

unofficial "partnership between large institutions and individual investors and homeowners" somehow operated to produce strikingly uniform results in a phenomenon involving hundreds of thousands of people over an interval of three decades. This movement evolved essentially "without zoning, without large-scale builders, and without public control of subdivision" and nonetheless produced the consensus which governed the creation of that environment which is recognized everywhere as "suburbia." [25]

This absence of legal regulations is another point of striking contrast with the District. As early as 1888 Congress passed a law requiring suburban developers to make their subdivisions conform to the street plan of the city. This was followed by the further stipulations of the Highway Act of 1893 and the creation of the Park Commission in 1901. Mrs. Green believes these three actions, together with coordinate policies formulated by the District Commissioners "constitute the first conscious attempt to guide the suburban growth of an American community along lines that would ensure harmony between new developments and the parent city." [26]

Warner was most impressed with the prominence of "small contractors and individual homeowners" as opposed to government initiatives or large scale developers. In the three suburban towns which he examined most closely—Roxbury, West Roxbury, and Dorchester—22,500 residential structures went up between 1870 and 1900. He found that at least 9,000 people were responsible for their construction. The largest single developer active in this thirty-year period built only 328 homes. The second most active landowner built only half that number. Warner's main explanation for this pattern of individualism is that there was a short supply of big capital available for local, long-term investment.[27]

---

[25] Warner, pp. 125, 4, 117ff. Because of the constraints on the small contractor builder, only a few basic house styles were risked with the resultant visual sameness. Warner is not entirely consistent on this point: compare his stress on variety, p. 68. Developers in Boston used 15–25 year covenants to assure conformity to stipulations as to structures and land use.

[26] Green, *Washington: Capital City,* p. 48. I have not mentioned Governor Shepherd's strenuous efforts at modernization in this narrative. Although they had a very large indirect influence on suburban growth, his "comprehensive plan of improvements" actually included very few efforts in the old County except for bridges over the Anacostia and some road grading to the north and east.

[27] Warner, p. 117. ". . . the main task of the speculator was to cut up the land into house lots, begin construction of streets, and find purchasers for the land. Only rarely did the speculators of this era follow the modern practice of purchasing land, setting out streets, and building houses in order to sell a finished land-house unit to the ultimate customer. Such a process required the tying up of more capital than most could command." (121)

MAJOR PRIVATE INITIATIVES IN THE TWO CITIES

The one notable exception to this pattern of individual or small-scale operators in this period in Boston was the development of the two miles of Beacon Street which lay within the borders of Brookline, Massachusetts. The transformation of this country drive into a French boulevard was the project of a syndicate headed by Henry M. Whitney. The West End Land Company began purchasing farms along the route in 1886.[28] The language of Mr. Whitney's publicist is worth reproducing.

> In 1886 Mr. Henry M. Whitney, who had become convinced of the magnificent possibilities of that section of Boston bordering on the town of Brookline, purchased large tracts of land along the line of Beacon street in the latter place, and shortly after formed a syndicate for its development. Having done this, he employed F.L. & J.C. Olmsted of Boston, to carry out the plans he had long cherished of connecting the two places named by a grand boulevard 200 feet in width.
>
> * * *
>
> The detailed plan of the grand boulevard is as follows: Average width, 160 feet; sidewalks on both sides, 10 feet wide; planting space for trees, 5 feet; driveway, 30 feet; trees, 5 feet; railways, 20 feet; trees, 5 feet. Length of boulevard, seven miles; total cost, about $227,000. About 1,300,000 square feet of land was required to widen the boulevard to its present width. Of this amount the West End Land Company gave 630,000 [sq.] feet, or about one half the quantity needed for the improvement, and Mr. Whitney pledged $100,000 individually for the project.[29]

After embarking on these grand improvements, however, it soon became evident to Whitney's syndicate "that the means of transporta-

[28] Warner, pp. 60, 125. Brookline was immediately adjacent to, not within, Warner's area of primary study. Whitney's father, Gen. James S. Whitney, was one of Brookline's most prominent citizens. The family moved from Boston to Brookline in the 1870's; their home was on the intersection of Beacon and Harvard Streets. John W. Denehy, *A History of Brookline, Massachusetts 1630–1900* (Brookline: Brookline Press Co.: 1906), p. 127.

[29] Hager, pp. 11–12. Hager may be forgiven for claiming all of Beacon street for his entrepreneurial hero. As a matter of fact, Beacon street had been steadily advancing westward as a "swell street" since the building of the Mill Dam across the Back Bay much earlier in the century. Its extension through Brookline had begun in 1850. For details and illustrations see Walter Muir Whitehill, *Boston: A Topographical History*, 2nd edition (Cambridge: Harvard University Press, 1968), *passim*. According to Denehy, the West End Land Company raised about one million dollars with which to make their land purchases. The cost of the transformation of Beacon Street into a parkway is usually given as $615,000 of which the town of Brookline was induced to pay $465,000. Charles K. Bolton, *Brookline* (Brookline, Mass.: C.A.W. Spencer, 1897), pp. 56–57.

tion . . . were entirely inadequate to convey the thousands who would naturally be attracted in that direction, and a street railway company was formed for the purpose of constructing a line from Boston to Brookline." [30] The resulting line ran down a tree-lined median on Beacon Street from the intersection of Marlborough Street and West Chester Park in Boston to the terminal at Chestnut Hill Avenue in Brookline and included two branch lines inside the town, making a total of about eight miles of track.

Mr. Whitney had very good political connections. The charter granted to him in 1887 by the state legislature in the "West End Bill" also contained the basis for a consolidation move whereby Whitney, with a capital base of $80,000, came into control of a traction empire valued in excess of seven million dollars.[31] He managed to preside over this profitable combine only until 1897 when a rival firm was capitalized to begin an even more ambitious era of coordinated public transportation.

Henry Whitney was an "ardent champion of the suburban city," but he was first of all a businessman. He and his colleagues realized a large and ready profit from their ventures. Although he spoke often and sincerely of the "moral influence" of the new commuter communities, he displayed no desire "to control the form and direction of this suburban expansion." [32] He left the making of that part of history to the individuals who purchased the lots made accessible by his West End Street Railway.

When one examines the place of Senator Newlands and the Chevy Chase Land Company in the concurrent history of suburbanization in the District of Columbia, one may first be struck by the parallels between the two ventures. But a closer investigation will reveal two significant points of contrast. First, the scale of Newlands' undertaking, both in absolute terms and even more so relative to the respective contexts of local development, was of a magnitude many times that of Whitney. Second, Newlands had the utmost interest in shaping the form and quality of the development facilitated by his land speculation and railway construction. In order to achieve that control, he was willing to forgo profit for himself and his investors for thirty years.

[30] There does seem to have been a prior company, the Metropolitan Street Railway Company, which held a franchise to build on Beacon Street. Reluctance to move quickly enough for his purposes or resistance to his schemes provoked Whitney to acquire controlling interest in that company. Denehy, p. 127. In any event, Brookline's population did increase from twelve to twenty thousand in the decade following the opening of the transit line.

[31] Hager, pp. 22–23. Whitney acquired five of the then existing lines in the metropolitan area.

[32] Warner, p. 26.

He had, or had at his disposal, the capital necessary to such a comprehensive, long-term undertaking.

A few words should be said by way of establishing the social and economic condition of Washington in the late 1880's which served as the context for Newlands' ambitious undertaking. Even the most otherworldly resident of the District must have been subject to some exhiliration on witnessing the unprecedented physical and economic expansion of the capital city in the closing months of the decade. The population was thirty percent larger than it had been ten years earlier. Builders and developers responded to that growth by making the District of Columbia sixth in the nation in 1889 in number of new houses constructed, many of them at last of "moderate size suitable for people of small incomes." [33] In that same year a new form of financial institution, the trust company, was chartered. Trust companies were indispensable to the kind of financing required for large-scale, long-term city building.[34]

The Board of Trade was founded the next year and immediately began its energetic promotion of civic advancement. Congress made its contributions to the municipal boom in 1890 by authorizing construction of a new post office and a new government printing office, by acquiring 2,000 acres for the creation of Rock Creek Park, and by appropriating $200,000 toward a new zoo. As if to symbolize the opening of a new chapter in local history, old Boundary Street was renamed Florida Avenue.

It was a big year in suburban real estate, especially along the Tenalytown electric street railway which was completed to the District line. On reaching that terminus, two spurs were immediately put under construction: west along Conduit Road to Glen Echo and north to Bethesda. A total of more than two hundred subdivisions were recorded: 156 in the old City, 7 in Georgetown, and 63 in the former County. But among all these invigorating signs of growth and development, there was one which overshadowed all that could be seen or remembered.

> The most notable transaction that has ever been known in the history of suburban property was the extensive purchase of land along the line of Connecticut avenue and for two miles beyond the District line by the representatives of the Sharon estate and others. The purchase of the land involved an expenditure of about $1,500,000. Under the same auspices

[33] The number of new houses that year was 4,048 according to the Census of 1890. See also "The Year at Home," *Star,* January 1, 1890.

[34] Washington Loan and Trust and American Security and Trust were both organized in 1889. On the founding of local trust companies and their significance, see D. M. Cole, *Banking in the District of Columbia,* (New York: William-Frederick Press, 1959).

the building of the Rock Creek electric road was begun, involving tremendous engineering work and an outlay of about a half million dollars. This road will be seven miles long and will be completed about May 1.[35]

This concise but respectful account of the most significant real estate development since George Washington "persuaded" the local farmers to go along with his scheme for the capital does not mention by name the principal agent in the business: Francis Griffith Newlands. That was not merely because Newlands had remained anonymous behind the straw men who made the numerous purchases of land in his behalf.

Newlands was a new face among the contingent of wealthy westerners who were usually referred to by local citizens as "the California syndicate," although they were here in their capacity as legislators from Nevada. The confusion was well founded; in this period Nevada was a virtual satrapy of California investors. This status was reflected in the fact that most of the Senators from Nevada in the first fifty years of its statehood were attorneys or financiers from San Francisco.[36] A special study could usefully be made of the unique role of the senatorial delegation from Nevada in the late Nineteenth Century expansion of the District.

William Sharon had served one term in the Senate, 1875–1881. He did not do a great deal of the Senate's business, but he did make some important land purchases here on the northwest edge of the old pedestrian city. His friend and senior colleague, Senator William Morris Stewart (1862–1875, 1887–1905), along with one of their San Francisco attorneys, Curtis J. Hillyer, had already invested $600,000 in land near DuPont Circle in 1871. Stewart's five-story "Castle," after

[35] "Washington in 1890," *Star*, January 1, 1891.

[36] Newlands, in this as in so many other respects, was significantly different from his colleagues and partners. Senator William Sharon, the father of Newland's first wife, never once visited Nevada during his entire term (1875–1881) and came to Washington only three times. Newlands by contrast moved his permanent residence to Reno in 1889 and was not elected to Congress until 1893. Moreover, during his 24 years as Representative (1893–1903) and Senator (1903–1917), he worked assiduously in behalf of his constituency, most particularly in his pioneering advocacy of large-scale irrigation and reclamation. He hoped to get Nevada out of its dependence on mining. Newlands' private life and public careers have been so thoroughly discussed by Arthur B. Darling in the introduction to his two-volume collection of *The Public Papers of Francis G. Newlands* (Boston, 1932), by Albert W. Atwood in his "The Romance of Senator Francis G. Newlands and Chevy Chase," *Records of the Columbia Historical Society of Washington D.C. 1966–1968* (1969), pp. 294–310 and *Francis G. Newlands: A Builder of the Nation* (Washington, 1969), and particularly by William Lilley in his brilliant, unpublished dissertation, "The Early Career of Francis G. Newlands 1848–1897" (Yale, 1965), that I will introduce only those facts necessary to the present narrative. Lilley should be consulted (pp. 188 ff), for example, for an understanding of the complex of reasons which led to Newlands' permanent relocation in Nevada.

serving for a time as the Chinese Legation, has given way to a branch office of the Riggs Bank. Hillyer's mansion is incorporated in the Cosmos Club.

No other state sent men to Washington with the requisite combination of wealth and passion for high-risk enterprises. Nor did any local entrepreneurs possess that combination. It was left to the Nevada contingent to translate Governor Shepherd's dreams of a metropolitan capital city into real estate. They were, for Washington, the bridge between the romantic capitalism of the Gilded Age and the monumental undertakings of the City Beautiful Movement.

This role was assumed in a conscious and forceful way by the youngest and newest member of the California syndicate, Francis Newlands. As early as 1887 he had advocated a program of improvements for San Francisco which he said would turn that frontier city into "the Paris of America." On moving to Nevada in 1889, he acquired 300 acres in and around Reno with the intention of executing a planned suburban development on the north side of that city. He started similar communities on property under his management in Burlingame, California and Phoenix, Arizona. Newlands was a personal friend of Frederick L. Olmsted and shared his views on the importance of pursuing only "well-considered, pre-established" plans. It was then only a natural extension of a long-held position when Newlands became the most ardent supporter of the 1901 McMillan Plan after Senator James McMillan's death in 1902.[37]

As it happened, the future Senator Newlands had spent his adolescence in Washington in the 1860's. However, after three years in the night school of the Law Department of Columbian College he had been admitted to the bar in 1869 and left for San Francisco in 1870. His personal charm and legal intelligence were soon rewarded, professionally and socially. Very early in his practice he became one of William Sharon's attorneys. In 1873 he married Sharon's daughter, Clara Adelaide. Following her death in 1885, he became trustee of the late senator's estate. After successfully defending the estate in various litigations, he devoted himself to the management of the considerable assets which had come to be at his disposal either directly through inheritance or as trustee. Among the holdings under his care were the old Sharon properties in Washington.[38]

---

[37] See, for example, Newlands' published Senate speeches of February 29 and March 21, 1904 on "The White House Restoration." In addition to his defense of the work of McKim in particular, he voiced a general tribute to the endeavors of Burnham and friends to restore high standards of architectural style in this country.

[38] A few facts give some idea of the size of Sharon's fortune. He was at one time the largest taxpayer in San Francisco and for many years personally dominated the economy of that city. He was the sole owner of the fabulous Palace Hotel. He made his first big

On a visit to the capital in 1886 or 1887, Newlands was possessed of a vision in which he saw Connecticut Avenue extended all the way into Maryland as the corridor for limitless suburban expansion. Apparently this vision came to him while standing in the cupola of the home of Colonel George Augustus Armes where he had gone for dinner as the companion of Senator Stewart.[39] Whatever the inspiration or its source, over the next few years Newlands' agents systematically purchased a total of 1,712 acres of land. His goal was to buy every parcel touching his projected avenue, if the price were at all reasonable. He did not in fact acquire all the land contiguous with the avenue and the line of the street had to be shifted somewhat in Maryland in order to by-pass some landowners who were holding out for too much profit. In 1890 he founded the Chevy Chase Land Company to receive

---

money in San Francisco real estate and then added to this his earnings as principal beneficiary of the Comstock Lode. During the mid-1870's his annual income was estimated to be $800,000. On Sharon's death all his property was in trust. Newlands was designated to receive one-third of the income from the trust (after his wife's early death that increased to two-thirds) and to serve as the sole trustee of the estate itself. The holdings of the estate in Nevada alone made Newlands the second largest property-owner in that state, but those holdings were said to be only a "small fraction" of the total estate. Lilley, pp. 166, 194. Sharon spent $160,000 on land around DuPont Circle. However, since the lots did not constitute a solid block of property which would allow uniform and comprehensive development, Newlands sold them in 1889—for approximately ten times the original purchase price. Lilley, pp. 207–208.

[39] Senator Stewart was both a partner in and a legislative friend of Newlands' venture. Stewart bought $300,000 of the first issue of Chevy Chase Land Company stock. But his supporting activities in Congress were perhaps more valuable, for example, in gaining a good charter for the street railway and in pushing the creation of Rock Creek Park. Not only did the presence of the park raise the value of nearby properties owned so largely by the Land Company, but at the same time, as Stewart so candidly expressed it, the action took "2,000 acres out of the market." Quoted in Lilley, p. 209. Armes later took credit for both the vision of Connecticut Avenue extended and the role of principal agent in purchasing the lands. George A. Armes, *Ups and Downs of an Army Officer* (Washington, D.C., 1900), pp. 605–613, 639, 683. Edith Claude Jarvis ("Old Chevy Chase Village," Montgomery County Historical Society, November 1969) accepts Armes' version. I am inclined to agree with Atwood (*Francis G. Newlands,* p. 31) that the principal intermediary was Edward J. Stellwagen, president of the Thos. J. Fisher realty company. Stellwagen not only succeeded Newlands as president of the land company on the latter's death, he was before that president of the Union Trust Company which was formed in 1899. Newlands needed such a corporate trustee in order to secure a large loan on his unimproved real estate from the Deacons Bank of Manchester, England. As for the origin of the vision, Newlands was famous for his conviction that "Everything in America grows to the West," unless blocked by some natural barrier (like the Potomac), in which case it would grow to the northwest. It is indisputable that Armes did have some preliminary role in the land acquisitions. I suspect that his great vanity led him to project a larger future for himself in the venture than others ever intended. His paranoid interpretation of his being phased out through the machinations of Stellwagen is consistent with his understanding of his multiple misfortunes as military officer, real estate broker, husband and father. Armes' diary-book is a fascinating record of realty transactions in the period, but his entries should always be read with circumspection.

title to all the properties from the straw men who had made the purchases for him.

At the same time his agents were concluding the accumulation of land between DuPont Circle and Jones Bridge Road, Newlands was taking steps toward its development. A Rock Creek Railway Company had been given a charter in 1888 for the construction of a street railway on what would have been Connecticut Avenue extended. However, they were never able to start building the line. In a series of transactions in 1890, Newlands became principal stockholder and president of the Rock Creek Railway.[40] (Stewart and Stellwagen were associated with him in this, too.) Construction began at once. The Chevy Chase Land Company was itself chartered to build the Maryland segment of the projected line.

Because of new ordinances forbidding overhead wires inside the old City limits, the lower section of this line was one of the first conduit or third-rail systems in the country. Two power plants were constructed: one for the downtown segment on Champlain Street, N.W., between 17th and 18th, the other and larger one at Chevy Chase Lake in Maryland. One of the most ambitious aspects of the entire venture, from an engineering point of view, was the grading and bridging required. The iron trestle bridge over Rock Creek at Calvert Street and the Klingle Street bridge were both constructed in 1891. In 1892 the first segment of the line went into operation.[41]

When the grading of the 150-foot-wide Connecticut Avenue was completed, Newlands deeded the street to the governments of the District and of Maryland. He was then ready to concentrate on the development of the central goal of this entire enterprise, a new kind of suburb for the nation's capital. It was to be a totally planned subdivision on 250 acres located just outside the District so that its residents would be able to vote. Chevy Chase Village, Maryland, was opened in 1893, the year in which the boom of the decade collapsed. "At the

---

[40] King, p. 28. It is commonly stated or implied that Newlands founded the Rock Creek Railway Company. However, the original minute books of the company, which are now in the collection of the Columbia Historical Society, record the developments as described in this paper. The charter which Newlands acquired was amended by Congress in a bill passed in 1891 which gave the Rock Creek Railway the right to purchase other transit lines in the District of Columbia or Maryland. No other charters had that provision.

[41] The route as finally laid out began at 7th and U Street, N.W., went west on U to 18th, up 18th to Calvert, across Calvert to Connecticut, out Connecticut to Jones Bridge Road. In 1895 Newlands' Rock Creek Railway Company acquired the Washington and Georgetown line and formed the Capital Traction Company with a combined capitalization of $12 million. The street railway continued to run on Connecticut Avenue until replaced by busses in 1935.

E. J. STELLWAGEN

Columbia Historical Society Collection

Edward J. Stellwagen by Clifford K. Berryman.

From Clifford K. Berryman, *Cartoons and Caricatures,* printed for H. B. Thomson by W. F. Roberts, Washington, D. C. Stellwagen was president of the Union Trust Company which was formed in 1899 and was president of Thos. J. Fisher & Co. See footnote 39.

close of the panic year of 1893, Newlands had spent $1,254,006 on land, $1,552,742 on grading, bridges, interest and taxes, and nearly $800,000 on developing Chevy Chase Village." [42]

It is an indication of the strength of Newlands' financial position that in 1893 he not only opened his new home on Chevy Chase Circle but purchased for himself the thirty-acre Woodley estate at a cost of

[42] Atwood, p. 38.

$140,000.[43] It was this kind of financial depth which made possible the long-term success of the entire venture. From the time of its founding down to Newlands' death, that is from 1890 to 1917, the disbursements of the Chevy Chase Land Company exceeded receipts by $172,000. The company paid no dividends until 1922. However, the company was perfectly situated to benefit from the expansionary period which followed World War I. Sales made by the company between 1918 and 1931 totalled seven and one-half million dollars.[44]

THE SUBURB OF CHEVY CHASE VILLAGE

Jane Jacobs has observed that a successful neighborhood always spreads, if not in terms of official boundaries then in the minds of those who perceive it. The success of Chevy Chase Village in this respect is demonstrated by the fact that when people today say they live in Chevy Chase they may mean any place from Albemarle Street north to Kensington, Maryland, and from Rock Creek Park west to Wisconsin Avenue.

One reason for this durable achievement in community building is that the original Village was a perfectly balanced expression of the paradoxical value of individuality among the successful elements of our society in the late Nineteenth Century. "The fixed purpose of the Chevy Chase Land Company was to provide for the National Capital a home suburb, a community where every residence would bear a touch of the individuality of the owner. . . ." But the condition of that touch of domestic individuality was "a big comprehensive plan" formulated by a man who "believed that the best results could be obtained only where things were done right." And while the Village "was designed and has been maintained to meet the requirements of discriminating people . . . that does not necessarily mean . . . people of great wealth." "The only restrictions imposed are those which experience has proven necessary in any residential section to maintain or increase values and protect values and protect property builders against the encroachment of undesirable elements." [45]

---

[43] *Washington Herald,* April 5, 1932. However, even Newlands had to make some choices as a result of the economic downturn in those years. He decided to forgo plans for a new planned community in Nevada rather than relinquish any part of his holdings in the District of Columbia or Maryland.

[44] The company continues to this day to be a major leaseholder and developer in the northwestern section of the city. Ninety-four percent of the stock of the Chevy Chase Land Company is still owned by Newlands' descendants or collateral heirs. Atwood, p. 42.

[45] "Chevy Chase for Homes." An illustrated brochure published by Thos. J. Fisher & Co. in 1917. I have not been able to see an original deed. Mr. Hunter Davidson, cur-

Newlands spent nearly one million dollars making sure that things were "done right" in his new settlement. He engaged an excellent professional staff. W. Kesley Schoepf was hired away from his position as assistant engineer for the District of Columbia. The New York landscape architect, Nathan F. Barrett, specified the trees and other imported and native plantings which give so much character to the town. The architect Lindley Johnson developed designs for a number of homes in order to establish an appropriate style and scale from the beginning. Barrett or Johnson laid out the first street plan. Alleys were proscribed. The broad streets were given "pleasant English and Scottish names." Samuel M. Gray as sanitary engineer presided over the development of a fine water supply and sewerage system. The land company drilled nearly twenty artesian wells and erected a handsome, 300,000-gallon water tower in 1895 just above Bradley Lane which served the community until 1934.

Newlands' team of professionals laid down certain general guidelines within which individual tastes were to flourish. Lots were sold with the stipulation that no home built on Connecticut Avenue could cost less than $5,000, no home on the side streets less than $3,000. Homes on the avenue had to be set back thirty-five feet, those on the side streets twenty-five feet. No lots could be less than sixty feet wide. Restrictive covenants allowed only single-family dwellings to be constructed. There were to be no commercial structures in the Village; stores would be located at a convenient distance down the avenue just inside the District line.[46]

The choice of a name for the whole venture followed the modern practice of picking up a distinctive local place name which antedates development. In the period of manorial settlement on the lands along the Potomac River, a 560-acre patent for "Cheivy Chace" was granted to Joseph Belt by King Charles I. Belt erected a brick manor house in 1725 which stood (on present-day Oliver Street) until 1907 when it was razed to make way for the development of Chevy Chase, D.C.[47] The name of the patent appears to have been derived from an old ballad which recounts a Fourteenth Century battle on the chase (French: chevauchée) or hunting grounds of Cheviot Hills between Scotland

---

rent president of the Chevy Chase Land Company, is of the opinion that the original sales were *not* covered by covenants governing resale privileges with respect to race of purchaser.

[46] An exception was made in 1961 when the Village extended its borders to the west in order to include the land where Saks Fifth Avenue intended to build. In that way the Village could regulate the architecture and landscaping of the new establishment.

[47] There is some confusion in secondary sources as to the size and date of this patent. Caleb Clarke Magruder's monograph, *Colonel Joseph Belt* (Annapolis, 1909), includes the text of the patent. The grant to Belt was later expanded to 1,000 acres.

and England. The modern word is then a conflation of two terms in the popular mind. In any event, it had the right tone, slightly foreign, for a better quality suburb.

Newlands' comprehensive planning vision included social institutions. A rather fashionable hunt club known as the Dumblane Club, which had been formed in 1885 and located in Tennallytown, came into financial and organizational difficulties. Newlands offered them Goldsborough Place (a property on the edge of his village) free of charge until they could buy and build to suit their means. When they accepted this offer to relocate in 1892 he also advanced them $1,000. They leased (1894) and later (1897) bought the old Bradley House Tract.[48] Nathan Barrett laid out the new club track. The club renamed itself the Chevy Chase Club and elected Newlands president. (Senator Stewart was on the Board of Governors.) George Ryder, whom Newlands had brought to the United States to teach his daughters to ride, became Huntsman and Henry M. Earle was the first Master of Foxhounds. When golf became popular some years later, the club put in a course.

The Chevy Chase Club came to have two hundred members by the close of the century, only ten of whom are listed as having Chevy Chase addresses. It was a suburban club for District gentlemen and their ladies (the latter having full privileges), but it clearly served its intended purpose for the developer. "The National Capital is no exception to the rule in every city of America, that the best suburban section is always surrounding or adjacent to the leading suburban clubs." [49]

Newlands' patronal concern extended to other more basic institutions as well. Very early the Land Company gave the residents of the community land on which to construct a school and paid the salary of the teacher.[50] The school was built on what is now called Western Avenue. Two of Newlands' daughters started a library for the community in 1896.

[48] The Bradley House is partially incorporated in the present club house. The Bradley farm was approximately nine acres. In 1903 the club purchased another 65 acres from the Land Company and added 117 more acres in 1908 through purchase of some land held by a trustee of the Bradley property. These and other details are from John M. Lynham, *The Chevy Chase Club A History 1885–1957* (Chevy Chase, Md., 1958). Today there are roughly 2,000 members with a reputed waiting list of a thousand. The Washingtoniana Room of the Martin Luther King Memorial Library has a good collection of the annual reports of the club.

[49] Quoted from The Thos. J. Fisher brochure. In 1909 the Columbia Country Club purchased 150 acres a short distance north of the Chevy Chase Club giving the area the benefit of two exclusive social clubs.

[50] This arrangement continued until 1898 when Congress agreed to pay for a schoolteacher. That action brought Miss Ella Given to head what was known as the E. V. Brown School which served the later Chevy Chase, D.C. community for years.

A group of Episcopalians who began meeting in the school in 1897 soon formed themselves into the congregation of All Saints Church. In 1901 the Land Company gave the parish land on the southwest arc of the circle for the construction of their church.

Once the Village had a plan, a name, utilities and incipient institutions the time had come to merchandize this new form of life. The Chevy Chase Land Company adopted for that purpose a method employed by real estate-street railway combines in many cities. They created an independent attraction at the end of the trolley line. Chevy Chase Lake, which had been developed in connection with the power plant which supplied electricity for the street cars, was put to other uses.

> An amusement park was designed around the lake and on hot summer evenings the open streetcars were filled to capacity; the passengers, unwittingly, were potential buyers of lots and houses in the Village! A bandstand was constructed which was a masterpiece of beauty and glamour! Its design was that of a mammoth seashell, with hundreds of electric lights sparkling from its interior, which was painted a pale and delicate blue. Some thirty or forty musicians of the United States Marine Band appeared each evening in full and colorful regalia. . . . For the last half of the program, which was dance music only, the musicians have walked down the hill from the bandstand to a large, rustic dance pavilion overlooking the Lake. . . .
>
> In addition to the concerts, which were free, there were other paid attractions, such as boating, bowling, horseback and pony riding. There was a gaily decorated merry-go-round for the children, a shooting gallery for the grown-ups, and enormous boat-swings that went high in the air. There were no games of chance, no rowdyism, but rather an atmosphere of dignity and quiet pleasure.[51]

The Spring Hotel was also constructed in the early 1890's just north of the Village on the site now occupied by the national 4-H headquarters. (Part of the original structure is incorporated in the facade of the main building.) The idea was that the people of the District of Columbia could take a five-cent trolley ride to the hotel and spend a pleasant weekend in the country.

In spite of all the care and expense invested in the Village, it did not fill up rapidly. Sixteen homes were built in 1894; a smaller number the next year. There were not quite fifty families living there by the end of the century.[52]

---

[51] Jarvis, p. 4.

[52] By 1915 there were 175 houses in the community. The real movement of people into Chevy Chase Village, as into other outlying sections of northwest Washington, took place in the boom years between World War I and the Depression. The 1970

The land company built the first four homes for its own executives, intending thereby to set the standards of homebuilding for subsequent residents. In this intent they were rather successful. An impressive but restrained residential character was achieved which did not require either large pieces of land or conformity to one style of architecture. Homes in the Village range from "A True California Bungalow Type" to the colonial house to the villaesque, with of course many representatives of the shingle style of the period.[53] The important point about these late Nineteenth Century suburban homes is, as Warner put it, that "they no longer depend upon rural nature or an estate-sized lot for their effect. Indeed they achieve their imposing quality by being large houses arranged in big masses on relatively small lots." And as a group they are situated so "as to produce for the public the gratifying view of a prosperous street." [54]

Although we are able to borrow the language of Warner's Boston study to describe many external features of Chevy Chase Village, a real divergence appears when we come to talk about the comparative fates of the two areas. History has been much more lenient with Chevy Chase Village than with most of her contemporary suburban communities. That is due in part to fortuitous circumstances and in part to intrinsic qualities of the Village.

In Warner's view, the success or failure of the streetcar suburbs "centered on the attempt by a mass of people, each with one small house and lot, to achieve what previously had been the pattern of life of a few rich families with two large houses [one in town and one in the country] and ample land." [55] Almost from the beginning Chevy Chase Village was a mixture of this middle class suburban phenomenon and the more aristocratic town-and-country gentle life which supplied the model for it. Some homeowners had several houses, not only in Washington but elsewhere in the country as well; some

---

Census reported a population of 2,265 which was down slightly from the 1960 figure of 2,405. These residents were living in 635 dwellings. The 1970 census reported 20 Negroes in the Village; these must be domiciled servants rather than property owners. This interpretation was supported by W. C. Austin, Village Manager, in a letter dated October 30, 1973. Mr. Austin also reported the annexation of two new sections at the southeast corner of the Village. This action in April 1972 raised the number of homes to approximately 700.

[53] The Thos. Fisher brochure contains numerous fine photographs of the homes. Each is accompanied by a caption, original in language or a folk saying, which shows the function of nature in the suburban ideology. For example: "Not Without Art, but Yet to Nature True," "In Chevy Chase Nature and Man have Combined Their Efforts with Charming Results," "He is Happiest be He King or Peasant Who Finds Peace in His Home."

[54] Warner, pp. 149–151. The average lot in Chevy Chase Village would be around or just under 10,000 square feet. There are no multiple family dwellings in the Village.

[55] Warner, p. 14.

stretched themselves financially in order simply to build a bungalow that met the requirements of the convenants. Chevy Chase Village is hardly what one would call heterogeneous, but it is a mixed community on the upper end of the general income scale.[56]

Warner used Roxbury highlands for his particular case study of the medium-to-high-priced community. This section had certain "unique qualities" which tested "the power of neighborhood conditions to retard the general flow of classes;" its experience showed "that neighborhood influence could at most delay for thirty years the general metropolitan patterns of population movement."[57] The power which Chevy Chase Village has exhibited to maintain its character for three-quarters of a century in the face of dynamic patterns of metropolitan population movement has several sources.

It was of course totally planned and tightly controlled from the start. More important than that, it was filled out while the controls of the original plan were still in effect. The fact that the right to self-government was secured from the state of Maryland has enabled the town to govern itself according to its exclusive interests.[58] Because of its location well in advance of the frontier of suburban expansion, coupled with the fact that the Chevy Chase Land Company controlled so much of the land between the city and the new suburb, the intervening development was much more harmonious than would have been the case in the event of haphazard development at the hands of dozens of speculators. And of course all commercial activity was banned from the Village.[59] Finally, over the years the social authority,

[56] This diversity of home values remains true. An examination of thirty sales recorded in *Lusk's Montgomery County, Maryland Real Estate Directory Service* for 1972 discloses that half of them were sold for between sixty and eighty thousand dollars. Five sold for less than fifty thousand, five for over one hundred thousand. There are several residential sections of metropolitan Washington for which the mean and median figures would be much higher. Related to this, it is interesting to note that the mean family income for the Village in 1969 according to the 1970 Census was $36,396. These facts indicate that the prestige associated with Chevy Chase Village is not derived from the cost of housing nor is cost of housing correlated with family income in the usual ratios.

[57] Warner, p. 69. The most appropriate comparison on this point would be between Chevy Chase and Brookline in order to take into account the important factor of municipal autonomy.

[58] The original charter was declared invalid in 1911. Since 1914 they have been incorporated with a form of government which combines elements of the old New England township and the modern city manager movement. They have their own tiny city hall, three-man police force, and set their own tax rate. C. Carroll Morgan, historical preface to the official handbook of *History, Ordinances and Regulations* published in 1965.

[59] At this moment in 1974 the Chevy Chase Land Company is lobbying for permission to develop intensively some commercial property which it owns in Friendship Heights. It will be a great irony if the founders thus contribute to events which by their very magnitude will inevitably break the Village's resistance to degrading change.

as it were, of the Village has tended to influence the quality of surrounding neighborhoods rather than the reverse.

CONCLUSION

Out of respect for Warner's complete study, as well as for the sake of a balanced historical analysis, one must not overlook Warner's strictures on the entire suburban movement in the last third of the previous century. After a most painstaking and sympathetic reconstruction of this remarkable social process, he concluded with an incisive list of negative outcomes when viewed from present perspectives. Chevy Chase Village does not escape the urban historian's indictment so easily as it has avoided the perils of that history which he studies.[60]

The achievement of the suburbs, namely, the creation of "a safe environment for half the metropolitan population," was also their failing. As the successful majority of the middle classes became progressively suburbanized they also became increasingly ignorant of the conditions of modern life in the cities. Most crucial of all, the carefully differentiated subdivisions left us with a society so utterly divided by classes and by separate political jurisdictions as to be virtually incapable of responding effectively to large forces of change which have confronted all cities in recent decades.

All of this could be said of Washington, only more so due to our correlation of class and ethnic segregation and the plight of a weak District of Columbia government surrounded by a plethora of state and local jurisdictions. The very strength of communities like Chevy Chase Village underlines the shortcomings of the age of individualistic capitalism in which they were generated. The fact that they remain the symbolic or even actual goal of ambition in our society indicates our failure to develop an alternative social philosophy and urban policy which would presuppose a sense of civic solidarity and a political will to achieve minimum conditions of the good life for all citizens in all sectors of the city.

---

[60] Perhaps the most well-known detractor on record was Frank Lloyd Wright. In connection with a trip to Washington in 1958, Wright was persuaded to address the Bethesda-Chevy Chase Chamber of Commerce Community Improvement Dinner at Kenwood Golf and Country Club. Of suburbs in general Wright said "the more fashionable, the more expensive, the worse they are" and he several times referred to Chevy Chase in particular as "a blighted area." *Star*, October 3, 1958.

Anacostia: Strength in Adversity

THOMAS J. CANTWELL

INTRODUCTION

During the time Pierre Charles L'Enfant's design was becoming a city, Anacostia was remote and rural. When the city became such, Anacostia became a suburb, developed as an alternative to city living. When Washington mushroomed into a major metropolis and political center, the open spaces of Anacostia were exploited to the fullest extent of their profit yielding potential. The Eastern Branch of the Potomac River, otherwise known as the Anacostia River, has separated Anacostia from Washington to the extent that it is often appropriate to speak of the two as separate entities. This paper seeks to show that this separation has played a predominant role in the development of the community of Anacostia.

The Post Office at the south end of the Eleventh Street Bridge officially became Anacostia, D. C., in 1849. In 1865 it was renamed Uniontown, D. C., after the real estate development scheme undertaken by the Union Land Company. On April 22, 1886, the name Anacostia was made official once more by an act of Congress.[1] Today Anacostia is a very ambiguous designation; in this paper it will refer to the entire area south of Pennsylvania Avenue, east of the Anacostia River.

Copyright, 1975, by Thomas J. Cantwell.

An earlier draft of this paper, "Anacostia: How Past History Accounts for Present Neighborhood," was delivered before the Columbia Historical Society on January 16, 1973.

The research for this paper began under a grant from the Carnegie Foundation to the Anascostia Neighborhood Museum of the Smithsonian Institution. I wish to thank Carolyn Margolis, research assistant, for her substantial contributions and Louise Hutchinson, research analyst, whose comments were invaluable. I also wish to thank John Kinard, director of the Museum, and Larry E. Thomas, director of the Anacostia Research Center, for their leadership while I was an employee and for their assistance and cooperation in the years of preparation since my employment.

[1] George C. Havenner, *Early History of Anacostia or Old Uniontown* (Washington, D. C.: The Printing House of Jas. C. Wood, n.d.), p. 3.

The Uniontown development and the Barry Farm Project, undertaken in 1867 by the Freedmen's Bureau, were the only two extensive development schemes until the last years of the Nineteenth Century. There were six of these developments south of Pennsylvania Avenue, and their limited scale preserved Anacostia's separation and rural character through the years until the 1940's. World War II marked the beginning of rapid development which continued through the 1950's and 1960's.

What began as an accident of geography has been reinforced over the years by governmental action. St. Elizabeths Asylum for the Insane was built in Anacostia in the 1850's. The Barry Farm Project was located here in the 1860's. Rather than have them camping among the monuments, governmental officials forced the Bonus Marchers to set up their encampment, Camp Marx, in Anacostia in the 1930's and the Vietnam Veterans Against the War in the 1970's. The Blue Plains sewage treatment facility and the sanitary landfill are in Anacostia. A disproportionately large share of the city's public housing is in Anacostia.

Neglect is a more subtle and more enervating reinforcement of separation. The things of a decent life, liveable housing, good education, employment opportunities, transportation, and sanitation services have been consistently denied to Anacostia, or provided only grudgingly. This pattern, too, has prevailed for a century.

To relieve the crowded living conditions of Civil War refugees in downtown Washington, free blacks and ex-slaves were sold lots in the Barry Farm Project and were given enough lumber to build a two-room house. The World War II developers were given an incentive to relieve wartime housing emergencies, insurance by the Federal Housing Administration covering ninety percent of the mortgage of approved complexes. Today there are too few private homes, too many apartment complexes, and too many mortgages on these complexes in default.

The freedmen of the Barry Farm Project bought the land and built their first school themselves at a time when people hotly debated whether they should have an education at all. During the era of segregation, black and white schools alike were seriously overcrowded.[2] Today the schools of Anacostia are still badly overcrowded and also subject to the ephemera of political fashions which infuse and then withdraw funds for special programs.

The freedmen who made the Barry Farm Project into a community accepted the uncertainty of meeting monthly payments on their home-

[2] *The Evening Star* (Washington, D. C.), January 16, 1941, sec. B, p. 1.

steads at a time when jobs for them were desperately few and wages were as near involuntary servitude as gainful employment. There have never been dependable centers of employment in Anacostia. Today's concerns are two: the concern for the quality of education which is such that jobs of a constantly increasing technical character are exceeding the grasp of Anacostians even farther, and the concern of an immobile population for whom jobs are becoming less accessible.

Getting roads graded and eventually paved were, in their times, problems comparable to getting bus and subway service today. It was difficult getting roads in Anacostia; it was difficult getting them paved and maintained. Today public transportation is poor, and it is difficult getting improved bus service. Metro's plans for Anacostia are minimal.

Sanitation services in Anacostia have been marginal, and at times have fallen below the margin. Public water hydrants were still in use in the 1940's.[3] The Fort DuPont Reservoir was sufficiently contaminated in 1943 to make people ill, and was alleged to have been unsafe for a ten year period.[4] Today "The Anacostia Suit", *Burner v. Washington,* seeks to gain a judicial opinion on the denial of public services by the governments, both District and Federal.

This is Anacostia, an anomaly and a consistency, a community that has been divided and disrupted yet one that maintains its spirit and sense of its own history. The Anacostia Neighborhood Museum's exhibits on Anacostia life are testimony to the disruption and neglect; the Museum and its research are testimony to the spirit.

EARLY HISTORY

The name Anacostia evolved from the name of the tribe of Indians who lived in the area, the Nacochtank. They were Algonquian, a linguistic classification of related languages.[5] The Algonquian tribes of the Middle Atlantic seaboard also had similar customs and cultures: they built similar houses, round-roofed, made of bent poles covered with branches and skins. They used similar weapons and tools, stone arrow points and axes, large wooden mortars and pestles for grinding grain. They ate similar foods, usually corn, cooked in similar ways, usually mush. They were agricultural people who supplemented their

[3] Harold Stern, interview at the Water Operations Branch of the Department of Environmental Services, Washington, D. C., November 1971.

[4] *The Washington Post,* May 8, 1966, sec. E, p. 5.

[5] In the same manner that Bantu is a classification of many African languages which are related, Algonquian is a classification of the languages of Indians who lived along the east coast of America. Just as there is no Bantu tribe in Africa, there was no Algonquian tribe here.

diet by hunting. Because of this it has been extrapolated that the customs, culture, and living conditions of the Nacochtank were not markedly different from those of the Algonquian people about whom we know considerably more through their contact with the first white people at Roanoke Island and the watercolors of John White.[6]

Captain John Smith was the first European to meet the Nacochtank. In 1608 he set out on an exploratory mission of the Chesapeake Bay region. Most of the tribes that he encountered along the journey up the bay and the Potomac River were hostile. Not until he reached the Washington area did he meet friendly tribes. One of them was the Nacochtank, a tribe of eighty men plus women and children.[7]

The next European to travel in the area is believed to have been Henry Fleet, a fur trader. After his arrival in 1631, Mr. Fleet explored the Potomac region and was either captured by or voluntarily lived with the Indians of a village on Piscataway Creek. Leonard Calvert, the brother of Caecilius Calvert, the second Lord Baltimore, found Fleet while exploring the area. Fleet returned to British society with Calvert.[8]

The British, represented by Lord Baltimore, claimed all of the territory in the area. As part of the British suzerainty, Catholic missionaries came to minister to the settlers and to evangelize the Indians. They latinized the name Nacochtank to Nacostines; later an "a" was prefixed, hence the name Anacostia. In 1662 Lord Baltimore granted to George Thomas the land which is now known as Blue Plains. Later he granted to Thomas the land which is now occupied by St. Elizabeths Hospital.[9] Lord Baltimore granted to John Meeks the Chichester Tract, part of which was to become the settlement of Anacostia (Uniontown).[10]

Following a period of intertribal warfare and wars between the Indians and the settlers, the settlers gradually gained the upper hand. During the last quarter of the Seventeenth Century, the Indians moved away from their traditional areas, and white people occupied the Anacostia area.[11] The Eastern Branch of the Potomac River had become more generally known as the Anacostia River, and the settle-

---

[6] William C. Sturtevant, interview at the Museum of Natural History of the Smithsonian Institution, Washington, D. C., November 1971.

[7] John Clagett Proctor, ed., *Washington: Past and Present,* 5 volumes (New York: Lewis Historical Publishing Co., 1930), Vol. 1, pp. 7–8.

[8] *Ibid.,* p. 17.

[9] Charles R. Burr, "A Brief History of Anacostia, Its Name, Origin and Progress," *Records of the Columbia Historical Society,* Vol. 23 (1920), pp. 167–179.

[10] Havenner, *Early History,* p. 2.

[11] Proctor, *Washington,* p. 38.

National Collection of Fine Arts
Smithsonian Institution

"City of Washington From Beyond the Navy Yard," aquatint, 1834, by William James Bennett after a painting by George Cooke.

This appears to be a view from the top of Morris Road, S. E. The Lombardy poplars lining the road to the farm house gave the name Poplar Point.

ment which stretched along Piscataway Road (now Martin Luther King, Jr. and Minnesota Avenues) was called Anacostia.

In 1790 President George Washington signed the act of Congress that established the new capital of the United States on the banks of the Potomac River. Thomas Jefferson, then Secretary of State, suggested that, for reasons of military security, the areas across both the Potomac and Anacostia Rivers be included in the District of Columbia.[12] It was done and thus did Anacostia become part of the new capital city.

RESIDENTIAL DEVELOPMENT

In 1854 three men, John Fox, John Dodler, and John vanHook, formed the Union Land Company, bought a tract of land at the south end of the Eleventh Street Bridge, subdivided it, named it Union-

[12] *Ibid.*, p. 10.

town, and offered the lots for sale to would-be suburbanites. John vanHook built his home on the southeast corner of 14th and W Streets, on the hill overlooking Uniontown. The residence was named Cedar Hill because of the stand of cedar trees, none of which are now standing.[13] The view from Cedar Hill is an impressive panorama of the city of Washington.

Uniontown's sales appeal was remarkably similar to the appeal of the suburbs in the 1950's and 1960's: large lots with room to have yards and greenery, away from the crowding, noise, dirt, and traffic of the city; and it was segregated. The articles of incorporation restricted sales to whites only.[14] There must have been some consternation ten years later when the Freedmen's Bureau developed the neighboring Barry Farm and offered large homesites for sale to Negroes.

Uniontown was bounded by Monroe Street (Nichols Avenue, now Martin Luther King, Jr. Avenue) on the west, Harrison Street (Good Hope Road) on the north, Taylor Street (16th Street) on the east, and Jefferson Street (W Street) on the south. The other streets were also named after presidents: Fillmore Street (13th Street), Pierce Street (14th Street), Adams Street (15th Street), Jackson Street (U Street), and Washington Street (V Street). The presidential names were changed in 1908 for use in other parts of town, and the usual numbered and alphabetical designations made Anacostia's street names consistent with the city-wide scheme.[15]

The Union Land Company experienced financial difficulties and failed. John vanHook's fortunes failed along with those of the Union Land Company, and he was forced to sell Cedar Hill in 1877. Frederick Douglass became the new owner.

Frederick Douglass was, without question, Anacostia's most prominent resident. When he moved to Anacostia, he was United States Marshall for the District of Columbia, the first black person to hold the position. In 1881 he became Recorder of Deeds for the District, and in 1889 he was appointed Minister to Haiti. After the war and emancipation, Mr. Douglass continued to struggle against the injustices to which black people were still subject. He understood the compromises and weaknesses in the Reconstruction legislation and its implementation. He also anticipated the reaction against Reconstruction. He continued to point out the discrepancy between ideals and practice, and he foresaw the long struggle for equality.[16] Douglass died on

---

[13] Burr, "Brief History," pp. 171–175.

[14] Havenner, *Early History,* p. 4.

[15] *Ibid.,* p. 3.

[16] National Park Service, United States Department of Interior, "Frederick Douglass Home" (Washington, D. C.: U. S. Government Printing Office, 1971), pp. 1–5.

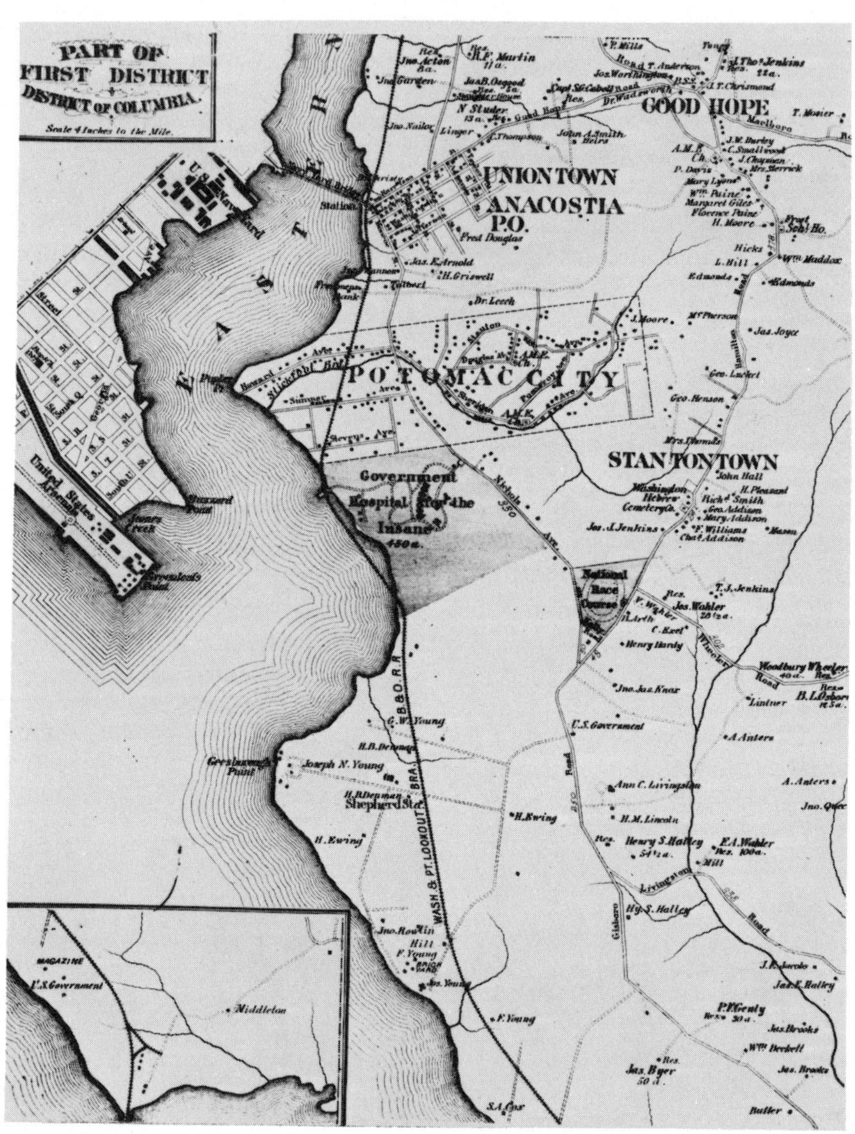

Anacostia Museum

Map showing Uniontown.

Uniontown was an undertaking of the Union Land Company, built next to the Anacostia Post Office at the south end of the Eleventh Street Bridge.

February 20, 1895, on his way to attend services at Campbell A. M. E. Church on Nichols Avenue. The Douglass Memorial Historical Association preserved the estate on Cedar Hill through the years and kept a caretaker on the grounds.[17] It was a large task, beyond their financial means. After years of this unassisted preservation, the National Park Service restored and refurnished the estate as a national monument and opened it to the public in 1972.

St. Elizabeths Hospital opened in 1855. Dr. Charles H. Nichols, a prominent figure in the field of mental health, was the first superintendent. Nichols Avenue was named for him.[18] Following the war, Nichols took an active interest in the neighboring Barry Farm Project. He observed the progress as the settlers built their new houses and wrote to the Freedmen's Bureau noting deficiencies in construction techniques and in the quality of the building materials.[19]

The hospital itself was almost entirely isolated from the neighborhood and the city. There was a farm, complete with a dairy herd, just south of the hospital grounds on Nichols Avenue where the patients worked and which supplied most of the needs of the hospital. There was even a railroad spur on which the hospital operated its own steam switch engine until 1967.[20]

The patients' contact with the neighborhood occurred as children walked through the grounds and talked with the patients. Though these conversations were from a barred cell window to the yard below, first name relationships developed. For the most part though, St. Elizabeths remained the walled-in hospital atop Asylum Hill.[21]

During and following the Civil War, refugees fled to Washington to start a new life. The Union had declared slaves to be contraband in order not to have to return escaped slaves to their masters. In April 1862 (nine months before the Emancipation Proclamation), Congress passed an emancipation act for Washington, and this made the city an even more attractive refuge for people fleeing slavery and the war. In

---

[17] Louise Hutchinson, interview at the Anacostia Research Center, Washington, D. C., August 1974.

[18] National Institute of Mental Health, U. S. Department of Health, Education, and Welfare, *Brief History of St. Elizabeths Hospital* (Washington, D. C.: n. p., 1971), p. 1.

[19] U. S. Bureau of Refugees, Freedmen, and Abandoned Lands, U. S. Department of War, *Register of Letters Received by the Assistant Commissioner for the District of Columbia,* 4 volumes, Old Military Records Division, Record Group 105, National Archives, Washington, D. C., Vol. 3, pp. 304, 386. (U. S. Bureau of Refugees, Freedmen, and Abandoned Lands, U. S. Department of War is hereafter cited as U. S. Bureau of Refugees.)

[20] *Brief History of St. Elizabeths Hospital,* p. 2.

[21] Edward Brazerol, interview at his home, 2113 13th St., S. E., Washington, D. C. November 1970.

1860 Washington's black population was 18,000; by the end of the war in 1865, it had grown to 31,500. By 1867 (when the Barry Farm Project began), it had increased to 34,700, a seven-year increase of ninety-four percent.[22] Living conditions became miserable: there was no housing or jobs for the people; food was scarce; poor sanitation caused dangerous health problems. Yet refugees continued to come to Washington. The white population, which at times had been openly sympathetic to the Confederacy during the war, was becoming restive with the increasing numbers of black people.

The United States Bureau of Refugees, Freedmen, and Abandoned Lands of the United States Department of War, the Freedmen's Bureau, was created by an act of Congress on March 3, 1865, to provide emergency food, shelter, and other necessities to the freedmen for one year after the end of the war. Subsequent renewals and supplements to the legislation broadened the Bureau's powers considerably. The Bureau gained the responsibilities of administering those states which had been in rebellion, insuring the civil rights of ex-slaves, and establishing schools and colleges. General Oliver O. Howard was President Lincoln's choice to be commissioner of the Freedmen's Bureau, and Lincoln's successor, Andrew Johnson, carried out these intentions.

General Howard had seen considerable service during the war both in the northern and western theaters. He resigned his teaching position at West Point to become a colonel in the Third Maine Regiment (Volunteers) and soon went to the war front. For his bravery at the First Battle of Bull Run, he was promoted in September 1861. At the Battle of Fair Oaks in June 1862, he lost his right arm and shortly thereafter was again promoted. He also fought bravely at Chancellorsville and Gettysburg. Following the Battle of Chancellorsville, he was charged with disobeying an order. General Howard denied receiving the order though a subordinate maintained that he had personally delivered it. A similar incident occurred at Gettysburg.[23]

In September 1863 General Howard was transferred to Tennessee where he subsequently commanded the right wing of Sherman's army on its march to the sea. For his participation in the western campaigns, he was promoted to brigadier general in the regular army (as opposed to volunteer) in December 1864. In March 1865 he was breveted ma-

---

[22] *First Annual Report of the Superintendent of Colored Schools for Washington and Georgetown, D. C., for the Year Ending June 30, 1868* (Washington, D. C.: Judd and Detweiler, 1870), p. 16.

[23] J. G. de R. H[amilton], "Oliver Otis Howard," *Dictionary of American Biography* (New York: Charles Scribner and Sons, 1931), Vol. IX, pp. 279–281. "Oliver Otis Howard," *Appleton's Cyclopaedia of American Biography* (New York: D. Appleton and Co., 1888), Vol. 3, p. 278.

jor general for gallantry at the Battle of Ezra Church and during the campaigns against Atlanta. In May 1865 President Johnson appointed him Commissioner of the Freedmen's Bureau. As the capstone to his military career, General Howard was awarded the Congressional Medal of Honor in 1893 for his bravery during the Battle of Fair Oaks.[24]

General Howard was a man of charisma and ideas. He approached his new position as commissioner with enthusiasm and set the machinery in operation. In February 1866 he appointed his brother, General Charles H. Howard, to succeed General John Eaton as the Assistant Commissioner for the District of Columbia and surrounding areas.[25]

The most immediate problem in the District of Columbia was the thousands of homeless, destitute refugees. To begin to meet this problem, four army barracks in the District were used as housing for 350 families. The confiscated Custis-Lee Estate was converted into an emergency refugee camp known as Freedmen's Village; it housed 350 families. Four barracks in Alexandria housed 111 families.[26]

These quarters met only a small fraction of the need, and thousands were unable to benefit from government emergency housing programs. Private real estate interests vastly increased the construction of shacks along the alleys in certain parts of town to rent and sell to refugees. The residents became known as "Alley Dwellers", and their plight was effectively ignored for half a century.[27] Acts passed in 1914 and 1934 outlawed the alley shacks after 1944 and created an agency to provide housing for these shamelessly exploited people. The agency was the National Capital Housing Authority which today figures prominently in the housing situation in Anacostia.

An endeavor of particular interest to General Oliver O. Howard was the Barry Farm Project which was undertaken as an experiment in developing home ownership among the refugees. Though it was quite successful, it appears not to have been attempted anywhere else. The plan dealt simultaneously with the severe housing shortage and with the restiveness of Washington's white citizenry, though with neither on a very large scale.

---

[24] *Ibid.*

[25] U. S. Bureau of Refugees, *Station Book of Civilians Employed in the District of Columbia, 1867–68,* Old Military Records Division, Record Group 105, National Archives, Washington, D. C., p. 151.

[26] *Idem., Report of the Assistant Commissioner for the District of Columbia, 1867,* p. 21.

[27] Federal Writers Project, *Washington: City and Capital* (Washington, D. C.: U. S. Government Printing Office, 1937), pp. 75–76.

Anacostia Museum

Map of Barry Farm after subdivision.

Following the Civil War, Barry Farm was bought for subdivision and sale to free-blacks and ex-slaves. Stickfoot Branch, now buried by the Suitland Parkway, rose in the steep wooded hollows and flowed into the Potomac near Poplar Point. Many present-day streets follow their original grades; this facilitates the locating of historical sites.

James Barry owned a 375-acre farm between Uniontown and St. Elizabeths Hospital. It was a truck farm growing produce for sale in the downtown markets. Barry himself lived in town and owned extensive holdings in the city.[28] The part of the farm east of Nichols Avenue was purchased by the Freedmen's Bureau in 1867, that west of Nichols Avenue was under lease until January 1, 1868, and was unavailable for sale until then.[29] Sections 1 through 7, east of Nichols Avenue, lay in the most distressing manner. The land was quite steep and almost entirely wooded.[30] For the most part it was unfit for cultivation, and a drive today in the area, along the streets, many of which are now as they were originally laid out, will reveal land which is too steep for the development that has been imposed upon it. Section 7, just east of Nichols Avenue as it ascended Asylum Hill, was mostly wooded except for the stretch along Nichols Avenue. It was more gently rolling land, suitable for cultivation. Sections 8 and 9 lay west of Nichols Avenue and were quite desirable for farming.[31] This was where Barry had raised most of his crops. It was these lots that were reserved for "race leaders".[32]

[28] "The Rambler," *The Evening Star,* February 11, 1917, sec. 4, p. 3.

[29] U. S. Bureau of Refugees, *Report for the District of Columbia, 1867,* p. 45.

[30] Adolph Boschke, "Topographical Map of the District of Columbia Surveyed in 1857–59," Geography and Map Division, Library of Congress, Washington, D. C.

[31] *Ibid.*

[32] Wade N. Carter, ed., Untitled notes of meetings of the earliest settlers of Hillsdale, 1921, p. 3.

On the other hand, many of those who were to become prominent members of the community, among them Mark McKenzie, Bartlett Matthias, and W. D. Harris, lived in the upland area.

The Freedmen's Bureau bought the Barry farm with monies that had been appropriated for school construction.[33] The skill of General Howard in manipulating the War Department bureaucracy may be imagined by his efforts to bring the Barry Farm Project to reality. He was able to persuade the appropriate politicians, perhaps justifying this shift of funds by pointing out that the profits from the resale of the subdivided farm would result in even more money being made available for school construction, thus yielding the double dividends of housing and schools. Special Order Number 61 of the War Department, on April 20, 1867, cleared the way for the Barry Farm Project "... with a view to relieving the immediate necessities of a class of poor colored people. . . ." [34] The lots were approximately one acre each and sold for $200 to $300, depending on location. Payments were divided into equal monthly installments to be completed by July 1, 1869. The first purchasers had twenty-four installments; those who purchased later had fewer and larger installments.[35] The Board of Trustees of the Barry Farm Fund oversaw the collection of monthly payments and the repayment of the education fund. The Rev. William H. Hunter, a Barry Farm resident, was chairman;[36] General Oliver O. Howard was treasurer; and John R. Elvans was secretary. General Charles H. Howard was a member of the Board.[37]

The venture was a success from the beginning. Almost immediately 180 lots were sold; an estimated ninety homes were completed before the winter of 1867.[38] The settlers formed a church, the Macedonia Baptist Church, and planned the construction of its building on a lot sold to Bartlett Matthias in section 3, probably lot 18.[39] The trustees of the church also planned the construction of more than one school, and in September 1867 asked the Freedmen's Bureau to supply lumber for the schools.[40] The community and the Bureau moved quickly, decided to build one school (on section 3, lot 30), and had one room ready for use in December 1867.[41] Peter Wilkinson, a settler and a carpenter, was the supervisor of the construction of the

---

[33] U. S. Bureau of Refugees, *Register of Letters Sent by the Assistant Commissioner for the District of Columbia,* 4 volumes, Old Military Records Division, Record Group 105, National Archives, Washington, D. C., Vol. 3, p. 401.

[34] *Ibid.* p. 461.

[35] U. S. Bureau of Refugees, *Register of Letters Sent by the Assistant Commissioner for the District of Columbia Concerning the Barry Farm,* Old Military Records Division, Record Group 105, National Archives, Washington, D. C., p. 2.

[36] *Ibid.,* p. 35.

[37] *Ibid.,* p. 32.

[38] U. S. Bureau of Refugees, *Letters Sent,* Vol. 3, p. 401.

[39] *Ibid.,* p. 284.

[40] U. S. Bureau of Refugees, *Letters Received,* Vol. 3, p. 210.

[41] *Ibid.,* p. 993.

school which was located at the top of Mt. Zion Hill,[42] approximately at the west corner of the present-day Douglass Junior High School on Douglass Road.

Living was especially precarious for ex-slaves in Washington during this post-war period. The promise of forty acres and a mule never materialized. Those who accepted this chance to become property owners were among the fortunate few who were able to do so. To preserve their opportunity they had to find and keep work, no mean accomplishment.[43] So the Barry Farm settlers worked at their jobs during the day to pay for their land and worked on their new homes at night and whenever else they could find time. In those days people worked a six-day, or at least a five and a half-day, week. Working on Sunday was not done, either from conviction or conformity. So building time available to the Barry Farm settlers was very limited. At night the hills and dales of the community were alight with the lanterns and fires of home builders.[44]

The Freedmen's Bureau provided each purchaser of a lot with enough lumber to build a two-room house, fourteen feet by twenty-four feet.[45] Those who wanted a larger house could purchase lumber, for cash, from the Bureau. In designing the standard house plan, the Bureau underestimated the amount of materials required.[46] This caused hardship on the homebuilders who were caught with winter near but no lumber to finish their roofs. A number of settlers purchased additional lumber; many placed small orders, no doubt to make up for the underestimate. Other orders were for substantial amounts. Peter Wilkinson had purchased three lots and ordered enough additional lumber to build a two-story house in which his family and also his son's family would live.[47] W. D. Harris placed four orders for additional lumber, the kinds and amounts of which indicate he was building a substantial house. Following a petition from a group of property owners to the Rev. William H. Hunter, Chairman of the Board of Trustees, asking that a road be graded to section 2, Harris, in turn, as spokesman for a group of citizens, wrote

[42] Carter, Untitled notes, p. 4.

[43] Gen. C. H. Howard, on January 5, 1867, in ceremonies at Freedmen's Village commemorating the Emancipation Proclamation, stated that there were too many freedmen there and that jobs in the area were very scarce. He went on to explain that the Freedmen's Bureau would arrange jobs in and transportation to other parts of the country and that only those who were gainfully employed could remain at Freedmen's Village. U. S. Bureau of Refugees, *Report for the District of Columbia, 1868,* p. 11.

[44] Carter, Untitled notes, p. 3.

[45] U. S. Bureau of Refugees, *Letters Sent,* Vol. 3, p. 138.

[46] U. S. Bureau of Refugees, *Letters Received,* Vol. 3, p. 148.

[47] *Ibid.,* p. 230.

to Assistant Commissioner Howard asking that the road be extended through section 3.[48] William J. Tolson bought additional lumber in such quantities as to indicate he planned a house with double the roof area of the standard house.[49] In 1868 Tolson's business failed; he was two months behind in his payments and in danger of losing his house and lot. General Charles H. Howard, as "Agent for the Board of Trustees", wrote General Oliver O. Howard, Treasurer, proposing a convoluted scheme which would save Tolson from forfeiture.[50] At least two other settlers did not fare so well. John Bundy, two months behind in his payments, was requested to personally return his contract to J. B. Johnson, Superintendent of the Barry Farm Project.[51] Similarly Henry Simms, two months behind in his payments, was notified that his lot was to be resold unless the payments were caught up within thirty days.[52] David H. Butler ordered lumber for a two-story house.[53] William Fractions built a two-story house and a back building.[54]

The Barry Farm Project was quite successful. Of 359 lots, fifty-nine remained unsold on October 1, 1868. There had been forty forfeitures. Lumber for 185 houses had been issued. The residents built their Baptist church and bought a lot for a Methodist church. They made a fund for school purposes, bought a lot, and built a school large enough for 150 pupils.[55] There had been some trouble collecting the monthly payments because some who had completed their payments early had had trouble getting clear title to their property. The experiment had developed into a cohesive community. Under the leadership of Solomon G. Brown, an employee of the Smithsonian Institution, Fred Smoot, and Mark McKenzie, the community adopted the name Hillsdale and formed the Hillsdale Civic Associa-

---

[48] *Ibid.*, pp. 36, 51, 94, 203, 259, 1049.

[49] *Ibid.*, pp. 533, 535.

[50] U. S. Bureau of Refugees, *Barry Farm*, p. 32.

William J. Tolson, lot 7 section 8, had paid $177.46 on a contract dated October 11, 1867. His business failed and he could not meet the payments for March and April 1868. He was liable to lose the improvements on the property valued at $150 unless he could raise $75 immediately. Gen. C. H. Howard in his letter dated April 30, 1868, recommended that "the Trustees of the Barry Farm Fund pay back to said Tolson $75 charging the same to his account.

"He will then have paid and the Treasurer will have in his possession, more than enough to have met his monthly payments, provided he had made them in amount not exceeding what is regularly required by the terms of our contracts."

[51] *Ibid.*, p. 19.

[52] *Ibid.*, p. 14.

[53] U. S. Bureau of Refugees, *Letters Received,* Vol. 3, p. 838.

[54] *Ibid.*, p. 880.

[55] U. S. Bureau of Refugees, *Letters Sent,* Vol. 4, p. 461.

Anacostia Museum

Solomon G. Brown.

Solomon G. Brown emerged as a leader of the new community of Hillsdale and was a founder of the Hillsdale Civic Association. He was an employee of the Smithsonian Institution.

tion.[56] The Association worked diligently for seventy-five years to get fundamental community improvements from a niggardly city government.

Older residents generally eschew the name Barry Farm in preference to Hillsdale. A public housing project was built in 1943 along Sumner Road and named Barry Farm. It was built to house war-

[56] Carter, Untitled notes, p. 4.

time newcomers, many of whom had lived in trailers across the river near the Navy Yard.[57] This intrusion and the old connotations of the name made Hillsdale the preferred name. The old residents of Anacostia are equally as particular about the name Anacostia.[58] To them Anacostia denotes only the area where the original Post Office stood, surrounded by the development that was, for a while, misnamed Uniontown.

HOUSING

The housing industry has been the dominant industry of Anacostia, beginning with the development of Uniontown and Hillsdale. With the exceptions of Garfield, another subdivision built by ex-slaves at the intersection of Good Hope Road, Alabama Avenue, and Naylor Road, and Twining City at the intersection of Pennsylvania and Minnesota Avenues, there was no further systematic development in Anacostia until the 1890's. Congress Heights and Randle Highlands (also known as East Washington Heights) were developed by Colonel Arthur Randle. To make sure his developments had transportation to downtown, Randle chartered and operated the first electric street car lines to cross the river, one out Pennsylvania Avenue and the other out Nichols Avenue.[59] Though he had a reputation for being a shrewd businessman, Randle may have pursued his ideas beyond reality; his fortunes fluctuated widely.[60] The Randle home, one of the most impressive in Anacostia, still stands next to the fire station in the 2800 block of Pennsylvania Avenue.

After this interlude, there was again no systematic development until World War II; this was the beginning of the total transformation of semi-rural Anacostia into a totally urban area. Only sixteen percent of the houses now in Anacostia existed before 1940. Thirty-eight percent of the houses have been built since 1950.[61] Since there has been little in the way of demolition and renewal, these statistics are reliable as an indicator of the area's development spurts.

The emergency demands for wartime housing gave the housing of the 1940's a character of its own. During the 1950's different influences came into play and in turn gave their character to Anacostia's development. The Southwest Urban Renewal and school desegregation

[57] Aloysius Briscoe, interview at the Anacostia Research Center, Washington, D. C., June 1972.

[58] Brazerol, interview.

[59] Havenner, *Early History,* pp. 6–7.

[60] Brazerol, interview.

[61] Office of the Mayor for Housing Programs, Government of the District of Columbia, *Washington's Far Southeast, '70* (n.p.: 1970), pp. 78–79.

Anacostia Museum

Nichols Avenue Trolley.

The trolley line that crossed the Eleventh Street Bridge and turned south on Nichols Avenue was built to serve Congress Heights, one of the developments of Col. Arthur Randle. This photograph was taken on Nichols Avenue at Talbert Street, S. E., near the present site of the Anacostia Museum.

were powerful influences in Anacostia's evolution. Three decades of public housing construction, through the 1940's, 1950's, and 1960's, provided a continuing undercurrent of neighborhood instability and decline. So today Anacostia has too many people crowded into too many apartment buildings which are crowded too closely to one another. Education suffers as a result of overdevelopment. Unemployment is a serious problem. Crime and drug abuse proliferate. The city government has not kept pace with the community's requirements for physical and social services.

World War II brought thousands of military personnel to Washington. Housing was extremely scarce, so much so that people were asked to rent out spare rooms in their homes as a patriotic gesture.[62] To stimulate construction of urgently needed housing, the Federal Housing Administration created a program which insured ninety percent of the mortgage of approved apartment projects. This program became infamously known as "FHA 608." Easy money and open space

[62] Leo Graves, interview at his home, 1746 Lamont St., N.W., Washington, D. C., January 1972.

so close to Bolling Air Force Base attracted developers. FHA accomplished its immediate purpose; housing was built. However, there were side effects that were either unforeseen or ignored.

The first side effect to manifest itself occurred during the construction phase. Because FHA insured ninety percent of the mortgage, a developer had only to inflate estimates and cut corners sufficiently and he would have no money of his own invested in the complex. This is alleged to have been done on a wide scale.[63]

A second side effect manifested itself more recently in the number of 608 mortgages that have passed into default. There are eight large developments, containing more than 1,600 housing units, abandoned by their owners with mortgages in default.[64]

The intervening years, between construction and default, provided owners with additional stimuli to abandon their properties. The first was the Southwest Urban Renewal Project in the early 1950's. This was followed in rapid succession by school desegregation in the mid 1950's. The continuing construction of public housing complexes intensified the tendency to make as much quick profit and then get out.

The Southwest area was an historical neighborhood dating from the Civil War era. It was here that many refugees settled after leaving the South. It was this area that bore the brunt of the anti-Negro riots of 1919.[65] The area had always been poor; it was a malarial swamp before it was a squatter town. Living conditions had not improved by the 1940's. The famous *Washington Post* photograph of the capitol dome framed by the squalor of a slum alley was taken in Southwest. A number of the houses did not have indoor toilets. However, there were a number of families who owned their homes. Thus the renewal displaced property owners as well as tenement dwellers.

The renewal had a reputation, even during its formative stages, as being prompted more by official embarrassment at a slum so close to the national monuments than by concern for those who lived in the slum. General U. S. Grant, 3rd, Chairman of the National Capital Park and Planning Commission, stated that the black people who were displaced by such improvement projects would be removed to the far reaches of Anacostia. Because of such injudicious remarks, the project was delayed until assurances of replacement housing in Southwest for the low income families who would be displaced by the

[63] Henry Petty, interview at the office of Neighborhood Development Center #3, 1016 Wahler Pl., S.E., Washington, D. C., March 1972.

[64] Office of Housing Programs, *Far Southeast,* pp. 84, 86.

[65] *The Washington Post,* July 19–25, 1919, passim.

Anacostia Museum

A Federal Housing Administration 608 development which has passed into default.

renewal were written into the plans.[66] Only a small percentage of these families were able to move back, and there is much bitterness that was caused by the government's breach of faith.

The integration of the District's public schools in 1954 and 1955 perhaps blunted a major housing crisis. White families fled to the strictly segregated housing of the suburbs. Anacostia's white population dropped from 82.4 percent in 1950[67] to 67.7 percent in 1960. By 1970 the population had experienced a complete reversal; it had become 85.97 percent black.[68] As a result of this racial change, privately owned apartment complexes which had been closed to black tenants became available to them.

The growing amount of public housing in Anacostia offered the refugees of urban renewal what the District of Columbia once offered

[66] Constance McLaughlin Green, *The Secret City* (Princeton, N. J.: Princeton University Press, 1967), pp. 279–280, 282–283.

[67] Bureau of the Census, U. S. Department of Commerce, *U. S. Census of Population: 1950,* Vol. III, Census Tract Statistics, ch. 59 (Washington, D. C.: U. S. Government Printing Office, 1952), p. 11.

[68] Office of Planning and Management, District of Columbia Government, *The People of the District of Columbia* (n.p., 1973), p. 2.

the refugees of the Civil War, a place to go and little else. Three public housing complexes were built during World War II, with a total of 943 dwelling units.[69] Two complexes were constructed during the 1950's: Stanton Dwellings in 1952, 348 units, and Highland Dwellings in 1954, 246 units.[70]

The decade of the 1960's continued the trend of the 1950's. South of Pennsylvania Avenue, 737 units were built or acquired as public housing.[71] The radical change in the racial make-up of the community coincided with a decline in maintenance of apartment properties. It was during the latter part of this decade that mortgages on FHA 608 complexes went into default.

Even though the quality of existing housing in Anacostia was declining markedly, new complexes continued to be built. Today eighty-five percent of Anacostia's housing is rental property.[72] Developers were able to gain indiscriminant variances from the zoning commissioners. Areas zoned for single family dwellings were rezoned for low-rise, "garden" apartments. Variances were granted to allow denser building concentrations; play areas were sacrificed; buildings were built up to the street; sidewalks were inadequate where they existed at all; drainage was allowed to find its own course.[73]

An example of such exploitative apartment construction is Ambassador Square on Stanton and Douglass Roads, known to the Hillsdale settlers as Mt. Zion Hill. The first units were available for occupancy in 1967, and there are now 523 habitable units.[74] The location is steep; buildings crowd each other and the streets; there are few sidewalks; erosion is dramatic.

The District Government is aware of this and many similar situations from its own report, *Washington's Far Southeast, '70,* and from the Anacostia Suit, which charges it along with agencies of the Federal Government with being derelict in their responsibilities properly to oversee and to control the zoning, financing, and construction of housing in Anacostia. In spite of its awareness, the local government in 1971 and 1972 permitted new construction by the Housing Development Corporation, a non-profit firm whose reason for existence is to bring some coherence to Washington's confused housing situation.

[69] National Capital Housing Authority, Government of the District of Columbia, *Annual Report, 1972* (Washington, D. C.: U. S. Government Printing Office, 1973), pp. 14–15.

[70] *Ibid.*

[71] *Ibid.*

[72] Office of Housing Programs, *Far Southeast,* p. 78.

[73] *Ibid.*, pp. 33–47.

[74] Elwood Mercer, interview at Ambassador Square Apartments, Washington, D. C., March 1972.

Anacostia Museum

"Sidewalks were inadequate, where they existed at all."

The Housing Development Corporation built a complex of medium income townhouses on the opposite side of the hill from Ambassador Square, which side is even steeper and even less suitable for development.

There are other, more prescient attempts to reverse the decline. Barnaby Gardens is an FHA 608 which went through default and was refinanced, rehabilitated, and revitalized as a condominium.[75] Park-

[75] Office of Housing Programs, *Far Southeast*, p. 87.

Anacostia Museum

"Drainage was allowed to find its own course."

chester Housing Corporation is another FHA 608 complex which went through default and was reorganized as a condominium. There has been partial success in this complex; only part of the buildings are currently operating as condominiums.[76] Others are still in default, having defaulted, in fact, on the refinanced mortgage.

The revitalization of housing in Anacostia is an extremely difficult task. Efforts have been as unsuccessful as they have been successful.

[76] *Ibid.*, p. 89.

Photograph by the author

Ambassador Square.

The steep north side of Mt. Zion Hill affords these units of Ambassador Square one of the fine vistas of the monuments of Washington. The erosion in the foreground is the grade of Douglass Road which has remained unfinished for years.

Anacostians have only limited control over the future of their houses. Bold steps are needed to discourage abandonment of buildings; to rehabilitate and demolish, to encourage occupant ownership, and to make mortgage and rehabilitation money available to low income families.

EDUCATION

Twining City, at the east end of the Pennsylvania Avenue Bridge, and Giesboro, located on a promontory in the Potomac River across from Haines Point which is now obscured by Bolling Air Force Base, were the first schools in Anacostia. They were for white pupils. The Hillsdale settlers built the first school for black pupils.

In 1871 the District of Columbia bought a two-acre site from Peter Wilkinson at the intersection of Nichols Avenue and Sheridan Road and built the Hillsdale School.[77] This building was used until 1913 when it was condemned. Birney School, named for James G. Birney, a leader of the anti-slavery movement who freed his own slaves and

[77] Carter, Untitled notes, p. 4.

Photograph by the author

The Housing Development Corporation venture opposite Ambassador Square.

The south slope of Mt. Zion Hill was developed by this venture of the non-profit Housing Development Corporation, ostensibly planned to attract middle-income families. The major problem in the area is the over-concentration of low-rise rental housing.

was the presidential candidate of the Liberty Party in 1844, was organized in 1889.[78] The building, still in use at the corner of Howard Road and Martin Luther King, Jr. Avenue, was built in 1901. It has been renamed Nichols Avenue School. The third Birney School is on

[78] Office of the Statistician, D. C. Public Schools, *Biographical Directory of the Public Schools of the District of Columbia* (n.p., revised 1953), p. 8.

King Avenue at Sumner Road. After the demolition of the Hillsdale School, Birney became the community center and meeting house.[79]

Garfield School, for the children of the freedmen who settled the Garfield community, was built in 1887. In 1909 it was razed and rebuilt in 1910 on its same site on Alabama Avenue.[80]

Of the eight schools, six for white children and two for black, built between 1881 and 1910, six are still in use: Congress Heights (1898), Orr (1900), Stanton (1903, rebuilt in 1950), Ketcham (1907), Nichols Avenue, and Garfield.[81]

There was no secondary school in Anacostia until 1935[82] when Anacostia High School was opened for white students who had until that time gone to Eastern High School. M Street School was the first public high school in Washington for black students, and this is where black Anacostians received their secondary education. The school served from 1891 until it was replaced by Dunbar High School in 1916.[83] The old M Street School is still standing and in use at 1st and M Streets, Northwest. It is now called Perry Elementary School.

Dunbar served the black community of Washington and of the entire nation for many years. The academically oriented students from Anacostia traveled across town either by trolley or more commonly by foot to attend Dunbar.[84] The quality of education was so high that people throughout the nation arranged to have their children educated there. Native Washingtonians who graduated from Dunbar include Dr. Charles Drew, the developer of the plasma method of preserving blood, and Senator Edward W. Brooke of Massachusetts.

Later, as other schools were built, Anacostia students crossed town to attend Cardozo Business High School at Ninth Street and Rhode Island Avenue, Northwest, and Armstrong Manual Training High School at First and O Streets, Northwest. There was no high school for black students in Anacostia until the Supreme Court desegregation decision integrated Anacostia High School in 1955.

The first junior high school in Washington opened in 1927. Anacostia's first junior school, Kramer, was built in 1943. Frederick Douglass, built in 1952 on the site of Hillsdale's first school, was

---

[79] *Annual Report of the Commissioners of the District of Columbia, Year Ended June 30, 1920,* 4 volumes (Washington, D. C.: U. S. Government Printing Office, 1921), Vol. 4, p. 255.

[80] Office of the Statistician, D. C. Public Schools, *Public School Buildings, Past and Present* (n.p., 1965), pp. 14, 26.

[81] *Ibid.*, pp. 13, 15, 18, 20, 29.

[82] *Ibid.*, p. 6.

[83] *Ibid.*

[84] Ethel K. Greene, interview at her home, 2643 Naylor Road, S.E., Washington, D. C., November 1970.

Anacostia Museum

A graduating class at Birney School.

Anacostia's first junior high school for black students.[85] Until Douglass was built, attending junior high school was particularly difficult. Some went to Shaw Junior High School at Seventh Street and Rhode Island Avenue, Northwest. Others went to Randall Junior High School at First and I Streets, Southwest, which was quite crowded. Crowding became so severe at Randall during the 1940's that the upper floor of Turner Elementary School at Alabama Avenue and Stanton Road was used as a junior high school from 1946 until 1950.[86]

The World War II years and those following were particularly difficult ones for Anacostians, both black and white. The wholesale construction of housing meant that great strains were placed on the school facilities. These strains continued until the new crisis of desegregation replaced overcrowding in public attention. Most Anacostians were not wealthy enough to send their children to private schools, so they moved. A large number of them moved just across the District line into Maryland. Prince Georges County is now a predominantly white working class area with a steadily growing black population.

Anacostians sustained a seven year effort between 1947 and 1954, working to have the segregated system of education outlawed. The

[85] Office of the Statistician, *Buildings*, p. 9.

[86] *Ibid.*, p. 21.

parents, churches, and civic organizations of Anacostia raised money for legal fees, organized groups to attend endless meetings, hearings, and planning sessions, and supported the parents and children who were plaintiffs in Anacostia's suit against segregation. The plaintiffs in *Bolling v. Sharp* were the families of James E. Jennings, Mrs. Sarah Bolling, and Samuel Briscoe. The Rev. S. Everette Guiles, then pastor of Campbell A. M. E. Church, provided leadership in sustaining community efforts in the movement. The plaintiffs' attorney was Charles Houston, a leading civil rights lawyer of the period. The suit brought by these Anacostians was not the one finally adjudicated by the Supreme Court in its historic decision of 1954. That case, *Brown v. Board of Education of Topeka, Kansas,* was in fact a composite of a number of suits from throughout the country, and the development of the case of the Anacostians who sued the District of Columbia Board of Education was important to the final ruling by the Supreme Court.[87]

Twenty years after segregation was outlawed, the schools, like the population, are overwhelmingly black, and they are still overcrowded. Eight elementary schools, two junior high schools, and one senior high school which compose the Anacostia School Project were operating at 150.8 percent of capacity in 1972. Eight other elementary schools in the area were operating at 168.3 percent of capacity in 1969.[88]

An indication of the pervasive problems of education in Anacostia is the drop-out rate. During the 1968–1969 school year, Ballou High School lost 232 students, 15 percent of its enrollment.[89] The implications of such a drop-out rate are far reaching: unemployment, crime, drug abuse.

The Youth Conference of the Southeast Coalition for Action, sponsored by the Frederick Douglass United Community Center in May 1972, formulated a list of recommendations which are indicative of the issues that youth feel must be addressed. The areas of concern include courses in black culture, vocational education, reading improvement programs, counselling, increased communication between the schools and the community, and youths serving as teacher aides.[90]

[87] The Rev. S. Everette Guiles, interview at Turner Memorial A. M. E. Church, Washington, D. C., June 1972.

[88] William Rice, interview at the Anacostia School Project, Washington, D. C., November 1971.

[89] *Ibid.*

The high school drop-out rate in the Watts section of Los Angeles has been placed at 29 percent, and some urban education experts do not consider a 15 percent rate to be alarmingly high. This may be a further measure of the problem.

[90] Report of the Youth Conference of the Southeast Coalition for Action (Frederick Douglass United Community Center, 1972), pp. 1–4.

The Anacostia School Project, a special program made possible by funds from the United States Office of Education, was begun in December 1968. The program endeavored to establish effective community involvement in and control over eleven schools in Anacostia. The primary issue that emerged from the Project's planning was reading. Part of the program to improve reading skills included extensive use of non-professional community residents as reading assistants, and a program to encourage and develop reading skills at the pre-school level. The project also proposed programs in environmental science, adult education, data processing, auto mechanics, and a street academy for dropouts. Funding such a far reaching program encountered resistance, and the Project dropped some of its proposals.[91]

Disagreements also arose over the roles that the Office of Education and the District of Columbia School Board should play in this experiment in community control. A third set of factors which played a significant role was that the program was designed and implemented during the administration of President Lyndon B. Johnson. The succeeding administration of President Richard M. Nixon reappraised the Project, revised it considerably, and cut its funding.

EMPLOYMENT

As an area of small residential communities among farms, Anacostia attracted few major employers. Livelihoods were gained from agriculture, from businesses which delivered the community's daily needs, and from working in the downtown employment centers.

Because of the size of the lots in Hillsdale, people were able to grow large gardens, often selling the produce in the downtown markets.[92] This situation prevailed until the 1940's and makes the growth of the last thirty years stand out in even greater contrast.

The businesses which developed in Anacostia and Hillsdale for the most part supplied the daily needs of the two communities. They also reflected the prevailing code of segregation. Anacostia's businesses were typical of a small town. Campbell's Hardware Store is still selling the tools and other wares that it sold in the rural, more self-reliant past. Curtis Brothers Furniture Store began as a hauling firm and grew into one of the largest furniture stores of the Washington area. The Anacostia National Bank prospered and moved across Nichols Avenue into a new building; then it merged with the National Bank of Washington in the 1950's. The original building is still recogniz-

[91] Rice, interview.

[92] George Trivers, interview at his home, 2529 Elvans Road, S.E., Washington, D. C., November 1970.

Anacostia Museum

Shipley's Pharmacy

Shipley's Pharmacy was on the ground floor of Douglass Hall at the corner of Howard Road and Nichols Avenue. Dr. Shipley is shown with his assistant.

able as having been a bank. On the new building, stains from the old brass lettering are still visible under the new name. The Anacostia Federal Savings and Loan Association, also begun as a community institution, merged with the Perpetual Building Association.[93]

The businesses of Hillsdale grew out of the necessities of segregation. Because some white businesses would not receive black patrons at all, black morticians, barbers, and beauticians became numerous. Mason's Funeral Home was licensed in 1902. Saunder's Barber Shop, the oldest now in operation, was opened in 1933. Other businesses which figured prominently in Hillsdale in the first half of the Twentieth Century included McKenzie's Sign Shop, Slaughter's Blacksmith Shop, Sayles Ice Cream Parlor, and a coal and ice company beside Douglass Hall.[94] The first drug store was opened by Dr. William E. Gayes in 1895.[95] Shipley's Pharmacy operated for many years and shared with Tignor's Law Office the ground floor of Douglass Hall at the corner of Howard Road and Nichols Avenue. The pharmacy of Charles Qualls, since 1941, has assumed the place in the community formerly occupied by Shipley's. A neighborhood grocery, Miller's Grocery, was owned and operated by a Jewish family. On the second floor, Max Miller had his law office. Miller's was across Nichols Avenue from Douglass Hall at Sheridan Road on the lot that had once been the playground of the Hillsdale School. It is now a Texaco gasoline station. The most successful black enterprise is Greenwood Moving and Storage Company. Founded in the 1940's, it has grown considerably in its thirty years. Today Greenwood trucks are a frequent sight in all parts of town.

The Navy Yard was an important employment center for Anacostians, both black and white. When ships regularly docked there, Anacostia was something of a navy town.[96] It has always been a predominantly blue collar residential area. A few residents were prominent Washington figures, for example, Frederick Douglass and Walter L. Fowler, who was the Director of the Budget for the District of Columbia. However most people were tradesmen and hourly wage earners. This perhaps explains, at least in part, why Anacostia has fared so poorly at the hands of local government.

The jobs downtown which were open to Hillsdale citizens were,

[93] Tracey Campbell, interview at Campbell's Hardware Store, 1300 Good Hope Road, S.E., Washington, D. C., March 1971.

[94] Esther Johnson, interview at the Anacostia Research Center, Washington, D. C., April 1971.

[95] *The Afro-American* (Washington, D. C.), May 12, 1956, p. 11.

[96] Larry E. Thomas, interview at the Anacostia Research Center, Washington, D. C., October 1971.

almost without exception, low-paying menial jobs: laborers and janitors. Messengers were higher level positions, and clerk positions were held by a fortunate few. John Dale, a respected leader of the Hillsdale community for several decades, after having worked at menial jobs for years, became a mail carrier. He also worked as janitor at the Anacostia National Bank.[97] The women who were employed downtown worked as charwomen and domestics. Some took in laundry to supplement the family income.

The black professionals of Anacostia worked exclusively within the black community: teachers, ministers, morticians, pharmacists, and lawyers. Clarence W. Tignor, whose office was in Douglass Hall, was admitted to practice law before the United States Supreme Court.[98]

With its semi-rural background and with real estate as its major industry, Anacostia has its own perspective on the manner in which the metropolitan area has been developing in the past two decades. Factors in Anacostia's employment future include the "white collar" character of Washington's economy, the effects of the Capital Beltway on the location of employment centers, the availability of public transportation, and Defense Department plans for redeveloping the Bolling Air Force Base.

Unemployment is a serious problem in Anacostia. The unemployment figures issued by the Department of Labor are based on the number of people who have applied for and are receiving unemployment benefits, with a statistical extrapolation as to the number of people who do not apply or are ineligible for benefits. Unemployment figures are not compiled regularly for Anacostia or any other specific locality within the metropolitan area; the decennial census is the only such source. There are, however, concrete indicators of the unemployment problem: more than 10,000 Anacostians receive welfare payments; more than 13,000 participate in the food stamp program; crime and drug abuse rates are high and are a constant concern to residents; the school dropout rate is fifteen percent a year. Everyone knows that unemployment is a serious problem, but no one can say exactly how serious.

Thirty-five years ago people could survive in Anacostia by raising produce and doing odd jobs. World War II created jobs in Anacostia at the Bolling Air Force Base, work for everyone. At the time no one sorted out the real employment picture. Most of the workers were transferred military personnel. After the war Bolling declined in im-

[97] John Dale, interview at his home, 2652 Nichols Avenue, S.E., Washington, D. C., November 1970.

[98] *The Washington Bee,* May 3, 1919, p. 1.

portance, and those who had been stationed there left, leaving Anacostia with no major source of employment for its swollen population.

Today in Anacostia the largest employers include the Naval Research Laboratory, St. Elizabeths Hospital, the public schools, and retail businesses such as Safeway grocery stores and Peoples drug stores. The professionals who work for these concerns, for the most part, do not live in the area; and for the most part, Anacostians are not prepared by education to occupy anything more than the lower paying positions.

Because its main business is government, Washington has a peculiar economy which requires particular abilities in its work force. Paperwork as the major product requires particular abilities in language: reading, writing, and spelling, the precise areas in which the Anacostia schools and students show very poorly. The applications of data processing to Washington's voluminous paperwork production requires mastery of the logic of the "new math," the ability to translate office functions, such as payroll and mailing lists, into mathematical functions which the computer can perform. The sophistication of the electronics of computers places new demands on the people who maintain and repair them; even the fuel systems of automobiles are being computerized. Washington's blue collar job market has always been limited, mostly to construction and automobile trades.[99] Today even the limited opportunities in these areas are demanding increasingly sophisticated preparation. In Anacostia where, as recently as the 1940's, people could subsist, the passage to technical and language competence is becoming more difficult.

Though Anacostia has always been separated, it has always been accessible. Students once walked to M Street School and Dunbar High School; people walked to work to save trolley fare.[100] The construction of the Capital Beltway, Interstate 495, has had profound effects on Anacostia's accessibility to jobs. In the greater Washington area, fifty-two percent of the families own at least one automobile. In Anacostia sixty percent of the families do not own even one automobile.[101]

[99] District of Columbia Manpower Administration, U. S. Department of Labor, *Manpower Directions in Metropolitan Washington, D. C., 1972–1980* (n.p., 1972), p. 19.

"The labor force of the Washington metropolitan area has been characterized as predominantly white collar. For the years in our forecast period (1972–80), white collar occupations account for 60 to 65 percent of total employment. Professional workers alone average 25 per cent."

All blue collar categories together are forecast to total 35.5 percent of the work force; on the other hand, clerical workers alone will compose 24.3 percent of the force.

[100] Ethel K. Greene, interview.

[101] Department of Urban and Regional Planning, George Washington University, *Transit Study—Far Southeast (Draft)* (Washington, D. C.: George Washington University, 1971), p. 16.

The Beltway was built to divert interstate traffic around the city; it has become a sixty-six mile main street. Industrial parks, vast shopping plazas, and other employment centers have distributed themselves around the circumference. This kind of development had the automobile as its *sine qua non,* and Anacostians do not have automobiles. Public transportation is designed primarily to take people downtown in the morning and take them back in the evening. This pattern is of little use to suburbanites who travel about the suburbs or to Anacostians whose transportation needs are almost exactly opposite to the design of public transportation.

The advent of the Metro subway system holds limited promise for Anacostia. Only one line is planned south of Pennsylvania Avenue, and it is scheduled during the next-to-last phase of construction, with a projected completion date of June 1978, subject to delay.[102] To serve a population of 126,000, this seems very little very late.

The United States Defense Department has extensive plans for redeveloping the Bolling Air Force Base area into a "Mini-Pentagon." The new development would include a complex of military office buildings, six thousand housing units for employees, a shopping center, a community center, four elementary schools, a junior high school, a senior high school, and other community buildings such as churches. The plans project that 20,000 jobs will be brought into Anacostia.[103]

Remembering the situation which prevailed during and following World War II, Anacostians are suspicious of these plans. A projected half of the jobs to be created will be for military personnel. The apparent self-contained nature of the development offers little promise for diversifying Anacostia's population and assisting in its economic development. Building new schools on the compound for these new residents will do little to improve the conditions in the overcrowded, existing schools. Integrating this area into Anacostia and providing jobs for Anacostians in Anacostia remains an effort against great odds.

Efforts to strengthen Anacostia's economy are being made by the Anacostia Economic Development Corporation, an indirect outgrowth of the 1968 riots following the assassination of Martin Luther

---

[102] William Fauntroy, interview at the Frederick Douglass United Community Center, Washington, D. C., November 1971.

[103] National Capital Park and Planning Commission, *The Proposed Comprehensive Plan for the National Capital* (Washington, D. C.: U. S. Government Printing Office, 1967), pp. 153–159.

These projected plans have been revised a number of times since their publication. Some concessions have been gained from the Department of Defense on behalf of housing for Washington. The isolated character of the military community does not appear to have been appreciably altered, however.

King, Jr., when a group of Anacostians organized the Anacostia Citizens and Merchants, Incorporated. ACM Inc. proposed to address the housing problems of the area, thereby attacking the root causes of such riots. It planned to replace the abandoned FHA 608 development, Barnaby-High Point, with townhouses. Though the project itself never became operational, a consciousness of the economic dilemma of Anacostia began to express itself in overt action. ACM Inc. did not improve the housing of Anacostia, but those involved in it came to concentrate their energies more directly on economic issues. The Anacostia Economic Development Corporation succeeded ACM Inc., based on cooperation between Anacostia businessmen, other Washington businessmen, and city planners.[104]

The Anacostia Economic Development Corporation provides technical assistance to developing businesses: identifying business opportunities, securing capital, working out real estate arrangements, advising on inventory, equipment, personnel, and bookkeeping. AEDC has assisted several businesses: Shabazz Bakeries, Diane's Restaurant, Congress Heights Hardware, and Tanners Dry Cleaners, among others. It plans a professional and commercial building at the corner of Martin Luther King, Jr. Avenue and Morris Road as a solid investment in the economic rejuvenation of the community.[105]

CRIME AND DRUG ABUSE

Until the 1950's Anacostians gave little thought to the security of their property or to their personal safety. The police station at the corner of Martin Luther King, Jr. Avenue and Chicago Street was built in 1901 and became Washington's Eleventh (and last) Precinct. Two Hillsdale residents were members of its force, William Stewart and Ernest Brooks. In those days the police officers were closer to the community they served, and the real crimes they dealt with were infrequent.[106] Most often they protected tomato patches from foraging neighborhood kids and performed other such services.[107]

Some Anacostians date the change from the influx of people displaced by the Southwest Urban Renewal. People became strangers to each other, and they began to lock their doors and their cars. The situation degenerated through the late 1950's and the early 1960's. The police became strangers, an alien white force imposing order on a

[104] Daryl Hill, interview at the Anacostia Economic Development Corporation, Washington, D. C., July 1972.

[105] *Ibid.*

[106] Thomas A. Brooks, interview at his home, 2401 Shannon Place, S.E., Washington, D. C., April 1972.

[107] Brazerol, interview.

Anacostia Museum

Officer William Stewart.

One of the Hillsdale residents on the force of the Eleventh Precinct, Officer William Stewart never rose above the rank of private.

resentful black community. The reorganization of the police department in 1967 and 1968 created one police district, the Sixth, for the entire area east of the Anacostia River, with headquarters in far Northeast, thus increasing the estrangement. An angry confrontation, a near riot, in 1966 dramatically revealed the intensity of the growing estrangement.

As crime and drug abuse rose dangerously and the hostility increased between the community and the police, the Seventh District was created south of Pennsylvania Avenue, the same area as the old Eleventh Precinct. A number of other measures have been adopted to control crime and the drug traffic. High intensity street lighting was installed and has been helpful in curtailing night crime. The number of officers and patrols has been increased; this, too, has significantly curtailed crime in some areas of Anacostia.

Controversial police powers, of dubious constitutionality, were enacted into law during the Nixon Administration with the intention of helping curb crime and drug traffic. One measure, repealed by the Congress in 1974, empowered the police, with a special warrant, to break into private buildings and dwellings without knocking. Another empowered the courts to detain an accused person without bail if the judge feels the accused may commit another crime while out on bail.[108]

The Narcotics Treatment Agency was created to institute a city-wide heroin treatment program which dispenses methadone to heroin users who come into the program either voluntarily, under the orders of a court, or as a condition of prison release. Methadone is a highly addictive drug, a synthetic relative of heroin. Unless an addict is given a decreasing dosage in order to withdraw completely, there is great danger of his becoming addicted to methadone, an addiction which many users and nonusers say is worse than heroin addiction. There is an important distinction to be made between methadone withdrawal and methadone maintenance. Unfortunately, much methadone treatment is maintenance, and the patients are only changing habits.

In Anacostia, the Southeast Neighborhood Action Board (SENAB) is addressing itself to the health problems of the area, and part of its concern is the drug abuse problem. SENAB operates a methadone treatment facility under contract with the Narcotics Treatment Agency and employs as counsellors ex-addicts and others who are undergoing methadone treatment. Its Juvenile Drug Program is a detoxification and abstinence program; no methadone is used. SENAB's first project was a community medical center which provides free medical services regardless of income; this was undertaken in cooperation with the District of Columbia Public Health program.[109]

The programs and legislation of the Nixon Administration greatly interrupted the flow of heroin, so much so that it is no longer the drug of choice among drug users on the streets. Crime statistics and drug arrests have shown a decline in Anacostia and are indeed welcome. Concern exists however over the powers which the police and courts now have and the reliance on these as a solution to the problem.

---

[108] Committee on the District of Columbia, U. S. House of Representatives, *Report on H.R. 16196* (Washington, D. C.: U. S. Government Printing Office, 1970), pp. 79–85, 104–109. *District of Columbia Code* (Washington, D. C.: U. S. Government Printing Office, 1973), pp. 1608, 1621.

A common response to inquiries regarding the unemployment problem was that crime is the only means left whereby undereducated, chronically unemployed people who feel the brunt of racial discrimination can support their families.[110] This is perhaps a rationalization, but it is a measure of the frustration and anger that Anacostians feel regarding their employment prospects. Also it may be an indication of a real solution to the crime problem.

PUBLIC SERVICES

Public services in Anacostia have perennially lagged behind those in the rest of the city. In the earlier years of the century, there was a difference between services in Anacostia and Hillsdale. When gas lines finally crossed the river, Anacostia had gas street lights while Hillsdale still retained the old oil lights.[111] Older residents recall vividly the lamp lighter carrying his ladder and torch, lighting the lamps in the evening, and then returning in the morning to put out the lamps and fill them for the next night.[112]

There were differences in street paving between the two communities, and also in sidewalks, in water service, and sewer service.[113] The Rambler in the *Evening Star* noted in 1891 the conditions in Hillsdale:

> The streets of Hillsdale have the appearance of being neglected by the authorities and inconvenience and discomfort are experienced by the residents as a consequence. The taxpayers are becoming restive under this neglect. Howard Avenue [sic], for instance . . . which is occupied by many residents on either side, is a mere country lane, not even provided with a sidewalk.[114]

Water piped into the homes came late in Hillsdale, primarily because most of its citizens could not afford the cost of installing the pipes from the street. The first water service came to Hillsdale because the privies began to pollute the wells. The city laid water mains and installed community hydrants, called "pumps" throughout the city. These pumps were used extensively until recently. The last one

---

[109] Benjamin Davis, interview at the Southeast Neighborhood House, Washington, D. C., February 1972.

[110] The inquiries were made during videotaped interviews conducted by the Anacostia Neighborhood Museum in various locales in Anacostia and also at the Employment Service office downtown.

[111] *Annual Report of the Commissioners of the District of Columbia for the Year Ending June 30, 1894* (Washington, D. C.: U. S. Government Printing Office, 1894), appendix, maps showing sewers, water mains, street lamps, street pavements, and street railways.

[112] Dale, interview.

[113] *Report of the Commissioners,* 1894, appendix, maps.

[114] "Roadside Sketches", *The Evening Star,* December 5, 1891, p. 7.

was removed from the corner of Jasper Road and 22nd Street only a few years ago.[115] The last community to depend on public pumps for its water supply was Marshall Heights off East Capital Street and Benning Road in far Northeast. These pumps were removed and water piped into the houses in the 1950's.[116]

Sewer service came to Hillsdale thirty to forty years later than water service.[117] The city provided a service through the Odorless Excavating Apparatus Company to clean out the privies. The name used came to be the "Odorless Apparatus Man." Though there are many humorous anecdotes concerning these men, they emerged as faceless men whom no one knew. They made a circle of their barrels to avoid being pestered by the neighborhood kids while they ate their bag lunches inside the circle.[118]

The Hillsdale Civic Association played a major role in pressuring the city to provide needed services. It worked long and hard to get streets paved, sidewalks built, street lights and traffic lights installed. Their last major effort was flood control. Stickfoot Branch, which now runs under Suitland Parkway, flooded regularly. It did considerable damage to the homes along Sheridan and Howard Roads, and finally claimed one life. The Association had been asking for many years that something be done.[119] Finally in the early 1940's, adequate drainage was provided during the construction of the Suitland Parkway.

In more recent years, different tactics have developed: lawsuits, confrontation, and political organization.

The Anacostia Suit is an attempt to get a judicial opinion regarding the responsibility of the local and Federal governments in providing services and in abiding by established guidelines. The accusations cover governmental decisions in rezoning, granting zoning variances, construction of public housing, and financing private, low-income housing. The suit charges that Anacostia has been denied adequate public services in education, refuse collection, police and fire protection, recreation, sidewalks, and public transportation.[120]

---

[115] Stern, interview.

Mr. Stern said that the pump was still in operation. A search at the site revealed nothing. A neighbor recalled its having been there in very recent times. She said that children used sticks to jam the mechanism open so that water would run all the time.

[116] Edith P. Greene, interview at her home, 2328 Pomeroy Road, S.E., Washington, D. C., May 1971.

[117] Stern, interview.

[118] Edith P. Greene, interview.

[119] William Underdue, interview at his home, 2510 Sheridan Road, S.E., Washington, D. C., February 1972.

[120] *Burner et al. v. Washington et al.*, "Amended Complaint for Declaratory Judgement and Injunctive Relief", Civil Action 242–71, U. S. District Court for the District of Columbia, pp. 4–24.

While the Anacostia Suit slowly makes its way through court proceedings, community organizations continually work to relieve the problems of Anacostia. Southeast Neighborhood House is the oldest such organization. Founded in 1930, its first headworker was Mrs. Marion C. Hope of Anacostia. It moved from its original location in the Capital Hill area to Anacostia in 1962. In 1965 with funds from the Office of Economic Opportunity, it initiated programs to aid tenants, welfare recipients, and youth. Protest demonstrations sought to focus attention on these neglected areas of social concern.[121]

In 1967 Congress Heights residents organized themselves through the assistance of Southeast House. Originally called C.H.A.S.E., the organization, since 1971, has been known as the Neighborhood Development Center #3. Ron Ely was instrumental in the successful development of the organization and was the first chairman of the Board of Directors.[122]

The organization worked diligently in the planning of the Highlands Public Housing Project and the Xenia Community School Project. Accomplishments have also been made in setting up a preschool program, an alcoholic rehabilitation program, and tenant councils.[123]

The Southeast Coalition for Action was an effort by the Frederick Douglass United Community Center. The Coalition endeavored to establish communication between the different agencies, programs, and people of Anacostia, especially with regard to matters relating to the youth.[124]

The Youth Council of the Coalition in May 1972 addressed itself to educational issues and attempted to communicate its findings to city officials, without success. As a result the Council worked to prepare in-depth research to support its findings and worked with other community agencies to provide services to youth.[125]

THE PARADOX

Anacostia is and has been a dynamic community. From its very beginning, the citizens have organized themselves to press for improvements and to meet problems. There have been varying degrees

[121] Zora Martin, interview at the Anacostia Neighborhood Museum, Washington, D. C., January 1972.

[122] Theresa Jones, interview at the Neighborhood Development Center #3, Washington, D. C., March 1972.

[123] *Ibid.*

[124] William Saunders, interview at the Frederick Douglass United Community Center, Washington, D. C., July 1972.

[125] *Ibid.*

Photograph by the author

"City of Washington From Beyond the Navy Yard," photograph, 1974, by Thomas J. Cantwell.

The view is from the top of Morris Road, S. E. Poplar Point has been obscured by the dredging of the Anacostia Flats.

of success. A visit to the area reveals the failures. The successes are not as obvious, but they are important. The construction of the Southwest Freeway raised the question of the relocation of the Southeast Neighborhood House. The Anacostia community organized itself to vie with other communities on both sides of the river for its services and was successful.

The competition was city-wide when the Smithsonian Institution sought a location for its planned storefront museum in an inner-city neighborhood. Anacostia, a second time, was successful in presenting its case. The Anacostia Neighborhood Museum is a most visible and viable institution of improvement in the community. Further it has become such through its own perseverance; the Smithsonian planned a storefront to show the accustomed kind of museum exhibits. The Anacostia Museum has showed the community to itself, and has served as a catalyst in a wide variety of endeavors aimed at improving the quality of Anacostia life.

A third time Anacostia presented its case and successfully gained a promising program, in the Anacostia School Project. President Johnson wanted to establish a model of urban education in Washington. Anacostia defined its educational problems and goals and designed a program which the Office of Education chose over those of other inner-city neighborhoods.

Though Anacostia has been exploited and ignored to the point that on the whole living conditions are miserable and the social problems overwhelming, the community consistently refuses to be destroyed. It seems that the worse the omissions and commissions by government and private interests, the more tenaciously Anacostians maintain their community spirit. It is a paradox. Some believe that adversity is good for you. If that be true, Anacostia is most assuredly good.

"Shelling the Citadel of Race Prejudice": William Calvin Chase and the Washington "Bee", 1882–1921

HAL S. CHASE

> Most white people in America are entirely unaware of the bitter and relentless criticism of themselves; of their policies in domestic or international affairs; their legal and political practices; their business enterprises; their churches, schools, and other institutions; their social customs, their opinions and prejudices and almost everything else in white American civilization. Week in and week out these are presented to the Negro people in their own press.[1]

Implicit in this statement is the reality of a segregated society based upon the oppression of one group by another. But the statement is a general one and may lack impact. Fortunately a specific history of the separation of black Americans and white Americans, and the oppression of black Americans by white Americans, in Washington, D. C. has been documented by Constance McLaughlin Green in her work *The Secret City*. As her title implies, however, that work is written from the perspective of a white American, for surely the "Secret City" was no secret to the black Washingtonians who lived in it. One purpose of this paper is to present an alternate view: to present a perspective from within the "Secret City" and so to lessen the error of mistaking the limits of one's own vision for reality.

For those who had eyes to see, William Calvin Chase shelled the citadel of race prejudice in the pages of his Washington *Bee* from 1882 until his death in 1921. His criticism of white American civilization was relentless and often bitter throughout the historical period which has been documented as "the nadir" of black American-white American relations[2] and it was characteristic of the content of the Afro-American press of his era. This journalistic protest stands in

[1] Gunnar Myrdal, *An American Dilemma* (1944), 908.

[2] Rayford W. Logan, *The Betrayal of the Negro* (1957), *passim*.

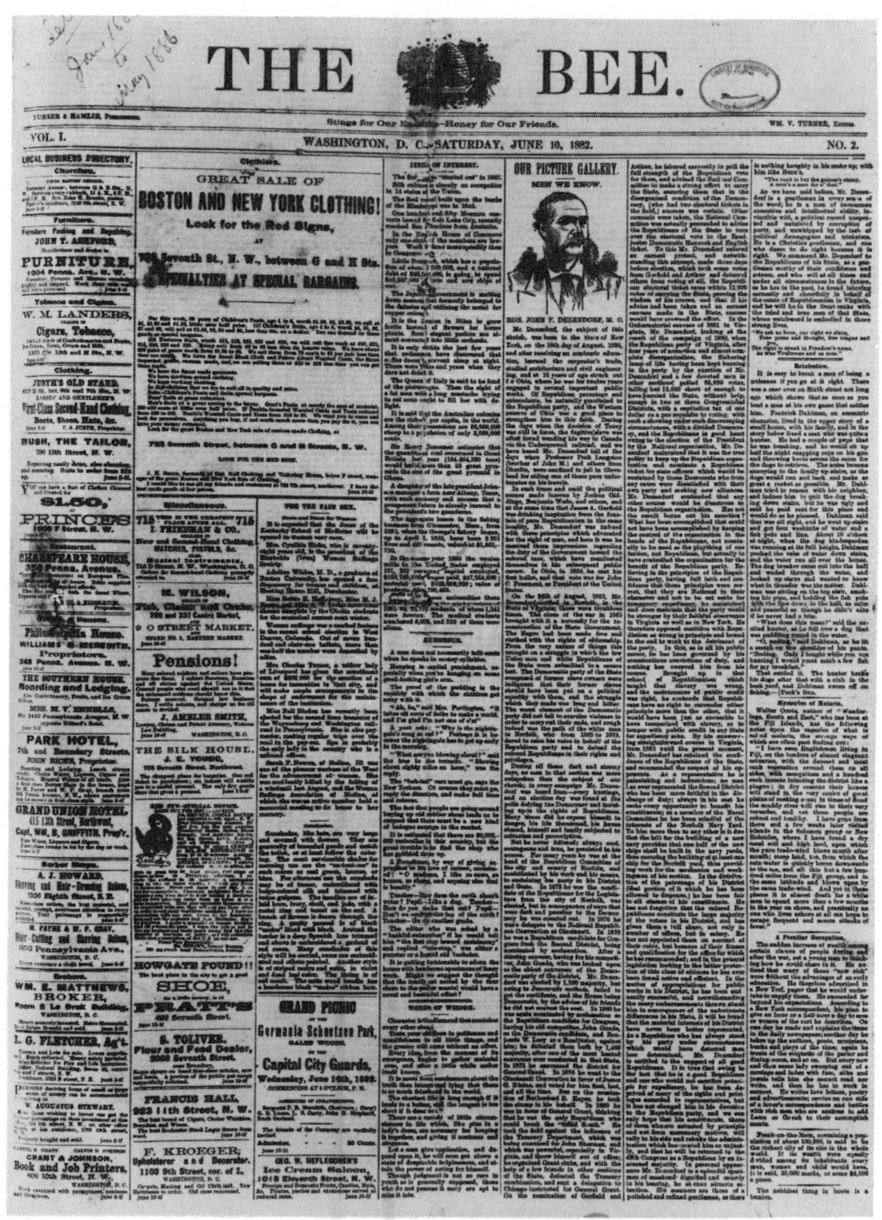

THE BEE.

TURNER & HAMLIN, Proprietors. — Stings for Our Enemies—Honey for Our Friends. — WM. V. TURNER, Editor.

VOL. I. — WASHINGTON, D. C., SATURDAY, JUNE 10, 1882. — NO. 2.

LOCAL BUSINESS DIRECTORY.

Churches.

Furniture.

Furniture Packing and Repairing.
JOHN T. ASHFORD,
Manufacturer and dealer in
FURNITURE,
1004 Penna. Ave., N. W.

Tobacco and Cigars.

W. M. LANDERS,
DEALER IN
Cigars, Tobacco,
1300, Cor. 13th and H Sts., N. W.

Clothing.

JUSTH'S OLD STAND,
LADIES' AND GENTLEMEN'S
First-Class Second-Hand Clothing,
Boots, Shoes, Hats, &c.

BUSH, THE TAILOR,
790 13th Street, N. W.

$1.50,
AT
PRINCE'S
1000 F Street, N. W.

Restaurant.

SHAKESPEARE HOUSE,
350 Penna. Avenue.

Philadelphia House.
Proprietors.
348 Penna. Avenue, N. W.

THE SOUTHERN HOUSE.
Boarding and Lodging.

PARK HOTEL,
7th and Boundary Streets.
JOHN BICKS, Proprietor.

GRAND UNION HOTEL,
415 13th Street, Northwest,
Capt. WM. B. GRIFFITH, Prop'r.

Barber Shops.

A. J. HOWARD,
Shaving and Hair-Dressing Saloon,
1100 Eighth Street, S. E.

H. PAYNE & W. F. GRAY,
Hair-Cutting and Shaving Saloon,
3072 Pennsylvania Ave.,
WASHINGTON, D. C.

Brokers.

WM. E. MATTHEWS,
BROKER,
Room 2 Le Droit Building,
WASHINGTON, D. C.

L. G. FLETCHER, Ag't.

W. AUGUSTUS STEWART.

GRANT & JOHNSON,
Book and Job Printers,
600 10th Street, N. W.,
WASHINGTON, D. C.

Clothiers.

GREAT SALE OF
BOSTON AND NEW YORK CLOTHING!
Look for the Red Signs,
AT
783 Seventh St., N. W., between G and H Sts.
SPECIALTIES AT SPECIAL BARGAINS.

Look for the great Boston and New York sale of custom-made Clothing, at
783 Seventh Street, between G and H Streets, N. W.
LOOK FOR THE RED SIGN.

Miscellaneous.

715 THIS IS THE CHEAPEST PLACE AFTER ALL. 715
I. FRIEDMAN & CO.
New and Second-Hand Clothing,
WATCHES, PISTOLS, &c.
ALSO,
Musical Instruments,
715 D Street, N. W. Washington, D. C.

M. WILSON,
DEALER IN
Fish, Clams and Crabs,
9 O STREET MARKET.

Pensions!

J. AMBLER SMITH,
WASHINGTON, D. C.

THE SILK HOUSE,
J. E. YOUNG,
706 Seventh Street, Northwest.

HOWGATE FOUND!!
The best place in the city to get a good
SHOE,
PRATT'S
409 Seventh Street.

S. TOLIVER,
Flour and Feed Dealer,
2000 Seventh Street.

FRANCIS HALL,
923 11th Street, N. W.

F. KROEGER,
Upholsterer and Decorator,
1103 9th Street, cor. of L,
WASHINGTON, D. C.

FOR THE FAIR SEX.

GRAND PICNIC
AT THE
Germania Schuetzen Park,
BY THE
Capital City Guards,
Wednesday, June 14th, 1882.
Admission, - - - 25 Cents.

GEO. W. HEFLEBOWER'S
Ice Cream Saloon,
1018 Eleventh Street, N. W.

ITEMS OF INTEREST.

HUMOROUS.

OUR PICTURE GALLERY.
MEN WE KNOW.

HON. JOHN F. DEZENDORF, M. C.

Microfilm Collection, Library of Congress

Front page of *The Bee,* Volume 1, Number 2, Saturday, June 10, 1882.

marked contrast to the view that Negro thought in 1880–1915 was accommodationist and it suggests that revision of this view is in order.[3] This protest of the black press has been largely neglected by historians despite the fact that primary data has been available since 1947 when Dr. Armistead S. Pride microfilmed many of the weekly black newspapers for the American Council of Learned Societies.[4] The lack of scholarly attention to the Afro-American press cannot be justified on the grounds that it was an insignificant institution; a social scientist so prestigious as Gunnar Myrdal has expressed the view in his work *An American Dilemma* that the press was the second most significant institution in the black community.[5] It is fortunate for historians of the District of Columbia that the files of the Washington *Bee* are substantially complete from June 1882 to January 1922.

The *Bee* was significant in its own day and its significance for historians is likely to increase with the passage of time. One of the foremost scholars of Afro-American history recently described it as "the powerful and influential *Bee*" and this evaluation is substantiated by the recognition which the *Bee* received in its own time. The *Bee*'s impact upon its readers is a different and more difficult question than its significance as an historical document. There is little data which reveals how its content affected its readers. There is, however, much in the pages of the *Bee* which reveals the intended effect of its content which in turn yields insights into the role it played in the black community.[6]

The Washington *Bee* served primarily "the Secret City" of Washington, D. C. But its presence in the nation's capital, which was a center for black political leaders and black intellectuals, gave the *Bee* a national role as well. One dimension of this role was as a source of information about the relationship of the Federal government to the national black community. Much of what follows, therefore,

[3] August Meier, *Negro Thought in America, 1880–1915* (1965), *passim,* but especially 7, 13–15.

[4] For neglect of the Afro-American press see James M. McPherson, et al, eds., *Blacks in America: Bibliographical Essays* (1971), 161, 293–4. There are fine monographs by Emma Lou Thornbrough, *T. Thomas Fortune* (1972), Stephen R. Fox, *The Guardian of Boston: William Monroe Trotter* (1970), and by the late Roi Ottley, *The Lonely Warrior: Robert S. Abbott* (1955) but all of these works neglect the content of the respective newspapers.

[5] Myrdal, *An American Dilemma,* 924. For similar assessments see Martin E. Dann, ed., *The Black Press, 1827–90* (1971), 13; and John Hope Franklin in Thornbrough, *Fortune,* vii.

[6] Meier, *Negro Thought in America,* 75; Frank L. Mott, *American Journalism* (1962), 794; I. Garland Penn, *The Afro-American Press and Its Editors* (1891), 290.

focuses upon the Federal government as a citadel of race prejudice. It should be remembered that Chase published the *Bee* in an era when a newspaper was the primary source of information for most Americans, black and white. The *Bee* was an institution of protest

against the various forms of white racism such as lynching, discrimination in the civil and armed services, the courts and public facilities. It was in fact, as Chase perhaps immodestly claimed in 1914, the protest of his generation of Afro-American journalists which prompted into existence such organizations as the National Association for the Advancement of Colored People.[7]

Chase's generation of black editors were similar to their counterparts in the white press in terms of "personal journalism." The character of the editor defined the content of his newspaper and Chase was no exception. Like many of his editorial contemporaries, William Calvin Chase was born in the decade 1855–1865; specifically, he was born February 2, 1854. Whereas many of Chase's journalistic colleagues were born into slavery, however, both Chase's father, William H. Chase, and his mother, Lucinda Seaton Chase, were free persons and there is evidence which indicates that they enjoyed middle class status. Both parents were literate and they owned their own home, a substantial three story brick structure which still stands at 1109 I Street, N. W. William H. Chase was a blacksmith, wheelwright and mechanic who had moved to Washington, D. C. as early as 1835 from nearby Maryland.[8] Lucinda Seaton Chase was a dressmaker and a member of the Seaton family of Alexandria, Virginia. Both were members of the socially prominent 15th Street Presbyterian Church, and Lucinda Chase became especially active in church affairs after her husband's accidental death in 1863.[9] She successfully raised her five daughters and one son and educated them all (except for one daughter who was rendered deaf by an early childhood disease). The fact that William Calvin Chase was born in a large urban center was unusual among his contemporaries and this urbanity and the fact of his free birth gave Chase a feeling of some superiority over those

[7] Constance McLaughlin Green, *The Secret City* (1967), 151; and Sterling Brown, *The Negro in Washington, D. C.* (reprint ed., 1969), 78. Myrdal, *An American Dilemma,* 908; Vishnu V. Oak, *The Negro Newspaper* (1948), 20; and Roland E. Wolseley, *The Black Press, U.S.A.* (1971), xiii. *Bee,* Jan. 17, 1914, 4.

[8] William J. Simmons, *Men of Mark* (1887), 118. Eighth Census (1860) District of Columbia, reel 102, Microfilm Room, National Archives, Washington, D. C. *Polk's Directory,* 1854–1864, Washingtoniana Room, Martin Luther King Library, Washington, D. C. See alphabetical listing for William H. Chase, 1109 I St., N. W., D. C. Records, Wills, Old Series 5070, Federal Records Center, Suitland, Maryland. A document in the probate papers substantiates that Chase resided in the District as early as 1835. The first city directory was published in 1854. See also Sixth Census (1840), reel 35, and Seventh Census (1850), reel 56, District of Columbia and Tax Books, A-L, 1839, 1840, 1845, 1850–63, National Archives, Washington, D. C.

[9] *Polk's Directory,* 1865–1893. *Bee,* Jan. 28, 1893, 2 and Jan. 8, 1921, 1. Sessions Records, 15th Street Presbyterian Church, mss, 482 and Session Book of 1st Colored Presbyterian "Register of Marriages," mss, 15th Street Presbyterian Church, Washington, D. C.

blacks who moved into the nation's capital during and after the Civil War.[10]

With the death of his father when he was nine, his chief childhood influence was that of his mother who was a woman of "commanding presence." Her strength of character, and the fact that Chase lived at home with his mother and his five sisters until he was thirty-two, suggests a strong maternal influence. Little is known of Chase's married life other than that he married Arabella V. McCabe in 1886. She was an only child, a graduate of the Preparatory Department at Howard, a writer of prose and poetry and a professional music teacher. In addition to contributing several serialized novellas to the *Bee,* Arabella assisted her husband with the administration of the *Bee.* She raised two children, Beatriz Lucinda, whose name further suggests a maternal influence upon Chase, and William Calvin, Jr. Both children attended Howard University and Calvin, Jr. was graduated from the college in 1910. Both worked for the *Bee,* Beatriz as a columnist and Calvin, Jr. as Business Manager. Beyond this apparent closeness there is little data on the family.[11]

Like his family life, Calvin Chase's education was not extraordinary. He attended a private school conducted by John F. Cook, Jr. and the Preparatory Department at Howard. Chase apparently completed the preparatory course, but did not enter the college. Later, however, he attended courses at Howard Law School in 1883–1884, but interrupted these studies to serve the Republican party in the presidential campaign of James G. Blaine in 1884.[12] In 1889 Chase was admitted to the bar in both Virginia and the District of Columbia. His education, like that of most of his colleagues, did not go beyond the secondary level. Chase was not a scholar, and one of his contemporaries described his academic inclination and that of many of his editorial generation with the statement: "He [Chase] displayed an appreciation of the real and practical, brushing aside theories for established facts." [13]

[10] For Chase's derogatory remarks on black immigrants to Washington, D. C. see *Bee,* Feb. 2, 9, Oct. 11, and Nov. 8, 1884, 2, 3, and April 4, 1885, 2.

[11] *Bee,* Jan. 30, 1886, 3. Tenth Census (1880), D. C., reel 122. Frederick D. Wilkinson, ed., *Directory of Graduates, Howard University 1870–1963* (1965), 236. Arabella V. Chase, *A Peculiar People* (1905). *Bee,* Aug. 25, 1883, 3, Nov. 10, 1883, 3, and May 15, 1909, 4. D. C. Records, *Index to Register of Birth,* Vol. 6, number 46605 and 51614. *Bee,* April 1905 to Aug., 1908, 1.

[12] Simmons, *Men of Mark,* 120–122. John F. Cook, Jr. was educated at Oberlin which was founded by abolitionists and thus young Calvin Chase was exposed to the protest tradition of Abolition. For the strong Abolition influence in Cook's school see Lillian G. Dabney, *The History of Schools for Negroes in the District of Columbia, 1807–1947* (1949), 15.

[13] *Bee,* Jan. 15, 1921, 4.

W. CALVIN CHASE.

Library of Congress

Photograph of William Calvin Chase published in *A Peculiar People* by Mrs. Arabella Virginia Chase, Washington, D. C., William Calvin Chase, Jr., Printer, 1905.

One of the facts of Afro-American journalism in Chase's era was its meagre financial return. Consequently Chase, like most of his contemporaries, pursued an additional occupation. In his case it was the law and the duties of some minor patronage position.[14] There was a dependent relationship between black journalists and politicians and political parties which accounts for some of the controversial content of the *Bee*. This relationship may also account for Chase's emphasis on political equality rather than social equality. It should be noted that Chase did not distinguish racial equality from political equality, but he did distinguish racial equality from social equality. Twice in 1885 he upheld acts of blatant discrimination by private institutions. The first occurred in January and involved the Harvard Club of Washington, D. C. which rejected membership applications of Richard T. Greener and Robert H. Terrell. Greener was the first black graduate of Harvard and in 1885 he was a professor at Howard Law School. Terrell was a teacher at the prestigious M Street High School. The second incident involved the rejection of W. H. Hart's application to the Columbia Law School of George Washington University. With logic similar to that of the Supreme Court ruling in *Moose Lodge No. 107* v. *Irves et al.* (407 U.S. 163) Chase reasoned that it was the right of a purely social club to dictate the terms of its membership.[15] Chase perceived the church also as a quasi-social institution and except for one ardent protest revealed in a cartoon in the *Bee,* he did not attack white congregations for their discriminatory practices. This cartoon was prompted by the exclusion of black American delegates from the annual meeting of the World Sunday School Convention held in Washington, D. C. in 1910 and the exclusion of black children from its parade.[16]

One of the most abhorrent features of white American racism between 1882 and 1921 was lynching. As the classic study by the National Association for the Advancement of Colored People reveals, the zenith of lynching occurred during the thirty year period, 1889–1918, which almost exactly parallels the era of the *Bee*. Chase witnessed the rise and decline of lynching and his response as an editor provides an insight into the role of the black press with regard to one of the most significant national issues which confronted black Americans in his time. Lynching was not a "local" issue in the District of Columbia. No lynching according to the NAACP oc-

[14] Emma Lou Thornbrough, "American Negro Newspapers, 1880–1914." *Business History Review,* XL (Winter, 1966), 474.

[15] *Bee,* Feb. 7, and Nov. 7, 1885, 2.

[16] *Bee,* May 28, 1910, 1, 4.

curred in the District of Columbia between 1889 and 1918. One of the foremost black writers on lynching has called the prominence given by black editors to stories and editorials on lynching a "terrific bombardment" which helped to create a "stupendous racial consciousness . . . which added mightily to the grim determination of Negroes to fight against mob-law." [17]

Another scholar has noted that the first records pertaining to lynching were published by the Chicago *Tribune* in the same year that the *Bee* was founded, 1882. There is evidence in the *Bee,* however, that Chase was aware of widespread murder, if not lynching, of Negroes in the South from 1865. In an interesting aside in an editorial denouncing General Alfred Pleasanton for his advocacy of an extermination policy concerning the American Indian, Chase wrote:

> extermination is a bad step. The democrats tried it on the colored race of the South and since 1865 have succeeded in murdering something like thirteen thousand.

In this editorial, one of Chase's first concerning lynching, the association of the South with the Democratic party and both with murderous acts against the Negro appears in a fully developed state.[18] To be sure, Chase's attacks on both the South and the Democratic party became more strenuous as lynching became more frequent, but this initial conception remained relatively constant in the years that followed.

In another early editorial, "Yazoo Murders," Chase wrote:

> It is a fact that the law in the South is but a shadow so far as the Negro is concerned, hence the sheriff and the whole legal fraternity must be put out of the way.

Chase counselled violent retaliation if legal justice could not be obtained:

> If these political assassinations and other murders continue, our advice is to fire the South, turn the rebel hole into ashes and let a reign of terror be witnessed.[19]

With the advent of the Cleveland Administration, Chase became more restrained and circumspect. In his coverage of the murder of thirteen Negroes in a courtroom in Carrollton, Mississippi, in 1886, Chase used an article from the *National Republican* which pro-

---

[17] National Association for the Advancement of Colored People, *Thirty Years of Lynching in the United States, 1889–1918* (New York: The Association, 1919), 32. Walter F. White, *Rope and Faggot* (New York: Arno Press reprint, 1969), 175–6.

[18] White, *Rope and Faggot*, 227. *Bee*, July 7, 883, 2.

[19] *Bee,* Jan. 5, 1884, 2.

claimed: "murder is the Democratic title deed to power" but in his own editorial he wrote:

> If we were to say measure for measure this great government would say we were endeavoring to excite the Negro to riot and confusion.

The following week Chase explicitly declared his lack of faith in the American judicial system:

> To be candid, we feel ashamed to acknowledge allegiance to a government so weak that when its citizens are killed by the dozens their relatives and friends can find no recourse to law.[20]

With the election of Benjamin Harrison and the return of Republican control over the Federal government, Chase escalated his essential theme of protest and agitation. His appeal in March 1889 for violent self-defense included words so unequivocal that they have been anthologized:

> Our condition demands . . . that when our homes are invaded the shotgun shall be the direct resort in their protection; when our rights are invaded the navy-six shall play as important part in their arbitrament as it does in their denial; that when our property is destroyed that the torch of retaliation shall be lighted and applied until devastation, destruction, blood, tears, misery and starvation shall teach our white oppressors that the colored man . . . can and will fight and die to assert his rights by the dreadful instruments of revenge.[21]

In the thirty years that followed, thirty years that the NAACP documented as a generation of lynching, Chase consistently devoted prominent space to the denunciation of this monstrous criminality. He continued the same themes, associating the South and the Democratic party with barbarism, making appeals to the majority to abide by the law, and advocating or praising self-defense by black Americans. During this period Chase became increasingly critical of the Federal government and its indifference to the rising tide of racial violence.

The most conclusive and telling data of a change in Chase's perception of the Federal government vis-à-vis lynching lies in the content of cartoons which appeared in the *Bee* after 1906. Cartoons did not appear regularly but were evoked by some act of violent aggression by white Americans against black Americans. They always ap-

[20] *Bee,* May 24, 1884, 2 re Danville murders. For the reprint from the *National Republican* and the accompanying editorial see *Bee,* March 27, 1886, 1, 2. For the candid editorial see *Bee,* April 3, 1886, 2.

[21] Dann, ed., *The Black Press, 1827–1890,* 118–119.

peared in the top center columns of page one and the cartoon which protested the East St. Louis "riot" of 1917 occupied the entire top half of page one.

One of the first cartoons was a response to the lynching of eleven Negroes in Hemphill, Texas, in June, 1908. It shows Uncle Sam standing and perspiring anxiously in front of a map of Texas on which is a blot labelled "Hemphill." Behind Uncle Sam stands a towering female figure in white robes labelled "Ethiopia." Her outstretched arm points to the blot and she asks: "What are you going to do about that Uncle Sam?"

That Uncle Sam represents the Federal government there is no doubt. That he is viewed as responsible for seeing justice done in such cases is also obvious. What is more tenuous is that Chase was shifting the blame for such racial violence from Southern prejudice to Federal inaction.[22]

Chase's intent in terms of blame is also ambiguous in a cartoon concerning the Coatesville, Pennsylvania, lynching of August 1911. Here a female figure of Justice is confronted by a smaller black male figure. Justice is at ease in a chair with all her symbols in disarray and disuse around her. She is laughing and above her on a wall is a map with a blot labelled "Coatesville." The black male figure remarks that he does not see anything so funny. Obvious in this cartoon is the reference to legal inaction which is represented by cobwebs that hang from the symbols of justice.[23] What is not clear is the association between legal inaction and the Federal government.

This link is forged in a cartoon evoked by the "riot" in East St. Louis in July 1917. The foremost scholar of this "riot" has concluded that it had a profound effect on black Americans all over the nation. Chase was no exception. The cartoon which appeared in the *Bee* was four columns wide and a half page high. In the background white men, women and children shoot and club black men, women and children amid burning buildings and in the presence of a blindfolded man dressed in a military uniform. In the foreground a kneeling black woman dressed in white robes (and reminiscent of both the "Ethiopia" figure of Hemphill and the "Justice" figure of Coatesville) holds the broken scales of justice in her hand. Reinforcing the theme of trampled justice, a building behind her labelled "Court of Justice" has a "CLOSED" sign on its door. Beside the female figure stands Uncle Sam with full military field pack, rifle and bayonet. Behind him is

[22] For the response to the Hemphill lynchings, see *Bee,* July 4, 1908, 4. For the cartoon, see *Bee,* July 25, 1908, 1.

[23] *Bee,* Aug. 9, 1911, 1.

the dome of the United States Capitol. He is holding a scroll on which is a bitter satire on the hypocrisy of the Federal government:

We have entered this war that
LIBERTY-JUSTICE
HAPPINESS
and
EQUAL OPPORTUNITY
shall be enjoyed by all the world.

Editorial comment concerning "southern influences" to the contrary notwithstanding, the caption of this cartoon, "East St. Louis Riot. This is American Civilization," is further evidence that Chase was moving away from the abolitionist view of placing the blame for racial violence solely on the South, and moving towards the view of protesting inaction by the Federal government.

The Federal government did respond to the wave of racial violence, but it was a year later and it came in the form of President Woodrow Wilson's appeal to the nation "to make an end of this disgraceful evil." To Chase, Wilson's appeal was "THE PRESIDENT'S GLANCING BLOW," and although Chase gave Wilson credit for denouncing lynching as a crime, he concluded, "it will not reach the lynchers of colored people in this country." [24]

In a cartoon evoked by rioting in Washington, D. C. in July 1919, Chase explicitly presented the law as an accomplice to violent white racism. The cartoon contains three figures: a large white male figure on the left labelled "Mob Law," a medium-sized policeman in the middle, and a small black man dressed in a business suit on the right. The policeman holds back "Mob Law" with the statement "Wait until I disarm him" and says to the black man: "In the name of law surrender your gun." To this the black man replies: "It is my only protection." [25]

Although this view of the role of Washington police was not one of Chase's major assaults on the citadel of race prejudice, it was not a special response evoked by the riot of 1919. Since his first years as editor of the *Bee,* Chase had criticized Washington police for the brutal way in which they often treated black Washingtonians. Chase

---

[24] Except for the impact which the East St. Louis violence had upon Chase, the content of the *Bee* does not support Rudwick's conclusions concerning the responses of Afro-American journals. There is no evidence that Chase considered the accounts of the "rioting" as inventions of the Southern press and he did not report that blacks retaliated. Elliott M. Rudwick, *Race Riot at East St. Louis, July 2, 1917* (Carbondale, Illinois, 1964), 63, 55. For the East St. Louis cartoon, see *Bee,* July 14, 1917, 1. For response to Wilson's appeal, see *Bee,* Aug. 3, 1918, 1, 4.

[25] *Bee,* Aug. 2, 23, 1919, 1.

was especially critical in 1885 when he denounced the acquittal of a white policeman tried for the fatal shooting of a black man, Addison Coleman, and at that time he rebuked the Chief of Police.[26]

It should be noted that Chase's denouncing police brutality could not have stemmed, as has been said, from his "having seen his father shot down in cold blood and his white assailant go unpunished." William H. Chase was accidently killed by Charles Posey, a black man.[27] It is possible that regardless of the race of his father's assailant Chase did hold the police in some way responsible, but it is more likely that his protest of police brutality was the product of a normal sense of outrage at such injustice.

Chase's second area of attack on the citadel of race prejudice was against the discrimination which the Federal government practiced in both its civilian and armed services. In one of his earliest editorials Chase denounced the use of government "messengers" and "laborers" as servants for the heads of government departments as a "new form of slavery." He was also throughout his career quick to defend the rights of black Americans who were dismissed solely because of their race. He was especially critical of Mr. McMichael, a United States Marshall for the District of Columbia, who fulfilled a pre-appointment pledge of discharging every Negro bailiff.

Chase was especially sensitive to discrimination in those civil service positions located in Washington, D. C. When a bill was pending in Congress to reduce the fee structure, and thus to reduce the income of the Recorder of Deeds for the District of Columbia, a position traditionally filled by black men since Frederick Douglass had been appointed by President Garfield, Chase raised the cry of "DISCRIMINATION AGAINST THE NEGRO." But in regard to both the Indianola, Mississippi, Post Office incident in 1902 and the appointment of William D. Crum as Collector of the Port of Charleston in 1902–3, he was relatively silent.[28]

When discrimination and segregation in Federal offices increased after the turn of the century, Chase became more vocal in his con-

---

[26] *Bee,* Aug. 22, Sept. 12, 19 and Oct. 17, 1885, 2.

[27] Green, *The Secret City,* 128. Records, District of Columbia, Metropolitan Police, Daily Precinct Returns, "Incidental Duties of the Dept." Nov. 24, 1863. National Archives, Washington, D. C. Records, District of Columbia Supreme Court, Criminal Docket 1, December term, case number 1032. *The Evening Star,* Nov. 23, 24, 1863, 2.

[28] For comment on "new form of slavery", see *Bee,* Dec. 30, 1882, 2. For attack on McMichael, see *Bee,* March 24, 1883, 3. For discrimination in regard to the Recorder of Deeds, see *Bee,* April 9, 1892, 2. Apparently, Chase did not comment on the Indianola affair but focused rather on a similar case in Wilson, N. C. For slight comment on the Crum appointment, see *Bee,* Dec. 13, 1902, 4.

demnation. In an editorial of September 3, 1904, he proclaimed the appearance of the first "Jim Crow" corner in the Bureau of Engraving and Printing, and in February of the following year he wrote that there was a "systematic effort" to "Jim Crow" the Negro in government offices. In 1908, he used a cartoon to attack "Southern Democrats still tainted with the 'Lost Cause' " for their attempt to pass a bill to impose segregation on the public transit system of Washington. Graphic ridicule of such segregationists as Representative (later Senator) James Thomas Heflin of Alabama appeared frequently in the *Bee* toward the end of the first decade of the 1900's.[29]

The high point of Chase's protest against white racism in the Federal government came during the Wilson administration. The sharpness of his attack stemmed from the administration's Southern Democratic character. Ten days after Wilson's inauguration, Chase issued "A WARNING" to black Federal employees which was, in essence, an admonition that the new administration believed that if one were black one should stay as far from white female employees as possible. Two weeks later, Chase wrote a personal letter to Wilson in which he asked:

> Is it true Mr. President that color is to be the primary cause for the displacement of Negroes from office no matter how efficient and that color will be the effectual bar to office of men whom God created with a darker skin than yours?

Wilson's only reply to Chase came a month later in the form of the dismissal of William K. Lewis from the Attorney-General's office and the dismissal of Ralph W. Tyler from the Auditor's office in the Navy Department. Chase castigated these dismissals and predicted that white Democrats would fill all the substantial positions held by blacks with the possible exceptions of the ministers to Haiti and Liberia. A scholar of segregation in President Wilson's administration notes that Chase's prophecy "was more than fulfilled by the end of Wilson's first term".[30]

Chase's protest against racial discrimination in the armed forces was as ardent if less continuous than his protest against racial dis-

---

[29] *Bee,* Sept. 3, 1904, 4, and Feb. 11, 1905, 4. For attack on segregation bill for D. C. transit, see *Bee,* March 12, 1908, 4. For attack on discrimination in the Interior Dept., see *Bee,* Oct. 7, 1909, 4.

[30] For "A Warning", see *Bee,* March 15, 1913, 4. Chase to Wilson, March 29, 1913, Woodrow Wilson Papers, Case File 152, Library of Congress. For dismissal of Lewis and Tyler and the *Bee*'s prophecy, see Kathleen L. Wolfgemuth, "Woodrow Wilson's Appointment Policy and the Negro," *Journal of Southern History,* XXIV (Nov., 1958), 461.

crimination in the civil service. The Spanish-American War was the first opportunity which Chase took to comment extensively upon the treatment of black Americans in the military. Six Negro regiments were established by law when the Army was reorganized on a peacetime basis in 1866. One scholar refers to the era from 1866 to the Spanish-American War as the "golden day" for the black soldier and notes that considerable controversy surrounded the recruitment, training and utilization of sixteen black regiments involved in the Spanish-American War. Chase plunged the *Bee* into the thick of this controversy as early as March 1898 by declaring:

> There is no inducement for the negro to fight for the independence of Cuba . . . when his own brothers, fathers, mothers, and indeed his children are shot down as if they were dogs and cattle.[31]

Two weeks later, he repeated the point under the banner "FALSE PATRIOTISM" by proclaiming:

> The cry of white America for war and their rush to enlist is false given their failure to protect the rights of citizens in the South.

By April Chase began to reverse this position by calling for a declaration of war and for the commissioning of black generals. When no black generals were forthcoming, he called for colonels. This retreat was counterbalanced by another editorial on the same page entitled "THE NEGRO MILITIA DISCRIMINATED AGAINST." When *The Daily Times* charged that "Negroes have shown no great display of patriotism" Chase counterattacked:

> the same prejudice that was exhibited against the enlistment of the negro in 1862 exists today

and

> A man would be a very big fool to show patriotism for a government that says she does not want a people . . . on account of color or previous condition.[32]

Chase was alert to slurs against the bravery of black soldiers. When

---

[31] Chase's first expressed interest in black soldiers concerned Civil War veterans and a movement to establish a monument to their service. *Bee,* Dec. 29, 1883, 2, Dec. 13, 1884, 2, and May 16, 1885, 2. Lawrence D. Reddick, "The Negro Policy of the United States Army, 1775–1945," *Journal of Negro History,* XXXIV (Jan. 1949), 18–19. *Bee,* March 5, 1898, 4.

[32] For "False Patriotism", see *Bee,* March 19, 1898, 4. For the call for war, *Bee,* April 2, 1898, 4. For "Negro Generals", *Bee,* April 30, 1898, 4. For "Colored Colonel" and discrimination against Negro militia, *Bee,* May 7, 1898, 4. For refutation of black lack of patriotism, *Bee,* May 28, 1898, 4 and June 11, 1898, 4.

some of the white press berated black soldiers for a disturbance in Tampa, Florida, in June 1898, Chase retorted, "only in the hotbed of prejudice and rebellion does complaint regarding black troops occur." When complaints arose elsewhere, as in the Washington *Post*, he was equally quick to condemn them. In response to reports from Cuba which cast aspersions on the bravery of black soldiers, Chase praised the black troops involved and berated the dismal promotion record of the army as a mockery to the valor and heroism of black soldiers. He denounced the lack of attention paid "THE FAMOUS 9TH CAVALRY" when it returned to Washington, D. C. from action in Cuba:

> Windows, doors, sashes and even chimney tops were decorated with flags and bunting in honor of the District soldiers who had made an excursion to Cuba and were greeted in their return to this city as heroes. But when the real soldiers visited the city, the famous black cavalry, not one of those white and black hot house plants would turn out.[33]

A more controversial event involving discrimination against black Americans in the armed forces was the so-called "Brownsville affair" which erupted in November 1906, when President Theodore Roosevelt summarily discharged three companies of black infantrymen for their alleged involvement in a "riot" in Brownsville, Texas. Chase, like most of his colleagues, was outraged and he protested Roosevelt's action for more than a year.[34] When the President released Special Orders Number 226 the day after the Congressional elections in 1906, Chase labelled the order "outrageous" and declared:

> Negroes are not fools, at least not all of them, and this after-election order is well understood by them.

The following week Chase exhibited the depth of his outrage by defiantly proclaiming:

> Jefferson Davis is more honored today than Theodore Roosevelt.[35]

Although ten years had elapsed, the memory of the "Brownsville affair" probably heightened Chase's criticism of the treatment of black Americans by the Federal government during World War I.

---

[33] For Tampa comment, see *Bee,* Aug. 13, 1898, 4; for Santiago comment, *Bee,* Aug. 13, 1898, 4; for rebuttal to *Post, Bee,* Sept. 10, 1898, 4; for comment in regard to 9th cavalry, *Bee,* Oct. 15, 1898, 4.

[34] L. N. Wynne, "Brownsville: The Reaction of the Negro Press," *Phylon,* XXXVIII (Summer, 1972), 153–60. Emma Lou Thornbrough, "The Brownsville Episode and the Negro Vote," *Mississippi Valley Historical Review,* XLIV (Dec., 1951), 469–93. *Bee,* Aug. 25, Nov. 10 and 17, and Dec. 1, 1906, 4, 1.

[35] *Bee,* Nov. 10 and 17, 1906, 4.

In any case, compared to the Spanish-American War, World War I presented a more extensive opportunity for criticism concerning the enlistment, training, utilization and bravery of black troops. Chase made the most of it. His comments must qualify the traditional view that the black press supported the war effort. Certainly Chase was not among those black editors who were "unequivocally" loyal in 1917–1918. As early as June 1916, Chase questioned the participation of black Americans in a European war on behalf of a government which had shown a decreasing inclination to protect their interests, which Chase saw as especially true for the black communtiy of Washington, D. C. where Wilson's dismissal and segregation of blacks in government offices had prompted Chase's vigorous protests. When blacks were placed in a segregated rear section of a preparedness parade, Chase declared that blacks had been " 'Jim Crowed' with a vengeance" and queried rhetorically: "How many in the parade last Wednseday would go to the front if they were called by their country? " The following week, under the editorial banner "BY WHAT AUTHORITY" he demanded of Emmett J. Scott where he derived the authority to claim that "one hundred thousand colored Americans are ready to go to war and defend their country." His criticism did not abate after Congress declared war the following April and with the discriminatory treatment of blacks in enlistment, training, and deployment in Europe, Chase's criticism became more frequent.[36]

In an editorial entitled "CARL VINSON" he delivered a blast at the young Representative from Georgia and his bill to segregate public transit in the District of Columbia:

> Read the bill that is reproduced in another column of the *Bee* and let the more intelligent American people decide for themselves and decide whether such acts are sufficient inducements for Colored Americans to volunteer? [37]

In July 1917, Chase wrote: "We know of no single instance where a colored man or colored committee has been called into the council of war" and he stated that he was "in the dark" concerning the government's policy for black troops. Following a declaration that "now is the time for the War Department to announce its plans for the organization of colored drafted troops," Chase announced the beginning of his own policy of "watchful waiting." [38] Chase was not appeased when Secretary of War Newton D. Baker wrote an open

---

[36] *Bee,* June 17 and 24, 1916, 4.
[37] *Bee,* April 14, 1917, 4.
[38] *Bee,* July 28, 1917, 4.

letter to Emmett J. Scott. The following week Chase took "respectful issue" with Baker's letter and noted several specific grievances. These included the retirement of Col. Charles Young, "our" highest ranking officer; the ordering of "our" only two other regular army officers to the Philippines and Liberia respectively; the stripping and chasing of black soldiers in Vicksburg, Mississippi; the denial of camp leave to black troops in Southern cantonments; the limiting of promotions for blacks and the limiting of line officers in black regiments. Chase remained sensitive to discrimination in the months that followed, and he delivered an especially sharp attack upon General C. C. Ballou when the General issued his Bulletin Number 35 which included the statement: "white men made the division [the 92nd] and white men can disband it." [39]

It is true that Chase and other black editors became more favorable towards the war effort after a conference in Washington, D. C. in June 1918, called by Emmett J. Scott who was a Special Assistant to Secretary of War Newton D. Baker. For Chase this lasted only six months and a month after the armistice he published the headline "TYLER EXPOSES AMERICAN DUPLICITY", the opening salvo in a barrage of criticism which appeared during the next three months. Chase exposed the existence of a pamphlet entitled *Secret Information Concerning Black Troops* which was circulated to French officers by white American officers. He also published articles based on the account of Sergeant Greenleaf B. Johnson of poor clothing, inferior rations, "Jim Crow" policies in mess halls and hospital wards, and the refusal of liberty passes to black troops when they were encamped near French towns.[40]

Another area of Chase's attack upon the citadel of race prejudice concerned judicial racism. As with his attacks on lynching and discrimination in the civil service and in the armed services, Chase became increasingly sensitive to the role of the Federal government after 1900. This is not to suggest that Chase was insensitive to judicial white racism earlier in his career. In 1883 he denounced Judge William Snell of the District of Columbia for "negro-driving, bull-whip decisions" and for courtroom comment which implied that black women were no more than cattle.[41] Chase's comments concerning the Supreme Court decision in the "Civil Rights Cases" in 1883 were subdued but his strongest statements may have appeared in those

---

[39] *Bee,* Dec. 8 and 22, 1917, 4. *Bee,* May 25, 1918, 4 and July 27, 1918, 1.

[40] John Hope Franklin, *From Slavery to Freedom,* 3rd ed. (1969), 475. *Bee,* Dec. 28, 1918, 1. For Sgt. Johnson's articles, see *Bee,* Jan. 11 and 18, 1919, 1.

[41] *Bee,* July 28 and Aug. 4, 1883, 2, 3.

issues of the *Bee* which have not survived. In June 1883, he noted the decision of a United States District Court in Texas concerning the treatment of colored citizens on steamboats and railroads, and he declared:

> The judge should not be allowed to set the rights of the Fifteenth Amendment to one side and call it a plaything that "Radicals put on paper to tickle the vain pride of Negroes with".

But when the Supreme Court rendered its famous decision in the "Civil Rights Cases" in October, Chase erroneously concluded: "The Supreme Court Jim Crow ruling will not affect us materially." He added that the Republican party was not responsible and, therefore, black voters should not take hasty actions. He did praise Justice John Marshall Harlan by name for his dissent, but he did not comment extensively on either the majority decision or Harlan's solitary dissent. Instead he reprinted excerpts from other black journals which opposed the decision.[42]

Missing issues of the *Bee* cannot account for Chase's mild response to the *Plessy* v. *Ferguson* decision in 1896. A possible explanation is that he followed the lead of the white dailies which showed little interest in the *Plessy* decision. While Chase did not go so far as to place his coverage of the *Plessy* decision in columns designated for railroad news, as did the New York *Times,* his editorial "WHY SHOULD WE CARE?" was a pragmatic call for political independence in the forthcoming election rather than a ringing rebuke to a racist judicial decision.

Chase was still indifferent the following week when he stated: "The United States Supreme Court decided a few days ago that the separate coach law was Constitutional." He then dropped all mention of the case. This scant acknowledgement of the significance of the *Plessy* decision was apparently general in the black as well as in the white press. Unlike the "Civil Rights Cases," Chase reprinted no excerpts from his contemporaries, and later studies of the *Plessy* decision do not show any extensive outcry from the black press.[43]

---

[42] For coverage of the "Civil Rights Cases", see *Bee,* June 23, 1883, 3, and Nov. 10, 1883, 2. Copies of the *Bee* are missing from Sept. 8 to Nov. 10, 1883, and it appears that it suspended publication during some or all of this period. If suspension was the case, the comments are mild for an initial opportunity to comment. If issues are missing, stronger statements may have appeared, for example in an account of the mass meeting held Oct. 22, 1883 at Lincoln Hall in Washington. For this meeting, see Brown, *Washington in the New Era,* 7; Thornbrough, *T. Thomas Fortune,* 47.

[43] Logan, *Betrayal of the Negro,* 211. *Bee,* May 23 and 30, 1896, 4. Otto H. Olsen, ed., *The Thin Disguise, The Turning Point in Negro History, Plessy v. Ferguson* (New York, 1967).

One explanation for Chase's mild reaction to discriminatory judicial decisions is that he did not view them as the cornerstones upon which a separate society was constructed. There is much evidence that he perceived the defeat of the Federal Elections Bill of 1890 as the rock upon which the House of "Jim Crow" was built. This bill involved what Chase perceived to be the crux of the problem between white Americans and black Americans: political power. It involved the disfranchisement of blacks in the South which meant a loss of power by the Republican party to which Chase belonged. But the Federal Elections Bill was even more. To Chase it was a symbol which represented the fulfillment of the meaning of the Civil War which to him was the redemption of the Republic from the twin evils of slavery and the Democratic party. He gave almost weekly coverage to the bill for almost a year.[44]

In late June 1890, Chase described the Elections bill as "this great and beneficient measure" in comparison to which "all others for the time being sink into insignificance." He viewed the bill as a remedy for "fraud, intimidation and murder" which threatened to "sap the foundations of representative government." In early July, Chase jubilantly reported the passage of the bill in the House by a strict party vote and wrote that speeches on the bill reminded him "of the days of Sumner, Stevens and Wade" and that "the destiny of a nation" rested upon the Senate. He tried to combat "rumors" that the bill would be defeated by Republican Senators absenting themselves or voting with Democrats and by the threat of a Democratic fillibuster on the McKinley tariff bill unless Republicans agreed to abandon the Elections bill. Chase's sensitivity to the politics of the Elections bill is indicated by the fact that all these "rumors" ultimately proved true. Moreover, Chase was sensitive to the Democratic strategy of labelling the Elections bill "The Force Bill" which he attacked as a ruse to deflect attention from violent white racism in the South which was the reason for the bill.[45]

Such extensive coverage concerning the issue of suffrage for black Americans clearly indicates Chase's belief that black political power was the most effective means of shelling the citadel of race prejudice. In this context, his ardent and graphic protest of lynching gains added

[44] Richard E. Welch, Jr., "The Federal Elections Bill of 1890: Postscripts and Prelude," *Journal of American History*, LII (Dec., 1965), 511. Welch argues that the defeat of the Federal Elections bill "more clearly marked the acceptance of Negro subjugation than the culmination of sectional reconciliation" and the content of the *Bee* supports this view.

[45] *Bee*, June 28, July 5 and 19, 1890, 2.

significance as does his protest of the irony of black Americans fighting to preserve the democracy of the United States. Even his most extensive coverage of judicial decisions was of "grandfather" clauses involving suffrage. Chase was a constant champion also of Home Rule for the District of Columbia throughout his career. In sum, his goal was equal political rights and towards this end his protests in the pages of the *Bee* were a precursor of W. E. B. Du Bois and the NAACP. Indeed, as the preceding evidence documents, there is reason to believe Chase's claim, made in 1914, that:

> It was the weekly newspapers, more than two hundred in number, whose strong, everyweek protests against the injustice heaped upon, the segregation aimed against the race that prompted into existence the NAACP. For thirty years courageous Harry Smith has been thundering against injustice through his Cleveland *Gazette,* for many years John Mitchell through his Richmond *Planet,* Ben J. Davis in his Atlanta *Independent* and Editor King in his Dallas *Express* right here in the heart of the South, have been protesting against the unjust restrictions hedged about their race. Uninterruptedly for thirty-three years the *Bee* has stood guard here at the nation's capitol shelling each week the citadel of race prejudice with facts and figures.[46]

[46] *Bee,* Jan. 17, 1914, 4.

Kate Field and "Kate Field's Washington": 1890–1895

MAURINE BEASLEY

On New Year's Day in 1890, a lively new weekly newspaper appeared in the capital. Bearing the name of its editor and publisher, *Kate Field's Washington* gave expression to the varied interests and individual views of a multi-talented woman who had been an actress, playwright, literary critic, lecturer, writer and journalist. Established in an era when it was an unusual achievement for a woman to found and edit a paper, the *Washington* was Kate Field's last and most ambitious undertaking and, like her other ventures, it met with only mixed success.

Kate Field liked to refer to her *Washington* as a "national newspaper." Through the five years of its publication, from January 1, 1890, until April 20, 1895, it skipped from one subject to another, attacking prohibition efforts and Mormonism, championing tariff and civil service reform, defending the rich while sympathizing with the poor, criticizing women's suffrage although eventually supporting it, recalling the days of the Civil War, writing of high society and promoting the arts. Its eventual demise may be attributed to its failure to achieve any clear and consistent character other than providing a forum for Kate Field's opinions.

Yet one theme emerged clearly and consistently: Kate Field's belief in the city of Washington, not only as the nation's political capital but as its center of social, educational and civic progress, and her determination to promote the city's growth and development. The yellowed pages of her *Washington* still provide a picture of the issues facing Washington at a time when it was considered a slow-moving cultural backwater. In a "Credo," published in the first issue, she outlined her belief in the future: "I believe in Washington as the hub of a great nation. I believe that the capital of a republic of sixty millions of human beings is the locality for a review knowing no sectional prejudices and loving truth better than poetry. I believe that 'men and women are eternally equal and eternally different'; hence I believe there is a fair field in Washington for a national weekly edited by a woman." [1]

Kate Field had never lived in Washington until she decided the capital would provide the scope needed for her venture. Fifty-one years old at the time she started her *Washington,* she had spent a lifetime traveling from continent to continent in pursuit of occupations, reforms and causes while supporting herself in a period when most genteel women depended on male relatives. Obviously an exceptional woman, Kate Field was the product of an unusual background.

The daughter of Joseph M. Field, an actor, journalist and theater manager, and Eliza Riddle Field, an actress, she grew up in St. Louis, receiving a sheltered Victorian upbringing in spite of her parents' financial troubles. After her father's death when she was eighteen, she became the ward of a millionaire uncle, Milton L. Sanford of Boston, husband of her mother's younger sister, Cordelia. The Sanfords introduced her to the select social circles of Boston and Newport, where they spent their summers, and took her abroad to Florence. Quickly becoming a youthful darling of the writers' colonly, she coquetted with the elderly writer Walter Savage Landor, took tea at the Brownings and flirted with Robert, charmed Anthony Trollope, twenty years older than she, and met George Eliot.

Yet she did not like to depend entirely on Sanford's charity. Before she left for Europe, she had persuaded the Boston *Courier* to pay her five dollars a column for a series of travel letters on her European experiences. Influenced by her literary friends to denounce slavery, she irritated Sanford, who favored the South.[2] When he threatened to cut off her allowance, she hunted up more journalistic work, sending back travel letters to the Boston *Transcript* and the New Orleans *Picayune.*

Returning to the United States on the eve of the Civil War, she mined her Florentine experiences, writing magazine articles on her old friends and theatrical criticism. During the Civil War she further antagonized Sanford by her fervent espousal of the Union, caushim to reduce the financial support he had continued to supply and to change his mind about making her his principal heir. Refusing to pine over the loss of a fortune, she traveled throughout the United

[1] *Kate Field's Washington,* January 1, 1890.

[2] Helen Beal Woodward, "Kate Field: The Woman in the Footnote," in *The Bold Woman* (New York: Farrar, Straus and Young, 1953), pp. 207–208.

States, writing letters on her experiences for Samuel Bowles' *Springfield* (Massachusetts) *Republican.* Seriously interested in an early-day ouija board, she published a volume on it entitled *Planchette's Diary* in 1868.

Beginning a successful career as a lyceum lecturer in 1869, she specialized in a laudatory description of Dickens, giving readings from his works, and in a "musical monologue," which ranged from a parody of a London dinner party to a Spanish song and dance. In the midst of writing two books, *Hap-hazard* (describing her life on the lyceum circuit) and *Ten Days in Spain* (an account of her trip to Spain during a revolution there), she embarked upon a theatrical career. Although critics politely told her she could not act after she starred in a New York play that failed, she persisted and performed in plays in this country and in England while trying her hand at writing drawing-room comedies.

In her whirlwind life of diverse interests, Miss Field seized upon an amazing new invention, the telephone. Reporting with gusto on Alexander Graham Bell's device, she received shares of Bell Telephone Company stock in appreciation for the publicity. They grew in value to a fortune of $200,000, but Miss Field lost heavily in the Cooperative Dress Association, a short-lived dressmaking venture to reform fashion by promoting simpler styles.

The restless search for fulfillment eventually led to the establishment of her newspaper. According to her friend and biographer, Lilian Whiting, "There had been nothing in Kate's entire life which had so concentrated her interest, and stimulated every gift and grace of her nature, as this enterprise of founding and conducting a national review of her own. She thought of it by day and dreamed of it by night." [3]

When Kate Field arrived in Washington in 1889 and settled at the Shoreham Hotel, then a new and most fashionable address, she found a city that had relinquished earlier dreams of becoming an industrial center and had come to realize that its future lay in providing services for the Federal government. That future looked promising. With a population of 230,392 in 1890, Washington was enjoying a real estate boom and experiencing the first of the suburban growth that was to mark its Twentieth Century development. Its social life, focused on the wealthy political and diplomatic set, attracted Miss Field who found

[3] Lilian Whiting, *Kate Field: A Record* (Boston: Little, Brown and Co., 1899), pp. 467–468.

it appealing that the city lacked the crudity associated with large-scale manufacturing and industry.[4]

With the same enthusiasm that she had shown for the telephone, Miss Field set out to publicize Washington. In her first issue she campaigned for Washington to be made the site of the World's Fair of 1893. Her argument, repeated in issue after issue, was that as Washington was the capital of the nation it was the logical place for the exposition. As she put it, "How can a fair be 'broadly national' unless it be held in the capital of the nation? Where have European Fairs been held? In London, Paris, Vienna. And why? Because they are the capitals of their respective countries and no self-respecting nation would dream of inviting the world to meet it at any other point than the seat of government." [5] In her enthusiasm to make Washington the site of the fair, Miss Field followed the lead of a group of Washingtonians who had begun to promote the idea in the late 1880's. Chicago won out in the competition for the fair and staged the brilliant Columbian Exposition of 1893. A gracious loser, Kate Field promoted the Chicago exposition with unflagging vigor.

In her first few months of publication, Miss Field began her efforts to improve the cultural level of the capital. A paragraph in a society column pointed out, ". . . the great drawback to living here is the absence of art in every shape. A few good pictures in the Corcoran Gallery do not make amends for the unspeakable horrors of the Capitol entailed upon a long-suffering people by ignorant Congressmen. An occasional concert and opera do not fill a void aching for melody." [6] But, optimistically, Kate Field saw a light in the darkness. She called attention to two recent concerts and noted, "When, however, Washington listens attentively and in large numbers to a symphony concert and a concert of American compositions in the space of one week, there is hope of better things." [7] She added, "Of course, it is not to be expected that everybody here will appreciate what such concerts mean in musical terms." [8]

On another occasion, she wrote "Bye and bye there will be music in more than one Congressman's soul, and critics will cease to point the finger of scorn at the Capital. Do they know that the Boston Symphony Orchestra gave four concerts here this season to crowded audiences? Are they aware that Washington already has its Choral Society sufficiently drilled to essay in public Mackenzie's 'Cotter's

[4] *Ibid.*
[5] *Kate Field's Washington,* January 22, 1890.
[6] *Ibid.*, April 2, 1890.
[7] *Ibid.*
[8] *Ibid.*

Columbia Historical Society Collection

Autographed photograph of Kate Field (1840–1896).

Saturday Night'? Do not the Washington Musical Club and the Wilhelmj Club give several concerts during the season?" [9]

Although a sincere devotee of art for its own sake, Miss Field never closed her eyes to its commercial possibilities. Applauding plans to erect a new Corcoran Art Gallery on Seventeenth Street, she pointed out that "the new Gallery will keep the best of company and increase the value of real estate in a part of the town which has never yet felt

[9] *Ibid.*, February 4, 1891.

KATE FIELD'S WASHINGTON

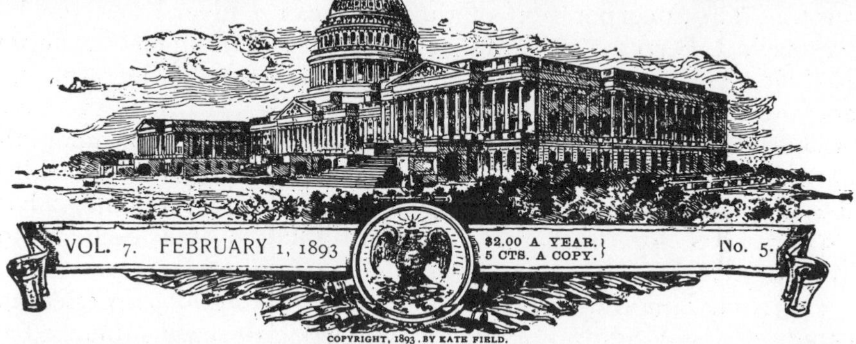

39 Corcoran Building, Washington, D. C.

COPYRIGHT, 1893, BY KATE FIELD.

Among the Articles in this Number are:

Pears'
Soap

What is wanted of soap for the skin is to wash it clean and not hurt it. Pure soap does that. This is why we want pure soap; and when we say pure, we mean without alkali.

Pears' is pure; no alkali in it; no free alkali. There are a thousand virtues of soap; this one is enough. You can trust a soap that has no biting alkali in it.

All sorts of stores sell it, especially druggists; all sorts of people use it.

A WORD TO THE WISE.

CERTAIN ADVERTISEMENTS FROM TRADE RIVALS,

who fear the phenomenal success of

Van Houten's Cocoa

in America, contain innuendoes against it, and appeal to the authority of

Dr. SYDNEY RINGER, *Professor of Medicine at University College, London. Author of the Standard "Handbook of Therapeutics."*

This eminent physician ACTUALLY writes as follows:—

"From the careful analyses of Professor ATTFIELD and others, I am satisfied that Messrs. VAN HOUTEN'S COCOA is in no way injurious to health, and that it is decidedly more nutritious than other Cocoas.—It is certainly "Pure" and highly digestible.

The quotations in certain advertisements from my book on Therapeutics are quite misleading and cannot possibly apply to VAN HOUTEN'S COCOA."

The false reflection on VAN HOUTEN'S COCOA *is thus effectually repelled and the very authority cited to injure it, has thereby been prompted to give it a very handsome testimonial.*

A Perfect Food....

Pettijohn's California Breakfast Food

Nourishing; palatable; delicate.

It has no equal as a Breakfast Food. In this food may be found Phosphates for the brain; Iron for the blood; Lime for the bones; Carbon in sufficient quantities to warm the body without burning the tissues, and all other elements necessary for the building and maintenance of a healthful, vigorous body and brain.

It cooks in 10 minutes. Ask your grocer for it.

the thrill of a 'boom.' "[10] In Kate Field's view, real estate development and cultural advancement would accompany each other.

Her genuine wish to see Washington become a center of learning also seemed mixed with a desire to sell building lots, as in her enthusiasm for the establishment of what is now American University and the adjacent residential area of Wesley Heights. In 1891 she wrote, "The incorporation of the American University is the last feature in Liberty's cap."[11] She noted that it would lie on the summit of "Wesley Heights, where Nature bids Art come to her arms and add the inspiration of human genius to the handiwork of the Great Architect"[12] and added a favorable notice of John F. Waggaman, the developer of Wesley Heights, who she wrote was retailing building lots at "wholesale prices."[13] Waggaman, in turn, frequently advertised his lots, for the bargain prices of $400 to $600 each, in the *Washington.*

In its championing of education, the *Washington* expressed the capital's long-standing hope for a national university supported by public funds. With her characteristic optimism, Kate Field lauded the establishment of Catholic University as well as American University and the expansion of Columbian University (now George Washington) into the field of graduate study. Convinced that the capital was destined to become a seat of scholarship, Miss Field seemed not to recognize that a number of competing institutions might guarantee only quantity not quality in education.

The *Washington's* interest in education and real estate appeared again in its praise for the Chautauqua located in the "magnificent amphitheater" at suburban Glen Echo.[14] Full page advertisements for the Chautauqua appeared frequently in the *Washington* and its news columns heralded its advent as "the beginning of a great people's great university."[15] When the cornerstone for the Chautauqua buildings was laid in 1891, Miss Field was on hand to participate in the ceremony and to testify to the "good work being done."[16] Chautauqua, she wrote, "is not for the rich; it is not for university men and women; it is for people dying of mental starvation."[17] Subsequently she outlined a diet that would relieve their distress: A series of

[10] *Ibid.*, April 29, 1891.
[11] *Ibid.*, June 10, 1891.
[12] *Ibid.*
[13] *Ibid.*
[14] *Ibid.*, May 13, 1891.
[15] *Ibid.*, June 24, 1891.
[16] *Ibid.*, May 27, 1891.
[17] *Ibid.*

lectures on "the Constitution, Hamilton, Jefferson, the War of 1812, John Quincy Adams, Jackson and the Capture of the Commonwealth." [18]

For those in search of a suburban home, Kate Field recommended a trip to Glen Echo to survey its scenic attractions. "It is the only new suburb I ever saw which did not offend the eye by its shabbiness and the taste by the intensely plebeian character of its recreations," she wrote.[19] "Glen Echo is lovely to look upon, easy to get to—now that the barge route is established—and comfortable to stay in after you are there." [20]

Kate Field dealt in superlatives. She employed her inexhaustible supply of adjectives to praise another suburb, Chevy Chase. "Nowhere are improvements in the suburbs of the Capital so apparent as in the direction of Chevy Chase, seven miles away in Maryland," she wrote in 1893.[21] "Thanks to the California syndicate a beautiful country has been opened to the public, and new rides and drives galore add to the delights of a winter at the Capital. A large hotel has been put up and charming cottages already dot the landscape." [22]

In addition to supporting Washington's expansion, Kate Field wrote column after column on the city's government, sights, history, and civic needs. Like journalists before and after her, she complained of congressional penury toward the District. She chided Congress for failure to build enough public schools and for inadequate support of the National Zoo, charging that "the death of twenty per cent of the entire collection of animals must be laid at the door of the Congressmen who voted to maintain a National Zoological Park and then failed to appropriate money enough to sustain it." [23]

The *Washington* opposed efforts to change the fiscal arrangement by which Congress appropriated half of the funds needed to maintain the District of Columbia and local tax-payers supplied half. When legislation was introduced in Congress to require the District to be totally self-supporting, Kate Field raised a familiar objection: It would be manifestly unfair since the capital lacked the right of self-government and the taxpayers "have no voice in saying who shall expend the money, or how much and for what it shall be expended." [24] The *Washington* complained of Congressional parsimony toward the

[18] *Ibid.*, June 3, 1891.
[19] *Ibid.*, June 8, 1892.
[20] *Ibid.*
[21] *Ibid.*, December 20, 1893.
[22] *Ibid.*
[23] *Ibid.*, February 28, 1894.
[24] *Ibid.*, May 16, 1894.

District and interviewed Representatives who chided their colleagues for cutting the District's requests for school construction, sewer improvements and street maintenance.[25]

Kate Field was a charter member of the Columbia Historical Society and was elected to its Board of Managers when the Society was organized in 1894. The *Washington* enthusiastically supported the society's formation and reported on its meetings. Although only a lukewarm feminist who did not endorse woman suffrage until 1893, Miss Field saw her prominence in the organization as a triumph for her sex. With an uncustomary touch of bitterness, she noted: "That women should be among the founders of this society and that they should also be elected to office, is a new departure for this District, where there are more women and less legal regard shown to them than in any other part of the Republic." [26] She did not amplify her remarks and her newspaper made no particular attempt to campaign for greater legal rights for women.

Perhaps it was Kate Field's consciousness of discrimination against herself as a woman which made her sympathetic toward the problems of the city's black population. Certainly she was not free from some racial prejudice. She largely accepted the stereotypes regarding blacks which were widely held among whites in the Washington of the 1890's. She referred to Isaiah T. Montgomery, a black delegate to the Mississippi Constitutional Convention, as a "Sambo of Mississippi." [27] An aristocrat in her tastes, Miss Field tended to look down on those she considered inferior and seemed, subconsciously at least, to put Negroes in this category. The *Washington* published numerous jokes in the then-popular Negro dialect that seem tasteless, offensive and pointless by today's standards. But judged by the mores of the late Nineteenth Century, Kate Field remained a friend of the city's growing black population that numbered 75,000 in 1890.

As the century ended much of the white press criticized Negro "shiftlessness" and stressed the race's high crime rate.[28] But in the *Washington,* Kate Field attempted to examine the social causes of problems in the black community. As she put it, "There never was a greater cruelty committed in the name of liberty than the sudden emancipation of millions of slaves without making any preparation for their subsistence. Brought up to depend on massa and mistress for food, clothing, medicine and thought itself, many of these poor

[25] *Ibid.*, April 18, 1894.

[26] *Ibid.*

[27] *Ibid.*, October 8, 1890.

[28] Constance McLaughlin Green, *Washington: Capitol City, 1879–1950* (Princeton: Princeton University Press, 1963), p. 101.

creatures were merely grown-up babies. That numbers should have drifted to the Capital was natural. Massa Lincoln freed them and Uncle Sam would take care of them." [29]

If Negroes were not able to find employment and provide for themselves, who was responsible? Clearly the Federal government in Kate Field's opinion. "What has the Government done to make these people self-respecting and self-supporting? Nothing." [30] What ought to be done? Kate Field had an answer:

> What have the Commissioners done? Nothing. What have white citizens done? Allowed their poor brethren to live like pigs in alleys where tenements should not be tolerated, and rear children to fill our streets with rowdies and our prisons with criminals. There should be an end to this great wrong, and the quickest way to end it is to establish my Labor Bureau. Already the District police know where the miserably poor congregate. A properly constituted labor bureau could consider cases individually and devise the ways and means of reform. The National Government pays half the District's taxes; being responsible for the negro's pitiable conditions; it should bear half the burden of this bureau, if not the whole.[31]

In advocating a labor bureau, Miss Field advanced a forward-looking proposal for a state-supported system of employment offices which was established in the United States in the Twentieth Century. She also exhibited more interest in the underlying causes of Negro poverty than did most white journalists of the time and seemed more concerned with recognizing individual differences among black persons than many of her contemporaries. To much of the white press, Negroes en masse represented a troublesome presence in the capital. Kate Field recognized social and economic distinctions among black people themselves.

An interview with C. H. J. Taylor, a Negro who was Recorder of Deeds for the District, was reported in one of the *Washington's* last issues. It quoted Taylor at length on the "four classes" of Negroes within the District. He stressed that the first three classes, composed of the wealthy, the professional, and the working blacks, compared favorably with their counterparts among the white population.[32] The last class Taylor referred to as the "unfortunates" who lived "literally from hand to mouth," lacked a "fixed abiding place" and had no skills with which to make a living.[33] In urging the government to

---

[29] *Kate Field's Washington*, January 25, 1893.
[30] *Ibid.*
[31] *Ibid.*
[32] *Ibid.*, February 16, 1895.
[33] *Ibid.*

provide "industrial schools and farms" to train the "vast army of idle persons," Taylor received the approbation of Miss Field, who added, "I have preached this doctrine until I am tired." [34] Subsequently the *Washington* printed a letter from the Rev. Walter H. Brooks, pastor of the Nineteenth Street Baptist Church, a prestigious black institution, thanking Miss Field for publishing the "fairly-written interview." [35]

Miss Field's concern for the black population was linked to her interest in improved hospital and sanitation services for Washington. She repeatedly urged establishment of a hospital for contagious diseases: "Remember that out of a population of 250,000 there are seventy-five thousand negroes, most whom live in shanties stowed away in alleys unseen by the casual observer. More peaceable people than these negroes cannot be imagined, but poverty and ignorance, for which they are not to blame, make them easy prey to disease, and the mortality among their children is very great. The presence of this lasting danger makes a contagious diseases hospital doubly necessary, but the void still exists and women protest in vain." [36]

In the field of education, the *Washington* called for more attention to black children. It reported enthusiastically on efforts by young white women to establish a free kindergarten for poor children, both black and white. The school, however, was not mixed—the benefactresses "hit upon the idea of letting the colored children come one day and the white children the next." [37]

Kate Field's views toward the poor reflected a sense of noblesse oblige rather than a commitment to change the existing social structure. The *Washington,* a well-printed 16-page publication, aimed at an upper-class audience and made exaggerated claims of its importance. Its miscellaneous character that may have led to the publication's failure can be seen by an examination of a typical issue.

In the issue of September 21, 1892, three articles attacked the Hamburg-American Packet Company for allowing cholera-stricken steerage passengers on one of its ships to spread the disease to first and second-class passengers. Other articles eulogized John Greenleaf Whittier, who had died on September 7, 1892, and commended plans for the inaugural reception of the forthcoming Columbian Exposition. Columns included a series of brief items headed "Noted on the Run," which described "completion of the electric road to (Washington's)

[34] *Ibid.*

[35] *Ibid.*, March 9, 1895.

[36] *Ibid.*, August 22, 1894.

[37] *Ibid.*

National Zoological Park" and a visit to the White House stables. "Roundabout News" contained a feature story on the Civil War career of a Confederate officer, and an editorial urged Washington to welcome Civil War veterans assembling for a reunion of the Grand Army of the Republic.

The back of the paper contained a short story, "Endurin' Er De War," in which an old and faithful slave lauded his master, and anecdotes entitled "The Rival Standards" that gave "Some Interesting Facts About the Stars and Stripes." Other items included the recurring column on "The Players," giving theatrical news, and odds and ends of news about prominent individuals headlined "People and Things." The issue also contained about two and one-half pages of advertising (the *Washington's* usual complement) for products such as patent medicines, California wines, Steinway pianos, Baker's cocoa, bottled spring water, and washing powders. An "educational directory" advertised boarding schools and military academies.

Kate Field claimed credit for numerous items of Congressional legislation. When she totaled up the accomplishments of her first year of publication, she listed a number upon which Congress had not acted. She admonished her readers:

> Remember that Congress has given to the world a National Yosemite Park two million acres in size, and do not forget the source of its inspiration. When Congress grants a charter to the National Conservatory of Music, think of the review which first pleaded the noble cause. . . . When the Copyright bill passes the Senate, recollect how the WASHINGTON has shouldered a gun, week after week, and fought those who would keep us a nation of pirates. When Mrs. Harrison throws open the White House for the first time to American artists, consider whence came the suggestion. If our coinage improves in design and our State militia organizations universally adopt the uniform and equipments of the United States army, bear in mind what pains the WASHINGTON has taken to enlighten the public on these points. If neglected Alaska secures land laws and her rightful place in the World's Fair, who will have worked so steadfastly for this tardy justice as the WASHINGTON? [38]

Kate Field's Washington came to an end with the issue of April 20, 1895. The mirror of her personality, it faded as her interest and health began to wane. Miss Field left Washington and journeyed as a newspaper correspondent to Hawaii. She died there of pneumonia in Honolulu on May 19, 1896.

Among those who mourned her death were her friends in the

[38] *Ibid.*, December 31, 1890.

Columbia Historical Society. The first volume of the Society's *Records* contained a tribute:

> Through her interest in national affairs Miss Field drifted to the national capital as the spark flies upward; her weekly review, "Kate Field's Washington," issued regularly from 1890 to 1895, constitutes one of the foremost American examples of personal journalism. Although she secured the aid of others in conducting this enterprise, the greater part of the work was her own, and the editorial and other items were characterized by such vigor, vividness and fearlessness as to render the review a peculiarly faithful mirror of men and events during the lustrum of its life.[39]

Kate Field's Washington deserves to be remembered as a pioneer attempt by a woman to edit a highly personal journal in the nation's capital. Hers was one of the first publications to undertake to bring the capital's local problems and concerns to a national audience, and it remains of interest to show how one intelligent and talented woman perceived life in the capital in the late Victorian era.[40]

---

[39] W J McGee, "Memorial of Kate Field," *Records of the Columbia Historical Society*, Vol. 1 (1897), pp. 172–176.

[40] David Baldwin, "Kate Field," *Notable American Women*, Vol. 1, p. 614. See also Mrs. Elden E. Billings, "Early Women Journalists of Washington," *Records of the Columbia Historical Society of Washington, D.C. 1966–1968* (1969), pp. 96–97.

The National Zoological Park: "City Of Refuge" Or Zoo?

HELEN L. HOROWITZ

In 1889 the National Zoological Park was established in Washington "for the advancement of science and the instruction and recreation of the people." [1] Prior to this founding, American conceptions of wild animals came out of three different forms of experience: the hunt, the animal show, and the zoological garden. Settlement of the continent by Europeans had involved the displacement, exploitation, and extermination of native peoples and animals. Some American fauna were merely in the way, nuisances or dangers to be eliminated. Others were economic boons as sources of food to sustain pioneers or as possessors of valuable fur to attract hunters and trappers. In either case the meaning of the wild animal was the same: the animal was the object of the hunt. It was the animal dead that was desired. Whatever pleasure was derived came from economic gain, personal security, or the thrill of the chase. The wild animal was hardly valued in and of itself.

Yet there were other kinds of animals—strange exotic beasts who inhabited other continents. From the early Eighteenth Century Americans had seen some of these wondrous creatures in traveling menageries that toured cities and towns. By the mid-Nineteenth Century, the great circuses and animal shows were gathering elephants, lions, tigers, and giraffes in large numbers to entrance, surprise, frighten, and titillate paying customers. Beyond their strangeness and beauty, the attraction of the wild animals in these shows was twofold: the animals were made to perform in ways that defied their wildness, went contrary to their nature, or endangered their trainers.

[1] This was the language of the bill establishing the National Zoological Park, first introduced April 23, 1888. Quoted in *The Smithsonian Institution: Documents Relative to Its Origin and History, 1835–1899,* complied and edited by William Jones Rhees (Washington: Government Printing Office, 1901), II, 1149. The Rhees compilation is the most convenient source for Congressional debate in the Nineteenth Century on the National Zoological Park.

Lions leapt through flaming rings and elephants held their massive feet above a man's head. Or the animals were odditites of nature. Displayed behind the bars of their small enclosures, wild animals were analogous to the freaks with whom they appeared. It was not really a different experience to look at the deer with the overgrown neck or the horse with black and white stripes than to look at Tom Thumb or the Connecticut Giantess. Americans obviously enjoyed such animal performances and displays for they were highly successful business operations.[2] Whether it be on stage or under a tent, Americans were willing to pay for their fun. Feeling about the animals was ambivalent, parallel perhaps to the attitude toward the stage celebrity. The animals were sources of curiosity and pleasure. Some, such as the elephant Jumbo, were well-known individuals. Yet the other side of fascination was contempt for the menagerie animal, perhaps the necessary tribute to a morality that scorned such amusement.

Well-traveled or more cosmopolitan Americans experienced wild animals through a distinctive medium, the zoological garden. Though one can find obvious precedents in the menageries of rulers, the display of wild animals in a public garden designed for recreation and enlightenment came only with the removal of the deposed king of France's collection to the Jardin des Plantes in Paris during the French Revolution and with the opening of the London zoo in 1828. By 1870 Americans could see the great German zoological gardens of Berlin, Frankfurt, Hanover, and Cologne, constructed on a monumental scale.[3] In such cities as New York, Cincinnati, and Philadelphia, Americans were attempting to recreate these European institutions within the limits of their means.

The Central Park Zoo in New York, founded in 1856, consisted of a menagerie, caged specimens of exotica gathered in a small section of the great park. While it may be seen as a refined version of an animal show, its placement and display suggest the Jardin des Plantes in Paris. Cincinnati, organized a decade later, was different. Resembling the recently developed zoo in Hamburg, Germany, decorative buildings to shelter animals were spaced generously along softly rolling grounds. It was a garden of delight. Well-dressed adults could stroll

[2] John and Alice Durant, *Pictorial History of the American Circus* (New York: A. J. Barnes, 1957), pp. 50–185 passim. For freaks, see pp. 55–56, 98–129.

[3] There is no adequate history of zoological gardens. Several sources, however, are useful: James Fisher, *Zoos of the World,* ed. M. H. Chandler and Vernon Reynolds (London: Aldus, 1966); Emily Hahn, *Zoos* (London: The Camelot Press, Ltd., 1968); Rosl Kirchshofer, ed. *The World of Zoos,* trans. Hilda Morris (London: B. T. Batsford, 1968); Gustave Loisel, *Histoire des ménageries de l'antiquité à nos jours* (Paris: Octave Doin et fils, 1912), III; C.V.A. Peel, *The Zoological Gardens of Europe* (London: F. E. Robinson & Co., 1903).

Library of Congress

The Traditional Zoological Garden in America.

"Birds-eye View of Cincinnati Zoological Garden," from the *Album of the Zoological Garden of Cincinnati*, Kreb's Lithographing Company, Cincinnati, 1878.

on sunlit days along its walkways into its animal buildings or its festive restaurant. In the guidebook of the Cincinnati Zoo the animals seem as civilized as their viewers, part of a peaceable kingdom to enhance the pleasure of a Sunday outing.[4]

Philadelphia, with a note of greater seriousness, undertook a similar enterprise. Here the model was London with its scientific society and educational goals. The buildings in Philadelphia were designed in a more romantic mode, communicating a sense of mystery and even foreboding. The animal kingdom took on an awesome aspect enhanced by impressive theatrical buildings within a wooded landscape. Still a place for adult recreation but an afternoon perhaps of melodrama rather than of comedy.[5]

Such zoos must have seemed like the parks in which they were set, delightful additions to urban life, sources of healthful recreation to the population. The animals themselves are almost secondary, elements of the landscape that interest and charm and an excuse for decorative garden architecture.

Beginning in 1888 the Smithsonian Institution in Washington attempted to establish an alternative way the public might experience wild animals. Established by the unanticipated bequest of an English scientist to lead to "the increase and diffusion of knowledge," the Smithsonian was, for several decades, largely a research institution. Its second Secretary, Spencer F. Baird, shifted emphasis to the development of the National Museum and the gathering of a collection of artifacts of natural history and ethnography.[6] Under Baird's Assistant Secretary George Brown Goode, a prominent ichthyologist, the National Museum grew from 200,000 specimens to more than three million.[7] What is significant is not just the size of the holdings but the understanding that guided acquisition. A museum had a dual function: it served to contribute to the culture of the public "through the display of attractive exhibition series, well planned, complete, and thoroughly labeled," and its study series served as the material base

[4] *Album of the Zoological Garden of Cincinnati* (Cincinnati: Drebs Lithographing Company [1878]).

[5] Arthur Erwin Brown, *Guide to the Garden of the Zoological Society of Philadelphia* (Philadelphia: Allen, Lane & Scott, Printers [1878]).

[6] Wilcomb E. Washburn, "Joseph Henry's Conception of the Purpose of the Smithsonian Institution," in *A Cabinet of Curiosities: Five Episodes in the Evolution of American Museums,* introd. Walter Muir Whitehall (Charlottesville: University Press of Virginia, 1967), pp. 106–166.

[7] Samuel Pierpont Langley, "Memoir of George Brown Goode, 1851–1896," in *A Memorial of George Brown Goode, Annual Report of the Board of Regents of the Smithsonian Institution,* year ending June 30, 1897 (Washington: Government Printing Office, 1901), II, 46.

for original investigation. As an adjunct to science the museum both stimulated research in particular areas and was a depository of record where would be placed specimens "upon which critical studies have been made in the past" and those which were "landmarks for past stages in the history of man and nature." [8] As a naturalist as well as museum administrator Goode saw his specimens as important to science not only as the basis of pure research but as of potential economic value.[9]

In 1882 Goode hired as chief taxidermist for the growing exhibition of mammals William Temple Hornaday, a young man who had distinguished himself on hunting expeditions in the Caribbean, South America, and Asia and who was currently achieving recognition for his naturalistic treatment of animals and his effort to place them in habitat settings. Reared on an Iowa farm, educated at the state college at Ames, Hornaday had served a fruitful apprenticeship at Henry Augustus Ward's Natural Science Establishment in Rochester, New York. Once in Washington Hornaday turned his attention to the larger North American mammals. Though with his love of the hunt he needed little excuse, the absence of adequate specimens provided him with the opportunity to travel to the Rocky Mountain West in search of bison. What he saw and learned changed the direction of his career and had a lasting impact on institutions concerned with the keeping and preservation of wild animals.[10]

The millions of bison which once roamed the continent were gone, systematically butchered. Hornaday's expedition financed by the Smithsonian required hard months of hunting to net twenty-five of the last hundreds remaining on earth. The finest specimens he mounted in a splendid habitat grouping for the National Museum. As hunter, naturalist, and social critic, Hornaday wrote on his return his tribute, "The Extermination of the American Bison." [11] The buffalo, once perhaps the most numerous quadruped in the world, was about to become extinct, lost to science and to humanity. It had not been

---

[8] George Brown Goode, "The Principles of Museum Administration," in *Ibid.,* 200.

[9] David Starr Jordan, "George Brown Goode," *Dictionary of American Biography* (New York: Charles Scribner's Sons, 1931), VII, 381–382.

[10] Fairfield Osborn, "William Temple Hornaday," *Dictionary of American Biography* (1958), Supplement II, 316–318; John Ripley Forbes, *In the Steps of the Great American Zoologist: William Temple Hornaday* (New York: M. Evans and Company, Inc., 1966) is a valuable children's book: one only wishes there were a documented version for scholars.

[11] William T. Hornaday, "The Extermination of the American Bison with a Sketch of Its Discovery and Life History," printed in *Report of the United States National Museum under the Direction of the Smithsonian Institution,* 1887 (Washington: Government Printing Office, 1889), pp. 367–548.

Smithsonian Institution Archives

Group of bison on exhibit in the National Museum of Natural History, shot and mounted by William Temple Hornaday, 1886–1887.

manly sport with its tests of courage and endurance that had exterminated the buffalo.[12] Literal armies of whites, Indians, and half-breeds had swept across the buffalo ranges totally destroying herd after herd.[13] The transcontinental railroad split the buffalo population in two; the Southern herd was wiped out between 1871 and 1875; the Northern, between 1881 and 1883. Had hunting been regulated, the buffalo could have provided an unending supply of excellent meat and warm robes. The extermination of the buffalo was accomplished with monumental waste: thousands had been taken for their tongues alone—then considered a gourmet's delicacy—and their bodies left to rot; of five buffalo taken in the Southern herd, only one hide ever reached the market.[14] The Federal government would now have to feed and clothe the Indians whom the buffalo had once sus-

[12] *Ibid.*, pp. 470–471.
[13] *Ibid.*, pp. 474–480.
[14] *Ibid.*, p. 497.

Smithsonian Institution Archives

Bison in the corral behind the Smithsonian Building before the establishment of the National Zoological Park.

tained. A combination of impersonal circumstances were at cause: the railroad, the technology of arms, the stupidity of the buffalo (Hornaday, though an admirer of the bison as "the grandest [ruminant] of them all" [15] was hardly sentimental about the victim: he was an animal of "phenomenal stupidity . . . his inoffensiveness and lack of courage leads one to doubt the wisdom of the economy of nature").[16] But there was also the human force, "man's reckless greed, his wanton destructiveness, and improvidence." And the failure of government to intervene to control the predator and protect his prey.[17] "With such a lesson before our eyes . . . who will dare to say

[15] *Ibid.*, p. 393.

[16] For impersonal causes and quote, see *Ibid.*, p. 465.

[17] *Ibid.*, p. 464.

that there will be an elk, moose, caribou, mountain sheep, mountain goat, or black-tailed deer left alive in the United States in a wild state fifty years from this date, ay, or even twenty-five?" [18]

George Brown Goode, Hornaday's superior, obviously approved of his taxidermist's work. Hornaday's expeditions to the West had also been sanctioned by Baird, toward whom Hornaday felt great admiration and gratitude.[19] With Baird's death in November 1887, Samuel Pierpont Langley, an astronomer, became Secretary of the Smithsonian. Under Langley's supervision Hornaday carried out his plan for a Department of Living Animals under the National Museum. No longer would the animals which had served as taxidermist models be killed or shipped away to zoos in Philadelphia or New York. They would now be maintained on the Smithsonian grounds and dedicated to the purposes of science and preservation. The Smithsonian became committed to extending its animal collections from the dead to the living.

Hornaday's cause became Langley's. The Smithsonian began its campaign for an area in Washington to be set aside for "a home and a city of refuge for the vanishing races of the continent," a national zoological park.[20] Hornaday was commissioned to survey the land in the area of Rock Creek for a possible site; and he began to solicit gifts or loans of bison from private collectors.

It took two sessions of Congress, 1888 and 1889, to authorize a Commission to establish a zoological park in Rock Creek. Strenuous debate ensued in the two years that followed about the method and amount of funding. In this whole period the arguments were stable, representing clear alternative understandings about the meaning of wild animals and their value in captivity. In the Congress certain Senators and Representatives became spokesmen for the Smithsonian Institution.[21] Under its aegis was to be established a national, scientific institution in which threatened North American species were to be sheltered in the hope that they would breed. It was therefore fitting that the Federal government be the only source of funds, that moneys be allocated for the acquisition of a collection, its appro-

[18] *Ibid.*, p. 391.

[19] See letters of Hornaday to Baird, esp. June 27, 1887, Incoming Hi-La, 1844–1887, f. Hon-Hot, Record Unit 7002, Smithsonian Archives, Washington, D.C.

[20] Langley to Samuel Dibble, Chairman of the Committee of Public Buildings and Grounds, House of Representatives, Jan. 18, 1889, printed in *Annual Report . . . Smithsonian Institution,* year ending June 30, 1889 (Washington: Government Printing Office, 1890), p. 28. Hereafter only the year of a regular annual report will be given.

[21] Especially William C. P. Breckinridge of Kentucky in the House, Justin S. Morrill of Vermont in the Senate.

Smithsonian Institution Archives

William Temple Hornaday with a bison calf, one of the first animals to form the nucleus of the National Zoological Park. The photograph was taken on the Smithsonian grounds in 1886.

priate housing, and its maintenance. There was no discernable difference between the collection of living animals in a national zoological park and the stuffed dead ones in the National Museum. Goals were the same, the advancement of science; the authority was the same, the Smithsonian; thus the means of support should be the same, Federal sponsorship.[22] While the national zoo would have a special relation to Yellowstone National Park as a source of animals, it was

[22] See, for example, speech of Breckinridge in the House, April 9, 1890, quoted in Rhees, ed. *Smithsonian Institution: Documents,* II, 1376–1379.

important that the zoo be located in Washington to be available to scientists for research.[23] (The Smithsonian's further hope that the zoo might serve "as a constant object lesson, under the eyes of the legislature," [24] a living lobby near the Capitol to assert the value of wildlife and the need for its preservation was discretely never stated on the floor.) Such were the arguments that won the Senate in the years of debate, 1888 to 1891.

However, in the House different voices were heard. Once a Representative rejected totally the notion that wild animals had any value beyond the chase: "this park might well furnish a very valuable and a very much appreciated entertainment to a large class of citizens of the District of Columbia, by providing a possum and coon hunting ground where they could go, in the old-fashioned way, at night, and hunt the possums and coons." [25] The more usual frame for condemnation of the zoo was that the Federal government had no business establishing an animal show. "A bear garden is to be established 'for the advancement of science!' . . . Barnum is to have a new rival in his 'animal industry.' " [26] One Congressman suggested that "hundreds of the people of my state would prefer, if this circus is to be inaugurated, that it shall be carried around . . . put on wheels. . . . Let us organize the menagerie, appoint the clown, get all the actors, and visit all the States and capitals of the country." [27] As well as objection based on opposition to the extension of the power of the Federal government that might increase taxes, those opposed to a national zoo —largely Democrats and Southerners—may have been expressing the limits of their experience of wild animals in captivity.

The majority in the House did not oppose a zoo but saw it as properly a local pleasure ground. Under the Organic Act of 1878 such District public works were voted on by Congress and supported one-half through Federal funds and one-half through District taxes. The park was not a proper way "to carry out James Smithson's bequest. The Government is being compelled by Congress to provide a 'zoo' for the city of Washington. . . . Every other city has to provide its own 'zoo.' " [28] When the Smithsonian's goals of preservation and science

[23] See, for example, speech of M. A. Foran of Ohio in the House, Sept. 12, 1888, quoted in *Ibid.,* 1161–1164.

[24] *Annual Report . . . Smithsonian Institution,* 1893, p. 27.

[25] Speech of Benjamin A. Enloe of Tennessee in the House, Feb. 10, 1891, quoted in Rhees, *Smithsonian Institution: Documents,* II, 1454.

[26] Speech by Benton McMillin of Tennessee in the House, Feb. 27, 1889, quoted in *Ibid.,* 1196.

[27] Speech of R. P. Bland of Missouri in the House, Sept. 12, 1888, quoted in *Ibid.,* 1164–1165.

[28] Speech by Joseph G. Cannon of Illinois in the House, Feb. 5, 1891, quoted in *Ibid.,* 1436.

were recalled they were labeled ideals; in reality, those who would actually use the park would be the residents of Washington who would visit it for the purposes of enjoyment.[29]

These were the arguments that determined Congressional action. The Senate maintained the Smithsonian position stoutly at the time of the founding of the park and during the initial debates over funding. But the House refused to compromise its stand and, to allow any zoo at all, the Senate had to accept the House's terms. By 1891 it was clear that any opposition was futile and that the form of the zoo was set. It was equally clear that the House would be most parsimonious with public money.

Until then Langley seems to have believed that the connection with the District of Columbia was merely a temporary arrangement. His plans for the park reflected these hopes. The National Zoological Park was to be unlike any zoological garden existing in America. In contrast to Cincinnati's thirty-six acres and Philadelphia's forty, the national zoo held over 166 acres "in the picturesque valley of Rock Creek. . . . Here not only the wild goat, the mountain sheep and their congeners would find the rocky cliffs which are their natural home, but the beavers brooks in which to build their dams; the buffalo places of seclusion in which to breed and replenish their dying race; aquatic birds and beasts their natural home." [30] Only a small section of thirty-seven to forty acres was to be open to the public, the rest was to be a preserve area where bison and elk and other North American mammals would live relatively free from man's presence and breed.[31] There would be within this reserved area space for scientific research, for medical care for the animals, and for the necessary administration.[32]

When the Superintendent of the Philadelphia Zoological Garden, Arthur E. Brown, was consulted by the Smithsonian, he could see no reason why such a park required the services of a landscape architect.[33] But Langley knew differently: he hired Frederick Law Olmsted to help him preserve and enhance the natural features of the park, to help him disguise the touch when the hand of man was necessary to protect animals or people or to provide facilities for

[29] See, for example, speech of J. H. Reagan of Texas in the Senate, Feb. 24, 1891, quoted in *Ibid.*, 1463–1464.

[30] Langley to Dibble, Jan. 18, 1889, printed in *Annual Report . . . Smithsonian Institution,* 1889, p. 28.

[31] Instructions with regard to the National Zoological Park, as decided upon to-day by the Secretary, Oct. 31, 1891, b. 51, f. 11, Record Unit 74, Smithsonian Archives.

[32] Langley planned a grouping of scientific activities around the administration building, Holt House, (Langley to Frank Baker, Dec. 10, 1890, b. 51, f. 13, Record Unit 74, Smithsonian Archives).

[33] Memorandum, June 18, 1890, b. 51, f. 10, Record Unit 74, Smithsonian Archives.

Smithsonian Institution Archives

Group surveying the grounds of the future National Zoological Park.

The four men in the center are, from left to right, Frederick Law Olmsted (in the light suit), Frank Baker, Samuel Pierpont Langley (facing the camera), and William Temple Hornaday.

them. Langley instructed that the accidental quality of the park be strictly maintained, that all natural ravines be respected, that there be straight lines, that fencing be disguised.[34] He followed quite literally the guidelines of the English landscape gardening school.[35] More so than Olmsted (or members of his firm) who could envision the larger design and who recognized that to accommodate the public it might be necessary to cut down a tree or alter the grade of a road. Langley stuck to detail and opposed any change in the existing natural terrain or vegetation.[36]

In terms of the American context Langley's plan for the park in its

---

[34] Langley to Baker, Oct. 31, 1890, b. 51, f. 11, Record Unit 74, Smithsonian Archives.

[35] That Langley's emphasis on naturalism involved a conscious aesthetic choice was brought out by his effort also to develop on the park grounds "a Jacobean garden, one of the features of which would be an old-fashioned 'maze' " (Langley to Baker, March 17, 1894, b. 52, f. 8, Record Unit 74, Smithsonian Archives).

[36] Baker to Olmsted, Olmsted & Eliot, Aug. 12, 1895, in Frederick Law Olmsted Papers, Manuscript Division, Library of Congress, Washington, D.C. Langley to Baker, April 29, 1893, b. 52, f. 6, Record Unit 74, Smithsonian Archives. Leonard H. Gerson his been most helpful in pointing me to relevant Olmsted material and in clarifying Olmsted's differences with Langley.

reservation of areas for breeding and in its naturalistic treatment is an innovation. But when one looks across the Atlantic at private estates there are clear precedents. Where Langley differed from his European contemporaries was in combining the game preserve with the zoological garden. Langley always understood that from certain points the public would be able to view the herds of American mammals. But in addition the National Zoological Park would have a section of the park where a collection of native and foreign animals would be on display in the more traditional fashion.[37] Since it was generally not expected that the zoo have significant funds for purchase, from the beginning it was planned to use the products of successful breeding as currency: young bison or elk might be exchanged for kangaroos or ostriches.[38] Among the first buildings sought in the appropriation was a tropical animal house, not unlike that of Cincinnati or Philadelphia, to be twice as costly as the shelter and fences for large ruminants.[39] This dual nature of the National Zoological Park was an extension into the area of living animals of Goode's understanding of a museum: through its study series and facilities it was to serve science; through its exhibition series it was to offer culture to the public.

The principle governing the design of the animal houses followed the Nineteenth Century notions of association. In the naturalistic setting of the park were to be buildings whose form carried "a suggestion of its character and of the habitat of the animals for whom it is designed." [40] Yet the words here are deceptive. They seem to signal a new departure in zoo architecture, but in fact they follow well-established lines. Langley did not mean that the structures resemble the desert plains or the Rocky Mountains, but rather that they assume the shape of the human dwellings in the area. The buffalo house thus took the form of a log cabin (somewhat ironically, given the buffalo's treatment by man). Langley was following the European tradition of zoo architecture that placed elephants in Indian temples, an effort at scene painting.[41] The importance of the decorative aspect was

[37] Langley sought non-American animals from the beginning (Hornaday to W. A. Conklin, April 3, 1890 [copy], b. 7, f. 1, letterpress p. 164, Record Unit 74, Smithsonian Archives).

[38] Hornaday to Carl Hagenbeck, Jan. 9, 1890 (copy), b. 7, f. 1, letterpress pp. 96–98, Record Unit 74, Smithsonian Archives.

[39] See "Explanations in detail of the estimates in the bill (S. 2284) for the expenses of the National Zoological Park for 1890–91," in Rhees, ed., *Smithsonian Institution: Documents,* II, 1345–1346.

[40] Langley to Baker, Oct. 18, 1893, b. 52, f. 7, Record Unit 74, Smithsonian Archives.

[41] David Hancocks, *Animals and Architecture* (London: H. Evelyn, 1971). See esp. pp. 110–111, on the Berlin zoo.

National Zoological Park

The lion house at the National Zoological Park, designed by William Emerson. Standing in the doorway is head keeper William Blackburne.

emphasized at the national zoo by being the sole responsibility of the architect, the Bostonian William Emerson, who furnished artistic sketches rather than plans.[42]

That Langley's initial design was shaped by a sense of the park as an extension of the National Museum of the Smithsonian became clear in 1891 when the Senate failed in its efforts to get the House to change the form of appropriation for the zoo. And this time those for whom animal collections conjured up circuses and menageries had their say. The appropriation regarded as absolutely necessary for park development and animal maintenance was halved, and it was expressly forbidden that any money be spent for the acquisition of animals.[43] Reality struck Langley and on March 4, 1891 he drafted a memorandum to the Smithsonian Regents that would critically revise his

[42] Langley to Baker, Nov. 20, 1890, b. 51, f. 12, Record Unit 74, Smithsonian Archives.

[43] The best discussion of the cut in appropriations is found in the Secretary's report, *Annual Report . . . Smithsonian Institution,* 1891, pp. 21–23; *Ibid.,* 1892, pp. 28–45.

National Zoological Park

Buffalo barn at the National Zoological Park.

plan for the National Zoological Park. The measure just passed had "the practical result of substituting for the scientific and national park (with subordinate features for recreation) . . . a local pleasure ground and menagerie." What followed from this is that there could be no animal preserves. Of the one-half to two-thirds of the park hitherto reserved, all, except that essential to animal protection, must be thrown open to the public. "The provision of preserves for large herds of native American animals, which formed an essential feature of the original plan, [was now] to be wholly abandoned." Money would have to be diverted from the building of permanent structures to cut roads, footpaths, and entrances into the park. The carnivora house would have to be cut down and no houses built as planned for birds, monkeys, or reptiles. The force of employees and watchmen was to be reduced. Whatever money could be saved should be spent for the acquisition of "interesting animals" before the Congressional prohibition on purchase should go into effect. Even if the growth of the collection might present difficulties in housing and feeding, additions were vital for "gifts can hardly be expected to come in to any extent until the collection is so impressive as to excite the enthusiasm of people who have such things to give." The very limited appropriation of $50,000 was to be spent "with the feeling that public approval of and interest in the work must be engaged as the most efficient agent in securing an increase in the annual appropriation." [44]

The Smithsonian Regents accepted Langley's memorandum, and it thus became, as he noted, "a general rule of action." [45] Gone were the elements of the National Zoological Park that made it different from a traditional zoological garden. Not only was the public to have access to the entire park but they should now be able to view the usual set of zoo animals. Downplaying its former concern with North American mammals, the National Zoological Park attempted to get those wild animals which defined a zoo in the public mind: lions, tigers, zebras, swans, polar bears. Its finest early animal was the Indian elephant Dunk given with a companion Golddust by James E. Cooper, proprietor of the Adam Forepaugh shows.[46] During the winter season of 1893–1894, the park accepted on loan seventy-three animals from the Forepaugh shows. This generated great popular interest, bringing to the park shortly after their arrival almost 30,000 visitors on a single Sunday.[47] What the zoo wanted was "interesting animals" that would be pleasing to the public,[48] or as Langley earlier put it, those that would make "some show." [49] The study series was forced to give way to the exhibition series.

Whether Hornaday would have forwarded or resisted these changes cannot be known, for by 1891 he was in Buffalo, New York, engaged in real estate ventures. He had felt forced to resign in May 1890, when Langley made it clear that the zoo was to be Langley's park, not Hornaday's.[50] Hornaday felt he could not remain as a "Superintend-

---

[44] Langley to Executive Committee, Board of Regents, Smithsonian Institution, March 4, 1891, b. 52, f. 1, Record Unit 74, Smithsonian Archives.

[45] Note added to Langley communication to Executive Committee, Board of Regents, Smithsonian Institution, March 4, 1891.

[46] *Annual Report . . . Smithsonian Institution,* 1891, p. 50. Golddust was actually on loan.

[47] Baker to Langley, Nov. 13, 1893 (copy), b. 8, f. 2, letterpress p. 677, Record Unit 74, Smithsonian Archives.

[48] Langley to Executive Committee, Board of Regents, Smithsonian Institution, March 4, 1891, b. 52, f. 1, Record Unit 74, Smithsonian Archives.

[49] Langley to Baker, Jan. 3, 1891, b. 51, f. 14, Record Unit 74, Smithsonian Archives.

[50] Langley stated his intended control over park development most clearly in a letter to George Brown Goode, May 7, 1890. Langley had already contracted both Olmsted and Emerson, and insisted that no development take place "even to the laying out of a foot path" without their approval and his own "personal knowledge and sanction" (b. 25, letterpress 5.1, pp. 9–12, Record Unit 34, Smithsonian Archives).

National Zoological Park

Ducks in winter.

ent of buildings and labor, or a head keeper," reporting to an Assistant Secretary, and powerless to shape development of the zoo which was to him "as clear as the noonday." [51] The substantive issues between these two powerful men may never be known. Doubtless there was the difficult adjustment for Hornaday, passionately devoted as he was to Baird, when his project was appropriated by the formal, stern Langley.[52] There were the new Secretary's efforts to gain authority over his subordinates.[53] Hornaday, too, may have been disheartened

[51] Hornaday to Langley, May 16, 1890, b. personal correspondence, 1890, 1895–96, f. National Zoological Park, Record Unit 7003, Smithsonian Archives.

[52] Even biographers sympathetic to Langley admit that he was difficult to work with, demanding of others, reserved, and formal. See, Cyrus Adler, "Samuel Pierpont Langley, *Annual Report . . . Smithsonian Institution,* 1906, p. 531–532; J. Gordon Vaeth, *Langley: Man of Science and Flight* (New York: The Ronald Press Company, 1966), pp. 54–62.

[53] Langley, May 10, 1890, had detailed Hornaday's responsibilities. The message was largely negative: Hornaday was to do nothing that committed the Secretary to any action; Hornaday could not receive letters or write "except under the authority and by the direction of the Secretary" (b. 25, letterpress 5.1, pp. 14–15, Record Unit 34, Smithsonian Archives).

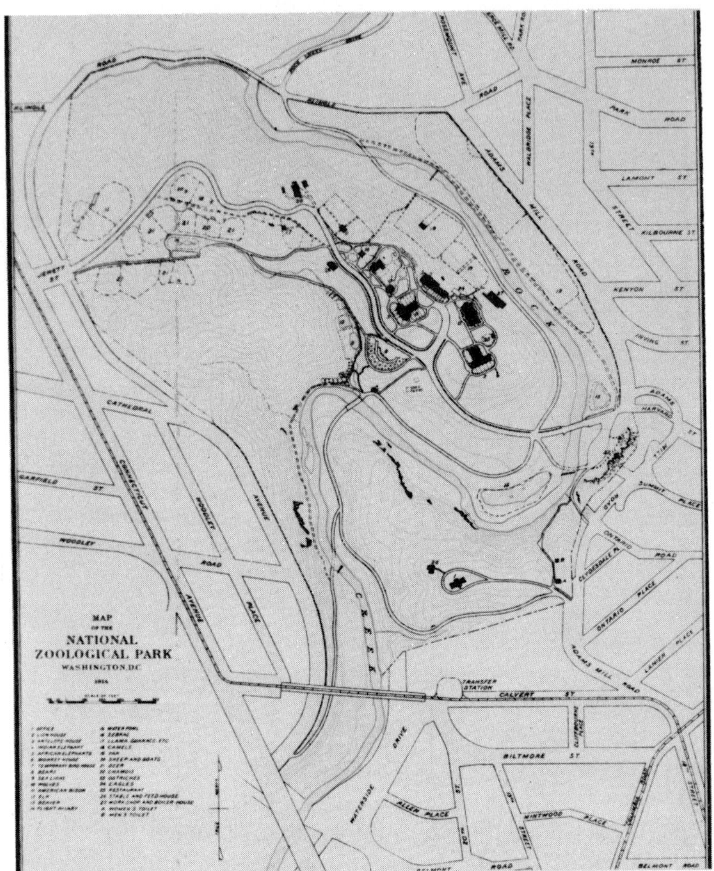

National Zoological Park

Map of the National Zoological Park, 1914.

The hope that three-fourths of the park would be range for North American animals threatened with extinction was not to be fulfilled.

by the actions of Congress, for he fully understood the implications of the District tax from the beginning, spelled out its meaning, and lobbied hard against it.[54] Finally, whatever his intentions in entering business in New York State, Hornaday was aware that a "big scheme" in zoological parks was afoot in New York City and advised another to attach himself to it.[55]

[54] Memorandum in Hornaday's handwriting (copy), b. 7, f. 1, letterpress pp. 130–32 (not dated, but between March 3 and March 8, 1890), Record Unit 74, Smithsonian Archives.

[55] Hornaday to [Charles] Hallock, April 17, 1890 (copy), b. 7, f. 1, letterpress pp. 181–

National Zoological Park

Picnicking and posing at the National Zoological Park, about 1912.

Langley acted quickly to fill the vacancy caused by Hornaday's departure, appointing as Acting Manager of the National Zoological Park Frank Baker, a specialist in comparative anatomy at the National Museum and professor of anatomy at Georgetown University. It was Langley's expectation that Baker would serve only a short time and be more responsible for supervising the construction of buildings than for the actual care of animals.[56] Baker's ability to act was severely restricted. Step by step through letters and memoranda Langley clarified that the Secretary's authority ranged from general guidelines to specific and minute detail, that Baker could make no

183, Record Unit 74, Smithsonian Archives. At the end of his life Hornaday drafted an autobiography. He saw his role in the founding of the National Zoological Park and his conflict with Langley in different terms than here presented. He credited himself with the origin and early success in getting Congress to appropriate funds; saw himself as having been betrayed by enemies; and remembered Langley as willful and cantankerous. With the exception of Hornaday's characterization of Langley, these recollections cannot be sustained by other sources. (See drafts for autobiography [1934], b. 15–16, William Temple Hornaday Papers, Manuscript Division, Library of Congress.)

[56] Langley to Baker, May 29, 1890, b. 51, f. 9, Record Unit 74, Smithsonian Archives.

National Zoological Park

Easter egg roll at the National Zoological Park, early 1900's.

move beyond day-to-day management without written authorization, and that Baker had only a very limited ability even to correspond in his own name.[57] Langley's domination of his Acting Manager was unremitting.[58] But, unlike Hornaday, Baker bore up, learned to satisfy Langley's demands, and little-by-little became an efficient bureaucrat asserting authority over his own staff.[59]

At the same time Baker also became a zoo superintendent, a title which he received on November 23, 1893, and was to hold until 1916.[60] Increasingly he worked at the park rather than at the Smithsonian building on the mall. He visited zoos in Cincinnati and Philadelphia,

[57] Notes of Verbal Instructions from Secretary Langley to the Acting Manager of the National Zoological Park, Jan. 9, 1891, b. 51, f. 14, Record Unit 74, Smithsonian Archives; Langley to Baker, April 30, 1892, b. 52, f. 4, Record Unit 74, Smithsonian Archives.

[58] Baker had no power to hire or fire, including the watchman who allowed Baker's son, who had run away from home, to sleep for a night in the elephant house (Baker to George Farquhar, April 28, 1892 [copy], b. 8, f. 1, letterpress pp. 415–16, Record Unit 74, Smithsonian Archives; Langley to Baker, June 17, 1892, b. 52, f. 5, Record Unit 74, Smithsonian Archives).

[59] Baker gave clear instructions that he, not the head keeper, was to receive all communications to the park (Baker to A. J. Hayward, Aug. 26, 1892 [copy], b. 8, f. 2, letterpress p. 32, Record Unit 74, Smithsonian Archives).

[60] Langley to Baker, Nov. 23, 1893, b. 52, f. 7, Record Unit 74, Smithsonian Archives.

National Zoological Park

Fording Rock Creek, early 1900's.

was surprised by their success, and learned from their directors.[61] Neither he nor Langley had known anything about the keeping of wild animals in captivity.[62] Here they were rank amateurs and had to inquire about the kind of enclosures, the effects of climate, the appropriate diet. In 1891 they hired as head keeper William H. Blackburne who brought to them his experience with animals gained in twelve years with Barnum and Bailey. Baker learned quickly and, as he did, he came to have a sense of the National Zoological Park quite different from that of Langley. Baker wanted a place that would please the public immediately, thus he found himself impatient with Olmsted and Emerson whose delays wasted valuable construction

[61] See, for example, Baker to Arthur E. Brown, Oct. 29, 1890 (copy), b. 7, f. 2, letterpress pp. 23–24, Record Unit 74, Smithsonian Archives; Baker to Goode, Aug. 25, 1890 (copy), b. 7, f. 1, letterpress pp. 370–376, Record Unit 74, Smithsonian Archives.

[62] They found that the bear yards while "picturesque and effective from the landscape architect's point of view" were too damp and too subject to the extremes of climate to be healthful for the animals (*Annual Report . . . Smithsonian,* 1892, p. 70); and the elephant barn should have been built near water (*Ibid.,* 1891, p. 50).

time.[63] He was concerned with public safety and convenience rather than with preserving naturalistic detail. Even before Langley's memorandum, Baker had wanted the zoo to get as many animals as possible including the foreign ones the public expected. Not only did he want examples for scientific comparison but he feared that when the National Museum's Department of Living Animals was moved to the park it would appear so small as to "make the whole scheme seem abortive and ridiculous." [64] Thus the changes in design that Langley outlined in May 1891, out of a sense of crisis, must have seemed to Baker sweetly reasonable.

While Baker accepted the form of the appropriations and its special tie to the District of Columbia, the drastically cut budget was another matter. Forced to give up hope for handsome buildings and to retire staff, Baker fought every retrenchment. Langley's commitment to the National Zoological Park was somewhat abstract, but Baker was there every day supervising work crews and responsible for the well-being of animals and public.[65] Initially the zoo dealt with the financial stringency by spending early in the fiscal year and getting additional money through a deficiency bill. Langley's precision, rectitude, and sense of economy could not tolerate such liberties, however, and he imposed on Baker strict limits, required monthly detailed budgets, and held him accountable for every expense. Baker was forced to comply. One senses, however, that within the limits Baker had to operate, he gradually learned how to satisfy his superior officer while pressing for the zoological garden that he wanted. He was gaining control over the park and becoming an accomplished zoo man to whom others turned for guidance.

Increasingly the National Zoological Park became Baker's. To the degree that it did it lost its distinctive qualities to become a modest zoological garden. By 1895, on the developed northeasterly segment of approximately forty acres, 520 specimens lived in a heated animal house, paddocks and barn for bison and elk, enclosures and thatched roof shelters for deer and llama, bear yards, elephant barn, prairie dog yard, waterfowl pond, and beaver valley. In contrast to the half-dozen or so substantial buildings evenly spaced throughout

---

[63] Baker to Arthur E. Brown, Oct. 29, 1890 (copy), b. 7, f. 2, letterpress pp. 23–24, Record Unit 74, Smithsonian Archives.

[64] Frank Baker, "The National Zoological Park," in *The Smithsonian Institution, 1846–96: The History of Its First Half Century,* ed. George Brown Goode (Washington: Government Printing Office, 1897), p. 457; Baker to Langley, Jan. 7, 1891 (copy), b. 7, f. 2, letterpress pp. 280–82, Record Unit 74, Smithsonian Archives.

[65] Baker to Langley, Sept. 28, 1891 (copy), b. 7, f. 4, letterpress p. 435, Record Unit 74, Smithsonian Archives.

Philadelphia's or Cincinnati's parks, Washington's zoo had only one solid, permanent structure.[66]

The National Zoological Park did have special potential, however. Because it was free, people enjoyed it during all phases of the business cycle. Its support for Federal and local funds meant it would never face the hard times, even bankruptcy, of its better equipped counterparts. And while only occasionally has Congress been generous, the National Zoological Park has been able to improve and build rather steadily and has thus been able to incorporate changing concepts rather than remaining essentially fixed by an early plan and set of buildings.

Despite his memorandum, Langley remained, as long as he lived, a force opposing the National Zoological Park's becoming a traditional zoological garden. He continued to fight for naturalistic detail, for emphasis of the collection of North American mammals, and for increasing the size of their paddocks.[67] And in his annual reports as Secretary of the Smithsonian he attempted to disguise the extent to which the National Zoological Park had come to resemble other zoos. He instructed Baker to "give prominence to the native races, keeping the others quite subordinate," [68] required him to strike out the name tropical house whenever it appeared (despite the fact that that was what it was), and rejected pictures showing animals visibly constrained for those of elk and bison where the fencing of the enclosures did not show.[69]

In 1895 Langley still recalled the hopes of 1889, hopes kept alive by the magnificent setting in Rock Creek Park. Alongside elements of a traditional zoological garden, what he had originally proposed for the National Zoological Park had been an alternative to the ways that Americans experienced wild animals. The animal was to be rescued from the hunter and given a protected area where it might replenish its stock. Here its primary value was not to have been exhibition either as an entertainer in an animal show or as part of a decorative setting. Its purpose was to have been merely to exist and breed—and only incidentally to be seen. The reason the national zoo was to be lo-

---

[66] Philadelphia's buildings had an estimated cost of $194,705 (*Annual Report . . . Smithsonian,* 1891, p. 22). I am grateful for the unpublished history of National Zoological Park construction, compiled by Sybil E. Hamlet, Office of Information, National Zoological Park, Washington, D.C.

[67] See, for example, Langley to Baker, March 23, 1895, b. 52, f. 10, Record Unit 74, Smithsonian Archives.

[68] Langley to Baker, received Dec. 20, 1894, b. 52, f. 9, Record Unit 74, Smithsonian Archives.

[69] Langley to Baker, Jan. 22, 1891, b. 51, f. 15; Dec. 21, 1893, b. 52, f. 7, Record Unit 74, Smithsonian Archives.

National Zoological Park

To keep the National Zoological Park naturalistic presented some challenges.

cated in Washington clarified its secondary purposes: the collection of animals would be available to scientists; and the animals could serve as a standing lobby for game protection. In this early effort at preservation of wildlife, the animal was important for its place in the natural order and for its value as an economic resource. Neither required emphasis on the display of the animal to the public.

Langley's plan was not to be realized. Saddled with a special relation to the District and its taxpayer, the National Zoological Park assumed the form of a traditional zoological garden. Limited by the meagre support of a reluctant Congress, it was only a minor affair, well below the scale of other gardens in the United States. Yet ironically it may have been the very stinginess of Congress that salvaged something of Langley's original plan. Though there were not the large herds of bison and elk breeding upon it, the land itself was left relatively unchanged, its wildness and beauty intact.[70] This may have been of some solace to Langley when he learned of the successful effort of the New York Zoological Society to realize what seemed

[70] In 1895 there were seven bison and fifteen elk (*Annual Report . . . Smithsonian,* 1895, p. 70).

like his design on a grand scale with a zoological park in the Bronx planned and directed by William Temple Hornaday. Yet while the Bronx zoo would establish large breeding areas for North American mammals, its plan would not be Langley's. To the members of New York's Boone and Crockett Club who brought the New York Zoological Park into being, preservation would take on a different note. These social leaders and sportsmen would attach symbolic values to threatened American wildlife, seeing in its demise the loss of the true America. And, paradoxically, they would celebrate America's rise to world power through the tributes of African and Asian animals. In both cases display would take on a new prominence and, unlike the Smithsonian scientists, these wealthy New Yorkers would have the means to realize their intentions.

Scientific Societies in Gilded Age Washington

J. KIRKPATRICK FLACK

"Voluntary scientific organizations," proclaimed W J McGee in 1905, "more than public appropriations and federal encouragement, have shaped scientific life in the national capital." [1] At least two easy inferences might be drawn from this large statement. One is that McGee, in a querulous way, was criticizing the scientific establishment by venting frustrations accumulated during twenty-five year's service in Washington's geological and ethnological bureaus. The other is that the context of his assertion—a memorial tribute to Marcus Baker, topographer and editor of maps at the United States Geological Survey—caused him to engage in rhetorical exaggeration. The two men had long been close associates in promoting national science and McGee felt deeply the loss of his intimate colleague. Yet here he was neither chiding official institutions nor mourning a friend; rather he was seizing an opportunity to celebrate a particular set of local societies. Therefore, instead of seeking presumptive evidence to discount McGee's statement, we should scrutinize his intriguing generalization for the light it casts on science and culture in the Capital City a century ago.

Such an analysis must begin with certain related questions. What institutions was McGee applauding? How and why had they come into existence? What purposes did they aim to achieve? Who were their members? Did it make any difference that they were located in Washington? And finally, what can we make of McGee's phrase "shaped scientific life"—does this mean the active advancement of

An earlier version of this paper was delivered before the Columbia Historical Society on December 18, 1973.

[1] W J McGee, "Tribute to Marcus Baker," *Records of the Columbia Historical Society*, Vol. 8 (1905), 187; there is no adequate biography of McGee, making it necessary to rely on the *Dictionary of American Biography* (New York, 1961), VI, 47–48, a memoir by his sister, Emma R. McGee, *Life of W J McGee . . .* (Farley, Iowa, 1915), and sketches published in various professional journals following his death in 1912.

science, and if so, how could informal structures have proven more instrumental than "public appropriations and federal encouragement"? The bases for answers to these points of inquiry can be found in archival and manuscript sources echoing the character of scientific development in late Nineteenth Century Washington.[2]

I

The years from the late 1860's onward witnessed a remarkable proliferation of literary and scientific associations at the seat of government. Though never noted as fertile ground for intellectual bodies, the banks of the Potomac now blossomed with an array of organizations existing to promote the increase of learning and culture. This happened within a brief time span; still, the process was evolutionary and its primordial stages contained few hints of what lay ahead.

As a matter of fact the first groups to make their appearance showed only a thin connection with subjects of the mind and objects of the imagination. These were the dilettante coteries known as "elegant circles." Nominally devoted to serious pursuits, the select company which attended Horatio King's literary reunions, the notables who made up the Washington Book Club, Salmon Chase's Club, and the Short Story Club, as well as the social luminaries who frequented Charles Eames's salon took greater delight in their fastidious image than in their dubious creative accomplishments. Gatherings were proper and decorous, the participants had high social repute, and the lectures were usually vapid. Occasionally there would be a memorable evening thanks to the presence of a professional author or journalist who happened to be visiting Washington. But perusing their literary remains one finds little of enduring merit, and on this basis it seems that Washington's "elegant circles" should be placed in permanent storage with the rest of the Gilded Age bric-a-brac.[3]

A more searching examination reveals that the "elegant circles" epitomized Washington's version of mugwump culture. Their nuclei

[2] See the "Essay on Sources" in my forthcoming book, *Desideratum in Washington: The Intellectual Community in the Capital City, 1870–1900*.

[3] Horatio King Papers, Manuscript Division, Library of Congress; First Washington Book Club mss, District of Columbia Miscellany Collection, LC; Washington *Evening Star, passim;* on Charles Eames's salon see LeRoy H. Fischer, *Lincoln's Gadfly, Adam Gurowski* (Norman, Oklahoma, 1964), 263; for a biographical account by his son see Horatio King, *Turning On the Light* ... (Philadelphia, 1895), 7–21; there are amusing sketches of "elegant circles" in L. de Hegermann-Lindencrone, *The Sunny Side of Diplomatic Life, 1875–1912* (New York, 1914).

BUREAU OF AMERICAN ETHNOLOGY
WASHINGTON

March 6, 1894.

Sir:

At the request of several gentlemen I have the honor to invite your attendance at a conference in the President's room of Columbian University, corner H and 15th streets, on Friday afternoon, March 9, at 4:20 p.m. The purpose of the conference is exchange of views as to the best means of gathering and preserving the history of the national capital.

Yours with great respect,

W J McGee

Mr. Marcus Baker,
U. S. Geological Survey,
Washington, D. C.

Columbia Historical Society Collection

Letter from W J McGee to Marcus Baker preceding the organization of the Columbia Historical Society.

consisted of people who, for the most part, regarded themselves as superior but unappreciated by the society at large; men and women inclined to read rapid social change as cultural malaise and who sought escape from its enervating effects. As with frustrated patricians in Boston and New York there was much laughing-up sleeves and looking-down noses at social gaucheries, and constant brooding over the erosion of traditional values. Yet Washington's mugwumps were not entirely despairing, and it was understandable that one of the brightest lights at Horatio King's reunions was the genteel reformer George William Curtis.

Like Curtis, the Washington mugwumps combined an adherence to genteel tastes and manners with a commitment to public responsibility. Part of their motivation for founding literary circles stemmed from the belief that Washington could be transformed into the cultural capital of the nation. Beyond this, however, they had scarcely any conception of how to proceed. Their aims were admirable, if extravagant: they sought to make their community "as well known as a centre of literature and art, as it is now recognized as the centre of statesmanship, law and science." [4] But how was this to be done? These first literary groups had no regular memberships, no meeting schedules, no publications, and not even official names. Refined as their guests may have been, they were so loosely knit that they lacked the most rudimentary characteristics of organization. Their sole possession was the singular geographical base from which they hoped to cast a nationwide radiance.

The brunt of their energy, therefore, was spent creating an impression of grandeur by drawing together an aggregation of congressmen, cabinet members, scientists, Supreme Court justices, and assorted public figures of stature. Even presidents of the United States might be included—though there is reason to believe that at the more exclusive salons this happened only as a last resort. Henry James's "Pandora," his satire of genteel Washington in the early eighties, depicts the most elegant of all elegant circles. In the center stand the fictionalized Mr. and Mrs. Henry Adams. They are appropriately named the Bonneycastles. Gathered about them is a collection of exquisite types, witty and clever people who thrive on the Bonneycastles's intimate soirees. The Bonneycastles's drawing room is the shining ornament of Capital society due to the brilliance of its guests, and only rarely is the president granted an invitation.

[4] I. Edwards Clarke, "The Conditions of Literature in Washington at the Time of the Founding of This Society," read before the Literary Society of Washington, January 21, 1899, Papers of the Literary Society of Washington, LC.

One of these occasions comes toward the end of a social season when Alfred Bonneycastle, in a fit of indulgence, decides, "Hang it, there's only a month left; let us be vulgar and have some fun—let us invite the President." [5]

Historians have customarily invoked such glimpses of the Gilded Age to underscore the contempt with which presidents were regarded, and to furnish proof of the insignificance of the lost men who occupied the White House between Lincoln and Theodore Roosevelt. Equally typical of the genre is a passage in Twain and Warner's *The Gilded Age* where the reader finds Laura, newly arrived in Washington, trying to impress her domineering hostess by discussing fashionable watering places. After the heroine mentions a nearby spa which she had assumed was quite acceptable Mrs. Major-General Fulke-Fulkerson snaps: "Nobody goes *there,* Miss Hawkins—at least only persons of no position in society. And the president." [6] Pertinent here is that Washington's literary groups sought personages of the highest possible order; that among such groups existed the feeling that because they were located in Washington they could induce a cultural renaissance of national proportions; that consequently they placed a premium on the image of style and grace; and that once this image was achieved it constituted their marrow and their source of vitality. Finally, their belief in the capacity of an elite of cultivated, dignified individuals to do good underpinned the confidence that sooner or later their vague conceptions of cultural improvement would be realized.

II

The more enterprising and serious-minded mugwumps soon proceeded to accomplish their self-appointed aims by developing intellectual bodies marked by greater clarity of purpose and a sense of urgency about matters of organization.

Illustrative of this was the way the founders of the Literary Society of Washington, which commenced operations in 1875, deliberately structured their group so that it would be less like a salon than an academy. There was a constitution, written by John G. Nicolay, providing for an organization of forty members. These were selected

---

[5] Henry James, "Pandora" (1884), *The Novels and Tales of Henry James* (New York, 1909), XVIII, 131; on the Adamses serving as prototypes for the Bonneycastles see J. C. Levenson, *The Mind and Art of Henry Adams* (Boston, 1957), 83–84, and Ernest Samuels, *Henry Adams: The Middle Years* (Cambridge, Massachusetts, 1958), 168.

[6] Mark Twain and Charles Dudley Warner, *The Gilded Age: A Tale of To-Day* (Hartford, 1873, 1902), 299.

according to their literary, artistic, or musical interest and placed in the appropriate category. Furthermore, the constitution established a five member executive committee, elected annually, which would appoint all other officers and committees, choose meeting sites, have charge of programs, and approve nominations for membership. When vacancies occurred new members could be installed only by securing two sponsors within The Literary and after receiving a unanimous vote of the executive committee. The reason why such stress was placed on the screening process was that every member was obliged to contribute, at least once a year, an original essay, poem, or translation. There was also a class of members designated as "honorary associates": the president and the chief justice of the United States, the speaker of the House of Representatives, the attorney general, and the secretary of the Smithsonian Institution. Indeed, such pains were taken to insure the presence of these public men that it soon became clear that The Literary was striving for official influence as well as social and intellectual distinction.[7]

This point was made explicit in 1888 by one of The Literary's most celebrated members, Madeleine Vinton Dahlgren. Mrs. Dahlgren appears strikingly reminiscent of Madeleine Lee, the protagonist of Henry Adams's *Democracy:* both were strong-willed and high-minded; both had lost distinguished husbands while they themselves were still in the prime of life; each engaged in philanthropy but restlessly sought more satisfying outlets for their reformist drives; ultimately, after shedding their widow's weeds, both tried to refine Washington society; and the two shared a fascination for the acquisition and manipulation of power.[8] Mrs. Dahlgren's definition of The Literary's purpose was an apt description of her own cultural view:

> This Capital is filled with representative men elected to mold the destinies of this great nation, as also with men chosen to represent other nations near us. It becomes then a center for forensic eloquence and of statecraft and diplomacy—shall it not as well become a focus of intellectual force in every domain, and thus exert a corresponding power over the national will in the various departments of human knowledge? But such influence, to be felt, must be aggregated. With this view our

[7] The constitution and other pertinent documents are included in the Papers of the Literary Society of Washington, LC; Helen Nicolay, *Sixty Years of the Literary Society* (Washington, D. C., 1934) and Thomas M. Spaulding, *The Literary Society in Peace and War* (Washington, D. C., 1947) provide historical data.

[8] Henry Adams, *Democracy, an American Novel* (New York, 1880, Signet edn., New York, 1961); Sarah G. Bowerman, "Sarah Madeleine Vinton Dahlgren," *Dictionary of American Biography,* III, 31–32; Charles Vandersee, "The Pursuit of Culture in Adams' *Democracy,*" *American Quarterly,* XIX (Summer, 1967), 239–248.

Society seeks a solidarity of interest for the scientist, the scholar, the writer, and the artist.[9]

The Literary Society did not forsake the mugwump's fixed principle of charming aloofness. Hence, Mrs. Dahlgren chose the adjective "suave," in characterizing the membership.[10] But at the same time it aspired to something greater than remaining just another polite circle. Its objective was to become the basis for a kind of intellectual establishment, to develop into an institution of broad culture that could take its place in an America which, at every turn, was growing more rationalized—or more "aggregated" as Mrs. Dahlgren would have phrased it. The Literary perceived that before intellectuals could influence national life it was first necessary to adopt the national mode of organization, to utilize the tactic of institutional development in order to achieve power. A corollary to this proposition was that key figures in the realm of politics be drawn into the orbit of intellectual organizations. While George William Curtis, defender of the genteel tradition, represented the "elegant circles" the Literary Society was personified by James A. Garfield, a member from almost its inception and The Literary's highest officer during his abbreviated term in the White House.[11]

III

In retrospect Garfield's Presidency seems scarcely more fleeting than the Literary Society's tenure of leadership among Washington's cultural organizations. From nearly the time of its birth The Literary was overshadowed by the several scientific groups which took shape between the Civil War and the turn of the century. This development could be seen as inevitable. First, there was no escaping the brute fact that the Literary Society suffered from a deficiency of talent with little likelihood that the condition could be remedied. As Washington matured into more of a company town literature's place in the scheme of things shrunk proportionately. On the other hand, there was good reason to assume that the role of science would expand. Second, while the Capital lacked a bona fide literati, its scientific population was increasing steadily. Government science was

[9] Madeleine V. Dahlgren, "Statement of the Purposes of the Literary Society" (1888), Papers of the Literary Society of Washington, LC.

[10] Madeleine Vinton Dahlgren to Carl Schurz, undated [1877/78?], XLVII, Schurz Papers, LC.

[11] Some of Garfield's impressions of the Literary Society are contained in unpublished portions of his Diary, Box 2, IV, Garfield Papers, LC; for The Literary's estimate of "The Sage of Mentor" see *A Tribute of Respect from the Literary Society of Washington to its Late President James Abram Garfield* (Washington, D. C., 1882).

fast becoming a conspicuous feature of American life. The result was that practitioners of science and those responsible for its support were bound to bulk larger in the Federal City. For reasons of quantity and quality, then, Washington's intellectual establishment would perforce be dominated by scientists.

Much of the early history of Washington's rise as a scientific center is summed up in the developmental pattern of Washington's Philosophical Society. With its roots embedded in Joseph Henry and Alexander Dallas Bache's pre-war Scientific Club, the Philosophical Society was destined to remain the city's premier institution in both age and prestige. At the outset it was nothing more than a loose collection of mathematicians, geodesists, army engineers, and astronomers, and there were so few of these that they had to augment their number as best they could. For instance when Hugh McCulloch came to Washington as comptroller of the currency he was invited to a meeting of the Scientific Club. He declined, apologizing that he was poorly versed in science. But Henry was insistent: "Finance is a subject in which the country is just now deeply interested," he assured McCulloch, "and the Club wants a member who knows something about it." [12] Over the course of a few years the situation changed dramatically.

Due to the establishment or enlargement of the Army Medical Museum, the United States Coast Survey, the Signal Service, the Lighthouse Board, the Naval Observatory, and the Patent Office, Washington's scientific corps had outgrown Henry's Club. As the literary circles were soon to discover, the times were ripe for more comprehensive organization, and in March of 1871 the old club was formalized into the Philosophical Society of Washington, "a society for the *advancement* of science." [13]

This fact and development suggested an organization of considerable scope which Henry spelled out as a "reflex influence upon every part of the United States." No time was lost in bringing forth a regular publication, and within a decade the *Bulletin of the Philosophical Society of Washington* was being received by major libraries and research institutions throughout North America and Europe; ex-

[12] Hugh McCulloch, *Men and Measures of Half a Century* (New York, 1888), 261–262; something of the character of meetings is rendered in George C. Schaeffer to Alexander D. Bache, Saturday, 1861, RH 2243, and Joseph Henry to Bache, December 11, 1861, RH 1501, Box 29, Henry to Bache, February 1, 1862, RH 1503, Box 30, Hugh McCulloch to Henry, February 17, 1870, RH 3492, Box 41, William J. Rhees Collection, Henry E. Huntington Library and Art Gallery.

[13] Joseph Henry, "Anniversary Address of the President of the Philosophical Society of Washington," November 18, 1871, *Bulletin of the Philosophical Society of Washington,* I (March 1871–June 1874), viii.

changes had been established with over a dozen royal societies and imperial academies; and to an increasing extent the Philosophical Society was emerging as a leading spokesman for national science. Scrupulous care went into the selection of members and the planning of meetings. Henry affirmed that while "comparatively few qualifications are necessary for admittance, no person is elected who is not supposed to have at least a high appreciation of science; has some familiarity with its principles, and is capable of doing something in the way of promoting the objects of the Association." [14] The standards set for meetings were equally rigorous. Twice a month between twenty and thirty members convened to hear and comment upon prepared papers. Contributions were of a high order and remarks from the audience that hinted of pedestrianism were coldly received. It was Henry's custom to open these sessions by reading from a volume of Royal Society *Transactions,* a fitting practice considering how the Philosophical Society endeavored to promote science on a national scale.[15]

Its impact was registered almost immediately through the founding of half a dozen Washington-based societies which in turn worked for the increase and diffusion of particular branches of scientific knowledge. First came the Anthropological Society in 1879, followed the next year by the Biological Society, then the Chemical and Entomological Societies in 1884, the National Geographic in 1888, and, in 1893, the Geological Society of Washington. Except for the last named group each emulated the Philosophical Society and published a bulletin or record of proceedings, thereby helping to transmit information and to strengthen ties between far-flung specialists. They jointly sponsored lectures at the Smithsonian as a means for inspiring a general appreciation of science, and these were so well received that one member wished some programs could be delivered "in the Senate Chamber, to Congress—it would be an admirable improvement on the ordinary methods of lobbying." [16] With their members drawn principally from public agencies, the specialized societies accelerated the trend of organizing government scientists so

---

[14] Joseph Henry, "Annual Address of the President," November 24, 1877, *Bulletin of the Philosophical Society of Washington,* II (October 10, 1874–November 2, 1878), 162.

[15] For published accounts of its history see William H. Dall, "The Origin and Early Days of the Philosophical Society of Washington," *Journal of the Washington Academy of Sciences,* VIII (January 19, 1918), 29–34; Francois N. Frenkiel, "Origin and Early Days of the Philosophical Society of Washington," *Bulletin of the Philosophical Society of Washington,* XVI (1962), 9–24; W. J. Humphreys, *The Philosophical Society of Washington Through a Thousand Meetings* (Washington, D. C., 1930).

[16] Cleveland Abbe to Thomas C. Mendenhall, April 24, 1897, Box 6, Mendenhall Papers, American Institute of Physics.

as to give them professional standing and make them more effective. But the scientific groups were not exclusively professional in that there were always places available for interested laymen. Here the societies took a cue from the mugwump circles by attracting socially promient persons and officials whose support was vital to national science. An illuminating statement in this regard is the advice given by Otis T. Mason, of the Anthropological Society, to Franz Boas, when the latter asked for suggestions about starting an ethnological association in New York: "You want patrons as well as talkers, men who like to see their names among intellectual people," counselled Mason. "Get the doctors, lawyers, architects, engineers, clergy, Rabbis, everybody interested. That is the way I greased the wheels of our now flourishing Anthropological Society." [17] Such contacts would serve not only to drum-up popular enthusiasm, but also as conduits to other departments of social existence.

After 1878, it was common for those in the Philosophical Society to be members of the Cosmos Club as well. Over half of the Club's founders came from the Society as did all its initial officers, and for years the Philosophical Society provided the core of the Club's membership. Both organizations refused to settle for anything less than excellence, yet the Cosmos Club gave excellence a broader gauged definition. Indeed, its intellectual range was as wide as knowledge itself, and, like the cosmos from whence its name was derived, the Club represented an orderly whole in which there was a place for everything. Samuel P. Langley elaborated on this feature by proposing as the Club motto, "Nothing human is foreign to me." [18] The objective of the Cosmos Club was not to promote culture directly, but to create an environment in which scientists, scholars, educators, public administrators, and their guests could meet socially at any time under pleasant surroundings. The subtlety of this motif was implicit in Simon Newcomb's injunction "that the bringing into closer touch of the academic and the political sides of Washington should be one of our great objects." [19]

All the while that such influence was radiating outward, there

[17] Otis T. Mason to Franz Boas, December 3, 1887, Boas Papers, American Philosophical Society.

[18] Address delivered by Samuel Pierpont Langley, in William A. DeCaindry (comp.), *The Twenty-Fifth Anniversary of the Founding of the Cosmos Club of Washington* (Washington, D. C., 1904), 21; this collection of documents should be supplemented by George Crossette, *Founders of the Cosmos Club of Washington, 1878* . . . (Washington, D. C., 1966) and Thomas M. Spaulding, *The Cosmos Club on Lafayette Square* (Washington, D. C., 1949); there are superb historical sketches by Kip Ross in issues of the *Cosmos Club Bulletin*.

[19] Newcomb, *Twenty-Fifth Anniversary*, 34.

were centripetal forces at work to give the several societies greater cohesion. In 1898, these combined to produce the Washington Academy of Sciences, an interlocking directorate for coordinating the affiliates' various activities. Basically this meant publishing a general directory of members, distributing notices for all meetings, taking over the cooperative lecture programs, sponsoring Washington conventions of the American Association for the Advancement of Science, and assisting the "scientific and other societies in matters of common concern." This was not the extent of its functions, however, for the Washington Academy was also honorific. Fifty of its members were elected at large as the "best qualified" individuals in the Washington community, and these were empowered to choose honorary members, "persons distinguished in science." The rest of the Washington Academy consisted of the regular members of its component groups.[20]

The organization of the Academy came as the fruition of Washington's scientific establishment. In stature its membership towered above those of the genteel circles, and it promised to become an effective mechanism for the advancement of science. It accommodated both amateurs and practitioners, while its structural form enabled it to bestow prestige on members and also function as an administrative body. In short, the Academy gave conclusive evidence of a flourishing intellectual community at the seat of government.

IV

The components of this structure were what caught W J McGee's attention as he took the measure of scientific Washington seventy years ago. By focusing on "voluntary scientific organizations," instead of the Academy itself, he forces the historian to probe beneath the surface and seek out the origins of the finished product. Obviously the whole was greater than the sum of its parts, but without these smaller bodies the larger creation would have been impossible and they remained vital to its continuance. In a metaphor which McGee would have appreciated, the Washington Academy resembled a homogeneous organism with the several affiliates making up its protoplasmic cells. As such they performed certain indispensable functions. By carrying out Henry's dictum that "public opinion in regard to scientific questions must eventually be determined by the authority of societies, journals, and individuals of established sci-

[20] Minutes of the Committee on Constitution, January 15 and 17, 1898; Minutes of the Joint Commission of the Scientific Societies, January 19 and 25, 1898, Washington Academy of Sciences Archives.

Columbia Historical Society Collection

W J McGee

Photograph published in *The McGee Memorial Meeting of the Washington Academy of Sciences held at the Carnegie Institution, Washington, D. C., December 5, 1913,* printed by the Williams & Wilkins Company, Baltimore, 1916.

entific reputation,"[21] they acted as a stimulus for professionalization. On another level, through their open lectures and standing invitation to laymen, they swelled the ranks of the patrons of science. And with their headquarters in Washington the scientific societies erected an institutional framework for the representation of intellectuals and men of specialized scholarship in government.

In McGee's view this latter point appeared as the most monumental contribution of all: Washington's societies had the effect of rationalizing the impulse for scientific and cultural advancement and imparting to it more of a public character. Where there might have been a welter of disparate scientific ventures functioning inefficiently, developing in haphazard ways and subject to the caprice of fortune for their success, there now was a unified body of interrelated organizations sustained, in part, through informal connections with agencies of the federal government. This, then, is the basis for McGee's observation that Washington's societies were instrumental in shaping "scientific life in the national capital." They consolidated Washington's men of science into a coherent whole, strengthening ties between them and giving them a keen awareness of corporate identity from which it was believed their collective influence would flow. Mrs. Dahlgren had earlier proposed a fusion of "intellectual force" and "statecraft" on behalf of the Literary Society, but her group was ill-equipped to act as the catalyst. Prior to that the elegant circles had yearned for Washington to take the lead in enhancing the quality of national life, but they were neither sufficiently organized nor professionally oriented to make this dream come true. As McGee understood, however, the scientific societies were specially suited to synthesize institutionalism, professionalism, and rationalization in a local intellectual community dedicated to the promotion of national culture.

[21] Joseph Henry, "Annual Address of the President," November 24, 1877, *Bulletin,* II, 162.

The Works of John Singer Sargent in Washington

CHARLES MERRILL MOUNT

By giving discipline to the disordered fabric of Impressionism John Singer Sargent (1856–1925) perfected the most sweeping artistic innovation since the Renaissance. That in addition he will be recorded as the most vigorous and versatile of watercolor painters there is no doubt. But in that final estimate which belongs to future centuries it remains a question whether his portraits will not take precedence. They compete with those radically original blends of metaphor, intimate impulse, and public statement, which characterize the best of his murals. We can only await the verdict of unborn generations and admire a creator whose intellectual powers equalled his manual skills and who allowed nothing to interfere with his primary responsibility. Simply but splendidly that was to art, the supreme sacrement of the adventurous and speculative imagination.

Conscious recognition of Sargent's supreme importance is suggested by the frequence and honored position of his works in Washington. After the exhibition assembled at the Corcoran Gallery in 1964, which first gave an electrifying glimpse of his real stature, and for which I was invited to act as *expert,* one might wish that were true. Certainly the White House and Capitol Building are not without examples of his work. The National Gallery, Corcoran Gallery, National Collection of Fine Arts, National Portrait Gallery, and Freer Gallery, boast pictures of the first rank. Despite an air of controversy surrounding their acquisition and partial dispersal, the hundred drawings still at the Corcoran Gallery remain a collection second to none. Even their somewhat embarrassing bronze *Turkey,* lone example of Sargent's skills in sculpture, forces an admission that this branch of his art is present. When portraits privately owned in Virginia are included the group becomes remarkable if no less fortuitous.

His position astride the Atlantic made Sargent an international figure and, as Rodin suggested, distinctly the Van Dyck of his time. His spectacular personal associations with the American Capitol nonetheless remained scant and brief. Nothing more profound than the arbitrary and individual impulse of museum directors, the personal taste of a First Lady, market conditions in drawings, or my urging that the Corcoran Gallery purchase the early portrait of *Madame Pailleron* to ensure its place in their exhibition, was responsible for this formidable collection.

To the credit side must be entered the superb quality of so many examples. Phases of the artist's thought and manner are present which can be seen nowhere else. Yet serious gaps remain. Among the portraits are none of those superb groups like the Hunter and Wyndham Sisters which display that special branch of Sargent's compositional fertility. Three watercolors are dissociated from the main stream of his art in that medium. And apart from preparatory drawings at the Corcoran Gallery the mural work on which Sargent expended the energies of mature and declining years is unrepresented. In this area it is worthy of note that brilliant preparatory oil studies recently were obtained by the Boston Public Library.

Lack of direction has been inherent in the collecting of Sargent's work in Washington. The collections should have begun in 1903, when amidst social and artistic fanfare the artist stayed at the White House to paint President Theodore Roosevelt. It was a visit momentous as that of Titian to the Emperor Charles V and one expects that the completed portrait, fairly choking with force and exuberance, would have stimulated the purchase of landscape and figure compositions. Instead, the portraitist's eminence over-shadowed his artistic worth. Sargent's 1917 visit when President Woodrow Wilson was committed to canvas saw a meager beginning. The Director of the Corcoran Gallery, C. Powell Minnegerode, acquired the splendid and misnamed *En Route Pour La Pêche*. Sargent evidently had forgot this early work, a part of his embarrassing early career in Paris as a *Salon painter*. His surprise permitted *The New York Times* to observe "it is proof of strength when a painter can look back some forty years and see that he was good."

Until three canvases in possession of Charles Lang Freer at Detroit were transferred to Washington in 1923 this remained the only Sargent on permanent view. Minnegerode himself, a pioneer in the skills by which museums are built, did much to alter that circumstance. His cellars were ready to store and re-pack Sargent's works returned from San Francisco's Pan-Pacific Exposition. Not only did Minnergerode

Corcoran Gallery

Oyster Gatherers of Cancale (En Route Pour La Pêche) by John Singer Sargent. Corcoran Gallery, Washington, D.C.

Acquired in 1917 by C. Powell Minnegerode, Director of the Corcoran Gallery, for the Corcoran's permanent collection, this luminous and graceful work, painted forty years earlier by the artist when he was 21, was Sargent's first picture on permanent display in Washington.

profit by exhibiting this prized collection (which included the world-famous portrait of *Madame Gautreau*) but he reported offers to buy pictures, none of which was accepted. When an ornament atop a frame was found loose his personal letter rang with concern. If evidence in the museum files can be trusted he provided Sargent the occasional typewriter or secretary when loose statements in the press required correction. And it was no small thing that under his auspices the completed portrait of President Wilson first was shown to the public.

A curiously sour fruit was born of this solicitude. Years after his death Sargent's surviving sister sent a gift of 191 drawings to the Smithsonian Institution which with a memorable fastidiousness refused them. Tales that they were carted about on offer to other Washington institutions are possibly exaggerated. At least I never personally have met the barrow boy. Eventually they found lodging beneath the Corcoran's ever hospitable roof. Whether legal title followed is a question never satisfactorily answered, especially in later years when

Photograph from the author

John Singer Sargent (1856–1925) in his Paris studio.

Sargent is shown with his portrait of *Madame Gautreau,* a pivotal work of his career, before it was sent to the Salon of 1884.

a quickened appreciation caused the Smithsonian to demand the drawings' return. The alarm that spread through the Corcoran can be imagined when the rival Director threatened that he would "come and get them"!

Roughly framed and hung row on row, for many years these drawings constituted a jumbled and over-powering decoration to back passages, stairways, and curatorial offices at the Corcoran Gallery. Accompanied by an Assistant Director and a stenographer in 1954, I identified enigmatic residues locked in a basement. Alas, a decade later 91 drawings and my notes no longer were at the Gallery. For the record, my fee from the exhibition was used to buy one of these charcoals in New York.

II

A full third of the thirty-six paintings by Sargent in the Washington area are from before the year 1884. Immediately the caveat must be entered that Sargent before he reached 28 was not the man known to us. These works do however provide an unequalled opportunity to examine a brilliant, sensitive, occasionally profound, always facile young painter. Trained in the latest French mode, using the new bristle brushes favored by his teacher Emile August Carolus-Duran (sable brushes always had been standard), he followed a bewildering variety of directions. So much was this the case each work was virtually unparalleled in his own career.

Carolus-Duran spent the spring and summer of 1877 at his country home near Fountainbleau. There he worked on an enormous ceiling decoration celebrating *The Triumph of Marie de Medici,* a somewhat specious event whose colorful depiction now is on a ceiling of the Louvre Museum. As his most favored pupil, Sargent prepared a study

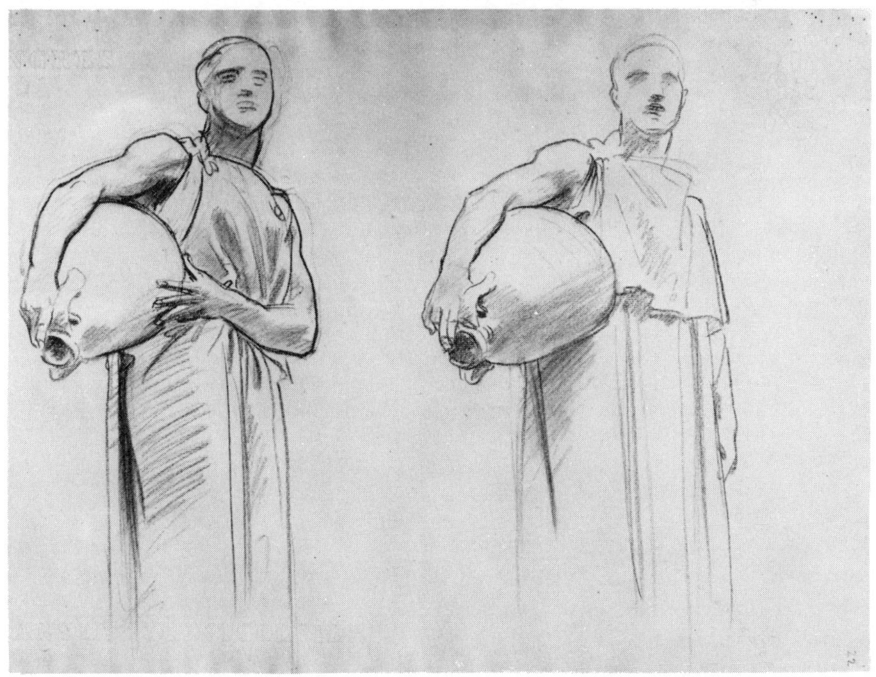

Photograph from the author

Charcoal drawing by John Singer Sargent. Formerly in the Corcoran Gallery, Washington, D.C.

A study for Sargent's murals in the Boston Museum of Fine Arts, he used only the arms from these two figures in his frieze of *Danaides*. In his final panel, the figures are maidens. Begun in 1916, Sargent's decorative work for the Boston Museum occupied him until his death. Drawing sold by the Corcoran Gallery.

Photograph from the author

Charcoal drawing by John Singer Sargent. Formerly in the Corcoran Gallery, Washington, D.C.

A study for Sargent's murals in the Boston Museum of Fine Arts, this charcoal demonstrated how he created a flying figure of Boreas, the cold north wind, from a model lying flat on his back. As employed in the mural the upper left corner became the bottom. The last group of murals was unveiled seven months after Sargent's death and no critical estimation of them has ever been attempted. Drawing sold by the Corcoran Gallery.

in possession of Roanoke College, Salem, Virginia. Mention of this canvas first was heard from Carolus' grandson in February 1961, and together we searched through the eccentric theatrical dressing rooms where the master's work is stored. Once found, together with an equally impressive companion sketch, it explained the large part Sargent had played in executing his teacher's decoration. (See *The Art Quarterly,* No. 4, 1964, pages 385–418.)

A fellow pupil and friend whose lodgings in Paris Sargent shared, J. Carroll Beckwith, also assisted work on this ceiling and recorded that hot summer of 1877:

> . . . One after another my camarades (sic) left the city until I was quite alone. I did not notice my loneliness much as my master was working

> upon his fresco (sic) and my services were valuable to him: frequently I passed several days with him at his country place at Montgeron and thus vanity kept me from getting blue. Nevertheless it was so hot in Paris and my work so irregular that I became impatient . . . Sargent and Lachaise were at Cancale and soon would be coming through on their way to the south. The morning of 21st Aug., 77, they awoke me early and said they should leave that night for St.-Germaine where Lachaise' family resided. Sargent was going to stay with him a few days and then go on to join his family at Chateau d'Oix in Switzerland. . . .

Sketches Sargent brought with him from Cancale that August morning showed interest in genre subjects. That pictures of humble people engaged in ordinary tasks enjoyed a respectable sale was doubtless their recommendation. At Cancale, on the Brittany coast, Sargent had entered directly into an established market created by Francois Feyen-Perrin and his brother Eugene Feyen, described jointly by

Photograph from the author

Charcoal drawing by John Singer Sargent. Formerly in the Corcoran Gallery, Washington, D.C.

This rain-spotted charcoal for a lunette of Hell, installed in 1916 at the Boston Public Library, demonstrates the persistence of an obsession. Its choleric head is taken direct from the female fury on the left of Bronzino's *Allegory* which intruded into every period and phase of Sargent's work after 1883. Drawing sold by the Corcoran Gallery.

Roanoke College, Salem, Virginia

Study by John Singer Sargent for ceiling decoration in the Louvre Museum by his teacher Emile Auguste Carolus-Duran.

At the age of 21 in 1877, Sargent assisted his teacher Carolus-Duran to execute a large ceiling now installed in Louvre, Paris. As this study shows, Sargent originated figures for the central part of the composition.

Benezit as "the official painter of the fisher-folk at Cancale." Their pubescent girls accompanied by children and older women traversing the wet sands to oyster beds, or returning with wicker hampers filled, was precisely the subject Sargent adopted.

That winter in Paris he developed from these sketches the many studies by which the Corcoran Gallery picture was evolved. Each figure had some debt to the Feyen brothers. Recognition that one leg of a blond child is direct from an older boy in a Feyen-Perrin canvas (former Luxembourg Collection) demonstrates this was no accident. Where Sargent excelled was in an artistry past reach of his sources. Figures strike a remarkably happy balance, move forward gracefully, and inhabit a sparkling and luminously atmospheric landscape such as rarely before had been coupled with figures. The touch of his brushes was exactly subordinated to its tasks but created an extra interest. Sent to the Salon of 1878, this stunning essay was awarded an *Honorable Mention.* Sargent's youthful mastery thus forced its own acceptance without indicating his true direction.

As his name suggests, John Singer Sargent was a member of the distinguished family which has figured continuously in the history of Massachusetts since early 1600's. Sailors, soldiers, bankers, a horticulturalist, and most recently a Governor and a Vice Presidential Candidate, have sprung from the line. From his mother came her maiden name, Singer, and it was this over-powering woman's taste for foreign travel that planted both his parents in Florence, Italy, where the artist was born January 12, 1856. Cut off from inherited wealth that flowed down other branches of his family, the artist grew up a perfect amalgam of his twin ancestry, shrewd, intelligent, and highly industrious like yankee forebears, touched with his Philadelphia mother's taste for the exotic. In the financially insecure first years of his career these twin heredities brought him twice to Venice, where in 1882 an essential stage in his career took place.

Efforts at genre like those undertaken at Cancale, and later in Capri and Morocco, had been so successful he launched into large-scale production of Venetian works. These followed a vein popularized by the Dutch painter Cecil van Haanen (born 1844). From 1873 when he took up residence at Venice, van Haanen had created a personal genre that memorialized the commonplace tasks of Venetian folk, frequently indoors and by winter. Unlike Sargent's other works of that trip, The National Gallery's *Street In Venice* is executed on wood. Begun in summer whose rosey tints it retains (shirt-sleeved figures are behind the principle group), completed in winter, this fascinating work hides a further surprise. Before serving its final purpose the panel had been used for a head still intact beneath the present surface. An x-ray reveals it sufficiently well to identify the model with the *Lady With A Fan,* in possession of Laurence Curtis.

Unique for that time and place, contrary to Sargent's overall intention at Venice in that year of 1882, this large canvas evidently was begun for submission to the Paris Salon. There it could announce to the largest possible audience that the painter of *Cancale* had prepared Venetian genre. Never completely finished (the signature reflects his script style a few years later) the *Lady With A Fan* was still at Venice awaiting shipment when the mass of smaller Venetian canvases met with buyer resistance in Paris.

Sargent was obliged to trade two of the Venice works to Bechstein for the piano which thenceforth graced his studio. One was given to

National Gallery of Art
Gift of the Avalon Foundation, 1962

Street in Venice by John Singer Sargent. National Gallery of Art, Washington, D.C.

Disturbed by his inability to sell numerous genre pieces painted at Venice, in 1882 Sargent abandoned it for a decade. *Street in Venice,* begun that summer, finished in winter, tells its own story. Close crackle proves siccatif de coutrai was mixed in the medium. Sargent included it in an exhibition of his works at Boston in 1888, when it was purchased for presentation to the architect Stanford White.

his landlord, Monsieur Lemercier, to whom it was inscribed. Another, from which a figure had been cut (!), was given to Fred Lawless. A further picture of the same group is inscribed to a friend named Litazia (?). A sixth would be presented as a wedding gift to Carroll Beckwith seven years later in New York. In the perspectives of 1882, such an unsuccessful venture could not be continued. The large canvas was abandoned at Venice to his relative Ralph Curtis and the mechanism of rejection consistent throughout Sargent's life came into play. He did not return to Venice for a decade nor ever again do serious genre work.

To a young man of New England ancestry who by necessity sought for stability in his affairs, portraiture had become the only reliable lucrative field. It is plain that he did not at first adopt it as his specialty. Earliest energies were expended on genre and exotic Salon pictures. *Fumée d'Ambre Gris* (1880) and *El Jaleo* (1882), each cunningly contrived to offer women in various forms of dress and frenzy, are typical of these large exhibited works. He had successes that were considerable, between which he experienced an occasional bloody repulse such as with the unsold Venetian subjects. Portraiture, the special province of Carolus-Duran, invariably came to his rescue. ". . . One of the best evidences of a portrait's success," commented his father, Dr. Fitzwilliam Sargent, August 15, 1879, "is the receiving by the artist of commissions to execute others. And John received six such evidences from French people. He was very busy during the two months we were in Paris."

Painted the following year, 1880, the infant *Peter A. Jay* exemplifies

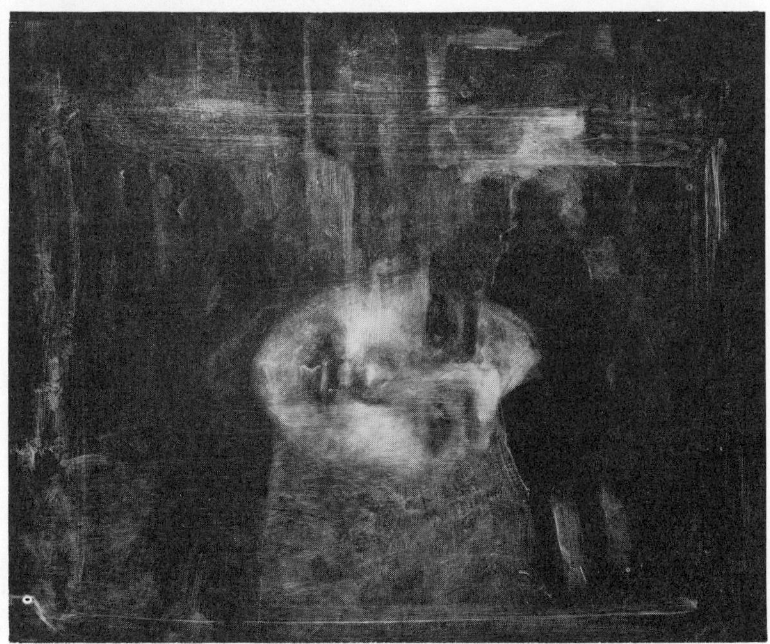

Photograph from the author

X-Ray of Sargent's Street in Venice.

This x-ray reveals the head, which appears still to be intact under the present surface, first painted on the panel. The model can be recognized as the same who appears in Sargent's *Lady With A Fan*.

Courtesy of Laurence Curtis

Lady With A Fan by John Singer Sargent. Lent by Laurence Curtis to the Corcoran Gallery, Washington, D.C.

Painted presumably for the Paris Salon, and left in Venice with Sargent's distant cousin Ralph Curtis, *Lady With A Fan* was Sargent's only effort at a life-size figure among his Venice work of 1882. Sargent's signature was added a decade later. The fan, and the hand holding it, are unfinished. The painting remains in the Curtis family.

these earliest efforts. Its thin facture, careful drawing, and enlarged eyes are typical of Carolus' own portraits of children. Methods had passed direct from master to pupil. Completed somewhat more colorfully than Duran might have done it, Sargent then let himself go in joyful cascades of white pigment which miraculously formed clothing.

As a good and practical French artist, catering to a clientelle of known tastes, Carolus idealized children, made women refined if not pretty, and conveyed men with cold distinction. Sargent instead had intensely personal reactions to each person he portrayed. His dowager portrait of *Mrs. Jules Vallé* is severe and restrained, as was appropriate. Areas surrounding eyes and mouth are simplified to conceal the worst ravages of age without disguising their result. Yet her attitude of mild resignation, as though cloaking a secret bitterness, is contrary to normal French notions of portraiture.

So too is the unimproved view Sargent took of Mrs. Vallé's daughter, Isabel. Painted in 1882 when he was twenty-six, this is a psychological document of unprecedented nature. Its statement of a girl who has reached woman's estate without so far coming into bloom is singularly delicate and appealing. At the dawn of his career Sargent is a miraculously sensitive medium through whose perceptions one sees and feels in a refreshingly natural way. That such pictures risked rejection (even when the subjects, like these, were distant relatives) is a part of their mystery. A further circumstance is that his range becomes more acute the less care he gives a portrait's technical apparatus.

For surely the most uniquely charming portrait of this early period is his sketch of *Beatrice Townsend,* painted as a gift to parents who commissioned pictures of themselves. Thinly and rapidly brushed, devoid of tricks and seemingly of thought content, it conveys the ravishing image of a glowing thirteen-year-old. Her ease and sparkling self-assurance contrast sharply with Isabel Vallé's tense introspection and illustrates Sargent's psychic range.

Another pair of early portraits, both ladies seen at full length, contrast even more strongly on the walls of the Corcoran Gallery. *Madame Pailleron,* chic wife of a Parisian playwrite, was put on canvas in 1879 when the 23 year-old Sargent stayed at Roujoux, her country home in Savoie. This visit was lightened for being mixed with calls on his parents nearby at St.-Gervais. Even so his ease was remarkable, as was his extraordinary proceedure while painting this large canvas out-of-doors and in unlikely flesh-tones tinted by green, mauve, and cerise. By other methods this typically patrician French face might have come upon the canvas with allure. Instead the out-door conditions eliminated shadows necessary to stress her fine lines and lofty

Collection of Mr. and Mrs. Paul Mellon

Miss Beatrice Townsend by John Singer Sargent. Collection of Mr. and Mrs. Paul Mellon.

The range of enchanted revelations that appear in Sargent's earliest portraits is demonstrated by this glowing sketch painted of *Miss Beatrice Townsend* (1870–1884) in 1882 when Sargent was 27.

eyes. Again we come upon the startling phenomenon of a youthful artist risking rejection. Certainly the more brief sketch he did of her mother, *Madame Buloz,* was received with reservation: "I see myself as I shall be in ten years, if God preserve me."

Nonetheless Madame Pailleron's portrait demonstrates that respectful attention to correct form typical of Sargent throughout his career. And here as elsewhere, once the head was executed a new and

Corcoran Gallery

Madame Pailleron by John Singer Sargent. Corcoran Gallery, Washington, D.C.

The work of a 23-year-old prodigy, Sargent's formal portrait of *Madame Pailleron* painted out-of-doors in 1879 at a country home in Savoie is distinguished by an improbable flesh of green, mauve, and cerise. Its purchase by the Corcoran was urged by the author to insure its presence in the 1964 exhibition of Sargent's work.

happier atmosphere took over. The brush describes drapery and hands in prodigies of improvisation. The gown is arranged into remarkably fine silhouette, and a landscape of mountain crocuses and garden terrace is seen with commendable aireal perspective. Probably the first outdoor portrait ever painted (in the sense of a formal "finished" work) it is both a vast credit to the young man who conceived it and a considerable artistic monument.

Four years had passed when *Mrs. Henry White* went to Sargent's new studio in the Boulevard Berthier. His reaction was immediate, masculine, and powerful. As shown at the Royal Academy of 1884 the product was an electrifying vision of truly regal distinction. Her head slightly tilted as though listening to distant conversation, the effect was of infinite aloof charm. Van Dyck's portrait of the Countess of Devonshire, then in the Bischoffsheim Collection at Paris, provided its basic design. Elements of long neck, sloped shoulders, and two hands (one with fan), once carried over, Sargent's extraordinary brilliance blazed forth.

The vast detailing of a complicated satin and tulle gown was wholly ignored. No hint of lace, embroidery, or other decoration reached the canvas. Even its ribbons, and bows which marked sleeves and trailed the fastening of a long waist, were indicated by staccato flourishes. Dancing and leaping, passing in long strokes, now striking rapid ripostes or scrubbing violently back and forth, the brush's magic transformed everything. Always the hallmark of Sargent's early intellectual prowess the silhouette became beautifully wavering, now firmly detached from and now sliding off into surroundings.

III

Great significance attaches to the fact that in both major works he exhibited in the year 1884, *Mrs. Henry White* at the Royal Academy in London and *Madame Gautreau* in the Paris Salon, Sargent misjudged taste. For all its beauty, criticism of the first was harsh: ". . . the painting is almost metallic; the carnations are raw; there is no taste in the expression, air or modelling," wrote *The Athenaeum,* with a final reservation, "but the work is able enough to deserve recasting."

Presumably at the insistence of his subject Sargent was forced to adopt that unpleasant suggestion. The angled head of the original portrait still peeks out from beside a more erect portrait with which he replaced it. The fan held in the lady's right hand was closed, after which he simplified the further silhouette and flowed turpentine washes over the shower of tulle cascading from her waist. The total effect, while evidently blunting the cutting edge of London criticism,

Corcoran Gallery

Mrs. Henry White by John Singer Sargent. Corcoran Gallery, Washington, D.C.

Sargent's *Mrs. Henry White,* exhibited at the Royal Academy in London in 1884 when the artist was 28, is the finest major work in his dazzling youthful style. After its exhibition it was altered by the artist and close examination shows the original head just to the left of the one brushed over it.

concentrated greater attention on the strongly stylized new head and masterly contours.

So far as the city of Washington is concerned, the climactic fusion of Sargent's youthful sensitivity and brilliance into devastating artistic genius took place off stage. He entered that fateful year 1884 a painter of exciting Salon pieces who had failed at genre. His haphazard portraiture revealed psychic transferences which enabled others to experience his own disturbed sympathies. A career of enchanted revelation lay ahead, had another more harsh destiny not overwhelmed him.

Two years before, when his *El Jaleo* was exhibited in Bond Street, he had travelled to London. At the National Gallery *Venus Disarming Cupid* by the Sixteenth Century Florentine painter Agnolo di Cosimo di Mariano, called Bronzino (1503–1572) attracted him. A complex and stilted allegory which still remains to be fully unravelled, its principle place is occupied by a nude figure quite unlike the soft matrons with which art teems. This slender figure whose breasts are small and hard is distinguished by an allure recognizeably real. Immediate response rose from Sargent's depths and its nature was only part artistic.

No other picture emits quite the same well-scrubbed and impeccably frozen sensuality. Sargent was sufficiently expert to see that this effect derived in part from the loss through cleaning of final rosey glazes which originally warmed an icy blue flesh. He knew too that Bronzino was the rage among generations of artists trained to appreciate the infinite grace of his rigid draftsmanship. And indeed, this Venus was a product of methods and criteria lost to our times. Her fine torso and legs may have originated with some living Sixteenth Century woman. Both arms were wrenched instead from previous works by Michelangelo: that at left from his Madonna Doni, a *tondo* painted about 1504 and now in the Uffizi Gallery. The trailing right arm is from a more hidden source, *Ezechias,* painted about 1511–1512 for a spandrel of the Sistine Chapel ceiling.

The American author Henry James, whom Sargent met at this period, permitted his heroine Milly Thrale to see through tears a Bronzino portrait which resembled herself. "And she was dead, dead, dead," the sentiment provided, adds an extra dimension to the shock Sargent felt before the Venus. Preoccupied by his London exhibition (which failed to generate any portrait orders), then the failure of his Venetian works, and the following spring by experiments in impressionism, Sargent never realized the Bronzino's potential until the summer of 1883.

Photograph from the National Gallery, London

Allegory (Venus, Cupid, Folly, and Time or Venus Disarming Cupid) by the Sixteenth Century Florentine painter and poet Agnolo di Cosimo di Mariano (Angelo Allori), called Bronzino (1503–1572).

Bronzino's *Allegory* in the National Gallery, London was, in the author's judgement, the single greatest influence on Sargent's style and career. From it Sargent took arms and hands for his portraits and some of its heads are found in Sargent's late murals. The most decisive factor was its use of line which fundamentally altered Sargent's personal vision.

Then it came with a rush. Now everything in some respect was related to that seminal allegory. Camped in Brittany, where he struggled to depict a Parisian beauty while flirting with the writer Judith Gautier, Sargent sketched the latter striking the pose of Bronzino's Venus. Even her fleshy head is forced to conform with the classic profile. Initially Sargent may have been attracted to Madame Pierre Gautreau by a profile that more nearly suited Bronzino's pattern. This latter was a sensuous young American whose childless marriage to a commodity dealer in the rue St.-Lazare centered on their vast third-floor apartment directly behind the Church of St.-Augustine. That he invited her to give him these sittings must be borne in mind. And between their sessions of work on the actual portrait, which took place in a country home near St.-Malo, he sketched a lamp-light portrait which stressed that likeness. Nature was given an assist in this respect, for he raised and artificially reduced the proportion of an ear as well as employing Venus' actual shoulders and extended arm.

Photograph from the author

Sketch of Judith Gautier by John Singer Sargent.

The first known use Sargent made of the Bronzino *Allegory* is this outdoor portrait sketch of the writer Judith Gautier in the summer of 1883.

To assess the disturbance in which he labored it is necessary to note that early in 1884 Sargent added distinction to another smartly cluttered image, of Mrs. Moore, by extracting Venus' trailing arm, reversing it, and in vigorous strokes scrubbing it to his subject's plump shoulder. The execution suggests she was not present when this virtuoso element joined her portrait. And as the picture was brought into agreement it became the tail that wagged the dog. His portrait of Madame Gautreau would follow the same route.

None of the preliminary drawings, all enhanced by the charm of her ample young beauty, suggest that Sargent was about to embark on a composition of the stark nature which grew on his canvas. Everything took second place to an extraordinary arm, reversed from Bronzino. Madame Gautreau's stunning profile harshly simplified and painted in Venus' icy tints, he filled letters with defenses against an inevitable

Photograph from the author

Sketch of Madame Gautreau by John Singer Sargent.

In this sketch of Madame Gautreau in the summer of 1883, Sargent was straining to emulate Bronzino.

criticism. "Do you object to people who are 'fardées' to the extent of being a uniform lavender or blotting-paper color all over? If so you would not care for my sitter. . . ." But whether he really referred to a voluptuous twenty-six year old, or his effigy of her, is a problem. As efforts to force her living glamor into an older mode became both obsessive and fatiguing he blamed her further: "Your letter has just reached me," he replied to a friend, "still in this country house struggling with the unpaintable beauty and hopeless laziness of Madame Gautreau." None of it should be accepted literally.

At the Salon of 1884 this picture made irreconcilable demands and attracted ridicule. By back corridors Sargent conducted his cousin Ralph Curtis to see it. The latter understandably was "disappointed in the color. She looks decomposed. All the women jeer." Audacious blue flesh, a composite of the Bronzino only sufficiently warmed to simulate life, was ascribed to cosmetics. The best joke of the day was to say the picture was a copy. "But of course. A painting after another piece that is painted is called a copy." Curtis recorded this bon mot, but possibly mistook its sophisticated double meaning. Had someone not recognized Bronzino's inspiration?

Genuine tragedy now surrounded Sargent. By struggling with a pictorial obsession he had created a masterpiece. Debatably the portrait of Madame Gautreau shall always remain his greatest work. At that moment however he was too far ahead of Parisian taste. Public reactions were opposed to his brilliant product and his reputation was ruined. ". . . We talked it over till 1 o'clock here last night and I fear he has never had such a blow. He says he wants to get out of Paris for a time. He goes to Eng[land] in 3 weeks. I fear there he will fall into Pre-Raphaelite influence which has got a strange hold of him . . ." Curtis wrote. Because the secretive Sargent neither identified the Bronzino which overpowered him, nor explained the real cause of objectionable traits in the Gautreau portrait, they were ascribed to a Pre-Raphaelitism which at least was contemporary and fashionable.

A previously unknown pen drawing made of himself conveys Sargent's introspection at this period. He had a tiger by the tail. The struggle was exhausting him, and in lowered brow and fixed eyes one recognizes the look of a fanatic. That this was strictly an interior view is shown by the affluent well-fed air so marked in Giovanni Boldini's parallel portrait. The American habit (unknown in Europe) of crossing an ankle over the opposite knee is employed to epitomize him, as Sir Hubert von Herkomer would use it again twenty years later.

In this same Boulevard Berthier studio which he turned over to

Photograph from the author

Self portrait, ink drawing, by John Singer Sargent.

This drawing of himself catches Sargent's introspection at the time of the ridicule of his work in 1884 at the Paris Salon.

Photograph from the author

John Singer Sargent by Giovanni Boldini.

None of Sargent's inner conflict is visible in this portrait by his friend Giovanni Boldini (1845–1931) to whom Sargent ceded his Paris studio at a considerably reduced rental in 1886.

Photograph from the author

Sargent's mother and his sister Violet by Giovanni Boldini.

After the unfavorable reception of Sargent's *Madame Gautreau* at the Paris Salon of 1884, his mother and 16-year-old sister Violet came to keep house for him. Sargent's friend Boldini recorded them playing duets on the Bechstein piano.

Boldini at Easter 1886,* the Italian made a revealing study of Sargent's mother and younger sister Violet playing duets on the Bechstein piano. He had asked that his sister Emily, equally artistic and nearly his own age, keep house in the absence of two servants recently discharged. Instead this more formidable duo arrived. Boldini especially noted sixteen-year-old Violet's freshness against a mother whom he found a horror.

No picture Sargent painted that year in England makes reference to the Bronzino. His Parisian repulse was a traumatic experience: "Just now I am rather out of favor as a portrait painter in Paris . . ." he wrote, and Sir Edmund Gosse recalled, "He was profoundly dissatis-

* New researches in Paris reveal that the peripatetic Sargent had no house furnishings and rented at 4,000 francs "with divers objects of furniture." Less of a vagabond and permanently settled at Paris, Boldini took it without the furnishings for 2,800 francs.

fied with Paris . . . determined to shake the dust of it off his shoes." The mechanism of rejection previously acting against Venice went far deeper. ". . . He talked of giving up art altogether. I remember him telling me this in one of our walks, and the astonishment it caused me."

Reasons were not hard to find. After failing in genre, and no longer producing costly Salon pieces (though *Carnation Lily, Lily Rose,* a vision of two girls lighting Japanese lanterns in a twilight garden, was begun at this moment) portraiture was still his single profitable activity. France had closed to him, "and he looked in vain," as Gosse recalled, "for any genuine invitation to stay in England. His sitters were all American birds of passage. . . ." "There is perhaps more chance for me there [in England] as a portrait painter, although it might be a long struggle for my painting to be accepted," Sargent observed. That he had been obliged to alter his Paris portrait of *Mrs. Henry White* did not bode well.

Gnawing away inside him all the while was an absolute knowledge that he had been right. And though memory of his scandalous fiasco returned over the years with appalling vividness, a photograph of the Bronzino accompanied him everywhere during an unhappy, unstable period of barn-storming. He painted the best people in the worst circumstances, obliged to brush likenesses in private homes and carriage houses throughout old and new England. At New York in 1888 he set *Mrs. Adrian Iselin* on canvas, "A portrait which claims and holds attention as few portraits of today do, a picture profoundly personal, full of character, vital in the extreme . . ." as contemporary criticism noted.

That he had found this model difficult is disclosed by the head's over-worked, enamelled surface. The figure he touched in more dexterously, as he always did, its black against ochre strengthening the hint of Frans Hals seen in a ruddy complexion. For a hand to link this erect body with an empire table he extracted from the Bronzino Cupid's graceful fingers indelicately carressing Venus' breast. "Only the clutch of tell-tale fingers on the ormolu mount of a nearby table betrays that this erectness demands an effort of will" observed the *Evening Post.*

Forceful reactions to sitters seen before 1884 remain constant. Extract the Empire table from *Mrs. Iselin,* reverse her figure, and she occupies the same spacial balance on an axis of the frame's lower member as *Mrs. R. B. Roosevelt, Jr.,* painted two years later. The enormous distinction is provided by their psychological make-up. The

National Gallery of Art

Mrs. Adrian Iselin by John Singer Sargent. National Gallery of Art, Washington, D.C.

After he left Paris, Sargent accepted invitations to paint likenesses wherever he could, often setting up his easel in private homes and carriage houses in England and the United States. One such portrait was *Mrs. Adrian Iselin* painted in New York in 1888.

large-eared red-faced matron exists in a different mental state from a girl holding orchids to her slender bodice as though following some embarrassing instruction.

That same year Cupid's indelicate hand was employed again for a

National Gallery of Art

Mrs. R. B. Roosevelt, Jr. by John Singer Sargent. National Gallery of Art, Washington, D.C.

Sargent's growing reputation in the United States as a portrait painter was enhanced by the virtuosity of such portraits as *Mrs. R. B. Rocsevelt, Jr.* painted in 1890.

portrait of *Miss Katherine Chase Pratt* and as always it brought instant success. "The attitude of maidenly unconsciousness, one hand resting on her side while the fingers of the other lightly and listlessly touch the circle of gold beads that clasp the throat, is 'felt' with a sensitiveness and artistic insight that are marks of a high order of creative work. There is much that is psychic in this interpretation of a human being" reported the *Review of Reviews.* Somewhere in the spontaneous complexity of his emotions was a sufficiently real resentment for this otherwise modest performance to be shipped from Massachusetts all the way to Paris' *New Salon.*

Emboldened, the artist slipped a trimmed and tapered version of *Madame Gautreau's* already famous arm into a portrait of Vanderbilt's daughter, *Mrs. Hamilton McKown Twombly.* Thereafter it became a mainstay, employed for *Mrs. Elsie Swinton, The Princess Demidoff, The Countess Clary-Kinsky, Mrs. Ralph Curtis, The Countess of Suffolk,* and everywhere in fact he required its note of perfect linear elegance. As late as 1902 in a group with two sisters Ferdinand Wertheimer assumes the position of Venus, just as Judith Gautier had done in 1883.

Portraits in Washington's public and private collections from Sargent's great maturity demonstrate the powerful personality which emerged from the crucible of the Gautreau-Bronzino scandal. The original road of his development was completely blocked out. No longer could he be merely a brilliant manipulator, nor even the straight-forward exemplar of elegant portraiture he had been when executing *Mrs. Henry White* (though at least one of her hands too was painted not from his sitter but Titian's *Entombment*). This early path was given over to his brilliant and facile friend Boldini. Sargent's own works grow in solidity and profundity. Superficially the cause can be attributed to the employment (past the turn of the century) of pigments without medium or perhaps his native American realism coupled with an increased awareness of suffering.

The real change is that Sargent had learned that painting is a craft of creating beautiful lines, shapes, forms, and textures. "I find as I grow older . . ." he explained, "that I care less and less about the painting of things 'just the way they look' and get more interested in—well something more in the nature of a Wedgewood plaque." Like Raphael and Rubens he had discerned that art feeds on earlier arts to refresh its vitality. Added to Van Dyck and Bronzino he regularly employed works by Boticelli, Perugino, Quentin de la Tour, Ingres, Gerard, Titian, Lelly, and Copley, with occasional dips into Rubens, Lawrence, Reynolds, and Tiepolo. And as his confidence in himself became a major artistic force the bold attack of his brush on so many canvases was plainly staggering. He had reached that last level of creative audacity that rushes beyond excellence into greatness.

By the turn of the century Sargent was an establishment figure in England and America, untouchable, doing what was expected of him with flair. About 1901 the small house at 31 Tite Street, Chelsea, was purchased, and he occupied it by breaking through a dining-room wall to the studio apartment at number 33, where for some years he had lived and worked. He now had available for portrait work two studios. The first, below in the old apartment, was covered by dark wood panelling purchased in France. The other, on the second floor of his house, was equally panelled, but painted white, and high, lofty, and airy. Some part of his prosperity was owed to Asher Wertheimer, a Bond Street antiques dealer who steered the most elegant part of his clientelle to Sargent. In return, from 1897 onward Wertheimer and his numerous family were made memorable in a succession of single portraits and groups.

A letter from Wertheimer's daughter Betty in possession of the National Collection of Fine Arts establishes that her portrait was executed in 1906, the year of her marriage. The most recent edition of my Sargent catalogue (Kraus Reprint Company, New York, 1969, page 456) noted the existence of a study head. More recently it appeared in London, dimensions somewhat altered and an inscription removed. Even were other evidence not conclusive its brevity and spontaneity would imply it to be the sole portion of the large portrait for which Miss Wertheimer actually posed. For like all the more considered portraits this was product of an astonishing pictorial conjuring that had begun with *Madame Gautreau*.

Comparison with the shoulders and bust of Francois-Pascal, Baron Gerard's portrait of *Madame Recamier* (Musée Carnavalet) demonstrates that Sargent drew them onto his own canvas direct. Presumably Betty Wertheimer's gown was in his studio. Yet the reclining form on which it appears is Madame Recamier. Arms, and a hint of an upper hand, are from the same source, as is the conceit of one shoulder on, one shoulder off, adopted for massive leg of mutton sleeves. At some point Sargent repented of the outdoor concept indicated by the sketch's light background and laid a darker tone onto his canvas. To preserve the head's stunning silhouette he then reverted to the original sky.

National Collection of Fine Arts
Smithsonian Institution

Betty Wertheimer by John Singer Sargent. National Collection of Fine Arts, Smithsonian Institution, Washington, D.C.

Painted in 1906, *Betty Wertheimer* is an example of the intense vitality Sargent gave his more decoratively conceived works. One is convinced that Asher Wertheimer's daughter was seated before the artist precisely as shown. Evidence indicates that she posed only for a study-head on another canvas.

Photograph from the author

Betty Wertheimer by John Singer Sargent.

Now in an English private collection, this life study of Betty Wertheimer appears to be the sole part of the work for the Smithsonian's portrait done from life. Sargent appears to have created Miss Wertheimer's devastating figure in the portrait by copying it direct from Francois Gerard's portrait of Madame Recamier.

IV

For my book *Monet* (New York, 1966) I defined Impressionism as *An art employing chemically constituted pigments to create a synthetic coloration and more powerful accents without the use of black or brown.* In the 1870's Monet had discovered a rough-shod method of painting with seven colors: white, yellow, orange, vermillion, alizarin crimson, verte emeraude, and ultramarine blue. Because whole gammas of gray and tan were impossible to find in these pigments Monet adopted the practice of using substitutes. Such approximations gave his pictures new lyric qualities and a sense of cleanliness older works did not possess. The capacities of these colors nonetheless were severely limited. Monet therefore devised synthetic accents by combining alizarin crimson with verte emeraude or ultramarine blue. These astonishing sizzling passages spluttered with an intensity unlike any seen before.

At Nice early in 1883 Sargent executed garden sketches that show his first use of the restricted Impressionist pallette with special hidden powers. From that point on his landscape work (but not his portraits)

Freer Gallery

Landscape with Goats by John Singer Sargent. Freer Gallery, Washington, D.C.

Beautifully articulated black goats add to this sparkling and richly painted Corfu scene. Unlike other Impressionists, Sargent in *Landscape with Goats* does not permit lavish pigmentation to lose the distinctive foliage of orange trees at left and olive trees at right. Impressionism has shed its limitations and come of age.

consistently employed Impressionism, which expanded from Monet's first awkward usages into a separate and full-fledged art form whose new intensity is seen in the Corcoran Gallery's *The Simplon.* "Mr. Sargent has constructed and modelled each rock as carefully and as subtly as he would the head of a statesman or the face of a child" commented *The Spectator* when this canvas appeared at the Royal Academy exhibition of 1910. "It is this basis of profound knowledge of form and design that enables the painter to give the more brilliant qualities of color and light force and enduring power."

Sargent had perfected an alternate approach to the *Cathedrals* where Monet blasted away all form and structure for this same research into light. The devastating force of Sargent's achievement is demonstrated by the fact that no criticism in the same terms could apply to a picture by Monet. The extent of his accomplishment, manipulating pigments without medium and preserving a strong fresh

Freer Gallery

Breakfast in the Loggia by John Singer Sargent. Freer Gallery, Washington, D.C.

Though really a luncheon with wine, *Breakfast in the Loggia* conveys the artist's own joy in flickering lights and atmosphere. The basic Impressionist technique remains intact but so refined by craftsmanship it is able to tackle any subject successfully. On the further bench are two more canvases. Sargent did four in and about this portion of the Villa Torre Galli at Florence.

color that did not hamper careful observation of trees' transparent foliage, and wonderfully articulated animals, can be seen in the Freer Gallery's *Landscape With Goats.* Possibly more ravishing still for cheerful luminescence and gusto is the same Gallery's *Breakfast in the Loggia* (though a large raffia wine fiasci suggests it was not breakfast these ladies enjoyed). Painted in the Florentine Villa Torre Galli it demonstrates how Impressionism's most exciting possibilities for the first time were exploited.

While Monet's roughened technique forced him to abandon figures in mature works, Sargent carried on with them through an advanced development. Expanding the capacities of Impressionism by extraordinary subtleties of observation in deep shadow, *The Weavers* is also a social document. Labor was not unknown to this transplanted New Englander who retained a work ethic in his nature. His first honor had come from depicting children employed to gather oysters. Later his

Photograph from the author

The Weavers by John Singer Sargent. Freer Gallery, Washington, D.C.

Sargent shared with Camille Pissarro (1831–1903) the only social conscience among Impressionist painters, selecting many of his subjects from the humbler laboring occupations. This interior of a textile mill in Spain suggests the ruggedness of conditions with notable reserve.

Photograph from the author

A Tyrolese Crucifix by John Singer Sargent. Formerly in the Corcoran Gallery, Washington, D.C.

Sold by the Corcoran Gallery, *A Tyrolese Crucifix* is another comment on the efficacy of labor. Sargent contrasts this craftsman's evident satisfaction with his horrifying art.

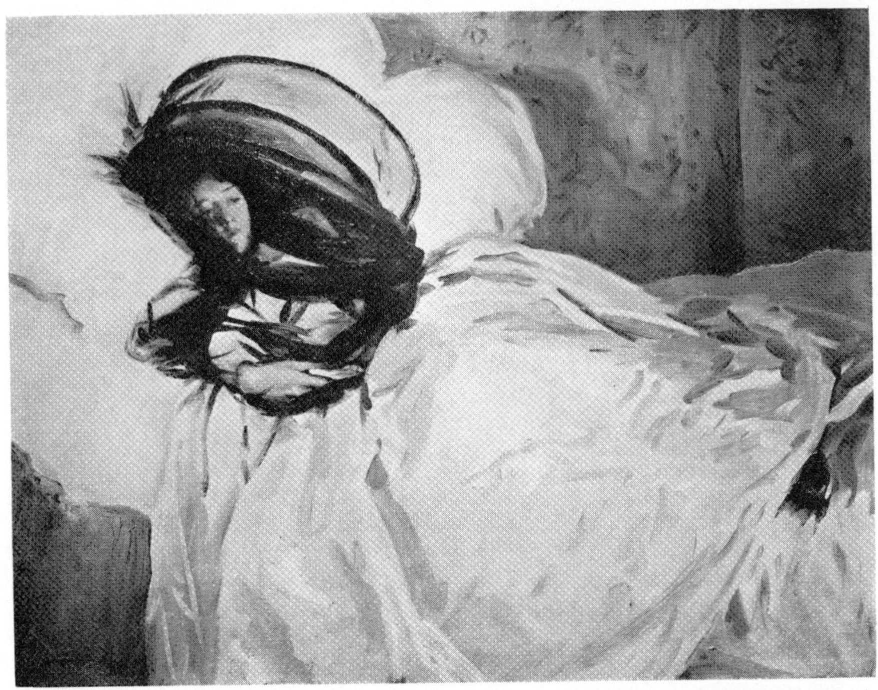

Photograph from the author

The Mosquito Net by John Singer Sargent. The White House, Washington, D.C.

A French cheese screen (garde manger) covered by mosquito netting is the humorous strategem that permitted Sargent's niece to sleep in infested continental hotels while Sargent pursued landscape motifs. The glistening skirt, excuse for an abstract pyrotechnical display of dense white pigment, is really its principal feature.

images of beggars, fruit sellers, water carriers, bead stringers, glass workers, wine pressers, indigo dyers, olive pickers, and a series of quarry stone cutters, indicated the broad spectrum of his sympathies. That these were the most oppressed of Europe's menial occupations was no accident for, with Camille Pissarro, Sargent shared the only social conscience in Impressionist ranks.

The *Tyrolese Crucifix* (formerly Corcoran Gallery) is more pointed in its analogies for straying close to the question of negative artistic values. This wood-carver is evidently a maker of religious images for churches and wayside shrines. His cherished masterpiece, a grotesque Memlingesque Christ, hangs outside for all to judge. Expressive of a curious understanding is the lack of pathos or any indication that the existence of this whittling man is not satisfactory. "I chronicle, I do not judge," Sargent's comment on his portraiture, applies here equally.

To transmute sumptuous abstract pigmentation into pictures of compelling luxury, thus arousing the tacile sense of each beholder, occupied another side of Sargent's personality. Thanks to Mrs. Richard Nixon, who hung *The Mosquito Net* in the family drawing-room at the White House, a pictorial form Sargent invented and made intensely personal is well represented in Washington. That to assist an afternoon nap his model has thrust over her head a remarkable contraption made of mosquito netting and an ordinary French cheese screen (*garde manger,* the original title) adds amusement. *Nonchaloire,* the National Gallery's equally luxuriant example might appear fortuitous were not the drapery so strongly reflective of this group's chief work, *Two Girls in White Dresses.* Now passed with an

National Gallery of Art
Gift of Curt H. Reisinger, 1948

Repose (Nonchaloire) by John Singer Sargent. National Gallery of Art, Washington, D.C.

Nonchaloire is one of two works in Washington representing the distaff side of Sargent's yearly landscape expeditions. Reserved for days of rain or excessive heat, these pictures probably are a related series and show inventive use of textiles. Their responsiveness to the mysterious romance of atmosphere is notable.

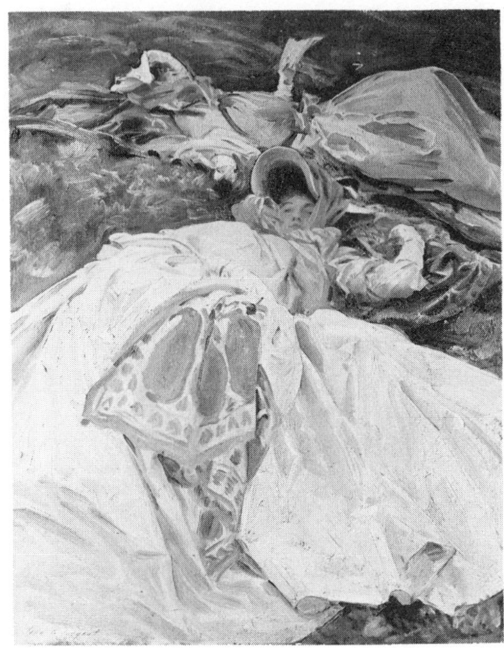

Photograph from the author

Two Girls in White Dresses by John Singer Sargent. Formerly in the Corcoran Gallery, Washington, D.C.

Most sumptuous and original of all Sargent's inventions for the display of the Cashmere shawl, *Two Girls in White Dresses,* after being shown in 1914 at the Corcoran Gallery, found its way back to England where, by probable error, it entered possession of the National Trust. In addition to fine draftsmanship, Impressionist color, and a dense pigment without medium, Sargent here makes astonishing use of perspective.

English private collection to the National Trust, in 1914 it too was seen at the Corcoran Gallery.

It seems incredible that Sargent's inexhaustible appetite for artistic experiment and permutations would not oblige him to attempt portraits in the Impressionist pallette. Logic implies that he did so, yet apart from his *Javanese Dancers,* and *Ellen Terry as Lady Macbeth,* all from 1889, which display the full impressionist armorey of limited pallette and synthetic accents, there are few notable pictures. Broadly speaking, his portraits were left a separate category for which older harmonies of umber and black remain in use. This did not prevent an influence from seeping through. From an early date, the clarity of flesh tones and brilliant tonality show Impressionist vision. Accents in his most conservative and darkest pictures often betray the presence of resonant combinations into which an Impressionist alizarin crimson is mixed. Resources available to the portraitist thus were essentially enlarged by additions from the Impressionist technique.

V

The two slightly disordered and expensively furnished London studios saw moments of unaccountable genius. An example is found in the portrait of *Mrs. William Crowninshield Endicott,* which can be traced through earlier stages and ultimately to the famous Quentin de la Tour pastel portrait of Madame du Pompadour. Elements of drapery from this French masterpiece are found early as the 1890 portrait of *Mrs. Augustus P. Loring.* But not until two years later, when painting *Miss Helen Dunham* in London, did Sargent essay a substantial revision of the La Tour into his own terms. Now the position of the head, neck, and tilted trunk, are carried over. More importantly, drapery masses are disposed according to its movements, flashes indicating the derivation of largest folds. Unaccountably the static original became intensely dynamic.

Henceforth in portraits of *Lady Agnew* (1893), which employed the hand of Bronzino's Venus, and *Mrs. Ian Hamilton* (1896) the concept of a woman in flowing skirt against a chair-back which fully occupies the picture's second plane was carried forth by felicitous variations. In 1898 the appearance of an unusually shy sitter caused revision of this successful formula. The same flowered chair was turned three-quarters right, permitting *Mrs. Ernest Franklin* to assume an askance position more suited to her personality. Her skirt unfortunately flowed out the lower right corner, losing what previously had been a central feature of these compositions. To counter-balance a bare center, Sargent moved in an Empire table with sphinx terminals on which he lay two books (an invention originating with Lawrence's Windsor portrait of Sir Walter Scott). The chair's insistent further contour was tactfully eliminated by an ill-defined cushion.

By 1901, when Mrs. Endicott appeared, the pattern for a distinctive and revealing portrait was ready. The sudden dignity it gained through dark harmonies demonstrates how fully the personality of Mrs. Endicott was a catalyst. This became more distinct when, four years later, repeating this remarkable and highly sophisticated pattern for a picture of the very fetching *Mrs. E. G. Raphael,* its effect became totally different.

Gravity that distinguishes *Mrs. Endicott* is carried over to the National Gallery's portrait of *Peter A. B. Widener,* done in the midst of that triumphant 1903 American tour. Its austere mood had become es-

National Gallery of Art
Gift of Louise Thoron Endicott, 1951

Mrs. William Crowninshield Endicott by John Singer Sargent. National Gallery of Art, Washington, D.C.

Unlike other great portrait painters who like Holbein and Van Dyck had a single mood, Sargent's flexibility is remarkable. Here he employs massive pigmentation and crisply painted eyes to convey the querulous and benign dignity of *Mrs. Willliam Crowninshield Endicott.* The mastery which permits him to define her arm by a single stroke drawn down its length is breathtaking.

tablished in the late 1890's for his three-quarter length male portraits. Partially it represented response to demand, but reflected also how the smart young painter of Paris was in middle age equating his art with qualities found in older works.

Nothing is present to distract from Widener's head, which, faced into shadows, and loaded with pigment, is a masterpiece of compact, knowing, and sympathetic execution. Even the two hands, which since Hals artists habitually enjoyed showing in full light, are deliberately cloaked in half-tone. Only here does one find the single reference to methods by which Sargent freed himself from restrictions. Extended against wood panelling by which he stands, Widener's further hand is the same previously used in London portraits of Lord Watson and Edward Wertheimer, and derives from Van Dyck's *Count Albert of Arenberg* at Apthorp House.

The silken swish of *Madame Gautreau's* skirt added grace to that most studied work. Loaded and tripping brushes brought sparkling joy to *Mrs. Henry White* and *Betty Wertheimer,* pictures conceived on principles diametrically opposed. The inimitable Gaelic grin of *Daniel J. Nolan,* which spread charm through the Corcoran Gallery from his death in 1921 to its sale in 1966, displays that same spontaneity. Done primarily of friends, these improvisations are among Sargent's most felicitous expressions. Painted in 1917, *Daniel J. Nolan* was the latest of Sargent's works in Washington.

After he restored an early picture for the artist, Nolan refused payment: "It's a tribute from one great artist to another!" Suggestion of a charcoal portrait was quashed by the thought it would not reach his descendants. "You see, my wife and I are both Irish, and in our household we sometimes have family discussions. Now, if she should throw her shoe at me, and it happened to go through your charcoal drawing it would be spoiled forever. But if it just dented an oil painting, I could always fix it up . . ." Nolan's widow had little else to sell after his untimely death.

Only occasionally did the same spirit of painterly bravado fill larger portraits. *Mrs. Joseph Chamberlain* is by no means an improvisation. Its head shows considerable stylization derived from English masters among whose works Sargent had then lived nearly twenty years. Reynolds, Romney, Gainsborough, Raeburn and Lawrence worked by established formulas, first creating a monochrome gray head which perfectly defined and modelled features. Over this preparation a transparent flesh tone was flowed, which, relieved of any necessity to provide definition so well established below, gave a glowing and uniform

National Gallery of Art
Widener Collection, 1942

Peter A. B. Widener by John Singer Sargent. National Gallery of Art, Washington, D.C.

Portraits like this one of *Peter A. B. Widener* can be considered Sargent's final mature statements. Profound in terms of skills and personal psychology, soberly considered, marked by fresh coloring and a massive pigmentation, it could not be confused with any other artist nor thought to belong to any other period.

National Gallery of Art
Gift of the Sitter, Mary Endicott Carnegie, 1957

Mrs. Joseph Chamberlain by John Singer Sargent. National Gallery of Art, Washington, D.C.

The remarkable self-assurance of *Mrs. Joseph Chamberlain* is made into a dazzling composition in white conveying Sargent's sensitivity to feminine charm. To enhance the effect of her posture, accessories and costume are treated with magical brevity.

color whose purity held abstract beauty. From it the strong accent of eyes sang forth, as did the flush of a maidenly cheek and lips' shining red.

To compete with this procedure while maintaining the integrity of his own direct technique required that Sargent limit shadows rigorously. His success was accentuated by the dark plume brushed into Mrs. Chamberlain's hair, like a whoop of joy at his accomplishment. To complete the canvas in this restricted gamma was a decision of courage, adequately rewarded by the sparkle and glow of a picture in which a mere half-dozen accenting strokes insure solid form.

Another phenomenon is disclosed by the picture of *Countess Szechenyi,* which for many years decorated her Washington home. The dark Vanderbilt features are conveyed, with more than a hint of feminine allure, in heavy-lidded eyes. An arbitrary decision to avoid outside compositional aid, which might have turned this beginning into something exciting, seems regrettable. The youthful Countess evidently stood as shown, hands clasped over the edge of some studio property which presumably was a polished stone mantel. (It appears also in the portrait of Lady Knaresborough.) This interested the artist more than a white frock, executed in dexterous but flaccid brushing from which his commonly masterly brio is absent. The sultry head might still have dominated a plain background but at last was overpowered by two balusters and a sketchy mass of foliage.

Already part of history, able to impose his values and mentality on patrons and public alike, Sargent's success with each portrait was dependent on a sympathetic nerve whose twinge was not always felt. The years that followed contain bewildering exercises in ambiguity. "In a breezy outdoor setting the three-quarter length figure of a smiling young lady is relieved against a background of sky and sea. White summer gown, décolleté, and fluttering draperies denote the action of a fresh wind . . . [Sargent] shows inimitable skill and dash in the rendering of the peculiar charm of young American woman-hood" commented *The Studio* when *Miss Mathilde Townsend* was first exhibited.

Overlooked was the perceptiveness which recorded languid eyes and a smile not wholly spontaneous. Such observation gives cautious depth to this flashing image without wholly explaining its air of intriguing bittersweet. An apparent spontaneity masks with what seriousness it was composed, or that Sargent consulted no less than four of the masters. Neck, shoulders, and bust, were taken from whatever source they were first found when employed for the 1894 portrait of Ada Rehan. So loosely grasping at a wind-blown shawl, the forward

Photograph from Grand Central Art Gallery, New York

Countess Szechenyi by John Singer Sargent. This 1906 portrait of Countess Szechenyi hung for many years in her Washington home.

The portrait's carefully conveyed head with its sultry look suggests accord between artist and subject. The flaccid drapery is a reminder that Sargent never employed assistants nor permitted anyone else to do menial work associated with his pictures. As Sargent grew older his fatigue sometimes was visible in his work.

National Gallery of Art
Gift of Mrs. Mathilde Townsend Welles, 1952

Miss Mathilde Townsend by John Singer Sargent. National Gallery of Art, Washington, D.C.

Sargent's portraits in the year 1907 exhibited an unparalleled inventiveness. He relaxed in this likeness of *Miss Mathilde Townsend* (Mrs. Sumner Welles) whom he painted like a splendid moth fluttering in the Edwardian twilight. (The composition was taken over by Sir William Orpen who made his fortune with it.)

arm and hand belong to the dead Christ in Titian's great *Entombment* (Louvre). Sir Peter Lely, whose sitters at one period are universally garbed in a similar crisply fluttering adornment attached between their shoulder blades, provided the drape. The further hand, and perhaps flashing passages for the drape too, came from Van Dyck's *Rinaldo and Armida* (Baltimore Museum) which in Sargent's time belonged to the Duke of Newcastle. The atmospheric sky is Lawrence's great Windsor portrait of *Archduke Charles of Austria,* or at least its disposition of lights and darks follows that pattern.

By enormous exertions Sargent created an image which recalls Scarlet O'Hara fluttering on the eve of catastrophe. A nimble, fiery performance, and possibly an unconscious projection of his own prewar world about to be dimned, it indicates the unique level of Sargent's accomplishment.

V

Psychologically and in his art Sargent presents problems of no ordinary kind. Merely to write about him requires an ability to dash back and forth between psychologic revelation and technical explanations, with abstruse references to forgotten procedures and the details of old masters. Three tragedies indicated in my *John Singer Sargent: A Biography* (W. W. Norton and Company, New York, 1955; Cresset Press, London, 1957; Kraus Reprint Company, New York, 1969) should not be minimized. The scandal that wrecked his youthful career in France haunted him throughout later triumphs. In middle life Yankee integrity precluded the practice of polite portraiture and after 1909, in a step without parallel, he abandoned this major branch of his art. Failure to marry a woman who would have made him happy created a loneliness and sense of personal isolation which embittered his final years.

Critically Sargent has been a Caesar judged by Walter Mitty standards. Called a pictorial journalist his special skills included selecting distinguished shapes from the past and forming bold new patterns of beauty. So convincing was he that for thirty-five years after his death the full nature of his art never was suspected. His career therefore is the greatest possible evidence that in art nothing is irreconcilable. Simultaneously he was an Impressionist and a muralist, a classic designer and a portraitist remarkable for aggressive credibility. And this last, the distinctive mark of a Sargent picture, is entirely the product of his mind. For much that he painted with such smart brilliance did not exist at all.

Awareness brings a new perspective. Compositions are inclined to reappear every few years so well dusted off, refurbished, and crisp in renewed visual impact, they lose nothing. With knowledge of his methods certain hands appear less well selected or cease to function in their compositions. Draperies, especially when they have been abbreviated, also become suspect. And this is only right, for in most instances (and contrary to general belief) sittings appear to have been devoted to heads and a general plotting of the figure. A limited assortment of hands and arms derived from improbable sources were then attached. Unfinished large portraits of *Madame Belleroche* (1884) and *Thomas Francis Bayard* (1897) remain at this stage before their introduction.

Anything resembling decorative treatment sent him searching through the masters. Annual excursions to the continent doubtless masked a persistent effort to replenish his small stock of pictorially effective patterns. Yet he seems never to have commented on the means by which his greatest works were composed. The name Bronzino seems never to have occurred in his conversation and his letters are barren of it. The door to one whole side of his genius thus was held firmly closed. Such surliness on the part of an aloof bachelor working long hours locked in his studios suggests an artistic personality akin to that of Reynolds, who also was at pains to hide his methods. But his special skills culling the past, the many forays into varied subjects, decorations, and new landscape methods, all imbued with personal gusto and astonishing vigor, show a more profound relationship to Rubens.

If there is a larger tragedy it is that a journeyman reputation for absolute credibility obscures the exalted nature of Sargent's creativity. True critical estimates require a scholarship equivalent to his own.

THE WORKS OF JOHN SINGER SARGENT IN WASHINGTON AND AREA

I. Drawings

100 drawings, mostly charcoal and related to the later murals (after 1912). Corcoran Gallery.

II. Sculpture

Turkey. Bronze. Corcoran Gallery.

III. Watercolors

Piazza, Venice (Two figures before the Church of the Frari; 1882) signed. Corcoran Gallery.

Gondola on Canal. Corcoran Gallery.

Mountain Brook. Capricorn Gallery, Bethesda.

IV. Portraits

Chamberlain, Mrs. Joseph (Mrs. W. Hartley Carnegie). 1902, London; 45 × 32 inches. Signed and dated. National Gallery.

Endicott, Mrs. William C. 1901, London; 64½ × 45⅛. Signed and dated. National Gallery.

Gosford, Mildred Countess of. 1908, London; 39½ × 29½. Signed and dated. The Hon. Patrick Acheson, Waterford, Virginia.

Guest, Mrs. Frederick. 1906, London; 58 × 38. Signed. Raymond R. Guest, Powhattan.

Iselin, Mrs. Adrian. 1888, New York; 60½ × 36½. Signed and dated. National Gallery.

Jay, Peter Augustus (as a child). 1880, Paris; 18 × 14¾. Signed and dated. Mrs. Peter A. Jay.

Lodge, Senator Henry Cabot. 1890, Nahant; 50 × 34. Signed. National Portrait Gallery.

Nolan, Daniel J. 1917, Boston; 26 × 20. Inscribed: To my friend Dan Nolan John S. Sargent. Sold by Corcoran Gallery (1966).

Pailleron, Madame Edouard. 1879, Savoy; 82 × 39½. Inscribed: John S. Sargent Roujoux 1879. Corcoran Gallery.

Reed, Thomas Brackett. 1891, Paris; 32 × 26 (cut down from full-length) Speaker's Lobby, Capitol Building.

Roosevelt, Mrs. R. B., Jr. 1890, New York; 64½ × 37½. Signed and dated. National Gallery.

Roosevelt, Theodore. 1903, The White House; 58 × 40. Signed and dated. The White House.

Szechenyi, Countess. 1906, London; 58 × 38. Signed and dated. Miss Cornelia C. Roberts.

Townsend, Beatrice. 1882, Paris; 32 × 23. Inscribed: to my friend Mr. Townsend John S. Sargent. Paul Mellon Collection.

Townsend, Miss Mathilde (Mrs. Sumner Welles). 1907, London; 57 × 36. Signed and dated. National Gallery.

Vallé, Miss Isabel. 1882, Paris; (three-quarter length). Signed and dated. Mrs. Robert Brookings.

Vallé, Mrs. Jules. 1882, Paris; 20 × 16. Signed and dated. Mrs. Robert Brookings.

Wertheimer, Miss Betty (Mrs. Euston Salaman). 1906, London; 48 × 37. Signed. National Collection of Fine Arts, Smithsonian Institution.

White, Mrs. Henry. 1883, Paris; 87 × 55. Signed and dated. Corcoran Gallery.

Widener, Peter A. B. 1903, Elkins Park; 58 × 38. National Gallery.

V. Works in Oil Other Than Portraits

1877 *Study for Carolus-Duran's 'Triumph of Marie de Medici'*, 32 × 25¾ inches, Roanoke College, Salem, Virginia.

1878 *The Oyster Gatherers of Cancale,* 31 × 48½. Inscribed: John S. Sargent Paris 1878. Corcoran Gallery.

Head of A Capri Girl, 18 × 14. Mrs. Martin Flett.

1882 *Street in Venice,* 17½ × 21, wood. Signed. National Gallery.

Lady with a Fan, 50 × 100. Signed and dated. The Hon. Laurence Curtis.

1908 *The Mosquito Net* (A Siesta), 22 × 28. The White House.

The Sketchers, 22 × 28. Virginia Museum of Fine Arts, Richmond.

1909 *Simplon Pass,* 28 × 36½, signed. Corcoran Gallery.

Landscape with Goats, 22 × 28, signed. Freer Gallery.

1910 *Breakfast in The Loggia,* 20¼ × 28, signed. Freer Gallery.

1911 *Nonchaloire,* 22 × 28, signed and dated. National Gallery.

1912 *Weavers,* 22 × 28, signed. Freer Gallery.

1914 *A Tyrolese Crucifix,* 36 × 28, signed, misdated 1915. Sold by Corcoran Gallery to Hirschl & Adler, New York.

George Biddle's Contribution to Federal Art

MARCIA M. MATHEWS

In 1944 American artists paid their President an unprecedented tribute—they gave an art exhibition in his honor. It was held at the Vanderbilt Gallery in New York and according to Moses Soyer was a huge, comprehensive affair the keynote of which was taken from Roosevelt's own words: "Only when men are free can the arts flourish and the civilization of national culture reach full flower."

In the tribute might well have been included one of the many exhibitors in the show, George Biddle, for it was he who had suggested to Roosevelt the idea of a government-sponsored art program. Roosevelt was not noted as a patron of art, especially modern art; the only art he thoroughly enjoyed was marine painting, because he loved ships and the sea. But he had a feeling for the underman and for social reform and the letter George Biddle wrote him on May 9, 1933,[1] suggesting that a school of mural painting might be used to improve the quality of American life, appealed to him.

"The artists of America," wrote Biddle, "are conscious as they have never been of the social revolution that our country and civilization are going through; and they would be eager to express these ideals in permanent art form if they were given the government's cooperation. They would be contributing to and expressing in living monuments the social ideals you are struggling to express."

Two weeks later George Biddle wrote in his diary: "Received a letter from Roosevelt in which he tells me he is enthusiastic over my idea of helping American mural painting and wants me someday to see Assistant Secretary of the Treasury Robert who has charge of reconstruction work. Tremendously elated over the idea. It looks at last as if something may come of it." [2]

---

[1] The communications between George Biddle and Franklin D. Roosevelt that are quoted from in this article are from the Franklin D. Roosevelt Papers, Franklin D. Roosevelt Library, Hyde Park, New York.

[2] Biddle's diaries, from which excerpts are quoted, are with the Biddle Papers, Manuscript Division, Library of Congress.

Neither he nor Roosevelt could have foreseen the vast national art program his idea would develop into or its impact on the American cultural scene. In less than four years the United States Treasury would have spent more money on art than all previous administrations thrown together.

The idea of government-sponsored art was not new. The Treasury had been established as a patron of art under George Washington when Alexander Hamilton was given charge of Federal architecture and the decoration of public buildings. But through the years the Treasury's role had been perfunctory and the various "Commissions" created from time to time to advise and recommend on Federal art were given little scope to promote new ideas. The place of art in the minds of most government officials was defined in the 1920's by President Calvin Coolidge's answer to the painter, Maurice Sterne, when Sterne commented that the United States was the only civilized country in the world that had no Minister of Fine Arts. "We have a Minister of Finance," Coolidge tersely replied, "Mr. Mellon." In 1933 the National Commission of Fine Arts, that had been appointed by Theodore Roosevelt in 1910, was considered by all but the most conservative artists as something of a troglodyte.

Fortunately it was George Biddle and not another artist of equally liberal ideas who wrote to President Roosevelt. They had known each other at Groton and later at Harvard and while not close friends —Franklin was three years older than George—theirs had been a pleasant relationship. George Biddle recalled it in a taped interview in 1964:[3]

> I'd known him very slightly, but probably enough so he remembered me. We both met at school; he was just leaving school and I was just coming there. We used to go to the infirmary together to get milk during the eleven o'clock recess in the morning. I was very small for my age and needed to put on weight. He told me much later that he had been sick and the doctors wanted to build him up. So we would chat a bit together, and I retained the memory of an older, friendly boy. He was Editor of the Harvard *Crimson* and once came back to talk about it to the editors of the school paper, of which I was one. Then I rowed on the school crew and once, back at school, he rowed on the graduate crew against us. And I met him once again at his mother's house, hobbling

[3] This comment by George Biddle, and all subsequent ones unless noted otherwise, are taken from typescripts made from a taped interview with the artist by Harlan Phillips, of the Archives of American Art, in 1964. The typescripts, located in the Archives of American Art in Washington, D.C., are an invaluable source of information not only for George Biddle but many aspects of Twentieth Century art.

down the stairs, just after his illness. So we had this relation, shared these memories of an older and a younger school boy.

There was another reason for Roosevelt's affirmative answer. George Biddle was one of the few members of his own social class he felt he could trust.

Roosevelt's intuition was right. George not only retained something of his early hero-worship of Franklin but knew what it meant to oppose one's own world of established values. He had suffered for five years at Groton and six more at Harvard trying to reconcile his creative self with his environment and had succeeded only after two physical breakdowns and his renunciation of a career in law for art.

Besides, he approved of Roosevelt's social reforms. He had a strong sense of moral justice, possibly inherited from his grandfather George Washington Biddle, one of the country's foremost lawyers, who had named George's father Algernon Sidney after the Englishman who, two years before the first Biddle had come to America in 1683, was convicted of treason and beheaded. Sidney had been refused a copy of his indictment, was denied counsel, and tried before a packed jury on the testimoney of a perjured informer of the Crown. By naming his second son after the convicted man, George Washington Biddle had evidently hoped in some way to balance the scales of justice.

Algernon Sidney Biddle, raised in the cultured Philadelphia of the Nineteenth Century, was a classical scholar as well as a highly successful lawyer but was subject to black moods of depression which may indicate that, like his son George later on, he had inner conflicts. He died when his four sons were still children, but George says: "My mother tells me my father at one time had thought of being a painter, wanted to be a painter, or sketched or something of that sort. And as a young child, when I from time to time had nervous breakdowns, or nervous illnesses, she encouraged me in painting."

George's real interest in art did not begin until much later—after his first year at Harvard Law School, when he was twenty-two years old and recuperating from one of his periodic illnesses. That year he spent six months on a cattle ranch, forty miles from the Rio Grande, where he worked for "cowboy wages." "I rode through the mesquite and at night, in the lea of the chuck wagon, sat round among the 'vaqueros,' listening to their 'corridos,' sucking and drinking in to my marrow this so different life from what I had experienced." [4]

Traveling through the wild beauty of the Mexican Sierras and

[4] From an article by George Biddle in the *American Magazine of Art,* August, 1929 (Vol. XX), p. 432.

Photograph by Peter A. Juley & Son
Courtesy of Michael Biddle

Winter on the Hudson by George Biddle. 1927. Oil. 36 × 36.

One of Biddle's "pleasant" pictures. "I don't like your unpleasant pictures, George, I like your pleasant ones," commented a friend who saw one of his water-colors at the Weyhe Gallery in New York in 1928.

living close to nature he learned more about life than Groton or Harvard could possibly teach—primarily, that conformity, method and long hours of study do not measure a man's mental capacity. For the first time a legal career began to appear drab and colorless and his mind turned seriously to art. Life, he believed, was the essence of art, not Sargent's art as seen on the walls of Widener Library, a pitiful, artificial reflection of life, but art that said something to people.

George Biddle was just beginning to catch his stride, to sustain himself on that "sturdy plane of being," as his brother Francis put it, which enabled him to achieve more of living and drew to him more devoted friends than is usual with men.

At the end of the year he returned to Harvard and completed his studies at the Law School, then passed his Pennsylvania Bar exams and, on September 11, 1911, sailed for Paris, putting all thoughts of a legal career behind him.

Paris was an exciting place for an artist, with all of the new art movements following briskly on the heels of one another—cubism, expressionism, futurism, vorticism, and others. George lived the artist's life of the Left Bank, traveled through Europe, made friends of artists, and painted. He studied at Julien's, but learned more from the American expatriate artist Carl Frieseke, who opened his eyes to the colorful world of the Impressionists, and from Mary Cassatt, a fellow Philadelphian, who showed him the exquisite meaning of line. The more he saw of the linear compositions of Cassatt and Degas the more he perceived line as the skeleton, the "rock-bottom basis" of all the visual arts. In 1919 he wrote in his diary: "One can learn to paint with a pencil; to produce the effect of atmosphere, matter and color . . . The great artists of the past century—Degas, Millet, Delacroix, Mary Cassatt all drew passionately."

With the outbreak of World War I, which temporarily shattered the art world, Biddle spent a winter in Rome before returning home to enlist in the First Reserve Officers training camp at Fort Niagara. He was married to Anne Coleman before going overseas, then for a year and a half was stationed with the United States Intelligence in France. But he saw enough of war to be repelled by its brutality. "War is a geat moral shock," he wrote in his diary on January 17, 1919. "It can only disorganize the creative impulse. . . ."

At the end of the war, and his brief marriage, he followed Gauguin's example and sailed for the South Seas—a step his friend Marsden Hartley said a few years later it would take him a long time to live down, just as it would the name Biddle. He remained in the Pacific for two years, living a solitary life in a remote village on Tahiti, readjusting his life, experimenting with media, and seeking an idiom of his own.

In 1921 he returned to the United States and for a year worked in New York in close touch with a group of talented, younger artists, some of whom—Marguerite and William Zorach, Eli Naderman and Gaston Lachaise—became warm and lasting friends. He continued working in various media, almost forsaking painting, and had

Corcoran Galley of Art, Washington, D. C.

At Ticino's by George Biddle. An oil painted in 1933, At Ticino's was acquired by the Corcoran Gallery of Art, Washington, D. C., in 1969.

Ticino's was a small restaurant run by Rosocco Ticino in Greenwich Village and was a popular meeting place for George Biddle and his artist friends during the depression. Morris Kantor and his wife and the artist Martha Ryder figure in the painting.

several shows in New York that were highly successful. But success came too easily and he returned to Paris. In December 1923 an exhibition of his Tahitian sculpture and decorations was held at the Gallerie Barbazanges and received good reviews.

Paris was again an "International Who's Who in Art," with Americans prominent in the lists—Adolphe Borie, Leo Stein, Marsden Hartley, Pop Harte, John Storrs, and others. Curiously, it was in this creative atmosphere, charged with the excitement of the "Ecole de Paris," that Biddle began to dislike French art. "It dawned on me at the end of three years that my natural predilection for something different was simply that I was an American." But it was several years yet before he conceived of a new, vital school of American painting based on American history and American ideals.

In 1925 he married again and for three years lived with his wife,

Jane Belo, in France, Cuba, Haiti, Puerto Rico and, for a year, at Croton-on-Hudson, New York. The marriage lasted happily until 1928, a year that was a turning point in his life, a year he made a prolonged visit to Mexico City.

Mexico had been a mecca for artists since the early 1920's when Diego Rivera, José Orozco and lesser Mexican artists—Montenegro, Pacheco, Atl and Siqueiros, forced into exile during the revolution for their radical ideas, had returned under the liberal leadership of President Alvaro Obregon to paint on the walls of public buildings themes from Mexican and Indian culture and dedicated to the philosophical idealogy of the revolution.

The art of these great muralists, strong in line design and passionate in expression, met a responsive chord in George Biddle. He spent six months with Rivera, talking with him, watching him paint his frescoes in the old *fresco buono* of the Italian Renaissance—the medium Michelangelo called "the work of men" and which had been practically forgotten until it was revived in Mexico. He compared the art of Rivera and Orozco with the wall paintings of Tarbell, Sargent, Blashfield, even Lafarge at his best, and concluded the United States had never had a real muralist. He thought of a mural as an entirely different art from painting. "It isn't just a bigger painting. In the first place, it has to embody an idea. And that's why a real mural, an important mural, can never be private. It's got to be for some wall which is the symbol of some public function."

The embodiment of the "social idea" in the art of the Mexican muralists was at variance with the Academic ideal of poetic beauty long popular in the United States and with Roger Fry's more recent theory of "significant form." But George Biddle had never liked Academic art or significant form. To him art was significant only as it was "an explosive, sub-conscious, vision of life," and life was not pretty; he had seen enough of it to know it was often unpleasant, ugly and, at times, deeply tragic.

His own art expressed this duality. A friend who saw one of his water-colors at the Weyhe Gallery in New York in 1928 commented: "I don't like your unpleasant pictures, George, I like your pleasant ones." It was a comment he heard repeatedly throughout his life. Biddle thought it a fair enough criticism "but I think of our civilization as a very complicated one, full of horror and full of beauty."

He left Mexico with the feeling that he had found his idiom. Before exploring it further, however, he wanted to establish roots in his own country. In the spring of 1929 he bought some land at Croton-on-Hudson, an area that he loved, and began building a home. He

Corcoran Galley of Art, Washington, D. C.

Lithographed by George Biddle. Spain: In Memoriam. Mussolini, Hitler: "Let her bleed a while longer."

wanted a house that was firmly constructed, with walls fifteen inches thick, and as few windows as possible, all facing south—a house that would answer his description of what a house should be: "a symbol of the withdrawing of the individual from the outer world into the privacy of his own thoughts and emotions."

This house, that he called "Ashacres" and renamed "Bittersweet" in 1950, was to be his home for the rest of his life. However far and often he traveled he always came back to it happily, feeling in its strong foundations and wooded acres the security and privacy he needed.

A few weeks after the house was completed he met a talented young Belgian-American sculptor, Hélène Sardeau, who was, he later wrote in his diary, "the sweetest thing that ever came into my life." They were married in April 1931 and the marriage, a most happy one, was lasting. Their only child, Michael, was born three years later.

Now that Biddle had a home and a wife to whom he was devoted, with his usual restlessness he felt a need to get back to Europe. For fifteen months he and Hélène lived in Ischia, Rome and a village on the edge of Abruzzi, where he worked furiously on oils, drawings, lithographs and ceramics. He did a fresco panel for the first exhibition of living American artists held at the Museum of Modern Art in New York, and was delighted when it was more highly praised by the critics than the rest of the show. He was even more delighted when Moises Saenz invited him to paint a fresco in Mexico City, and was shattered when the offer fell through.

While Biddle was abroad the shadow of Hitler grew darker, United States Steel spiralled downward, and the Democratic Convention took place in Chicago. In his diary he wrote: "Bill Bullitt writes from the Berkshires. He's been seeing something of Franklin this summer and thinks he's a swell guy."

By the time the Biddles returned home in the fall of 1932 the United States was deep in the depression. George was moved by the suffering he saw and by the plight of many of his artist friends, but, even so, the depression was to him less ominous than was Fascism. His fear, shared by many thoughtful Americans, was that the depression would act as an agent for the repression of freedom as it had in Germany.

Nevertheless, through the gloom he saw a hopeful sign—museum attendance in the United States was at an all-time high. Having no money for anything else, great numbers of Americans were for the first time looking at art. The moment seemed to Biddle ripe for the establishment of a school of mural painting, modelled on that of Mexico, which would have meaning and purpose. With the inauguration of Roosevelt as President his hopes soared. The National Commission of Fine Arts, committed to the pseudo-classical art of the Eighteenth Century, he knew would not be receptive to his plan but Franklin, he believed, would listen.

Before writing him, though, he discussed his idea with Bruce Bliven, Susan LaFollette, Stark Young, Walter Lippmann and other liberals whose views he valued and who, he hoped, would give his project a boost. They were enthusiastic.

Biddle talked to Henry Varnum Poor, a Croton neighbor and fellow artist, whose views on art and whose integrity he trusted. They agreed on artists for the project—Maurice Sterne, Boardman Robinson, Thomas Benton, Reginald Marsh, Edward Laning, John Steuart Curry and, possibly, Grant Wood. They thought the group should eventually be self-selective but wanted to start with artists who shared similar views on modern art and who had the same social concerns. Money, Biddle insisted, would become a "grab swill" unless the artists worked for "plumbers' wages" as the Mexican muralists did. Once

Photograph from the author

Arab Prisoners Burying Their Dead by George Biddle. 1944. Oil. 16 × 20.

This painting, made from one of his war drawings, expresses Biddle's feeling that war had the romance and physical beauty "of an automobile accident, of a slaughter-house, of an earthquake, of a vessel pounding on a reef."

the project was effectively working he expected it to provide a groundswell for similar projects in other parts of the country.

In June, Biddle went to Washington to talk to Assistant Secretary of the Treasury Lawrence Wood Robert, Jr. and learned that Congress had the money to decorate the new Justice Department and Post Office buildings but was reluctant to spend it on a "luxury" like art. To win support for his idea Biddle wrote up his proposal, called "A Revival of Mural Painting," and sent copies to Robert, Secretaries Frances Perkins and Harold Ickes, Assistant Secretary of Agriculture Rexford G. Tugwell, Mrs. Franklin Roosevelt and a few others. In summary, he stated three things were needed to give impetus to a mural school:

1. A few social-minded, creative artists of the first rank, representing the modern movement, and experienced in mural painting.

2. The assignment to them by the government of public wall space on which to express the social ideals of the government and the people.

3. The understanding that in the personal expression and technical execution, the artist be given as complete freedom as possible.

Mrs. Roosevelt sent her copy of the proposal to Marguerite LeHand, the President's personal secretary, with a memo: "Please ask President to whom this should be referred. It is not new—a little like the old Italian idea and has possibilities, I think."

Roosevelt forwarded the proposal to the Commission of Fine Arts, whose duty it was to advise on questions of art when asked to by the President or any committee of either House of Congress. Its report was unfavorable. The artists proposed by Biddle, in the Commission's estimation, were "painters of easel pictures of incidental nature" and represented a style of art unharmonious with established art traditions. The shortcomings of each artist were enumerated and the project condemned as a whole.

Roosevelt sent the report on to Biddle with a personal note:

> Dear George,
>
> The enclosed from the Fine Arts Commission speaks for itself. It does not sound very encouraging about mural painting.
>
> Sincerely yours,
>
> Franklin

Biddle thought he detected in the President's words a note of caution but permission to go ahead. Tactfully, he wrote the Commission a letter, giving proof that the artists were highly respected members of their profession and were experienced muralists. He also went to see Eugene F. Savage, the one painter-member of the Commission, and Savage conceded that his criticism had been based on a misunderstanding of the artists' goal.

Assistant Secretary Robert was impressed with Biddle's plan, the more so as he knew it had the President's backing. On August 15, 1933, George wrote in his diary: "A very reassuring letter from Robert who will try to shove our idea through, notwithstanding the Commission. Happy for the first time in a fortnight."

Biddle won the support of Charles Borie, the architect of the new Justice Department building, who, like himself, came from an old Philadelphia family, and whose brother Adolphe had known George in Paris. Borie had designed his building with large wall spaces and was delighted at the thought of getting murals for them.

His greatest help, though, came from Edward Bruce, an expert on monetary policy who had come to the Treasury Department in 1932

Courtesy of Tamas Breuer

George Biddle and Amanda, 1969. Photograph by Tamas Breuer.

and was a good friend of Assistant Secretary Robert. Bruce was a man of unusual and varied talents who, according to Biddle, "loved Chinese painting better than anything in life" and was a pretty good artist. But Bruce's chief talent was as an organizer and promoter. When he learned from Robert of the possibility of getting government patronage for a national art program he was elated and in October 1933 began holding meetings in his Washington home to discuss ways and means of getting the project going. With the strong backing of such influential people as Mrs. Roosevelt, Justice Harlan Fiske Stone, Rexford G. Tugwell, and Mrs. Juliana Force of the Whitney Museum of American Art, Robert appointed a committee of art experts to act as sponsors of the project. When the Treasury refused to release funds, Bruce and Biddle together went to see Public Works Administrator Harold Ickes and Ickes agreed that money might be given to art from the $400,000,000 he had transferred from the Public Works Administration to the Relief Administration of Harry Hopkins. Hopkins saw no more reason to deny relief money to artists than to plumbers and he allocated $1,039,000 to the project.

Mural art was now "in"—but not in the form Biddle had envisaged. His original idea to get a fine school of mural painting, beginning with a group of hand-picked artists, had turned into a much broader program—or programs, since ultimately there were four—on a very different basis. This was to help all needy artists during the depression.

George Biddle was not averse to the change of direction nor was he opposed to Bruce as coordinator of the project, although he would have handled some aspects of the program differently had he been in charge. His main objective had been realized—to see mural painting in public buildings which would express the democratic ideals of America in terms of contemporary art and subsidized with government money.

The first national art relief program, the Public Works of Art Project, was established in December 1933, under the supervision of the Procurement Division of the Treasury Department, with Edward Bruce as head of the Advisory Committee on Fine Arts. It had a short life, lasting only until June 1934, when the Civil Works Administration, which funded it, came to an end.

In October 1934 a new program was initiated, called the Section of Painting and Sculpture—later, the Section of Fine Arts—also under the jurisdiction of the Treasury and with Bruce again in charge. This program was closer in spirit to Biddle's original idea, for its primary aim was not to offer financial relief to artists but to obtain the best talent available through anonymous competition. Biddle did not like the idea of competition which, in his estimation, favored mediocrity over genuine talent, but his idea of a self-selective group was considered undemocratic by members of the Section.

The two projects represented opposing views. One saw need as the primary consideration; the other, quality of art. The conflict between the two views was partially, though inadequately, resolved in 1935 by the creation of two additional art programs: the Treasury Relief Program, 1935–1939, and a much broader project that included music, drama and writing, as well as art, which operated until 1943 under the Works Progress Administration.

It was the Section of Painting and Sculpture, with its emphasis on talent, that enabled George Biddle to complete part of the mural work he had planned for the Justice Department. For the two most important new buildings in Washington—the Justice Department and the new Post Office—the announced method of selecting artists by anonymous competition was by-passed. Instead a committee of museum directors and artists, *hors concours,* was asked to submit names of painters and sculptors who, in their opinion, were best qualified for the work. The artists were then asked to submit sketches of their proposed murals for consideration by the Section staff and, out of courtesy, by the Commission of Fine Arts. Of eleven painters chosen by the Committee to decorate the Justice Department building eight were from Biddle's original list: George Biddle, Henry Varnum Poor, Maurice Sterne, Reginald Marsh, John Steuart Curry, Boardman Robinson and Thomas Hart Benton. The others were Leon Kroll, Eugene Savage and Rockwell Kent.

Biddle's sketches were the first ones submitted to the Section, probably because, having previously worked on thematic subject-matter for the entire building, he knew exactly what he wanted to do. His mural, designed for the fifth floor stairwell just outside the Law Library, consisted of five panels in which he contrasted the beauty and order of a society controlled by justice with the misery and ugliness of one where injustice prevails. The panel for each side of the stairwell depicted scenes of ghetto and tenement life in which the pale, pinched faces of the subjects indicate the exploitation of human beings by industry. Under the left panel he placed a quotation from Oliver Wendell Holmes's *Common Law:* "The life of the law has not been logic, it has been experience." Under the right panel, he placed a quotation from Louis D. Brandeis's opinion in *Burns Baking Company* v. *Bryan:* "If we would guide by the light of reason we must let our minds be bold."

For the wide wall in the stairwell he composed three panels: a large central panel represented a happy, healthy, well-clad farming family seated around a dining-table, well supplied with food; on each side were scenes of farmers working at congenial chores. Beneath the panels he underscored his theme with the words: "The sweat-shop and tenement ordered with justice of tomorrow."

Using the Italian Renaissance custom of including self-portraits or those of friends or relatives in their frescoes, Biddle used his brother Francis, later to be Attorney General, as the model for the central figure at the table, and Edward Rowan, Assistant Director of the Section, for that of the man hanging up his coat.

The Section staff accepted the sketches but with some reluctance. They feared public reaction to Biddle's caustic social comment as well as his style of modified realism. The Commission of Fine Arts was less open-minded. They turned the sketches down unequivocally on the grounds that they were crudely and grotesquely drawn, gaudy in color and, above all, "intrinsically un-American and ill-adopted to express American ideas and ideals."

The matter hung fire for several months. Finally, on March 16, 1934, Biddle wrote in his diary: "At last I can count on success. And we must have a united front and make it a success. Liberal art in America can't afford to have this first effort a failure." It is to the Section's credit that in spite of the Commission's veto, and their own reluctance, they advised Biddle to proceed with his work.

Biddle spent two years on the mural—one year at Croton working on the cartoons and another in Washington on the frescoes themselves. He was never happier than in the excution of this work. Sometimes he started work before dawn and continued on until evening. "I gathered myself in a concentration of purpose . . . I experienced a feeling of elation, of mastery of my medium of faith in the outcome of the two years preparation and work." [5]

Looking at his mural today one is impressed with its colors, subdued rather than "gaudy," and with its social relevance. Olin Dows, one of Biddle's least strong supporters on the Section in 1934, recently wrote: "After revisiting the Washington murals this winter I feel that both our own and the Commission's lack of enthusiasm in Biddle's case has not been justified by time. His mural stands up very well indeed; it is personal, has character in its color and design, and is interesting in subject. It looks better to me now than many paintings I preferred thirty years ago."

With the completion of his mural Biddle's connection with the Federal Art Program came to an end. He left Washington in the fall of 1936, and from then on, until the attack on Pearl Harbor and the entry of the United States in World War II in 1941, he says: "I saw nothing of what was going on in the mural picture in Washington. I'd hear about it, but no personal contact."

For two years after leaving Washington Biddle and his family lived in Colorado Springs, then moved to California. During this time he wrote his autobiography, *An Artist's Story,* which has become, as Frank Jewett Mather predicted on its publication in 1939, an increasingly valuable document on the generation that bridged the First World War.

Biddle sent Roosevelt a copy of the book and the President read it with interest, particularly the part that dealt with the years at Groton. He wrote Biddle: "I like the book—it is beside my bed and I have read the first hundred pages. It is a good thing for Groton and the world that you wrote that chapter."

Roosevelt and Biddle met infrequently but their limited corre-

[5] George Biddle, *An American Artist's Story* (Boston: Little Brown and Co., 1939), p. 287.

National Archives

Department of Justice Fresco by George Biddle. Panel at right end of stairwell.

Biddle believed a public mural should express the meaning of a building just as a spire describes the meaning of a church. The subject matter for his mural, "Society Freed Through Justice," was suggested to him by Judge Harold M. Stephens, then Associate Justice of the United States Court of Appeals for the District of Columbia.

National Archives

Detail from the preceding.

Many of the faces in Biddle's mural were portraits of friends, sometimes painted with a kind of puckish humor. The young man with glasses is not identified.

National Archives

Department of Justice Fresco by George Biddle. Panel at left end of stairwell.

Sweatshop and tenement scenes done in a realistic manner were new to American mural art, long dominated by academic ideals. But Biddle believed his realistic treatment of contemporary themes had its anchor in American tradition.

National Archives

Detail from the preceding.

Biddle, like F. D. R., had an intuitive feeling for the victims of injustice, though unlike the Mexican muralists he rejected the idea of art for political propaganda.

National Archives

Department of Justice Fresco by George Biddle. Center panel, main wall of stairwell.

The model for the central figure of this panel was the artist's brother, Francis Biddle (1886–1968), then Chairman of the National Labor Relations Board and later Attorney General. The model for the man hanging up the coat was Edward Rowan, Assistant Director of the Section of Fine Arts of the Treasury Department.

National Archives

Detail from the preceding.

This charming study of a woman and child is probably of the artist's wife, Hélène Sardeau, and their son, Michael John.

National Archives

Department of Justice Fresco by George Biddle. Right panel, main wall of stairwell.

Biddle was impressed early in his career by the art of Mary Cassatt. Her influence is apparent in the simplicity and amplitude of his modeling.

National Archives

Detail from the preceding.

Biddle took liberties with perspective and proportion, as did the early Italians, when he thought it would enhance his compositional effect.

National Archives

Department of Justice Fresco by George Biddle. Left panel, main wall of stairwell.

"All art is a re-statement, or re-creation, or criticism... conforming to a certain rhythm or design."

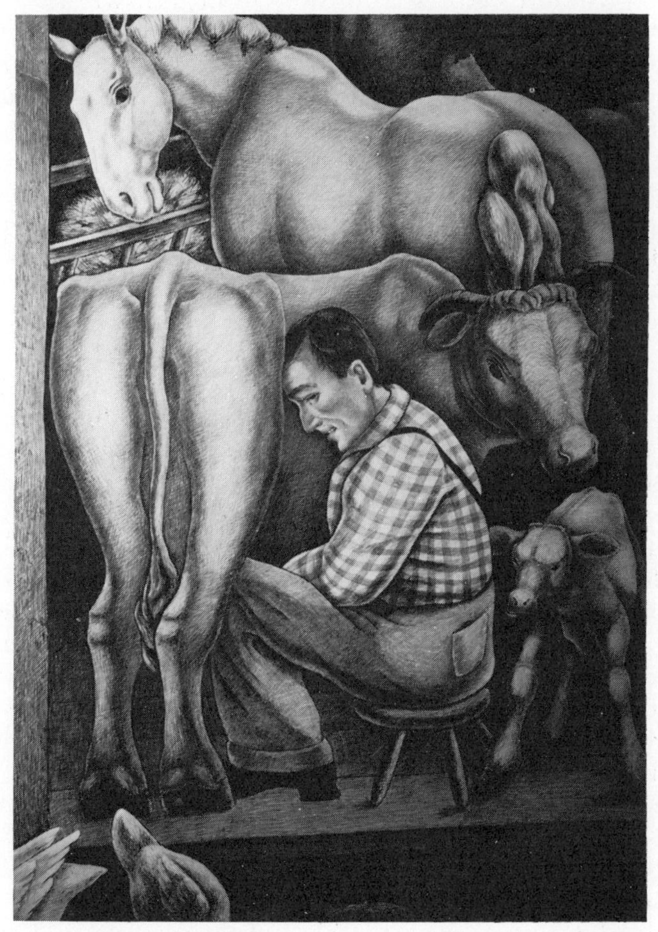

National Archives

Detail from the preceding.

Biddle believed, as did Michelangelo, that drawing is the basis of painting. His reliance on line in the creation of form is apparent in this detail.

spondance, beginning in 1933, reveals a warm feeling of friendship. Biddle says: "I never wrote him a letter—I wrote him some eight or ten in all—without getting an answer from him within a week or two . . . It showed two things—first of all, the utter loneliness that we've heard about so much from anybody in that position. And, secondly, the bitterness he felt about his own class and the comfort he got from anyone in that class, no matter how little he knew of him, whom he felt was loyal."

Perhaps their strongest bond was their mutual hatred of Fascism. On the occasion of Roosevelt's Navy Day radio speech of October 27, 1941, Biddle wired him from California: "Your splendid talk on Nazi arms and our defense policy is the most important American declaration of our generation."

It was the war that brought Biddle back to Washington and involved him in another Federal art program. He returned in 1943 after spending a year in Brazil working jointly with his wife on a mural for the National Library at Rio de Janeiro.

In 1943 Biddle was fifty-eight years old, too old for combat duty. But it went against his grain to be a passive spectator in a war he believed was just and necessary and he was happy when in January 1943 he learned from Lieutenant General Brehon B. Somervell of a request by Major-General Frederick H. Osborne, of the Special Services Division, to form a "select group of artists to be dispatched to active theaters to paint war scenes." A few months later Biddle was Chairman of the War Department's Advisory Committee that selected twenty-three artists to report the war and, not surprisingly, a few months later was himself among those on their way to Tunisia. *Newsweek* magazine dubbed him "the Ernie Pyle of the Brush." A comment made to him by a young officer in Tunisia, "I don't rightly see how the Army can let you old men, who served in the last war, go over to Sicily," proved a poor estimate of George Biddle.

He arrived in time to report the last of the fighting in Tunisia but had not yet reached Sicily when an economy-minded Congress killed the $125,000 art program. Fortunately, *Life* magazine took it over and for the next few months, during some of the most heated fighting of the Italian campaign, Biddle was in the thick of the conflict. His drawings, and the paintings he later made from his drawings, are some of his "unpleasant pictures," but they are also some of the most individual and moving records made of the war. "I wanted the human faces, the suffering, the death," he wrote, "and I wanted all the little incongruities which made war seem like *Alice in Wonderland* played in a madhouse."

His wife Hélène, at home in Croton with their young son, knew how much it meant to George to be associated with the army that was fighting for what he believed in, and she was patient and encouraging. In a letter on November 4, 1943, she wrote: "Knickerbocker in his column described your crossing the Volturno river at 3 a.m.—wading and swimming—with the moonlight above and adds that 'you should know better at your age' . . . Everyone is astounded at the many experiences you are having—and full of admiration. Of course I too . . . But I miss you." [6]

Biddle returned home in December 1943, happy with the prospect of doing a mural for the *Corte Suprema,* or Justice building, in Mexico City. He was given the commission through a Guatamalan poet, a friend of Biddle's sister-in-law in Washington, who had spoken favorably of his work to Mexican friends. The subject of Biddle's Mexican mural was "The Cannibalism of War," inspired by his recent experiences and conceived as a strong indictment of man's inhumanity.

By normal standards Biddle was no longer young when his Mexican mural was completed. He was nearly sixty, but as active, as gregarious, as deeply interested in his work and as productive as ever.

For the next twenty-seven years, until the last year of his life, he continued to work on art, to write books, to travel, to follow the literary, political and artistic trends that affected American life.

The paintings, lithographs, block-prints and silverpoints that he exhibited in this country and abroad reveal remarkable execution and wide-ranging interests—from his bird and flower silverpoints, done with exquisite charm, to his several drawings of "The Peaceable Kingdom," macabre and grotesque commentaries on death.

Travel was a part of Biddle's life and though he loved "Bittersweet" better than any place on earth he felt the need periodically to refresh his eye with new sights and new impressions. In 1959 he went around the world and wrote and illustrated *Indian Impressions,* one of his many books.

His last connection with Federal art was from 1950 to 1954, when he served as a member of the National Commission of Fine Arts, his old enemy in Washington, to which he brought new vitality. He knew that Congress, after the war, was in no mood to give patronage to art but he continued to hope that eventually a new program, under the direction of a Federal bureau of art, would become a part of the United States government.

He was sorry to see American art follow European trends as closely as they did in the 1950's and 1960's, for he believed in "regionalism"

[6] From the Biddle Papers, Manuscript Division, Library of Congress.

in art, though not in a narrow sense. "I think most art is regional," he said in 1964, "It always has been. The French Impressionists were all regional artists. Claude Monet was more of a regional artist than anybody I know . . . You very, very seldom get an artist that is above the thing we call regionalism. Michelangelo was, Blake was . . ."

Biddle himself was "regionalist" in his feeling for America and its institutions. He was often defeated in his efforts to establish his ideas in governmental thinking about art, but defeat did not embitter him. He met it with the same grace that he met success. There was in him, as his brother Francis said, "a tough belief in himself" that sustained him through failure, yet did not inflate him through his years of success.

The present author has an unforgettable memory of George Biddle in his last years. He was saddened deeply by the death of his wife, Hélène Sardeau, in 1969, but at his summer home on Cape Cod, "Hog's Back Hollow," he continued to mow his lawn, clip his ancient poodle Amanda, and take a daily dip in the ocean. His faith in himself and in American art were what they had always been. He died, on November 8, 1973, at "Bittersweet."

The Economic Development of Washington

Opening Remarks at the Columbia Historical Society Washington Economic History Institute

HOMER TOPE ROSENBERGER

The type and extent of the economic development of Washington, D. C. comprises a fascinating story. That story focuses on two major activities, government operations and local tourism. Together these two activities carried in their wake prosperous real estate, building construction, banking, merchandising, hotel businesses and lobbying activity. That fascinating story is being documented today by the five persons who will address this distinguished audience.

Naturally, most of Washington's economic development took place in the Twentieth Century. As late as the 1850's the Capital was a "sea of mud." Until the first decade of the 1900's the District of Columbia was almost rural in appearance and in atmosphere.

Unique in the history of national capitals, the city of Washington has had a unique economic development. Located in an area that was almost primitive, its main street, Pennsylvania Avenue, laid out in 1796, passed through marshy ground called the great Serbonian Bog. In the summer of 1800 the seat of the Federal Government of the United States was removed from Philadelphia to Washington, with the Post Office Department in the vanguard. That Department had nine employees and established itself in three rooms approximately fifteen feet square, at Ninth and E Streets, N. W., on June 11, 1800. Pennsylvania Avenue remained unfit for travel until Thomas Jefferson's Administration as President of the United States, 1801–1809.

From such humble beginnings the Federal Goverment and its city

Delivered at the Columbia Historical Society Washington Economic History Institute, September 19, 1973.

grew, rather steadily, until the Civil War. Almost immediately after that devastating conflict the city reached out to Georgetown which had previously been a port of significance with shallow-draft sailing vessels from England, France, and the West Indies tied at its docks.

World War I brought hordes of people to Washington in 1917 and in 1918 to handle war assignments. Many of those people remained. The great expansion of the jurisdiction of the Federal Government during the Administration of President Franklin D. Roosevelt, 1933–1945, the time of the Great Depression, and then of World War II, brought large numbers of people to the city to work for the Executive Branch.

From the end of World War I to the present day the increasing number of Federal buildings, the various monuments and museums, and the budding Twentieth Century grandeur of the city, resulting largely from the resurrection of the L'Enfant dream by the 1901 Plan of the McMillan Park Commission, brought a steady stream of tourists. The vast operations of the Federal Government caused an endless number of trade associations to establish their headquarters offices at the seat of government in order to be at the scene of decision.

After World War II the powerful position of the United States throughout the world and the location of the International Bank for Reconstruction and Development (World Bank) and the International Monetary Fund in Washington caused the city to become the center of numerous business ventures of international significance. However, to the present day, manufacturing and commerce within the District of Columbia have been only a small part of the city's economic activity. The focus continues on government operations and tourism.

At the opening of this Institute it seems appropriate to point out that during the seventy-nine years that the Columbia Historical Society has been serving the city of Washington the Society has had excellent cooperation from the city's leading businessmen. Here are a few examples. Theodore W. Noyes, editor of the Washington *Star,* was a founder, officer, and donor of the Society. Charles Carroll Glover, president of Riggs National Bank from 1896–1924, was an active member of the Society from 1899. John Bell Larner, president of the Washington Loan and Trust Company, 1917–1931, was the editor of the Columbia Historical Society for twenty-six years, from 1905 to 1931. Allen Culling Clark, one of the founders, the secretary, and a trustee of the Equitable Life Insurance Company of the District of Columbia, was president of the Columbia Historical Society from

1916 to 1943. Today, Colonel William H. Press, who organized this Instiute, is one of the most useful members of the Columbia Historical Society's Board of Managers. He served the Board of Trade of Metropolitan Washington for 35 years, from 1936 to 1971, and was its Executive Vice President, except for three and a half years in military service during World War II, from 1941 to 1971. On August 7, 1973, the President of the United States appointed Colonel Press as Chairman of the National Capital Planning Commission.

We hope each of you will enjoy this Institute. It is the first attempt to present a comprehensive view of the economic development of the Nation's Capital.

Some Aspects of Washington's Nineteenth Century Economic Development

JOHN NOLEN, JR.

The heritage that was to be given to Washington in 1791 was a remarkable one, unparalleled in its time. It was to be a new city and capital worthy of a great nation yet to be. A site was to be selected and a plan designed objectively appropriate to this destiny. To arrive at such decisions would require great vision, political ingenuity, skill and perseverance by its creators. To give effect to these goals a plan had to be created that would envision the city's needs over time and be an inspiration to accomplishment. And the plan had to be so implemented as to survive. Such were the qualities inherent in bringing into being America's national capital. How well they served to make Washington what it is today is ingrained in its history.

The location and boundaries for the Seat of Government, as it was first defined, were the decision of President George Washington within the limits prescribed in the Residence Act of July 16, 1790. He chose a site at the head of navigation on the Potomac, with boundaries of the ten mile square embracing the ports of Alexandria and Georgetown and the terminus of the Potomac Canal which he had started in 1786 as the gateway to the west. He was influenced in this decision by the expectation that, as the Seat of Government of a great nation in the making, the city would naturally become "a great commercial emporium."

The L'Enfant Plan was an original design and the product of an objective genius that required a century fully to appreciate. The Congress House and the President's House were given the prime sites and a pattern of streets and public reservations devised that would accommodate at other prominent locations "the different Grand Edifices and

---

Delivered at the Columbia Historical Society Washington Economic History Institute, September 19, 1973.

[for] the several Grand Squares or Areas of different shapes" which were listed for specific uses in his marginal "Observations Explanatory of the Plan." These included sites for a City Hall, a National Church, and Statues, Columns or Obelisks which would be focal points for memorializing the achievements of individuals from the different states. The Squares and Avenues would also provide situations for the grand Federal Improvements. In short, the plan was conducive to a wide distribution of public uses and resulting spread of benefits.

While the lines of the plan were unalterably fixed by President Washington's astute agreement with the nineteen original proprietors, Pierre Charles L'Enfant's equally important recommendations for implementation were forgotten after his dismissal following his quarrel with the Commissioners. Instead of selling a limited number of lots at locations where initial development was desired and improvement would be more likely, the Commissioners attempted to market the government's 10,000 lots, first by an unsuccessful auction, then in discounted quantities to syndicates, with the sole objective of raising money for constructing public buildings. The result was widespread speculation in land, bankruptcy of the syndicates, and foreclosures on such a scale as to inhibit for years to come development at the most desired locations. Scatteration also delayed the financing of paving and walks which would have been more readily provided for a concentrated early settlement.

EARLY ECONOMIC FORCES

The mainstay for the early economy was the expenditure by the government for its public buildings and the confidence thus established for private investment. In addition, of course, the ongoing government activities and payroll and the many visitors to Washington were a constant stimulus and stabilizer when all other economic activity was at a low ebb, a condition that existed for several decades prior to 1840. A tabulation of the number of government employees in Washington, the population at roughly comparable times, and the houses and shops constructed in the preceding decade reveals some interesting correlations (see page 526).

The initial efforts to secure brick construction were ineffectual as it would appear that more than half the houses constructed up to about 1855 were of wood, after which brick dominated. During roughly this same period, the incomplete total of pavement laid was about 60 miles.

One of the retarding factors in the slower growth rates between 1820 and 1850 was the difficulty in financing public improvements,

Census	Population	Government Employees		Houses	Shops
		Number	Percent of Population		
1800	14,093	131	0.9	(372)	
1810	24,023	535	2.2		
1820	33,039	603	1.8	2,028	129
1830	39,834	666	1.7	1,038	130
1840	43,712	1,014	2.3	895	173
1850	51,687	1,533	3.0	2,367	148
1860	75,080	2,199	2.9	1,938*	94*
				8,261	674

Government employees are for year following census.

Houses and shops are for decade preceding census, and are taken from the Session Annals.

* To 1853 only.

principally paving of roadways and walks and their drainage and lighting. Beginning in 1802, there was a local government with a mayor and a board of aldermen and council with power to tax and expend for such improvements. However, the needs were great and the taxable resources small. The Federal Government made no contribution except where Federal reservations were involved and for Pennsylvania Avenue. Costs that could not be managed were for the Washington Canal connecting Georgetown and deep water on the Eastern Branch and the investment of $1,000,000 in the Chesapeake and Ohio Canal stock which Congress had authorized. Four repeated efforts to obtain Federal assistance between 1835 and 1858 brought no fiscal relief so that at the outbreak of the Civil War the Nation's Capital was termed a shabby town with mediocre dwellings and cattle and swine roaming the muddy or dusty streets.

Nevertheless in this depressed period the groundwork for substantial economic expansion was taking place. Simultaneously on July 4, 1828, there were ceremonies inaugurating the construction of the Baltimore and Ohio Railroad in Baltimore and of the Chesapeake and Ohio Canal in Washington. Although the Baltimore and Ohio tracks were laid to a depot at 2nd Street and Pennsylvania Avenue by 1835, Congress did not allow steam engines to enter the city until 1852, horse drawn cars being brought from the city line for the intervening seventeen years. But in 1835 contractors for conveying the mail by stage between Baltimore and Washington were allowed to carry it on railroad cars provided that stages would convey it if received too late to make the rail connection.

Another substantial force in this early period for later economic growth was the almost continual and ever expanding expenditures on

Federal buildings. The Capitol was under some stage of construction until the end of the Civil War, and such monumental buildings as the Treasury, Patent Office, and original Post Office were undertaken. For the local government in this early period there were the original Hadfield city hall and court house and the jail and penitentiary. Then in the 1840's and 1850's, the Smithsonian Institution, Armory, and Washington Monument were begun, with private finances, on the Mall, which was then graded, fenced and landscaped by the government. Congress also replaced the old Pennsylvania Avenue macadam with cobbles and in 1842 lighted it with lamps which were turned off, however, when Congress was not in session. Finally the Washington Aqueduct was started in 1853 and completed ten years later. Gas became a public utility and though privately financed the government was initially its only customer.

A subject for special documentation not covered here is the development of external travel and commerce prior to 1860. This was the period when stage coach, canal, and railroad were in evolving competition, toll roads and bridges were being built, and the ports of Georgetown and Alexandria were at their peak. Washington was at the crossroads and perhaps could have benefitted as greatly as had been anticipated if the city had not been handicapped by the inadequacy of its own financial resources and the failure of Congress to give it the support or authority it needed.

DEVELOPMENTS IN THE LAST THIRD OF THE CENTURY

The Civil War marked and brought about great changes in Washington. An entirely new base, or point of departure, for physical, economic and social growth had been building up which the conditions brought about by the war undoubtedly accelerated. In addition, the political outlook and attitude toward the Nation's Capital became altogether different and things began to happen.

Foremost among the forces that were to stimulate change was that of internal transportation. In many respects, Washington pioneered in this field and prospered by it. A brief account of the streetcar system that resulted will illuminate the growth that followed the war.

The "City of Magnificent Distances" early developed the need for some form of public transportation. Unpaved streets made the omnibus a difficult operation under pre-war conditions. With this need, and the prospect of its military value in mind, Congress readily granted a charter, on May 17, 1862, to the Washington and Georgetown Railroad to construct three lines for the first horse drawn streetcar operation. One line was to run between Georgetown and the Navy

Yard via the Capitol grounds, and the others on 7th and 14th Streets. The gauge was to be that of the Baltimore and Ohio Railroad and the company was given six months to complete it. This it did ahead of time, completing the Capitol-Georgetown line in the prescribed 60 days with a force of 100 men. The entire operation was an immediate financial success. By July 1, 1863, with a five cent fare and free transfers, it took in a quarter of a million dollars and paid a $45,000 dividend. It operated 4,000 daily car miles with 490 horses, 70 cars, and a five minute headway.

A second charter was granted to the Metropolitan Railroad Company, on July 1, 1864, for a line extending through what is now the central business district. Over the ensuing years, extensions to both these original operations were made and many additional charters for lines by other companies were obtained from Congress. By 1890, a network of lines covered not only the old city but outlying portions of the District of Columbia with further lines projected into Maryland.

Great changes then took place. Experiments were underway with various kinds of electric operation and even with compressed air. Congress disapproved of further horsedrawn lines on the Capitol grounds, and prohibited overhead wires in the old city. In the early 1890's, the Washington and Georgetown Company converted to cable car operation. However, a disastrous fire, on September 29, 1897, destroyed the company's power house at 14th and E Streets, ending the cable operation.

Several years previously the Metropolitan Railroad Company had begun construction of an underground conduit system, developed by General Electric, and its success led the way for the conversion of all central lines to electric conduit operation by the end of the century.

During this decade there were many consolidations into what became the two main operations in the early Twentieth Century—the Washington Railway and Electric Company and the Capitol Traction Company. The suburban electric railways also were born in this decade. There can be no doubt that the street railways were a prime factor in the economic growth of Washington in the late Nineteenth Century.

With such enterprise in meeting the internal transportation need, it is not surprising that unprecedented growth took place. Between 1860 and 1870, population increased by 75 per cent, from 56,620 to 131,700, more in rate and numbers than in any other decade in the

Nineteenth Century. About half of this increase was due to a large influx of colored population as it was then identified. During the next three decades, however, rates of increase as between whites and blacks were about even, so that the proportion of white and black population appeared to stabilize on a two-thirds—one-third basis. By 1900, the District population had nearly quadrupled its prewar numbers, closing the century with a total of 278,718 persons.

This large population growth was accompanied by an even greater economic expansion. The value of manufactures of the District had doubled in the decade preceding the war, to nearly $5,500,000; by 1890, the value had increased seven fold to nearly $40,000,000. There were then 2,295 manufacturing establishments employing more than 23,000 persons receiving wages of nearly $15 million. An analysis made at that time indicated that very little of the manufactured product was sent out of the city. Chief items were the products of bakeries, building of carriages and wagons, clothing, engraving, flour and grist mills, painting and papering, plumbing and gas fittings, printing and publishing. Each of these industries produced more than a million dollars worth of goods or work. Obviously, such goods as were made were those which would be consumed by an expanding, thriving city.

The same source reported that the wealth of the city as revealed by the market value of real and personal property had increased from about $14 million in 1850 ($271 per capita) and $41 million in 1860 ($547 per capita) to $344 million in 1890 (nearly $1,500 per capita) at which time it was well above the United States per capita figure of $1,036. Truly this was, in sharp contrast to the pre-war doldrums, a period of great economic growth.

At the local government level also there were significant and far reaching changes. The formation of the territorial government in 1871 and the ensuing unprecedented program of public works under Governor Alexander R. Shepherd was able to overcome in three short years some of the deficiencies of decades past and lay the basis for the great expansion then in the making. Although the program amassed a debt of $24 million, it established the need for a strong local form of government which, with substantial Federal assistance, would be capable of dealing with city problems. The Commission form of government was thus created in 1878 and a 50-50 formula for sharing costs incorporated in it.

By then, the Washington Aqueduct had been bringing water from Great Falls for nearly two decades and horse cars were well established. The city had extended beyond its original boundaries and growth outside was uncontrolled by any plan. In their annual report of 1887, the District Commissioners, commenting on the melee of subdivisions north of Florida Avenue, candidly stated:

> The streets go nowhere and connect with nothing. They are narrow and not even straight within the limits of the park itself. The designer of its plan seems not to have had a single well considered idea, and if still in existence should not be again permitted to experiment with matters of importance. . . . If, as has been subtly contended, the configuration and architecture of a city has a moral influence upon its residents, the rectification of the irreclaimable obliquity of the streets is manifestly desirable for more than physical reasons.

Such conditions called for strong corrective action. Subdivision regulations were immediately promulgated and by 1893 Congress had authorized the establishment by the District Commissioners of a Permanent System of Highways Plan for the area of the district beyond the original city. The legislation provided for extending the principal Avenues of the L'Enfant Plan and a network of proposed highways to which all recorded subdivisions were required to conform.

The 1890's produced other examples of the exercise of a forward looking public conscience by the Congress that was to have lasting benefit to the National Capital. Rock Creek Park was acquired and the cost divided 50-50 between the United States and the adjoining property owners who were assessed benefits. Potomac Park resulted from a transfer in 1897 of Federal lands reclaimed with river and harbor appropriations during the preceding fifteen years.

So it was that, in celebration of the 100th anniversary of the Government's moving to Washington, the Senate Committee on the District of Columbia was authorized "to consider and report to the Senate plans for the development and improvement of the park system of the District of Columbia." Under the leadership of Senator James McMillan of Michigan, a commission of nationally known experts produced a report which proposed a revival of salient features of the L'Enfant Plan that had been forgotten, such as the Mall, a monumental design for the grouping of public buildings, and extension of the park system into the surrounding area, that would be worthy of the Nation's Capital. While this plan was never given any formal sanction by the Congress, it became an authoritative reference document for major decisions on development in the first half of the Twentieth Century. So, with a look ahead, ended a remarkable first century for the Nation's Capital.

POSTSCRIPT

This brief account of selected aspects of Washington's Nineteenth Century economic development has suggested the need for a chronological reference document listing the major events and landmarks in the city's history. This could be a concise but authoritative work, with references to sources of which there are many. A companion to this might be a series of monographs on the development of specific fields of economic activity such as banking, real estate, construction, business and industry and, most important, the entrepreneurs of Washington.

A Summary of Twentieth Century Economic Development of the District of Columbia and the Washington Metropolitan Area

ROGER W. ALLEN

Years of research and volumes of written material would be required to do justice to the Twentieth Century economic development of the District of Columbia and the Washington Metropolitan Area. For this reason I have restricted this paper to a summary and have leaned heavily upon work done by others in years past.

I. THE WASHINGTON ECONOMY TODAY

Perhaps an economic profile of Washington today is in order before discussing Washington's economic progress in this century.

The natural consequence of being the Nation's Capital is that Washington is a legal, legislative, administrative, and defense command post with supporting staffs, research groups, and important communication requirements to every part of the United States and the world. Because Washington's economy is dominated by steadily growing, service-oriented industries—most notably, government and tourism—it has a broad stable base, making it practically recession-proof which, in turn, makes the area attractive economically.

Over the years, as the nation has become more urbanized and has gained in population, industry, wealth, and international prestige, the federal government has assumed increasingly larger responsibilities. As a result, government employment in the Capital has grown steadily. Government salaries in the District alone are now over one and one-half billion dollars a year. In total, government accounts for almost 40 percent of all employment and over 50 percent of all wages in the District. This means good income and secure employment for many

Delivered at the Columbia Historical Society Washington Economic History Institute, September 19, 1973.

area residents. And, as this income is eventually poured into the economy in the form of consumer purchases, it tends to strengthen secondary industries like entertainment, automobile services, and food and retail outlets in the area. The government also benefits the area in that its unsurpassed research facilities, libraries, personnel and available funds attract a high proportion of scientific firms, particularly research and development groups, to Washington. A total of 405 private such "think factories" and 42 government laboratories are in and about the city now. The number of private research and development firms has more than doubled since 1960 and they have an estimated payroll of $659 million annually. In addition, many national businesses open offices in the District to foster political contacts and to stimulate government contracts. So an important secondary influence of the federal government in the Capital is the underlying strength it gives the area's economy. Since demands on government are likely to continue growing in the future, the outlook for continued expansion of government, the Capital's major industry, is good.

Similarly, the District's second largest business, tourism, is a vital, growing component of the economy. Last year a record number of tourists—nearly 18.2 million—visited the Nation's Capital. They pumped $700 million dollars into the area's economy. Some 720 conventions in the area brought 650,000 delegates to Washington last year. Future estimates of tourist activity indicate excellent growth during the 1970's. Estimates of the number of tourists in the area for the 1976 Bicentennial celebration range from 29 million to 40 million, with spending estimated at more than $1 billion. The National Visitor's Center at Union Station and the Eisenhower Convention Center will update the city's facilities for handling the growing numbers of tourists and conventioneers. Redevelopment of Pennsylvania Avenue, rejuvenation of the city's downtown retail center, new buildings at the Smithsonian Institution, and the Metro system will all make Washington a more attractive tourist center.

The rest of the District's economy is basically tailored to the needs of tourism and government. The largest manufacturing industry is printing and publishing—over 330 firms (not including the giant Government Printing Office) employ 15,600 persons to produce the reams of graphic, documentary, technical and informational materials which result primarily from government operations. In addition, the city has become a major transportation center, processing thousands of visitors annually and acting as a distribution hub for five surrounding states.

As a result of its stable economy and good transportation facilities, Washington rates as a top marketing area. D.C. citizens consistently have a higher per capita income than any of the states and the average family spends about a third more on retail goods than other families nationally. Last year retail sales topped $2.3 billion in the District alone. Banking activity, measured by the value of checks processed, has more than tripled in the past thirteen years and shows no sign of slowdown. Bank debits grew 21 percent last year.

Associations are a big business in the Washington area. Estimates put the number of national associations with offices in Washington between 1,500 and 1,600 (including trade, professional, and labor unions). These local offices employ over 50,000 persons and spend over one-half billion dollars annually. The movement of national associations to Washington has gained momentum in recent years, with today's number 50 percent above the 1,014 in 1961. Many have moved from New York to take advantage of cheaper office space and operating costs. Growing involvement with Congress and government regulatory agencies and the need for convenient access to government sources of information also have prompted much of the movement.

Businesses that want to be in the center of activity and enjoy a large market are locating in the District. Construction of office buildings has been expanding rapidly in recent years. Much of this construction represents new businesses in the area as well as replacement of older buildings by established firms. Construction of government office buildings (FBI, Federal Triangle, Bureau of Printing and Engraving, etc.) has also contributed to the building boom. A recent survey revealed a low vacancy rate, indicating a high level of use for the area's office space. With the "no-growth" stances in some of the suburbs affecting office buildings as well as housing, an increasing trend toward planning office buildings within the District may develop.

In addition to the expansion in office building, there are numerous redevelopment projects throughout the District to make the city a better place in which to live. Population in the District has declined slowly since 1950 and now amounts to 748,000 persons, compared to 802,200 in 1950. On the other hand, the Washington Metropolitan Area has been one of the fastest growing of the major metropolitan areas in the United States. Urban renewal in the District got underway in 1953. Currently the city's urban renewal areas cover about 3,400 acres and contain about 140,000 people. The Southwest and Columbia Plaza projects are virtually complete and current emphasis is being placed on the Neighborhood Development Program—covering Shaw,

Downtown, H Street, N.E., and 14th Street, N.W. Much of this work is centered around rebuilding and rehabilitating the three corridors damaged during the April 1968 riots. Work is underway on Fort Lincoln—a "New Town in Town" project. The Nation's Capital is setting an example in trying to coordinate participation by government and private agencies and citizens. The organizational work is tedious, but the overall benefit to the city and her residents should be immense. Advances have already been made in employment and educational opportunities. The District's first public institutions of higher education were opened in 1968 and have expanded at a rapid pace. Both institutions are embarking on building programs: Washington Technical Institute plans a group of buildings at Van Ness and Connecticut Avenue, and Federal City College has plans for two new campuses—one near Mount Vernon Square and the other in Fort Lincoln New Town. In the employment field, District businessmen surpassed their quota by finding 14,311 summer jobs for needy youths. These jobs were supplemented by 12,300 jobs offered by the District government and 5,000 jobs offered by the federal government. This indicates the extent of active, concerned community effort to better conditions in the city.

The regional metropolitan transit system will boost the Capital City's economy in the years to come. Construction on the 97.7 mile system began in late 1969 and the first section is scheduled to open to the public in mid 1975. An all-out drive is being made to have at least 24 miles of the system in operation for the 1976 Bicentennial celebration. Top priority is being given to the extension of service to the Dupont Circle, National Airport, Silver Spring, and Stadium-Armory stations. Estimated annual passenger capacity by 1990 is 350 million. More than a third of the system will be located in the District. With connections to suburban areas, Metro will shorten commuting time and relieve traffic congestion, thus allowing continued increases in the number of people working in the District.

In summary, the outlook for the District and the Metropolitan Area economies is bright. There is every reason to anticipate continued growth in the major businesses of government and tourism. Office building is growing, numerous urban renewal style programs are underway and job placement and education for the under privileged are receiving top attention. Furthermore, the city can expect to grow as the urban hub of a large, fast growing, wealthy metropolitan area as promises of rapid transit are fulfilled. As the country grows, so will grow the importance of its Capital City.

II. GROWTH SINCE 1900

Now I would like to discuss Washington's growth since 1900 in terms of population, employment, income, construction, tourism, cultural activities, higher education, communications, sports and gross product.

A. Population

Since 1900, the population of both the District and the Washington Metropolitan Area has grown faster than the population of the United States. And, as the following table portrays, of the three areas the Washington Metropolitan Area has been the fastest growing.

Population Growth Rate 1900 to 1970

D.C.		Washington Metropolitan Area		U.S.	
Total	Average Annual	Total	Average Annual	Total	Average Annual
171%	1.4%	578%	2.8%	167%	1.4%

However, looking at growth of the three areas over the entire 1900–1970 period hides several important developments. First, from 1900 to 1940 the District and the Washington Metropolitan Area grew at

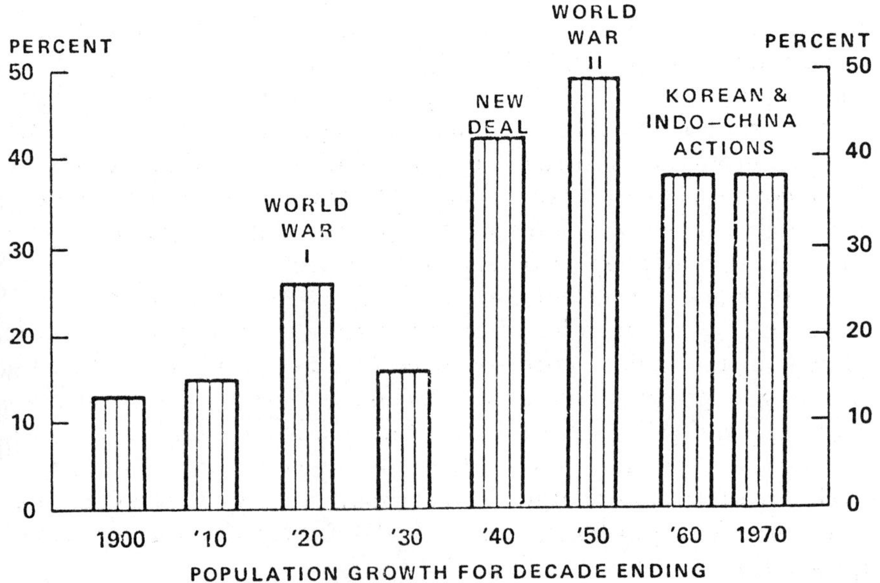

the same average annual rate, 2.2 percent. Second, since 1950 the District's population has declined almost 6 percent or an average of about .2 percent a year. Third, there have been periods of major growth in the Washington Metropolitan Area in this century.

As the chart above shows, since 1900 there have been four periods of vigorous growth in Washington: (1) World War I, (2) New Deal, (3) World War II, and (4) the Korean and Indo-China actions. All these periods were characterized by sharp increases in federal civilian employment.

B. Employment

1. Federal civilian employment has increased in every decade since 1900 except one:

Washington Federal Civilian Employment
(D.C. only prior to 1941)

Year	Millions	Percent Change
1901	28.0	—
1910	38.9	39
1920	94.1	142
1930	73.0	−22
1940	139.8	91
1950	223.3	60
1960	239.9	7
1970	321.0	34
1972	328.1	2

Source: Manpower Statistics Division, Civil Service Commission. Parts of Fairfax County, Va., and Montgomery and Prince Georges counties, Md., included from 1941 through 1949; D.C., Arlington and Fairfax counties, Va., Falls Church and Alexandria, Va., Montgomery and Prince Georges counties, Md., included beginning in 1950; Included Fairfax City beginning in 1964; Included Loudon and Prince William counties, Va., beginning in 1967.

2. Total employment data for the Washington Metropolitan Area have been available only since 1954. From then until 1972, Washington Metropolitan Area employment increased from 675,600 to 1,353,200 or 100.3 percent (D.C. Manpower Administration). During the same period, District employment increased from 481,000 to 627,600 or 30.3 percent (C&P Telephone Company, Business Research Division).

3. During the same period, Washington Metropolitan Area and District unemployment rates were consistenty lower than that of the

United States:

Unemployment Rates
Percent of the Civilian Labor Force

	D.C.[1]	Washington Metropolitan Area[2]	U.S.[3]
1954	3.9	2.9	5.5
1957	3.8	2.5	4.3
1960	4.2	2.6	5.5
1963	3.9	2.5	5.7
1966	3.8	2.4	3.8
1969	3.8	2.3	3.5
1972	5.1	2.9	5.6

[1] Source: C & P Telephone Company, Business Research Division
[2] Source: D.C. Manpower Administration
[3] Source: U.S. Bureau of Labor Statistics

C. Personal Income

Personal income statistics first became available for Washington in 1929. Between then and 1972 the District's per capita personal income increased from $1,292 to $6,383 or 394 percent. During the same period, U.S. per capita personal income increased 535 percent. For many years the District per capita personal income has been greater than that of any of the fifty states. Interestingly, in 1929 the District's per capita personal income was 83 percent above that of the United States; today it is 43 percent above. Also in 1929, the District's per capita personal income was 17 percent above that of the Washington Metropolitan Area; in 1971 it was 11 percent above.

Per Capita Personal Income

	District	Washington Metropolitan Area	U.S.
1929	$1,292	$1,101	$705
1940	1,198	Not Available	590
1950	2,221	2,018	1,496
1959	2,927	2,679	2,161
1970	5,466	4,968	3,933
1972	6,383	Not Available	4,478

Source: U.S. Department of Commerce

In 1929, total personal income in the District was $624,000,000; in 1972 it was $4,976,000,000—an increase of 690 percent. During the same period, U.S. total personal income increased from $85.9 billion to $996.6 billion for an increase of 1,060 percent.

D. Construction

1. Development of the General Concept:

According to the original plan for Washington by L'Enfant, Capitol Hill was to be the center of activity. Thomas Jefferson suggested the Mall. By the end of the 1890's, knowledgeable Washingtonians had come to see the city's future as forever tied to her status as national capital. Service to the U.S. government, to sightseers in the capital, or to citizens promised a more stable and satisfactory source of livelihood than could costly attempts to develop manufactures and shipping. A 1901 Commission employed planners Charles F. McKim and Daniel Burnhaur and landscape architect Frederick L. Olmsted who made the plan for the Federal Triangle, a new center of Government between the Capitol and the White House. In 1962 a new Commission was appointed to survey problems of Pennsylvania Avenue, where majestic buildings of the partially completed Federal Triangle on the south contrasted with deteriorated buildings on the north. They emerged with the concept that the Government sector of the Nation's Capital is inextricably linked with the city of Washington and its people and that all future building should be under that concept—public and private buildings should not be separated.

2. Some Major Development Areas:

In the early 1900's much of the building was in the vicinity of the Capitol, plus several buildings on 17th Street. Although the Lincoln Memorial was built in the 1920's, the business revival in the District after World War I was marked by an expansion of private building—apartment houses, luxury hotels, office buildings, private housing. Mounting demand for office space was due chiefly to Secretary of Commerce Herbert Hoover's far-ranging programs which encouraged national trade associations to set up headquarters in Washington. The New Deal era saw a spectacular proliferation of government building, with concentration in the Federal Triangle area, while in the 1940's before World War II the State Department rose in Foggy Bottom and National Airport and the Pentagon were built across the river in Arlington. Recent construction in the city has seen a great concentration of office buildings in the area west of the White House near Connecticut Avenue and K Streets and the rise of large apartment complexes in Foggy Bottom near the Kennedy Center.

The first conscious attempt to guide suburban growth of an American community came in 1888 when Congress passed a law requiring suburban developers in Washington to lay out subdivisions in conformity with the street plan of the city. The ever-increasing housing shortage resulted in a push out from the District when business began to revive in the 1930's. Arlington, one of the first suburbs to expand, attracted middle-class householders and the well-to-do went to Chevy Chase. The National Institutes of Health attracted people to Bethesda and the overflow from the District pushed Silver Spring's growth and affected Prince Georges County. The Resettlement Administration opened the planned community of Greenbelt, Maryland, and private entrepreneurs started Clarendon, Virginia, in Arlington County. In Georgetown old federal houses were changed from slums to fashionable neighborhoods. After World War II the economic competition from the suburbs became formidable. The 1960's saw the development of complexes of office and apartment buildings such as Rosslyn and Crystal City, and huge shopping centers such as Montgomery Mall, Seven Corners, Tyson's Corner, and Landover. Large shopping centers continue to proliferate, spreading farther and farther out from the District.

3. Government Construction:

From the very beginning government has provided the major thrust to District construction. This was particularly true in the 1930's when a burst of government building took place during the depression and New Deal at a time when private construction had all but ceased. The volume of construction in the 1930's is suggested by a listing of projects completed during the period.

Completed Major Government Structures—Washington 1931–1940

Structure	Date Completed	Structure	Date Completed
Water Gate	1931	Justice	1935
Memorial Bridge	1932	Supreme Court	1935
Civil Service Commission	1932	Interior	1936
Commerce	1932	Tomb of Unknown Soldier	1936
Senate Office Building	1933	Federal Reserve	1936
House Office Building	1933	National Gallery	1937
Agriculture	1934	National Archives	1937
Interstate Commerce	1934	Federal Trade Commission	1938

Source: *Your Government Guidebook*, R. D. Stevens

4. Residential Construction:

Since housing-starts statistics are not available for the District, building permits may be used as a reasonable proxy. Five-year averages were computed. As the following table shows, District building activity has beeen reasonably stable from 1909 (when the data first became available) to the present, with the exception of three or possibly four five-year periods. That the average for the most recent five-year period, 1968–1972, is lower than for the depression period, 1931–1935, is disturbing.

Building Permits—D.C.

Period	Annual Average
1909–1912[1]	6,377
1913–1917	4,219
1921–1925[2]	5,104
1926–1930	4,268
1931–1935	2,015
1936–1940	6,178
1941–1945	6,315
1946–1950	5,042
1951–1955	4,084
1956–1960	3,029
1961–1965	5,892
1966–1970	2,529
1968–1972	1,402

[1] a four-year period
[2] data for 1918 thru 1920 not available

Source: 1909–1917, *Clay Working Industry and Building Operations In the Larger Cities*, U.S. Geological Survey, Department of the Interior; 1921–1955, *Housing Construction Statistics 1889 to 1964*, U.S. Department of Commerce; 1955–1972, Construction Statistics Division, Bureau of the Census.

5. Office Building:

The Washington Metropolitan Area demand for new office space in recent years has been insatiable. In 1970 building permits for $135.3 million were issued for new office buildings; in the four-year period, 1966–1970, the total was $545.4 million, well over half a billion in just four years. In spite of this, the vacancy rate does not seem to be a problem.

Washington Metropolitan Area Value of Office Building Permits

Period	Millions
1954–1957	$87.0
1958–1961	233.9
1962–1965	278.5
1966–1969	506.7
1967–1970	545.4
1970	135.3

Source: U.S. Commerce Department

E. Tourism and Convention Business

In 1960 there were 450 conventions in Washington attended by 375,000 delegates. In 1972 there were 720 conventions attended by 650,000 delegates. (Reliable convention data do not exist for the first half of this century.) Tourism includes visiting sightseers from within the District, from any of the fifty states, or from any foreign country. The number of visitors to the Smithsonian is considered a good measure of sightseeing visitors and records of the number of such visitors by fiscal year are available back to 1900.

Visitors to the Smithsonian by Fiscal Year 1900–1972

1900	358,587
1910	458,370
1920	759,979
1930	1,894,987
1940	2,505,171
1950	2,675,970
1960	6,831,600
1970	13,714,200
1972	14,989,800

Source: Smithsonian Institution

It is estimated that the total visitor spending in Washington amounted to $700 million in 1972. It is a very important industry indeed.

A paragraph on early tourism from *Washington: Capital City, 1879–1950* by Constance McLaughlin Green shows early recognition of the importance of tourism, an importance which has increased over the years.

> . . . Yet yearly the flood of visitors ready to spend money in the capital rose. By 1908 Washingtonians were learning to recognize the arrival of spring less by the appearance of crocuses and daffodils than by the fleet of victorias and sightseeing wagonettes manned by megaphoned guides which lined up near the White House. By 1916, next to government business and real estate, the tourist trade ranked as Washington's chief financial asset.

F. Communications

1. Newspaper:

Newspapers and journals of varying types sprang to life in Washington from its very beginning. *The National Intelligencer,* the first daily paper of importance, was established in 1800. By 1902 nearly 900 newspapers had come and gone. Washington's current daily newspapers are two that survived. The *Star* was established in 1852 and the

Post in 1877. The daily *News,* established in 1921, was combined with the *Star* to become the *Star News* on July 11, 1972. There are also two suburban dailies, the *Northern Virginia Sun* and the *Alexandria Gazette,* and several weeklies including the *Montgomery Sentinel, Arlington Globe,* the *Potomac Observer* and the *Prince Georges County News.*

2. Telephone:

In April 1878 George C. Maynard secured an exclusive license to use, and to lease to others for use, Bell telephones in the District of Columbia and the territory in Maryland immediately adjacent. The company was known as the National Telephone Exchange. The District had one of the first central telephone offices in the United States at 1423 G Street in December 1878. By 1879 there were 400 telephones operated by the company.

In 1883 the Chesapeake and Potomac Telephone Company was incorporated in New York. At that time there were 2,354 telephones in operation (896 in the District and the rest in Maryland). By 1900, there were 4,426 telephones in the District and adjacent Maryland and there was a second central office on B Street (now Constitution Avenue).

By the end of 1972 there were 955,952 telephones and 115 central offices in the District and 2,589,543 telephones and 318 central offices in the Washington Metropolitan Area.

3. Radio and Television:

Washington's first AM radio station was WIL which operated for two-hour periods broadcasting music. In 1921 WPM began "full-time" operations and in 1946 the first FM station, WINX, went on the air. Today there are 25 AM and 19 FM stations operating within the Washington Metropolitan Area.

Washington's first VHF television station, WRC, Channel 4, began broadcasting on June 27, 1947, and the first UHF station, Channel 26, WETA, started in 1961. Today there are four VHF stations and three UHF stations, including two educational stations, operating in the Washington Metropolitan Area.

G. Cultural Activity

At the turn of the century few considered Washington a center of creative art although enthusiasm for copying works in the Corcoran Gallery led to the establishment of the Corcoran School of Art in 1888. The collections at the Smithsonian increased in the early 1900's and in 1920 the Phillips Gallery opened and came to be known to connoisseurs the world over. In the New Deal era Public Works art projects encouraged original art. In 1941 the National

Gallery on Constitution Avenue, containing the Mellon and Kress collections, opened. We now also have the National Portrait Gallery (in the old Patent Office Building on G Street) and soon will have the Hirshorn Sculpture Gallery.

In music Washington lagged behind other large cities. A week or two of opera by a touring company was Washington's quota. Composers and artists were discouraged by lack of a public concert hall. The Coolidge Auditorium of the Library of Congress was completed in 1925 to provide chamber music concerts. Radio broadcasting and new concert series in the 1920's widened the city's interest in all music. In black Washington in the 1920's music was a cultural cement; Washingon jazz bands made the city known for its syncopation. The National Symphony Orchestra under Hans Kindler was formed in 1931 and concerts were played at Constitution Hall; in 1935 the symphony began outdoor Water-Gate concerts which were continued until the blackouts during World War II. Opera and ballet were performed at Lisner Auditorium, and concerts were continued at Constitution Hall, but until the addition of Merriweather Post Auditorium in Columbia, Wolf Trap Farm, and—the crowning addition—the Kennedy Center, there was not adequate housing for a well-rounded musical bill of fare.

In the 1920's there was a new emphasis on basic research. The National Research Council gradually supplanted the Smithsonian as a prime mover in scientific research, the Department of Agriculture Graduate School opened in 1923, and the Brookings Institution, the American Council on Education, and the American Council of Learned Societies in 1927. The Library of Congress attracted scholars and gifts to the Library permitted the establishment of chairs of American history, the fine arts, aeronautics, Spanish and Portuguese literature and other subjects.

Part of the magic of Washington has always been the awareness that questions of world importance are part of the capital's day-to-day business. At least in round about fashion, the scholar, the lawyer, the labor leader at his union headquarters, or the scientist working with a research and development firm might find himself contributing an iota to the formulation of significant policies. The humblest Washingtonian rarely escapes some sense of brushing against great events and great people.

H. Higher Education

Washington is a very active center of higher learning. In 1900, 3,000 persons were enrolled in eight institutions in the metropolitan area. Enrollment has grown to about 170,000 students in 33 institutions of higher learning in 1972. Suburban enrollment has expanded rapidly in the past two decades as community colleges and branches of other universities have grown. These colleges attract a large number of part-time students. The largest institution in the metropolitan area is the University of Maryland at College Park. The larger institutions and approximate enrollments are shown in the following list.

The Larger Institutions of Higher Education in the Washington Metropolitan Area

Institution	Approximate 1972 Enrollment
University of Maryland	35,000
George Washington University	15,000
Northern Virginia Community College	14,000
American University	13,500
Montgomery College	13,000
University of Virginia	10,000
Prince Georges Community College	8,200
Federal City College	7,600
Catholic University	6,700
Georgetown University	6,300
Howard University	5,500

Source: Washington *Star-News*, September 1972

I. Sports

1. Baseball:

The Washington baseball team is said to be the oldest team in the nation. It was called the National Baseball Club and organized by a group of government clerks in 1859. In the 1890's when the National League cut its teams to 8, the Senators, always at the bottom of the league, were dropped. In 1901 the American League was organized and the Senators admitted. Griffith Stadium opened in 1912. The Senators won the World Series in 1924 and won the American League Pennant in 1933. In 1971 Bob Short, owner of the team, took it to Texas. Currently efforts are being made to acquire another team.

2. Football:

The Redskins came to Washington from Boston in 1937. They won the World Championship in both 1937 and 1942 and were Eastern Conference Champions in 1940, 1941, 1943, and 1945. Then, after many years of disappointment, Vince Lombardi became the head coach in 1970 and the Redskins had a winning season. The present head coach, George Allen, came to Washington in 1972. In his first season the Redskins won their conference and went on to the Super Bowl (where they were defeated by the Miami Dolphins). Prospects look good for another winning season.

3. Other Sports:

Currently a sports colosseum is being constructed at Largo, Maryland which will be home for a National Hockey League team and a National Basketball Association team. Upon its completion, Washington will have (if it acquires a new baseball team) local representation in all four major national sports leagues.

In addition, golf is a strong sport in Washington with approximately sixty courses in the Washington Metropolitan Area. Tennis is also a popular Washington sport with hundreds of courts, including many indoor facilities, and many strong programs.

J. Gross District Product

Up to this point we have been discussing the growth of individual economic series such as population, construction, and tourism. Some broad all inclusive measure of the District's economy is needed.

The Chesapeake and Potomac Telephone Company in 1961 developed a method of estimating the Gross District Product in the same framework as the Gross National Product. Gross District Product figures are available from 1950 to the present and they are directly comparable to national data. In 1971 a similar measure was developed for the Washington Metropolitan Area and figures were developed for 1957 thru 1971. The following chart compares the economic growth of the District, the Washington Metropolitan Area, and the United States in terms of their respective gross production indexes.

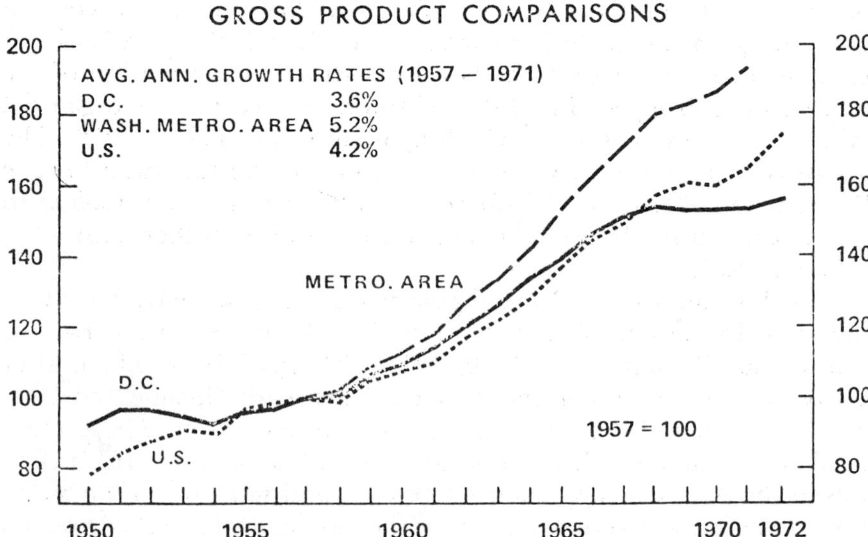

The chart shows that the Washington Metropolitan Area's economy has been growing more rapidly than that of either the United States or the District. The District's economy is the slowest growing of the three. The year 1957 is 100 for plotting purposes because Washington Metropolitan data started with 1957; for the same reason the annual growth rates are based on periods beginning in 1957.

III. ECONOMIC CHANGES OVER TIME

This century has witnessed some important changes in Washington's economy. Four of these which will be discussed briefly in this section are:

1. Decline in the relative importance of government
2. Changing character of transportation
3. Development of retail outlets in the suburbs
4. Rising proportion of blacks in the District

Perhaps only the first of these is peculiar to Washington. Certainly the changing character of transportation is a worldwide development. And the shift of retail outlets to the suburbs and the rising proportion of blacks in the central city reflect trends national in scope.

A. Decline In The Relative Importance of Government

Since 1954, when total employment data became available for the Washington Metropolitan Area, the relative importance of federal civilian employment has fallen from 33.7 percent of total employment to 23.9 percent in 1972. This represents a decline in relative importance of 30 percent.

Federal Civilian Employment as a Percent of Total Washington Metropolitan Area Employment

Year	Percent
1954	33.7
1957	31.4
1960	28.2
1963	27.6
1966	26.6
1969	25.3
1972	23.9

Source: D.C. Manpower Administration; Federal Civilian Employment figures for Suburban Areas from U.S. Civil Service Commission

The Government sector product in relation to the total gross District product has also been declining since 1953.

Gross District Product Relative Importance of Major Sectors

	Percent of total GDP		Change
	1953	1972	
Government	41.3	31.0	−10.3 pts.
Finance-Insurance-Real Estate	17.9	23.5	+5.6
Services	13.7	18.0	+4.3
Trade	14.8	10.3	−4.5
Communications-Public Utilities	3.3	6.6	+3.3
Contract Construction	3.0	6.3	+3.3
Manufacturing	3.5	2.8	−.7
Transportation	2.5	1.5	−1.0
	100.0	100.0	

Source: The C & P Telephone Company, Business Research Division

As the table above shows, the principal shifts among the major sectors were Government and Trade declining in relation to total Gross District Product with Finance-Insurance-Real Estate, Services, Communications-Public Utilities, and Contract Construction rising.

B. Change In The Character of Public Transportation

1. Trolley to Bus to Metro:

For the following items I am indebted primarily to the Washington *Post* and to the book *100 Years of Capital Traction: The Story of Streetcars in the Nation's Capital* by Leroy O. King, Jr.

In the 1880's and 1890's there were 15 separate transit companies operating in the city and suburbs. Included in the service were three mail cars, the last of which ceased operation in 1913.

In 1899 the Capital Railway Company (name changed to Washington Railway and Electric Company) acquired by purchases and receivership virtually all major railway systems in Washington except Capital Traction Company.

In 1909 the Metropolitan Coach Company started experimenting with gasoline motor buses.

In 1913 all its horse-drawn buses were withdrawn in favor of gasoline buses.

In 1915 the Metropolitan Coach Company went bankrupt and buses disappeared until the organization of the Rapid Transit Company in 1921.

In 1922 Capital Traction and Washington Railway and Electric branched out into the bus field.

In 1925 the Washington Rapid Transit Company was bought by the North American Company.

There were many early abandonments in the 1920's, victims of the rising popularity of automobiles.

In 1933 the Capital Transit Company was born of the merger of Washington Railway and Capital Traction and all street railways were under one management for the first time.

In 1936 the Washington Rapid Transit Company, sole remaining independent operator, was sold to Capital Transit.

In 1947 Capital Transit routes covered 426 streetcar and bus miles. It had 1,082 buses, the largest privately owned bus fleet in one city in the United States, and 824 streetcars (509 streamlined and 315 conventional type).

In 1949 Louis Wolfson, of Jacksonville, Florida, gained control of Capital Transit.

In the summer of 1955 Capital Transit was struck for higher wages and Wolfson refused to bargain unless the Public Utilities Commission guaranteed the company a rate increase. Congress enacted Public Law 389 giving the District Commissioner the right to settle the strike and revoking the Company's franchise effective August 14, 1956. The law also specified a new owner would have to provide an all-bus system.

October 1955 was set as the date for bids on the Capital Transit system. Not a single bid was received. A search for a buyer was ended when O. Roy Chalk, a New York financier, bought the system assuming title on August 26, 1956 under the new name of D.C. Transit.

Many citizens objected to the abandonment of the trolley but the first major conversion to buses came on September 7, 1958, and January 3, 1960 saw the next major conversion.

On January 28, 1962, buses replaced the trolleys of the 14th Street and U Street lines and Washington became an all-bus town.

Some Washington trolleys operated later in Fort Worth, Texas; Barcelona, Spain; and Sarajevo, Yugoslavia. Several are relics, one was sold to General Electric, and the rest were scrapped or sold for non-transit use.

In December 1969 work was started on Metro, the regional metropolitan transit system. The first section is scheduled to open to the public in 1975.

In January 1973 Metro purchased D.C. Transit, and in February purchased the other bus lines providing local bus service within the Washington Metropolitan Area (AB&W and WMA) so that today there is a single regional metropolitan transit system.

2. Chesapeake and Ohio Canal:

The Chesapeake and Ohio Canal was begun in 1828, at the same time as the Baltimore and Ohio Railroad. It was to promote western trade and establish Washington as a commercial center. But trade went to Baltimore instead. By the time of the Civil War Washington's only rail connection with the North was through Baltimore. By the 1850's there was no longer any real expectation of Washington becoming a commercial center.

The Chesapeake and Ohio Canal was abandoned in 1924 and was purchased by the government in 1938. It is now maintained as a National Monument. The 22 miles of the canal between Georgetown and Seneca were fully restored. No water was fed into the remaining 160 miles. In 1972 hurricane Agnes did much damage to the restored part and it has not yet been repaired.

3. Automobile:

The enormous growth in the number of automobiles is, of course, not peculiar to Washington but is a phenomenon national in scope. Neither the growth of automobile registrations in the District nor the growth of registrations in the Washington Metropolitan Area alone indicates the magnitude of the problem. The problem is compounded by the fact that such a high percentage of these cars are driven to work locations in the District every day.

The following table shows the growth in auto registrations in the District since 1910.

Automobile District Registrations

Year	Registrations
1910	6,320
1930	159,000
1950	195,000
1970	257,000
1972	264,000 (estimated)

Source: D.C. Department of Motor Vehicles

The following excerpt from Constance McLaughlin Green's *Washington: Capital City, 1879–1950* shows vividly that today's traffic problems are not new to the Washington area.

> . . . In 1921 and 1922 many people still walked to and from work, but, as population spread further and further, more people drove or rode. Gas fumes and the menace to life and limb from the rush of moving vehicles took most of the pleasure out of walking. In spite of a new regulation requiring applicants for driving permits to pass an examination, the installation of additional traffic lights, and somewhat stricter enforcement of the 22-miles-an-hour speed limit, "vehicular casualties"

mounted. The nearly 9,400 accidents of 1925, to be sure, fell to 4,138 in 1928, but in the interval motor vehicle registrations rose and by 1930 topped 173,600, not counting commuters' or tourists' cars. Drivers unable to find legitimate parking spaces in the heart of the city left their cars all day on the Elipse below the White House, on the Mall about the tempos, or in a fenced-off area of Potomac Park. "The entire Mall," protested the Fine Arts Commission, "has become an open-air garage. . ." In 1929, only 34.3 percent of the people who rode to work in downtown Washington used public conveyances; in Kansas City and Milwaukee, cities with the next smallest number, the figures stood at 45.5 and 50.3 percent, respectively. What the Board of Trade called the "best municipal government" in the United States was unable to provide an answer.

A traffic jam on Armistice Day in 1921 pointed up the need for Memorial Bridge. A formal procession to Arlington Cemetery was delayed by a two-hour traffic tie-up on the approaches of the highway bridges over the Potomac.

. . . A number of dignitaries did not reach the cemetery at all. Late that afternoon the Fine Arts Commission met to recommend immediate enactment of the legislation necessary to start work on the new bridge. . . . As the bridge was an integral part of the Park Commission plan for the river end of the Mall, Washingtonians committed to the "city beautiful" ideal drew a deep breath when Congress accepted the designs submitted in 1924: a stone bridge of simple flowing lines placed slightly below the Lincoln Memorial, above it a water-gate for boats and a plaza with parkways radiating from it, and on the far shore a second bridge over the Virginia channel and the intervening Columbia island to an imposing entrance into the cemetery.

Still another quotation from Mrs. Green's *Washington: Capital City* describes the continuing traffic problem in the 1930's:

Meanwhile parking problems constantly worsened. A long report of 1930 prepared at the instance of the Park and Planning Commission, the metropolitan police, and a half-dozen business organizations had proposed the use of the interior courtyards of the Federal Triange and under- and above-ground tiers of parking space at the rear of other office buildings, but in 1941 the downtown section of the city had only two or three big garages. Installation of additional parking meters and prohibition of leaving cars standing along much-travelled stretches of streets during rush hours made no dent on the problem. As long as twice as many people as in other big American cities persisted in driving their own cars into the business district, the chances of arriving at a solution looked dim. Only wartime gasoline rationing would provide a reprieve.

Today we have more than 300 parking garages in the District, and many parking lots, providing off-street parking for thousands of cars. Nevertheless, at any given time one can experience difficulty finding a parking space for his car. And just as we have had traffic jams since the early days of the automobile, we have them today. In spite of new bridges, a circumferential highway, coordinated traffic lights, one-way routes, improved streets and highways, and helicopter traffic reports, rush hour traffic jams occur frequently, even in good weather, and without fail in bad weather. The number of cars continues to increase at the same or a faster rate than our solutions to traffic problems.

The best hope for any permanent traffic solution is the development of a convenient, adequate, fast, safe mass transit system. It is to be hoped that Metro will be such a system.

4. Airplane:

A discussion of transportation would not be complete without recognition of the growing importance of air traffic.

The Washington Metropolitan Area is served by three major airports. Since National was opened in 1941, air travel to and from Washington has been increasing at a very high rate. In 1950 Friendship, located about halfway between Baltimore and Washington, was opened with the purpose of serving both communities. Then in 1962 Dulles International Airport was opened.

At first air transportation was used for the most part by businessmen and the more sophisticated travelers. As it became evident that this mode of travel was safe it became a widely accepted way to travel. Through the years planes have become faster, larger, more independent of weather, and more comfortable. Terminal facilities have become more efficient and comfortable. All of this has increased the appeal of air travel.

The following table shows the number of flights in and out of Washington by the three major airports in 1963 and 1972.

Flights to and from Washington through National, Friendship, and Dulles Airports

Airport	Flights (000)		Passenger (000)	
	1963	1972	1963	1972
National	294	331	5,464	11,122
Friendship	160	219	1,147	2,894
Dulles	91	209	667	2,517
Total	545	759	7,278	16,533

Source: Federal Aviation Administration

In addition to the large public airports, there are many small airfields for private planes. These have developed because the number of commercial flights at the major airports make it impossible also to handle all their private plane flights. Private plane ownership has increased as more businesses and individuals discover its convenience.

C. Development of Retail Outlets In The Suburbs

As I have said, the District rates as a top marketing area because of its stable economy, good transportation facilities, and high per capita income. This has been true for many years.

Retail trade figures became available for the District in 1929 and for the suburbs in 1948. In 1948 suburban sales accounted for 25 percent of total Washington Metropolitan Area sales. Since that time, suburban stores have been accounting for a larger and larger proportion of the Metropolitan Areas total sales. In 1972 suburban stores accounted for 70.5 percent of the total.

Suburban shopping centers were at first very modest with only a few specialty stores. Today's shopping centers offer complete shopping convenience with scores of specialty stores and usually one or more branches of the large department stores. Such centers are usually readily accessible from the circumferential highway or from other main automobile routes and they provide acres of free parking. Such shopping centers account for the increasing relative importance of suburban retail trade.

The following table shows this change in relative importance.

Retail Trade——Total Sales

District of Columbia and Washington Metro Area ($ Millions)

	D.C.	Washington Metropolitan Area	Percent of Metropolitan Area	
			D.C.	Suburbs
1929	$332			
1939	403			
1948	1,103	$1,471	75.0	25.0
1958	1,304	2,502	52.1	47.9
1967	1,603	4,731	33.9	66.1
Source: Census of Business				
1969	$1,746	$5,552	31.4	68.6
1972	2,317	7,848	29.5	70.5

Source: *Sales Management Magazine, The Survey of Buying Power*

In the early days of this century, Washington as a retail center was not considered to be in the forefront as the following quotation from Mrs. Green's *Washington: Capital City* suggests:

Shoppers were delighted when Isadore Saks opened his fine clothing store [in 1888] and S. Walter Woodward and Alvin Lothrop [in 1880] a department store modelled upon Wanamaker's of Philadelphia and Marshall Field's of Chicago. But despite advertisements of the latest Parisian pelisse, Washington, as one disappointed young woman noted, was not "a brag shopping place." Wholesale firms were few.

The same cannot be said today. Woodward and Lothrop is just one of many department stores now in the Washington area, among them Garfinckel's, Hecht's, Lord and Taylor, J.C. Penney, Saks Fifth Avenue, and Sears. In addition, Bloomingdale's of New York and Neiman Marcus of Texas are planning Washington stores. As for wholesale firms, according to the Department of Commerce's County Business Patterns there were 1,123 in the District and 2,394 in the Washington Metropolitan Area in 1970, certainly enough to qualify Washington as an important wholesale center.

D. Rising Proportion of Blacks in the Central City

The rising proportion of blacks in the central city is not peculiar to Washington. It began in the 1920's in many cities and is perhaps related to the wider ownership of automobiles. The trend has accelerated in recent decades and in the District reached 71.1 percent in 1970.

The following table indicates that this trend is due not only to a drop in the District's white population but also to a somewhat faster black population growth rate in the 1920's, 1930's and 1940's and to a continuing rapid growth of black and a gradual decline of white population after 1950.

District Population Mix 1900–1970

	Total (000)	White (000)	Black		Other Races	
			(000)	Percent of Total	(000)	Percent of Total
1900	278.7	191.5	86.7	31.1	.5	0.2
1910	331.1	236.2	94.4	28.5	.5	0.1
1920	437.6	326.9	110.0	25.1	.7	0.2
1930	486.9	354.0	132.1	27.1	.8	0.2
1940	663.1	474.3	187.3	28.2	1.5	0.2
1950	802.2	517.9	280.8	35.0	3.5	0.4
1960	764.0	345.3	411.7	53.9	7.0	0.9
1970	756.5	209.3	537.7	71.1	9.5	1.3

Source: Census data, 1900–1970

In spite of a 215 percent increase of whites in the Washington Metropolitan Area since 1940, the increase of blacks in the same period has been even greater, 229 percent. The percent of increase of other races was the largest of the three, 1,928.

Washington Metropolitan Area Population Mix 1940–1970

	Total (000)	White (000)	Black		Other Races	
			(000)	Percent of Total	(000)	Percent of Total
1940	907.8	692.4	213.8	23.6	1.6	0.2
1950	1,464.1	1,121.9	337.8	23.1	4.4	0.2
1960	2,001.9	1,502.4	487.2	24.3	12.3	0.6
1970	2,861.1	2,124.7	703.7	24.6	32.7	1.1

Source: Census data, 1900–1970

IV. RECAPITULATION AND FORECAST

In this century Washington has outstripped the United States and other major metropolitan areas in rates of population growth, unemployment, per capita income, and tourism. It has enjoyed a dynamic construction industry in federal buildings, private office space, and more recently mass transportation. Impressive progress has been made in the provision and use of cultural and higher educational facilities and the area seems to be on the threshold of having teams in all four major national sports leagues. Such dynamic growth as the Washington Metropolitan Area has enjoyed has required at least equal growth in communications, including newspaper, telephone, radio and television.

In this century we have seen a better balanced economy but one still dominated by the federal government and tourism. We have seen the disappearance of the trolly, an increase in automobiles and busses and related traffic problems, the growth of air travel, and most recently the birth of Metro, our future mass transit system. And we have seen, duplicating national trends, the growing relative importance of suburban retail sales and a rising proportion of blacks to whites in the central city.

I believe the outlook for the District and the Washington Metropolitan Area economy is bright. There is every reason to anticipate continued growth in the major businesses of government and tourism. Office building is growing, numerous urban renewal programs are underway, and job placement and education for underprivileged are receiving top attention. The city can expect to grow as an urban hub of a large, fast growing, wealthy metropolitan area as promises of rapid transit are fulfilled. As the country grows, so will the importance of its Capital City.

The Development of the Business Sector in Washington, D.C., 1800–1973

WALTER F. McARDLE

INTRODUCTION: THE LOCAL PERSPECTIVE

The District of Columbia is unique in the western world. European and North American colonial towns and cities grew up on a foundation of trade and commerce. Latin American centers were placed near the hinterland of ranches, farms and mines to permit their control by the royal emmissaries of the Spanish crown. Washington is like neither. The new capital of a young republic was fairly carved from the wilderness as the permanent meeting place for Congress and the seat of the Federal government. L'Enfant's plans for the capital embodied the sensibilities of a proud new country: national purpose and dignity were expressed in a series of broad avenues and streets angled to create a plethora of splendid parks and gardens, the sites for grand national monuments.

The fact that the subsequent development of the capital diverged from L'Enfant's plan suggests the presence of political, social and economic factors that determined the course of development in the rapidly growing nation. We have already been made mindful of the degree to which these international, national and regional factors greatly influenced the overall development of the Nation's Capital. It is now our task to try to appreciate some of the distinctly local factors that have also played a most significant role. Despite the dominant Federal purpose and character of the city, the story of the founding and development of Washington is tightly interwoven with the significant commercial possibilities of the selected Potomac River area. It is to these local features of commercial development that I would like to turn our attention in what must be a very brief review of Washington's business sector since the city's founding.

Delivered at the Columbia Historical Society Washington Economic History Institute, September 19, 1973.

I. A CAPITAL OF COMMERCIAL POTENTIAL

The decision to locate the capital at its present site was a political one, the compromise in 1790 between Thomas Jefferson and Alexander Hamilton. It is most significant, however, to recall that commercial factors played a major role in that political decision. These commercial considerations were evident in nation-wide competition for the capital site and in the arguments made in support of the Potomac River site.

In its first years the United States temporarily located its capital in no less than eight different cities. The decision in 1783 to establish a permanent seat of government triggered one of the most vigorous conflicts in the annals of Congress, fraught with sectional animosity that at times threatened to disrupt the Union. For seven years the debate went on, north and south each seeking to enhance its position by securing the location of the national capital. Behind the bitter sectional competition lay the conviction that the Federal establishment promised a lasting commercial base for any small town, just as it would enhance the prestige and wealth of any established city and, indeed, of the entire region in which it was located. Thus Jefferson, George Washington and James Madison urged a site on the Potomac River in the hope that a southern capital would spark an economic revival in the south which had suffered in the Revolution and with the economic downturn in conflict-ridden Europe.[1]

Kingston, New York's initial offer to receive the national government, was quickly followed by bids from: New York City; Boston; Philadelphia; Annapolis; Yorktown, Reading and Lancaster in Pennsylvania; Trenton, New Jersey; Newport, Rhode Island; and Williamsburg, Virginia. In the end, Jefferson and Hamilton arranged their famous compromise over the Secretary of State's supper table in New York: in return for Hamilton's aligning northern support for a southern capital, Jefferson agreed to lobby for federal assumption of the debts incurred by the states during the Revolution. The embodiment of the compromise, the Residence Act of 1790, authorized President Washington to create the new capital on any ten-square-mile site between the mouths of the Eastern Branch (also known as the Anacostia River) and the relatively small but navigable Connocheague River forty miles to the north.[2]

---

[1] John Claggett Proctor, ed., *Washington: Past and Present* (New York: Lewis Historical Publishing Co., two volumes, 1930), p. 33. Hereafter cited as Proctor, *Washington*.

[2] Constance McLaughlin Green, "Washington, D.C." in *Encyclopedia Britannica*, 1970, Volume 23, p. 254. Hereafter cited as Green, "Washington, D.C."

President Washington's choice of the precise Potomac River site reflected both practical considerations and complementary commercial expectations for the new capital. Washington shared the widely felt need to place the national capital on a navigable waterway and in a geographical location fairly central to Georgia and New Hampshire. Washington also envisaged a capital that would inevitably compare with the largest European cities.[3] Accordingly the capital had to be located below the tidewater to assure its accessibility to coastal and ocean-going vessels, the era's major transportation forms. While corn and tobacco fields, orchards and woods covered most of the ten square miles surveyed by Andrew Ellicott in 1790, the lower Potomac region was also attractive because it had already evidenced a significant degree of commercial potential. This was a key consideration in view of the condition of near insolvency in which the nation then found itself. President Washington probably hoped that local commercial activity would make the Nation's Capital essentially self-sufficient.[4]

The President was aware that the city of Georgetown had stood on the heights of the Potomac, upstream from the site of the new capital, since 1751. Incorporated in 1789, the little river port flourished as a shipping center for Maryland and Virginia tobacco. In 1800 Georgetown's population of 4,900 far exceeded the new capital's, and a half-dozen wide streets of attractive brick houses, taverns, churches and the Georgetown Seminary lent the village a settled and prosperous air. The Potomac area boasted another firmly established village in Alexandria, five miles down the river at the edge of Washington's southern boundary. By 1790 the village's Scottish merchants had built a network of roads into the lower Shenandoah Valley enabling them to capture most of the export trade in Virginia wheat and flour. The prosperity and confidence of Alexandria's 5,000 residents was visable in beautiful pre-Revolution houses and in the villagers' feeling that the transfer of the Federal government to the Potomac promised a bright future of continued commercial expansion.[5]

Alexandria's success encouraged President Washington in his belief that the Potomac River offered relatively easy access to the beckoning lands of the trans-Allegheny West and that a capital below the Mason-Dixon Line would attract "foreigners, manufacturers and settlers to Virginia and Maryland . . ." In a letter to a friend in 1791, Washing-

[3] Constance McLaughlin Green, *Washington: Village and Capital, 1800–1879* (Princeton: Princeton University Press, 1962), pp. 6–7. Hereafter cited as Green, Washington, 1800–1879.

[4] *Ibid.*

[5] *Ibid.*

ton declared that the capital would become "the greatest commercial emporium in the country." [6] Finally, the sectional interests of Washington, Jefferson and others blended with their commercial and political designs as both founding fathers looked forward to a "shift southward [of] the [national] center of both population and power" once the new capital had been firmly established on the Potomac River.[7]

II. THE INTRODUCTION OF A COMMERCIAL SECTOR: 1800–1875

At President Washington's request, Major Pierre Charles L'Enfant, a young French engineer who had served in the American Revolution, agreed to prepare a plan of the new capital. While primarily providing for the broad streets and large gardens required of a grand capital, L'Enfant also anticipated the two commercial sections characteristic of any great city: first, the shore of the Eastern Branch, its deep navigable water permitting the development of what promised to be the city's commercial center and second, the Capitol Hill where an arcade to accommodate shops should stretch due east from the Congress.

L'Enfant's vision of a luxuriant, vibrant national center, with its necessary commercial element, was slow to materialize in the first seven decades of the capital's life. During the initial decades, the rawness of the new city tempted many Congressmen to proclaim their preference for a return of the Federal establishment to Philadelphia. A tendency to pessimism in those early days was heightened by the initially small presence the national government made in the Potomac area: the federal government numbered no more than 131 employees when it officially transferred to Washington in 1800, hardly the basis for immediate substantial commercial activity. At the same time, Congress—after granting city charters to Washington, Georgetown and Alexandria—left the municipalities largely to fend for themselves. Lack of significant Federal support plagued two generations of Washingtonians whose city lacked the paved streets, water and sewer systems, and other conveniences beyond those that small local taxes could support.[8]

Despite such continual handicaps, Washington gradually began to take on the air and form of a small but established seat of government and commerce. In 1801 Congress created a court system for the city and defined Washington County above the Potomac and Alexandria County to the south (each subject to state laws). At the area's center,

---

[6] Washington Topham, "Business Washington" in Proctor, *Washington,* p. 689.

[7] *Ibid.,* p. 690.

[8] Green, "Washington, D.C."

TABLE 1

Population: Washington, D.C., 1800–1970

Year	Population
1800 —	3,210
1820 —	13,274
1840 —	23,364
1860 —	61,122
1880 —	177,624
1900 —	278,718
1920 —	437,571
1940 —	663,091
1960 —	763,956
1970 —	756,510

Source: Census Bureau

the capital's population steadily increased: (see Table 1) 3,210 in 1800; 8,208 in 1810; 11,299 in 1818. Scattered Federal buildings began to rise along the Mall and Pennsylvania Avenue, the basis for a substantial construction sector as well as a flurry of early hand speculation; the latter activity proved disastrous for occasional speculators but might be viewed as the antecedent of the real estate sector that was to become one of the crucial areas of local development. Work on the Capitol was nearly continuous, the predominance of slave labor on that project attesting to the limited size of the city's work force as well as to Washington's distinctly southern environment. By 1819 the government—still numbering less than a thousand employees—had erected or was occupying 43 public buildings.[9]

At the same time, the city's private sector began to take form. The recurrent neglect of the Federal government left Washington's private sector to develop much of the infrastructural framework for commercial activity. Thus early private initiatives often took the form of elements of rough transportation systems, such as the collection of bridges that sprang up at points across the rivers where turnpikes unwound to Alexandria, Bladensburg and the Montgomery Courthouse. These first bridges, planned and constructed largely or entirely by business interests, included the "chain Bridge" erected over the Potomac in 1801 with iron link supports to prevent its being washed away. Such enterprises were designed to support increased regional trade and to return a profit by means of tolls—25 cents for a man and horse, a dollar for a horse and carriage. In addition, by 1800 several

[9] Washington *Post, A History of the City of Washington: Its Men and Institutions,* Allan B. Slauson, ed. (Washington, D.C., 1903), p. 45. Hereafter cited as Washington *Post, History.*

commercial wharves had been constructed on the Potomac and Anacostia.

Federal support was lent for a series of costly canal projects first undertaken in 1807. By 1816 the small Washington Canal, navigable for boats drawing three feet of water, formed a water connection between the Potomac and Eastern Branch. Thomas Law, a Washington resident and the project's promoter, was permitted to charge tolls, but was required to turn over "net profits in excess of 15% of the sum expended" to the capital's Mayor and City Council. A second canal passed above Georgetown at the Little Falls and bore most of the flour used in and exported from Washington. The area's major waterway, the Chesapeake and Ohio Canal, was begun in Washington with much hope in 1828. The C and O Canal was not completed, however, until 1850 by which time its six-feet deep channel (costing $11 million) had been largely outmoded by the advent of iron railways.

On the very day in 1828 that the President of the United States turned the first sod on the great C and O Canal, the first rail was laid on the western outskirts of Baltimore for a line that was to stretch from the Atlantic to the Ohio River. Baltimore's successful railroad venture guaranteed for that city control of much of the vast interior trade that some Washingtonians had cherished fond hopes of monopolizing with their canal. By 1835 Baltimore and Washington were linked by rail, despite the opposition of the promoters of the C and O Canal. The popularity of the new rail line added to the chagrin of Washington's canal promoters who, in league with the city government, had incurred enormous debts to realize their ambitions. Alexandria, burdoned by canal construction costs, pleaded its case for incorporation into Virginia in 1846 and gained retrocession to the state in that year.[10]

The gradual development of bridges, roads and railways lay the foundation for growing mercantile and manufacturing sectors in the Nation's Capital. In 1803 the city housed 21 "merchants" and 32 "shopkeepers," primarily keeping drug, hardware and drygoods stores, groceries, hotels, restaurants and bookshops. By 1819 there were 129 shops apart from dwellings, typically in two or three story structures of frame or brick.[11] In that year, three banks, a single insurance office, 7 printing offices and 2 daily newspapers (including the widely read

[10] Edwin Melvin Williams, "The Mayoral Period: 1802–71" in Proctor, *Washington,* pp. 103–6.

[11] Washington *Post, History,* p. 45. There were 2,028 dwelling houses, of which 925 were of brick; of these brick houses, 221 were three stories high and 541 were two stories. None of the frame houses were over two stories.

National Intelligencer) sufficed to transact and record city business. In 1819 the assessment on real and personal property in the city was $6,430,615, and the amount of taxation, at the rate of one-half of one per cent, was $32,015.[12]

Manufacturing

Manufacturing arrived in the capital in 1800 in the form of Wilson and Handy's furniture shop. A nail factory followed, opening on F Street in 1803. A variety of small enterprises operated in the city's first decades, some flourishing, others sputtering and occasionally dying, by the 1830's. By then the city had housed manufacturers of hats, threshing machines, a producer of fire engines, another of cotton spinning machinery, and makers of rolled iron, knit stockings, window glass, flour, and, towards the close of the Civil War, paper and envelopes.[13]

In 1820 a census of manufacturing listed 29 different kinds of manufacturing concerns in operation in Washington (including Alexandria and Washington Counties). The concerns ranged from one-man establishments to the brick kiln, run by Thomas Crown in the city's first ward, where 71 men were employed. Richard Davis, a Georgetown clothing manufacturer, employed 50 workers. Edgar Patterson was another leading employer with 35 men in his Alexandria blanket mill and 28 in his Georgetown paper mill. Russell V. Bartlett employed 27 people in his Georgetown carriage factory, and Ezra Kinsey 20 in his Alexandria tannery. Zachariah Smart was another large employer: 16 workers made woodenware and flour barrels in his Georgetown shop.[14]

The largest number of manufacturing establishments in 1820 were involved in boot and shoe making (22). There were 8 tanning operations, 6 tailoring establishments, 6 brick kilns, 6 carriage factories, 3 cigar factories, 4 stoneware and pottery makers, 3 bakeries (specializing in crackers and ships-bread), 2 candle and soap makers, 2 sugar refineries, a brewery and several mills of various sorts.[15]

The 1820 census also lists wages averaging $249 a year and ranging from the highly paid brewery workers (who made $570 annually but were employed only six months each year) and bakery workers ($517 annually) to saddlers ($84 annually) and millers ($75 a year). Wage

[12] *Ibid.*, pp. 45–7.

[13] *Ibid.*, pp. 253–4.

[14] Orville Z. Tyler, "The Census of Manufactures of 1820 in the District of Columbia," unpublished manuscript, copy in Columbia Historical Society Library. Hereafter cited as Tyler, "1820 Census of Manufactures."

[15] *Ibid.*, p. 6.

scales varied greatly according to the individual employer. Four different tanning establishments, for example, paid wages of $333, $220, $175 and $190 annually.[16]

Among the enterprises enumerated in the 1820 census, the largest by capitalization were the $35,000 sugar refineries in Alexandria and Washington County. The combined enterprises of George Patterson, however, reached a total of $75,000 with his woolen blanket factory in Alexandria and flour mill in Georgetown. J. D. Barry's tannery in Washington was capitalized at $20,000. The total capital reported for all manufacturers was just over $275,000.[17]

The largest manufacturing enterprise in 1820 was, for some unaccountable reason, excluded from the census cited above: in 1801, Henry Foxall had decided to follow the Federal government from Philadelphia to Washington to set up the Columbia Foundry, the source of most of the heavy American guns used in the War of 1812 as well as the Mexican War.

But Foxall's great foundry was located just above Georgetown and Washingtonians with an eye to their own commercial development took a keener interest in the prospects for the Government's new Navy Yard. The deep water running close inshore along the Eastern Branch made its banks the logical place for the Navy Yard (as well as merchants' wharves and warehouses). As American interests began to run headlong into British hegemony on the high seas, the development of a half dozen major naval centers—including one in the capital—took on a high priority. By 1806 an arsenal and barracks had been constructed as more Federal funds were expended on the Washington Navy Yard than upon any other yard. By 1811, 280 men labored on the construction of three new gunboats in the Navy Yard's 900-foot long workshop. Improvements on the yard continued and in 1820 a frigate was on the "stocks" where a 74-gun battleship had just taken form. Settlements of workmens families inevitably rose around the Washington Yard while private rope-making and gunpowder establishments dotted the vicinity.[18]

The Center Market

Another hub of activity in the capital was the Center Market, until recent decades Washington's most important merchandising institution. In 1801 Dr. William Thornton, architect of the Capitol, pre-

[16] *Ibid.*, p. 10.

[17] *Ibid.*, p. 13.

[18] Washington Topham in Proctor, *Washington,* pp. 694–5; and Tyler, "1820 Census of Manufactures." Interestingly, the Navy Yard was also omitted from the 1820 Census.

sided over the public meeting that voted to erect a market-house on the south side of Pennsylvania Avenue between 7th and 9th Streets (the site initially suggested by President Washington in 1797). Thenceforth the Center Market opened on Tuesdays, Thursdays and Saturdays and was the principal factor in the movement of the city's business center from the Capitol Hill down to Pennsylvania Avenue. The market's established place in city life was strengthened by its use as the seat of municipal government after 1802 when the District Government commenced operations. Potential market sellers were also attracted by the annual rental fee of $10 per market stall. The growing popularity of the Center Market encouraged gradual reclamation of nearby swampland; the market stood at one of Pennsylvania Avenue's lowest points and early chroniclers of market day activities occasionally noted shoppers tossing stones to scatter wild ducks that had settled on the wet market grounds.[19]

The Center Market gradually became the city's produce supply center, with most of the beef and other farm goods coming by ox-drawn wagon from Prince George's County. While the market lost the municipal buildings to the Judiciary Square in the 1820's, it remained the center of business, profiting by the increasing use of Pennsylvania Avenue. Stagelines from Georgetown and Baltimore terminated near 7th and Pennsylvania at the renowned Brown's Hotel. Washington residents crowded the market stalls and daily promenaded along Pennsylvania Avenue where sidewalks near Market Square sometimes measured thirty feet in width. In the 1830's the first permanent (macadam) surfacing of Pennsylvania Avenue and the admittance by canal of smaller steamboats as high as 7th Street gave Center Market further importance. By 1870, 40-odd firms were located in the immediate neighborhood of Center Market while more than 100 butchers, green-grocers, butter and egg merchants, bakers and fish dealers rented stalls in the market itself.[20]

Police headquarters and the Perseverance Fire House located near the Central Market in 1839. Washington's Whigs noted the market's

[19] Washington Topham in Proctor, *Washington*, pp. 696–703.

[20] Within the 7th Street and Pennsylvania Avenue neighborhood were 2 agricultural implements firms, 2 groceries, 8 dry goods stores, 2 drug stores, several commission houses, the St. Marc's and Avenue Hotels, the Bank of Washington, 2 insurance companies, several saloons and eating places, the Canterbury Theater, a junk shop, a wood and coal yard, a sash, door and blind company, a hat and shoe store, a furniture store, a photographer, a millinery, a carpet firm, a gymnasium, a horse bazaar, an iron foundry, a fish dealer, and a flour and seed store. Market stalls were held by 48 butchers, 33 green-grocers, 11 butter and egg merchants, 7 bakers, and 4 fish dealers. Proctor, *Washington*, pp. 702–3.

central location in erecting a log cabin and 107-foot high liberty pole in front of the Center Market in the midst of the 1840 presidential campaign. In 1842 the introduction of outdoor lamps along Pennsylvania Avenue extended the daily activity of the increasing number of stores located in the Center Market area. In 1850, the recently chartered Washington Gas Light Company introduced brighter gas lamps creating an imposing "white way" from the Capitol to the White House. Before the outbreak of civil war intervened Congress had planned to replace the original market-house, by then a somewhat dilapidated long, low frame structure with whitewashed walls and moss-covered roof; new construction was to include a grand entranceway to release the flood of wagons on market days that blocked the broad expanse of Pennsylvania Avenue from 7th to 11th Streets.[21]

1840–1875

Despite the retrocession of Alexandria to Virginia, Washington's population grew steadily in the pre-Civil War years. In 1840 the capital's population was 23,364 and Washington was gaining new residents at the rate of 500 a year. In the next decade the population rose three times as fast; by 1850 the city had 40,000 inhabitants. The growing population made itself felt in increasing demands for municipal services. The real estate tax rate in 1860—75 cents on $100—was the highest that the City was empowered to make and reflected, in turn, Washington's large and growing debt ($831,000 at the outbreak of the Civil War). The tax levy and debt accumulation generally represented attempts at public improvements that Congress refused to finance. Such local efforts were limited and through the 1860's Washington remained effectively sewerless, while dependent for water entirely upon a series of scattered springs within the city. Until 1845 Pennsylvania Avenue was the capital's only paved street, and that had been accomplished only at Federal expense. In that year 7th Street, by virtue of its distinction as one of the principal business streets, became the first thoroughfare paved by the city authorities, with cobblestones laid between H Street north and Virginia Avenue. No further paving was done until 1852 when the roadway was cobbled on the north side of Market Square, between 7th and 9th Streets.[22]

The Civil War proved a major impetus to Washington's growth and development. With the outbreak of the conflict, the city's population suddenly doubled to more than 80,000 persons as the capital

[21] *Ibid.*

[22] *Ibid.*, p. 704.

became the principal supply depot of the Army of the Potomac, a great hospital center, and the source of government contracts. By 1870 the capital's population exceeded 109,000 persons and 5 banks and 8 newspapers served the city. In the course of the war, more than 40,000 former slaves poured into the capital. Federal government employment during the war years doubled to 7,184. The city teemed with soldiers, horses, supply wagons and the construction of new banks, hotels, theaters, additions to government buildings and a ring of new forts around the city. To a significant extent, however, the war-time capital was overburdened, the rare paved streets cut to ribbons by army wagons, the unpaved ways trampeled into dust and mud by cattle herded through town to graze on the Mall as part of the military food supply. The widely deplored condition of city streets, in combination with the presence of a sizeable Negro population, prompted occasional proposals in Congress that the capital be moved to a Midwest location.[23]

Washingtonians, while alarmed at the talk of abandonment by the Federal establishment, remained confident that the city could develop into a modern capital. Most confident of all was a long-time civic leader, Alexander Robey Shepherd. In 1865 Shepherd had been instrumental in the organization of some fifty city merchants into a "Board of Trade of the District of Columbia" that lobbied Congress for the consolidation of the cities of Georgetown and Washington.[24] In 1871 Shepherd took charge of the Board of Public Works and effectively ran the city's affairs when territorial status was granted in that year and Georgetown's separate status was abolished. Under Shepherd's driving leadership, the face of Washington was transformed; "the city of mud and dust" became a series of magnificent stretches of paved, well-lit streets lined with shade trees. In addition, more than eighty miles of underground sewerage were laid.[25]

By 1875 Washington had finally become the national showplace envisaged by L'Enfant and Washington—but only at an enormous cost. Within three years of the granting of a form of self-government, Washington was bankrupt with debts amounting to more than $18 million, partly because Shepherd had simply disregarded expense in his determination to carry out his "comprehensive plan of improvement".[26]

---

[23] Green, "Washington, D.C.," p. 255.

[24] H. W. Crew, *Centennial History of the City of Washington, D.C.* (Dayton, Ohio: United Brethren Publishing House, 1892), p. 417. Hereafter cited as Crew, *Centennial History*.

[25] Green, "Washington, D.C.," p. 255.

[26] *Ibid.*

III. AN ERA OF COMMERCIAL EXPANSION: 1875–1900

The collapse of the first experiment in home rule threatened to dampen the extension of the growing commercial sector in Washington. The reinstitution of complete Federal control seemed to promise that the Federal establishment would continue to set the pace of over all development. Through the post-Civil War period of massive industrial and intensive mercantile development in a number of cities, Washingtonians favored comparatively small-scale private enterprise. Washington's small-scale, light-industrial orientation was in part a natural response to the continued dominance of the Federal government. The stability ensured by the Federal establishment and its regular payroll stood in marked contrast to the unsettling—often frightening—environment of industrialized cities where employment and incomes fluctuated with alarming frequency. But Washington also lacked both the natural resource base and the large supply of surplus skilled labor common to the great commercial centers that emerged after the Civil War. The enormous harbor and port facilities of Baltimore, Philadelphia and New York, as well as their recurrent inflows of skilled and semi-skilled immigrants, outstripped the capacities of the Potomac River and Washington's more modestly sized population.

In any event, the District of Columbia, in the wake of the much needed facelifting provided by Shepherd, did evidence increasingly varied and extensive commercial activity in the three decades after the Civil War. The Center Market's continuing preeminence as the retail core was emphasized in 1872 with the opening of large new market-houses on 7th, 9th and B Streets; 666 stalls covering 60,000 square feet were available. The average monthly rental for a market stall was $8.35.[27] Earlier, in 1869, the third annual meeting of the Board of Trade heard a report stating that in the previous year 740,000 bushels of wheat had been received in District mills and manufactured into flour. The arrival of 500,000 bushels of corn also pointed to Washington as an important milling center. Trade in building materials had encouraged several shipping interests to run

[27] It should be noted that by the 1890's Washington contained in addition to Center Market seven other—and much smaller—markets. The North Liberty Market at 5th and K Streets, N.W. was a one-story building covering 41,600 square feet with 284 stalls renting at $5.90 each. Riggs Market on P Street between 14th and 15th Streets, N.W. was a one-story frame structure covering 9,100 square feet with 187 stalls renting at $3.56. Similar market-houses stood at 21st and K Streets, N.W. (the Western Market); High Street between 1st and 2nd Streets in Georgetown; Bridge Street (the Georgetown Market); and 7th and C Streets, N.E. (the Eastern Market). Crew, *Centennial History*, pp. 419–20.

the fourty-two hour route between docks in Georgetown and New York. By 1865 the Atlantic Steamship Company had three steamers in a Washington-New York passenger service with a round-trip fare of $13. Shipbuilding was undertaken by private establishments in 1851, complementing the continuing work at the Navy Yard. Else-

TABLE 2

Manufacturing and Allied Enterprises in the District of Columbia, 1880 to 1900

	1880	1890	1900
Building materials and construction			
No. of establishments	251	565	744
Persons employed	1,718	7,321	7,322
Wages, salaries	596,042	4,734,360	4,186,013
Capital investment	755,505	4,602,692	7,425,342
Value of product	1,904,206	12,543,013	13,928,690
Food and beverages			
No. of establishments	82	99	119
Persons employed	283	858	1,092
Wages, salaries	124,842	518,995	666,683
Capital investment	559,040	2,192,020	3,510,117
Value of product	2,053,843	3,827,437	4,010,971
Clothing			
No. of establishments	37	140	208
Persons employed	237	967	904
Wages, salaries	102,850	512,318	475,989
Capital investment	115,550	601,173	648,813
Value of product	386,415	1,170,353	1,526,326
Printing & engraving			
No. of establishments	30	69	146
Persons employed	2,645	4,593	7,419
Wages, salaries	2,175,578	3,733,469	5,994,588
Capital investment	2,118,800	3,270,306	6,953,043
Value of product	3,775,478	6,121,703	9,254,032
Other (mostly handicrafts)			
No. of establishments	571	1,422	1,507
Persons employed	2,254	9,665	10,039
Wages, salaries	935,300	5,123,122	5,123,878
Capital investment	1,933,631	18,198,898	23,443,930
Value of product	3,762,374	15,668,931	18,947,603
Totals			
No. of establishments	971	2,295	2,754
Persons employed	7,146	23,404	26,776
Wages, salaries	3,924,612	14,622,264	16,477,151
Capital investment	5,552,526	28,865,089	41,981,245
Value of product	11,882,316	39,331,437	47,667,622

Source: Census of Manufacturers, 1880–1900; Green, *Washington: Capital City, 1879–1950.*

where along the river fronts, wholesale dealers in salt built large warehouses at Water Street in Georgetown.[28]

Manufacturing

The variety and expansion of commercial activity was also evident in the census reports dealing with manufactures. (See Table 2 and footnote 31.) The 1880 census listed 971 manufacturing and allied establishments (including government manufacturing establishments),[29] employing 7,146 persons and turning out finished products valued at $11.8 million. In 1890 almost 2,300 establishments were enumerated, employing 23,477 persons, paying $14.6 million in wages and producing goods valued at $39.3 million. In 1900 maufacturing establishments numbered 2,754 with nearly 27,000 workers (5,771 in public printing operations) and finished products valued at $47.4 million (of which $6.5 million was accounted for by public concerns).[30] Thus between 1880 and 1900 the number of manufacturing concerns tripled, employment nearly quadrupled, wages and salaries rose five times, capital investment increased about seven-fold and production value rose four times.

The 1890 census of manufacturers reported 120 different kinds of industries; 40 of these industries employed fewer than 10 men each and 4 employed more than 1,000 men each; of the latter, there were 3,597 men in printing and publishing firms, 2,482 in carpentering, 1,204 in brick and tile production, and 1,134 in paper hanging and painting.[31]

[28] Washington Topham in Proctor, *Washington*, p. 706.

[29] Government manufacture in 1890 consisted primarily of: lock and mail-bag repair shops of the Post Office Department; the public printing office; the Bureau of Printing and Engraving; Navy Yard ordinance and ordinance stores; carpenter shops operated by the War, Navy and Treasury Departments. For these government operations capital employed, $7.5 million; wages paid, 3.8 million; cost of materials, $1.8 million; value of product, $5.9 million; employees, 4,592. Crew, *Centennial History*, p. 438.

[30] *Ibid.* The Census did not distinguish between public and private manufacture until 1890.

[31] Crew, *Centennial History*, p. 439. The 25 principal industries in 1890 were:

Industry	Employment	Wages (aggregate yearly)
Bottling	208	$118,957
Brick and tile	1,204	442,929
Carpentering	2,428	1,754,367
Carriages and wagons	290	160,170
Confectionary	349	165,907
Engraving on steel	997	849,332
Flour and grist mills	149	85,718

The classes of businesses each of which had more than 100 establishments in 1890 were boots and shoes (232), carpentering (171), painting and paper hanging (156), women's clothing (146), and men's clothing (116). The classes of business each of which annually "used more than one million dollars" in 1890 were carpentering ($2.9 million), flour and grist mills ($1.4 million), and printing and publishing ($1.3 million).

Significantly the pattern of manufacture of the period 1880–1900 remained approximately the same in succeeding decades as is shown in Table 3. The categories of printing and publishing, food products and baked goods and beverages ranked the same among all manufactures—in terms of value of production—in 1967, 1927, and 1880.

The Board of Trade

By 1889 the mercantile trade of Washington was sufficient to support a permanent Board of Trade. The original Board of Trade, organized by Alexander Shepherd, had disappeared at some point between 1871 and 1875 in the hectic days of territorial government. The new Board of Trade's officers included Myron M. Parker, president, S. W. Woodward, first vice-president, B. H. Warner, treasurer, and Alexander O. Anderson, secretary. The initial Board of Trade Directory listed thirty-one members. As stated in its by-laws, the new Board was intended to promote "the consideration of, and action upon, mat-

Industry	Employment	Wages (Aggregate yearly)
Foundry and machine shops	311	172,297
Furniture	161	94,028
Iron Work	309	186,412
Malt liquors	120	82,422
Lithographing & engraving	127	79,568
Planed lumber, sash, doors and blinds	440	258,438
Marble and stone work	391	305,631
Masonry	661	537,180
Painting & paper hanging	1,134	748,728
Paving & paving materials	878	404,523
Plastering & stucco works	237	148,093
Plumbing and gas fitting	646	432,567
Printing and publishing	3,099	2,494,406
Printing and publishing, newspapers	498	389,731
Saddlery and harness	106	58,636
Tinware	424	259,120
Tobacco products	159	83,279
Watch, clock, jewelry	126	83,224

TABLE 3

Leading Manufacturers in the District of Columbia: Number of Employees and Units, Rank by Value of Production, 1880–1967

	1880	1927	1967
All industries			
No. of establish.	971	503	593
Employees	7,146	9,519	23,100
1. Food products			
No. of establish.		40[a]	46
Employees	[b]	852	4,400
Rank		2	2
2. Bread, bakery products, beverages			
No. of establish.	82	95	18
Employees	283	1,543	1,700
Rank	3	3	3
3. Printing and publishing			
No. of establish.	30	173	328
Employees	2,654	2,391	14,800
Rank	1	1	1

[a] Includes coffee, ice cream, nuts, meat in 1927, and "food and kindred products" in 1967.

[b] Categories (1) and (2) are combined.

Source: Census of Manufactures and Allied Enterprises, 1880; Census of Manufactures, 1927 and 1967.

ters concerning the commerce, prosperity, and advancement of the material interests of the National Capital, and the dissemination of information relating thereto." To these ends, the Board of Trade created a variety of committees to deal with such matters as taxation and assessments, railroads, transportation, commerce, public buildings, parks and reservations, streets and avenues, charities, public health, water supply, improvement of the Potomac River, universities, bridges and insurance. By the turn of the century, the Board counted among its membership the day's most prominent business firms and individuals.[32]

Mercantile Washington in 1900

The Board of Trade's membership at the turn of the century gives a useful indication of the form and extent of the period's business activity both in wholesale and retail trade (reviewed here) and in what became one of the capital's leading fields of activity, banking and finance (reviewed in a subsequent section).

[32] Crew, *Centennial History,* p. 439.

The experience of Samuel W. Woodward, first vice-president of the Board of Trade, and Alvin M. Lothrop particularly suggests the course of retail development in the last decades of the Nineteenth Century. In 1880 Woodward and Lothrop established the Boston Dry Goods House in an unpretentious building, number 705 Market Place. Not long after, the need for larger quarters led the store to be moved to 921 Pennsylvania Avenue, still comfortably within the city's retail center. In 1887, however, the business had continued to expand to the extent that a third location was needed. Determined to secure space that would allow for future expansion, Woodward and Lothrop decided to leave the principal business street—Pennsylvania Avenue. Despite many warnings that a move out of the established retail core could prove disastrous for the store, Woodward and Lothrop's quickly thrived at its new location at 11th and F Streets. Other merchants soon followed and F Street gradually assumed the position as the city's newest business center. By 1900 Woodward and Lothrop's was eight stories high and covered most of the block from F to G Streets and from 10th to 11th Streets. By 1898 Woodward had developed the interlocking interests typical of a leading Washington businessman: in that year he was a member of the executive boards of the Board of Trade and the YMCA, was director of the National Metropolitan Bank, president of the Colonial Fire Insurance Company, and a member of the board of directors of the Washington Loan and Trust Company. Similarly Lothrop was vice-president of the Union Savings Bank and director of the Equitable Building Association.[33]

The turn-of-the-century Board of Trade membership included other notable business firms and figures. C. G. Cornwell, for example, was well known as the founder of one of the city's leading grocery establishments, C. G. Cornwell and Son. The firm was located at 1412 Pennsylvania Avenue in a five-story brick building and advertised "a full and complete line of imported and domestic luxuries, fancy and staple groceries, and wines and liquors." William Frederick Gude finished courses at Washington's Spencerian Business College before opening what soon became the city's premier floral business in 1887; the firm of A. Gude and Brothers had salesrooms at 1224 F Street, N.W.

In 1882 Edwin Spottswood Clark opened what was soon the capital's major furniture and carpet house, the firm of Clark and Davenport, at 12th and F Streets, N.W. By 1900 J. Maurry Dove had developed a small supply depot on the Georgetown wharf into one of the

[33] Washington *Post, History,* Chapter 21.

city's leading supply centers for coal. The J. Maurry Dove Company established branch yards throughout the city to receive coal brought in by water and rail; no less than five officers of the coal company claimed Board of Trade membership in 1900. The firm of Johnson Brothers, however, operated an even larger fuel supply business. O. Perry Johnson and Charles H. Johnson, graduates of Georgetown University, operated a wide network of offices, making deliveries of coal and wood directly from railroad yards and wharves; the firm reportedly owned and operated the largest kindling wood factory south of New York.

The manufacture and sale of musical instruments was another major business undertaking about 1900. The city's acknowledged master of piano sales and manufacture was the Washington branch of the national Bradbury Piano Company which opened at 1103 Pennsylvania Avenue in 1879. In 1887 the successful operation erected its own building a block up on the Avenue where 75 of the famous Bradbury pianos could be seen on display on the first of the building's four floors. The success of the Bradbury piano with Washington society was credited to W. P. Wickle's management of the Washington showrooms.

Paper products supply was another major business activity at the turn of the century. The firm of R. P. Andrews and Company and the E. Morrison Paper Company carried complete stocks of paper, stationery and printing supplies. The R. P. Andrews Company employed 52 people, including 5 traveling salesmen, and was the city's sole agent for pulp and paper companies in West Virginia, Virginia, Maryland and Pennsylvania. These major paper suppliers supported another leading Washington industry, printing and bookbinding. In 1900 the capital's largest printing and binding firm, Gibson Brothers, operated a plant at 1238 Pennsylvania Avenue. Nearby, at building number 1230 on the Avenue, Andrew Butler Graham operated one of the country's most complete photo-lithograph establishments. Like many of his successful Washington counterparts, businessman Graham was identified with a number of institutions including the Arlington Fire Insurance Company (which he directed), the Riggs Insurance Company, and the Union Trust and Storage Company. By 1900 the Southern Printers' Supply Company, with offices, warehouse and shop on 10th Street, was also a major source of printing machinery and supplies.

In other lines of endeavor about the time of the capital's centennial, Arthur A. Chapin and George D. Saks operated Chapin-Saks, wholesalers of butter, eggs, cheese and ice, and were proprietors of a large cold storage plant in an immense warehouse at 974 Louisiana Avenue in the center of the city's wholesale produce markets. In 1900 Chapin-Saks was reported to be the largest wholesale firm in its line south of New York. Another major produce enterprise, Golden, Love and Company, also operating on Louisiana Avenue, was Washington's leading caterer. The George W. Knox Express Company, founded in 1894, was one of several major private transport companies operating at the turn of the century. The Purity Ice Company operated its plant at 5th and L Streets, N.W., employing a fleet of horse-drawn wagons and carts for deliveries. The company's founder, John Evans McGraw, proudly advertised that his steadfast refusal to collaborate with the ubiquitous ice trust permitted Washingtonians to receive ice at prices even "within the reach of the poor".

A sampling of mercantile Washington at the turn of the century may be rounded out by mention of the capital's primary brewing establishment, the Abner-Drury Brewing Company. Founded in 1871, the company plant was located on 25th Street between F and G Streets, N.W. at a point overlooking the Potomac. The capital's local brand beer, "Old Glory," was, the Washington *Post* assured readers in 1898, "favorably known to almost every inhabitant of the District of Columbia and endorsed for its purity and strengthening qualities by the medical profession everywhere." [34]

Hotel industry

The post-Civil War expansion of commercial activity was also reflected in a series of grand hotels. The success of the Willard Hotel—formerly the renowned City Hotel, purchased in 1858 by Henry Augustus Willard—probably set the example for W. W. Corcoran who constructed one of the capital's most sumptuous hotels, the Arlington. The new hotel covered the entire square on Vermont Avenue from H to I Streets. Prior to the Arlington's opening in 1869, Washington's hotel accommodations—at $2.50 to $4.50 a day—were generally felt to be "both primitive and limited" particularly in comparison "to the more improved methods then in vogue in New York and the larger capitals of Europe." [35] The Arlington enjoyed immediate success, a growing number of city residents giving up their houses to take up permanent residence in the hotel. At the same time visiting diplomatic parties occasionally made use of the hotel's widely adver-

[34] *Ibid.*

[35] *Ibid.*, pp. 293–4.

tised "Diplomatic Suite" consisting of 32 rooms. The popularity of the Arlington's cuisine is said to have caused Congress to rearrange its hours of adjournment to conform with the hotel's five o'clock dining hour.[36]

In 1890 the Raleigh Hotel opened its doors at the corner of 12th Street and Pennsylvania. T. J. Talty, the former manager of enormous Chicago hotels, came to the capital to make an international reputation as an innkeeper. Talty's efficient direction helps to explain the decision to more than double the number of Raleigh bedrooms to 300 within two years of the hotel's opening. In 1898 a half million dollars was spent to refurbish the old Shoreham Hotel on the corner of 15th and H Streets; the result was "a masterpiece of the builder's and decorator's art" including, in the tradition of the great hotels, an elegant and heavily patronized dining room.[37]

In time many of the original grand hotels were replaced. The original Shoreham gave way to an office building; the Arlington fell before the Veterans' Bureau. By 1930 new hotel names were widely known: the Wardman Park (with 1,500 rooms) at Woodley Road near Connecticut Avenue; the Mayflower (with 1,100 rooms) on Connecticut Avenue; the Carlton located in the day's most prominent residential boulevard on 16th Street (at K Street); the Burlington near Thomas Circle; and the Pennsylvania, Grace Dodge, Commodore, Congress Hall, Harrington, Grafton, Annapolis, Lafayette, Ambassador and others. According to the Hotel Association of the District of Columbia, Washington in 1928 ranked sixth in hotel accommodations in the nation. The Hotel Association estimated that hotel property in the capital represented a total investment in 1928 of about $45 million, including: the Mayflower, $4.7 million; the Wardman Park, $3.6 million, the Willard, $3.7 million; and the Raleigh, $2.1 million, among others. By 1930 the capital contained 77 hotels with 13,465 bedrooms, 43 dining rooms, 5,172 employees, and a total payroll of $4.8 million.[38]

Building trades

The substantial construction of the post-Civil War era, visible in immense hotels, private residences and public buildings, supported a significant building trades sector. Dean of the city's builders, about 1900, was Thomas W. Smith, the characteristic "self-made" man who

[36] *Ibid.*, p. 295.

[37] *Ibid.*

[38] Proctor, *Washington*, pp. 783–5. Also Washington Board of Trade, "A Survey of Washington and its Environs," 1930, pp. 66. Hereafter cited as Board of Trade, "Survey."

founded in 1874 what became one of the Mid-Atlantic region's largest lumber manufacturing and supply centers. In the 1890's Smith displayed his wares in a building at the corner of 1st Street and Indiana Avenue; in addition Smith's mill and lumber sheds stood at the foot of New Jersey Avenue and a lumber drying kiln stocked more than 100,000 feet of lumber at an Anacostia location. The lumber yard of Church and Stephenson Company covered the entire block at Maryland Avenue, 8th and 9th Streets, S.W. The capital also housed a number of architectural and building firms, three brick companies, the B. F. Smith Fireproof Construction Company, the Washington Granite and Monumental Company (at 11th Street and New York Avenue), the appliance firm of S. S. Shed Company (on 9th Street), (several plumbing establishments including the city's largest, James Noland and Sons (established in 1882 at 1722 14th Street), and the capital's leading paver, the Crawford Paving Company, founded in 1871.[39]

Banking and finance

It was characteristic of that era of commercial growth and self-made men that stores and companies should carry the names of their founders and that their portraits, unfailingly with beards and mustaches, should fill the pages of volumes celebrating the centennial of the founding of the National Capital. The leading figures of banking and finance were similarly noted, for while banking had strong historical antecedents the post-Civil War era brought its own financial order. By 1930 Washington contained 12 national banks, 7 trust companies, and 22 savings banks.

The oldest of the national banks, the Bank of Washington, opened its doors in 1809 and within two years was under charter from Congress. In 1886 it became the National Bank of Washington and erected its own banking house three years later. In 1907 it absorbed the Central National Bank, boosting its capital to more than one million dollars. By 1929 the National Bank of Washington possessed resources totaling $12.6 million.[40]

The early need for additional banking facilities in Washington was partly satisfied in 1814 when the Bank of the Metropolis opened its subscription books for 25,000 shares at a par value of $20. The bank was originally located on 15th Street near the Treasury Building and endeared itself with General Andrew Jackson in 1815 by

[39] Washington *Post, History,* Chapter 22.

[40] John B. Larner, "History of Banking in the District of Columbia," in Proctor, *Washington,* Chapter 18; and Washington *Post, History,* Chapter 18.

making the loan that permitted the financing of Jackson's successful New Orleans military campaign. As President, Jackson privately patronized the Bank of the Metropolis in addition to making it one of the depositories of United States funds in place of the Bank of the United States. In 1865 the Bank of the Metropolis reorganized under the new National Banking Act as the National Metropolitan Bank. At that time its capital was $350,000. By 1928 the bank ranked second among the city's national banks in the amount of deposits held, $18.1 million.

The total deposits of the National Metropolitan Bank in 1928 were exceeded only by the Riggs National Bank. Washington's preeminent banking institution began in 1836 as a tiny exchange and brokerage business on Pennsylvania Avenue near 15th Street owned by William W. Corcoran, the son of a prominent Georgetown family. In 1840 Corcoran formed a partnership with George W. Riggs, also of an established Georgetown family. While their considerable banking talents yielded a respectable business by 1845, it was the purchase of the assets of the defunct Bank of the United States that lent the firm of Corcoran and Riggs an unmatched aura of prestige. The partnership proceeded to use land-warrants (obtained in its purchase of assets of the Bank of the United States) to develop one of the capital's leading financial houses. Corcoran subsequently enhanced the firm's fortunes by successfully marketing bonds to finance the Mexican War. It was not until 1896 that the firm became a public bank with a national charter, authorized to do business as the Riggs National Bank. Thenceforth, under the direction of its president, Charles C. Glover, the Riggs Bank rapidly expanded: between 1896 and 1903 the bank's total resources jumped from $3.8 million to $14.8 million. By 1928 the bank's resources had increased over 800 percent to $56.9 million. At that time the bank had 8 branches including its headquarters at Pennsylvania Avenue and 15th Street, N.W. Glover retained an active role in the bank through 1930 and was largely responsible for securing Rock Creek Park as a public preserve, for choosing and securing the site of the National Cathedral, and for helping to institute a plan to reclaim hundreds of acres of land for residential development near the Rock Creek in the increasingly popular northwest section of the city.

A number of smaller but active national banks were organized in the decades following the Civil War: the Second National Bank in 1872, with $7.9 million in resources in 1928; the Columbia National Bank, chartered in 1887, with $5.4 million in resources in 1928; the

National Capital Bank of Washington, 1889, $2.3 million; the Lincoln National Bank, 1904, $20.4 million; the District National Bank, 1909, $12.6 million; the Federal American National Bank, 1913, $15.8 million; the Franklin National Bank, 1914, $4.7 million; and the Liberty National Bank, 1917, $4.4 million.

By 1890 trust companies had been active in other cities for a quarter century. In that year Washington interests were finally able to obtain Congressional authority to establish trust companies in the capital, although it was stipulated that such companies should be under the immediate supervision of the Comptroller of the Currency and subject to the same inspection by national bank examiners as the national banks. Trust companies were required also to have initial capitalization of one million dollars. In 1928 seven trust companies, with a total of $86 million in deposits, were functioning in the District.

The Washington Loan and Trust Company became the pioneer trust company after the passage of the new trust law in 1890. Washington's trust companies were the only trust institutions in the country chartered under an act of Congress and accountable to supervisors of the Federal government. Such distinctions allowed the Washington Loan and Trust Company quickly to dispose of capital stock of a million dollars. Near the turn of the century the company erected a massive, granite, nine-story building at the corner of 9th and F Streets, N.W. which was widely credited with bringing an immediate impetus to that lagging but important business section of the city. In 1902, under the direction of two of the Board of Trade's most venerable members, John Joy Edson and John Augustus Swope, 1,300 safe deposit boxes had been rented, at the cost of about $3 a piece, at the Washington Loan and Trust Company; a substantial amount of real estate had been accumulated in the bank's position as executor and trustee, necessitating the creation of a separate real estate department. In 1928 the trust company listed total resources of more than $19 million.

Although the Washington Loan and Trust Company was the city's pioneer trust firm, it was closely followed by the American Security and Trust Company. In its first year of operation, American Security and Trust had deposits of about $271,000. By 1928 the company's deposits had $31.1 million. This expansion was partly the result of its consolidation in 1919 with the Home Savings Bank, then the city's second oldest and largest savings bank with some 40,000 depositors. The acquisition of the Home Savings Bank gave the American Security and Trust Company branch banks in the central, northeast and southwest sections of the city. In 1907 the storage business of the company had expanded enough to lead to the creation of a separate entity, the Security Storage Company, to handle that element of the trust company's business. At about the same time, the American Security and Trust Company took up main quarters in the northwest corner of Pennsylvania Avenue and 15th Street, N.W. The presence of the American Security and Trust Company, Riggs National Bank, the National Savings and Trust Company and the U. S. Treasury made of 15th Street and the Avenue the city's financial center.

The National Safe Deposit Company was chartered by a special act of Congress in 1867. Its incorporators included Alexander Shepherd and George W. Riggs. For two decades after 1870 the National Safe Deposit Company and the National Savings and Trust Company shared the same building. In 1892 the two companies merged, taking the corporate name of the National Safe Deposit, Savings and Trust Company, soon shortened to National Savings and Trust Company. In 1928 the National Savings and Trust Company reported resources of $17.2 million and deposits of $13.3 million.

In 1900 the Union Trust Company was chartered and opened on F Street. Seven years later the company moved to its newly completed quarters at 15th and H Streets, N.W. By 1928 the Union Trust Company had deposits of $9.2 million. In 1912, 1913 and 1922 additional trust companies were formed. In 1929 the first of these, the Continental Trust Company, reported resources totaling $4.3 million and deposits of $3 million. The Munsey Trust Company began auspiciously in 1913 by absorbing the five branch banks of the United States Trust Company. By 1928 the Munsey Trust Company had resources amounting to $8.9 million and deposits of $4.8 million. The Merchants Bank and Trust Company, chartered in 1922, gradually expanded with the absorption of other established banks, including the Merchants Bank, the Citizens' Savings Bank, the Dupont National Bank, and the Exchange Bank of Washington. In 1929 the Merchants Bank and Trust Company had resources amounting to $11.1 million and total deposits of $9.3 million.

By 1929 Washington also housed 22 savings banks. The McLachlen Banking Corporation became the first savings institution in 1891, locating at 10th and G Streets, N.W. in a three story dwelling. In 1912 the bank's original house was demolished and a nine story office building erected in its stead. In 1928 the McLachlen Banking Corporation had resources totaling $2.3 million. Between 1903 and 1917,

TABLE 4

Categories of Manufacture with More Than $1 Million in Production Value, Washington, D.C. 1927

Industry	Number of Firms	Employees	Value of Products
Printing and publishing, newspaper and periodical	88	1,189	23,671,701
Bread and other Bakery products	66	1,221	10,567,203
Slaughtering and meat packing, whlsale	8	356	7,703,792
Printing and publishing, book and job	85	1,202	6,341,453
Ice cream	19	347	3,874,164
Coffee and spice, roasting and grinding	6	48	2,085,943
Beverages	22	185	1,468,774
Ice (manufactured)	9	108	1,398,871
Structural and ornamental iron and steel work, not made in rolling mills	11	224	1,355,669
Planing-mill products	6	198	1,050,100
All industries	503	9,519	90,389,537
Public Utilities			104,474,886
Capital Traction Co.			17,606,000
Washington Railway and Electric Co.			32,012,700
Washington Rapid Transit Co.			766,574
Potomac Electric Power Co.			25,523,000
Washington and Georgetown Gaslight Cos			14,459,612
Chesapeake and Potomac Telephone Co.			14,107,000

Source: Census of Manufactures, 1927, Bureau of the Census.

seven additional savings banks opened their doors: the Potomac Savings Bank of Georgetown; the East Washington Savings Bank, at 312 Pennsylvania Avenue, S.E.; the United States Savings Bank, at 14th and U Streets, N.W.; the Washington Mechanics Savings Bank, in southeast Washington; the Bank of Commerce and Savings, at 8th and G Streets, N.W.; the Anacostia Bank, at Nichols and U Streets, S.E.; the Seventh Street Savings Bank, at 7th and N Streets, N.W.; the North Capital Savings Bank, at 731 North Capital Street; the Industrial Savings Bank, at 11th and U Streets; the Security and Savings Commercial Bank, at 7th and G Streets; the Northeast Savings Bank, at 800 H Street, N.E.; and the Washington Savings Bank, on 10th Street, N.W. at Grant Place. In most cases, these savings banks each listed, in 1925, total deposits in the range of $465,000 to $3.5 million; the Security Savings and Commercial Bank listed deposits of $6.1 million.

Between 1920 and 1925 still another seven savings banks were chartered: the Mount Vernon Savings Bank, at Mt. Vernon Place and 9th Street, N.W.; the International Exchange Bank, at 5th and H

Streets, N.W.; the Chevy Chase Savings Bank, at 5530 Connecticut Avenue; the Bank of Brightwood, on Georgia Avenue, N.W.; the Prudential Bank, at 715 Florida Avenue; the Woodridge-Langdon Savings and Commercial Bank, at 2027 Rhode Island Avenue, N.E.; and the Morris Plan Bank, near 14th and H Streets, N.W. In addition, the Departmental Bank was organized in 1904 by an enterprising government clerk whose short-term loans became popular with fellow government employees. Deposits in all these banks ranged from about $322,000 to $3.6 million.

By 1901 the extensive and expanding activities of the banking sector led John Joy Edson and Charles C. Glover to take the lead in forming the District of Columbia Bankers' Association. For a number of years Washington's financial leadership occasionally gathered in the Willard Hotel. In 1919 the uncertainties of the early post-war period brought the city's bankers together in what was to be the first of a series of annual conventions. In 1930 the Association numbered 40 members with 24 branches, total resources of over $310 million, and deposits of over $250 million.[41]

Before leaving the financial sector, mention should be made of the District of Columbia League of Building and Loan Associations founded in 1892. By 1930 the League listed 19 members whose resources had more than doubled in ten years to total $59.9 million, with loans outstanding on real estate of approximately $57.5 million. In that year the percentage of real estate loans as a part of total assets was higher in the District than anywhere else in the country, the Washington percentage being about 94 and that of the country 91.5.[42]

IV. BUSINESS WASHINGTON IN 1930

As the steady increase in banking activity has already hinted, the first three decades of this century saw Washington's population rise rapidly, from 278,718 in 1900 to 331,069 in 1910. The impact of World War I on government employment caused the city's population to soar. By 1920, 437,571 persons resided in the capital. (See Table 5.) In 1930 the District's population of 485,716 ranked 14th among American cities. Persistent growth was reflected in the seven-fold increase in assessed valuation of taxable property (between 1900 and 1930) to $1.2 billion. Steady growth was also manifest in the rise in total bank deposits, from $31.2 million in 1900, to $317 million in 1930.[43]

---

[41] Frederick P. H. Siddons, "A History of the District of Columbia Bankers' Association," in Proctor, *Washington,* Chapter 29.

[42] C. Clinton James, "Building and Loan Associations," in Proctor, *Washington,* Chapter 30.

[43] Board of Trade, "Survey."

TABLE 5

Paid Civilian Employment of the Federal Government, Washington, D.C., 1816 to 1957[1]

Year	Employment
1816	535
1841	1,014
1851	1,533
1861	2,199
1871	6,222
1881	13,124
1910	38,911
1917	48,313
1919	106,000
1925	67,563
1930	73,032
1935	108,673
1940	137,940
1945	264,770
1951	265,980
1957	236,330

[1] Beginning in 1950 includes all suburban jurisdictions; 1941–1949 includes only parts of Fairfax County, Virginia, and Montgomery and Prince George's Counties, Maryland; prior to 1941 D. C. only. Source: *The Statistical History of the United States from Colonial Times to the Present.*

Tax rates and receipts also suggest the growth trends. Between 1900 and 1930 the real estate tax rate rose from $1.50 to $1.70 per hundred dollars, with revenues climbing from $2.6 million to $19.7 million. Gasoline tax receipts suggest increasing incomes, mobility, and growing attachment to private automobile ownership and usage. While the gasoline tax remained 2 cents per gallon between 1925 and 1930, the number of gallons sold doubled to 88 million gallons, the number of gasoline companies nearly tripled to 47, and tax receipts increased from about $821,000 to nearly $1.8 million. In 1930 there were 149,179 passenger cars registered in Washington and 17,132 trucks and delivery cars. That on a typical shopping day fully 42 percent of shoppers in the central business district traveled downtown by private car was already creating alarm among Washingtonians concerned with parking and traffic congestion; the Automobile Parking Committee of Washington identified over 40 points within the central business district that were "congested", that is, where automobiles slowed down to less than 15 miles per hour between intersecting streets.[44]

[44] *Ibid.*

Government sector in 1930

The District of Columbia remained primarily the seat of Federal government and that was clearly the city's single leading industry. The assessed value of Federal property in 1930 was $530 million and of District government property $58 million (a grand total of $588 million in comparison to the $1.2 billion value of all taxable property). The Bureau of Printing and (Engraving, the Government Printing Office, and the Washington Navy Yard were the main sources of employment and income among the District's industrial plants. The Bureau of Printing and Engraving employed more than five thousand persons in 1927. The Government Printing Office employed over 4,000 workers in the annual production of almost 60 million books, bulletins and other publications. The Naval Gun Factory at the Washington Navy Yard employed another 4,000 persons in a plant valued at about $50 million.[45]

The advantages of the continuing presence of 71,500 Federal and 4,500 District civil servants remained sharply etched into the awareness of the city's business community. In 1929 the Board of Trade stated that "it is doubtful if any other large community can boast of such stability of income to its residents as can Washington. This is in view of the large number of salaried Government employees here and the general solidity and permanence of established businesses and industries which are not affected by fluctuating industrial conditions outside the city. . . . The Government salary payroll is little affected by general business conditions." In 1928 that payroll amounted to $127,300,000 or about $74 per person in every two-week pay period. The capital's status as a major tourist center was further encouragement to support local public sector development that precluded "the smoke and industrial litter of the average industrial town." [46]

Private sector-manufacture

Despite the large and continuing presence of the Federal establishment, Washington's business community hardly needed reminding that private industry was the means of livelihood for two-thirds of the capital's 242,475 working people (in 1925). The industrial census of 1927 (see Table 4) listed 503 manufacturing plants (not including government operations) making 175 different products and employing 9,519 persons.

Still the relatively limited nature of Washington manufacture was

[45] Proctor, *Washington,* pp. 708–10.

[46] "Facts About Washington" in Proctor, *Washington,* p. 709.

hardly disputable and, in fact, had never been after the Civil War when the nation's major industrial centers took their form—a form most Washingtonians were quick and determined to reject. Of Washington's 503 plants in 1927, only 38 could be characterized as "heavy" industry and they involved only 701 workers. The remaining 465 plants were "light" industry and employed the bulk (8,818) of the manufacturing labor force.

The small-scale character of most of Washington manufacture was also clearly portrayed by the 1927 industrial census. The leading industrial element—printing and publishing—included 173 establishments employing 2,391 workers, about 15 men in each plant. The second major industrial category, bread and other bakery products, included 66 establishments employing 1,221 persons, about 20 workers per establishment. The manufacture of beverages ranked third, with 22 establishments and 185 employees. Ice cream production ranked fourth with 19 establishments and 346 employees. In all of the city's 503 manufacturing establishments, 9,514 wage-earners were employed—about 18 per plant—in the production of products valued at $90.4 million in 1927. Only 8 individual manufacturing categories produced goods valued in excess of $1 million.[47]

In 1880, however, the value of production of all the city's manufacturing concerns, including government operations, had been just $11.9 million. Thus in 1930, Washingtonians had some reason to feel that the capital's manufacturing base was growing and at least relatively substantial. To the city's production value of $90.4 million (1927) could be added the $10 million in product value of 107 plants in the outlying areas. The product of government plants was estimated at about $100 million in 1928. This grand total of $200 million (excluding utilities) of production value for the Washington area was sufficient to place it 32nd among the nation's 93 largest industrial centers (over 100,000 population) listed by the Bureau of the Census in 1927. In this view, Washington ranked ahead of Camden (New Jersey), Columbus, Seattle, St. Paul, New Orleans, Syracuse, Hartford, Houston and Wilmington (Delaware) among others.[48]

Other private enterprise

In 1930 real estate and building and construction were probably Washington's major private industries. While the capital ranked 14th in population, it was among the first ten in construction in the

[47] Proctor, *Washington*, pp. 710–12.

[48] *Ibid.* It was also noted that the combined capitalization of the city's utilities in 1927 was more than $104 million with about $10 million paid in wages and salaries in the year.

post-World War I decades. In accordance with the 1920 zoning ordinance, there were (in 1930) approximately 842,000 feet of commercial frontage of which 47,000 was in the downtown business district. In the same year there were 1,623 stores in the central business district of which 203 (12.5 percent) were vacant. There was approximately 2.3 million square feet of office space in the capital, of which 15.7 percent was unoccupied in the fall of 1930. The city's large transient population element had encouraged the construction of 1,440 apartment buildings containing 39,848 units by 1930. One- and two-family dwellings numbered 90,051 in 1930 with about a third of the homes owner-occupied. Forty building firms employed 1,528 people in the city and had a 1929 payroll of $2.4 million; 64 general contractors and 93 subcontractors employed 5,606 workers on a payroll of $10.1 million.[49]

Most of Washington's 313 wholesale firms in 1930 were confined to the distribution of products within the city. Occasional houses were located in the capital for the purpose of distributing goods through southern states. The wholesale establishments employed a total of 4,469 persons and had a total payroll of $7.9 million; 125 firms were engaged in food and tobacco products; 48 in hardware, electrical, plumbing and sporting goods; 21 in automotive products; and 19 firms dealt in machinery, equipment and supplies.

Washington's warehouse business in 1930 was also essentially local in character. Consequently warehouse space tended to be limited; a firm requiring warehouse space generally constructed buildings to fit its needs. There were 11 warehouses in 1930 employing 130 workers and providing 189,473 square feet of space.[50]

The capital's retail sector included a core of department stores, ten in 1930. These large stores employed 6,225 persons and had a payroll of more than $8 million. Net sales amounted to $45.9 million in 1929. There were also approximately 60 national chains operating 950 stores in the city; the chains employed 4,436 people with a payroll of about $6.4 million and annual net sales (1929) of about $64 million. Among the chain enterprises, grocery and meat firms were dominant in terms of number of stores (549), employees (1,672), and net annual sales ($32.1 million). Filling stations ranked second (141 stations), followed by shoe stores (62), drug stores (59), womens clothing shops (24), and variety and general stores (15).[51]

In addition a large number—4,287—of specialty stores operated in the city about 1930. These stores employed a total of 14,401 persons on a payroll of $23.3 million while registering net sales in 1929 of about

[49] Board of Trade, "Survey," p. 65.
[50] *Ibid.*
[51] *Ibid.*

$191.8 million. Exclusive groceries and meat markets ranked first in number of stores (1,820), employment (2,939) and sales ($49 million); they were followed by clothing establishments (593 stores, 2,744 employees, $31.5 million in sales), automotive firms (432 excluding gas stations, 3,354 employees, $43.9 million in sales), and general and variety stores (138, employing 136, with sales of $2.1 million); "other" stores numbered 979 with 3,725 employees and net sales of $46.9 million. The census figures strongly suggest the "small business" orientation of the 1930's: the typical chain and specialty store employed 3 or 4 persons (with the exception of drug and variety stores where 10 to 25 people were often employed).[52]

Despite the growth of the chain store movement and the expansion of the outer limits of residential Washington, the Center Market retained its importance as a shopping center. The more than 250 market dealers continued to be regularly patronized by city residents, many of whom had begun to make the trip to market in private cars.[53]

By 1930 the Nation's Capital had become an increasingly attractive location for professionals, both as individuals and in associations. In that year over 500 national associations had offices in the city, of which more than 100 had their national headquarters in Washington. The latter group included the United States Chamber of Commerce, the American Dairy Federation, the American Drug Manufacturers Association, the National Board of Farm Organizations, and the American Federation of Labor. Teachers (3,234) composed the city's largest category of professional individuals, followed by lawyers and judges (2,415), trained nurses (1,818), engineers (1,287), physicians and surgeons (1,227), designers, draftsmen and inventors (1,041), realtors (972), musicians and music teachers (930), and authors, editors and reporters (838).[54]

The city's substantial professional population was reflected in Washington's role as an educational center. By 1930 over 2,400 pupils paid about $900 in annual tuition and fees to attend one of ten "specialized educational institutions" (providing training in art, music, electrical engineering, workshop skills for the blind, "self-expression", and physical education). In addition, 18 commercial schools (business administration, applied arts, hotel and secretarial training) housed 5,335 students in 1930. Finally, 12 colleges and universities had a student population of 17,722.

The city was well supplied, as noted earlier, with hotel accommoda-

[52] *Ibid.*
[53] Proctor, *Washington,* p. 703.
[54] Board of Trade, "Survey," p. 66.

tions by 1930. Washington contained 77 hotels with 13,465 rooms and 43 dining rooms, employing 5,172 persons with a payroll of $4.9 million. Washington also contained 605 restaurants and eating places employing 4,164 persons with a payroll of $3.7 million.[55]

In 1930 Washingtonians looked forward to significant industrial and commercial development. The president of the Washington Electrical League, while recognizing that Washington's principal industry was "the business of Government administration," advocated a search for "the lighter industries, such as food products, clothing, novelty factories, printing and publishing, and light machinery and fabricating plants." Ample space for expansion seemed available: the city then had 6,727 acres zoned for industrial and commercial purposes of which only 1,789 had been used.[56]

V. EXTENSION OF THE FEDERAL ESTABLISHMENT: 1930–1945

The successive incidence of economic depression, international conflict and post-war political developments between 1930 and 1945 made Washington the unrivalled national center of social and economic reform and military planning and the international political capital of the non-communist world. Through the 1930's a host of new Federal agencies—including the Social Security Board, the National Labor Relations Board, the Public Works Administration and a dozen other planning and administrative units—gave Washington a national position far exceeding that of earlier years. During World War II the capital became the center for planning and supply operations for the Allied forces and the extensive control of the wartime economy further enhanced Washington's role as the nation's administrative center. The advent of Cold War divisions required Washington to maintain a central political as well as diplomatic role on an international scale.

The capital's growing importance drew large numbers of new residents into the city. Washington's population increased more than a third (to 663,091) when the city was the "New Deal Capital" in the 1930's. Between 1940 and 1950 the population jumped 21 percent to 802,178. Federal employment, as shown in Table 5, reached 264,770 in 1945 and 265,980 in 1951.

Such population and employment trends permitted the Washington community to weather the Great Depression better than most cities; then, as perhaps never before or since, the capital realized the benefits of the stability provided by the Federal presence. In 1934 the cash

---

[55] *Ibid.*, pp. 30–32, 56.

[56] Proctor, *Washington*, p. 713.

from $9.5 million in government paychecks circulated through Washington shops and markets every two weeks. Compared to salary reductions averaging 50 percent in other cities, the 15-percent Federal pay cuts introduced in 1933 were slight and 10 percent of the 15 was restored in July 1934, the rest the following spring. Retail sales in the capital managed to rise 22 percent between 1929 and 1939, although much of the increase was registered after 1933. The number of retail establishments rose 21 percent in the depression decade, from 5,815 establishments to 6,893.[57]

VI. THE POST-WAR ERA: THE CHALLENGE OF METROPOLITAN DEVELOPMENT

The nearly three decades since the close of World War II have seen a dramatic spatial alteration involving the District of Columbia—the growth of a major metropolitan area. From the viewpoint of the capital's business community, metropolitan development has brought a mixture of blessings and recurrent challenges. While the growth, for example, of suburban residential neighborhoods has created new shopping centers to compete with the city's retail centers, the demand for downtown office space has fairly exploded: between 1959 and 1971, 186 office buildings were constructed, giving the capital 17.9 million square feet of office space. Much of the demand for new space has been accounted for by Washington's "hidden industry", the associations; by 1960 the continuing influx of learned societies and association headquarters had made Washington the capital of all major American interests and aspirations. Associations now employ over 50,000 people and spend some $500 million annually in the District. There are approximately 1,100 trade and professional associations in the city, and 1,600 such groups when religious and philanthropic associations are included.[58] The influx of professionals who tend to reside in the suburbs and work downtown has encouraged massive use of private automobiles, to the extent that the environment of Washington is threatened with serious deterioration: the incidence of car ownership (of Washingtonians alone) per 1,000 population grew from 264 in 1955 to 352 in 1971 when 263,998 cars were registered in the city.[59]

---

[57] Constance McLaughlin Green, *Washington: Capital City, 1879–1950* (Princeton: Princeton University Press, 1963), pp. 88, 257–83. Hereafter cited as Green, *Washington, 1879–1950*. Also Census of Retail Trade, District of Columbia, 1940.

[58] Green, *Washington, 1879-1950,* p. 501. Also Chesapeake and Potomac Telephone Company Company Business Research Office, *Business in Washington,* various issues.

[59] Mayor's Economic Development Committee, "Policy Perspectives for the District of Columbia," unpublished manuscript, p. 28.

The renovation of Georgetown and renewal of southwest Washington have tended to slow down—but not reverse—a distressing trend: the exodus of white middle-class families to nearby suburban developments and the complementary tendency for new business enterprise to locate in outlying areas where land availability, lower crime rates and more favorable tax structures have been strong drawing points. While this trend to suburbia is common to all American urban areas, government policies of Federal agency centralization have encouraged suburban growth in the Washington area by relocating some major research facilities and administrative offices in Maryland and Virginia. Thus as many middle-class families have followed Federal and private jobs to the suburbs, Washington's business community has witnessed the decline of the city's central residential position. In 1920 the District contained 76.5 percent of the persons living in the metropolitan area; in 1950 the city contained 61.6 percent. By 1970 the number had dropped to 26 percent.[60]

Suburbanization is also reflected in the near parity with Washington banks (in terms of total deposits) reached by suburban banking institutions. Significantly, however, Washington's largest banks continue to rank among the major financial institutions on both a regional and national basis: District banks reported a record $3.3 billion in deposits in 1972, an increase of 10 percent over 1971. Last year the Riggs' Bank became the area's first to gain over one billion dollars in deposits.[61]

The District of Columbia remains the place of work for fully 62 per-

[60] Green, "Washington, D.C.," p. 258.

[61] Washington *Post,* January 4, 1973. Total bank deposits, District of Columbia, as of December 31, 1972 were:

Riggs National	$1,006,249,331
Amern, Security & Trust	870,908,576
Natl Bank of Wash	405,747,260
Natl Savings & Trust	276,171,124
Union Trust Co.	236,983,408
First National	172,238,986
Madison National	88,724,800
Security National	69,845,266
D. C. National	44,420,355
McLachlen Bank	41,035,991
Industrial Bank	33,418,316
Public National	28,106,044
National Capital	27,767,248
United Community	19,186,031
Total deposits	3,320,801,936

cent of the area's Federal government civilian employees. The most current census figures show that Washington's black population has recently had the highest employment rate of any of the nation's largest metropolitan areas: 96 percent of the city's black labor force was steadily employed in 1970. The median income of all Washington families increased (including allowance for inflation) 65 percent between 1949 and 1969; in 1969 Washington's median family income was greater than that of Atlanta, Boston, Baltimore, Cleveland, and St. Louis and the median income of black families was greater here than in all of those cities and Milwaukee and San Francisco. The aggregate personal income of all Washington residents rose 70 percent between 1949 and 1959 to $2.9 billion. This solid income base permitted the District Government revenues to rise, to provide crucial public services, at an annual rate of about 10 percent in the last decade, from $251 million in 1960 to $641 million in 1970.[62]

While the central position of the District of Columbia has, to some degree, given way to a national trend towards suburban development, the capital is increasingly aware of the potentials of effective regional cooperation. In the decade of the 1960's the Washington Metropolitan Area was the fastest growing region in the nation, rising from 10th to 7th ranking in the decade.[63] The creation of the Washington Metropolitan Council of Governments and the Washington Metropolitan Area Transit Authority (1962) have promised renewed attention on the District's traditional role as a retail, employment and residential center. The efforts of a half dozen technical assistance groups, the Board of Trade, the Chamber of Commerce, and the District Government's newly created office for business and industrial promotion also promise further retail and light industrial development for the entire Washington community.

The Nation's Capital continues as one of the country's leading centers of tourism, conventions, research and education. Approximately 18.3 million tourists visited the capital last year (up 3.4 percent over 1971), making Washington second only to New York as a national sight-seeing center. The presence of headquarters of national organizations led the capital to serve as host to 725 conventions in 1972 involving about 700,000 delegates. The promotion of scientific research during World War II laid the foundation for one of the na-

[62] Chesapeake and Potomac Telephone Company Business Research Office, *Business in Washington,* various issues; and Financial and Statistical Report, D.C. Government, 1972.

[63] Washington Center for Metropolitan Studies, *Metropolitan Bulletin,* Number 2, 1971.

tion's most significant "research and development" centers: the number of these companies grew from 7 in 1940 to 50 in 1960. Complementary development in nearby suburbs has made Washington first among the nation's metropolitan areas in the number of scientific persons employed per 1,000 population (these include scientists in government service).[64]

Washington's continuing role as an educational center is suggested by the fact that in recent decades the Washington Metropolitan Area has had the highest educational attainment level of adults 25 years of age and over of any of the nation's largest metropolitan areas. In 1970 the city's university population numbered 64,443. The first of the city's nine general colleges and universities was founded in 1789 as Georgetown Seminary to train young men for the Roman Catholic priesthood. The school was later chartered by Congress as the Georgetown University. In 1821 the Columbian College was founded by a group of Washington Baptists. Benefitting from a small congressional endowment in 1831 and a gift of one million dollars from William W. Corcoran in 1871, the university (later renamed after George Washington) acquired its own campus a few blocks west of the White House. The Catholic University of America was founded in 1887 to serve as the center of American Roman Catholic education. The American University was chartered in 1893 by a group of Washington Methodists who pooled $100,000 to purchase a large wooded tract above Georgetown. The 90-acre undergraduate campus went largely unused until after World War I as the university maintained a downtown center that included a graduate school, the Washington College of Law, and schools of business and public administration; by 1967 the transfer of graduate facilities to the uptown campus had been completed.[65]

Howard University was chartered in 1867 to provide for the higher education of Negroes. While originally intended as a biracial institution, that goal had been abandoned by the 1890's and Howard's student body remained all Negro until after World War II. The university is supported primarily by annual Federal appropriations administered through the Department of Health, Education and Welfare. Since 1968 the Washington Technical Institute has been the

---

[64] Green, "Washington, D.C.," p. 260.

[65] *Ibid.,* p. 261. 1970 student enrollment: American University, 15,211; Catholic University, 6,113; D.C. Teachers, 2,980; Dumbarton College of Holy Cross, 354; Federal City College, 6,038; Gallaudet, 799; George Washington University, 14,998; Georgetown, 8,189; Howard, 8,892; Oblate College, 70; St. Paul's College, 95; Trinity College, 744. American Council of Education, *American Universities and Colleges,* W. Todd Furniss, ed., Washington, D.C., 1973.

city's primary vocational training center. Gallaudet College, located in northeast Washington at Kendall Green, began in 1857 as a school for deaf-mutes. Its first director was the son of Thomas H. Gallaudet, who introduced into America the use of sign language for teaching deaf-mutes. Gallaudet was the first school in the nation to provide higher education for the deaf. The Federal City College opened its doors in 1968; Washington's land grant college has already attracted more than 6,000 students. The District of Columbia Teachers College has a student population of about 3,000. The city also has two

TABLE 6

Selected Industrial Distribution by Employment and Units, Washington, D.C., 1948 and 1970

Industry	Employees (Total #)	Number of Units	Total Employees under 20
Construction			
1948	21,182	1,303	1,057
1970	18,589	736	—
Manufacturing			
1948	16,382	542	395
1970	23,991	652	—
food products			
1948	4,468	78	31
1970	3,139	35	—
printing, pub.			
1948	8,801	269	207
1970	15,109	332	—
Transportation & other utilities			
1948	22,529	369	199
1970	30,123	451	—
Wholesale trade			
1948	20,966	1,513	1,282
1970	20,535	1,105	—
Retail trade			
1948	74,720	4,841	4,318
1970	63,305	3,267	—
Fin., insur. real			
1948	23,732	2,655	2,431
1970	36,350	2,931	—
Services			
1948	46,344	5,737	5,317
1970	133,209	7,080	—
Total			
1948	227,646	17,480	15,621
1970	326,584	16,495	—

Source: County Business Patterns, District of Columbia, 1948 and 1970, Department of Commerce, Bureau of the Census.

women's colleges—Trinity College and Dunbarton College of Holy Cross—and two seminaries for the Catholic priesthood. The National War College and the Industrial College of the Armed Forces are also located within Washington, on the grounds of the former Washington Arsenal. The United States Army medical department also maintains a research and graduate school in the capital.[66]

The continuing role of education reflects the major developments in the capital's post-war structure of economic activity. (See Table 6.) The growing importance of services industries (where higher educational attainment is generally characteristic) is seen in the jump in employment in that sector—from about 46,000 persons in 1948 to more than 133,000 in 1970. Similarly, another highly professional sector—containing banking, finance, insurance and real estate—increased by a third in employment. Suburban shopping center competition is apparent in the small decline in the capital's retail trade sector in employment and in the number of firms in operation. Yet the capital's other traditional strengths continue in force. Manufacturing, employment and the number of firms have risen, with food products and printing and publishing categories retaining their leading positions.

Manufacturing is a solid base of employment and income but a relatively small factor in the capital's total employment in 1970 of more than 326,000 persons. The postwar era continues the pattern characteristic of the capital since its founding. The Federal establishment continues to determine the overall environment of the seat of national government although business activities provide employment and income for a substantial part of the city and metropolitan population. The development of a major metropolitan area challenges the citizens of the city and of its neighboring suburbs to realize the continuing retail, tourist, research, educational and light industrial possibilities of the urban center and to increase the delivery of those services in which the capital has become a national leader.

SELECTED BIBLIOGRAPHY

American Council of Education, *American Universities and Colleges,* W. Tood Furniss, ed. Washington, D.C., 1973.

Chesapeake and Potomac Telephone Company Business Research Office, *Business in Washington,* various issues.

Census Bureau, Department of Commerce, U. S. Government, various reports.

Crew, H. W. *Centennial History of the City of Washington, D.C.* Dayton, Ohio: United Brethren Publishing Co., 1892.

Green, Constance McLaughlin. *Washington: Village and Capital, 1800–1878.* Princeton: Princeton University Press, 1962.

[66] *Ibid.*

Green, Constance McLaughlin. *Washington: Capital City, 1879–1950.* Princeton: Princeton University Press, 1963.

Green, Constance McLaughlin. "Washington, D.C." in *Encyclopedia Britannica,* 1970, Volume 23.

Proctor, John Claggett, ed. *Washington: Past and Present.* New York: Lewis Historical Publishing Co., 1930. 2 volumes.

Tyler, Orville Z. "The Census of Manufactures of 1820 in the District of Columbia," unpublished manuscript, copy in the Columbia Historical Society Library.

Washington Board of Trade, "A Survey of Washington and its Environs," compiled by Rufus Lusk, Inc., 1930.

Washington Center for Metropolitan Studies, *Metropolitan* Bulletin, various issues.

Washington Post. *A History of the City of Washington: Its Men and and Institutions.* Allan B. Slauson, ed. Washington, D.C., 1903.

Washington's Regional Development

WALTER A. SCHEIBER

We have explored today many of the forces and events which have shaped the development of Washington. These forces and events have resulted in what Philip Hammer has called the "open-ended" economy of this area—an economy subject to a variety of international, national and local stimuli. These forces have combined to produce a metropolitan community rich in resources and diversified in character. It is this development of Washington into a regional entity far broader than that envisaged by Congress in 1790 that I would like to address in the next few minutes.

DEFINING THE WASHINGTON REGION

First let me define what I mean by "the regional development of Washington." I am speaking here of the region in its fullest context—physical, economic, social and political. Washington as a community has evolved from a small, single-purpose town into a metropolis of major size, economic scope and cultural diversity.

The Washington region is the residence of more than 3 million people. It encompasses an area of some 2,900 square miles in two states and the District of Columbia. During the last two decades it has been one of the country's fastest growing urban centers. Metropolitan Washington is now the eighth largest metropolitan area in the United States.

The Washington region provides employment for more than one and one-quarter million workers, three-quarters of whom are not federal workers but part of a growing army of service, finance, trade, manufacturing and other business employees. The Washington region is today one of the country's richest market areas. It has the highest median family income of any metropolitan area, total personal income of $15 billion and retail sales in excess of $6 billion annually.

Delivered at the Columbia Historical Society Washington Economic History Institute, September 19, 1973.

I wish to express my appreciation to Stuart W. Bendelow, Senior Economist, Metropolitan Washington Council of Governments, for his assistance in the preparation of this paper.

With growth in numbers and economic strength, Washington has broadened its cultural composition to include many ethnic communities with a wide range of interests and resources. These have enriched the urban character of the region and brought many new features to the area. Because of its size and interests Washington now supports numerous cultural activities that were previously available only in other metropolitan centers such as Philadelphia and New York.

Economically Washington is no longer confined to the District of Columbia but penetrates a broad band of counties in Maryland and Virginia and in some instances West Virginia, Pennsylvania and Delaware. It is this transition in size, complexity and specialization that typify the evolution of Washington from a small city into a factors we have discussed earlier, national development, international metropolitan region.

Granted much of Washington's growth was initially due to those events and urbanization. But accompanying this growth has come a level of independence apart from outside forces that has given Washington an economic character of its own. The fact that the Washington region is a market of some 3 million persons, who are highly-educated, predominantly professionally employed, with incomes well above the national average, means that it is able to support a variety of commercial and social activities that were previously imported or nonexistent. This facet of the metropolitan economy has grown rapidly in recent years, becoming a greater and greater force in shaping the form and direction of local development. The prospects for the future appear even greater than those of the past.

Let us examine those factors and trends that have thus far shaped the regional development of Washington.

REGIONAL GROWTH TRENDS

Forty-years ago, in 1930, the metropolitan area of Washington contained just over 700,000 inhabitants, 70 percent of whom lived in the District of Columbia. Suburban development that existed at that time was clustered along the borders of the District in small communities such as Bethesda, Wheaton, Takoma Park, Seat Pleasant, Mount Rainier and similar areas in Maryland and across the Potomac in Alexandria and the nearby portion of Arlington County. For the most part these were residential clusters whose economic livelihood was directly tied to that of the central city although some pre-dated the founding of the national capital as trade centers on their own and some had been developed as retreats from the city.

In 1930 three-quarters of the region's jobs were located in the District of Columbia. The downtown core was the dominant center of employment, commercial business and social activity. Streetcars, buses, railroads and walking were the principal modes of commuting to work. Mass transit was utilized to a much greater extent in 1930 than it is today. The automobile was then an expensive form of transportation unavailable to many. The area's highways were relatively few and rough outside the central city. A broad range of housing opportunities existed in the District, much of it within walking distance of the core.

During the 1930's Federal efforts to revitalize the American economy focused a good deal of attention on Washington. Federally-sponsored projects and programs brought new activities and more jobs to the Nation's Capital than ever before. During this time the role of the Federal Government assumed a greater responsibility in overseeing and managing the nation's economic growth. With this expanded responsibility came increased potential for new business and an extension of service activities in Washington. Between 1930 and 1940, the Washington region added some 300,000 new residents, surpassing the million mark in total population. Close to 60 percent of this growth was within the District of Columbia. Following the inauguration of Franklin D. Roosevelt in 1933, the area witnessed the expansion of many Federal agencies and the creation of new departments which brought new Federal workers and their families to Washington. New Deal economics and the build-up of the country's military power resulted in roughly a doubling of Federal employment in the region during the decade of the 1930's.

During the 1930's and through most of the 1940's Washington's economic structure actually became more specialized as the Federal sector increased in size and influence. In 1930 Federal employment represented 22 percent of all metropolitan jobs; by 1940 this proportion had risen to 32 percent and in 1950 it stood at 35 percent.

While the economic profile of Washington was becoming more specialized during the 1930's the first major thrusts toward regional growth were also taking place. The mid-thirties witnessed the beginning of the suburbanization of Washington. The lure of the suburbs along with the automobile and the FHA mortgage spurred the growth of housing in adjacent areas of Maryland and Virginia. The area's first "new town", Greenbelt, Maryland, was developed under Federal leadership during this period. Still the vast majority of the area's economic activity and influence was centered in downtown Washington. So was the majority of the area's cultural and social activity. But as the suburbs began to grow so did the responsibilities, functions and influence of new suburban governments. Suburban residents looked to their new jurisdictions to provide needed public services such as schools, police and fire protection and sanitation. Their focus of attention was thus divided between the jurisdiction in which they worked and the one in which they lived.

A host of trade and personal service activities followed the flow of new residents into suburban Maryland and Virginia. These activities provided the economic base for the emerging suburban jurisdictions.

Suburbanization continued strong until 1941–1942, when material shortages stemming from the war effort sharply curtailed new housing construction. But following World War II suburban growth resumed its rapid pace, stimulated by returning GIs and the pent-up demand for housing resulting from the war. The desire for single-family detached housing pushed development well into the surrounding countryside. By 1950 metropolitan Washington had grown to more than 1.5 million inhabitants, almost one-half of whom now lived outside the District of Columbia. The 1950 Census of population expanded its definition of the Washington Metropolitan Area to include Arlington County, Virginia.

The United States had emerged from World War II as the dominant world power. Our efforts to manage both national and international affairs fostered another surge in Federal employment, not only in Washington but through the entire United States and abroad. In 1950 the total Federal work force numbered almost 2 million, double the level just prior to World War II.

Between 1940 and 1950, Federal employment in the Washington area increased by over 83,000, totaling over 223,000 workers by the end of the decade. At this time the Federal sector composed 35 percent of the area's total work force. This was the highest level of specialization the Washington economy had reached since World War I and a level from which it has slowly been receding.

Let me qualify that observation by adding that even though the metropolitan employment profile is shifting it does not mean that Federal influence is proportionately declining but merely that it is taking on new forms and exerting its influence in more subtle ways. In addition to stimulus from the Federal Government, the effects of size and geography have more recently played a vital role in metropolitan development.

Having amassed a population of 1.5 million people in 1950, the Washington region achieved a level of economic independence. Previously many products and services that had been imported from other cities could now be economically produced or provided locally to satisfy local market demands. The number and variety of these activities have risen with the growth of the area's consumer market.

The geographic location of Washington at the southern end of the Eastern megalopolis and between the industrial Northeast and the rapidly developing Southeast makes it an advantageous location for firms serving the entire east coast region. Consequently, during the decade of the 1950's Washington became one of the fastest growing metropolitan areas in the United States; the fastest east of the Mississippi. By 1960 Washington ranked as the tenth largest metropolitan area in the country, a substantial rise from its position of sixteenth in 1930.

By 1960 two-thirds of the region's population and one-third of its jobs were in the suburbs of Maryland and Virginia. The metropolitan area now contained in addition to D.C. some 66 separate elected, governmental units plus several dozen special purpose agencies and authorities. These governmental units often acted independently of one another and in some cases in conflict. The unity of structure and identity that usually prevails in a metropolitan area lying within one state did not initially exist in the Washington area but is one that was slowly to be fashioned.

There again we see how the specialized purpose of the National Capital, the absence of any physical resource base, and the political fragmentation of the area has influenced its development as a regional entity.

By 1960 the Washington Metropolitan Area had developed not only the physical and economic attributes of an urban region but was beginning to conceive a unified community of interest. Suburban communities were no longer just the bedrooms of the central city but were fast becoming economic units, units with their own economic base. The basic structure of these new suburban economies were still linked to the Federal City. Just as a branch plant operates separately from its headquarters office but is functionally related to and influenced by the decisions of the home office, so the suburban communities around Washington related to the functional elements of the core economy. Evidence of this relationship is present in every segment of community activity from employment to housing, from school financing to local politics. Enlightened elected officials in the Washington region recognize the interjurisdictional relationships present and are working to utilize this relationship as a vehicle to find solutions to mutual urban problems. The nurturing and development of this process has been significant in instituting a sense of regionalism and mutual cooperation in the Washington Metropolitan Area. I feel this has been an important step in the development of metropolitan Washington as a regional entity.

During the 1960's a number of events occurred which had a significant impact on the regional development of the Washington area. The inauguration of the Kennedy Administration in 1961 saw the beginning of another surge upward in Federal activities and employment levels in Washington. While the full impact of these policies and programs on local Federal employment levels were not felt until the mid- to late-1960's, the net effect was a one-third increase in Washington's primary economic sector between 1960 and 1970. The stimulus created by this Federal increase generated considerable expansion in other local economic sectors, in local employment and in local population growth. Some of the side effects of that growth surge continue to be felt in the metropolitan area.

But Federal job increases were not the only causal factor; new Federal policies relating to the national economy, foreign trade, business regulations, civil rights, social programs, the Vietnam War, environmental concerns and a host of others resulted in a new and closer relationship between government, business and the general public. All of these drew more attention to the Nation's Capital as the center of national and world power and as a prime location from which to influence or respond to Federal actions.

Furthermore, decisions by the Federal Government in increasing Federal pay scales and in locating Federal work facilities have had a profound effect on the Washington region. The pattern of metropolitan growth, the composition of that growth and its inherent costs have all been influenced by these Federal decisions. This situation exemplifies the Federal sector's strength in shaping Washington area development patterns. It is still the underlying factor in the growth of the Washington region.

While Federal employment increased by one-third during the 1960's, all other employment in metropolitan Washington was expanding by two-thirds, or double the Federal rate. The most significant increases were in Services, Finance, Insurance and Real Estate, Trade and local government sectors. Thus by 1970 the Washington region had grown in size to be the eighth largest metropolitan area in the country. Its population and work force provided the foundation for an economic region far greater than that area officially designated by the Office of Management and Budget as the Washington SMSA.

The distribution of the growth that occurred between 1960 and 1970 greatly enlarged the physical size of the urban region. Of the 425,000 new jobs added to the metropolitan economy over the decade 80 percent were located in suburban Maryland and Virginia. Where as recently as 1950 the District contained three-quarters of the region's jobs, by 1970 its share was less than one-half. Employment activity once concentrated was now dispersed. The major factors prompting or encouraging this dispersal were many: the low cost of suburban land, improved highway access (most notably headed by the completion of the Capital Beltway), improved communications and the Federal policy of leasing commercial office space resulting in the shift of numerous Federal jobs to the suburbs.

During this period virtually all of the region's increase in total population took place in the suburbs. Growing job opportunities, availability of housing, and efforts to avoid the ills of urban living—both real and imagined—helped concentrate growth in the suburbs. The bulk of the region's new residents, in-migrants who comprised over half the region's total growth, found the suburbs more attractive and more commensurate with their desires for a community environment. Added to this was the sizeable number of families and individuals who changed residences between local jurisdictions. Within the Washington region, for every one person moving in from outside the region and estimated 1.3 moved within the region.

These population shifts changed the size and character of Washington's individual communities. The suburbs increased in size and affluence while the city increased in the number of elderly residents and the young. Accompanying these shifts were numerous problems such as overcrowded public facilities in some areas, under-utilized facilities in other areas, utility shortages, traffic congestion and pollution. Moreover these population shifts have not reduced the disparities between jurisdictions but have in some cases intensified them, reinforcing the necessity to find mutual, interjurisdictional solutions to what have become regional problems.

Through all of this Washington has developed into a region of distinct character, exceptional in quality and highly specialized in nature. No other region has so high a level of family income or educational attainment, nor so low a level of unemployment and manufacturing. Nowhere is the specialized nature of the Washington region more vividly portrayed than in the personal earnings statistics reported by the Department of Commerce. Here the amount of personal income received by local residents from various sectors of the economy is identified. For example, Detroit's primary function and major earnings' generator is the automotive industry; Pittsburgh's is steel, and so on. Most of the country's more than 200 metropolitan areas derive the largest share of their income from manufacturing and are classified primarily as industrial centers.

Some metropolitan areas have grown in response to other economic forces, developing as specialized centers of a non-manufacturing nature. Examples of such centers are Atlanta, as a trade and transportation center; New York, as a service center; and San Francisco, as a government and trade center.

Most apparent from an examination of these statistics is the prominence of government as the major earnings' generator in metropolitan Washington, at twice the level that is found in any other region. The Federal Government is to Washington what manufacturing is to Detroit or Pittsburgh. It is the dominance of this function that has given Washington its unique character as a city and a metropolitan area.

SOME OBSERVATIONS ON THE FUTURE

I have attempted to trace the course and character of metropolitan Washington's regional growth. How we have developed and achieved our present status is certainly interesting but from my viewpoint as a planner and former city manager the challenges that lie ahead are clearly the most demanding. At this point I would like to share a few observations with you on the future development of the Washington region.

Undoubtedly Washington will continue to grow in size and influence through the remainder of this century. The rate of growth will probably be less rapid than that experienced during the 1960's. We as a region have come to recognize the need to plan for growth and to measure its value in terms of how it impacts the total urban environment. The impact of this position will surely influence the direction and character that future metropolitan development takes.

What are the forces with which we will be dealing? What trends are now discernible? One certainly is the growing concentration of headquarters offices, lobbies, associations and special interest groups in the region. As the Federal role of managing the national economy and protecting the environment expands, a continuing flow of individuals, groups and firms will move toward Washington to assist or influence Federal decisions.

Supportive business and service activities will also expand to provide the goods and services needed by government, private business and the general public. These include a broad range of activities including retail trade, personal services, real estate, financial houses, educational institutions, and local government.

Tourists and convention activity will increase rapidly, particularly with the expansion of overnight accommodations and exhibition facilities.

There is reason for confidence that the economic strength of Washington provide it with good prospects for development.

The most perplexing problem facing this region is where growth will occur. Recent studies by several local governments have shown that the location and character of development is as much a factor as as is the amount of growth. Thus the ability to influence the type and distribution of growth is critical and is a subject which we are currently examining.

Several forces are at work here. One is the location and improvement of the region's highway network. A second is the construction of metro which will significantly reshape the distribution of the region's growth and activity. Third is the growing convergence of the Washington and Baltimore regions. The economic ties between the two have grown closer over the past decades. Their economic functions overlap as do their commuting patterns. As the corridor between the two centers develops, the distinction between the two becomes more obscure.

The future holds great potential for the Washington region. It is a potential which judiciously managed and shared can improve the economic prosperity and quality of existence of every metropolitan citizen.

The Christian Heurich Brewing Company, 1872–1956

GARY F. HEURICH

It was exactly 100 years ago this year that German-born immigrant Christian Heurich took control of his first brewery. This was on 20th Street, just a matter of a block from here. It was in 1872 that Mr. Heurich went into partnership with Paul Ritter who, at the time, was brewmaster in the Seeger brewery in Baltimore. On the advice of Mr. Ritter, Mr. Heurich withdrew $1,000 of the $2,000 he had invested in the Building Association of Washington in order to buy a brewery. Of several breweries that were offered for sale, Mr. Heurich and Mr. Ritter considered the malt house Denmead in Baltimore. They decided against this, however, for it had a mortgage of more than $8,000 and another of more than $2,000 at 10 percent interest, roughly equivalent now to some $70,000. They finally decided on Schnell's brewery and tavern on 20th Street. The lease for the brewery was $150 a month and $1,500 was spent on furnishings. In October 1872 Mr. Heurich and Mr. Ritter took over the business, lock, stock, and beer barrel.

Mr. Ritter and his wife took over the tavern, the visiting with the customers, and the bookkeeping. It was Christian Heurich who made the beer. This included the processing of the hops, malt, and yeast, the brewing, the putting of the beer in barrels, and the storing of the barrels in the cellar. Much of the time Mr. Heurich worked 18 hours a day.

As business picked up, Mr. Ritter was the one praised for the good beer. Since Mr. Heurich was in the back brewing the beer and not mingling with the customers, he got no credit for it. As time went on, discord set in between Mr. Heurich and Mr. Ritter.

I would now like to quote from the translation of Christian Heurich's autobiography the reason for the dissolution of the Heurich and Ritter partnership:

I discovered, let's call it a stupidity, which the partner had committed

Delivered before the Columbia Historical Society on February 20, 1973.

and which aroused my distrust. He now tried to get rid of me, and he set a trap for me; I let him get caught, and took over the business.

After the partnership was dissolved on August 2, 1873, Mr. Heurich took care of everything and did the work of six persons. He was not discouraged, however, because he knew success was "just around the corner". More and more customers came to Heurich's tavern and beer sales increased steadily. It became necessary to enlarge the cellars to store more beer. In 1876 Mr. Heurich bought the mortgage on the property and also two adjacent lots on which he built wagon sheds. In 1877 Mr. Heurich had the brewery modernized and hired a former sailor to perform the duties of boilerman who continued in that position until 1915. Also in 1877 Mr. Heurich brought two of his brother's sons over from Germany to whom he taught the brewery business.

As beer sales continued to increase, Mr. Heurich was forced to use a waiting list for customers.

From the profits on the sale of his beer, Mr. Heurich was able to increase his real estate holdings considerably. One of these was the old Arlington Brewery which, however, he did not use as a brewery. In 1880 Mr. Heurich hired Charles Meyer who became another trusted employee in the position of chief bookkeeper and secretary until his death in 1914.

As a result of the enormous workload Mr. Heurich carried he suffered a breakdown in 1881. To relieve some of the pressure he gave his nephew the position of brewmaster. However his health did not improve and under directions of his physicians he took a cure in Carlsbad.

In 1883 Christian Heurich had his first problems with labor unions. He purchased from Jenks and Co. some materials needed in brewing beer. The unions threatened to blacklist him if he did not countermand the purchase from Jenks and Co., a company which did not hire union workers. Mr. Heurich called a meeting between the two parties involved to talk it over. After attending the meeting for a while, and being unable to make head nor tail of the talk going on, he explained that he had not come to America to become a slave and then left the meeting. Mr. Heurich left for Europe on a previously scheduled trip. The workers then proceeded to abstain from patronizing the customers, making matters worse. More meetings were held between the retailers and the workers. When Mr. Heurich returned from Europe he settled the matter once and for all. He compromised and stated, and I quote, "Our purchases will only be made from firms

Photograph from the author

Christian Heurich at his desk in 1940 at the age of 97.

employing union members, but I am allowed full liberty with the brewery workers."

In 1884 the nephew to whom Mr. Heurich had given the supervision of the brewery operation was injured while pitching barrels and became incapacitated for work. He died two years later because of the injury. Mr. Heurich was forced, in 1884, because of the accident, to hire a new brewmaster. The new brewmaster was Carl Eisenmenger who held that position until 1898. One day in 1898 he approached Mr. Heurich and demanded a raise. Mr. Heurich asked him what he would have to do if he (the brewmaster) died. Mr. Eisenmenger answered that Mr. Heurich would have to get a new brewmaster. To that Mr. Heurich replied, "Consider yourself dead."

In 1888 Christian Heurich had his hands full. The Young Women's Christian Association was trying to get the Congress to pass a prohibition law in Washington and Mr. Heurich made arrangements for the negotiations to be made public. In the same year there was also a movement to drive the brewery from 20th Street. To prepare for this Mr. Heurich bought several blocks of land in what was then called the Isherwood area. This location had large water springs which were suitable for a brewery. Nothing became of either of these two incidents.

On December 31, 1890 the brewery was incorporated and its name was changed from Christian Heurich's Brewery to the Christian Heurich Brewing Company.

The year 1892 was an exciting one for Christian Heurich. While he was staying at his Bellevue Farm he was informed one morning that a large fire had broken out in the brewery. This was not the first fire but it was definitely the worst. In 1875 there was a fire caused by a chimney spark which ignited a shingle roof and caused damages amounting to several thousand dollars. In 1883 there was a fire in the horse stable caused by a worker who was smoking which also caused damages amounting to several thousand dollars. This third fire in 1892 was caused by an explosion in the malt mill and it proceeded in all directions causing great damage. To the malt alone the damages totaled $20,000. For a while there was a question as to whether the business could go on because the fire had gotten as far as the cellar and had damaged the beer in storage. Mr. Heurich, however, resolved the problem and the brewery continued to make and sell beer.

This last fire and the need for a completely fire-proof brewery, similar to the concrete fire-proof mansion that was in the process of being built for him, would not leave his mind. He considered three building sites for such a brewery. The first was the property already owned by him in Isherwood. The second was a block in the neighborhood of the Tidal Basin near the Bureau of Engraving and Printing. The third was block 22 in Foggy Bottom on the Potomac. He chose the third. Block 22 is where the John F. Kennedy Center for the Performing Arts and the approaches to the Theodore Roosevelt

Memorial Bridge are today. Construction was started in the spring of 1894 and the building was finished in time for brewing to begin in the fall of 1895. The brewery buildings were probably the most solid in the country. Mr. Heurich personally supervised the concrete work and the buildings were susceptible only to dynamite. The only drawback was that it would not be economically feasible to make changes. That is why the brewery buildings remained idle during prohibition.

After the brewery was completed five months were needed for the transition of operations. The beer in the old brewery had to finish aging at the same time that brewing began in the new. The change-over took its toll on Mr. Heurich and he went to Europe for another rest.

In 1897 Mr. Heurich bought the rest of Block 22 and started a beer bottling business.

On a pleasure trip in 1900 to visit the Paris World Exhibition Mr. Heurich learned that his beers had been awarded a bronze and a silver medal. In 1905 they won a gold medal at Liege, Belgium, and in 1907 a gold medal at the Jamestown Exposition in Virginia.

In 1908 the battle for prohibition in Washington troubled Christian Heurich. He could see no reason to prohibit a popular and he believed very healthful beverage. He wrote in a letter of his to a friend:

> Since the bible teaches that Christ changed water into wine, I do not have to make excuses for the selection of my trade.

In 1909 the local breweries won the battle, for the time being, and business continued to flourish until about 1913 when it reached a peak and leveled out.

In 1914 an old ice plant in the original building was converted into a storehouse for beer and a new ice plant was built adjacent to the original brewery.

Two kinds of ice were produced, can ice and plate ice.

Can ice was made by pouring water into slightly tapering 300-pound capacity cans and inserting a small brass tube through which air was blown in order to keep the water clear as it froze and to bring the impurities to the center of the can. After the water was frozen the tube was taken out and the impure water, which was not frozen, was pumped out. Water was then poured into the hole in the center and frozen. The 300-pound blocks of ice were cut up by a delivery man or "ice man" into smaller blocks for refrigerators.

Plate ice was made by filling big sections of a tank and then cir-

Photograph from the author

Stock Certificate of the Christian Heurich Brewing Company, capitalized at $800,000 in 1890.

The building pictured on the ceritificate is the brewery at 1229–1235 20th Street, N. W.

culating the water as it froze to keep it clear and pure. When the water was frozen the ice was taken out and placed on its side and then cut up by large circular saws into 300-pound blocks for big refrigerators used for commercial purposes.

Prohibition was enacted in 1918 in Washington and Mr. Heurich was at a loss as to what to do with the brewery buildings. He considered an alcohol-free apple cider and anticipating prohibition he bought apples in the amount of $10,000 in 1917 to try the product on the beer drinkers of the time. But a strange thing happened. The cider fermented despite pasteurization to an average of six percent alcohol. Four weeks remained before prohibition and the brewery sold one third of the entire stock. The brewery did not deliver the cider and people flocked to the brewery cellars to pick it up after word got around of its high alcohol content. It was said that one limousine which came to get cider belonged to the White House.

During the years of prohibition, 1918 to 1933, the brewery produced ice only. Parts of the building were rented out as storage space.

On April 7, 1933, Congress enacted legislation allowing beer to be produced up to an alcoholic content of 3.2 percent. Even though 3.2 beer was legal in April, Mr. Heurich took his time, unlike some brewers, in producing the first beer. He said that he wanted to make it good, not fast. His first beer was not put on the market until August 2, 1933, his 60th anniversary as a brewer.

During prohibition the rest of the stock of the apple cider was kept refrigerated in closed containers awaiting the time that the 6 percent cider could again be sold. In 1933, however, the vats in which the cider was stored were needed for the aging of beer and since 6 percent was above the legal limit, something had to be done with the cider. Mr. Heurich made the decision, despite good offers from vinegar companies, to dump the entire 60,000 gallons into the Potomac, remarking that nothing ever made under his supervision was going to end in vinegar.

When prohibition was repealed only two breweries were left in Washington of the five before prohibition. Mr. Heurich was skeptical as to whether two breweries would be able to supply the demand for beer since Washington's population had increased. It came as a surprise to him to discover that there were not nearly so many beer drinkers. During prohibition much illegal boot-legged hard liquor was available and after repeal many people stayed with stronger beverages. Beer sales did increase slowly.

In 1933, after attending a World Series game, Mr. Christian Heurich, Jr. and his party decided to go to the brewery. While they were being served beer in the yard just outside one of the doors to the office, Chief Engineer Claude Price came running out and said, "There's a holdup in the office." Thinking he was joking everyone laughed. He went back inside and returned to say, "There really is a holdup." Mr. Heurich, Jr. went into the office followed by the rest of his party and saw the last of four of the office employees getting up off the floor.

It was later learned that Dutch Misunas, leader of the Tri-State gang, and an accomplice had entered the lobby of the office and forced the switchboard operator at gun-point to open the connecting office door. All of the employees were forced to lie on the floor while one of the robbers picked up a canvas bag which contained the day's receipts. The employees were told to stay on the floor for five minutes after the robbers left. The police were then called and a few minutes later a Brinks truck which was to pick up the receipts arrived at the brewery.

Several months later Dutch Misunas was caught in California and brought back to the District of Columbia. A few days later Misunas, accompanied by two detectives, came to the brewery. After having a few beers and signing the guest register, he explained how the brewery was cased and how they pulled the job off. He was later convicted.

Little happened after 1933 except that the brewery got back into full swing and resumed producing its fine beers. In 1940 the ice operation was closed.

On March 8, 1945, the brewery employees learned that at 12 minutes after 11 o'clock the previous night, their president and founder had passed away. Christian Heurich, 102 years old and suffering from a cold, had gone to the office until nine days before his death. Mrs. Heurich finally persuaded him to stay home. During those nine days

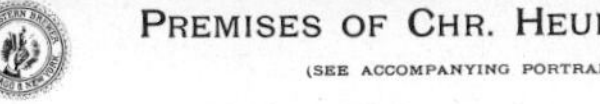

Photograph from the author

The Christian Heurich Brewing Company at 1229–1235 20th Street, N. W.

A large illustration published as a supplement to *The Western Brewer* of August 15, 1883, shows the major remodeling which was completed in 1881.

Mr. Heurich's cold turned into acute bronchitis. That and exhaustion took the final toll on him. Out of respect for him the brewery was closed on the day of his funeral.

When Mr. Heurich was alive he held the distinction of being America's oldest active brewer and since his death no one has surpassed him.

Throughout his life Mr. Heurich did not draw a salary but the year that he turned 100 he was voted a $25,000 bonus by the Board of Directors. Whenever he had a case or barrel of beer sent to his home he always paid for it and insisted that the employees do the same. Whenever Mr. Heurich had a glass of beer he would always set the glass on the radiator to warm it.

At the first meeting of the Board of Directors after the founder's death, his son Christian Heurich, Jr. was elected president of the company.

In 1946 the brewery workers union became a part of the Teamsters Union which demanded increases in wages which were not granted. The brewery workers went on strike which lasted a little over three weeks after which a compromise settlement was reached.

In 1949 the brewery was producing a product under the name of Champeer. In New Jersey a brewery was producing a product under the name of Champ Ale. The New Jersey company filed an injunction suit to stop the use of the Champeer name. Christian Heurich, Jr. succeeded in getting the injunction dissolved but agreed that after the last of the stock was sold the name would not be used. This ended the brewery's only major suit.

So far I have not discussed how beer was made at the brewery. I will turn to that.

First rice or corn grits were placed in a pressure cooker, used to increase the temperature. Some 6,500 pounds of grain were stirred by large paddles to mix it thoroughly. At the same time 13,500 pounds of malted barley were put in a mash tub after it had been ground or cracked in a malt-cracking mill. Malted barley is barley that has been allowed to sprout to a certain point and the sprouts nipped off. This malt was also stirred by large paddles. The purpose of the pressure cooker and the mash tub is to turn the starch in the grain into sugar so it can later be fermented into alcohol and carbon dioxide.

Next the corn grits or rice were added to the mash tub and this was all stirred, requiring about an hour. The grain was then allowed to settle for about half an hour and the liquid, which is known as wort, was drained off through a false bottom in the mash tub, slowly so as not to stop up the strainer, into troughs where it could be checked for speed and purity. From here it went to the brew kettle where the steam jacket around the kettle boiled the wort. This is also where the hops were added, before the kettle was completely full, and while the wort was boiling. The whole transferral and cooking process took about three hours.

From here the wort was pumped into the hop jack where the hops were strained out. It was then run over the cooler and from this point on the wort was kept cool. It was pumped over the cooler into large wooden vats in the fermenting room where the yeast was added. Twenty-four hours later when the process of fermentation, the process of turning sugar into alcohol and carbon dioxide, had begun, the wort went into smaller fermenting vats which were temperature controlled. Because fermentation gives off heat the temperature had to be kept at about 38 degrees or the brew would ferment too rapidly. The brew remained there about seven days, where the yeast settled on the bottom of the vats, and was then pumped into storage vats for a three-month stay.

There are two kinds of yeast used in brewing, one is for making ale, the other for making lager beer. The yeast used in ale rises to the top of the vats, while the yeast used for beer settles to the bottom. Only one type of yeast can be used in one brewery, otherwise the spores of one yeast will contaminate the other.

Photograph from the author

The Christian Heurich Brewing Company at 25th, 26th, D and Water Streets, N. W.

This picture postcard shows the 26th and Water Streets sides. The taller building is the brewhouse on the corner of 25th and Water Streets. These brewery buildings housed the Washington Wax Museum and the Arena Stage between 1956 and 1961.

After storage the beer is filtered and carbon dioxide is added. The old method of adding carbon dioxide was known as the Kraüsen Method in which the brew was allowed to ferment in tightly sealed vats so that carbon dioxide would be in the beer after the fermenting process was over. The new method is to ferment some of the beer in closed vats and draw off and cool the carbon dioxide to liquid form. It is then added in its gaseous form to the beer after storage and filtering.

After the carbon dioxide was added the beer was pumped to the Rack Room where it was put in kegs, to be draft beer, which was then kept constantly refrigerated until it was sold to the customer, or was pumped to the Bottling Department where it was put in bottles and cans. Then the bottles and cans were sent through the pasteurizer and they were ready for sale. The brewery produced 13 different beers under 47 different labels in its 83 years of existence. The different beers were Champion, Home Brew, Boxer, Capital, Champeer Malt Liquor, Heurich's Lager, Old Georgetown Bock Beer, Old Georgetown Ale, Old Georgetown Beer, Maerzen, Bock, Senate Beer, and Senate Ale.

With World War II the population of Washington grew rapidly. Many new residents brought with them their own preferences in beer. The sale of beer distributed in Washington by such large companies as Pabst, Schaeffer, and Anheuser-Busch increased to the detriment of the locally made product. Although the total consumption of beer increased, and many Washington natives felt that the "home town" product was superior to the "imported" ones, the sale of Heurich's beer declined.

In 1956 because of the decline in sales and because of the knowledge that the government would seek to acquire the site of the brewery for the approaches to the new Theodore Roosevelt Memorial Bridge, the decision was made by the Board of Directors, of which Mrs. Christian Heurich, Sr. was a member, to stop brewing beer and in 1960 the decision was made to liquidate and dissolve the Christian Heurich Brewing Company.

The Heurich brewery was not the only one affected by population changes and the growth of larger breweries. At the close of the Civil War in 1865 there were 1,269 breweries in the United States. In 1934 after the repeal of prohibition there were 725. In 1970 there were 154. In 1971 there were 76. In 1972 the number had dropped to 65. The trend is toward a very few very large and powerful breweries.

In 1961 the government condemned and bought the brewery buildings and the surrounding property. During the preceding five years the buildings were rented as warehouses and for a while the gymnasium at the brewery housed the Arena Stage drama group.

In the fall of 1961 the ice house was torn down with some considerable difficulty. The first try in which 650 sticks of dynamite were used failed. The ice house walls consisted of two brick walls with one foot of granulated cork between them. The cork absorbed the impact of the dynamite. The dynamite, thought to be enough to level the building, managed only to fell three walls. Christian Heurich, Jr. told reporters at the time, "When my father built something, he didn't build it to come down easily." A crane with a wrecking ball was brought in to finish the job.

In the spring of 1962, the main brewery building was torn down with even more difficulty than the ice house. Again, the wrecking ball was used and with the last swing of the giant steel ball went the remains of a dream so strongly believed in by a poor immigrant boy. Down went the symbol of what a strong-willed man could build with hard work and brains, a man who was the epitome of highest ideals.

Reminiscences by Dorothy Clark Winchcole: "Do You Remember—?"

DOROTHY CLARK WINCHCOLE

Do you remember riding on the large open street cars to Glen Echo or Cabin John (six tickets for a quarter)?

Do you remember taking a street car ride out to dance at Chevy Chase Lake—or perhaps walking down those thirty-six steps in Georgetown to take the trolley to Great Falls?

Do you remember the Sunday school picnics in Rock Creek Park?

And do you remember when Quentin Roosevelt came to the Force School in his pony cart? And when nearly everyone was excited about the winning company in the annual High School Cadet's drill?

Do you remember the horse-drawn ice-wagons on the hot summer days? The ice was lifted by large cleavers, weighed, and then carried dripping to the customers. There were also the Huckster and the "Watermelon Man."

Or do you remember the hot summer nights; sitting on the front porch and watching the Lamp Lighter, with his little ladder, make his rounds like a human fire-fly?

Do you remember having a chocolate soda in Huylers at 12th and F Streets, or going to Reeves for pie, and meeting several people you knew on F Street?

And do you remember coming outside—along with your neighbors —in the middle of the night, to give the News Boy five cents for an "Extra Paper"—to learn the latest report on the sinking of the *Titanic?*

Do you remember walking through "Peacock Alley" in the Willard Hotel and then going out onto the Avenue to watch the election returns on the *Post* building?

Do you remember the snow storm during the Taft inaugural—or the rain during FDR's second inauguration?

Do you remember the hilarious excitement at the Treasury Building when World War One ended?

Do you remember seeing Lindbergh at Dupont Circle on the balcony of the Patterson House with President Coolidge?

And do you remember waiting on the Avenue to see King George of England, and his lovely queen? She carried a parasol because of the intense heat.

Although the City has changed—for better and for worse—it is always a good thing to *Remember!*

Reminiscences by Emil A. Press: "Growing Up In Swampoodle"

EMIL A. PRESS

About a year ago the Columbia Historical Society was treated to Frank Taylor's presentation of life on Capitol Hill at the turn of the century.[1] Many favorable comments indicated that the subject was of unusual interest to our members and your program committee concluded that similar dissertations should be presented from time to time for other areas of the city. It was your program committee's idea that Brother Bill and I jointly recall the scene where we grew up in Swampoodle and adjoining areas.

The generally accepted limits of Swampoodle were the City Post Office and Union Station on the south, tracks of the Washington Terminal on the east, Florida Avenue on the north, and North Capitol Street on the west.

Actually, I was not born in Swampoodle, as was Bill. My birthplace was 47 Q Street, N.W., a building that is still standing. There are no markers of any sort to commemorate the big "goings on" of August 26, 1904. I was totally unaware of another important event that took place a little later and, as the crow flies, within 100 yards of number 47—the birth of Eleanor, my wife.

A little background concerning our family. Mom and Pop were immigrants from Denmark. They met each other in Washington and married. They spoke Danish at home and, when I was about 4½ years of age, I spoke it as well as any brat of that age in Copenhagen. At that point, they suddenly switched to English to prepare me for school. They became very proficient and in 1910 enrolled me in the Twining School on 3rd Street, N.W.

Shortly after my birth, the family moved into Swampoodle, in which, during daylight hours, streets were subjected to heavy traffic

Delivered before the Columbia Historical Society on December 17, 1974.

[1] Frank A. Taylor spoke before the Society on April 16, 1974. The editor hopes to obtain a manuscript from him for publication in a future volume of the *Records*.

(for that time) in the form of heavy horse-drawn vans hauling goods generated by the B & O Freight Yards, the Chapin-Saks ice cream plant at 1st and M Streets, N.E., the coal yards along 1st Street, N.E., with such familiar names as Griffith, Chapman, Marlow and Agnew and, upon its completion, the City Post Office. At the close of business each afternoon and on Sundays and holidays, with automobiles practically non-existent, the streets became playgrounds.

I recall vividly how, during snows, rags and burlap sacks were wrapped around horses hoofs to prevent slipping and enable the animals to haul their heavy loads. In about 1911, we saw the first chain-drive solid-tire truck in operation.

Environmentalists would have had a field day with the conditions that residents then considered normal. In those days all railroad locomotives to Union Station, including the many Washington Terminal switchers, were coal fired and constantly contributing to the pall of smoke over the area. In addition, the District of Columbia manufactured asphalt for street paving in a plant that occupied the width of New York Avenue, at a point just north of Florida Avenue, and was a worse offender than the railroad. Only our mother's dogged Scandinavian insistence on cleanliness made conditions tolerable.

During the Society's recent walking tour of the Pension Office and Judiciary Square,[2] one of our members mentioned the snow storm during the inauguration of President Taft. My earliest recollection as a child was of troops marching from the B & O Freight Yards to the inaugural parade in the heavy snow. Later in the day they returned. Actually, the distance traveled was approximately three present day parades, every inch on foot—no busses or trucks as used by modern troops.

That inauguration also gave me my first insight on intoxication when, shortly after the parade, four soldiers passed our house, one on each corner of a stable door carried horizontally. A fifth man was on the door with two scrub buckets of beer. I couldn't understand why they staggered all over the street until my mother explained that the men were "full" and the beer "had gone to their toes."

Old Swampoodle was well supplied with "open-air" summer movies. Rio Grande Park, on the corner of North Capitol Street and New York Avenue, was the start of the Crandall movie empire. At the time, Mr. Crandall operated a livery stable on adjoining alley property.

Standard Park was on North Capitol Street between O and P

[2] The Society's seventh walking tour was conducted on Sunday, September 22, 1974.

Streets. It moved to Bates Street when the Liberty theatre was constructed on North Capitol Street and soon closed permanently. At Truxton Circle, which was at North Capitol Street and Florida Avenue, we had a park and theatre operated by Coblentz, the druggist. He named both Truxton, and when it rained shows were moved indoors to the theatre.

The Liberty was a neighborhood moving picture house patronized by residents of Swampoodle as well as Eckington, High View, and Bloomingdale. Every Saturday morning we were in the mob seeking to deliver weekly programs to these areas. It was a door-to-door operation that paid seven movie tickets for placing about 300 programs. It was a most wonderful opportunity, to one in a family of limited means, to enjoy pictures starring Francis X. Bushman, Beverly Bain, William Farnum, Wallis Reid, Fatty Arbuckle and others of that era.

Does the name Leo Rocca mean anything to any of you? Some of you may recall him as having a Dodge Agency on Connecticut Avenue opposite the old Bureau of Standards. As a young man, in about 1919, he operated a gasoline filling station and accessory shop on a triangular lot formed by New York Avenue and N Street, just east of North Capitol Street. He also had a row of about six tin garages, one of which was rented by my father for, I believe, $3.00 a month. Rocca expanded and for many years operated the Triangle Ford Agency in an enlarged plant on the site formerly occupied by the Rio Grande Park.

Persons born in the early years of the Twentieth Century have witnessed developments in science and engineering far exceeding accomplishments in any other similar period. Among these was the telephone, of which there were relatively few in Swampoodle and none in any residences in our section. The corner grocer had a pay phone that was used by the neighborhood to make and receive calls. On incoming calls the grocer, a most patient and cooperative individual, would dispatch a messenger to summon our folks to the phone. I don't know why the phone number has stayed with me all these years—North 2404.

Another new fangled contraption was the radio, or wireless. In about 1913, we made a trip on three nights each week to Hasselbusch's bakery on P Street, west of North Capitol, to buy black German rye bread as it came out of the oven at 10 p.m. The oven was an old-time one from which the coals were removed so that the bread might bake on the hot brick. On one occasion, we were permitted to hear the 10 o'clock time signal from Arlington as received on a United States

Army receiving set. This really gave us something to talk about to our envious playmates, some of whom began accompanying us to the bakery so they might hear the signal.

With the entry of the United States in World War I, war fever was rampant in Swampoodle and other areas of the city. A group of high school cadets under the leadership of Vincent Callahan organized a marching team of some 75 youngsters in the 10 to 15 year age group. They were drilled in the "school of the soldier" as well as squad and platoon movements. The outfit became quite proficient and at the end of each evening would march, everyone counting one, two, three, four, past the New York Apartments (New York Avenue west of 1st Street) where Callahan's best girl lived. I have no recollection of anything being done to promote the war effort and the whole thing disintegrated after several weeks. Callahan became a Vice President of the National Broadcasting Company.

Incidental to the construction of Union Station, Florida Avenue in the vicinity of 4th Street, N.E. was lowered to pass through the viaduct beneath the terminal tracks. Subsequently, in 1908, the Capital Traction Company began service on its new tracks on Florida Avenue and 8th Street, between New Jersey Avenue, N.W. and Pennsylvania Avenue, S. E. Each unit of equipment was comprised of two four-wheel cars painted green. Open cars with running boards were used in summer, closed cars in winter.

This car line was a big asset in keeping up with the Washington Baseball Club. We would sit on the curb waiting for the cars carrying those who had attended the game and would learn the score, the batteries for the day and particularly what about Walter Johnson. I believe it was more fun though not as convenient as tuning in to today's radio or television.

Reminiscences by William H. Press: "Another View of Swampoodle"

WILLIAM H. PRESS

My life began at 43 O Street, N.E. nearly seventy years ago. About four years later we moved around the corner to First Street, N.E., at the foot of Eckington Hill, across the street from an undeveloped triangle between our home and the B & O Freight Station. This area, the intersection of First Street, New York Avenue—which ended at Florida Avenue, and Eckington Place, was the center of the world for me until I went way up town to 7th and Rhode Island Avenue to attend McKinley Tech High School in the building which is now "shameful Shaw Junior High School."

In the 'teens Washington City was still quite undeveloped with many open rural areas north of Florida Avenue. The B & O Freight Station was the major neighborhood development. East of it was the Patterson tract, as it was then called, extending along Florida Avenue to Gallaudet College and up the hill to the raidroad. On the hill was Brentwood, a stately mansion almost in ruins. Nobody seemed to pay it any mind despite its historical significance which would easily qualify it as a Category One Landmark today.

This mansion was built by Robert Brent, the first mayor of Washington City, who was appointed by the President. It was designed by Latrobe and started in 1816. Brent built it for his daughter who was married to Joseph Pearson, a Congressman from North Carolina. For a while the estate was called Pearson according to printed reports. Pearson's daughter, Elizabeth, married Carlyle Patterson and that accounts for it being called the Patterson Tract when I was a youngster. It was a fascinating area.

Brentwood was unbelievably large and ornate for the kids who lived in modest homes in the neighborhood even though it had been through a big fire and had been stripped of its accouterments. In the early 'teens it was deteriorating rapidly and Emil and I felt that this

---

Delivered before the Columbia Historical Society on December 17, 1974.

was a terrible thing. But we put the blame entirely on the bums who rode the freight trains and camped out in the railroad yards.

Behind Brentwood was the Brent mausoleum. It was broken into frequently. Coffins were opened, bones were spread around, and silver coffin handles and anything else of value seemed to have been purloined—as we assumed—by the railroad bums.

Brentwood must have been a bit closer to Florida Avenue than the Rock Creek Ginger Ale factory is today. Behind it was an extensive "tall tree" wooded area. We'd go there in the spring and pull down great limbs of dogwood. At other times of the year we cut other flowers and blackberries which were peddled around the neighborhood.

In the banks along the railroad—where New York Avenue is today—were wonderful clay deposits which we kids would dig out and take home and fashion into elegant sculptures.

Coming down the hill past the mansion to Florida Avenue we went through large open fields where we picked daisies by the thousands which could be sold for 5 cents or 10 cents a bunch especially at one of the nearby cemeteries around Decoration Day. This open area was also a fine kite-flying place for the very fancy kites we learned to make at an early age. On Easter Monday it was well used for rolling eggs. There was always a sizeable turnout of neighborhood people who either didn't want to walk to the White House or spend the money to ride there on the streetcar with those expensive 5 cents fares.

The circus always came into the B & O Freight Yards, where the performers stayed on sleepers, and they pitched tents on the Patterson tract at about 5th and Florida Avenue N.E. (where the farmers market is now). Before World War I the circus parades started at Eckington Place and went up Pennsylvania Avenue where they were enthusiastically viewed by the schoolchildren who were dismissed to see all the wild animals.

Our daisy farm was inoperative during most of World War I and for a while thereafter because the War Department built and operated Camp Meigs on the Patterson tract between the railroad and Gallaudet College. Here volunteers and draftees were processed and began training, some housed in tents and some in the standard temporary military barracks put up by the Quartermaster Corps. I understand that Sidney Hechinger got his start as a building wrecker by getting the contract to dismantle Camp Meigs.

At the Florida and New York Avenue corner of the Patterson tract was the D. C. Government's asphalt plant which had to be removed when New York Avenue was later cut through to Bladenburg Road.

Across the street along the streetcar tracks at the foot of Eckington Hill was an extraordinarily interesting place of business. It was a restaurant catering to the black teamsters who hauled freight from the B & O yards across the street, and coal and ice from a string of coal yards along First street to M street, N.E. including W. W. Griffith, Agnew Coal Co., J. Maury Dove Co., and W. H. Marlowe.

Keith Sutherland, a tall mustachioed Negro with a wide brimmed black felt hat, was the owner, cook, cashier and waiter. His restaurant was about a 9 by 12 foot sheet metal structure having a completely open east side. Benches lined the other three inside walls and provided seats where the customers could eat their baked beans ("1,049 beans to the plate") or devilled crabs.

Sutherland was a philosopher and, as I see it now, a public relations expert. Periodically he whitewashed the three outside walls and then completely covered them with printed comments about current events, religion, his fine food, and other items which took his fancy.

West of the railroad was Eckington. Roughly it was bounded by the tracks, Florida Avenue, North Capitol Street, and Rhode Island Avenue. Much of it was purchased in 1815 by Joseph Gales who with W. W. Seaton owned the *National Intelligencer*. Gales became a City Councilman in 1827 and Mayor of Washington City in 1828. In 1830 he built a magnificent house on Eckington Hill which became a welcome port of call for many statesmen, cabinet members, and visiting notables.

Fifty five or sixty years ago this was a suburban area with wooded groves and many open fields where Judd & Detweiler and Peoples Drug Stores now are as well as the McKinley High School. I served the *Evening Star* route from 2nd and R Streets out to 6th and Rhode Island Avenue. Almost all the residents were subscribers and I delivered about 100 papers a day through the entire Eckington section.

I first went to Twining School on Third Street, N.W., between N and O. On the way home I recall sitting on the curbstone and watching the brick-laying on the Dunbar High School which was under construction. Within the past year Twining School was demolished and work was begun on a new Dunbar High School. In the 6th grade I attended Eckington School, which still stands, and, in the 7th the Emery School on Lincoln Road, which was named after the last Mayor of Washington before Mayor Walter Washington.

In our neighborhood in the early 1900's most youngsters didn't receive allowances from their parents. To get spending money and for entertainment—before the days of radio and television—a significant portion of our out-of-school time was devoted to working for neighbors and neighborhood small businesses and to being juvenile entreprenuers.

My *Evening Star* route which paid me about $5 a month was important until I went to Tech High School-it was steady income. We also sold newspapers on the street cars during rush hours by getting on at one stop and getting off at the next corner and then riding back on a car going the other way. This, of course, was by sufferance of the motorman and conductor. The big money in the newspaper business was selling "extra papers" for 10 cents when the daily editions were 2 cents or 1 cent.

Naturally we cut grass and shovelled snow from time to time. We also collected junk. Newspapers could be sold at a junk shop about a block away as could scrap iron, lead, brass and the like. There was recognized and realized potential when the circus came to town and when inaugural and other parades were held. The transients in sleeping cars at the B & O yards were pretty good customers for lemonade, snowballs, and other refreshments.

But for steady and reliable income I had several customers for two or three years who paid me a weekly retainer. During the summer with my *Evening Star wagon* I hauled ice for them. Chapin Sacks' Ice Plant was at First and M Streets, N.E. and I would go there and get a 10 cent block of ice for each customer every day. I substantially undercut the commercial ice wagons which served the whole town. In the winter I sifted ashes. Every house and flat had a coal stove which needed to be shaken down well every day and have the ashes removed. But in addition I sifted the ashes and recovered the bits of coal which had not been burned and put them back in the coal bin.

The Liberty Theater, where Kate Smith and other youthful performers appeared on Amateur Nights, printed a handbill every week listing each night's movie. They were delivered to every house or apartment in its market area every Saturday. We, the deliverers, received seven passes a week for our labors.

Our neighborhood was a charming conglomerate. My parents came over from Denmark. Some families were German or Irish, and many of them, particularly those working on the streetcars, came from Culpepper or Vienna, Virginia, or Frederick County, Maryland. There were twenty five or thirty families of Italians on Decatur Place, most of whom worked on the railroad.

We saw many Negroes though few of them were neighbors. A few families lived in an alley behind us, several more were on N Street between North Capitol and First Street, N.W., and there were other black settlements scattered around, a block here and an alley there.

Though our family was of modest means, we always had many good books, stereoptican views, and fine red-label Victor records. Both our parents were elegant cooks and knew how to entertain our friends in sumptuous style. Before prohibition, two quarts of red wine were left behind the vestibule door every week and in the early 1920's I was sure my father was far and away the best beer and wine maker in town.

Chain stores were just beginning to be formed. All families within a block or so dealt with the corner grocery store and with one of the neighborhood drug stores. Bargains were offered quite regularly by hucksters selling vegetables, watermelons, cantaloupes, and fish. A wagon came by weekly to sell kerosene for the coal-oil lamps and for starting the kitchen coal range. Armenian rug and statuary peddlers hawked their wares from door to door. Those were the days when one could make many of one's purchases on the front door step.

One of our finer institutions was Bloomer's Drug Store at North Capitol and R Streets. They had one of the first victrolas with a horn sticking out of the window. It was said that Mr. Bloomer originated the ice cream sundae even though he first called it a "friday." He lived above the store and could be roused at night by the night bell rung at the drug store entrance. When there were few telephones and automobiles this was a great convenience for those who became ill or got a bad toothache.

The Washington Temple: A New Landmark

FRANK MILLER SMITH

The Washington Temple, a magnificent edifice that dominates the northwest skyline of the Nation's Capital, brings something entirely new to this world center.

It is a unique structure built by The Church of Jesus Christ of Latter-day Saints (Mormons) in which the sacred ordinances of their religion are conducted. Although the outer dimensions would permit it, the building is not a church, chapel or tabernacle in which the faithful gather for Sabbath services. It is a House of the Lord in which those who are worthy come to be married for eternity; to be sealed to their families; to be baptized for the dead and to participate in other ordinances given to the Saints through their Prophets by heavenly revelations.

It is the eighteenth such temple built by the "Mormons" and the only one now in use in the United States east of the Mississippi. It will serve the Saints in a Temple District created January 18, 1969, which includes the eastern portion of the United States and Canada. At the time the Temple was being constructed there were 300,000 members of the Church in that area, and it was the fastest growing church in the country.

The Temple rises 288 feet to the tip of the golden statue on its foremost spire above a knoll in Kensington, Maryland, on the northern stretches of Rock Creek Park. It is a diamond shaped, marble sheathed structure of concrete and steel built to sustain the severest of earthquakes. It is topped by six spires coated with 24 carat gold fused into the embossed, porcelainized steel from which they are formed.

Topping the eastern spire is the statue of the angel Moroni. It is 18 feet high and finished in gold leaf. It was cast in bronze in Italy and sculptured by Dr. Avard Fairbanks of Salt Lake City, Utah.

Located on the highest spot of the 57 acres purchased by the

Photograph from the author

View of the Washington Temple from the highway.

Church in 1962 for $850,000, its sylvan setting provides an ideal spot for construction of a "Monument to Spirituality," as the Temple has been called.

The building required 173,000 square feet of Alabama marble to cover it. It is 248 feet long, 136 feet wide and has a total area of 160,000 square feet.

Although it carries with it the essence of the Salt Lake City Temple, which has become a Mormon symbol around the globe, it is of a distinct modern feeling.

The sylvan setting chosen for its availability, yet protected from commercial encroachment, has been maintained by preserving the surrounding array of many of the native trees including poplar, oak, beech and maple.

Augmenting the native trees and shrubs, approximately 108,000 square feet around the Temple has been landscaped, while on the south side there is a reflecting pool 106 feet long and 52 feet wide. It is built in the same elongated diamond shape as the Temple. On the south end of the mall a fountain sends a single jet of water 30 feet up from the center of a stone basin eight and a half feet in diameter. The water overflows from the center basin to an outer basin 32 feet in diameter. This decorative feature will be illuminated at night.

Looking at the building from the outside with its heavily ribbed walls, it appears to be without windows; but between the ribs, the marble has been shaved to ⅝ths of an inch, permitting a glowing light to pour through the walls in the daytime from the sunlight. At night light shines through from inside. On the east and west ends there are faceted glass windows made of inch-thick colored glass chipped on the edges to refract more light. These W-shaped panels are seven feet wide and run from the ground to the top of the Temple. The colors change from reds and oranges at the bottom to colors of light tone such as blue, violet and white as they stretch upward.

The angel Moroni, whose statue tops the building, was the last of a long line of prophets in the early Americas. Moroni's writings, translated by the Prophet Joseph Smith, comprise the Book of Mormon which is accepted as holy scripture by the members of The Church of Jesus Christ of Latter-day Saints.

One of the unique features of the Temple is that it was opened to the public for free tours from September 17 to November 2, 1974, then closed until dedication ceremonies were held November 19, 20, 21 and 22, 1974.

Following the public preview of the Temple and its dedication, only those members of the Church deemed worthy to participate in the sacred ordinances performed within its walls are permitted to enter.

Approximately 750,000 persons of all creeds, colors and nationalities walked through the main entrance into the Annex, and across a glass enclosed 90 foot bridge that leads directly inside the Temple itself, during the preview.

Here they paused in the reception room to scrutinize the only painting in the building. It is a mural depicting the Second Coming of Jesus Christ.

This mural covers the large curving rear wall of the reception area. It was executed by the artist John Scott of Ridgefield, Connecticut. Early in life he began doing illustrations for various Sunday School publications. During World War II he served as artist-correspondent in Europe for the U. S. Army publication, *Yank*. He has been commissioned by the Church of Jesus Christ of Latter-day Saints to execute a number of religious paintings.

The painting depicts Jesus decending to the earth where a multitude is gathered with the righteous to the right of him and the wicked on his left. In the background on the right is the Temple, and on the left the burning cities of the wicked.

The building has seven levels. Below the reception area is the baptismal font. Above there are five floors of offices, dressing rooms, ordinance rooms, a beautifully appointed celestial room with a 37 foot vaulted ceiling, and the solemn assembly room on the top level. The dedicatory services for the Temple were held in the latter room.

The fourth floor of the Temple includes six ordinance rooms, each of which can accommodate 80 persons. It is estimated that approximately 3,000 members of the Church can participate in the Temple sessions each day.

The interior colors change from walnut paneling and carpets of deep blue on the lower floors to the use of more and more white with traces of gold as you ascend to the upper levels. The celestial room, with white ceiling and white walls, is carpeted in a very pale apricot gold. Plants provide the only other color.

Visitors were impressed with the quiet dignity and richness of the interior—the blending of the colors, the sparkling elegance of the chandeliers, the fine materials and splendid craftsmanship that exudes from every direction.

Special attention was given to the bronze doorknob plates on all the interior doors. They feature a three-dimension casting of the east or west temple facade. The three spires extend above the doorknob.

The design of the main entrance doors and the sliding gates at the north annex entrance is of special significance. As described in *The Ensign,* a magazine published by the Church:

> Eight bronze medallions by Latter-day Saint sculptor Franz Johansen portray the Big Dipper and North Star, the earth, the planets, the moon, the stars, cocentric circles representing eternity, the traditional sun face, and seven cocentric pentagons representing the seven dispensations. These designs are symbolic of the creation, mortality, and the degrees of glory. Triangular ribs that arch from the top to the bottom of the medallions like a much segmented orange are a distinctive feature.

Photograph from the author

Baptistry of the Washington Temple.

The baptismal font rests on the backs on twelve oxen, symbolic of the ancient twelve tribes of Israel. Ordinance work performed in the temple includes vicarious baptisms for ancestors and eternal marriages.

"Patterns of the celestial bodies sculpted on these medallions have a different expression every hour of the day," according to Brother Henry Fetzer, "because the shifting sunlight strikes the striations at different angles."

In the Baptistry, the baptismal font rests on the backs of twelve life-sized oxen statues as it did in Solomon's Temple in ancient Israel. It is here that living proxies are baptized by immersion for the dead.

The building also includes rooms for the endowment ceremony where instructions are given about man's eternal journey before birth, through mortality and after death.

Marriages for eternity are performed in rooms beautifully appointed and decorated in lovely soft colors. Each such room contains mirrors that repeat and repeat the scene, symbolic of the eternity of the ordinance binding bride and groom.

It is in these rooms also that husband and wife of marriages performed outside the Temple are sealed for eternity and children are sealed to their parents.

The building also contains administrative offices, waiting rooms and dressing rooms, laundry, kitchen and dining facilities.

In a special issue of *The Ensign,* a brief history of its development recounts:

> When Elder Ezra Taft Benson, now President of the Council of Twelve (governing body of the Church), became the first president of the Washington Stake in 1941, he and each succeeding group of stake officers spoke often of the day when a temple would be built to serve the members of the Church living in eastern North America, just as other temples serve the Saints in the western United States, Canada, Europe and the South Pacific.
>
> Fifteen years ago, desire began to move toward reality. When Milan D. Smith was called as president of the Washington D.C. Stake in 1957, more than 90,000 members of the Church lived in the eastern half of the United States. Church membership and resources in the area had grown considerably. At the first meeting of the new stake presidency, Robert W. Barker, then a counselor to President Smith, suggested that the first business on the agenda should be to seek land for the Church, including acreage for a temple.
>
> President Smith was later asked to meet with the First Presidency on November 6, 1960, to make a formal presentation on the desired temple project. At a meeting of the First Presidency and the Council of the Twelve on November 14, 1960, approval was given for a temple to be constructed in the area.
>
> After consultation with Church leaders in other stakes and in the mission areas in the eastern United States and Canada, approval was given to negotiate for land. The 57-acre parcel where the Temple now stands was one of the two sites initially suggested and was purchased in 1962 for $850,000.
>
> The real work of designing, building and financing the Temple started in 1968. Ground breaking ceremonies were held on December 7, with 4,500 Church members gathered at the site to watch President Hugh B. Brown of the First Presidency turn the first shovel of earth. He was joined by Elder Ezra Taft Benson of the Council of the Twelve and President Paul H. Dunn of the First Council of the Seventy.
>
> Soon after the groundbreaking on January 18, 1969, the First Presidency announced the creation of a new temple district and the appointment of a temple committee, with President Smith as chairman. The Temple District included all of the United States, east of the Mississippi River, and eastern Canada.

The design of the Temple is the work of four architects selected by Emil B. Fetzer, Church Architect and designer of the Provo and Ogden Temples.

Each of the four architects, Harold K. Beecher, Henry P. Fetzer, Fred L. Markham and Keith W. Wilcox, drew up sketches which were considered in committee meetings headed by Brother Markham. Out of these consultations grew the design for a hexagon with towers on the corners which was finally elongated into a diamond shape. This design was then approved by the First Presidency.

Later the group was jointed by Architect Gerrit Timmerman who added to the design and then became the architect on the site during the construction period.

Workmen began to clear the temple site on May 28, 1971, and a "Completion Ceremony" was held September 9, 1974.

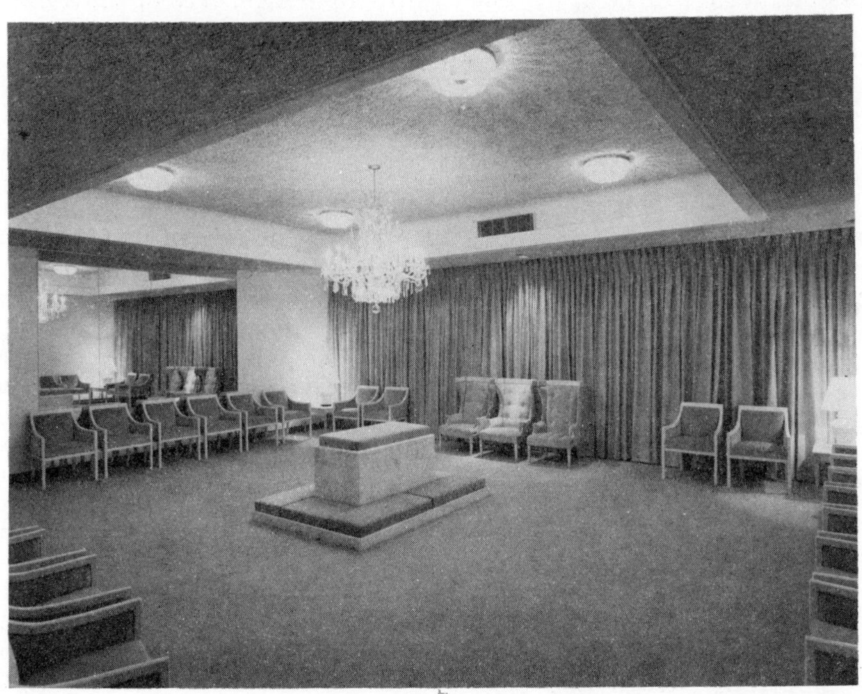

Photograph from the author

Sealing Room in the Washington Temple.

In the sealing room a couple being married kneel at the altar for marriage for both "time and eternity." Mormons regard marriage as an eternal partnership of man, woman, and their creator, with family ties carrying over to the next life if the individuals are worthy.

Three hundred distinguished guests attended the "Completion Ceremony" held outside on the steps of the east front of the Temple.

Spencer W. Kimball, President of the Church, presided at the ceremony. He was accompanied by his First Counselor, Marion G. Romney, who conducted the program and Elder Gordon B. Hinckley, a member of the Council of the Twelve.

"Temples to the true and living God," President Romney declared, "are built only under His direction, built to His plan and the work in them is carried on as revealed by Him.

"We have no finer buildings in the Church than the temples. A Temple is a House of God. It belongs to God. It is His dwelling place. It is a place where God reveals His presence to His faithful Saints."

In his address President Kimball told the audience that more temples would be built by The Church of Jesus Christ of Latter-day Saints in the future.

"We're a temple-minded people," he said. "We believe in eternity. We believe in permance.

"When we build a temple, we build it forever; when we perform temple ordinances, we perform them forever."

During the ceremonies, President Kimball directed and participated in the sealing of the cornerstone in which was placed a time capsule.

The capsule—a copper box 8 by 24 by 24 inches—was filled with historical documents obtained from the U. S. Archives.

These documents and the other material included:

A copy of Brigham Young's presidential appointment as territorial governor of Utah. The appointment, dated September 8, 1850, was signed by President Millard Fillmore and his Secretary of State, Daniel Webster.

An album of photographs showing the construction of the Temple and the groundbreaking ceremonies.

The Standard Works of the Church and copies of the books *Jesus the Christ, Articles of Faith* and *House of the Lord.*

A copy of the *Deseret News* of September 7, 1974; the *Church News* of June 8, 1974; and copies of the Church magazines, *The Ensign, The New Era* and *The Friend.*

The Washington Star-News of September 8, 1974, the *Washington Post* of September 9, 1974, and the September 8, 1974 issue of *Potomac Magazine.*

Also a copy of the Declaration of Independence, the Bill of Rights and the Constitution, an American flag flown over the Capitol, a

Photograph from the author

Mural in the WashingtonTemple, "The Second Coming of the Savior" by John Scott.

copy of the *Congressional Record* and photographs of the General Authorities of the Church, local Church leaders and the Temple Presidency.

The enormous task of preparing for and directing this preview of the Temple fell on the shoulders of the local temple committee among others, headed by President Julian C. Lowe of the Oakton, Virginia Stake who succeeded President Smith. Serving with him were President William D. Ladd of the Washington D.C. Stake, President J. Russell Smith of the Silver Spring, Maryland Stake and President Paul Thompson of the Annandale, Virginia Stake.

These men spread the work among 1,400 volunteer workers from the membership in this area. Men, women and their children responded to the call for help at all hours of the day and night—first to get the Temple cleaned and ready for the thousands of visitors and secondly to handle the streams of visitors each day.

At the beginning of the public tours on September 17, 1974, the Temple was opened on Mondays from 9 a.m. to 5 p.m. to permit groups from various organizations such as other churches, schools, civic, fraternal, industrial, social and patriotic organizations to come at specified times, by reservations.

The Temple was closed Monday evenings because of the practice of the Saints to hold Family Home Evening programs on each Monday. This program, when the families of the Church gather in their homes to spend an evening together, is considered of such importance that no other event is permitted to interfere with it.

Tuesdays through Saturdays the Temple was open from 9 a.m. to 9 p.m. with tours starting every ten minutes. Tickets were distributed by the hundreds of thousands all over the continent and some in Europe.

It soon became apparent that all those who wished to see inside this magnificent edifice could not be accommodated on the original schedule and the hours from Tuesday through Saturday were extended to from 7:30 a.m. to 10:30 p.m. Still the demand for tickets continued to increase, and finally the First Presidency of the Church permitted the public preview to continue for five more days until Saturday, November 2, 1974, when the last tour was clocked in at 10:30 p.m.

The visitors were greeted at the entrance to the Temple Annex and presented a brochure containing pictures and a brief text about the Temple while their tickets were collected. They were guided around the stained glass screen that separates the Annex from the bridge leading inside the Temple. After they passed over the bridge, they were halted temporarily at the Temple entrance while a taped message briefly explained the Temple and what they were about to see.

The visitors walked through the Temple from bottom to top without further explanations of what they saw until, at the end of the tour as they walked outside, they were greeted by scores of workers stationed at the exit to answer questions. Information booths were scattered around the Temple grounds where other information in written form could be obtained.

Comfortable couches and chairs were available at various spots along the tour, and the visitors were urged to rest if they became tired until they wished to join the tour again.

Elevators were ready for use by the elderly and those who could not walk the steps from floor to floor. Wheelchairs were provided for those who needed them.

A special ceremony was held Friday, October 18, 1974, when Donald Trowbridge De Roche, a tool and die maker of Baltimore, Maryland, arrived at the entrance to become the 500,000th person to visit the Temple since it was opened to the public.

The De Roche family was escorted by Elders J. Rick Carter and Lee Yates directly to a room off the Temple entrance where they were welcomed by Temple President Edward E. Drury, Jr. and his two counselors Wendell G. Eames and Byron F. Dixon.

President Drury presented Mr. De Roche with a copy of the *Book of Mormon,* a record of the Mormon Tabernacle Choir's greatest hits and a bound volume of the Church magazine *The Ensign*.

Elders Carter and Yates then took the family on a special tour.

When they first entered the Temple, Mr. De Roche, upon being asked what he thought of it, said: "Fantastic. Fantastic."

After he had made the tour he was asked the same question and replied: "Unbelievable."

Both Mr. and Mrs. De Roche said that they were extremely impressed by the friendliness of everyone they met during their visit. Mr. De Roche's comments were typical of many who visited the Temple.

After the last tour was held on November 2, preparations began to put the Temple in shape for the four days of dedication ceremonies.

President of the Church Spencer W. Kimball voiced the dedicatory prayer at each of the ten sessions held during the dedication November 19 through November 22.

At each session the program included music by soloists and several choirs chosen from Canada and the eastern seaboard of the United States. Talks were also given at each session by members of the General Authorities of the Church and local church leaders.

Admission to the exercises was by ticket only and only those members of the Church who were considered worthy of entering the Temple for this sacred ceremony were issued tickets after an interview by their bishop.

The Temple was opened for a limited time in December for marriages and other ordinances, and on January 2, 1975, it began full-time operation.

Approximately 600 workers, most of them on a part-time basis, are required to meet the daily demands of those who flock to this House of the Lord from all over the globe.

These workers are under daily direction of the Temple Presidency headed by the Temple President Edward E. Drury, Jr.

Mrs. Drury serves as Matron of the Temple, overseeing matters relating to the women and children who come to the Temple.

The Drurys are not strangers to this area. Previous to his calling to the temple position, President Drury was mission president for three years of the Delaware-Maryland Mission. He was released from this position in July of 1973.

Photograph from the author

View of the Washington Temple.

Prior to that he was manager for 23 years of Friden Division of Singer Company, Denver, Colorado, and Salt Lake City, Utah, before retiring.

As a young man he served on a British Mission. He was bishop of the Denver First Ward and president of the Denver Stake for 21 years. He also served on the Priesthood Home Teaching Committee of the Church and as a Regional Representative of the Church's Council of the Twelve.

Mrs. Drury was born in Salt Lake City, Utah. She attended Denver University. She has served in various capacities as a teacher and counselor in the Church.

The Drurys were married in the Salt Lake Temple. They have two daughters and a son.

Wendell Geddes Eames of Silver Spring, Maryland, serves as President Drury's First Counselor. President Eames was formerly president of the Washington, D. C. Stake of the Church. He was born in Preston, Idaho, May 30, 1917.

He was active in the Boy Scouts and in 4-H Clubs in his early years. He became a four-palm Eagle Scout, and through the 4-H Clubs he received a scholarship to the University of Idaho where he received a degree in political science. He also attended New York University and Northeastern University.

After a stint in private industry he joined the Federal Bureau of Investigation in 1940. He served the FBI as special agent in Mississippi, Pennsylvania and Washington, D.C. Later he became the Bureau's Records and Management Officer. After 20 years with the FBI, he was appointed director of the National Driver Registration Service which he organized and administered in the U. S. Department of Commerce. In 1965, he received the department's Silver Medal for this work.

Before becoming president of the Church's Washington Stake, he served in various other capacities including bishop of the Washington Ward located at Sixteenth Street and Columbia Road in northwest Washington.

The chapel in which this ward meets was the first meetinghouse of The Church of Jesus Christ of Latter-day Saints erected in the Capital.

President Eames is married to the former Nedra Cole of Fairview, Idaho. They have one son.

Serving as President Drury's Second Counselor is Byron Fife Dixon of Arlington, Virginia.

President Dixon was born in Downey, Idaho, July 9, 1908. He was married in the Logan Temple to Mabel Patra Hackney and they have two children.

President Dixon graduated in 1938 from the University of Idaho. He also studied accounting at the Benjamin Franklin University. He holds B.C.A., M.C.S., and C.P.A. degrees. He was a practicing Certified Public Accountant in Washington from 1940 until 1970. He has also been a Professor of Accounting and Associate Director of Benjamin Franklin University.

During his service in several positions in the Church, he has been a counselor in the Potomac Stake, bishop of the Arlington Ward and a member of the Washington Stake High Council.

In conclusion, it may be well to mention another unique feature of this temple—this "monument to spirituality." It was fully paid for before the building was well under construction. It is a rule of the Church that its chapels and temples cannot be opened for use until all bills for the project have been paid.

The Washington Temple cost approximately $15,000,000. The goal for collection from the Saints in the Washington Temple District was set at $4.5 million. The remainder of the money came from the general tithing collection of the Church.

Members of The Church of Jesus Christ of Latter-day Saints consider it an honor and a privilege to contribute to the construction of the chapels, temples and other buildings necessary to the practice of their religion.

The local temple committee, first headed by President Milan Smith now presiding over the mission in London, and later chaired by President Julian Lowe, found that the members in the District were ready to make sacrifices, if necessary, in order that the goal would be reached.

The first contribution to the Washington Temple was made even before the land was bought or the Temple authorized.

Nicholas Perry, President Barker recalls, had left the United States sometime before World War II to set up an assembly plant in eastern Europe. The venture was successful until his business was confiscated by the Nazis when the war broke out. Mr. Perry escaped with his wife and daughter to the Washington, D.C. area.

Through the Alien Property Custodian, several years later, Mr. Perry receiver partial payment for his holdings that had been seized in Germany. A short time later he went to see President Milan Smith and said: "I understand that you hope we can build a temple here. Soon you will be raising money to pay for it. I want to contribute." He thereupon made the first contribution.

Many stories can be told of children who saved their baby-sitting pay for the Temple and adults who gave up vacations and other pleasures so that they could have the privilege of helping to build a House of the Lord.

Now that it has been built and is in full use, it is opened to the faithful to participate in the sacred ordinances from Tuesday through Saturday. It is closed on Sundays, when the Saints worship in their chapels and other meeting places, and on Mondays.

Although the Temple is not open for public worship, hundreds of visitors still come to see the beautiful grounds and to get a close-up view of the magnificent structure.

An Information Center is under construction nearby where those who come may learn more about the Temple and those who belong to The Church of Jesus Christ of Latter-day Saints.

Presidents of the Society, 1894–1974

Joseph M. Toner (1825–1896)	1894–1896
John A. Kasson (1822–1910)	1897–1906
Alexander B. Hagner (1826–1915)	1906–1909
James Dudley Morgan (1862–1919)	1909–1916
Allen C. Clark (1858–1943)	1916–1943
F. Regis Noel (1891–1952)	1944–1946, 1948–1950, 1952
H. Paul Caemmerer (1884–1962)	1947–1948
Frederick S. Tyler (1882–1951)	1951 (President Elect)
Laurence F. Schmeckebier (1877–1959)	1951–1952
U. S. Grant, 3rd (1881–1968)	1952–1968
Homer T. Rosenberger (b. 1908)	1968–

Officers and Managers of the Society, 1973, 1974

1973 OFFICERS

President. . . . . HOMER T. ROSENBERGER
First Vice President. . . . . WILCOMB E. WASHBURN
Second Vice President. . . . . CORNELIUS W. HEINE
Secretary. . . . . VACANT
Treasurer. . . . . WILLIAM L. ELLIS
Curator. . . . . ELDEN E. BILLINGS
Chronicler. . . . . MAURICE P. MAHONEY
Librarian. . . . . ROBERT A. TRUAX
Editor. . . . . FRANCIS C. ROSENBERGER
Executive Director. . . . . R. J. MCCARTHY

1974 OFFICERS

President. . . . . HOMER T. ROSENBERGER
First Vice President. . . . . WILCOMB E. WASHBURN
Second Vice President. . . . . CORNELIUS W. HEINE
Secretary. . . . . EDWARD F. GERBER
Treasurer. . . . . WILLIAM L. ELLIS
Curator. . . . . MARK G. GRIFFIN
Curator of Prints and Photographs. . . . . ROBERT A. TRUAX
Chronicler. . . . . MAURICE P. MAHONEY
Librarian. . . . . PERRY FISHER
Editor. . . . . FRANCIS C. ROSENBERGER
Executive Director. . . . . R. J. MCCARTHY

MANAGERS

Term Expires January 1974

Mrs. Anita Heurich Eckles
Herman R. Friis
Christian Heurich, Jr.
Francis D. Lethbridge

Term Expires January 1975

Leo Bernstein
Herbert P. Ramsey
Miss Edith Ray Saul
Robert A. Truax

Term Expires January 1976

O. Kenneth Baker
John V. Hinkel
Elmer L. Kayser
William H. Press

Term Expires January 1977

Mrs. Benjamin C. Evans, Jr.
Henry H. Glassie
Frederick D. Hunt
Francis C. Rosenberger

Term Expires January 1978

Robert R. Ayers
Christian Heurich, Jr.
Mary Mitchell
Emil A. Press

Index to Subjects

Index to Illustrations

Index to Authors

Comments on the 45th volume, *Records of the Columbia Historical Society of Washington, D. C., 1963–1965,* illustrated, xx, 513 pages

JOHN BEVERLEY RIGGS in *The Pennsylvania Magazine of History and Biography:* "This volume has an excellent balance, and its well-researched papers are a valuable addition to any bibliography on the City of Washington."

ALBERT W. ATWOOD: "It is not only admirable, it is superb. Well printed, good type, good paper, good pictures and contents of inestimable value to anyone interested in D. C. history."

LEONARD CARMICHAEL: "Splendid work as editor."

DOROTHY CLARK WINCHCOLE: "The new volume of the Columbia Historical Society Records is one of the best—if not the best—we have ever had."

Virginia Quarterly Review: "Contains much information difficult to find in other sources."

P. W. FILBY in the *Maryland Historical Magazine:* "A wealth of information on the Washington area."

The Journal of Southern History: "There are many interesting illustrations."

MATTIE RUSSELL in *The North Carolina Historical Review:* "Illustrations greatly enhance the articles."

Cosmos Club Bulletin: "Altogether an impressive and fascinating book for those attracted by the never-ending ramifications of local history."

Comments on the 46th volume, *Records of the Columbia Historical Society of Washington, D. C., 1966–1968* illustrated, xviii, 467 pages

Virginia Quarterly Review: "This 46th separate volume maintains the Society's high level of interest and information in its papers. Its range of topics is wide—transportation, society, economics, music, journalism, and the presidential wives. All are treated exhaustively, while many have been illustrated with enough rare material to enhance not only the record but the research value of the individual article. It is remarkable, but encouraging, that a local historical society, especially in a city with as shifting a population as Washington's, can produce such distinguished work."

ELMER LOUIS KAYSER: "A distinguished volume."

DOROTHY CLARK WINCHCOLE: "Each new volume of the Records seems to surpass the former success."

OLIVER W. HOLMES: "This volume seems better than the last and I hardly thought that the last could be made better."

HERMAN R. FRIIS: "The best of any the Society has ever had."

MARJORIE RISK DAVISON: "The best yet published."

MELVILLE J. BOYER in *Pennsylvania History:* "Valuable local and national historical contributions."

P. W. FILBY in the *Maryland Historical Magazine:* "The whole volume is heartily recommended."

THOMAS C. PARRAMORE in *The North Carolina Historical Review:* "Distinguished and useful series."'

HERMAN SCHADEN in the *Washington Star:* "The book is a credit to the Society's recently celebrated 75th anniversary."

ADVERTISEMENT

Comments on the 47th volume, *Records of the Columbia Historical Society of Washington, D. C., 1969–1970,* illustrated, xxxv, 570 pages

CARL BERNSTEIN in *The Washington Post:* "The current 47th volume is the best in decades. It contains many fine scholarly contributions and some intriguing reading. Almost all the 26 contributors are historians, anthropologists or curators. Their writing is excellent at best and serviceable at worst. Their topics, with a few exceptions, should be of interest to anyone more than remotely concerned about this city's past and future."

Virginia Quarterly Review: "How is one to choose from the riches of this volume, riches which turn from a study of personalities to the institutions those personalities developed or managed. This splendidly produced volume shows no slackening in the scholarship being produced in the nation's capital and, indeed, serves to astonish the reader with the variety and depth of the capital's cultural life. We are now promised a biennial compilation of the papers instead of a triennial one as in the past. It is a welcome change."

HENRY H. DOUGLAS in *Echoes of History:* "One is equally amazed at the energy and ability of Francis Coleman Rosenberger, the editor of this and four preceding volumes."

CAROLYN ANDREWS WALLACE in *The North Carolina Historical Review:* "If the volume has a concentration other than the District of Columbia, it is the field of cultural history. More than half the essays deal in some way with art, architecture, libraries, publishing, and literature. Most were written by specialists, and a number display mastery of style as well as subject matter."

Military Affairs: "Another of the society's superb anthologies of articles devoted to the history of the nation's capital. Essays relevant to military history include two on the role of military officers in non-combat endeavors . . ."

HARRY M. MEACHAM in the *Richmond News Leader:* "Of enormous importance, not only to historians, archivists, and Virginians whose forefathers played such an important role in establishing and developing Washington, but also to all Americans who want to know the history of the nation's capital."

WELFORD D. TAYLOR in the *Richmond Times-Dispatch:* "Francis Coleman Rosenberger, perhaps better known to Virginia readers as editor of the *Virginia Reader,* has edited and introduced each of the five collections with his usual degree of insight and precision."

Cosmos Club Bulletin: "Much in association with Cosmos Club . . . six Club members have contributed essays."

PAUL R. BAKER in *The Journal of American History:* "The book is handsomely designed with over 200 illustrations."

The Journal of Southern History: "Well-illustrated volume."

MELVILLE J. BOYER in *Pennsylvania History:* "It is a privilege to review a publication of the cultural and historical magnitude of this latest edition."

P. W. FILBY in the *Maryland Historical Magazine:* "The volume will greatly interest its members—not always the case with society publications—and the range of subjects represented will attract many other readers. The editor and the Society are to be congratulated on continuing the series so ably and efficiently."

DANIEL P. JORDAN in *West Virginia History:* "The scope ranges from the 1790's to the present, is interdisciplinary, and covers subjects of concern to specialists and laymen alike."

DUMAS MALONE, Author of *Jefferson and His Time:* "A very valuable source book."

FREDERICK GUTHEIM in *Capitol Studies:* "By comparison with the publications of other state and local historical societies, most of which receive a considerable measure of assistance from tax-supported sources, the high historical and editorial standards maintained by Dr. Rosenberger in this more distinctly private endeavor are worthy of special commendation. . . . Here are eminently readable essays, well-illustrated and presented in a balanced, skillfully edited collection. Through its pages one is introduced to Washington the national capital city, as well as Washington the distinctively local community."

Comments on the 48th volume, *Records of the Columbia Historical Society of Washington, D. C., 1971–1972,* illustrated, xxv, 846 pages

CONSTANCE MCLAUGHLIN GREEN: "The new volume of the *Records* is a triumph. It is exactly what I had always hoped the Society would produce one day but until now had not achieved wholly."

RICHARD R. DUNCAN in *The Virginia Magazine of History and Biography:* "A tour de force of what a local historical society is capable of publishing."

KENNETH R. BOWLING in *The North Carolina Historical Review:* "The sixth and best volume he has edited. Rosenberger has invigorated the *Records* and placed them on a high level."

GEORGE GREEN SHACKELFORD in *The Maryland Historical Magazine:* "Under his auspices, the *Records* have attained an enviable place."

MILLARD K. BUSHONG in *West Virginia History:* "A valuable chronicle of personalities, institutions, and events relating to the history of the nation's capital."

The Journal of Southern History: "A rich lode of material both for the history of the area and many other aspects of American history."

Editorial in *The Washington Post:* "The current volume is the 48th in the society's series, and those who have enjoyed the society's high standards for historical scholarship in the past will find the most recent edition—846 pages—a continuation of that excellence. A richness of information is contained, revealed both in the writing and in the illustrations. The current editor of the series, with six volumes to his credit, is Francis Coleman Rosenberger."

JOHN MCKELWAY ("The Rambler") in *The Washington Star-News:* The reading is relaxing and interesting and particularly so for those who become curious about, say, a statue or park or painting they might pass from time to time."

HARRY M. MEACHAM in *The Richmond News Leader:* "Over the years, historians have come to lean heavily on these publications."

The Progress-Index, Petersburg, Virginia: "The treatment is scholarly. People, institutions, and social and economic subjects are represented. The essays are of high quality."

LEONARD RAPPORT in *History:* "A most attractive volume, with good paper, good typeface, good design, good illustrations, and attractive binding and endsheets. It has more than twice as many pages as most earlier volumes and has an 18-page double-column name index."

HENRY H. DOUGLAS in *Echoes of History:* "These profusely illustrated volumes are truly a monument to the editor."

ELMER LOUIS KAYSER: "It is a truly noble volume, both in physical appearance and editorial excellence."

Virginia Quarterly Review: "Once again the Columbia Historical Society of Washington has issued a volume of papers. This time, although a year has been lopped off the usual three-year interval between publications, the book itself is almost twice as large as the last. Not only must the energy of the Society be praised, but its intelligent selection of material is of a continuing and astonishingly high standard. Since it is impossible to choose a favorite from the thirty-four articles, they must be praised together, a very easy task, for they are universally interesting whether they are on politics, biography, or shipbuilding."

DONALD JACKSON, Editor, *The Papers of George Washington:* "It is outstanding, as always, for its diversity, scholarship, and its remarkable collection of illustrations."

L. H. BUTTERFIELD, Editor, *The Adams Papers:* "These volumes are becoming more and more useful to our enterprise and along with a great number of other scholars we are most grateful."

H. G. NICHOLAS, *Rhodes Professor of American History and Institutions, New College, Oxford:* "What a pleasure it is to be introduced to such a handsome series, beautifully produced and full of interesting material."